CORPORATE CONCENTRATION
AND PUBLIC POLICY

PRENTICE-HALL ECONOMICS SERIES

E. A. J. Johnson, Editor

CORPORATE CONCENTRATION AND PUBLIC POLICY

Second Edition

HARRY L. PURDY

Research Director
British Columbia Electric Company, Ltd.

MARTIN L. LINDAHL

Professor of Economics, Dartmouth College

WILLIAM A. CARTER

Professor of Economics, Dartmouth College

NEW YORK • PRENTICE-HALL, INC. • 1950

To
Our Students
in
Economics Eleven

Preface to the First Edition

This book is devoted to the problems and public policies arising from the concentration of economic power in the United States. No attempt is made to cover the whole field of social control of industry: the study is confined to monopoly and monopolistic competition in the general field of industry. It describes the development of the modern large corporation and the public controls which have been designed to protect investors and to remove corporate abuses; it traces the developments in a considerable number of industries which have been characterized by concentration and coöperation; it reviews American public policy with respect to trusts and administrative control of the competitive process; and it considers proposals for invigorating our traditional policy against monopolistic elements in the economy, and the alternative policies of government price regulation and government ownership and operation.

No original or revolutionary doctrines with respect to economic theory or public policy are advocated. The purpose has been simply to collect the available materials relating to these extremely important economic and social problems and to present them in a manner that will be helpful to students of social science. New light has been thrown upon the operation of the modern economy by recent investigations of the Temporary National Economic Committee and the permanent administrative bodies in Washington. But numerous decisions concerning proper public policy remain to be made. No ready answers have been found to the problem of fashioning implements that will assure the maintenance of the system of competitive individualism. It is our conviction, however, that the system has merits that are much to be desired and that our efforts should be directed to its preservation and betterment.

We are greatly indebted to the many outstanding scholars who have studied and written in the field. Acknowledgments have been made throughout the text. But our debt is especially great to Professors Arthur R. Burns, Frank A. Fetter, Milton Handler, and Myron W. Watkins. We have also benefited from friendly discussion with our colleagues in Dartmouth and wish particularly to mention Dr. Nelson Lee Smith, now chairman of the Board of Investigation and Research, Transportation

Act of 1940, and Professor Bruce W. Knight. We wish finally to record our appreciation of the kindly assistance rendered by the staff of the Baker Library of Dartmouth College.

Hanover, New Hampshire

Harry L. Purdy
Martin L. Lindahl
William A. Carter

Preface to the Second Edition

In this edition the materials treated in the original volume have been brought up to date. This has required an expanded discussion of the interpretation and application of the Sherman Act and public control of discrimination under the Robinson-Patman Act. Some new material has been added to the industry studies relating particularly to petroleum, nickel, and automobiles. The treatment of the sulphur industry has been expanded and the chapter used as a vehicle for the analysis of international cartels.

No reorganization of the contents of the book has been attempted. For pedagogical reasons, the industrial monopoly cases are separated from the industry cases relating to oligopoly and coöperation by the discussion of public regulation. For those who wish to consider all the industry cases illustrating the various degrees and types of concentration in one block, the discussion of public regulation may readily be deferred. Neither has the theoretical analysis of oligopolistic markets been expanded. Excellent treatments of the refinements of the theory of oligopoly and monopolistic competition are available in text form for those interested in these aspects of the problem.

We are indebted to many people for comments and suggestions for the improvement of the book, all of which have been considered carefully in this revision. We are especially appreciative of the suggestions made by Professors Joe S. Bain, Francis M. Boddy, Frederic B. Garver, and Shorey Peterson, and to our colleagues in Dartmouth, Professors Joseph S. Ransmeier and Earl R. Sikes.

H. L. P.
M. L. L.
W. A. C.

Preface to the Second Edition

Contents

xi

PART III

PUBLIC REGULATION OF MONOPOLY AND COMPETITIVE PRACTICES

PART IV

OLIGOPOLY AND INDUSTRIAL COÖPERATION

CONCLUSION

POSSIBLE PUBLIC POLICIES

Introduction

1

American Economic Individualism: Achievements and Processes

As America set out on her course of political independence, she subscribed to the philosophy of economic individualism that was gaining rapid acceptance in England. The trade restrictions of the English government had been irritating in the colonial period, and the Constitution reflected the interest of the commercially important middle class in freedom of enterprise. Without exception, leaders of American thought espoused the individualistic system. Alexander Hamilton did wish to use government interference in the form of the tariff to force the growth of American manufacturing, but he valued highly the driving force of self-interest in the economic sphere. His desire for a strong central government did not lead him to seek any material interference with the initiative and discretion of "the assiduous merchant, the laborious husbandman, the active mechanic, and the industrious manufacturer."[1] And the manufacturer, the western settler, and the laborer who frequently came to America to escape religious and economic repression in Europe, readily joined in acceptance of the *laissez-faire* philosophy. The bright lustre of individualism was dulled by unemployment and pauperism after 1807, but its essential virtues were seldom questioned save by some easily ignored "lunatic fringe."

To the mind of the early nineteenth century it seemed that the proper rôle of government was only to protect and organize the institutions of capitalism. The framework of the individualistic system—private property, free exchange, freedom of contract, freedom of enterprise—developed vigorously under the aegis of political democracy. Exceptions to the *laissez-faire* attitude were made to serve the general rule. In 1815, the recommendations of President Madison for tariff protection justified it on the score that import duties would protect the tender individualism of American industry against the older and more rugged individualism

---

[1] *The Federalist* (Hallowell, Maine, 1826), Vol. XII, p. 64.

found in other countries. Madison had no doubts as to the wisdom of the accepted theory "which leaves to the sagacity and interest of individuals the application of their industry and resources."[2] The individual, left free to direct his labor, his ability as an enterpriser, or his capital, could surely be trusted to advance his own interests, and incidentally, the public interest also. The individual would prosper only as he contributed to the economic development of the country. Sufficient control of the producer would be found in competition, which would preserve the identity of the private and public interests by preventing personal gains for the inefficient or the monopolist. Protected by the institutions of capitalism, individuals would be driven by self-interest to organize and develop the productive capacity of the country.

THE ACHIEVEMENTS OF AMERICAN CAPITALISM

Much had to be done in the new nation. America found in economic individualism not only a satisfying freedom, but a means of achieving a spectacular economic development. In any critical study of American capitalism it is especially important to appreciate the achievements of the system. On the one hand, we must not sit quietly, immersed in self-satisfaction, when grievous faults can be seen and possibly remedied. But on the other hand, we must not become so absorbed in the pathological that we ignore the healthy elements. In our analysis of the faulty control of production under economic individualism we must not overlook the really great achievements of American enterprise. To do so would lead to serious errors in our conclusions.

The history of the past one hundred and fifty years shows a truly great story of individuals undertaking the tremendously complicated task of directing American enterprise and resources into the varied fields of industry, exchange, commerce, and agriculture; undertaking the discovery of new tools and new methods of manufacture; and developing improved forms of business organization and more efficient producing units. The achievements and the processes of the system are readily seen in the economic growth of the United States.

Early Development

Until about 1812 American enterprisers, composed in the main of merchant capitalists, turned their attention largely to foreign trade. They did, however, start a textile and an iron industry, particularly in New England and the Middle Atlantic States.

---

[2] James D. Richardson (editor), *Messages and Papers of the Presidents*, Vol. I, p. 567.

Political disturbances inaugurated by the French Revolution and our participation in another war with the British slowed down the early economic development. But, despite the vagaries of war, foreign political upheavals, and the trade cycle, the United States made economic progress. A great ocean commerce grew up. Banks and banking developed and foreign and domestic trade expanded. The corporation as an institution began to play its part in the American economy. Economic development was stimulated, perhaps often over-stimulated, by the speculative spirit of American citizens—a spirit which continues to show itself on the slightest provocation. And continually the opportunities found in commerce and manufacture were decreasing the former emphasis upon agriculture.

Though foreign trade grew rapidly after 1815, it developed certain features that served to direct the attention of individuals to other fields.[3] The post-war deflation of prices in Europe and America cut heavily into the sale of Oriental cotton and linens in the Western market. As silk hats replaced beavers, the fur trade in Europe experienced a real shift in demand. At the same time, in America, the cost of furs was rising as the exhaustion of nearby sources of supply drove fur traders deeper inland. Far-sighted American merchants of the type of John Jacob Astor, John P. Cushing, T. H. Perkins, and Messrs. Bryant and Sturgis were withdrawing from foreign trade.

A temporary decline in mercantile profits was a potent factor in shifting resources and men from commerce to industrial pursuits. For example, Cushing participated in railroad and canal development. Astor found real estate and banking attractive. Sturgis, Bryant, and others entered the fields of banking or industry.

As the leaders moved from the category of merchant capitalists, a valuable specialization appeared: enterprisers concentrated on special fields of industry as the corporation allowed business units to be organized on a larger scale and management became more specialized.

For a time conflicting views on the proper scope for the corporation retarded its use. Among state legislators there were those who agreed that liberal grants of charters would stimulate industry and promote industrial progress. But others, taking a more cautious point of view, wished to confine corporate charter privileges such as limited liability to those enterprises which would directly advance public welfare and the interests of the state. Into this category fell banks, turnpike, canal, and, at times, insurance companies. As a result, in industries where private gain was more manifest than public benefit, corporations were given

---

[3] N. S. B. Gras and H. M. Larson, *Casebook in American Business History* (New York, F. S. Crofts & Co., 1939), p. 668.

"limping" charters and denied the important feature of limited liability.[4] The increased size of the business class eventually made its weight count in legislative assemblies, and ultimately limited liability became a widely accepted legal feature. Through the same business influence special acts of the state legislature ceased to be necessary for incorporation, as the supervision of incorporation was handed over to some state officer who operated under a general act prepared by the legislature. This so-called general incorporation was introduced by Connecticut in 1837.[5]

While business activity "bucked" the many economic cross-currents to be found in a new country endowed with great natural wealth, the growth of population and its westward movement proved an encouraging factor. Moreover, it was supplemented by the Federal Government's liberal policies with respect to both immigration and land. The growth and expansion of population widened markets, giving them both depth and breadth. And individual enterprise sought and found solutions as growth created innumerable problems.

One restraining feature was the high cost of transportation. In 1821, it cost as much to convey a ton of merchandise thirty miles inland as it did to carry it from Europe to the United States. Freight charges between Philadelphia and Pittsburgh were eight dollars per hundredweight; moreover, freight moved slowly.[6]

Thanks to the pioneer work of Morey, Fitch, Fulton, and Livingston, propulsion by steam offered a partial solution to the water transportation problem. And in 1824 the Supreme Court made a significant contribution when it ruled that the regulation of commerce on interstate waterways was a province of the Federal Government.[7] As a result, the practical monopolies held by certain steamboat interests were broken and the way was opened for enterprisers.[8] Meanwhile public effort was

---

[4] Shaw Livermore, "Unlimited Liability in Early Corporations," *Journal of Political Economy*, Vol. XLIII, No. 5 (October, 1935), p. 686.

[5] New York had passed such a law in 1811, but limited general incorporation procedure to *manufacturing*. The Connecticut law permitted incorporation for "any lawful purpose," not through the special negotiations with the legislature in establishing the corporate contract, but through simple application to a designated state official who scrutinized the articles of incorporation to assure himself that they were within the general law of incorporation. *Cf.* A. A. Berle, Jr., and G. C. Means, *The Modern Corporation and Private Property* (New York, The Macmillan Company, 1933), p. 136.

[6] B. H. Meyer (editor), *History of Transportation in the United States before 1860* (Washington, D. C., Carnegie Institution of Washington, 1917), pp. 88–90.

[7] Gibbons *v.* Ogden, 9 Wheaton 1 (1824).

[8] New York State had granted to Robert Livingston and Robert Fulton and their assignees the exclusive right to navigate for a stipulated number of years all waters within the state with boats moved by fire or steam. Gibbons was licensed under United States laws to carry on coasting trade and was plying the waters falling under the Livingston-Fulton franchise which had been assigned to Ogden. The Supreme Court held the New York law repugnant to the commerce clause of the Constitution.

directed toward the development of canals. New York State built the Erie and Champlain Canals. Pennsylvania connected the Great Lakes and Pittsburgh with Philadelphia and the anthracite coal fields. Farther west, in Ohio, Indiana, and Illinois, ambitious projects were undertaken.

Railroads, in an experimental stage, showed promise. As they proved their worth they attracted capital through the medium of the corporate device. Commercial interests in Boston, New York, Philadelphia, Baltimore, and other metropolitan centers invested heavily and successfully despite panics, depressions, and falling prices. Central markets were linked together and railroad lines were projected into tributary areas. Between 1830 and 1850, over seventy-three hundred miles of railroad line were built, largely in the New England and Middle Atlantic States and in Ohio, Michigan, and Indiana. The capital goods industries expanded to supply transportation with its requirements.

In private hands, banking moved forward rapidly though often disastrously. The First and Second Banks of the United States came and went. In the older eastern cities and in the New England region less banking trouble was experienced than elsewhere. In other areas less restraint was shown and the mortality rate was exceptionally high. Private bankers and exchange brokers increased remarkably in importance.[9] They had much to do with the issue of and the trade in securities, though they could hardly be classified as investment bankers. They performed also the function of transferring funds from one part of the country to another, besides acting as agents for both the borrowers and lenders.

In marketing, new opportunities were seized and new ways of doing business were developed. Wholesalers thrived and specialization in retailing increased greatly in the larger market areas. The actual pattern varied for different communities. In small villages and towns the general store was characteristic. In the larger inland cities wholesale and retail establishments were combined. In New York, A. T. Stewart's department store heralded the approach of a marked change in the retailing of consumer's goods.

Technological Advancement

Under the encouragement offered by the patent law, men were busy with inventions. The Constitution had foreseen the aid which government might bring to the improvement of economic techniques, and had provided that:[10] "The Congress shall have the power to promote the

---

[9] Cf. Gras and Larson, op. cit., p. 676.

[10] This constitutional power granted the Federal Government in Article I, Paragraph 8, ended the conflict, confusion, and uncertainty of the earlier arrangement where each colony had granted patents independently of the others. The Articles of Confederation had continued this unsatisfactory lack of system and centralization.

progress of science and useful arts by securing for limited times to authors and inventors the exclusive right to their respective writings and discoveries."

The first law passed in 1790 was amended three years later and then fundamentally changed in 1836.[11] As it now stands after a number of revisions the law gives the patentee, or his heirs or assigns, for a seventeen-year period the exclusive right to make, use, or sell the invention or discovery throughout the United States.[12] It confers on him also the right to restrain others from infringement by taking action in the United States courts through injunctive proceedings and recovery of damages for unauthorized use.

Near the close of the eighteenth century, Oliver Evans produced a high-pressure steam engine more suited to American conditions than the heavier and bulkier English machines.[13] In 1833, the Reverend Doctor F. W. Gussenheim invented and patented a method of smelting anthracite coal by a blast of heated air. Within two decades, anthracite smelting exceeded charcoal smelting in the nation's output of pig iron. Since the Lehigh, Delaware, Schuylkill, and Susquehanna valleys had easy access to rich deposits of anthracite coal, they became the real centers of an expanding iron industry.

In Newburyport, Massachusetts, in 1790, Jacob Perkins invented a nail-making machine which soon superseded the laborious hand methods of nail production. And forty years later, Ichabod Washburn developed a wire-drawing machine which became the basis of the great wire industry in Worcester, Massachusetts. This machine aided substantially in making practical the telegraph when the talents of Samuel F. B. Morse, Joseph Henry, Alfred Vail, and Ezra Cornell combined to invent it.

Simeon North, the farmer who turned munitions-maker, and Eli Whitney, inventor of the cotton gin, were other notable contributors. They

---

[11] Cf. G. A. Weber, The Patent Office, Institute of Government Research, Service Monograph No. 31 (Baltimore, The Johns Hopkins University Press, 1924), p. 4.

[12] The salient provisions of the present law may be listed under the following heads: subject-matter of patent; application for patent; rights of patentee, and relation of patent to competition.

Under subject-matter, the applicant must establish conception, novelty, and utility of any art, machine, manufacture, or composition of matter or improvement thereon, under certain rigid conditions provided to protect others as well as himself.

The application for a patent includes six parts: petition; assignment of power of attorney to the patent attorney representing the applicant before the Patent Office; specification, describing the invention as revealed by the drawings; the official drawings giving different views of the invention; the inventor's claims for his invention; and finally, the oath that the applicant believes that he is the original and first inventor of the thing for which he is soliciting a patent grant. Cf. Floyd F. Vaughan, Economics of Our Patent System (New York, The Macmillan Company, 1925), pp. 23–27.

[13] E. C. Kirkland, A History of American Economic Life (New York, F. S. Crofts & Co., 1939), p. 309.

introduced the principle of interchangeable parts and precision methods in firearms manufacture, and set the stage for the adoption of this principle in other industries. Agriculture benefited when the inventions of Jethro Wood, John Deere, Obed Hussey, and others revolutionized agricultural machinery.

Not all the inventive genius, however, was confined to the native stock. Much advancement came from the transplantation of talent from Europe. For example, the textile industry's rapid development owed much to Samuel Slater, who slipped out of England with his mind full of information which, when applied to our infant cotton textile industry, eventually earned him a place of eminence in cotton manufacturing.

One could go on almost indefinitely to enlarge on the manifestations of inventive genius and the human instinct for workmanship in the United States. The product must stand as one of the great contributions made by economic individualism in this early period.

The Civil War had both a retarding and a stimulating effect on American economic development. As is true of all major wars, total or partial destruction of man-power and wealth produced immediate and continuing economic and social losses of great magnitude. The distortions which an economy must endure as it is transformed from a peace to a war basis and then back to a peace basis bring consequences which vary in seriousness, depending upon the stage of economic development of the countries involved. In this instance, great opportunities and a vigorous individualism made possible a rapid recuperation, particularly in the industrial states north of the Mason-Dixon line.

In one way the war had contributed to further industrialization. The drain of man-power into war service left industry understaffed. And the unprecedented demand for certain types of products necessary to equip and feed the army and navy emphasized the need to mechanize production. Men of wealth turned their attention and resources to meet this situation and profited thereby. For example, Colonel Gordon McKay financed a new type of shoe-stitching machine. To encourage its use he introduced the royalty-leasing system to shoemakers. Introduction of this machine process in the shoe industry helped greatly in supplying the Union armed forces with footwear. Similar growth of mechanization occurred in cotton textiles, pig iron production, and farm implement manufacture. Goods produced in large factories owned by companies managed by corporate boards were becoming more and more common. While government efforts were turned to remedy weakness in the banking system revealed by the war, private enterprise attacked the problem of transportation. Deficiencies in transport were revealed during the war and were accentuated by the growing needs of Western settlers who were pouring into the lands beyond the Mississippi. The public was land-value conscious, and governmental land policy whetted the appetites of a wealth-gathering people.[14] Consequently it was not difficult to arouse public interest and support in laying a wide-flung railway network. The public attitude was encouraged by a capitalist group which had made large profits from the Civil War. The accumulations of war days sought new channels of investment, so with characteristic energy American promoters and capitalists took advantage of the favorable circumstances.[15]

The era after the Civil War witnessed a great exploitation of natural resources. Up to about 1870 the concentration of anthracite in northeastern Pennsylvania and the heavy transportation costs confined industrial development largely to the Northeastern section of the country. But industry learned to use cheaper bituminous coal not only to produce steam power for industry and transportation, but also for the gas it yielded for lighting and heating purposes. With soft coal abundantly available in the Appalachian plateau which stretches from Alabama to Lake Erie, and with heavy deposits in the Mid-Western states, industry began to spread out.

In 1859, Colonel Drake discovered oil in Pennsylvania. When the properties of this product proved it a good illuminant there occurred a mad rush of prospectors to Western Pennsylvania. A great new industry was born, and great fortunes awaited the more careful exploiters. At first, attention was directed to the production of kerosene from petroleum. Later this product was to be relegated to the background by gasoline, fuel oil, and various grades of lubricants when the internal combustion motor became important.

The Lake Superior iron resources, discovered by government surveyors in 1844, were rapidly developed. Roadbeds and trackage were laid inland from the Great Lake ports, and high-grade ore poured from this great region which harbored one of the richest iron ore beds known to man.

Coal, oil, and iron, basic to industrialization, were made available to a population eager to develop and use them. In addition, further technological developments appeared.

Henry Bessemer, an Englishman, developed the Bessemer (acid) process of steelmaking. Later improvements by the Thomas-Gilchrist (basic) process allowed phosphorous or sulphur-bearing iron ore to be used. These methods were followed shortly by the Siemens-Martin

[14] This land policy was exhibited by a series of acts such as the Homestead Act of 1862, the Mineral Land Act of 1872, and the Timber and Stone Act of 1878, which aimed to transfer natural resources from public to private hands at low prices.
[15] William Z. Ripley, *Railroads: Finance and Organization* (New York, Longmans, Green and Co., 1915), pp. 370–384; Stuart Daggett, *Railroad Reorganization* (Cambridge, Mass., Harvard University Press, 1908), Chap. 10; E. G. Campbell, *The Reorganization of the American Railroad System, 1893–1900* (New York, Columbia University Press, 1938).

open-hearth process, so named from its German and French inventors. These changes were timely for transport and for industry.

In other fields technical progress was no less startling and significant. Production of refrigerator cars revolutionized the meat-packing industry. Tool machines in great variety were improved. The grinding machine, the emery wheel, and other important machines which worked with automatic precision combined to push forward with great speed the important machine tool industry. A telegraph line spanned the continent east and west in 1861, and Cyrus Field laid the first Atlantic cable in 1866. Alexander Graham Bell's telephone became of practical importance and its use spread rapidly and widely after a brief period of public skepticism. Meanwhile men like Edison and Westinghouse, in experiments with electricity, laid the foundation of a great electric industry.

Associated with this period were men whose names have gathered fame or notoriety for one reason or another. In railroading, Jay Cooke, Jay Gould, Cornelius Vanderbilt, Edgar Thomson, E. H. Harriman, James J. Hill, W. B. Ogden, Henry Villard, and Leland Stanford are best known. Industry had John D. and William Rockefeller, Andrew Carnegie, Henry Frick, H. O. Havemeyer, Cyrus McCormick, William Deering, Herman and Philip Armour, Gustavus Swift, Gordon McKay, E. I. du Pont de Nemours, and John W. Mackay. In merchandising, the leaders were John Wanamaker, A. T. Stewart, and Marshall Field. In banking, J. P. Morgan, Jay Cooke, George Fisher Baker, and James Stillman were most prominent. And the great speculators, men of the type of Daniel Drew, Benjamin P. Hutchinson ("Old Hutch"), Jacob Little, Israel Freyer, Daniel Reid, Joseph Leiter, and John W. ("Betcha-Million") Gates made splendid news copy from time to time with their daring market activities and their personal idiosyncrasies.[16]

Business Organization

The organization of business did not escape unchanged. Marketing methods in particular were re-shaped. John Wanamaker and A. T. Stewart emphasized customer service and the single price as they expanded the department-store method of merchandising.[17] In 1872 Montgomery Ward and Company opened a mail-order house in Chicago to meet the needs of the farming community, and its trade grew rapidly.[18] The chain-store movement had appeared in 1858 with the establishment of the Great Atlantic and Pacific Tea Company, and twenty years later

---

[16] Cf. Miriam Beard, A History of the Business Man (New York, The Macmillan Company, 1938), pp. 628–632.

[17] Cf. Gras and Larson, op. cit., pp. 479 ff.

[18] Allan Nevins, The Emergence of Modern America (New York, The Macmillan Company, 1927), p. 172.

it grew in importance when F. W. Woolworth started his "Five and Ten" chain. The James Butler grocery chain appeared in 1882 and S. S. Kresge's variety chain followed it in 1885.[19] Meanwhile, marketing experiments in other lines were attempted, in order to circumvent the wholesale organizations in the channels of trade. Thus, one shoe manufacturing firm, W. L. Douglas and Company, in 1876 established a chain of retail shoe stores, thereby cutting out entirely the wholesalers of its products.[20]

In marketing, many producers began to increase the emphasis placed on attempts to differentiate their products from those of competitors. Sellers had always attempted to attract custom by the offer of special services to the buyer. A friendly personal service, favorable credit terms, or other inducements had frequently established a producer and the goods he sold in a distinctive position in a market. As modern advertising developed, increasing efforts were directed to this end. Greater attention has been given to packaging and to the offer of varying qualities of the product and supplementary services attached to it. In the sale of many goods, such as clothing, frequent changes in public taste have been fostered and individual companies have been able to set off their product as distinct from that of other companies by maintaining a style leadership. Frequently these developments have brought valuable information to buyers and have broadened the markets for many products so as to allow production to be organized on a larger and more efficient scale. Unfortunately, however, they have brought heavy costs on many industries as expenditures are made for advertising or style changes that bring little or no benefit to the buyer.

While marketing was being revolutionized after the turn of the century, products continued to be improved, and costs and prices were lowered in numerous instances as factory processes and methods supplanted the handicrafts. In the great changes that have occurred there has been not so much a disappearance of old industries as a transformation through improved product and increased productive capacity. What has proved even more spectacular, however, has been the great increase in new industries based either on the technical development of old industries or on completely new inventions and discoveries. Thus, the high-speed gasoline motor invented by Gottfried Daimler in the eighties had its American adaptations and development in the twentieth century. It became first the basis of a great new automobile industry and later the foundation of a lusty young aviation industry, following the initial success of the Wright brothers' flying machine at Kittyhawk, N. C., in 1904. The telephone, another nineteenth-century invention, has become

---

[19] *Encyclopaedia Britannica* (14th edition), Vol. V, p. 190.
[20] N. S. B. Gras, *Business and Capitalism* (New York, F. S. Crofts & Co., 1939), p. 199.

a widely used and highly developed present-day mechanical marvel. It has taken its place beside the earlier telegraph. Similarly, radio communication has appeared, bringing with it an entirely new industry which tends to complement rather than displace other forms of communication. Likewise the chemical industry has made great advances in the manufacture of a large variety of synthetic products. Nor should we lose sight of the great advances made in business machines, without which business organizations of the present day would be subject to almost insuperable difficulties in handling payrolls, correspondence, and business records. Perhaps the most startling innovation of all time is the development of atomic energy under the stern stress of World War II. Although we have witnessed the devastating military results of this new force, its full impact on our social, political, and economic institutions is yet to be realized.

These developments, in which economic individualism has played no small part, have had varied effects on our economy. On the one hand, they have frequently provided the opening of new opportunities for the individual. On the other hand, they have forced him to take advantage of the new opportunities by making the older ones relatively less attractive. Thus, the shift in demand from carriages to automobiles forced carriage-makers to abandon their industry largely and turn to automobile production or to other things. Moreover, the introduction of the new product created other new demands. For example, the popularity of the automobile brought demands for better roads, for convenient wayside gas stations, restaurants, and sleeping accommodations. And established industries, like the rubber goods industry, found their markets enlarged with the demand for automobile equipment and accessories.

As these changes have taken place, men have been quick to provide new organizational methods to handle the problems of mechanical development and large-scale operations. Specialization has become more minute, and group effort has changed the activities of individuals. In numerous instances technical and commercial researches are no longer undertaken by individuals but by groups of individuals, any one of whom is perhaps more amply supplied with the tools for research and scientific investigation than he could be by his own efforts. In making these things possible the business corporation, including the holding company, has served well, being highly proficient as a mechanism for raising capital funds upon which such group activities are dependent.

THE PLANNING MACHINERY OF CAPITALISM

In the historical record it is possible not only to realize something of the achievements of the American system, but also to discern the tasks that face any system of control. Firstly, it must determine how the productive resources of the country are to be allocated to the various producers. Secondly, it must provide some means to force the individual plants or producing units to operate efficiently. Thirdly, the size of business organizations resulting from a combination of individual plants must be set at an economic size. Fourthly, the resources spent on planning must be held to a minimum in order that production may be as great as possible.

The Allocation of Resources

While capitalism utilizes the individual as the instrument for economic planning, it uses the guiding force of costs and prices to direct production. If producers are competing for profits, and entrance into the various fields of production is open, costs of production would allocate natural resources, labor, and capital as directed by the wishes of buyers who make their desires known through price offers.

If the products of a number of producers are homogeneous in the sense that they appear to be the same to buyers, it is possible to think in terms of an industry in which a considerable number of independent companies of similar size and efficiency are producing to satisfy the demand for a commodity. If these conditions were present the commodity would sell at a price which covers the unit cost of the individual firms when they are operating at their point of lowest cost. Any price above this figure would bring in added firms, and any lower price would make impossible the continued existence of the producing companies. If differences in efficiency exist between firms, the commodity must sell for a price sufficient to cover the costs of those least efficient firms that are just needed to produce the quantities taken by purchasers. None of these marginal firms could continue over a long period of time to take less than cost. If losses were suffered, investment would be forced to withdraw from the field until lower-cost firms became marginal and the reduced output could sell at prices that covered costs. Superior or intra-marginal firms would accept this same price and enjoy certain profits from their superiority. Besides, the products of the several producers are not distinctive, so the demand for the product of any one producer is perfectly elastic—that is, if any firm asked a price above this cost-determined price it would make no sales. As a result of the competitive situation, costs set a price that serves as both a minimum and a maximum.

The cost which any one producer incurs in the production of a commodity would be a function of the amount of product he could get out of the labor, capital, and natural resources he would use and of the prices he would pay for these factors of production. Furthermore, their prices would be determined by what all producers would pay for them. Under perfect competitive conditions, producers would pay a price equal to whatever the factors of production were worth to marginal producers in their respective industries. It appears that the value of the factors to one industry would be the cost which another industry must pay to get the use of these or similar factors. So, if any one industry should grow to such a size that its last increase in the used factors of production turned out a commodity which could sell exactly at cost, then this industry would be of "ideal" size. The resources producing the marginal supply of the commodity in question have a value in this particular field just equal to what they would have in other fields. In such a case, resources would have been allocated among all the various industries in the most efficient way possible.

It is only in the abstract that we can describe this process as working with thoroughness and precision. But this does not mean that it has not directed American enterprise. The whole economic history of the United States reveals that one field after another has been exploited as it showed profitable prospects. It is not by chance that railroads were extended when the expansion of industry rendered existing roads inadequate. Neither, in various periods, were resources poured into the heavy industries by chance. When the prices that could be obtained for the products of the heavy industries yielded or promised to yield an income sufficient to pay the cost of attracting resources from other fields, their expansion occurred.

Plant Efficiency

Prices and costs also drive the individual to work for the second objective of production control, the efficient operation of individual plants. A number of plant factors affect costs and thereby are brought in under the control of the competitive planning device. If location is important to the efficiency of a plant, its influence on costs will force an enterpriser to develop the best available sites or suffer severely from the competition of lower-cost producers. Similarly, the pressure to reduce costs would drive each producer to improve his methods of management and his technical processes. Improvements, resulting in lower prices, would be rewarded with increased sales and larger profits. Any enterprise which failed to keep step would lose profits and possibly would be forced out of the industry. Furthermore, since the purchasing power of the consumer is limited, competition brings pressure on industry as a whole to improve its technical methods. The elasticity of demand for shoes may be such that lower prices would persuade the consumer to spend a larger portion of his income on shoes and a smaller part on gasoline, or hats, or excursions on the railroad.

The mere adoption of improved techniques will not improve the efficiency of plants unless plant size is properly adjusted. Where technical methods are simple a small plant will allow production to be carried on efficiently, but in many industries elaborate specialization calls for large capital investments. For example, in 1905 only a number of hand tools and a few machines were required in the best automobile plants. Today, however, the specialized production of various parts of the car and the intricate assembly system require a large investment in plant and equipment. In every industry there is a certain size demanded by technical methods. Firms below this *optimum size* cannot take full advantage of large-scale methods and will suffer in competition with larger producers. For most industries there is probably a fairly wide range over which size may vary without adverse effects on costs. And as plants are built beyond this scale they will reach a point where added capital does not yield a corresponding increase in producing capacity. In this case the largest firms would suffer in competition with the smaller ones.

When proper amounts of capital are assembled, costs may then be influenced by the amount of labor and materials combined with that capital. At any one time the capital may be considered a fixed factor, and a certain proportion of these variable factors must be combined with it to bring operations to the point of maximum efficiency. If production were started with part of the plant unused, costs would be high for two reasons. Firstly, the total of fixed costs would have to be spread over a small output. The fixed cost borne by each unit of the product (average fixed cost) would be high. In other words, the capital would not be utilized fully. Secondly, the cost in labor and materials to produce each unit of the product would be relatively high. If more variable factors were added, output would increase more than proportionately, and the cost for variable factors borne by each unit of the product (average variable cost) would be reduced.

These two costs will not continue indefinitely to respond so favorably to increases in the scale of operations. In fact, they soon start to move in opposite directions. As soon as the point of diminishing returns is reached, the average variable cost starts to rise. At this point the output per laborer is greatest. Then, as more men are employed, the output increases, but not proportionately. For example, the expenditure for labor may be increased 10 per cent and the output 8 per cent. The same phenomenon would be true for materials, and the average variable cost would increase as soon as operations were pushed into the stage of diminishing returns. The average fixed cost reacts more favorably. The total fixed cost stays the same and is spread over the larger output, so the amount laid on each unit of the product continues to decline. This would go on until further attempts to increase the output would so crowd the plant with variable factors that the total product would actually decline.

At any one scale of output the total cost of each unit of product (average cost) is obtained by adding the average variable cost and the average fixed cost. It would appear, then, that as the scale of operations grows past the point of diminishing returns this average cost will be pulled downward by the average fixed cost and upward by the average variable cost. The pleasing influence of the former diminishes and the influence of the latter grows until some point or range of operation is reached where the average cost is at its lowest point. Here the plant is at its *optimum scale,* where it has combined the fixed and variable factors in ideal proportions.[21]

If all the firms in a field of industry were on an equal footing, they would be forced to operate at their optimum scale, and their average cost would be the same. Subtle inequalities between firms do appear, and give rise to the concept of marginal and intra-marginal companies. The latter may safely and economically push their production past the least cost point. A simple illustration might show a superior firm operating at its optimum scale with an output of one hundred units and an average cost of one dollar, while the article sold at one dollar and ten cents. It is making an abnormal profit of ten cents on each of one hundred units. But it can do even better. The added cost directly attributable to the production of one more unit (marginal cost) would be one dollar and three cents. This unit would be produced because there is a profit of seven cents to be made on it. Output could be increased by the use of more labor and materials until the marginal cost equalled the selling price. Although its operations are profitable, the company would not proceed beyond this point. To do so would entail producing some units that actually cost more than their selling price. The competition of marginal and intra-marginal firms would prevent it from obtaining any better price. Concern for its profits would stop its growth at the point where marginal cost was equal to the selling price. Here its superiority over marginal firms has forced it past the ideal proportioning of fixed and variable factors. But as long as the superiority exists, it achieves the most efficient use of the factors at this point. The marginal amounts of labor and materials yield a value equal to their cost.

Combination Economies

The size of business organizations also tends to be shaped by costs under competitive conditions. Various economies may be realized when

---

[21] In time the superior firm would increase its fixed plant so that it would be operating at its optimum scale. If some relatively scarce factor prevented the increase, its value would be written up by an amount equalling the capitalized value of the excess profits, and the least cost point would be shifted.

plants are combined under one business. Costly management may be employed and its expense borne by a large concern. Plants may be located at strategic points near to varied sources of raw materials or near various market centers. Integration of various steps in production may be achieved by vertical combinations that result in a coördination not possible between separate companies. And horizontal combination of plants in the same stage of production may bring economies through purchasing raw materials or marketing finished goods in large volume; through support of research by the large combination; through plant specialization that may adjust production in certain plants to particular local market conditions or may allow steady operation of most of the plants while a few bear the cost of fluctuating demand; through a specialization of plants that allows a saving of freight as plants are decentralized through major market areas. Where gains from these sources are realizable, the competitive pressure to reduce costs tends to bring about an efficient combination of plants.

Product Differentiation

In this competitive process buyers are pictured as turning to a group of sellers for satisfaction of their demand for some product. In many industries, however, producers have not been content to accept the lack of distinction between their goods and those of competitors. They have tried to make the buyer view their products as distinctive and not merely as part of the output of a whole industry. Patents, copyrights, advertising, style changes, and many other devices have been used in pursuit of this objective. If the individual seller is successful in persuading a significant number of buyers to think not merely of coffee when they want their breakfast drink, but to think of "Malkins' Best," he has made an important competitive move against other producers in the same field. He can now raise the price of his product above the levels of other coffees without losing all his sales to competitors—that is, the demand for his product is no longer perfectly elastic. In this case, any analysis of the economic planning effected by the competitive system must center attention on the individual firm and not on the industry. In effect, each company producing a differentiated product becomes a more or less distinct "industry."

Where products are homogeneous the individual company is forced to set its price at the going price level, which is determined by demand and supply conditions beyond its control; and if it wishes to make as large profits as possible, it is forced to adjust its production to the current price level. But when the seller is able to persuade buyers that his product is a distinctive one, he is able to set his price with some independence. In other words, he can now raise his price above the current level for outwardly similar products and suffer only a limited loss in sales. This inelasticity of demand will probably vary at different price levels. Sales may fall off very slightly for small increases in prices and then may decline materially for further increases.

For the demand condition that exists at any one time the seller will fix his price so as to maximize his profits. As he restricts output below the competitive amount, where his costs are equal to the current price, he finds that he can demand higher prices without an equal increase in unit costs. He cannot restrict too far, or he will find that the unit cost of production is rising too rapidly, or that a sizable profit per unit of product is being made but sales are curtailed so much that the total profit is diminished. He will cut his production only to the point where his total profit is greatest. The price, of course, will be above the competitive level and production will be restricted below the "ideal." However, if competitors are making vigorous efforts to differentiate their own products, the price increase and the consequent injurious restriction of production will tend to be small. A small number of buyers may view the product as unique, and the inelasticity of their demand may be high, but sales sufficient to allow an efficient scale of operations will have to be made to a mass of buyers who have a very limited belief in the distinctiveness of the product.

Over a period of time the producer may change the expenditures he makes on the various forms of non-price competition. He may alter the intrinsic qualities of the product, the packaging or other elements in its appearance, the supplementary services he offers, the distinctive styles he tries to develop, the amount of sales promotion and advertising. For the sake of simplicity, it may be assumed that he views the price he charges as fixed. If so, these competitive efforts will change both the demand for his product and the cost of it. His objective then will be to adjust these selling expenditures so that his total profits will be as large as possible. They will be greatest when any additions to sales expenditures will just increase his receipts by an equal amount.

In actuality, many producers who are not selling at conventional prices will be adjusting their prices, the character of their commodity, and their expenditures for advertising and so forth, at one and the same time. The adjustment becomes more complicated, but the results are essentially the same. Output will be restricted below the ideal amount expected under conditions of price competition, and resources that could be used in producing goods and services will be expended on the non-price competitive effort. There are, however, powerful competitive forces residing in these varied efforts. There is every reason to believe that the pressure of selling costs will exert pressure on producers to minimize their production costs. The one inescapable harm lies in the restriction of sales which product differentiation permits.

Conclusion

Competition requires a great deal of the individuals who wish to use it as a planning device. Intelligence and a considerable concern for their economic affairs are demanded of consumers. Without these qualities the system lacks any satisfactory direction. With them, production is guided into the channels desired by consumers with purchasing power, and the distortion that may be developed by non-price competition will not be of great importance. On the production side, enterprises must possess a knowledge of present and future economic opportunities, and resources must be transferable from one employment to another as opportunities are revealed. In spite of imperfect conditions, competition has effected a truly remarkable development of American industry. The imperfections, however, have made it yield far less satisfactory results than might have been realized.

2

The Faults of American Economic Individualism

While economic individualism achieved great results, it fell far short of perfection in organizing American production. Serious faults appeared even in the period before the Civil War, when the economic field possessed characteristics very favorable to the operation of the competitive system. Business units were relatively small and techniques relatively simple; entry into various fields of enterprise was open and competition was protected. Market weaknesses arising mainly out of poor transport allowed small local monopolies to exist in many industries and many localities. Imperfect knowledge regarding production methods and markets was responsible for waste that reached staggering proportions in recurring business depressions. By 1860 a half-dozen serious business collapses had occurred. One of the most severe, that of 1857, was preceded by a serious over-expansion of railroad-building and marked speculative growth in the exploitation of natural resources, and was made worse by banking excesses. Five thousand business failures and the unemployment of labor and capital were evidence of an unfortunate waste.[1]

Agriculture also suffered, partly from the faulty operation of economic individualism and partly from mistaken public policies. Individualism led too often to the appropriation of land for the purpose of speculation instead of production. As late as 1890, homesteaders had directly acquired less than three and one half per cent of the land west of the Mississippi. Most of it fell first into the hands of railroads and speculative land syndicates. It was sold to native and immigrant settlers at prices which, though relatively cheap, helped to saddle unnecessarily heavy debts on a large section of the population.

The tariff added to the farmer's troubles by increasing the cost of materials he bought and injuring the foreign market for his products. Frequent gluts in the produce markets, the high cost of credit arising from an unsatisfactory banking system, exorbitant and discriminatory

[1] Ernest L. Bogart, *Economic History of the American People* (New York, Longmans, Green and Co., 1930), p. 383.

railroad rates, and the abuses perpetrated by produce middlemen and the "livestock ring" in Chicago made the competitive system far from satisfactory for the farmer.

After the Civil War, improvements in communication and transport and in banking made possible the removal of some of the faults of the earlier period. But as markets widened, competition reached a peak of activity, only to develop new faults. In industry, trade, and finance, the emphasis was on speed and quick action. The tactics of land-grabbing, so much a part of the westward expansion, were carried over into business activity. "Beat the other fellow to it" was the slogan in business. So few checks existed to control the excesses of business that a number of state governments were corrupted by business interests. Competition deteriorated in quality as it grew in intensity. Deception and unfair tactics in both old and new forms were common. They served both to increase brute economic strength and to bolster the economically weak. Whether or not they read Darwin and Herbert Spencer, business men in general subscribed to the philosophy of the survival of the fittest. And the fittest were too frequently those with the most economic power and the least conscience.

Certain economic phenomena contributed to this survival philosophy and to the intensified economic rivalry. War and post-war inflationary conditions were not long sustained, and 1873 brought a panic which affected every operation of finance and commerce. The panic proved, however, to be merely the beginning of a quarter-century of seething economic and social ferment of wide-spread significance. Railroad construction had proceeded too rapidly,[2] and heavy industries had pushed into a stage of over-investment along with the railroads. Aided by the corporation, business leaders had gone too far in their search for the alleged economies of larger-scale production. When prices fell like plummets in 1873 there arose a great cry for inflation. But the Grant administration succeeded in staving off this demand, and an outgoing Republican Congress in 1875 passed an act to resume gold specie payments. Fortunately, by the time specie payments were actually resumed in 1879, foreign trade had improved markedly. The decline in prices at home, occasioned by the resumption of specie payments, and the European crop shortages of 1879 and 1880 boomed American exports and aided in the retention of gold and its importation from abroad. In spite of this, the downward trend of prices continued until well into the 1890's. Declining prices and the pressure of overhead costs served to sharpen competition to such an extent that even powerful individuals sought eco-

---

[2] Railway mileage owned and operated in 1860 was 30,626 miles; in 1870, 52,922 miles; in 1880, 93,262 miles; and in 1889, 161,276 miles. *Statistical Abstract of the United States* (Washington, D. C., U. S. Government Printing Office, 1916), p. 272.

nomic safety in group action. And they found in combination a very comfortable haven.

The Growth of Coöperation

Group action revealed itself in various ways. In its most elementary form it appeared first as the "gentlemen's agreement" to forego or limit competition. But too many business men of that era were lacking in the required gentility. They threw aside the gentleman's mask whenever a good opportunity appeared and took advantage of other gentlemen. Groups of supposed competitors then tried written agreements to restrict competition. These pools, however, broke down also. The courts held that the agreement was not a legal contract and could be broken with impunity. When prices broke in 1873 and continued downward, the strain on these agreements became too great. It became obvious that stronger bonds must be forged. The Rockefeller oil group found an answer in the trustee device. By inducing a sufficient number of share-holders in competing organizations to lodge their shares in the hands of a small group of trustees and accept in exchange trust certificates, a small set of leaders gained complete control of an industry. This device served nicely until it was subjected to legal attack by several states on the ground that it exercised a power not granted to corporations in their charters.[3] By the time this attack was made, however, revenue-hungry states, competing for business in corporation charters, made it possible for corporations to be formed for the sole purpose of holding shares of stock in other corporations. A wide opening was made for the gathering of hitherto competing companies under one consolidation.

As the 1890's drew to a close, there were present a number of conditions which, by favoring economic concentration, led to attacks on competition. Widening markets and continued technological progress encouraged consolidation into larger business units. The corporation lent itself to relatively easy acquisition of the large capital sums needed. Large investments in fixed plant, machines, and other expensive equipment reduced the number of competing firms, while they eventually made it more difficult for new firms to enter a field. In addition, overhead costs were made much heavier and threatened to generate extreme and unruly competition. Coöperation seemed the wiser course. Corporate promoters and powerful financiers foresaw the possibilities and were ready and willing to take advantage of their opportunities. The holding company device was available to make consolidation comparatively simple and effective. Public interest was divided. On the one hand, the laborer, the farmer, and the small investor wished to benefit from the

---

[3] Some of the better-known trustee devices in operation in this period, in addition to the Standard Oil Trust, were the Whiskey Trust and the Sugar Trust.

alleged economies of larger-scale production through lower prices and through increased dividends from corporate successes. On the other hand, they feared the consequences of concentrated economic power.

The Tariff and Patent Laws

Public policies in this period were contradictory. This was exemplified by the attempts to apply the Sherman Act to restore competition while, at the same time, Congress passed the Dingley Tariff of 1897 to insulate domestic markets against foreign competition.

Unfortunately the patent law was also injuring competition. The patent privilege confers a monopoly, but only on a specific invention. It was based on fundamental ideas of competition: that individual initiative and enterprise should be encouraged through the offer of patent rewards for significant improvements in industrial techniques.[4] It was intended to stimulate competition by encouraging rival inventions.[5]

As the United States developed industrially, a process in which inventions played a significant part, patent privileges began to be used as a method or screen to accomplish things hardly consistent with the competitive system. One investigator has labelled the patent as the greatest single monopolistic device of recent decades.[6] Many others in less extreme statements have indicated generally similar attitudes.[7]

The pool, a typical form of combination in the decades immediately after the Civil War, was employed by patent owners, as well as others, in attempting to eliminate competition. Through the patent pool, former competitors participated in the patent privileges according to some arrangements acceptable to all the participants.

Defects of the pooling arrangements led competitors often to seek outright ownership of all patent rights relating to a particular industry. This was accomplished in various ways. One method allowed a corporation to acquire plants, patents, and other properties of its competitors through purchase. Another method was to buy only the patent rights of individuals and companies. Some companies, as the Eastman Kodak, combined the two methods, buying all the properties of some companies and only the patents of others.

Unfair competition—a phrase peculiarly difficult to define satisfactorily —has appeared in various forms while linked to the legitimate patent monopoly. It has taken the form of forcing the rental or purchase of the

---

[4] Floyd L. Vaughan, *Economics of Our Patent System* (New York, The Macmillan Company, 1925), pp. 23–27.

[5] Oldfield Committee on Patents, H. R. 1161, 62nd Congress, 2nd Session, p. 2.

[6] Mortimer Feuer, "The Patent Monopoly and the Antitrust Laws," *Columbia Law Review*, Vol. XXXVIII, No. 7 (November, 1938), p. 1146.

[7] E.g., Vaughan, *op. cit.*, p. 34; Senator O'Mahoney of the Temporary National Economic Committee, *The New York Times*, July 17, 1939.

patentee's *unpatented* articles as a requirement of purchase or lease of patented articles. In other instances purchasers of patented articles have been required to submit to pricing policies dictated by the patentee. In addition, competitors of patent-holders have been threatened with infringement suits or have been injured in other ways.

The Combination Movement

A wave of combination swept over the country between 1897 and 1904. Railroaders Hill and Harriman in the West and the leaders of the New York Central and the Pennsylvania Railroads in the East purchased control of many of the lesser independent railway lines. But railroad combinations were dwarfed by the horizontal and vertical combinations that appeared in the industrial field. Between 1899 and 1901 two hundred industrial combinations, with a total capitalization of ten billion dollars, were formed. Among the giants was that combination of combinations, the United States Steel Corporation, with a capitalization in excess of $1,400,000,000. Others of great size were the Standard Oil Company of New Jersey, Consolidated Tobacco, International Harvester, American Can, American Locomotive, National Packing, International Mercantile Marine, and the United Shoe Machinery Company. In some instances, combination was accomplished through the medium of the pure holding company through exchange of controlling securities. In others, it resulted from outright fusion of companies through merger, amalgamation, or purchase of assets.[8]

In 1904 a Supreme Court decision adverse to the Northern Securities Company, a railroad holding company alleged to be violating the Sherman Act, brought an end to a combination movement which had about exhausted itself.

From 1904 to 1920, few industrial consolidations of real importance took place. Exceptions should be made for General Motors, established in 1908, and for such consolidations as Paramount-Famous-Lasky (1916), Union Carbide and Carbon (1917), and Sinclair Consolidated Oil (1919). Investment bankers had carefully culled the industrial field and then had turned their attention to merchandising securities in the public utility field. Moreover, Theodore Roosevelt and his successors, Taft and

[8] By merger is meant a transfer of assets from one or more corporations to another already in existence. The transferring corporations lose their identity and disappear. By amalgamation is meant the creation of a *new* corporation. It acquires the assets of the corporations amalgamating with it. The old corporations are then dissolved. Where outright purchase of assets is involved, the selling corporations dispose of their assets to a corporation directly. The selling corporations may then remain mere shells, or they may be dissolved later according to statutory provisions. *Cf.* J. C. Bonbright and G. C. Means, *The Holding Company* (New York, McGraw-Hill Book Company, 1932), pp. 27–28.

Wilson, were applying the Sherman Act to industrial combinations. In 1911, the apparent governmental success in the Standard Oil and Tobacco cases[9] gave a setback to corporate combination. And in 1914 another apparent check on corporate combination appeared in the form of Section 7 of the Clayton Act.[10] This section made it illegal for one corporation to acquire the stock of another corporation similarly engaged, where the effect of the acquisition would be to lessen competition substantially between the two companies or create a monopoly in interstate commerce. Later developments proved that the section served merely to increase the purchase of the physical plants of competitors in place of the proscribed stock purchases.[11]

As these checks appeared, corporations turned to other forms of combination, namely: (1) the community of interest, a loose understanding based solely on common interests, and (2) the trade association. The latter, the more important of the two, may be defined as a non-profit organization formed for mutual advantage by independent competitors who produce or distribute similar goods and services.

The trade association had its American origin as early as 1854. Up to 1890, however, these associations developed in a sporadic and desultory manner. After 1890 they moved ahead with greater rapidity and attained the dignity of business institutions.[12] Their activities were widened in scope. They supported permanent offices and full-time officials. There was a tendency to deëmphasize coercive policies. They embraced eagerly the "new competition" which largely consisted of price controls by so-called open-price associations.[13]

The factors contributing to the growth of the association movement are varied. On occasion since 1890, the main driving force has been the desire to formulate and put into practice uniform policies concerning labor relations. On other occasions, over-stimulated competition has forced competitors to seek relief through association. Sometimes unruly competition has been sufficient excuse for coöperation to attain monopoly profits. At times the Federal Government has fostered their creation and development directly. This was the case in the First World War. Military success depended on economic success, which in turn meant that the government must deal with agencies representing whole

---

[9] Standard Oil Company v. U. S., 221 U. S. 1 (1911); U. S. v. American Tobacco Company, 221 U. S. 106 (1911).

[10] Act of October 15, 1914, 38 Stat. 730.

[11] Cf. Bonbright and Means, op. cit., p. 74.

[12] National Industrial Conference Board, Trade Associations: Their Economic Significance and Legal Status (New York, National Industrial Conference Board, Inc., 1925), p. 12.

[13] A. J. Eddy's book, The New Competition (New York, D. Appleton Company, 1912), was greatly responsible for the popularity of the "new competition."

industries rather than single units of industry.[14] Federal legislation has favored trade association growth. This has been true in no small measure in the case of the Webb-Pomerene Act of 1918, which permitted export associations to organize and operate exempted from anti-trust laws, providing they did not injure domestic competition. In spite of this provision, they have not been sufficiently well supervised to prevent injury to domestic competition. To a still greater degree the National Industrial Recovery Act of 1933 fostered associations in the formulation of codes of fair competition. Various Federal agencies also have pushed them. As Secretary of Commerce, Herbert Hoover gave them his official blessing and aid in the early 1920's. The Federal Trade Commission, through its conferences with industries, has encouraged them. And in addition to all these stimuli which have been present at one time or another, there has been the genuine urge to attain lower costs for public benefit through coöperative effort in research, marketing, and the like.

The forces which have restrained trade association development during this period have been less numerous and less potent. Anti-trust laws have struck at them, but the objects of the attacks have been particular activities, not the form of organization. Economic depression has taken its toll occasionally as shrinking markets and mounting costs have shattered morale. At times the popularity of associations has waned when some of them have exhibited short-sighted economic greed, thereby incurring public ill-will.

On balance, however, the stimuli for association development have proved stronger than the deterrents. Trade associations exist by the thousand at the present time. They stand along with corporate combinations as major organizational elements in the modern pattern of the American economy.

Renewed Combination

For several reasons industrial corporate combination moved forward again in the 1920's. Firstly, the Supreme Court asserted in the United States Steel case that the mere size of a corporation was in itself no violation of the Sherman Act.[15] Secondly, a restoration of the Republican party to national political power brought a milder use of the anti-trust laws. Thirdly, economic rejuvenation after the immediate post-war depression of 1920–1921 encouraged the movement. Investors were receptive and investment bankers were eager to respond to their clients' moods.

Between 1921 and 1928, in manufacturing and mining industries

---

[14] Cf. J. H. Foth, *Trade Associations: Their Services to Industry* (New York, The Ronald Press Company, 1930), pp. 21–22.

[15] U. S. *v.* United States Steel Corporation, 251 U. S. 417 (1920).

alone, nearly 4,800 concerns disappeared through merger or direct acquisition. Recorded mergers numbered approximately one thousand in this short span of years.[16] Some of the outstanding corporate combinations were the Allied Chemical and Dye Company, Drug, Inc., Texas Corporation, National Dairy Products Corporation, Pullman, Inc., Crown Zellerback Corporation, American Radiator and Standard Sanitary Corporation, and the Gulf Oil Corporation. These were all huge combinations with depreciated gross assets (as of January 1, 1929) ranging between one hundred million and four hundred and sixty million dollars.[17]

In the 1930's there was a decline in the movement. The stresses and strains of economic recession and stagnation did not offer much encouragement to investment bankers or their prospective clients. Corporation finance in this dull period was confined largely to refunding and reorganization—to sloughing off obligations rather than acquiring them.

Following World War II, however, another great surge of corporate growth and concentration has appeared. Old giants have added to their industrial and financial flesh, and new giants have been born. For example, war-built, government-financed plant has been added to the sinews of the United States Steel Corporation, Bethlehem Steel, and the Republic Steel Corporation. Likewise, International Harvester acquired several war-surplus plants to increase its capacity to produce agricultural machinery. In the electrical machinery field, the two leading corporations, General Electric and Westinghouse, have snapped up most of the war-surplus plants. Only in aluminum has the pattern of war-surplus-plant disposal varied. Here a new corporation—Kaiser-controlled Permanente Metals Corporation—has entered. And Reynolds Metals has improved its position relative to the Aluminum Company of America.[18] The merger movement, underway since 1940, has accounted for the disappearance of more than 2,450 formerly independent manufacturing and mining companies with total assets amounting to over five billion dollars.[19]

This post-war merger movement has extended into practically all phases of manufacturing and mining. It has been especially prevalent in such industries as food and beverages, textiles and apparel, chemicals (including drugs), non-electrical machinery, petroleum, and transportation equipment. In form it has been predominantly horizontal with a

[16] These figures are derived from the Hoover Committee Report, *Recent Economic Changes* (New York, McGraw-Hill Book Company, 1929), Vol. I, Table 12, p. 186. See pp. 179–188 of this volume for an elaboration of the data.
[17] See Bonbright and Means, *op. cit.*, Table 2, pp. 77–78.
[18] *Cf.* Harrison F. Houghton, *The Progress of Concentration in Industry*, Papers and Proceedings of the American Economic Association, American Economic Review, Vol. XXXVIII, No. 2, (May, 1948), pp. 88–89.
[19] Federal Trade Commission, *The Merger Movement; a Summary Report* (Washington, D. C., U. S. Government Printing Office, 1948), p. 1.

fair amount of vertical and conglomerative (non-related products) integration.

Two outstanding developments are to be noted in this movement. In the first place, large corporations have been purchasing small companies. Fully 93 per cent of the firms acquired since 1940 had assets of less than five million dollars each. And nearly 30 per cent of the companies merged since 1940 have been absorbed by corporations with assets in excess of fifty million dollars. In the second place, inroads have been made into the traditionally "small business" industries, such as the textile and apparel field and the food and beverage field.[20]

Once again the international military struggle for political and economic power has intensified the growth and relative importance of mammoth business organizations and the decline in the relative position of the small, independent business firms.[21]

Concentration in Other Fields

Consolidation in the field of banking and finance has lagged. Though bankers have long had their nation-wide banking association, many of its members have been the supporters of unit banking. Supporters of unit banks have persistently fought against developments that promised to concentrate banking power. Despite this opposition, however, mergers have experienced an upward trend since the turn of the twentieth century.[22] The pace of consolidation quickened considerably after the First World War. The depression years of the 1930's accentuated the merger movement and the importance of the giant banks. In 1935, the thirty largest banking corporations (a fraction of one per cent of our banking system) held 34.3 per cent of the country's banking assets outside of the Federal Reserve banks. And seventeen life insurance companies accounted for 81.5 per cent of the assets of all life insurance companies.[23]

Labor organization has made most of its progress in the past half-century in the fields of mining, manufacture, and transportation. The movement has waxed and waned. The American Federation of Labor made steady progress from 1900 through the period of the First World War. Others were less fortunate. But numerous strikes in the immediate post-war period brought labor organization into ill repute. Membership

---

[20] *Ibid.*, p. 5.

[21] *Cf.* Senate Document No. 206, *Report of the Smaller War Plants Corporation to the Special Committee to Study Problems of American Small Business* (Washington, D. C., U. S. Government Printing Office, 1946), Chap. 3.

[22] See John M. Chapman, *Concentration of Banking: The Changing Structure and Control of Banking in the United States* (New York, Columbia University Press, 1934).

[23] U. S. National Resources Committee, *Structure of the American Economy* (Washington, D. C., U. S. Government Printing Office, 1939), p. 103.

shrank noticeably, while the great depression placed labor in a most precarious position. In 1933, the National Industrial Recovery Act restored some of labor's fading prestige, until the Act was declared unconstitutional. The use of the company union, largely employer-controlled, and the employers' effective anti-union campaigns offered further serious threats to organized labor. Out of this situation rose the CIO (Congress of Industrial Organizations), under the militant leadership of John L. Lewis of the United Mine Workers.[24] New strength was injected into the movement to organize labor, particularly along industrial lines, to offset the concentration of capital control in industry. And, in 1935, a sympathetic political administration in Washington helped matters along by passage of the National Labor Relations Act, administered by a National Labor Relations Board. Organized labor now numbers slightly more than fifteen million in a total working force of sixty million. Though labor gains in the 1930's have been partially checked by the Taft-Hartley Act of 1947, the ability of organized labor to keep "take-home" pay within sight—if not ahead—of post-war price changes will enhance among unorganized workers the popularity of unionization and group action. But despite the gains of labor in recent years the percentage of gainfully employed persons on the membership rolls of labor organizations is still relatively small—approximately 25 per cent.

In agriculture, since the turn of the century, organizational development has proceeded haltingly along several lines. Units like the Grange and the Farm Bureau have joined farmers less for economic than for social, educational, and political purposes. In their capacity as political organizations they have imitated industry and labor. They have constructed powerful national lobbies designed to obtain through politics what economic organization, or lack of it, has failed to accomplish in the market-places.[25] Another phase of organization has taken the form of coöperatives to purchase supplies or to market farm products in a more orderly fashion. A few of these coöperatives have reached mammoth size. For example, the California Fruit Growers Exchange in 1930 controlled 85 per cent of the citrus fruit of California and spent hundreds of thousands of dollars in advertising. A third organizational form is found under the heading of corporation farming. It has been encouraged

---

[24] Owing to policy disagreements, Mr. Lewis abandoned the CIO in 1942. He affiliated his United Mine Workers with the American Federation of Labor in 1946 only to disaffiliate a year later.

[25] The Farm Bureau was instrumental in securing cohesion among a small group of mid-western Congressmen to form a Farm Bloc in 1921. Since that time, by astute political trading, this bloc has brought about the passage of numerous Federal Acts of varying value to the farmers. See Fred A. Shannon, *America's Economic Growth* (New York, The Macmillan Company, 1940), p. 722; also William Allen White, *The Changing West* (New York, The Macmillan Company, 1939), p. 64.

by the wider adoption of capitalistic methods. Conclusive proof of its advantages is not yet apparent, however, so the development remains insignificant. A variant of this third form is to be found in chain farming. As large life insurance companies, by mortgage foreclosures, have become outright farm owners, they have used a system of carefully supervised tenancy to obtain the income once derived from mortgage interest. Despite these developments, farming remains largely individualistic in organization. Sole proprietorships of small size predominate. There were nearly seven million farm units in 1935, and 99 per cent of them employed less than five persons each.[26]

Small enterprises also predominate in retail trade, construction, and service lines. In retail trade, small independent stores account for a large percentage of all retail sales. But mail-order houses, chain stores, and large department stores have encroached heavily on this field since the turn of the century. A goodly segment of the construction industry is still in the hands of small builders such as those found in villages and towns. Most service industries are small-scale, though exceptions, such as the motion-picture industry, are becoming more numerous.

Changing Attitudes and New Controls

As concentration spread through American industry the competitive system met increasing criticism. Doubts as to its unqualified virtues were crystallizing even while the development of the West and the advances of industry and transport were creating strong social sanctions for the system. As the nineteenth century advanced it became evident that more than a "lunatic fringe" were regarding competitive individualism with deep suspicion and concern.

Politically influential groups recognized the faults of the system, but they never reached any agreement to abandon its control of production. Each injured group visualized its particular devil and demanded his extermination or control. For example, the farmers' devils were the railroads and the produce market monopolists. To Henry George and his followers the landlord, with his land monopoly and unearned increment, was the satanic obstacle barring the way to economic welfare and progress for the common man. On the other hand, some, like Henry Demarest Lloyd, newspaper and magazine writer, struck dramatically at industrial monopoly in various places, belaboring in particular the Standard Oil Company and the grain-marketing system. Labor groups perceived their devil in the form of all firmly entrenched capitalist employers and sought to improve their lot by organization and mass action. Capitalists retaliated against labor by enlisting the use of the court injunction to prevent anticipated property damage.

[26] U. S. National Resources Committee, *op. cit.*, pp. 103, 384.

As the decade of the 1880's drew to a close, however, it became increasingly apparent that the public would not be satisfied unless Federal laws were passed to relieve the country of dangerous excesses in the field of transportation and industry. State constitutional and statutory provisions designed to meet these problems were proving a public disappointment.[27] The impotence of political subdivisions and the increasing evidence of concentrated economic control, accompanied by business leaders' irresponsibility and indifference to public welfare, were establishing the psychological foundation necessary for a broader public acceptance of centralized Federal control over economic affairs.

The increase of public controls after 1870 shows the ability of powerful and articulate factions in the electorate to get some measure of remedial legislation. But it does not reflect any general willingness to abandon the basic elements of the competitive system. For instance, there is no evidence of any wide-spread acceptance of socialistic doctrines. In the main, where the forces of competition have proved destructive, wasteful, or unworkable, most citizens of the United States have preferred to meet the problem by accepting government regulation of private business property rather than government ownership.

Through constitutional and statutory provisions a number of states, before 1890, gave their support to the maintenance of competition by prohibiting monopoly and attacking its various forms and practices. The Federal Government added the Sherman Anti-trust Act in 1890. And Congress further showed its will to support competition in the Clayton Act, passed in 1914, which made it a duty of the Federal Trade Commission to attack certain trade and combination practices that tended to lessen competition substantially. Our later study will show that these controls have enjoyed only a partial success in attacking monopoly and almost none in their attempts to make the restraints of gentlemanly "competitors" give way to competition. But the public intention to retain the general system is none the less clear. Immediate evidence to this effect appears in the vigorous use of the Sherman Act since 1935—except for the years of World War II, 1941-1945,—and in the grant of additional powers to the Federal Trade Commission in 1938.

A number of controls have sought to correct the imperfections of the competitive order. Public systems of unemployment and old-age insurance have laid support of the unemployed worker on industry. Certain socially undesirable results of competitive inequality have been checked by factory regulation, regulation of working hours, workmen's compensation laws, and minimum wage laws. The character of acceptable competition has been defined in pure food and fair trade practice laws. Cer-

---

[27] Cf. H. R. Seager and C. A. Gulick, Jr., *Trusts and Corporation Problems* (New York, Harper & Brothers, 1929), Chap. 17.

tain forms of unfair competition have been attacked by the Federal Trade Commission and by state commissions. Since 1935 the Securities and Exchange Commission has set standards that must be maintained in the sale of new securities and has regulated trading practices on organized security exchanges. These controls inevitably do re-define the institutions of the individualistic system. The personal rights of private property and freedom of enterprise and exchange are not the same as those of a hundred years back. In general, personal freedoms are being constrained by public controls as it becomes apparent that the old definitions do not yield satisfactory results. But there is still no sign that the basic control of competitive individualism is being vitiated by these changes.

It is true, however, that in a number of important fields not even a doubtful and troubled faith in competition has been able to survive. Here public interference has assumed a different rôle. It has been designed to replace the competitive control and not merely to supervise it. It has appeared in two general forms—public utility regulation and government operation.

Faults in the Operation of the Competitive System

In spite of public controls, the theory of economic individualism is not translated into action without the appearance of serious faults.

A first fault lies in the presence of a great deal of irrational economic behavior. Capitalism does not require us to be economic men perpetually in search of purely economic objectives to the exclusion of all else. But it does require that producers and consumers have an interest in economic values and arrive rationally at economic decisions. If they fail in these respects they will be responsible not only for personal losses but for the faulty operation of the competitive machine. Consumers will support inefficient firms, and producers will ignore the direction of prices and costs to the injury of their profits. The former are probably the worst offenders. Their individual purchases are commonly small, they are offered a pleasant but bewildering number of choices, and they are subjected to conflicting claims from a variety of sellers. On the whole, producers are more experienced in buying and selling, but they undoubtedly miss profitable opportunities through carelessness or inertia. The worst result probably grows out of the exploitation of a confused and careless consumer, whereby the sale of shoddy articles and the use of deceit and misrepresentation are made more profitable than efficient manufacture and marketing.

A second fault appears in the form of imperfect knowledge. Our economy is not static. Planning must allow for changes such as population growth, altered consumer habits, and new technical processes. If production is to be adjusted to demand, both present and future opportunities must be known to producers and consumers. Knowledge of current conditions and accurate prediction must be available to all, or mistakes will be made. For the producer, prediction is particularly difficult. He must be able to forecast how dynamic changes promise to affect his industry, and also how his competitors view these changes and how they are going to react to their own predictions. It is obvious that our forecasts have often been faulty, but it is equally obvious that capitalism has adjusted itself to tremendous dynamic changes in spite of many mistakes. The general cost of imperfect prediction is to be found in prices that rise above those of perfect competition as a payment for risk. A more serious "cost" is the waste of labor and material resources that occurs in periods of business depression.

A third imperfection consists in a considerable measure of indivisibility in the factors of production. If one of the factors, say capital, is organized in large segments that cannot be easily split, it will cause two troubles. First, it may lose the mobility that is necessary if resources are to be transferred so as to equalize their marginal productivity in various employments. A large accumulation of specialized capital is moved out of an industry by the owner's refusal to replace it as it is used up. As a result, the rate of depreciation, which may be very slow, will generally determine the speed with which it can be transferred to other uses. Second, other factors, such as labor, may be divided into many completely separate units and a faulty wage level may result from the concentration of capital. Inequality in bargaining power might allow wages to drop below the marginal productivity of labor. The value of labor in the general field of industry would not shape the labor costs of the one industry, and labor would be used in uneconomic amounts. Not only the laborer but the whole organization of industry would be injured. The capitalist, however, may not be the only sinner. The tables may be turned and combinations of labor may do corresponding harm in forcing owners of capital or materials to take less than their value.

All these imperfections permit errors to endure for long periods. The corrective forces that are at work, however, in most cases, finally achieve an approximation to the desired results. Frequently, the producers of some commodity are found turning it out in quantities that the demand will not take except at prices below cost. Clearly some of the materials and labor would have greater value in other fields of industry, but they are not re-allocated for a long time. The losses incurred by such producers do tend to bring about some curtailment of production. In time, resources move from the over-developed industry into other fields until something near a proper allocation is achieved. Similarly, imperfections may permit poor techniques and bad proportioning of the factors to exist for years in individual plants. At the same time, however, strong forces are operating to prevent these inefficiencies from being flagrant and general.

Faults in the Structure of the Competitive System

In a number of American industries, unfortunately, still more serious faults seem to have grown out of the development of large corporations. Competitive individualism requires firms to be small, relative to the size of the whole industry. Small business units will assure two necessary conditions. First, those who have invested property in an enterprise and are interested in its efficiency can take an active part in its affairs. Their private interest coincides with the public interest in efficient production, and they can be trusted to set the business policy of the enterprise. Second, the small firm assures a large number of producers in each field and goes a long way toward creating the competitive independence that is needed.

To the early nineteenth-century economist the business unit was a small personal venture most commonly organized and directed by an individual or a set of partners. Today, the corporation has become the typical business form, and in many industries we must recognize the fifty-million-dollar corporation as a small organization. In the steel industry, for example, the assets of ten outstanding companies range between one hundred million and two and two-tenths billion dollars. The petroleum industry possesses twenty companies with assets of over one hundred million dollars. Similar conditions are found in a number of important fields. Close to 40 per cent of the business wealth of the country is administered by enterprises with assets of over ninety million dollars.

Under these circumstances the whole logic of traditional economic theory is weakened. In the first place, profits do not continue to assume the key rôle assigned to them. They are supposed to go to the property-owner in return for the risks he has borne and for his efficiency in running a business. In these large corporations the investor is still legally entitled to all the residual return, but he no longer appears to direct the affairs of the business. Thousands of stockholders are found in each of these giant concerns, and control of business policy has slipped out of their hands. Some other group, frequently composed of the management officers, has taken over their planning duties. Economic and legal theory, then, is found sanctioning payments to property-owners for services they do not perform. This problem, and the manner in which the modern corporation has been adjusted to it, comprises the first large section of this study.

In the second place, as large corporations appear, competition cannot be relied on. It persists in disappearing in too many industries. From at least one point of view the capitalistic system is a strange one. It places its regulative force, competition, in the hands of the enterpriser who is constrained and harassed by this very competition. It is not surprising, then, if the producer feels that his interests will be well served by the lessening of competition. And the appearance of a few large firms in an industry provides favorable ground for the growth of monopolistic elements. In a number of industries single firms have risen to a position of monopoly control to challenge the validity of the competitive theory. The second section of the study deals with this problem.

In other fields, the monopoly of a single firm has not appeared, but various forms of coöperation between a few large corporations have restrained and altered competition. In the production of steel, petroleum, anthracite coal, industrial alcohol, cement, and other commodities a leading firm or group of firms has organized a "gentlemanly restraint" which has virtually eliminated price competition. In meat-packing, in the production of copper, in the hardwood industry, understandings have kept at least the large firms in a conventional position that price competition is seldom allowed to disturb. This problem, the decline of price competition, comprises the third section of our study.

PART I

The Modern Corporation

3

The Modern Corporation: Its History
and Characteristics

Introduction

It is generally agreed that the corporation is our most important form of business organization. Data from the Bureau of Internal Revenue, filed through December 31, 1946, indicate that in 1945 there were in the United States 454,462 corporations (33,335 inactive) distributed as follows: mining and quarrying, 9,144; manufacturing, 82,189; public utilities, 21,138; trade, 124,442; service, 37,904; finance, insurance, real estate and lessors of real property, 143,289; construction, 12,801; agriculture, forestry, and fishing, 6,528; businesses non-allocable, 17,027. Though greatly outnumbered by the personal forms of business organizations, that is, by proprietorships and partnerships, the corporation in other ways is the dominant business unit, except in agriculture.

If we base relative importance on the percentage of national income produced by various business forms, we readily see the outstanding place of the corporation. In mining and quarrying it accounts for approximately 96 per cent of the contribution of this industry to national income; in manufacturing, 92 per cent; in transportation and other public utilities, 86 per cent; in trade, 63 per cent; in finance (banking, insurance, real estate, and so on), 56 per cent; in service (professions, amusements, hotels, and so on), construction, and various miscellaneous fields, 33 per cent each; and in agriculture only 6 per cent.[1] Exclusive of government contribution to national income, the corporate share averages slightly in excess of 62 per cent of the total.[2]

Viewed from another angle, the corporation again looks impressive. In the boom year, 1929, there were approximately 211,000 manufacturing

---

[1] Twentieth Century Fund, Inc., *Big Business: Its Growth and Place* (New York, The Twentieth Century Fund, Inc., 1937), Table 3, p. 17.
[2] *Ibid.*, p. 1.

39

establishments in the United States, of which 48 per cent were incorporated. Corporations employed 90 per cent of the wage-earners engaged in manufacture and produced 92 per cent of the value product. Similarly, corporations made up 53 per cent of the wholesale marketing establishments. They employed 80 per cent of the full-time employees and produced 74 per cent of the total net sales. In the retail field, corporations only accounted for 16 per cent of the number of establishments, but they employed more than half the full-time employees and accounted for nearly 50 per cent of the total net sales.[3] Moreover, data from the sixteenth census indicate that while the number of manufacturing establishments in the United States shrank from 211,000 in 1929 to 184,000 in 1939, the relative position of the incorporated business unit increased from 48 per cent of the total number of manufacturing establishments to 52 per cent, approximately. Between 1929 and 1939 in the wholesale and retail trade there have been no significant changes in the relative importance of the common forms of business organization.[4]

It is evident, therefore, that in most lines of economic activity the corporation is being utilized as the most typical business organization. Through this unit, individuals contribute their funds by the purchase of shares. To make this possible, however, the organization is incorporated, that is, the state approves and acknowledges its charter or certificate of incorporation, which explicitly outlines the purposes of the organization, the nature of the shares to be issued, the rights and relations of those who participate in the organization, and so forth. By incorporation this business form is conveniently endowed with a legal personality and entrusted with many of the legal rights and powers of a natural person. The organization, in its own name, but under the general direction of a board of directors chosen by the owners, operates the business. It enters into contracts with others. It sues and is sued in its own name. It buys and sells commodities, employs or discharges workmen, and pledges its properties to lenders.

The corporation, however, has not always enjoyed its present important economic position. Its dominance and popularity have been achieved only after a long struggle which has been marked by an increasing appreciation of its merits by business men and by the decline of public antipathy toward it.

---

[3] Data derived from the U. S. Department of Commerce, Bureau of the Census, *Fifteenth Census of the United States*, 1930. *Manufactures*, 1929, Vol. I, Table 2, p. 95. *Distribution*, 1929, Vol. II, Wholesale Distribution, Table 8, p. 92; Vol. I, Retail Distribution, Table 12A, p. 89.

[4] U. S. Department of Commerce, Bureau of the Census, *Sixteenth Census of the United States*, 1940. *Manufactures*, 1939, Vol. I, Table I, p. 229. Census of Business, Vol. II, *Wholesale Trade*, 1939, Table S, p. 26. Census of Business, Vol. I, *Retail Trade*, 1939, Part I, pp. 35 and 71.

BRITISH BACKGROUND

In eighteenth-century England business organizations were for the most part simple in structure and personal in nature. Sole proprietorships predominated. For legal and economic purposes the individual owner and his business were identical. Partnerships were also numerous. The need to collect more capital or the need to divide important management tasks among several owner-participants as the scale of business operations increased gave the partnership considerable popularity. Frequently organizations sprang up in the form of *unincorporated* joint-stock associations.[5] These were nothing more than sprawling partnerships; although they called themselves companies and issued transferable shares, they operated without benefit of Crown or Parliamentary recognition through formal incorporation by charter grant. Unlike corporations, they were not given any exclusive trading privileges. Nor could they sue or be sued except in the name of all their members. And the members had unlimited liability, that is, the individuals and not the business unit were responsible for the debts of the enterprise. At the same time, however, incorporated business units were not unknown.[6] They were even then handling considerable amounts of the business wealth of eighteenth-century England.[7]

Public reaction against the unincorporated associations aided the growth of the incorporated companies. The Bubble Act of 1719, a criminal statute enacted by Parliament in response to public demand for the restraint of the stock promotional excesses of the times, had considerable effect on the development of business organization.[8] Striking vaguely at

---

[5] The joint-stock device, based on a stock of freely transferable shares owned by a relatively large number of people, had been transplanted from the Continent to Britain in the sixteenth century. See A. B. Dubois, *The English Business Company After the Bubble Act, 1720–1800* (New York, The Commonwealth Fund, 1938), p. 1.

[6] The corporation idea was not new at the time. In England its roots go back to the gilds and boroughs of medieval life. Its business application first appeared in the overseas trading ventures in the sixteenth and seventeenth centuries. It had been applied to mining enterprise in Germany by the beginning of the fifteenth century.

[7] Dubois, *op. cit.*, p. 85.

[8] The term "bubble" came into use in the eighteenth century to describe the speculative undertakings of the period. One of the most famous was that connected with the South Sea Company. This company was incorporated in England in 1711. In exchange for the assumption of a portion of the public debt it was to receive a monopoly of the British trade with South America and the Pacific Islands. Later it received a monopoly of the slave traffic with Spanish America. In 1719, it offered £7,567,500 to the government, in return for which it was to assume responsibility for the entire public debt of £30,981,712. The government, however, would pay the company interest at the rate of 5 per cent for seven years and 4 per cent thereafter. Persons holding present claims on the government in the form of terminable annuities would be persuaded to exchange them for stock in the South Sea Com-

the unincorporated companies, it sought to control the excessive issue of shares by making void and illegal such things as acting or presuming to act as a corporate body without legal authority from either the Parliament or the Crown. It definitely made incorporation a privilege and not a right. But, since the Act was ambiguous, it was not effective for very long. It succeeded in retarding free association through unincorporated joint-stock companies only for a relatively short time. Consequently, by 1825, when the Act was repealed, the unincorporated English companies were quite important.

Perhaps the outstanding result of the Bubble Act was to focus attention on formal incorporation or the process of obtaining government recognition of the legal existence of the corporate body of associates. The numerous petitions for charters of incorporation in England during the eighteenth century indicate that the corporate concept in business, wherein men might participate in enterprise apart from their principal occupation by purchase of fully transferable shares in a business organization, was soon to rival the proprietorship and partnership business forms. That British business men had a keen appreciation of the practical value of the corporate form as a means of operating enterprises on a larger scale is apparent in the reasons they advanced in their petitions for the privilege of incorporation. Some emphasized the value of the corporate right to hold property directly in the corporation's own name. Others stressed the legal right to sue and be sued. On other occasions, satisfactory delegation of powers to a directorate was alleged to be best arranged under corporate organization. Delegated powers were considered necessary, even then, for the efficient management of large-scale industry, which was on the rise during this period. At times, the greater possibility of permanence was brought forward as an advantage of incorporated over unincorporated enterprises.[9]

Limited liability, or restriction of financial responsibility to the capital voluntarily invested in the company, was only infrequently invoked as a reason for incorporation. Though it had made its appearance in the seventeenth century, it was seldom introduced into the calculations of

---

pany. The stock was to be issued at a high premium in order to dispose of a large amount of these annuities or annual government payments.

Public excitement over the South Sea Company led to other stock promotion schemes, particularly by unincorporated companies, in a variety of wild undertakings. Speculation began to increase rapidly. The price of South Sea shares rose tremendously. Meanwhile the insiders withdrew. When this became known the share prices dropped precipitately. Parliament investigated and found an unsavory situation. Government officials were fined and imprisoned for their parts in the scheme. Directors' estates were confiscated. Yet losses were heavy for those who had exchanged their government claims for South Sea Company shares. See Willard L. Thorp, "Speculative Bubbles," *Encyclopaedia of the Social Sciences* (New York, The Macmillan Company, 1930), Vol. III, pp. 25–26.

[9] Dubois, *op. cit.*, pp. 89–91.

lawyers who advised business clients under the Bubble Act during the eighteenth century.[10]

Though incorporation was definitely a privilege to be sought and prized, and business men had a keen sense of its usefulness and efficacy, contemporary observers were less aware of its possibilities. No less a person than Adam Smith, in discussing institutions for facilitating commerce, said:[11]

> The only trades which it seems possible for a joint-stock company to carry on successfully, without an exclusive privilege, are those of which all the operations are capable of being reduced to what was called a routine, or to such uniformity of method as admits of little or no variation. Of this kind is, first, the banking trade; secondly, the trade of insurance from fire, and from sea risk and capture in times of war; thirdly, the trade of making and maintaining a navigable cut or canal; and fourthly, the similar trade of bringing water for the supply of a great city.

Smith's observations were correct in the sense that corporate organization did fit these types of business ventures particularly well, but he failed to perceive the full possibilities which the Industrial Revolution was to offer the corporate form in other lines of endeavor. The advancement of technology and large-scale enterprise was ultimately to bring vast changes.

THE BUSINESS CORPORATION IN AMERICA

In colonial America at the beginning of the eighteenth century, industry had made but little advancement. That which existed could be operated by sole proprietors without great difficulty. Travel was difficult and markets were narrowly restricted. Hence domestic business ventures had little need for large amounts of capital. Moreover, the colonial mind was largely agrarian, and from time to time it revealed a considerable hostility to business. Privilege through charters was especially feared by the common folk.[12] They were inclined to associate the chartered company with monopoly.[13] And the extension of the principal provisions of the Bubble Act to the American colonies in 1741 deterred the development of unincorporated joint-stock companies.

As the eighteenth century advanced, the total number of formal in-

---

[10] *Ibid.*, pp. 93–97.
[11] *An Inquiry into the Nature and Causes of the Wealth of Nations* (second edition, Oxford, Clarendon Press, 1880), Vol. II, p. 340.
[12] This was carried to such lengths on occasion that sentiment was expressed in Boston in 1714 against incorporation of the town. See Robert A. East, *Business Enterprise in the American Revolutionary Era* (New York, Columbia University Press, 1938), p. 26; also Simeon E. Baldwin, "American Business Corporations Before 1789," *American Historical Association Report*, 1902, Vol. I, p. 273.
[13] Shaw Livermore, *Early American Land Companies* (New York, The Commonwealth Fund, 1939), p. 67.

corporations of colonial business, religious, educational and political bodies increased. In this development, though, the commercial or business enterprise did not predominate. This was attributable to several factors: first, it was costly to obtain a royal or parliamentary charter; second, the legal status of a colonial charter was uncertain; third, limited liability, now such a valuable feature of incorporation, was not generally available to business enterprise; and finally—and perhaps most important of all—the necessity of applying to the state for a charter did not jibe precisely with popular notions of free association.[14]

The Evolution of the Incorporation Process After the Revolution

The War of Independence changed the situation considerably. American business men were thrown on their own in the organization of business and in the collection of capital. Closer economic relations were established, particularly among those who congregated in the growing centers of Boston, Philadelphia, and New York.[15] And business expanded markedly. The war disposed of the British Bubble Act and the several states assumed the power to grant corporate charters. Unincorporated joint-stock companies could now be organized without restraint, also.

Though it was not entirely compatible with existing ideology, the several states adopted the British legal conception that to obtain corporate capacity was a *privilege* and not a *right*.[16] Consequently, a peculiar development took place in the young American economy. On the one hand, by special acts of state legislatures, a limited number of business corporations were formed. For the most part, they were turnpike, bridge, canal, dock, water, fire, banking, and insurance companies—the type for which Adam Smith said the corporate form was adaptable.[17] On the other hand, many unincorporated companies were formed which the courts persisted in calling partnerships though, in fact, they were essentially corporate bodies which had not sought the privilege of *bona fide* incorporation by charter grant. Many early American land companies were of this type.[18] Although in need of comparatively large capital contributions and unified control, these companies did not seek incorpora-

[14] *Ibid.*, Editor's Introduction, pp. xxiii and xxv.

[15] *Cf.* Joseph S. Davis, *Essays in the Earlier History of American Corporations* (Cambridge, Mass., Harvard University Press, 1917), Vol. I, pp. 178–179.

[16] For a brief, clear statement of the development of the English concept which so greatly influenced American legal thought, see Charles C. Abbott, *The Rise of the Business Corporation* (Ann Arbor, Mich., Edwards Brothers, Inc., 1936), pp. 12–13.

[17] Up to 1800 only 335 profit-seeking corporations had been chartered in the United States. About 2 per cent of this number were formed during the colonial period. Nearly 90 per cent were chartered after 1790. *Cf.* Davis, *op. cit.*, Vol. II, pp. 21–29.

[18] See Livermore, *op. cit.*, pp. 133–214.

tion, because state legislatures were still reluctant to grant charters except to businesses associated primarily with public welfare rather than with private profit.

Out of this situation emerged a struggle between business interests and the state as to whether incorporation was a right open to all who wished to promote legitimate business interests or a privilege to be granted or withheld as state legislatures saw fit.[19]

As the pace of economic development quickened, business interests, as distinct from agrarian, became more influential. Business groups began to exert increasing pressure on legislatures to make the incorporation process easier and incorporation a right available to all legitimate businesses. They wished to dispense with a procedure that forced them to submit elaborate petitions to the legislature praying for the right to incorporate and adopt a corporate seal. Too frequently prolonged hearings, political bargaining and jockeying were involved.[20] Such methods were time-consuming and fraught with uncertainty. To be sure, there were social advantages where each incorporation meant the passage of an act through the legislature. The legislature or a legislative committee could scrutinize carefully the proposed arrangements. In the articles of incorporation the purposes of the corporation and the powers granted to it and its management could be carefully defined and limited. Retention of this legislative procedure could be a real protection to the general public and to the corporate creditors. And to a lesser extent it protected shareholders, although as a rule they were expected to fend for themselves. Eventually, however, state legislatures yielded to the demands of business men for easier incorporation and to the increasing pressure of other legislative business that was crowding the calendar. Gradually general acts of incorporation were passed. These laws made it possible for business men to obtain corporate charters by simply submitting prescribed information to the proper state official in accordance with the content of the incorporation law.

Laws that approximated general acts of incorporation for business purposes were passed by North Carolina in 1795 and by Massachusetts in 1799.[21] And in 1811, a New York statute made it possible for any five or more persons who wished to form a manufacturing corporation to realize their desires by filing with the Secretary of State a document which had been signed and acknowledged before a justice of the Su-

---

[19] This clash has been perpetuated by the failure of the legalistic mind, so enveloped by precedent, to adjust quickly to changed social and economic conditions. This is still apparent in the survival of the fiction-concession theory of the corporation. For a discussion of this and other theories of the corporation, see N. S. Buchanan, *The Economics of Corporate Enterprise* (New York, Henry Holt and Company, 1940), pp. 36–45.

[20] Livermore, *op. cit.*, p. 224.

[21] Davis, *op. cit.*, Vol. II, pp. 17–20; Abbott, *op. cit.*, p. 45.

preme Court of the state or other designated officials. When this certificate, which contained such data as the name of the corporation, the number of shares of stock, the number and names of the managing trustees, and the place or places of business activity, was properly filed, the signers were considered a "body corporate and politic" for twenty years. Such associations were given full corporate powers, including the right to sue and be sued and the right to buy, sell, and hold lands and other property. Capital of such corporations could not exceed one hundred thousand dollars. Shares were to be freely transferable, with one vote for each share. Liability was limited to the amount of the capital invested. Voting by proxy, that is by delegated authority, was permitted. The stockholders elected trustees who managed the affairs of the company and passed by-laws. Though the New York law represented progress to the business group, it was not until 1837 that a general statute was passed allowing incorporation for any legitimate purpose.[22]

To Connecticut goes the distinction of taking this final step. Other states then soon followed its lead. By 1850, a number had adopted the general incorporation principle.[23] The gradual infiltration of the corporate form into the economic scene and into the public conscience succeeded finally in breaking down public resistance built on fear of monopoly and special privilege. The eighteenth-century American philosophy of economic equality was reflected in these enabling acts which have made freedom of incorporation one of our fundamental political institutions.[24] Once this freedom was established, the course of legislative development ran to further easement of the incorporation process and to the extension of corporate rights and privileges.

The Liberalization of State Laws of Incorporation

At various times different states have assumed the lead in making the incorporation laws more liberal. New Jersey was one of the first to pursue the deliberate policy of encouraging the collection of capital for business purposes through the medium of the corporation.[25] In 1846 it made a general provision allowing limited liability. About twenty years later it provided that any company organized under the New Jersey law might carry on a part of its business outside the state, and have one or more

---

[22] W. C. Kessler, "A Statistical Study of the New York General Incorporation Act of 1811," *Journal of Political Economy*, Vol. XLVIII (December, 1940), p. 877.
[23] Berle and Means, *op. cit.*, p. 136.
[24] *Cf.* Baldwin, *op. cit.*, p. 274.
[25] For a more complete account of the evolution of the New Jersey law to 1900, see Edward Q. Keasbey, "New Jersey and the Great Corporations," *Harvard Law Review*, Vol. XIII (1899–1900), pp. 198–212, 264–278.

offices and hold real estate and personal property outside the state, providing a statement to that effect was made in the certificate of incorporation. In 1875 the state constitution was amended so as to forbid the grant of special charters of incorporation. The legislature was directed to pass general laws under which corporations would be organized for every lawful business or purpose. And to make it easier for corporate directors to expand their business, the law provided that corporate shares might be exchanged directly for acquired property. Incorporators were relieved of the necessity of filing public notice of intention to incorporate. It was no longer necessary to petition any government official for leave to incorporate. The law also dispensed with limitations on the amount of capital stock to be authorized and issued under the terms of the charter.

In the 1880's New Jersey made several more changes. It introduced the corporation filing fee and the annual franchise tax, and introduced into its law that extremely important provision which allows corporations to hold and dispose of stocks of other corporations. A year later this portion of the law was revised and clarified and became the means by which many of the great holding companies of the 1890's and 1900's were formed.

In the latter part of the 1890's New Jersey again made several revisions in its laws to encourage the use of the corporation. It removed limitations on the duration of the corporate charter. It provided for the issuance of different classes of stock. It provided legal protection to stockholders and officers of domestic and foreign corporations against suits within the state upon personal liability arising under corporation laws of other states. It allowed all corporations, save railroads and canal companies, to lease their properties and franchise to any other corporation provided the consent of two-thirds in interest of the stockholders was obtained. And to assure better operation of the corporate organization, incorporators were authorized to define and limit the powers of the several parties in a corporation, the directors, officers, and stockholders. Thus the incorporation certificate became not only a record but also an instrument recognized by the state as controlling the actions and relations of the parties to the corporate organization.

This summary of the nineteenth-century development of the New Jersey corporation law in no sense tells the complete story. It suffices to show, however, that this state went far toward encouraging the use of the corporation as an association for business purposes. And under the rules of interstate comity, whereby states reciprocate favors extended to the institutions which they create, New Jersey corporations might exercise beyond state lines the liberal powers conferred upon them for use at home.

Effects of New Jersey's Liberal Policy

The effects of New Jersey's policy of easement were twofold. It encouraged prospective incorporators outside the state to seek New Jersey charters to avoid the heavier restrictions placed on corporations by most other states.[26] It also encouraged some states to imitate New Jersey in order to put themselves on a stronger competitive basis for incorporation business which, through filing fees and annual franchise taxes, was becoming a source of considerable state income. Delaware, formerly a strict state, re-vamped its laws of incorporation in 1899 and featured three things: simple procedure in corporate formation; low corporate fees and taxes; and the grant of those statutory powers and privileges which business men considered desirable.[27] As a result Delaware's incorporation business grew quite steadily from 1899, when it chartered 421 corporations, to 1929, when it approved 7,537 charters.[28] In the latter year Delaware received $3,300,698 from incorporation fees and $2,270,296 from corporate franchise taxes. These receipts constituted approximately 42 per cent of the state's total revenue of $13,109,398. Though more corporations may be chartered annually by other states, Delaware leads in the incorporation of large interstate business organizations. In 1932 Delaware was the state of incorporation of 209 (34 per cent) of the 606 industrial companies listed on the New York Stock Exchange. It was also the state of incorporation of 191 (38 per cent) of 503 industrial companies listed on the New York Curb Exchange.[29]

The present Delaware law is plentifully supplied with provisions which depart radically from the more strait-laced provisions of earlier state laws. Thus, any kind of stock may be issued. These shares may or may not carry voting powers. They may also be shorn of the preëmptive right—the right of the stockholder to subscribe to similar new stock

---

[26] Between 1888 and 1904, 192 out of 345 companies with capitalizations in excess of $1,000,000, formed from a combination of two or more individual companies, took out New Jersey charters. In 1899 alone, 61 of 83 such combinations were organized under New Jersey laws. See R. C. Larcom, *The Delaware Corporation* (Baltimore, Md., The Johns Hopkins Press, 1937), pp. 13–14.

[27] *Ibid.*, p. 15.

[28] This represents the peak year of activity for the State of Delaware. The annual average from 1930 to 1947 has been 2,395 incorporations and the range has been from 912 in 1942 to 5611 in 1930. In 1947 Delaware issued 2,787 certificates of incorporation. Annual income from incorporating taxes and fees and from annual franchise taxes since 1929 has ranged from a low of $2.7 million in 1937 to a little more than $5 million in 1930. In 1947 Delaware received about $3.8 million from these sources. (The foregoing figures are for calendar years and are derived from data obtained from the Office of the Secretary of State in Delaware.)

[29] The statistical data are drawn from Larcom, *op. cit.*, Chap. 7. At this point it is appropriate to note that Delaware's popularity increased notably after 1913, when New Jersey passed the "Seven Sisters" Acts which made more strict its incorporation and anti-trust laws. Loss of popularity and revenue led the state ultimately to repeal these restrictive measures.

issues before they are offered to others. The loss of this right may be important to stockholders who desire to retain their proportionate interest in the corporation. The state does not burden the re-sale of securities with a transfer tax. For the convenience of the directors and stockholders it is permissible for their meetings to be held outside the state. Stock of no par value (as opposed to stock with a nominal or stated face value) may be issued. And directors may, if they wish, allocate to the corporate surplus account a part of the money received from the sale of no-par stock. In itself this privilege is not an evil, but like so many of the liberal provisions of incorporation laws, it is subject to abuse. The failure of the directorate to designate such a surplus as a paid-in surplus might mislead prospective investors to think it was derived from real earnings. The law does not require directors to own stock in the company to qualify for the directorate. While this may be a convenience for the corporation, it is possible that the directors, having none of their own capital at stake, may be less careful in decisions involving policy. Probably the most lenient provision of the law is that charters may be approved which allow directors to issue new stock, change the terms of stock which has been authorized but not yet sold, retire preferred stock, and change the company by-laws without obtaining the stockholders' consent.

Many other states have followed the liberal policy of New Jersey and Delaware. The principle of interstate comity and the competition for incorporation business tend to make the liberal laws of these states the common standard. For small intrastate businesses this trend is of little consequence. Such organizations will seek charters at the capital of their home state. But where business is large, varied, and interstate in nature, the liberality of the general incorporation laws, the costs of incorporation, and the annual financial outlays for the franchise become strong determinants in selecting the state of incorporation.[30]

Incorporation Process

As a rule, state statutes outline the general methods of procedure for the alliance of natural persons into a corporate body. The details of formation are, however, the work of the incorporators, who may proceed

---

[30] When Standard Brands, Inc., sought a charter in 1929 it chose to obtain it from the state of Delaware. It paid an organization fee of $43,050. Had it chosen to incorporate in Arizona the fee would have been $85; in Nevada, $2,100; in Maine, $43,050; in New Jersey, $210,000; and in New York, $1,050,000. In some states it would not have had to pay any annual franchise tax. In others, this burden would amount to a considerable sum. In Maine, for example, Standard Brands would have had to pay annually $52,525. The Delaware law limits the annual franchise tax to a maximum of $25,000. The "bargain-counter" rates of some states did not appeal to Standard Brands, apparently. The company probably feared that states with such rates would not be likely to have any well-settled body of corporation law on which to depend. The uncertainties involved more than offset the lure of low costs.

with or without expert legal advice. Should incorporators elect to use the expert services available in one form or another, the process of incorporation is reduced to a simple procedure.

The principal task of incorporation lies in the formulation of the charter. This document serves a triple purpose. Firstly, it is the device by means of which express and implied legal relations between the business associates are established. Secondly, it serves, when approved by the state, as a notice to the public that the state and the business group have reached an agreement concerning the rights, privileges, burdens, and responsibilities accorded a corporate body by law. And finally, it serves as documentary evidence of the true nature of the business organization which is about to do business with the public.[31]

Where the corporate enterprise is the brain-child of investment bankers, as is often the case, the details of the corporate charter are drafted by skilled lawyers retained for that purpose by the bankers. Both parties, through long experience, are acquainted with the procedure.

Where incorporation is undertaken by the immediately interested enterprisers, the non-specialist lawyer may be employed, or it is possible to turn to organizations which make incorporation procedure a special profession. There are several well-known organizations which supply this service. They are minutely informed on the merits and demerits of incorporation in each of the several states. For a fee, they will design and procure for the incorporators a charter from the state whose incorporation laws and fees are most suited to the incorporators' purposes and purses. The incorporators need only specify in general terms the corporate powers they desire, the corporate name they wish to adopt, the types of securities to be issued, and the other general provisions to be included in the charter. The specialists do the rest. Once the terms of the charter are agreed upon, the process is merely one of clerical routine. Usually the state or its official representative remains passive up to the point where the charter or articles of incorporation are completed and presented for approval. Then the state official charged with the duty of charter examination scrutinizes the document for irregularities. Should any be found, the appropriate corrections must be made, after which the charter is approved and the proper fees are paid.[32] Completion of these matters gives undeniable corporate legal status to the body of business associates.

The state-approved certificate of incorporation is the company charter. Within this document are to be found these important provisions, pre-

---

[31] *Cf.* Calvin Crumbaker, *Organizing and Financing Modern Business* (New York, John Wiley & Sons, Inc., 1939), p. 91.

[32] The charter or certificate of incorporation is usually made in triplicate. One copy is left on file with the proper state official. One goes to the office of the clerk of the county in which the corporation elects to maintain its principal office. The third is retained by the corporation.

sented usually in the following order. Firstly, there is the name of the corporation. Selection of a name is a matter of business judgment. Incorporators must exercise care so as not to duplicate or closely approximate the name of an existing corporate organization, if they wish to avoid delay and difficulty. Next, the location of the principal office within the state is designated, since it must serve as the focal point for the receipt of notices and the service of legal papers. Some states allow the incorporators to name a legal representative within the state to serve the corporation for these purposes. Then there follow the purposes for which the corporation is to be established. These must be set forth clearly. Restricted terms may be used, or broad blanket clauses. It is important that the corporate powers should have sufficient coverage to avoid later charges of corporate acts *ultra vires*, that is, of acts which are not legally valid or are illegal because the company had not provided for them in its charter. Such acts may lead to embarrassment by charter revocation or at least to the necessity of charter amendment.[33] A statement of the amount of capital stock and the number of shares into which it is divided usually follows the statement of purposes. If there is more than one type or class of stock, each type or class must be described with all its varying features.

Stocks are evidences of ownership in a corporation. Usually they are divided into two categories, preferred and common. There may be variations in this standard pattern. As the title indicates, preferred stocks enjoy some preferences over common stocks. They bear a stated rate of income when paid, though if they are designated *participating preferred* they may receive something more. Preferred dividends must be paid before dividends for the accounting period are paid to the common stockholders. If the preferred stock is labeled *cumulative,* unpaid dividends must be paid, together with the amount of the current dividends, before the common stockholders are paid. In event of the dissolution of the corporation, the preferred stockholders are entitled to a stated principal sum before the common stockholders participate in the distribution. Preferred stockholders may or may not have voting power. This power may be denied to them completely, or it may be granted to them fully along with the common stockholders, or it may be a power which accrues to them under conditions wherein their immediate interests are vitally affected.

Common stocks represent proportional interests in the residual ownership of the corporation. The stock certificate is the basic instrument from which many variants have developed. Unless otherwise stated,

---

[33] How careful corporation lawyers are to avoid these contingencies is apparent from a perusal of the blanket charter of the United States Steel Corporation. See A. H. Stockder, *Business Ownership Organization* (New York, Henry Holt and Company, 1922), pp. 573–581.

common stocks carry full voting power, that is, one vote per share. It was customary to issue common shares at a par value, that is, a nominal or face value, such as $10 or $100, inscribed on the certificate. Twentieth-century finance has introduced no-par stock, a share that has no nominal or face value inscribed on the certificate, but represents a certain proportion of the number of shares issued. Common stock has the residual claim on the earnings and assets of the corporation. Modern finance has introduced also the non-voting common stock. Where this type is used, it is customary to designate this stock as Class A common and to call the voting shares Class B common.

Whatever the capital stock plan may be, the certificate of incorporation should clearly state for each type or class of stock its rights in the payment of dividends, its participation in assets in event of dissolution, its voting rights, and other important protective provisions.

Corporations also raise money through their capacity to borrow. Usually, in the charter, provision is made for the power of the corporation to pledge its properties for debts incurred and to issue bonds.

Bonds are claims of creditors on the issuing corporation. If the bonds conform to standard pattern, they usually have certain unqualified rights, such as the right to fixed interest payments on definite dates and the right of repayment of a fixed principal sum on a fixed date. They may or may not be protected by specific assets of the corporation. For example, a railroad equipment trust bond is a credit claim against the railroad which issued the bond. The bondholder is protected by a claim on specific railroad equipment held in trust to satisfy his claim, in event the railroad cannot otherwise meet its bond obligations. On the other hand, a debenture bond offers no specific security to the bondholder. It is backed by the general credit of the issuer corporation. Bondholders do not have any voice in management, nor do they have direct interest in the assets or the profits of a corporation beyond their own immediate claims. There are a host of types of bonds issued by corporations. Their descriptive titles serve to identify them only roughly. Prospective holders of these claims should scrutinize the terms of contract carefully and not rely simply on titles.

Many state laws require that incorporators reveal how much of the authorized stock they themselves have subscribed. Many also set a minimum amount to the stock actually sold and paid for before the corporation may begin business. In Delaware, for example, one thousand dollars is sufficient.

It is usual for states to insist that within the charter shall be recorded the names and legal residences of the incorporators and directors. Some states require only the names and addresses of the original incorporators. Where the incorporation process is professionalized, this information has less significance than formerly, since the incorporators are frequently "dummies" for the principals. Clerks of the legal counsel caring for the details of incorporation often serve in this capacity. The principals assume direction after the corporation is duly organized. It is customary also to state in the charter its official duration. Many states issue perpetual charters. Others limit them to specified periods, but make charter renewal relatively easy. Any other special stipulations may be included in the charter. It is important, however, that the charter should be drawn up in simple terms and constructed in strict accordance with the general incorporation laws of the state. Details relating to the operation of the company should be relegated to the corporate by-laws.

The corporate by-laws are a set of working rules or regulations by means of which the corporation operates within the powers it has obtained in its approved charter. These rules are adopted at the first meeting of the newly organized corporation, and they guide the corporate directors thereafter. Included in the by-laws are such fundamentals as these: regulations for the issuance and transfer of shares; the time and place of stockholders' meetings, the method of stockholder notification, quorum requirements, and methods of voting; election and qualification of directors;[34] the time, the place, and quorum requirements for the directors' meetings; officers to be elected by the directors; the duties and limitations imposed on the activities of such officers; standing committees within the board of directors, and the duties and activities of such committees; and finally, such things as dividend declaration and distribution, care of cash and bank deposits, debt limitations, and the like.

Given a set of working rules, the directors of a business corporation will usually meet monthly, or oftener if circumstances warrant it. The volume of work varies with the type of business, the size of the company, and the general and special economic conditions which affect the company's operations. Normally, directors' duties are confined to employment of important corporate officers, ratification of important contracts, approval of budgets, examination of plans for operation or expansion, the distribution of profits, and examination of the results obtained by the hired corporate officers. Since the directorate oversees the corporation and its operations, it assumes real responsibility. The directors are subject, therefore, to civil liability for certain faults, such as gross negligence, issuance of false information, and allowing the corporation to function beyond its corporate powers. And they may be subject also to criminal action for committing fraud, larceny, or embezzlement.

From the foregoing paragraphs, it is clear that the procedure which establishes the legal and administrative framework of the corporate organization has been reduced to the simplest terms. Such complexities as do arise are not so much the product of organizational form as they

---

[34] Some states require persons to own qualifying shares of stock to be eligible for a directorship; other states do not.

are the outcome of the vastness of the undertakings proposed. Simple and restricted objectives foster simple and clean-cut relations, whereas complex and unrestricted objectives produce contrary situations.

From the viewpoint of business enterprisers, the popularity of the corporate organization or of any other business form depends in particular on its usefulness in meeting the initial and continuing problems of organization.[35] In the main these problems can be stated summarily in the following fashion: (1) burdens and responsibilities which derive from the formation of the business enterprise, and (2) the organizational problems arising from the maintenance and expansion of the venture.

These broad problems in turn break down into a series of lesser problems which are evident in the following questions: How to organize with the minimum expense and legal difficulty? How to reduce to a minimum the burdens of taxation and governmental regulation which relate to the form of business organizations? How to minimize the liability of the owners of the business venture? In what ways is it possible to facilitate the acquisition of the necessary initial capital, and of additional capital when needed? Which organizational form will contribute most to the smooth operation of management in the event of large-scale development? Which form will contribute most to business planning? The merits and demerits of the common business forms of organization reflect the answers to these questions.

FACTORS AFFECTING THE CHOICE OF
BUSINESS ORGANIZATION

The so-called personal forms of business organization, the proprietorship and partnership, appear to have an advantage over the impersonal corporate form by being comparatively easy and inexpensive to organize. The sole proprietor has no problem or expense related to the form of organization. He simply acquires a location, invests his capital in the necessary equipment and supplies, and opens his doors for business. With slightly more difficulty a partnership may be established. No written contract need be formulated, but it is customary and wise to draw up a carefully stated written agreement known as the articles of co-partnership. Such a precaution reduces the risk of later friction which might arise to impair the success of the organization. A properly conceived partnership will be protected, therefore, by an agreement which carefully deals with such fundamental matters as capital contributions and

---

[35] In some instances choice of business organization is limited by law. For example, in New York State, incorporation is forbidden to the professions of law, medicine, and dentistry. On the other hand, it is required that commercial banking be undertaken only by corporate organizations.

their payment by the respective partners, duties of the partners, methods of accounting, provisions for periodic financial statements, compensation of the partners for services rendered, division of the profits and losses, duration of the partnership, and methods of partnership termination. The services of a competent lawyer experienced in drafting the articles would represent the main organizational expense.

The incorporation process is likely to be somewhat more arduous and expensive, despite the fact that the burdens have been reduced by state competition for the incorporation business and by professionalization of the incorporating process. There remain more legal formalities attached to incorporation, and filing fees and annual taxes must be paid.[36] These accepted but inconvenient requirements not infrequently cause business men to choose the informal, personal types of organization rather than the corporate form. This is especially true for small ventures.

It is quite possible that proprietorships and partnerships may be subject to public regulation. But the nature of the enterprise and not the form of organization is responsible for this. On the other hand, when a group of business associates adopts the corporate form, the state always requires that it recognize the existence of the convenient artificial personality by scrutinizing and approving the proposed charter. And the state imposes upon the corporation the duty of filing reports and paying corporate taxes and fees of various kinds. Moreover, the corporation must keep rigidly within the express powers stated in its charter and within the powers implied under the general incorporation laws of the state. Furthermore, a corporation has no legal standing outside the state of its incorporation unless it takes special steps to qualify itself. This may involve further burdens in the form of licenses, reports and taxes. In contrast, sole proprietors and partners are natural persons with full citizenship. They are not subject to these burdens. One must recognize, however, with respect to the corporation, that the principles of self-interest and interstate comity operate to keep the onerous burdens of public regulation within reasonable bounds. Hence, in this phase, the advantages of the proprietorship and partnership forms do not become unduly emphasized.

The corporation far outdistances its rivals in the matter of ownership liability for business debts. In a proprietorship a single individual contributes all the ownership funds. Consequently he takes all the gains, and he alone bears all the losses. His liability is unlimited, that is, even his non-business property is subject to legal attachment to pay his business creditors if his business assets are insufficient. In the partnership the burden of unlimited liability for business debts is even more serious.

---

[36] The variation in these fees and taxes has already been indicated. Other tax burdens of increasing importance are the state and Federal taxes on corporate incomes.

Ordinarily each partner is liable for the business acts of the other partners. Where the business and the number of partners is large, and the personal fortunes and investment in the partnership vary greatly among the partners, the unlimited liability feature is fraught with danger, particularly for the more well-to-do partner.[37] On the other hand, the corporate form imposes no such burdens or dangers on the stockholders. Liability is limited to the amount of each stockholder's investment.

In respect to the collection of capital funds for starting the business establishment, all the burdens and responsibilities attaching to each form are significant. The disadvantages of the corporate form, however, appear to be more than offset by the limited liability feature. And this is not the complete story. Except when the business enterprise is financially insignificant, the corporation offers exceptional advantages in raising capital. It can present to prospective investors a wide range of corporate securities—stocks and bonds. To fit the purses and investment inclinations of almost every type of person, these securities may be issued in convenient denominations, degrees of power and participation in the enterprise, and the like. Moreover, most securities are readily transferable, so that the owner or the lender can easily withdraw from his position by the legal sale of his security. Ordinarily this has no effect on the corporation, since it operates under the principle of perpetual succession, whereby the organization itself legally survives despite many changes in its owners.

In contrast, in collecting capital funds the proprietorship is limited to the personal savings of the proprietor and to such funds as he may obtain from credit-lending agencies. It is true that in obtaining credit his unlimited liability may be a real advantage, provided he has not placed his non-business property beyond legal attachment. But the limitations involved in capital acquisition are obvious. Hence proprietorships are restricted to such enterprises as require relatively little capital. Furthermore, transference of ownership is more difficult where this form is used. Prospective purchasers are likely to be fewer where ownership means a considerable outlay in a single project, an actual direct and active participation in the business enterprise, and unlimited liability for the business debts.

While the partnership is superior to the proprietorship in collecting

---

[37] A partner with fifty thousand dollars in personal assets and five thousand dollars at stake in a partnership could suffer badly should the partnership meet with financial disaster, especially if his co-partners were less well-off. Such a partner would be well-advised to enter into a limited partnership agreement whereby his personal liability would be limited to the amount of his investment. There are two difficulties in this arrangement. Firstly, some partner or partners must assume unlimited liability in any case. Secondly, such a partnership must be formed under the state statutes rather than under the common law, so as to record publicly the limited liability feature in order to protect creditors who might otherwise be misled.

its initial capital because it can tap the resources of more than one person, it is inferior to the corporation. The liability disadvantages of the partnership are such that well-to-do prospective participants are hesitant to enter the partnership and risk their personal fortunes. Moreover, the inclusion of too many partners with small investments results in an unwieldy organization. Therefore, partnerships, like proprietorships, will be most popular where the enterprise is to operate on a comparatively small scale.

Another factor which detracts from the popularity of investment in a partnership is the uncertainty of its legal existence. The death, withdrawal, bankruptcy, or legal disability of a single partner brings an end to the partnership agreement. Such a contingency might force the liquidation of the business and impair the investments of the other partners. No such problem arises under the corporate form of organization, which, other things being equal, promises greater permanence of life.

Business organizations not only need initial capital to get under way, but they also may need additional capital funds for expansion and development. Such funds may be accumulated from earnings, but success frequently depends on tapping other sources. Successful businesses can get such funds from either or both of two sources: (1) from banking institutions and other short-term lenders, and (2) from investment or long-term capital markets.

By its very nature, the proprietorship is limited largely to the short-term lending agencies.[38] But, because the liability of the proprietor is unlimited, he is likely to receive more favorable consideration from the short-term lending agency than would a corporation with equal net business assets engaged in the same business. As explained earlier, this is because the proprietor's non-business assets may be attached to satisfy the creditors' claims in case the business itself becomes incapable of meeting its obligations.

The partnership has similar advantages and disadvantages in acquiring more capital funds. It may, however, if the present partners are willing, add a new partner.[39] Legally, this means a new partnership and a new agreement to fit the added member into the co-partnership arrangement. Though this is an awkward procedure, it does offer a way to get additional funds while retaining the same fundamental form of organization.

The same advantages are attached to the corporation in raising additional funds as in raising initial capital. What this form lacks in short-

[38] The sole proprietor can seek long-term loans, of course, by mortgaging personal or business property. Such procedure would weaken his borrowing capacity in the short-term market.

[39] New partners must be acceptable to all the present partners under the legal principle known as *delectus personae*. This is a limiting factor in adding new capital to an established venture.

term borrowing capacity, as compared with the personal business forms with their unlimited liability, it more than offsets by its ability to tap the investment market. Securities may be issued in types and unit sizes that will appeal to a wide range of investors. Through the organized market mechanism, the public has a clearer picture of the past earnings of the issuer corporation, as well as of the earnings that prevail in that particular field of economic activity. And, moreover, if an investor is displeased with his choice, he has much less difficulty in disposing of his investment.

The form of organization may aid in or interfere with management. For example, in the partnership where each partner is a general agent, interference with each other's functions may develop. Even where precautions are taken to outline carefully each partner's duties in a written agreement, this may still occur. And even though a partner is acting beyond the scope assigned to him, outsiders can hold the partnership or the other partners legally accountable. On the other hand, if the partners tried to hold each other legally accountable it would become necessary to dissolve the partnership. In the case of the proprietorship, the proprietor is, of course, master of his own enterprise. He makes his own decisions, defines the duties of his subordinates, and limits their activities. Because he is dealing with subordinates, rather than with equals as is the case in a partnership, he can always wield the "big stick" of dismissal over those who assume too much authority. In the corporation, responsible management can be made more or less flexible. As a rule, owners delegate governing power to the directors to select the corporate officers, who then choose the executive personnel. Responsibility can be centralized or divided and subdivided as circumstances warrant.[40] The corporation also possesses another advantage for management. The fact that many states will endow a corporation with a perpetual charter is extremely helpful in drawing up long-term contracts and laying out other long-range plans, so necessary in a capitalistic enterprise. This advantage does not accrue to the personal forms of business organization.

THE CORPORATION AND ECONOMIC WELFARE

If the general economic welfare is promoted fully, our relatively scarce means of production must be utilized with the utmost efficiency. In any given stage of technological development this is accomplished best when the scarce resources are distributed among their various uses in such a fashion that no greater production of the desired things could

[40] It is quite possible that corporate organizations can develop into an unwieldy bureaucracy. See Temporary National Economic Committee, *Bureaucracy and Trusteeship in Large Corporations*, Monograph No. 11, Washington, D. C., 1940.

result from a different arrangement. This applies to the distribution of the productive factors within an industry as well as between industries. That form of business organization which contributes most to this end, and aids in technological development as well, is the form which holds forth the most promise to society.

In many respects the corporation assumes the rôle of the most promising contributor. It collects capital more easily than do other forms, and thus aids the development of the economics of larger-scale production. Through information derived from the market mechanism that has been established to assist the ready transference of corporate shares, the public should be better able to estimate the rates of return on investment that are derived from the different fields of economic activity. Normally the more personal forms of business organization keep this information secret. In the case of the corporation the presumption is that, through the information yielded by corporate reports, the investor is better equipped to select the places where productive resources should flow to yield the public a higher total of human gratifications.

The corporate mechanism, however, has not been an undiluted blessing. At times investment returns have been obscured. The sale of new securities too frequently has resulted in the victimizing of an ill-informed public. Market manipulation of the prices of old securities has decreased the usefulness of market quotations as guides for new investment. And other failures have impaired the effectiveness of the corporation in organizing production. But the larger social problems of the corporation have not grown out of its faulty operation as much as out of its very merits. These have made possible the organization of huge business units, and in the process their internal characteristics have been altered so as to remove owners from the position of control which they are assumed to possess in the theory of competitive individualism. Their removal creates a basic social problem unless their planning function is assumed successfully by some other interest in the corporation. The growth of giant concerns also has changed the relations between corporations. At times the corporate form has offered the means by which single firms have grown to dominate whole industries. Or where growth has stopped short of that extreme it has left so few firms in an industry that competitive controls have been weakened greatly.

4

The Character of Ownership in the Modern Large Corporation

Very large corporations have not only become a well-established feature of the American economy, but promise to be of increasing importance. In studying the growth of non-financial corporations[1] between 1909 and 1929, Berle and Means conclude that companies with gross assets in excess of ninety millions of dollars increased in size two or three times as fast as the average.[2] And in the severe depression following 1929 the large companies gained further ground. The following table shows that as a group they suffered some loss in assets but did better than the smaller enterprises.

Table 1

ASSETS OF NON-FINANCIAL CORPORATIONS, 1929–1933[3]

	Total Assets in Millions of Dollars		
	1929	1931	1933
The 200 largest[a]	98,597	101,662	95,617
All others	100,832	76,766	72,104
Total	199,429	178,428	167,721
Percentage importance of the largest	49.4	57.0	57.0

[a] Corporations with gross assets (less depreciation and depletion) of sixty-seven millions or more.

Depression obviously does neither the large nor the small company any particular good, but at least in this instance of a very severe depression the large enterprise stood the strain comparatively well.

[1] These include all corporations except those in commercial banking, insurance, investment, and the trust field.
[2] Berle and Means, *op. cit.*, p. 40.
[3] National Resources Committee, *The Structure of the American Economy* (Washington, D. C., U. S. Government Printing Office, 1939), Part I, Table VII, p. 107.

It seems almost certain that a larger and larger rôle will be played in the American economy by these giant concerns. It must be through the instrumentality of such organizations that much of our economic planning is effected. And if competitive individualism exists to regulate economic affairs in any large part of our economy, it becomes apparent that the individual is frequently a corporate being of great power and size. Private enterprise has in many sections of the economy fallen into a corporate scheme that dwarfs the individual and even rivals many political units in wealth and strength. The market, so important in the theory of competitive capitalism, has been affected by the great power of individual sellers and buyers and by their great scope. More and more semi-finished goods and many services are not being bought and sold on the market, but are kept from the raw material to the finished article under the administrative control of large concerns. Size in itself need not be objectionable, but the power of many corporate units is so great that their affairs cannot help being of public concern. So many aspects of our life are affected that control of these giants cannot remain wholly the private affair of powerful management officers and owners.

The generally accepted economic thought of the nineteenth century gave to the private property-owner an important duty in exchange for certain indulgences. The owner was left relatively free to direct his property as he wished and to enjoy the income it produced. It seemed logical to give this considerable grant of power to the individual. The economic benefits he sought for himself came as he contributed to the production of needed goods and services. The owner of an enterprise committed his capital to certain risks and benefited only from the residue of income left after labor, raw materials, and borrowed capital had been paid for. If his planning brought sufficiently valuable goods and services to the market, he was rewarded with prices that more than covered his costs; the residual income was his reward. Adam Smith and his immediate successors, however, viewed the owner as operating in close contact with his business. Today many owners collectively subscribe the property for huge corporate enterprises and are far removed from any experience in the affairs of their enterprise.

When the owner attempts to take some part in controlling his business he frequently is dwarfed by the corporate mechanism. While legal and to a certain extent economic theory still views control of business as resting in his hands, he frequently has delegated most of his duties to boards of directors and his control over these boards is only passive. And directors, in their turn, not uncommonly are forced by the complexity of the business to hand control over essential matters to management officers. The owner may be so far removed from essential affairs that tasks assigned to him in nineteenth-century thought may be far beyond his scope and he may have permanently abandoned them. His functions, however, are necessary ones and must be assumed by some group if production is to be carried on. As a result, the extent to which the owner has lost control and the present location of that control are matters of general social concern.

The Two Hundred

In a study of the ownership of the two hundred largest non-financial corporations in American industry, the Securities and Exchange Commission has thrown a great deal of light on the character of ownership and the extent to which stockholders actually control large corporations.[4] In 1937, these companies individually had balance sheet assets of over sixty million dollars and their combined assets came to seventy billion dollars. Their dividends of two billion dollars made up 45 per cent of the dividends of all non-financial corporations, and their assets represented a similar percentage of the wealth of such corporations.[5]

In the following list of the two hundred we find ninety-six manufacturing companies that dominate most of the important lines of manufacture—about one-third of the chemical industry, one-half or more of petroleum refining, autos, steel, non-ferrous metal industries, and important branches of the machine industries. There are twenty-nine railroads owning approximately one-half of the assets of all railroads, and forty-five outstanding electric power, gas, and water companies possessing about the same importance in their field. The thirty great retail and service organizations included in the list do not dominate their fields to the same extent. Although the motion-picture industry, chain stores and mail-order houses are important exceptions, most industries producing consumers' goods such as beverages, textiles, leather and the like show the large corporation holding only about 10 per cent of the total corporate assets.[6]

In addition to the 1937 figures compiled by the Securities and Exchange Commission, figures are supplied also for the fiscal year ending on or about December 31, 1947, to show the changes in dollar values in ten years.[7] No attempt has been made to adjust values to price level

---

[4] Banking, insurance, investment and trust companies were excluded, as well as companies in bankruptcy or receivership and subsidiary corporations having less than sixty million dollars' worth of stocks in the hands of the public.

[5] Temporary National Economic Committee, *The Distribution of Ownership in the 200 Largest Non-financial Corporations*, Monograph No. 29 (1940), p. 4 (hereafter cited as T. N. E. C., *Monograph* No. 29).

[6] Attention is called at this point to the merger movement taking place in the food and beverage, textile and apparel, and other fields since the end of World War II. See Chap. 2.

[7] The 1947 data are derived from Standard and Poor's and Moody's investment manuals.

changes. Substitutes for companies that have disappeared from the list for one reason or another have not been inserted, although there are many that qualify in the sixty million-or-more dollar asset class.

EXTRACTIVE AND MANUFACTURING

Industry and Company	Total Assets in Thousands of Dollars on or about December 31 1937	1947
Agriculture:		
United Fruit Co.. $	186,774 $	258,446
Coal mining:		
Glen Alden Coal Co......................................	145,093	102,185
The Lehigh Coal & Navigation Co........................	80,428	75,516
Philadelphia & Reading Coal & Iron Co. (Reorganized 1945).	83,104	45,944
Pittsburgh Coal Co. (Became by merger in 1945 Pittsburgh Consolidation Coal Co.).............................	139,537	147,367
Other extractive industries:		
Texas Gulf Sulphur Co.................................	62,900	79,061
Food and related products:		
Grain milling and baking:		
National Biscuit Co................................	124,023	154,313
Dairy products:		
The Borden Co.....................................	122,435	206,187
National Dairy Products Corporation..................	202,807	276,943
Meat packing and allied industries:		
Armour & Co. of Delaware } merged 9/24/43	210,478	
Armour & Co. (Illinois)	329,964	420,887
Cudahy Packing Co.................................	85,871	93,670
Swift & Co..	319,961	437,148
Wilson & Co., Inc...................................	90,011	139,801
Canning and preserving:		
California Packing Corporation.......................	65,408	81,621
Sugar Refining:		
The American Sugar Refining Co......................	118,193	132,585
Miscellaneous:		
Corn Products Refining Co............................	110,622	145,622
General Foods Corporation...........................	76,054	207,082
Standard Brands, Inc................................	77,647	134,602
Tobacco products:		
The American Tobacco Co.............................	274,023	646,754
Liggett & Myers Tobacco Co..........................	183,607	366,247
R. J. Reynolds Tobacco Co............................	180,721	390,182
Beverages:		
Distilleries:		
National Distillers Products Corporation..............	64,467	209,553
Schenley Distillers Corporation.......................	82,462	278,474
Other beverages:		
The Coca-Cola Co..................................	76,295	167,997
Textiles and textile products:		
Cotton and wool:		
American Woolen Co...............................	65,200	117,579
Lumber and lumber products:		
Weyerhaeuser Timber Co.............................	140,280	166,540
Paper and allied products:		
Crown Zellerbach Corporation........................	104,550	129,000
International Paper & Power Co.......................	258,143	252,533
Printing, publishing, and allied industries:		
Hearst Consolidated Publications, Inc..................	128,021	148,122

Industry and Company	Total Assets in Thousands of Dollars on or about December 31	
	1937	1947
Chemicals and fertilizers:		
American Cyanamid Co. .... $	69,863	$ 206,618
Allied Chemical & Dye Corporation.....................	233,432	574,818
E. I. du Pont de Nemours & Co........................	699,139	1,438,115
Union Carbide & Carbon Corporation..................	292,595	649,109
Drugs, medicines, toilet preparations, and soap:		
Colgate-Palmolive-Peet Co.	68,734	102,726
The Proctor & Gamble Co.	144,529	242,263
Petroleum refining:		
The Atlantic Refining Co.	186,213	329,645
Consolidated Oil Corporation (Now Sinclair Oil Corporation)	352,319	591,280
Continental Oil Co.	104,351	209,224
Empire Gas & Fuel Co. (Subsidiary of Cities Service Co.)....	413,941	278,972[8]
Gulf Oil Corporation.	560,399	929,169
Mid-Continent Petroleum Corporation.	65,383	115,648
The Ohio Oil Co.	138,856	163,773
Phillips Petroleum Co.	212,454	439,289
The Pure Oil Co.	178,442	244,540
Richfield Oil Corporation.	87,135	109,180
Shell Union Oil Corporation...........................	380,203	533,912
Socony Vacuum Oil Co.	905,213	1,261,974
Standard Oil Co. of California.	596,334	876,185
Standard Oil Co. (Indiana).	735,079	1,268,104
Standard Oil Co. (New Jersey).	2,060,816	2,995,990
Sun Oil Co.	128,401	212,829
The Texas Corporation (Now The Texas Co.).	614,793	1,115,345
Tide Water Associated Oil Co.	203,773	262,801
Union Oil Co. of California.	165,516	271,827
Tires and other rubber products:		
The Firestone Tire & Rubber Co.	166,192	324,394
The B. F. Goodrich Co.	135,436	246,722
The Goodyear Tire & Rubber Co.	194,933	407,845
United States Rubber Co.	179,117	348,341
Leather and leather products:		
International Shoe Co.	83,625	108,730
Building materials and equipment:		
Building materials and supplies:		
Pittsburgh Plate Glass Co.	118,124	206,671
United States Gypsum Co.	65,180	132,497
Building equipment:		
American Radiator & Standard Sanitary Corporation....	165,825	153,458
Crane Co.	108,667	129,411
Iron and steel:		
The American Rolling Mill Co. (Now Armco Steel Corporation).	145,845	248,792
Bethlehem Steel Corporation.	715,810	948,758
Inland Steel Co.	158,326	243,724
Jones & Laughlin Steel Corporation.	219,643	341,329
National Steel Corporation.	204,453	292,361
Republic Steel Corporation.	364,659	455,061
United States Steel Corporation.	1,918,729	2,162,613

[8] From balance sheet of 12/31/46. Company data not shown separately in recent years.

Industry and Company	Total Assets in Thousands of Dollars on or about December 31	
	1937	1947
Wheeling Steel Corporation.......................... $	123,551	$ 158,487
The Youngstown Sheet & Tube Co.....................	220,641	260,331
Non-ferrous metals:		
Aluminum Company of America......................	236,567	430,118
The American Metal Company, Ltd....................	68,090	93,016
American Smelting & Refining Co.....................	151,991	255,568
Anaconda Copper Mining Co.........................	592,825	637,462
Climax Molybdenum Co..............................	81,022	67,086
Kennecott Copper Corporation........................	354,497	540,612
National Lead Co...................................	99,035	162,854
The New Jersey Zinc Co.............................	88,681	88,581
Phelps Dodge Corporation...........................	196,479	250,550
United States Smelting, Refining & Mining Co...........	71,480	75,136
Machinery and tools (including electrical):		
Industrial machinery and tools:		
Allis-Chalmers Manufacturing Co....................	110,636	213,751
The National Supply Co............................	73,864	86,949
United Shoe Machinery Corporation..................	126,740	104,859
Agricultural machinery and implements:		
Deere & Co.......................................	108,105	228,900
International Harvester Co..........................	427,074	620,119
Electrical machinery and equipment:		
General Electric Co................................	423,177	1,026,865
Westinghouse Electric & Manufacturing Co...........	227,455	601,632
Radio:		
Radio Corporation of America.......................	89,373	216,196
Office equipment and machinery:		
International Business Machines Corporation...........	74,219	184,270
Miscellaneous:		
Singer Manufacturing Co...........................	163,637	205,790
Automobiles and parts:		
Automobiles and trucks:		
Chrysler Corporation...............................	188,803	487,200
Ford Motor Co. (Delaware).........................	704,923	1,025,733
General Motors Corporation.........................	1,227,322	2,575,986
Other transportation equipment:		
Railroad equipment:		
American Car & Foundry Co........................	91,793	145,674
Pullman, Inc......................................	263,653	196,550
Miscellaneous manufacturing industries:		
American Can Co...................................	178,218	249,568
Continental Can Co................................	134,409	206,830
Eastman Kodak Co.................................	179,387	359,846
Owens-Illinois Glass Co............................	87,562	162,086
Total extractive and manufacturing..................	$25,198,929	$40,104,609

MERCHANDISING

Chain Stores:		
The Great Atlantic & Pacific Tea Co. of America.........	184,621	322,849
S. S. Kresge Co....................................	123,453	182,544
S. H. Kress & Co...................................	75,873	88,955
J. C. Penney Co....................................	81,413	222,841
Safeway Stores, Inc.................................	71,864	134,788
F. W. Woolworth Co................................	221,747	325,030

Industry and Company	Total Assets in Thousands of Dollars on or about December 31	
	1937	1947
Department stores:		
Gimbel Bros., Inc..	$ 83,281	$ 131,450
R. H. Macy & Co., Inc......................................	96,322	129,324
Marshall, Field & Co..	83,534	99,704
Mail-order houses:		
Montgomery Ward & Co., Inc..............................	213,189	530,041
Sears, Roebuck & Co.......................................	284,073	711,175
Wholesale, commission, and brokerage:		
Anderson, Clayton & Co....................................	91,096	213,537
Total merchandising.....................................	$ 1,610,466	$ 3,092,238

TRANSPORTATION

	1937	1947
Railroads:		
The Atchison, Topeka & Santa Fe Ry. Co.................	1,104,210	1,256,605
Atlantic Coast Line R. R. Co..............................	310,132	371,936
The Baltimore & Ohio R. R. Co...........................	1,114,155	1,186,425
Boston & Albany R. R. Co.................................	67,783	62,909
Carolina, Clinchfield & Ohio Ry...........................	68,199	69,394
The Central R. R. Co. of New Jersey......................	170,582	183,163
The Chesapeake & Ohio Ry. Co. (In 1947 acquired the Pere Marquette Ry. Co. by merger.).........................	673,622	736,913
The Delaware & Hudson Co................................	225,136	194,918
The Delaware, Lackawanna & Western R. R. Co. (In 1945 acquired Morris & Essex R. R. Co.)....................	174,428	294,801
The Great Northern Ry. Co................................	761,399	792,059
Illinois Central R. R. Co...................................	643,566	613,489
Kansas City Southern Ry. Co..............................	133,508	156,742
Lehigh Valley R. R. Co....................................	209,337	180,251
Louisville & Nashville R. R. Co............................	447,897	475,483
Morris & Essex R. R. Co. (see above).....................	89,759	
The New York Central R. R. Co............................	1,639,180	1,731,545
The New York, Chicago & St. Louis R. R. Co.............	273,825	292,170
Norfolk & Western R. R. Co...............................	479,261	574,644
Northern Pacific Ry. Co...................................	784,689	828,670
Pennsylvania R. R. Co.....................................	2,011,606	2,220,598
Pere Marquette Ry. Co. (see above).......................	155,733	
Reading Co...	385,865	350,358
Southern Pacific Co..	581,223	661,949
Union Pacific R. R. Co.....................................	1,094,581	1,155,240
The Virginian Railway Co..................................	154,248	160,724
Western Maryland Ry. Co..................................	166,996	189,316
Western Pacific R. R. Corporation.........................	114,446	127,844
Total railroads...	$16,017,495	$15,868,146
Other transportation:		
Street railroads:		
Hudson & Manhattan R. R. Co...........................	122,319	116,110
Miscellaneous:		
General American Transportation Corporation...........	104,163	131,802
Total other transportation...........................	$ 226,482	$ 247,912

COMMUNICATION

	1937	1947
Telephone and telegraph:		
American Telephone & Telegraph Co......................	3,859,293	4,597,029
General Telephone Corporation............................	71,894	156,393
International Telephone & Telegraph Corporation..........	514,097	426,894

Industry and Company	Total Assets in Thousands of Dollars on or about December 31	
	1937	1947
New England Telephone & Telegraph Co.................. $	253,884	$ 345,707
The Pacific Telephone & Telegraph Co. (Acquired So. California Telephone Co., 1947).........................	369,382	796,194
Western Union Telegraph Co...........................	304,528	320,787
Total communication............................... $	5,373,078	$ 6,643,004

SERVICE

Service:

Amusements:

	1937	1947
Loew's Inc..	142,554	229,853
Paramount Pictures, Inc.............................	120,219	185,589
Warner Bros. Pictures, Inc..........................	177,545	178,048
Total service..................................... $	440,318	$ 593,490

ELECTRIC, ETC.

Electric light, power, heat, water and gas companies:

Holding:

	1937	1947
American & Foreign Power Co. Inc. (Reorganized 1947 under P. U. H. Co. Act.)..........................	700,376	702,440
American Gas & Electric Co..........................	441,094	528,830
American Power & Light Co. (New reorganization plan to S. E. C. 4/3/48.)................................	768,511	800,526
American Water Works & Electric Co. (In liquidation by S. E. C. order; American Water Works Co, successor.)..	358,446	159,985
Central & Southwest Utilities Co. (Changed to Central & Southwest Utilities Corp. Corporate simplification under P. U. H. Co. Act. 1947).........................	188,772	208,205
Cities Service Co. (Property divestment 1947 under P. U. H. Co. Act.)...............................	1,099,472	899,585
Columbia Gas & Electric Corporation (Under integration proceedings, name changed to Columbia Gas System, Inc.)..	596,324	276,612
Commonwealth & Southern Corporation (Dissolution proceedings underway.)............................	1,132,316	1,123,076
Electric Power & Light Corporation (Dissolution proceedings underway.)................................	682,498	549,883
Engineers Public Service Co. (Dissolution effected 5/31/47.)	341,290	
Federal Water Service Corporation (Dissolved in 1941, and successor company dissolved under P. U. H. Co. Act.)	175,666	
International Hydro-electric System (In liquidation.)....	516,906	78,829
Lone Star Gas Corporation (Dissolved 1943. Successor, Lone Star Gas Co.)..............................	129,429	102,774
The Middle West Corporation (Dissolution proceedings underway under P. U. H. Co. Act.).................	407,960	
National Power & Light Co. (In liquidation.)...........	548,022	
New England Gas & Electric Association (Recapitalized in 1946.)...	93,686	62,268
New England Power Association (Became New England Electric System, 6/3/47.).......................:	362,303	374,123
Niagara Hudson Power Corporation...................	559,735	471,690
The North American Co. (Structure simplified 1947–1948 under P. U. H. Co. Act.)......................	795,214	309,476
Northern States Power Co. (Delaware) (liquidation proceedings underway.)...............................	264,976	260,254

Industry and Company	Total Assets in Thousands of Dollars on or about December 31	
	1937	1947
Pacific Lighting Corporation............................	$ 153,319	$ 194,263
Philadelphia Company (Corporate simplification under-way in 1947 under P. U. H. Co. Act.)................	336,079	286,252
Public Service Corporation of New Jersey (Dissolved under P. U. H. Co. Act, effective 7/1/48.).................	556,570	
Standard Gas & Electric Co. (Integration proceedings, P. U. H. Co. Act.)..................................	810,957	526,728
United Gas Corporation..............................	265,685	267,948
The United Gas Improvement Co. (Divestment proceed-ings, P. U. H. Co. Act.).............................	764,757	74,598
The United Light & Power Co. (Liquidated 1947 under P. U. H. Co. Act.).................................	507,017	
The West Penn Electric Co...........................	247,181	303,625
Operating-holding:		
Commonwealth Edison Co............................	682,181	751,146
Consolidated Edison Co. of New York, Inc.............	1,264,905	1,158,872
Long Island Lighting Co. (Simplification proceedings underway.)..	130,606	89,382
Pacific Gas & Electric Co............................	641,251	820,004
The Peoples Gas, Light & Coke Co....................	171,069	152,612
Operating:		
Boston Edison Co....................................	164,088	179,511
The Brooklyn Union Gas Co..........................	111,118	92,013
The Cincinnati Gas & Electric Co.....................	127,872	122,049
The Cleveland Electric Illuminating Co................	125,663	179,424
Consolidated Gas, Electric Light & Power Co. of Baltimore	151,606	187,499
Consumers Power Co.................................	235,209	299,293
The Detroit Edison Co...............................	304,256	339,181
Duke Power Co......................................	157,924	181,374
Duquesne Light Co..................................	198,435	157,828
The Kansas City Power & Light Co....................	76,055	84,079
Philadelphia Electric Co.............................	390,777	471,009
Southern California Edison, Ltd. (Became Southern Cali-fornia Edison Co. in 1947.).........................	357,117	381,050
Total...	$19,094,693	$14,208,296
Unclassified companies:		
Koppers United Co. and Koppers Co. (Consolidated) (Merged into Koppers Co., Inc. in 1944.).....................	343,162	101,507
Total unclassified companies.......................	343,162	101,507
Grand Total...................................	$69,002,459	$80,859,202

The Character of Ownership in the Two Hundred in 1937

In making possible the growth of these powerful economic units the security system of the corporation has made corporate shares the common form of business wealth for the individual. And two somewhat contradictory developments have occurred in the share ownership of these large companies. On the one hand, a great many small investors have contributed capital, so that ownership has come to be very widely dispersed. But on the other hand, in many cases, a few large investors are responsible for the concentration of sizable blocs of shares in the hands of a few people.

For corporate industry as a whole there are many evidences of widely dispersed stockholdings. In the United States about one person in fifteen owns one or more shares. The most reliable estimates place the number of owners between eight and ten millions, and they split their investments into about twenty-four millions of individual blocs or shareholdings.[9] Since 1927 the number of shareholders has increased more rapidly than the number of new shares, so that the general trend toward wider dispersion and smaller individual holdings seems to be continuing.[10]

Dispersion is very marked among the two hundred. In 1937 their 208 issues of common stocks were broken up into slightly over seven million shareholdings. With the total value at twenty-eight billions of dollars the individual shareholding was small, being worth about four thousand.[11] Since one person may own a number of shareholdings, it is not clear how many individual owners there were, but it is possible to make a rough estimate. For all corporations it appears that on the average the individual stockholder owns a share or more in three different issues. If this same condition exists for the stock of the two hundred, it will mean that the seven million shareholdings are spread into the hands of approximately two and one-third million people.

In 1937 with 641,308 common stockholders, the American Telephone and Telegraph Company had the largest number of owners; but over half the stock issues of the large companies had between ten thousand and one hundred thousand stockholders.[12]

It follows that many individual holdings must be small. The Securities and Exchange Commission found that about 83 per cent of the total number of all common shareholdings consisted of less than one hundred shares. And at the prices of December 31, 1937, nearly half the shareholdings had a value of five hundred dollars or less.[13] Under 5 per cent of them had a value above five thousand dollars. Companies ranging in capital size between two hundred and five hundred million show less than the average proportion of small holdings, while those below two hundred million and those above five hundred million have slightly more than their share of small holdings. The importance of the stock market

---

[9] A shareholding is a bloc of one or more shares of one issue of stock, either owned beneficially by one person or registered on the books of the corporation in the name of one person. Since in a small percentage of cases the names listed on the books of the issuing corporation are not those of the beneficial owners but those of brokers, banks and trustees, the dispersion of ownership is actually greater than would appear from a study of registered stockholdings.

[10] T. N. E. C., *op. cit.*, pp. 16 ff.

[11] *Ibid.*, pp. 23 ff.

[12] *Ibid.*, Table 25, p. 286. As of December 31, 1947, the A. T. & T. Company had 723,374 common stockholders, an increase of about 80,000 in ten years.

[13] *Ibid.*, Table 22, p. 282.

in the dispersion of stocks is apparent. The percentage of the small holdings is greater for common stocks listed on the exchanges than for unlisted stocks.

Preferred stock ownership shows slightly less dispersion.[14] The 196
issues, with a market value on December 31, 1937, in excess of five
billion dollars, were divided into 1,394,000 shareholdings. On the average the distribution is obviously wide, but shows only one-fifth of the
issues with over ten thousand owners as against three-fifths for common stocks. And the value of individual holdings is slightly greater. The
percentage of shareholdings with a value under $500 was about 10 per
cent less than in the case of common stocks. Since 90 per cent of the
shareholdings were in lots of less than one hundred shares as against
only 83 per cent for common stocks, the greater value per shareholding
reflects a higher average value for preferred stocks.

While there is this wide dispersion of common and preferred stocks
among many small owners, there also exists a markedly unequal distribution of the shares among the individual shareholdings. There are
many small holdings, but a relatively few large holdings frequently contain a high percentage of the total shares. The following chart illustrates
this condition.[15] The diagonal line would represent the situation if all
the individual shareholdings were of equal size: 10 per cent of the shareholdings would contain 10 per cent of the total value of the shares outstanding; 50 per cent would contain 50 per cent of the total value, and
so forth. The actual distribution of ownership is quite different. For
common stock issues, 10 per cent of the individual holdings contain
over 80 per cent of the total value of outstanding common stocks; 35
per cent of the holdings contain nearly 95 per cent of the total value.
Ownership of the preferred issues is less concentrated, but is still far
away from an equal distribution.

Study of a number of representative companies shows that the degree
of concentration varies markedly for different stock issues. The common
stock of the Inland Steel Company is much more concentrated than that
of the United States Steel Corporation and the Bethlehem Steel. Ownership is heavily concentrated in the United States Rubber Company, but
much less so in the B. F. Goodrich Company. Others where a high degree of concentration is particularly noticeable are E. I. du Pont de
Nemours and Co., the Singer Manufacturing Company, Standard Oil of
New Jersey, Gulf Oil, Shell Union Oil Company, and Sun Oil Company. Common stocks of the New York Central and the Norfolk and
Western Railroads are heavily concentrated, while those of the Union
Pacific and the Pennsylvania are more evenly distributed. Among the

[14] *Ibid.*, Table 28, p. 289.
[15] *Ibid.*, Chart V, p. 41.

Table 2

CONCENTRATION OF OWNERSHIP OF STOCK IN 200 LARGEST
NON-FINANCIAL CORPORATIONS

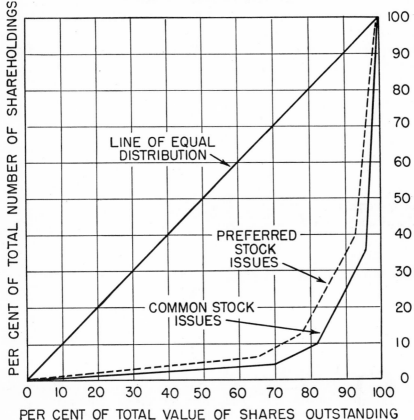

three large tobacco companies the holdings also vary considerably, with the R. J. Reynolds Company showing the greatest concentration and the American Tobacco the least.

In spite of a great deal of individual variation it appears that for half the 208 common stock issues only 1½ per cent of the total of individual shareholdings is needed to make up a majority of the common stock outstanding.[16] For three-quarters of the issues it is only necessary to assemble 2½ per cent of the shareholdings to collect a majority vote. In only a very few cases does it take over 5 per cent to make up a majority of an issue.

Since 94 per cent of the stock issues of the two hundred have over ten thousand owners, these percentages, though small, still might spread

---

[16] Since a broker or other recorded owner may be holding one bloc of stock for several beneficial shareholders, these percentages would be higher if recorded in terms of beneficial shareholdings.

majority control over a sizable body of investors. If 2½ per cent of the
owners make up a majority of the shareholdings in a company, and
if there are fifty thousand shareholdings of approximately the same size,
majority control would rest in the hands of 1250 people. But the marked
inequality in the size of shareholdings makes a considerably greater concentration. This is apparent in the following figures, which show the
importance of the twenty largest blocs of stock in the different issues of
the two hundred.

THE VALUE OF THE TWENTY LARGEST RECORD HOLDINGS IN 208
COMMON STOCK ISSUES AS A PERCENTAGE OF TOTAL VALUE[17]

Manufacturing Companies.................................... 26.7%
Railroads.. 24.9%
Electric, Gas and Water Utilities............................. 45.3%
Others... 17.3%

Holding companies account for the particularly heavy concentration
of ownership in the public utility category, and the presence of the
American Telephone and Telegraph Company in the fourth category
explains much of the smaller percentage found there.

With stock values so unevenly dispersed, it is inevitable that a number of specific issues will be held mainly by the twenty largest stockholders. The Securities and Exchange Commission found twenty owners
with 50 per cent or more of the outstanding shares in over one-fourth
of the 208 common stock issues, with 30 to 50 per cent in over one-sixth
of the issues, and 10 to 30 per cent in one-third.[18] In only forty-six issues
did the twenty largest owners fail to hold 10 per cent of the outstanding
shares.

In general, the preferred issues show the same picture, although the
concentration appears slightly less than for common stocks. It is worth
noting that the large holders have not concentrated their holdings in
those preferred issues that carry the voting privilege. One hundred and
eleven of the 196 preferred stocks had full voting rights and 68 had
contingent rights, but large shareholdings were not particularly concentrated in these issues.

Character of Control in the Two Hundred

The dispersion and concentration of stock ownership have had important effects on the control exercised by owners in the large corporations. By electing boards of directors, stockholders are supposed to set
the broad policies of corporations. In general, the wide dispersion of
stocks has made it difficult for great numbers of owners to keep up with

[17] T. N. E. C., *op. cit.*, Table 4, p. 73. Holdings of banks, brokers, etc., are excluded where beneficiary was not disclosed.
[18] *Ibid.*, Table 5, p. 81.

the affairs of the corporation, and has made it impossible for many to attend annual meetings where policy may be debated. As a result, a great many stockholders never exercise their right to vote, and many merely turn their vote over to others to be cast at the meetings of the stockholders. At the same time, the presence of a few large holdings coupled with the wide dispersion of the remaining shares makes it easy for minority groups of owners to maintain a control out of proportion to their ownership.

In studying the two hundred, the Securities and Exchange Commission found between 1937 and 1939 that in only forty-two companies did the majority of the voting stock exercise control.[19] In nine of these, single families held a majority of the stock, and in six others a multiple-family majority control was present.[20] The most obvious examples of the former exists in the Ford Motor Company, where three members of the family own all the voting stock.[21] The Jones and Laughlin families give their names to and own control of the Jones and Laughlin Steel Corporation. The complexity of ownership arrangements that may exist is illustrated in the case of the Singer Manufacturing Company, where three families (Clarke, Bourne and Singer) were beneficial owners of nearly half the voting stock, which was spread over two dozen family trusts, one family holding company, and several direct holdings.

In almost three-quarters of the cases of majority control the stock was owned by other corporations. For example, the American Telephone and Telegraph Company held over half the voting stock of the New England Telephone and Telegraph Company and the Pacific Telephone and Telegraph Company. The Shell Union Oil Company appeared as a heavily controlled subsidiary of the Royal Dutch Shell. Three of the large railroad companies and over a dozen of the large electric, gas and water utilities were under the majority control of other corporations.

Minority control in varying degrees was found in ninety-seven of the companies.[22] Thirty-seven of these showed a "predominant minority" controlling between 30 and 50 per cent of the voting stock. Family control of the E. I. du Pont de Nemours Company rested safely on ownership of 44 per cent of the common stock. And the Mellon family held over 34 per cent of the common stock of the Aluminum Company of

[19] *Ibid.*, pp. 14, 86–87.
[20] The Commission found very few cases where a single individual or corporation was the dominant stockholder. Usually several holdings voted and acted in unison to make up the majority control. Such holdings were designated as a single "interest group" and in some cases were owned beneficially by one person but held through separate instrumentalities such as trust funds, estates and personal holding companies.
[21] Another example is the Great Atlantic and Pacific Tea Company of America, in which the Hartford family owned all the voting common stock through a family holding company, the New York Great Atlantic and Pacific Tea Company, Inc.
[22] T. N. E. C., *op. cit.*, p. 107.

America.[23] Three families (Field, Simpson and Shedd) held a predominant minority of the stock of Marshall Field and Co.

Corporations, particularly in the public utility field, were the predominant minority control in seventeen of the thirty-seven cases. The Electric Bond and Share Company held such control over the American Power and Light Company, the American and Foreign Power Company, Inc., and The National Power and Light Company. The Standard Gas and Electric and the United Corporation were other important holding companies. The American Light and Traction Co. and the North American Co. coöperated to maintain a safe working control over the Detroit Edison Co.

The Commission found forty-seven companies controlled by a "substantial minority" where control was exercised by interest groups owning between 10 and 30 per cent of the outstanding voting stock. Family groups in manufacturing and merchandising businesses made up half the group. The Crane, Colgate, Firestone, Gimbel, and other families gave their names to firms and held control over their policies through ownership of less than 30 per cent of the voting stock. Other well-known companies and families in the group were Pullman, Inc., (Mellon family); International Harvester (McCormick); United States Rubber Co. (du Pont). And the Rockefeller name was attached to five—The Ohio Oil Co., Socony Vacuum Oil Co., and the Standard Oil Companies of California, Indiana, and New Jersey.

Although the percentage of total voting shares was rather small in some of these cases, control seemed to be firmly held. It undoubtedly rested at least in part on the coöperation of the management with the dominant family. When stockholders receive notices of annual meetings from the management and are asked to assign their votes to a proxy they frequently drop the slip into the waste-paper basket, but many do return proxies, so that a bloc of votes rests in the hands of a committee named by the management and presumably friendly to the management. Where the minority owner has little more than 10 per cent of the voting shares, his position might be challenged by an unfriendly management.

In seventeen cases a "substantial minority" required the continued coöperation of several families, such as apparently exists between the Widener, Elkins, Dula, and Ryan families as minority holders in the Liggett and Myers Tobacco Company. In one case an English finance corporation, Selection Trust Co., owned 24 per cent of the common shares of The American Metal Co., Ltd., but the Hochschild, Sussman,

---

[23] Other examples of predominant control by a family group were: Cudahy Packing Company (Cudahy family), Deere and Co. (Deere family), Pittsburgh Coal Co. (Mellon family), Pittsburgh Plate Glass Co. (Pitcairn family), R. H. Macy and Co. (Straus family), S. S. Kresge Co. (Kresge family and Kresge Foundation), Western Pacific Railroad Co. (A. C. James family).

and Loeb families with only 14 per cent were represented in the management and apparently controlled the company.

Corporations controlled twelve of the two hundred through holdings of 10 to 30 per cent. These were all found in the railway and public utility fields, except for the General Motors Corporation. With 23 per cent of its common stock in the hands of E. I. du Pont de Nemours and Co., it fell under the control of that company. The Commonwealth and Southern Corporation, which has been noticeable for its quarrels with the TVA, is directed through a 19 per cent control of its stock by the American Superpower Corporation and the United Corporation.[24]

Even smaller holdings than 10 per cent seem in a few cases to constitute control.[25] In Swift and Company the Swift family owns a small percentage of the outstanding voting stock, but has sufficient representation in the management to suggest that it is in control. Other instances of the same condition appear in American Can Co., the Crown Zellerbach Corporation and Warner Bros. Pictures, Inc.

We finally come to a group of sixty-one companies where there is no evidence of ownership control. Three of these are railroads leased to other roads and hence controlled by them.[26] For some of the others it is possible that there is an ownership control that could not be located by the Securities and Exchange Commission. But it seems safe to say that there are at least fifty companies, one-quarter of the whole, in which owners do not perform their directive function. That rôle has been taken over by the chief officers of the corporation, who can maintain their position by use of the proxy machinery of the corporation.

Recent Growth

Reference to the table of the two hundred companies and their balance sheet data as of the end of 1947 will show that growth in the dollar value of assets has been greatest in the *extractive and manufacturing* category. There have been much smaller increases relatively in *merchandising;* in *communication;* and in the *service* categories. In *transportation* and in *electric (etc.) utilities* there has been a decline in the dollar amount of assets, especially in the public utility field where the effects of the Public Utility Holding Company Act of 1935 are being felt. Total assets of the two hundred have increased from $69 billion at the end of 1937 to almost $81 billion at the end of 1947, approximately 17 per cent.[27] The growth picture in real assets, as opposed to assets in dollars, is not clear, however, owing to such things as the depreciation of

---

[24] For the present status of The Commonwealth & Southern Corporation, see S. E. C., *Fourteenth Annual Report*, pp. 64–65.

[25] T. N. E. C., *op. cit.*, p. 109.

[26] Boston and Albany Railroad Co., Carolina, Clinchfield and Ohio Railway, and the Morris and Essex Railroad Co.

the dollar, the acquisition by some firms of war surplus properties at figures far less than cost, individual accounting practices relating to the revaluation of assets in a period of dollar depreciation, and so forth. It would appear, however, that the giant firms have not exhibited any real symptoms of economic anemia since the days when they fell under the scrutiny of the Temporary National Economic Committee. The picture will no doubt be presented more precisely when the Federal Government makes another of its periodic investigations of the growth of big business.

Conclusion

It is evident that large corporations possess great importance in the organization of American industry, and all indications point to an even greater rôle for them in the future. And as they have developed, they have spread their securities over a great number of small owners, and have at the same time dropped important blocs of stocks into the hands of a few owners. As a result, a great deal of economic power has fallen into the hands of a few people, and many owners no longer exercise any directing control over their property. The general situation developed in this chapter is summarized in the following table:

Table 3
TYPES OF CONTROL IN THE TWO HUNDRED

Controlling Group	Type of Control: Number of Instances				
	Majority	Pre-dominant Minority	Sub-stantial Minority	Small Minority	No Dominant Owner Group
Single family..............	9	13	13	8	
Multiple family............	6	6	17	5	
Family and corporation......		1	5		
Single corporation..........	22	14	6		
Two or more corporations....	5	3	6		
Totals.................	42	37	47	13	61

Where a few giant concerns dominate a field of industry and where these companies are under the control of a few people, competition may

[27] Actually in 1947 the number of companies involved is less than two hundred, since no new giants were included in the table to offset the disappearance of some of the original companies through merger, consolidation, dissolution, etc. For this reason the $81 billion of assets is an understatement.

be seriously threatened. On the one hand, the presence of a few large concerns may make price competition rather dangerous for them. And on the other hand, the existence of a small number of individuals in control of them may make coöperation very easy. In our later studies of single-firm monopoly and monopolistic coöperation we will find that these factors have been and are important. In our present concern for the functioning of corporate industry, we are forced to notice that frequently the ownership of property has been divorced from control of business. In practice many owners have surrendered their control to a minority of the stockholders or to management officers. In theory we have been satisfied with the economic results of owner control, but it is quite possible that minority control and management control may not give as satisfactory direction to business as majority control would. It is possible that the great mass of disfranchised owners may be injured and industry suffer through the loss of investor confidence in corporate industry. Or our economy may suffer in the case of management control because the rewards for efficient direction of industry go to property owners who are not responsible for that efficiency. These considerations make up the subject-matter of the inquiries pursued in the following chapters.

5

Minority Control

In an address before the American Bar Association at Chattanooga in 1910, Woodrow Wilson observed that, in most of our states, the holders of less than a majority of voting shares in a corporation were in an extremely unsatisfactory position. As shareholders they contributed to the corporation, yet they did not enjoy the property rights which they expected from their contribution. Often confronted with a "like it or lump it" attitude on the part of the majority or the management, they had no recourse, if dissatisfied, except to dispose of their stocks in the market, even though they might be forced to take a loss.

MINORITY PROTECTIONS

Wilson's comment was an over-statement of the defenseless condition of minority interests. Corporation law has aimed to protect the supposedly vulnerable minority. It is an accepted rule that the will of the majority, present and voting at meetings, shall prevail in the determination of corporate policy. But it is also an accepted rule that the majority stockholders and the corporate management which the majority has installed in office are bound to exercise both diligence and good faith in the conservation of the property of the corporation. Moreover, the majority cannot legally act beyond the powers of the corporate charter. And they must exercise diligence to protect the interest of the minority.[1] Failure of the majority to exercise reasonable diligence entitles minority stockholders to seek relief through courts of equity. Likewise an *ultra vires* act undertaken by the majority and any act tainted with fraud are grounds for equitable relief if the dissenting minority chooses to act.[2] A majority of stockholders, for example, cannot legally appropriate or divert to themselves, either directly or indirectly, the assets of the cor-

---

[1] Backus v. Finkelstein, 23 Fed. (2nd) 531 (1924).
[2] Lebold v. Inland Steamship Company, 82 Fed. (2nd) 351 (1936); Wabash Ry. Co. v. American Refrigerator Transit Co., 7 Fed. (2nd) 335 (1925).

poration to the injury of the other stockholders. Nor can the majority dispose of the rights of a corporation against the protest and to the injury of the minority. While the law recognizes reasonable, proper and lawful expenditures made at the behest of the majority, it will not support the payment of debts for which a corporation is not liable, even though the majority of the stockholders has approved such payments.[3] In short, the courts will protect the minority from majority actions which defraud or inflict unequitable conditions on the minority. But the court protection does not go so far as to permit a minority group to estop majority action clearly favorable to the corporation as a whole.[4]

In addition to these protections the minority stockholder is in the position of any other stockholder who possesses voting power. He is entitled to be properly notified of the meetings of the stockholders of the corporation. He has a right to attend such meetings, vote for the election of officers, and pass judgment on any fundamental changes which might vitally affect the corporation and its future. He has the right to participate in the profits and dividends according to the provisions laid down in the corporate charter. He has the right to share equitably in the residual assets upon dissolution. And he has the right to examine the books of the corporation. Generally all stockholders of the same class stand on equal footing as to their corporate rights and liabilities.

These protections may seem adequate, yet they may not be. Technically, the minority stockholders do have these rights and are afforded protection from the injurious acts of the majority shareholders and the management. Actually, however, these rights and protections may not be so clearly apparent and available to the minority stockholders. This has been the case frequently where corporations were large and many stockholders, possessing small amounts of stock, were widely scattered. The stockholder's imperfect knowledge of the law and all its technicalities has bred fear of litigation. Small stockholders, when injured, have tended to avoid legal entanglements, and have sought questionable relief through the stock market by sale of their stock, rather than risk satisfaction of their claims by legal proceedings.

THE MODERN LARGE CORPORATION AND MINORITY INTERESTS

It seems, however, that since the turn of the century, far from being a weak group needing more practical protection, in many instances the

---

[3] 18 Corpus Juris Secundum, 1194.

[4] Thus the erection of a toll bridge across a bay might necessitate the dissolution of a ferry company heretofore successfully serving the surrounding community. A minority could not successfully oppose the dissolution so long as they were treated equitably.

minority has actually assumed the powers of the majority. As we have shown in the previous chapter, in 50 per cent of our two hundred largest non-financial corporations, shares are so widely dispersed that a minority interest may exercise powers far beyond those normally attributed to it. With ownership of less than one-half the voting shares, for example, the Mellons control the policies of the Aluminum Company of America, and other family groups, the du Ponts, the McCormicks, and the Swifts in a similar ownership position exercise control over E. I. du Pont de Nemours, International Harvester, and Swift & Company respectively. This is quite contrary to the presumption long maintained in legal and economic theory that the ultimate power over corporate industry rested in the hands of the owner or owners who possessed a majority of the voting shares. The new development has raised new problems as regards the control and direction of the business affairs of the corporation. Now if anyone needs better legal protection, it may well be the widely scattered holders of the majority of the voting shares.

Minority Control

Immediate corporate control lies in the hands of the corporation's board of directors. Within this group majority rule prevails, and corporate policies are formulated to be laid before the management as a guide to general administration. Ultimate control is lodged in those individuals (interest group) or that individual who, either by actual ownership of a majority of the voting shares or by influence over the owners of a majority, can elect a majority of the board of directors. The ultimate control is exercised annually to establish the immediate control. Between annual meetings the immediate control may reign supreme in the determination of corporate policy, since the shareholders can no longer remove directors at will.[5] Minority control is the power of the holder or holders of less than a majority of the total voting stock to elect a majority of the board of directors, who presumably are cognizant of and always subservient to the will of the minority interest which elected them.

The possibilities of control by a minority interest become more apparent when it is realized that at an annual meeting of a corporation a quorum does not necessarily require the presence of a majority of the stockholders or a majority of the voting shares.[6] Provided no action

---

[5] There are exceptions, of course, since statutes, charters, and by-laws may empower stockholders to remove directors at any time for cause. See W. W. Cook, *The Principles of Corporation Law* (Ann Arbor, Michigan, The Lawyers Club, University of Michigan, 1925), pp. 360, 371. It should also be noted that the threat of removal has a strong influence when made by powerful stockholders.

[6] *Ibid.*, p. 332.

of an *ultra vires* nature is taken, the action of the majority of the attending quorum is as valid as the action of a majority of all the stockholders.[7]
Since this is so, the minority control under discussion assumes greater
stature. The du Pont family, for example, has control over 44 per cent
of the voting shares of the E. I. du Pont de Nemours Company.[8] If less
than 88 per cent of the voting stock is present, actually or through proxy,
at the stockholders' meeting, the 44 per cent minority interest easily becomes a real working control, *i.e.*, it is as effective as an outright majority
of all voting shares. And, providing there is management coöperation,
it is conceivable that a 10 per cent or even smaller minority interest
can dominate the action taken in an annual meeting. This latter condition
appears to prevail in such organizations as Swift & Company, Crown-
Zellerback Corporation, American Can Company, National Lead Company, and Warner Brothers' Pictures, Inc. The chance that the minority
interest will become a real working control varies directly with the
coöperation of management and inversely with the interest and intelligence shown by the other shareholders with voting powers. If, outside
the minority interest, the shareholdings are widely held in small amounts,
the minority interest can count on stockholder inertia, indifference, and
ignorance to strengthen its hand.

When a particular minority interest is opposed by another minority
group the control will eventually be lodged in the hands of that group
which exhibits the greater ability to solicit the proxies of the scattered
small shareholders. It is apparent, also, that since the existing board
of directors or management establishes the machinery for soliciting
proxies, a particular minority interest should have the support of management or be prepared to wage a proxy battle with a recalcitrant management. Such a battle is likely to be decided on the basis of popular
prestige and financial strength.[9]

Special Legal Devices As Aids to Minority Control

In addition to the general conditions conducive to minority control,
there are specific legal devices which minority interests may use to obtain control. Weighted or multiple voting stock contributes to this end.
Here one class of stock is given more than one vote per share, while
another class is given a single vote per share, or one class is given a
single vote per share, while another class is allowed but a fractional

---

[7] *Ibid.*, p. 333.

[8] Securities and Exchange Commission, *The Distribution of Ownership in the 200
Largest Non-financial Corporations* (Washington, D. C., 1940), p. 83.

[9] The outstanding case of this sort was that of John D. Rockefeller, Jr., *v.* Col.
Robert Stewart of the Standard Oil Co. of Indiana, in 1928–1929.

vote per share. Judicious holding of blocs of the weighted voting stock, combined with the general conditions contributing to minority control, assures control by a minority interest. One of the best known instances of this technique of lodging control in the hands of special interests was the case of the Cities Service Company. This corporation issued both preferred and common stock, but gave each share of preferred stock one vote, whereas each share of common had but one-twentieth of a vote. By this arrangement H. L. Doherty & Company, with an investment of $1,000,000 (one million shares of preferred at $1.00 per share, par value) controlled 27 per cent of the total votes that could possibly be cast at a stockholders' meeting.[10] Since the number of preferred stockholders was about 81,000 and common stockholders totaled nearly 378,000, the concentrated Doherty voting power was fairly secure in its control. This arrangement permitted a million-dollar stock investment to control a consolidated capital structure of a billion and a quarter dollars.[11]

Another device to which minority control sometimes turns is the voting trust. This is essentially a stock-pooling agreement whereby a group of individuals within a corporation for a specified period—usually not more than ten years—deposit their stock with designated trustees to hold and vote at the corporation's meetings. In exchange the stockholders receive voting trust certificates as evidence of the transaction and as claims on dividends and other rights. This is the usual and perhaps most important method of securing majority control for a limited period of time. But it can be and frequently is used to solidify a minority working control. Promoters and investment bankers, for example, have used it to secure responsibility for and uninterrupted management of new corporations.[12] By retention of a sizable minority bloc of stock which they transfer to a trustee group, the bankers can dispose of the majority of voting shares and still be reasonably assured of corporate control until the new venture has proved its worth. According to one authority[13] this has been its principal use, although it has been popular also in corporate reorganizations.[14] In recent years the trustee device has been used by dominant stockholders to award income to their family

[10] B. Graham and D. L. Dodd, *Security Analysis* (revised edition, New York, McGraw-Hill Book Company, 1940), p. 806, note 65.

[11] J. C. Bonbright and G. C. Means, *The Holding Company* (New York, McGraw-Hill Book Company, 1932), pp. 113–114.

[12] A. S. Dewing, *Financial Policy of Corporations* (third edition, revised. New York, The Ronald Press Company, 1934), p. 387; *ibid.* (fourth edition, revised, New York, The Ronald Press Company, 1941), Vol. I, p. 120.

[13] *Ibid.* (third edition, revised), p. 389.

[14] H. G. Guthmann and H. E. Dougall, *Corporate Financial Policy* (New York, Prentice-Hall, Inc., 1940), p. 695. For other uses see M. M. Bergerman. "Voting Trusts," *Yale Law Journal*, Vol. XXXVII (1928), pp. 445–467.

beneficiaries while the control, such as the right to sell, exchange, or vote shares, is lodged in the hands of trustees.[15] Insurance against the loss of family domination of the affairs of certain corporations is thus provided.[16] Occasionally the actions of a strong and aggressive minority have caused the scattered holders of a majority of the voting shares to band together by means of the voting trust to defend themselves.

The voting trust has received conditional legal approval from the courts. In general the courts approve or disapprove after examination of the purposes and results attained by the device.[17] Where stockholders have voluntarily transferred their right to hold and vote stocks to trustees for a limited period of time, the courts do not consider it a restraint on the alienation of private property, that is, there is no restraint where the transfer is not complete and the stockholder later regains title. Nor is it considered in opposition to public policy as a restraint of trade so long as the stocks are those of a single corporation. And it is not an illegal separation of ownership from voting power if no fraud is to be observed.[18]

Many states in their corporation laws now permit the use of the voting trust, though most of them make no statutory provision for it.[19] Usually the duration of the trusteeship is limited to ten years. As in the case of some courts, certain states have recognized that the continuity of management and policy to be had through the voting trust arrangement for a limited period of time is a valuable advantage for the corporation as a whole.

It is not uncommon, however, for trustees to prolong the trusteeship by renewal of the agreement. Some state laws make extension very easy. Berle and Means cite the case of the Interborough Rapid Transit Company voting trust, which was renewable for five successive periods of five years each without further action by the holders of the voting trust certificates.[20] On their own volition, the trustees could thus maintain their control over the affairs of the company. Even though continuance of the trust agreement beyond the original period may be valuable, it is only reasonable to insist that the holders of the voting trust certificates should retain the power to vote on its renewal.

---

[15] Securities and Exchange Commission, *op. cit.*, p. 76.

[16] The same objective has been reached through the medium of the personal holding company.

[17] For the attitude of the different state courts and the Federal Court, see Cook, *op. cit.*, pp. 351–355.

[18] Cook, *op. cit.*, p. 355.

[19] In our states, dependencies, and the District of Columbia, twenty-two of these governmental units make statutory provisions for the voting trust; thirty do not, and one declares it illegal. *United States Corporation Manual* (42nd edition), New York, U. S. Corporation Company, 1941.

[20] Berle and Means, *op. cit.*, p. 78.

Legal Devices Which Magnify Minority Control

In addition to those legal devices which have aided minority interests to exercise corporate control, there are two devices which greatly magnify minority power and extend it far beyond what one would expect from the actual amount of ownership of corporate shares. These two devices are the holding company and the non-voting share.

The holding company came into prominent use in the 1890's. It is a corporation which is permitted to hold stock of other corporations for the purpose of control of the subsidiaries which it thus draws together. The importance of this device is so great, however, that its discussion is reserved to a special chapter.

Non-voting stock is largely a phenomenon of twentieth-century corporate finance. During the period of active combination by means of holding companies between 1898 and 1903 there were no important limitations on stockholders' voting rights.[21] While there were several instances of restrictions on the voting power of preferred stock, non-voting common stock was very rare. The International Silver Company was one of the first corporations to use non-voting common.[22] Organized in 1898, it made its common stock non-voting until January, 1902. Thereafter its common stockholders were entitled to one vote for every two shares held.

The practice of issuing non-voting preferred and non-voting common became more wide-spread with the passage of time.[23] The loss of voting power by preferred stockholders was considered but an offset to the preferences they enjoyed over common stockholders with respect to dividend distribution and prior participation in residual assets upon corporate dissolution. The loss of voting rights by common stockholders can be charged to stockholder indifference to their property rights, to the desires and motives of corporate promoters and investment bankers who were willing to take advantage of stockholder indifference, and to the liberalization of the incorporation laws of the several states.[24]

In the late 1920's the loss of stockholder voting rights became serious enough to attract the attention of various students of corporation law and finance.[25] Attention was called to the extreme use of the device by

---

[21] W. H. S. Stevens, "Stockholders' Voting Rights and the Centralization of Voting Control," *Quarterly Journal of Economics*, Vol. XL (May, 1926), p. 354.

[22] *Ibid.*, p. 355.

[23] *Ibid.*, p. 361. Dr. Stevens listed American Tobacco, Liggett & Myers, R. J. Reynolds, Dodge Brothers, McCrory Stores, Pan American, Pierce Oil, and Gabriel Snubber as having issued large blocks of non-voting common stock.

[24] Corporation lawyers and financiers played an important part in this liberalization program.

[25] W. Z. Ripley, "More Power to the Bankers," an address before the American Academy of Political Science in October, 1925, republished in *The Nation*, Vol. CXXI (December, 1925), p. 618; "From Main Street to Wall Street," *Atlantic Monthly*, Vol. CXXXVII (January, 1926), p. 94; A. A. Berle, Jr., *Studies in the Law of Corporation Finance* (Chicago, Callaghan and Company, 1928), Chap. 3.

Dodge Brothers and the Industrial Rayon Corporation. Dodge Brothers, Inc., issued 1,500,000 Class A, non-voting, common stock and 500,000 Class B voting common. Industrial Rayon went even further. It distributed to the public 598,000 non-voting shares of Class A common, while 2,000 shares of Class B common held the exclusive voting rights.[26]

As Professor Berle maintained, the emergence of this device has amounted to something more than a change in form. Heretofore, where corporations with widely scattered stockholdings have been dominated by holders of a substantial and concentrated minority interest without the aid of a legal device of any sort, there has always been a latent power resting in the holders of a majority of the voting shares if they choose to act together.[27] Through the use of non-voting shares, however, this latent power is destroyed, and a minority in ownership can control corporate affairs unmolested. In the Industrial Rayon Corporation, for example, 1001 shares of B voting common were necessary for control of the majority voting power, instead of more than 300,000 if all of Industrial Rayon common had had equal voting power.[28] Similarly, one share in excess of 250,000 of Dodge Brothers Class B common amounted to a clear control of that company. But, what is even more striking, in these days of widely scattered holdings control of a majority of voting shares is not necessary. A substantial minority may be just as effective, thus reducing control to an even smaller fractional part of the total ownership interest.

MINORITY CONTROL AND CONFLICTS IN INTEREST

No matter where control lies, it gives a certain group power over positions, salaries, business patronage, disposition of earnings, purchase of new assets, and the use and disposition of corporate property. Although control should be exercised always for the benefit of the entire organization in its multiple relations between majority and minority

---

[26] W. Z. Ripley, *Main Street and Wall Street* (Boston, Little, Brown and Company, 1927), p. 87.

[27] A. A. Berle, *Studies in the Law of Corporation Finance* (Chicago, Callaghan and Company, 1928), p. 43.

[28] In fairness to the Industrial Rayon Corporation its subsequent financial history should be given. The Corporation increased its non-voting Class A common from 598,000 to 998,000 without increasing its Class B common. On June 1, 1928, however, its authorized stock was reduced to 200,000 shares, all of one class, with voting power. An exchange was made at the ratio of five of the old of each class for one share of the new voting common. Later the number of voting shares was increased to 1,200,000. See *Poor's Industrial Manual*, 1939, pp. 2288–2289.

At the end of July, 1939, the M. A. Hanna Company of Cleveland, Ohio, was the largest single shareholder, with 112,800 shares, or 14.9 per cent of the total outstanding. See Standard Statistics Co., Inc., *Revised Description*, March 28, 1940.

owners, management, labor, creditors, and the general public,[29] frequently it is not. Interests definitely conflict. Moreover, where the amount
of investment is relatively small as compared with the power of the
control group, the chances of conflict are increased.

Members of the control group may place themselves on the board of
directors and appoint themselves to important offices at exorbitant salaries regardless of competence. In a small mining company, for example,
a single family held a predominant minority control by carefully voting
in concert at the annual meetings of the corporation. The family vote
usually exceeded a majority of the stock present and voting at the meeting. In its dominant position the minority ownership interest elected
directors from its own ranks. These directors in turn dominated the
board. They appointed themselves chief officers of the corporation. As
directors they approved and appropriated for themselves such large
salaries as to consume the entire income of the corporation and encroach
upon its capital assets. Obviously this policy, if continued, would be
injurious to the creditors and to the remaining stockholders. It was only
stopped when stockholders sought relief through legal action.[30]

Control may make leases or award contracts on extremely favorable
terms to companies in which the control group has a greater financial
interest. A classic instance of this involved the Shepaug Company, a
short-line Connecticut railroad.[31] A small group of associates acquired a
substantial interest in the railroad company. They then established a
voting trust to solidify control. Thereupon they elected themselves
directors and appointed themselves officers. Definitely in control, they
awarded railroad construction contracts to a company also under their
personal control, on terms they knew were oppressive and injurious to
the railroad company and its shareholders. Though this voting trust
involved a majority control rather than a minority, it demonstrates
admirably what may be done in either case. A stockholder complaint
and legal suit fortunately restrained the culprits. The court voided the
questionable contracts and permanently enjoined any further action to
execute them.

By its influence over a docile directorate, a control group may manipulate the distribution of earnings in such a fashion as to divert earn-

---

[29] For a more detailed statement of the various segments of interest in a corporation, see R. A. Gordon, "Financial Control of Large-Scale Enterprise," *American
Economic Review, Papers and Proceedings,* Vol. XXIX, No. 1 (March, 1939),
pp. 88–90. See also P. M. O'Leary, *Corporate Enterprise in Modern Economic Life*
(New York and London, Harper and Brothers, 1933), Chaps. 3–6.

[30] Decatur Mineral Land Company *v.* Palm, 113 Alabama Reports 531 (1896).
Cited by William H. Spencer, *Casebook of Law and Business* (New York and
London, McGraw-Hill Book Company, 1939), pp. 574–580.

[31] Bostwick *v.* Chapman; Starbuck *v.* Mercantile Trust Company, 60 Conn. 553
(1890).

ings entirely from certain classes of stock. Or control may not go quite
so far, but far enough, however, to allow one class of stock to participate
unfairly in the corporation's earnings. The practice is facilitated by the
general lethargy of the stockholders; by the bewildering variety of stocks
with varying powers and participation rights which some corporations
issue under our liberal incorporation laws; and by the complete and
absolute powers which corporate charters under some state laws grant
to boards of directors. Inequitable treatment is possible where the corporate capital structure includes non-cumulative preferred stock and the
minority control, holding a substantial interest in the common stock,
insists that the directors pay no dividends from the current year's earnings or from earned surplus. The holders of non-cumulative preferred
stock then lose forever the dividends due them for that year. In the
following year dividends may be declared for both classes of stock. The
preferred, however, would get only the fixed rate for the current year,
whereas the common stockholders would benefit from all the undeclared
dividends of the previous year as well as participate in the earnings of
the current year.[32] It is the rule rather than the exception that non-
cumulative dividends are seldom paid unless payment is necessitated by
the desire to declare dividends on common stock.[33]

The power to injure the majority which circumstances may place in
the hands of a minority interest is suggested by a recent case of deception
by a predominant minority stockholder.[34] In this instance, in the solicitation of proxies, he asked for stockholder approval of a contract which
would pay him a substantial salary as president of the corporation, for
ratification of the corporation's purchases of its own common stock, and
for approval of an arrangement which would permit him to purchase
stock in the corporation at a price substantially under the market price.
He did not inform the other stockholders that he was a dominant stockholder. Neither did he tell them that the other directors on the board
held no stock in the corporation, and that hence he was practically free
to dictate the terms of the contract. Furthermore, he did not inform the
stockholders that the shares purchased by the corporation were at private

---

[32] An example may be of value to the student. Assume that a corporation has
outstanding $2,000,000 in 6% non-cumulative preferred stock and 50,000 shares
of common (par value $100). Assume also that the earnings of the current year
available for distribution are $700,000. The preferred stock should get $120,000
and the common stock $580,000, or $11.60 per share. All dividends, however, are
passed. The following year the corporation's earnings again reach $700,000. The
total available for dividends is now $1,400,000. The directors declare a dividend
and distribute all the earnings. The non-cumulative preferred stock gets but $120,-
000 and the common stock gets $1,280,000. It is obvious that the $120,000 which
the preferred stockholders should have received in the previous year is in the
current year being distributed to the common stockholders.

[33] Graham and Dodd, op. cit., p. 171.

[34] Securities and Exchange Commission, Fourth Annual Report (Washington,
D. C., U. S. Government Printing Office, 1938), pp. 69–70.

sales at prices sometimes as high as $20.00 per share above the market price at the time of purchase. Fortunately for the stockholders, public authority forced the disclosure of the full facts.

While lack of interest of the majority of shareholders may be blamed in allowing these minority abuses, the situation should not be dismissed so easily. Short of monopoly, there has been strong public support of large-scale enterprise. Capital has been sought from the savings of small investors whose major interests lie elsewhere than in the actual business operation of the corporation in which they hold a small equity. The average small investor is mainly interested in income from his investment. His confidence in corporate industry may be severely shaken by the manifest ability of a minority interest to further its own welfare at his expense.

On the other hand, while it is true that a strong minority interest may use its control in undesirable ways, it is likewise a fact that it may serve to protect the rank and file of shareholders from exploitation from other sources by its alertness and vigorous action. The well-known struggle between John D. Rockefeller, Jr., who held a strong minority interest in the Standard Oil Company, and the Company's Chairman of the Board, Colonel Robert Stewart, is a good example of the protective nature of a dominant minority interest.

The incident originated from an investigation by the United States Senate of the Teapot Dome oil scandals involving leases made by government officials with oil companies during the Harding administration. Incidental to the main investigation, the affairs of the Continental Trading Company, a Canadian concern, were investigated. Though the Trading Company was not connected with the lease scandals, the investigation revealed that this company was operated by some officials of the Prairie Oil & Gas Company and the Sinclair Crude Oil Purchasing Company, subsidiaries of the Standard Oil Company of Indiana. The Trading Company contracted to buy crude oil from a Texas oil company. It then immediately resold it at a substantial profit per barrel to the two Standard of Indiana subsidiaries.

Colonel Stewart was requested by the Senate Committee to testify concerning the affairs of the Trading Company which dealt with and had officers in common with his subsidiaries. Stewart at first refused but later complied. His uncoöperative conduct before the Senate Committee incurred the displeasure and then open disapproval of Rockefeller, who sought unsuccessfully in 1928 to deprive the Colonel of his seat on the board of directors of the Standard of Indiana. Later Mr. Rockefeller requested Colonel Stewart to resign. Stewart refused, whereupon Rockefeller launched an intensive campaign to gather enough proxies to defeat Colonel Stewart at the 1929 annual meeting of the Standard of Indiana.

At Rockefeller expense, Winthrop Aldrich, prominent New York banker and member of the Rockefeller proxy committee, sent a seventy-two-page letter to all the stockholders of Standard of Indiana, stating the Rockefeller case. In this letter, among other things, reasons were given why Colonel Stewart was no longer qualified to remain in his position of trust as Chairman of the company's board of directors. The Colonel had failed to use his power as chief executive to prevent certain officials in subsidiaries of the Standard from participating in and personally profiting from contracts made by these subsidiaries with the Trading Company, in which they also had a definite interest.[35] Furthermore, even though he was acquitted of Senate charges of perjured testimony and contempt, the Colonel's actions and attitude toward his Company, the public, and public authority destroyed stockholder confidence.

Supported by his fellow-directors, Colonel Stewart fought the Rockefeller challenge vigorously. About a month prior to the annual meeting, the directors declared a 50 per cent stock dividend and an extra cash dividend of fifty cents in addition to the regular quarterly dividend of sixty-two and a half cents per share. The extra cash dividend was larger than any preceding extra dividend by 100 per cent. Furthermore, the directors voted that the additional stock (of the stock dividend) was to receive the extra and the regular quarterly cash dividend. In other ways the directors also worked hard to procure stockholder proxies and support for Colonel Stewart.

When the annual meeting was held in the huge auditorium at Whiting, Indiana, it was found that Mr. Rockefeller was the victor. He had procured the votes of 5,510,313 shares of stock, representing 15,204 individuals. Colonel Stewart had 2,954,963 shares, which represented 31,337 owners. Over 7,648,000 shares were represented by proxy and about 817,000 shares by holders who personally attended the meeting. Less than 10 per cent of the shares outstanding were without any representation either by person or by proxy.

Another instance of a minority interest offering protection to a scattered majority occurred during the First World War. In this case a minority voting trust had been formed. Its purpose was to hinder German agents who were intent on buying up the stock of a company manufacturing submarines for the British navy.[36] The obvious object of German stock ownership was to interfere with the American company's policies

---

[35] In its short life the Continental Trading Company made more than $8,000,000 from its venture without capital or risk and with little effort. The company records were then destroyed and its officials departed to foreign lands to escape interrogation. For fuller details, see Mammoth Oil Co. v. U. S., 275 U. S. 47–51 (1927).

[36] Frost v. Carse, 91 N. J. Eq., 124, 108 Atl. 642 (1919). This voting trust was protested as illegal. The New Jersey Court of Errors and Appeals upheld the arrangement in this instance. The attitude of state courts toward this type of voting trust is divided. See Bergerman, op. cit., pp. 459–463.

and production program as soon as they got control of sufficient shares to become a real power in corporate meetings. The results would have been bad not only for the British but also for the stockholders of the corporation.

The foregoing illustrations serve to show how control—and in these instances, minority control—may be exercised for evil or for good purposes. It is apparent, however, that the law cannot prohibit control. It must always be present in some form. Consequently, protection from abuses of control must be devised if it is not already available.

PROTECTIONS AVAILABLE TO THE WIDELY SCATTERED HOLDINGS OF THE MAJORITY STOCK

At the present time there are several direct protections offered to the scattered shareholders of a majority of the voting stock. In the first place, they are protected if the holders of a dominant minority interest are blessed with a high sense of moral values. Secondly, protection is present when the probabilities are large that injury to the dominant shareholder's investment in the company may exceed in amount any monetary gains which might accrue from the dominant interests' unethical conduct or illegal action. Thirdly, protection and relief may always be sought through the courts to control dominant group actions which may be injurious to the corporation as a whole and hence injurious to the complaining stockholder group.[37]

This latter protection is recognized in the doctrine of the dominant shareholder. The law does not dispute or forbid the power of control, but it does place some checks on it. The courts have recognized the right of shareholders to combine to get an outright majority of the total potential voting shares or to get a minority "working" control in order to direct a corporation's policies and development. And the courts recognize the right of a single stockholder to do likewise. On the other hand, the courts have not been willing to allow a control group complete freedom in wielding its powers. Directors are expected to act freely and independently in the best interests of the corporation, and not solely for the interests of the particular group that placed them in office. As a judge in the United States Circuit Court of Appeals, William Howard Taft clearly enunciated the doctrine of the dominant shareholder. Taft condemned contracts made by a dominant shareholder with his own company for his own profit. The validity of such contracts, however, must be questioned by the company's other stockholders or bondholders or by the

---

[37] Courts are not likely to interfere in matters involving managerial judgment. In cases involving fraud, *ultra vires* acts, and intentional inequities, the courts will act to relieve complainants.

company itself.[38] Subsequent cases indicate that the courts not infrequently cut through form to substance. And where it is apparent that control is being improperly exercised by a dominant shareholder through dummy directors, the courts attempt to set matters right.[39] They place responsibility where it rightfully belongs.

Although these protections are valuable, they are insufficient. There is need for the removal of or restrictions on the special legal aids to minority control, and for the elimination or control of those devices that magnify it.

Methods to Curtail the Control of Minority Interests

The use of weighted or multiple voting stock should be restricted. If used at all, weighted voting power should be permitted only for a definite and well-publicized purpose. For example, its use might be restricted to contingencies which clearly threaten the rights and expectations of preferred stockholders. In such circumstances, since common stocks of a corporation exceed in number the outstanding preferred shares, the preferred stockholders could more adequately protect their particular interests. And the arrangement is excusable, perhaps, when used temporarily by investment bankers to retain control of a new corporation until it has demonstrated its ability to stand on its own feet. Always, however, the arrangement and its purpose should be clearly set forth and limited to a reasonable period of time.

The voting trust has sufficient merit to warrant its continued use in industrial corporate finance. It should be strictly limited in time, as is the case under present state laws permitting its use, and renewal should not be made easy. The holders of voting trust certificates should always retain the power to vote on the renewal of the trust. Furthermore, the trust should publicly acknowledge its responsibility for management of the corporation. Where promoters and bankers use the device as a means to control a dominant minority interest in a new corporation, it is doubtful whether renewal of the trust should be permitted beyond the first contract period.

Stockholders should never be completely deprived of their right to vote at corporate meetings. The complete loss of voting rights is as undesirable in the economic sphere as in the political. The transfer of the right temporarily should be sufficient to permit flexibility in corporate finance, as is the case in proxy voting and in the use of the voting trust.

It is encouraging to note that, despite the fact that many state incorporation laws permit the issue of non-voting stock and courts have

---

[38] Central Trust Company v. Bridges, 57 Fed. 753, 766 (1893). In this instance the dominant stockholder held a majority of the voting stock.

[39] For a more extended development, see Berle and Means, op. cit., pp. 235–238.

declared that its issue is not contrary to public policy,[40] our leading security exchanges, the New York Stock and the New York Curb, have taken a stand against non-voting stock. They deny listing privileges to new issues of common stock without voting rights.[41] And, among the states, Illinois has set a good example by an express grant of voting rights to stockholders. Corporations chartered in Illinois cannot deprive their stockholders of these rights.[42]

SUMMARY AND CONCLUSIONS

The position of the minority interest in our modern corporation has shifted considerably in the last three or four decades. The problem of protections for minority interests from the actions of the majority have been superseded by the problem of protection for the widely scattered majority.

Minority control has sprung from a combination of circumstances. The increasing size of corporations has scattered shares of stock widely among many shareholders. A very large proportion of these shareholders are either unable or unwilling to take an active interest in the affairs of their corporations. Consequently their voting power is not represented at corporate meetings, or it is entrusted through proxies to the control group which elects a "coöperative" directorate. Furthermore, certain artificial devices, such as weighted or multiple voting stock and the voting trust, have been utilized by minority ownership interests to assume control. And often power is magnified by means of non-voting shares and the holding company device.

Although they need not, the results of minority control may prove unfortunate for the scattered mass of stockholders. On the other hand, the presence of a strong minority may insure the small holders of widely dispersed shares against injuries contemplated by unethical management. This protection may spring from the honesty and integrity of the minority or from its own interests in the corporation. And, of course, courts of equity are available to protect stockholders who may be harmed through injuries inflicted on the corporation by a control group.

These protections do not appear to be sufficient. At times minority interests can and do take unfair advantage of their power to control corporate affairs. The temptation to exploit the weaknesses of others is often too great to resist. Since the temptations cannot be removed by

---

[40] See A. S. Dewing, *op. cit.* (fourth edition), Vol. I, p. 129, citing the following state court cases: St. Regis Candies, Inc., *v.* Hovas, 117 Texas 313 (1928); and Smith *v.* San Francisco, etc., R. R., 115 Cal. 584, 606 (1897).

[41] Berle and Means, *op. cit.*, p. 76.

[42] United States Corporation Manual (42nd edition, New York, U. S. Corporation Company, 1941), pp. 552–554.

simply calling upon control interests to assume greater responsibility for the welfare of the widely dispersed and impotent holders of corporate stock, the sensible procedure is to remove or restrict the use of those devices which aid or magnify the powers of the minority control interest. The organized stock exchanges have already taken a progressive step by refusing to list new issues of non-voting stock. And at least one state, Illinois, has shown itself to be equally enlightened.

The corporation is an important institution in a highly industrialized and complex economic society. Its usefulness must not be impaired by abuses which severely shake the confidence of small savers in the desirability of saving and investment in corporation securities. The effects are particularly bad when exploitation of the many is accomplished by a few in power.

6

Management Control

NATURE AND PREVALENCE OF MANAGEMENT CONTROL

A Securities and Exchange Commission study reveals that about sixty of our two hundred largest non-financial corporations have such a wide dispersion of ownership that no owner or small group of owners is able to exercise control by virtue of voting strength.[1] Barring a few exceptions, control lies in the hands of the managerial group, that is, the board of directors and the principal officers of each of these corporations.[2]

Among the companies where no definite ownership control is to be found are many of America's leading business organizations. In the segment of industry classified as the utility field there are, for example, the American Telephone and Telegraph Company and the Consolidated Edison Company of New York, Inc.; in railroads, notably the Pennsylvania, the Southern Pacific, the Union Pacific, and the Atchison, Topeka and Santa Fe; in mining, the Anaconda Copper Mining Company; in manufacture, Bethlehem Steel, United States Steel, Eastman Kodak, General Electric, Westinghouse Electric, Paramount Pictures, Goodyear Tire and Rubber, B. F. Goodrich, Radio Corporation of America, and the Union Carbide and Carbon Corporation; in merchandise distribution, Montgomery Ward and Company, Inc. It is interesting to note that more than half of the sixty companies are manufacturing concerns. Only a few are found in the publicly regulated utility fields.

It has been customary to consider management as composed of two groups of individuals, the directors and the principal officers. The former, elected by the stockholders from the stockholder group and serving usually without salary, formulate the broad general policies of the com-

---

[1] Securities and Exchange Commission, *The Distribution of Ownership in the 200 Largest Non-Financial Corporations* (Washington, D. C., 1940), p. 79.

[2] The exceptions are certain railroad companies which are leased lines and are, therefore, under the control of the companies leasing them. In some instances, investment banking houses and trust companies exercise a considerable degree of influence, if not complete control, over policies even though their stockholdings are small.

pany. They appoint the corporation's principal officers, who are to administer the daily affairs of the corporation in a manner consistent with the policies laid down by the directors. Periodically, in behalf of the stockholders, the directors examine the results of the company administration and approve or disapprove the acts of the principal officers.

Where management control prevails, the situation departs quite radically from this customary arrangement. Actually the salaried officers represent a major portion of the board of directors, in influence if not always in numbers. In some directorates there are no stockholders serving without some other official connection.[3] In some cases directors do not even hold stock in the corporation. In these instances we observe that both policy formation and the surveillance of administration are performed by the same group of men. Such a management group is situated very much like that famous and delightful character, Pooh-Bah, in the Gilbert and Sullivan operetta, "The Mikado." It was Pooh-Bah who—at a salary—found it difficult to untangle himself from his many conflicting but consolidated functions as First Lord of The Treasury, Commander-in-Chief, Attorney-General, Chancellor of the Exchequer, Groom of the Back-Stairs, and so forth. After the fashion of Pooh-Bah, the management group often finds its position intriguing and profitable.

PERPETUATION OF MANAGEMENT CONTROL

The basic factors which permit perpetuation of management control are as follows: (1) the wide dispersion of stock ownership; (2) the docility and indifference of shareholders generally, especially if their dividends are received with some degree of regularity; (3) the expense involved if any stockholder seeks to organize opposition to oust management; (4) the strategic position of management in its control over the machinery by means of which votes are gathered, and (5) the changes in corporation laws and their application which have diluted the strength of the stockholders.

As previously stated elsewhere, when corporations were very much smaller, and their capital structures were simpler, stockholders were more intimately associated with corporate control. Shareholding meant an active ownership interest, an intimate participation in the ultimate direction of corporate affairs through a controlled management. The shareholder guarded his relative position. At an early date the courts, under common law interpretation, protected the shareholder by recognizing his

---

[3] In 1934 this was true of the American Tobacco, Liggett & Myers Tobacco, and the R. J. Reynolds Tobacco Companies. All of their directors in that year held official positions in their respective corporations. Cf. National Recovery Administration, Division of Review, *The Tobacco Study* (Washington, D. C., 1936), p. 14.

right of preëmption.[4] According to this doctrine, it will be recalled, every shareholder in a corporation had a right to maintain his *pro rata* share of control or voting power and his *pro rata* share in corporate assets. He could participate in additional issues of stock on a basis determined by the ratio of his present holdings to the total number of shares outstanding. As a holder of a particular class of stock, his position in the corporation was seldom disturbed except by his own consent.

Consequently the stockholder had more lively and definite interests in his corporation. He expected, and in fact, he demanded that the corporation's management operate the company so as to earn the highest possible profit without undue risk of its assets. He insisted that the management distribute profits equitably among the limited classes of stock according to their charter status. If profits were retained in the business, the amount must not exceed the needs of sane expansion and the maintenance of adequate reserves to stabilize dividend payments and to meet contingencies. And finally, he expected that his stock would be kept easily saleable at a price which reflected fairly its present earning power and future expectations.[5] His more intimate knowledge of his corporation's affairs, moreover, gave him a clearer idea of what would be a fair market price.

While it is true that shareholders still retain these fundamental interests, it is likewise true that their power to realize them by their own actions has waned appreciably. Dilution of their power has proceeded as the corporate organization has attained greater and greater size. The search for corporate capital has scattered ownership far and wide in relatively small amounts. The significance of any single shareholder has declined, and he has become docile and indifferent. Even if he had not, the expense of battling with management is beyond the financial capacity of an ordinary shareholder. Only a Rockefeller can wage a successful struggle against an arbitrary management fortified with a strong corporate treasury.[6]

The position of the shareholder is weakened further by the strategic position of management in its control of the machinery by means of which proxy votes are gathered. The management group appoints the proxy committee, subservient to management, to prepare a proxy statement to be sent at company expense to shareholders with voting rights. Many shareholders ignore the proxies and, moreover, do not attend the stockholders' meetings. Others sign them obediently and thus turn their voting power over to those who are sure to approve reëlection of the present directorate. Until recently there has been little public regulation

---

[4] Gray *v.* Portland Bank, 3 Massachusetts 363 (1807).
[5] *Cf.* Berle and Means, *op. cit.*, p. 121.
[6] See above, pp. 88–90.

of the information contained in proxy forms or public supervision over proxy solicitation. Frequently shareholders have granted voting powers all too blindly.[7]

Under pressure of corporate management and corporate legal counsel, shareholder strength has been diluted greatly by certain changes in corporation statutes. In part this has been hastened by the necessities of finance problems; in part, by the desires of management to have a free hand.

The old common law right of preëmption has become but a shadow of its former self.[8] Under the corporation statutes of some states it may be, if so provided in the corporate charter, either waived entirely or limited greatly.[9] Furthermore, where a corporation is acquiring new properties, it need no longer offer new stock for sale, first to its shareholders and then, if necessary, to the public. Direct exchange of stock for property may be made without regard for preëmptive rights. In addition, some courts have limited the right of preëmption to those cases where the shareholders must approve a charter amendment to increase the corporation's authorized stock. Thus limited, the exercise of the right may be easily avoided at the outset by petitioning the state for the authorization of many more shares than are likely to be issued when the corporation is first established. It is obvious that these methods of diluting ownership strengthen the control of management.[10]

In recent years another device has appeared in the form of the option warrant or stock purchase warrant.[11] This financial instrument entitles its possessor to purchase from the corporation at specified prices a stated number of shares of its authorized but unissued capital stock of any class or classes whenever he sees fit to exercise his option. Not infrequently the right is unlimited in its duration. Under the Delaware laws, for example, corporate directors are given wide latitude in the use of this instrument. While the arrangements for stock warrants may be definitely stated in the certificate of incorporation, they need not be.

---

[7] For companies whose securities are listed on the organized exchanges the Securities and Exchange Commission now formulates rules and regulations relating to proxy solicitation. These regulations will be treated in a later chapter.

[8] It may be argued that this common law doctrine was pronounced when rarely more than one type of stock was issued and that present-day corporate structures practically preclude its application. If one accepts the complicated corporate structure as desirable and necessary, the validity of this argument must be recognized. On the other hand, there are those who believe corporate capital structures are unnecessarily complex.

[9] Cf. R. C. Larcom, The Delaware Corporation (Baltimore, Md., The Johns Hopkins Press, 1937), pp. 35, 40. See also Berle and Means, op. cit., p. 146.

[10] For a number of cases where management undertook deliberately to wrest power from shareholders by ignoring preëmptive rights, see H. S. Drinker, Jr., "The Preëmptive Rights of Shareholders to Subscribe to New Shares," Harvard Law Review, Vol. XLIII (1930), p. 599, note 34.

[11] 36 Delaware Laws, 1929, Chap. 135, Sec. 6.

The various provisions relating to the amount, the time of issue, limitations as to duration, price and so forth may be determined in a resolution adopted by the corporation's board of directors. In either case, the rank and file of shareholders are unlikely to be aware of the situation which permits the issuance of an instrument that is basically opposed to their best interests.[12]

Under some state laws, corporate capital structures are no longer fixed. Relations between various groups of shareholders are subject to change without great difficulty. This is accomplished by including in the charter the power to amend the corporate contract as it relates to rights, preferences, participations, etc. Successful accomplishment, to be sure, depends usually on the mobilization of a majority vote to validate any proposed change and on legal support by the courts in event the action is contested. On this matter, however, the courts are divided. Some maintain that the relations between classes of stocks are fixed in the charter and therefore are not subject to change. Others take a contrary view. In the main, however, the courts permit changes to be made providing the results are beneficial to all parties involved, or at least, are not injurious to any particular class of shareholders.[13] But until all courts follow this pattern of interpretation, or until state statutes are improved, shareholders in some corporations will be left in a state of uncertainty as to their future position in their respective corporations.

Even more damaging to the shareholder's fixed position in the corporate structure are the provisions in state statutes which allow corporations to be set up with "blank" stock.[14] Stock is authorized, but its voting powers, preferences, participations, and other rights are not indicated in the certificate of incorporation. Rather, the power is given to the directorate to determine these matters by resolution. A corporation, for example, may issue common stock and authorize the issue of preferred stock, but leave it entirely to the directors to decide what rights and participations shall be attached to the preferred stock when it is issued. In these circumstances, with so much depending on the action of the directors, those who buy the common shares take considerable risk.[15] It is apparent that, if necessary, management control may use this power to perpetuate or strengthen its own position.

It is apparent that the basic factors which serve to perpetuate management control, buttressed as they are by artificial devices used to

---

[12] *Cf.* Graham and Dodd, *op. cit.*, pp. 644–647.

[13] Yoakum *v.* Providence Biltmore Hotel Co. *et al.*, 34 Fed. (2nd) 533, 547 (1929); Berle and Means, *op. cit.*, p. 150.

[14] Rev. Code of Delaware, Chap. 65, Par. 13 (as amended by the Act of March 22, 1929).

[15] A. A. Berle, "Investors and the Revised Delaware Corporation Act," *Columbia Law Review*, Vol. XXIX (1929), pp. 563, 589 (1929).

dilute or vitiate ownership power, have left shareholders in a greatly changed position. Their interests have become expectations dependent largely on the decisions of the management group. Their attention has drifted to the securities markets and the daily price quotations. Their position approaches that of creditors—bondholders—without the creditors' protections. Without control, without knowledge, without abiding interest in corporate affairs, shareholders may be exploited easily by unscrupulous management.

THE DANGERS OF MANAGEMENT CONTROL

Where management is the master of the corporation, management and stockholder interests may conflict. Management may wish to pay itself larger compensation than it deserves. It may desire to increase the size of the enterprise in order to acquire more prestige, power, and compensation when further increases in size are economically unjustified. It may accomplish this size objective by a niggardly dividend policy. To preserve its vested interest the management group may continue to operate a corporation when its affairs should be immediately wound up, either in part or entirely, in order to prevent or to minimize shareholder losses. Management may withhold from shareholders the information which is rightly theirs, or it may delay the release of information until the "insiders" have profited by it.

Given these possibilities by which management can selfishly serve itself, together with the conditions which have separated ownership from control, we can see that a high sense of management ethics is about the only real protection stockholders have had in the past in our management-controlled corporations. This is especially true where directors and officers are identical groups, for in this circumstance there is no adequate system of checks and balances to insure the interests of shareholders. Need for new capital and fear of litigation have been deterrents, to be sure, but it is questionable whether either has been, in particular cases, a very important factor in forestalling abuse. The investing public soon forgets, and litigation is more remedial than preventive.

Management Compensation and Stockholder Interest

It has only been within the last decade that detailed information has been made available regarding the compensation received by the management of large corporations. Heretofore, compensation policies and practices were not matters of open discussion even in the annual meetings of stockholders, the legal owners.[16] But occasionally there came to light through court cases some facts that caused stockholders and the public in general to wonder at the ethics of business leaders. Sometimes income tax cases exposed the true state of affairs.[17] In other instances the facts were disclosed because certain stockholders objected to what seemed to them to be excessive compensation payments to management.[18]

In the case of the Botany Worsted Mills, for example, each of the directors was an executive officer or manager of a department within the organization. For this each received annually a modest $9000 salary. In addition they participated in the distribution of the net profits. This latter arrangement went through several changes, but from 1908 to 1917 the director-officers received 30.08 per cent of the annual net profits. From the very beginning (1890), under the by-laws of the company, the board determined the total amount of profits and the aggregate amount payable to the directorate. Until 1917 the highest annual amount the board members paid themselves, exclusive of salaries, was $693,617. In 1917 they increased their compensation to $1,565,739 in addition to the $90,000 total salary outlay. Each of the ten directors received about $165,000 annually.

The Federal Government protested against this entire amount being regarded as an ordinary and necessary expense of management. It generously allowed slightly over $782,000 as a fair extra compensation. This amount, incidentally, exceeded by $100,000 any previous payments to the Botany Mills management. The Supreme Court in upholding the claims of the Federal Government stated:[19]

. . . it is clear that extraordinary, unusual and extravagant amounts paid by a corporation to its officers in the guise and form of compensation for their services, but having no substantial relation to the measure of their services and being utterly disproportional to their values, are not in reality payment for services, and cannot be regarded as "ordinary and necessary expenses" within the meaning of the section (Par. 12a, Revenue Act of 1916); and that such amounts do not become part of the "ordinary and necessary expenses" merely because the payments are made in accordance with the agreement between the corporation and its officers.

Although, in this case, there was no stockholder protest against the payment of these sums as executive compensation, it is clear that the Court felt that the executives were overpaid by about $780,000. Since

---

[16] John C. Baker, *Executive Salaries and Bonus Plans* (New York and London, McGraw-Hill Book Company, 1938), p. 1.

[17] See U. S. *v.* Philadelphia Knitting Mills Co., 273 Fed. 657 (1921); Botany Worsted Mills *v.* U. S., 278 U. S. 282 (1929).

[18] For example, Heublein *v.* Wight, 227 Fed. 667 (1915), 238 Fed. 321 (1916); Rogers *v.* Hill, 289 U. S. 582 (1933); Rogers *v.* Guaranty Trust Co., 60 Fed. (2nd) 114 (1932).

[19] Botany Worsted Mills *v.* U. S., 278 U. S. 292 (1929).

this excess was considered taxable income instead of expense, it belonged really to the shareholders.

For many years the leading manufacturers of tobacco products, such as the American Tobacco, Liggett & Myers, and R. J. Reynolds Companies, have used salary and bonus schemes for the payment of their chief executives.[20] The details concerning the American Tobacco Company were brought to light in court by a stockholder protest.[21] In 1912, the stockholders, presumably acting in good faith and according to their best judgment, approved a management compensation plan whereby the president and vice-presidents of the Company were to receive 10 per cent of the annual earnings in excess of $11,369,000.[22] The 10 per cent was to be divided according to plan, i.e., 2½ per cent to the president and the remaining 7½ per cent to the several vice-presidents. The increasing prosperity of the American Tobacco Company brought its chief executives handsome returns. Their peak was reached in 1930, when President G. W. Hill received $168,000 in salary, $243,470 in cash credits, and $842,508 as a bonus.[23] The vice-presidents also fared very well, with total compensation during the year exceeding $500,000 each. The bonus payments in 1930 were twice as large as in 1929.

Regardless of the apparent regularity of the arrangement, the Supreme Court maintained that, against the protest of a shareholder, a rule or by-law cannot be used to justify payments of sums as salaries so large as to amount to spoliation or waste of corporate property. It cited with approval the dissenting opinion of Judge Swan of the Circuit Court of Appeals, in which he said: "If the bonus payment has no relation to the value of services for which it is given, it is in reality a gift in part, and the majority of the shareholders have no power to give away corporate property against the protest of the minority."[24] As a result of this case the company entered into a new plan of "incentive compensation" for its officers in 1933.

Management has sometimes operated compensation schemes without revealing the details to the stockholders.[25] This was illustrated in a minority stockholder suit in 1931 against the officers and directors of the Bethlehem Steel Company. The shareholders sought to compel an accounting of bonus payments and a refund to shareholders in event the amounts paid out were deemed excessive. The facts revealed that, over

---

[20] See Reavis Cox, *Competition in the American Tobacco Industry* (New York, Columbia University Press, 1933), pp. 305–311.

[21] Rogers v. Hill, 289 U. S. 582 (1933).

[22] Cox, *op. cit.*, p. 309.

[23] 289 U. S. 582, 585, note 2.

[24] Rogers v. Hill, 60 Fed. (2nd) 109, 113.

[25] In the steel industry a number of corporations had bonus plans. Very few had been approved by stockholders, and information to stockholders about them had been very scanty. *Cf.* Baker, *op. cit.*, p. 155.

a twenty-year period, about $36,000,000 had been paid in bonuses with-
out stockholder approval. The sums paid up to 1928 were equal to
approximately 80 per cent of the dividends paid to shareholders. Between 1925 and 1928 the common stockholders received no dividends
at all, due to the directors' expansion policy, whereas the chief executives
received $6,800,524 in bonuses. Slightly less than half this amount went
to Eugene Grace, President of the Company.[26] It was also revealed that,
between 1918 and 1930, Mr. Grace received an average annual bonus
of $814,993 in addition to his salary of $12,000.[27]

Settlement of the suit was accomplished out of court. Mr. Charles
M. Schwab, Chairman of the Board, succeeded in placating the disturbed shareholders. They agreed to a new plan in which the executive
officers and officer-directors were to receive higher salaries and continued
participation in earnings, though on a slightly lower scale. In the future
the directors' annual report to the shareholders was to specify the total
compensation paid to management. This plan was modified later, and
the rate of management participation in profits was again lowered.
Despite the changes, the Bethlehem Steel management receives generous
annual compensation.[28]

Not infrequently management benefits by allotment of purchase warrants or options to buy unissued stock at prices below the market quotation. The American Tobacco Company utilized such an arrangement,
and options of great value were given to various officers. President G.
W. Hill, for example, was allotted options on 32,370 of the 56,712 shares
in the first distribution made under his company's plan. Mr. Hill had
the privilege of buying shares at $25.00 each. At the time of distribution
of the options the market price for the shares was $112.00. In other
words, the differential meant millions of dollars to Mr. Hill and a considerable dilution of the stock values to shareholders.[29] In the case of
the Electric Bond and Share Company, not only was management permitted to buy stock at a price far below the market, but later when
the market price dropped below the subscription price, the officers were

---

[26] *The New York Times*, March 21, 1931, p. 27.
[27] *The New York Times*, March 4, 1931, p. 23. Full details about the bonuses
paid each year to each of the twenty-one participating executives are given in
this account.
[28] See Standard Statistics, *Individual Corporation Descriptions*, Vol. I, No. 14,
revised May 24, 1940, p. 12; Securities and Exchange Commission, *Selected Information Reports*, No. 1, Steel Producers, New York, 1938, Table xiv, p. 61.
[29] *Cf.* "The American Tobacco Company Bonus Plans," *Notes*, *Harvard Law
Review*, Vol. XLVI (March, 1933), pp. 829–830. It is obvious that by exercising
the stock warrants additional shares are issued, and they share in future earnings
and have a *pro rata* share in assets if and when distributed. Consequently, other
outstanding shares lose some of their value. As a matter of fact, the mere presence
of stock purchase warrants may depress the price of issued shares even before the
warrants are exercised.

not compelled to pay for their subscribed shares. Such sums as they had paid in were returned to them.[30] Beyond a doubt such privileges are unfair, though unfortunately they are not illegal. Under some state statutes directors may not only have the sole power to issue such warrants, but may also be unrestricted by any controls.[31] In corporations where the managerial group may exercise these privileges unrestrained, shareholders obviously are at a great disadvantage. Not only are their stock values lessened, but their *pro rata* control, little as it may be, is further diluted.

Business Expansion and Management—Stockholders' Interests

Management's unrestrained control over corporate dividend policy may lead to unwise business expansion.[32] This may prove to be merely poor judgment on the part of the director-officers, or it may be impelled by greedy motives. In the latter case management expects to enjoy greater prestige, power, and higher compensation as the size of the enterprise increases.[33] Compensation does seem to be affected by the size of the corporation, as measured by assets. Irrespective of earnings, the larger companies generally pay higher total compensation to officers than do the smaller companies.[34]

While reinvestment may lead to greater business volume for an enterprise, it does not necessarily follow that the increased business will add more than proportionately or even proportionately to its earning power. A vital factor in the outcome is the connection between the present size of the enterprise and the optimum size in that particular industry under the existing demand conditions. Firms which are under the optimum size should expand if the opportunity is present, in order to take advantage of the lowest possible unit costs of production and sales. On the other hand, firms which have already attained the optimum size certainly should not. Knowledge of this relation is probably not profound in many instances. Hence there is all the more reason that such information as is available should not be vitiated by management's personal motives. Perhaps the wiser course for management to follow, if it can lay aside personal interests, is to subject the question of expansion to market analysis and investor judgment. In other words, expansion should be undertaken in the main by the sale of new issues in the

[30] Graham and Dodd, *op. cit.*, p. 598.
[31] See A. A. Berle, Jr., "Investors and the Revised Delaware Corporation Act," *Columbia Law Review*, Vol. XXIX (1929), pp. 563, 570.
[32] For an excellent theoretical discussion of dividend policy and the expansion of business enterprise, see Norman S. Buchanan, *The Economics of Corporate Enterprise* (New York, Henry Holt and Company, 1940), Chaps. 9 and 11.
[33] *Cf.* Graham and Dodd, *op. cit.*, p. 378.
[34] Baker, *op. cit.*, pp. 238–239.

market-place, rather than through reinvestment of earnings. While this might be somewhat more expensive in the short run, nevertheless, the combined judgment of less biased individuals would doubtless reduce the ultimate cost to the firm and its shareholders and employees by protecting them against unwise expansion.

Numerous studies have attempted to show the correlation of profits and the size factor in industry.[35] The Twentieth Century Fund study, covering the years 1931–1933, indicates that when the gauge of profitableness was the ratio of net income to net worth (capital, surplus, and undivided profits), or total profits to total investment (net worth plus borrowed capital), large corporations that made profits did so at lower rates than smaller corporations. Likewise, larger corporations that realized losses experienced them at lower rates than smaller firms; thus the range between profits and losses was narrower in the larger than in the smaller corporations. When the profitable and unprofitable corporations were combined, the corporations in the giant class made the best showing.[36] It is also interesting to note that, despite the more favorable showing of the larger corporations, the percentage of net income paid in dividends increased with the increasing size of the asset classes studied.[37] This seems to indicate a general awareness by directors of large corporations that persistent reinvestment may ultimately defeat its own purpose.

When the problem is considered in terms of particular industries, however, the picture is less favorable to firms in the largest size class. A study of the automobile industry, covering the period 1919–1927 and including the greater part of the industry, reveals that in no year did the largest firm earn the highest profit on invested capital. Over the entire period the largest firm stood fifth in average earnings. The firm

---

[35] R. C. Epstein, "Profits and the Size of the Firm in the Automobile Industry, 1919–1927," *American Economic Review*, Vol. XXI (1931), pp. 636–647; H. B. Summers, "A Comparison of Rates of Earning of Large-Scale and Small-Scale Industries," *Quarterly Journal of Economics*, Vol. XLVI (1931–1932), pp. 465–479; R. T. Bowman, *A Statistical Study of Profits* (Philadelphia, Pa., University of Pennsylvania Press, 1934); W. A. Paton, *Corporate Profits as Shown by Audit Reports* (New York, National Bureau of Economic Research, Inc., 1935); Twentieth Century Fund, Inc., *How Profitable Is Big Business?* (New York, Twentieth Century Fund, Inc., 1937); W. L. Crum, *Corporate Size and Earning Power* (Cambridge, Mass., Harvard University Press, 1939).

[36] Twentieth Century Fund, Inc., *op. cit.*, p. 159; Crum, *op. cit.*, p. 335. Professor Crum's study indicates that, considering all corporations, the larger the corporation the higher the rate of return, on the average, for the six-year period 1931–1936. There is extreme variability in the rate of return, from the smallest size class to the largest. This variability is accounted for by the deficit corporations, *i.e.*, those experiencing losses. In the case of the income corporations, *i.e.*, those showing a net profit, the rate of return does not vary greatly. Such variations as there are indicate that the smaller corporations have a higher rate of return than do the larger ones. See Crum, *op. cit.*, p. 32.

[37] Twentieth Century Fund, Inc., *op. cit.*, p. 162.

which consistently enjoyed the highest return was one which corresponded closely to the median size in the industry.[38] In the steel industry, data on the average cost of sales, net profit from operations, and net profit after the deduction of all charges indicate, for the four-year period 1934–1937, that the giant United States Steel Corporation with its two billion dollars of assets did not do so well as the average of twelve companies, including U. S. Steel, whose data were examined.[39] Some of the smaller companies such as Bethlehem Steel, National Steel and Inland Steel, with assets ranging downward from seven hundred to one hundred million dollars, had better records.

It is apparent from these various studies that the decision to expand is not a simple one to make, and it must be vexatious to all corporate managers save those who are very callous or expect to profit personally by corporate expansion.

Business Liquidation and Management—Stockholders' Interests

Management may also continue to operate a business when it should recommend that the shareholders consider a complete or a partial liquidation to avoid or minimize shareholder losses. Management may be reluctant to do this, however, for at least three important reasons. Firstly, it knows that the property values of the enterprise will shrink considerably in the process of liquidation. Secondly, it may sincerely feel that the foundations of the business can be reconstructed and profit-making resumed. Or, thirdly, it may prefer to mark time, receive its wages of management as long as possible, and then abandon the venture to its fate when there is no other alternative. The fair method, however, is to submit the problem to the shareholders.

An excellent instance of proper procedure is illustrated by the actions of the management of the Hamilton Woolen Company.[40] The company had experienced operating losses which depressed the market value of its shares well below their probable liquidating values. Since continued losses might wipe out shareholder capital, the management outlined the situation, gave the arguments for and against continuation of the business, expressed its own opinion, and requested the shareholders to make the decision. The shareholders voted to continue operation under new leadership. Once more profits were realized. The market price of the shares rose above their liquidating value. After a few years, however,

---

[38] Epstein, *op. cit.*, p. 639. In 1920 the median was $180,000,000; in 1927, $53,-000,000. The median average annual investment for the whole period was roughly $29,000,000.

[39] Securities and Exchange Commission, *Selected Information Reports*, Report No. 1, *Steel Producers* (New York, 1938), Table V(a), p. 23, and Table XII, pp. 53–55.

[40] Graham and Dodd, *op. cit.*, pp. 603–609.

losses reappeared and stockholders had to face the old problem. On this occasion they voted to discontinue. The properties were sold and shareholders received $40.00 per share, which was exactly equal to the market high of 1929 and but $10 per share under the book value for 1933.[41]

Management-Stockholder Market Relations

The fountain-head of information concerning current success or failure is under the control of the corporate directors. They keep closed or turn the dividend spigot as their judgment dictates. The individual directors and leading officers are, therefore, always the first to know what the collective action of management is. Since the market value of shares responds to good or bad news concerning a company's success or failure, it is obvious that management can profit in the market-place if it wishes to take advantage of its preferred position. The late Judge Gary, Chairman of the Board of the United States Steel Corporation, had a method to combat this temptation. He required the directors to remain in the board room after an announcement of dividend policy until the news had been transmitted to the stock exchanges. All corporate director-officers, however, are not so restrained or so endowed with a sense of moral obligation.

In the case of the General Asphalt Company, for example, two of the directors used their intimate knowledge of the plans and condition of their company in an attempt to profit personally in a stock exchange pool which they helped to organize.[42] Prior to the formation of the pool the company had paid no dividends on its common stock for some time. It proposed, however, to simplify its capital structure and resume dividends. With this advance knowledge these directors, through the pool, bought up blocs of stock at an average price of $80.00 per share. By the time the stockholders had been informed of the simplification plan and the proposed resumption of dividends, the common stock had risen to $94.25 per share. For some time thereafter the company continued to pay dividends, even though current earnings did not hold up to dividend requirements. The pool participated heavily in these payments. Ultimately, however, it wound up with a net loss due to the effects of the market crash of October, 1929.[43]

---

[41] For a sketch of the liquidation results, see Poor's *Industrial Manual*, 1935, p. 3102. Book value is ordinarily computed by adding together all the tangible assets, subtracting all liabilities and stock issues ahead of the common stock, and then dividing the remainder by the number of common shares outstanding.

[42] *Stock Exchange Practices*, Senate Report No. 1455, 73rd Congress, 2nd Session, p. 67.

[43] See testimony of John L. Weeks, Hearings Before the Committee on Banking and Currency, United States Senate, 72nd Congress, 1st Session, *Stock Exchange Practices*, Part II, pp. 541–542.

Governmental investigation has disclosed other instances, notably Anaconda Copper, Fox Film, and Fox Theatres Corporation, where directors, officers, and principal stockholders have partaken of pool operations in the shares of their own companies.[44] While it may be true that these operations do not necessarily inflict harm on the particular corporations, they do injure particular shareholders who unwittingly dispose of their shares of stock. Furthermore, this violation of a relationship between directors and shareholders, which is coming more and more to be considered fiduciary, brings into disrepute the useful corporate device.

While management should not use its preferred position to profit in the market-place, it does not follow that it should not properly take a protective interest in the market price of its corporation's shares. One of the main interests of shareholders lies in the marketability of their shares. Marketability includes not only a place to sell the shares readily, but also the ability to dispose of them at a fair price, that is, at a price which reflects the combined market judgment of the value of the shares as revealed by the true condition of the corporation. Not infrequently certain market forces establish unduly high or unduly low prices for a particular stock. When discrepancies of this sort are great and persistent, a frank statement of the facts by the management of the corporation would go far to rectify a condition dangerous to the shareholders.[45]

MANAGEMENT CONTROL AND SOME FUNDAMENTAL CHANGES

The growth of management control and the abuses that have developed under it have centered attention on some fundamental changes not found to the same degree in the corporation problems discussed in earlier chapters. There we dealt with the dominance of particular *ownership* groups which have reached their position of control, or have had their powers magnified, by various convenient devices. In those instances certain groups of owners had final control over the corporation. They might also have been directors and officers, but the fact remains that they, as owners, had the power of decision over policies which affected their varied interests. Whether or not it paid them to sacrifice their ownership interests for their management or other personal interests, nevertheless they retained the ownership power to make the decision. In the case of management control, however, managers have no ownership interest, or have so little that ownership and ownership income as

---

[44] *Senate Report*, No. 1455, p. 68.
[45] *Cf.* Graham and Dodd, *op. cit.*, pp. 601–603.

personal determining factors in corporate business policy and administration may be ignored.

The passiveness of shareholders, accentuated by management's unwillingness to render a full account of its stewardship, has brought about a complete separation of ownership from control. As we have already indicated, stockholders' attention has been diverted largely to the marketplace and daily quotations on their stocks. Knowledge of and interest in the underlying organized property values has been sadly lacking among corporate shareholders. In these circumstances officers have in many instances forgotten that they are employees working for the corporation. Rather, they have often worked largely for themselves. Directors, whose primary legal duty is to serve in the best interests of the owners, in their dual capacity as officers and directors have overlooked their basic function. As managing officers they have encouraged the notion that shareholders are not entitled to all the profits of enterprise, a notion which as directors they should have discouraged. Too frequently they have ignored the interest of minor employees and the general public. In some of these large quasi-public corporations, management has acted as if it were a trusteeship solely for itself, as if it were a perpetual totalitarian business *élite* rather than a group of stewards working for the interests of stockholders, employees, and the general public.

The changing emphasis on the functional nature of private property and profits, due to the separation of ownership and control, gives unscrupulous management wherever it is present a personal interest in monopoly profits. The impelling reason for seeking complete monopoly in any field or for strengthening and expanding the monopoly elements in any market area is no longer solely a matter of ownership reward. Rather, monopoly is sought in order to distribute a good share of monopoly gains among a few managers on the one hand, while reducing their managerial worries of competition on the other.

The development of management control and the appearance of opportunities for personal gain have made the ever-present problem of monopoly all the more difficult to handle. Where management control is found in railroad and public utility corporations, the problem is one of lesser degree than in the case of industrial corporations. For in the former fields we have accepted the wastefulness of competition as an inherent characteristic and have substituted the problems and social costs of public regulation for the problems and social costs of nonregulation. Under the special surveillance of state and Federal regulatory authorities, management has less chance, and therefore less incentive, to acquire for itself rewards over and above the competitive rate of return. In the case of industrial corporations, however, coming only under the general run of state and Federal anti-trust laws and supplementary legislation, management is subjected to less rigid controls. And the application of these controls is made more difficult as market policies are determined and executed by a small group of self-perpetuating managers. At best the discovery and proof of overt acts in violation of anti-trust laws has been difficult. Under the conditions of management control in our large industrial corporations, where managements of competing corporations may cultivate close personal contacts with each other, it becomes even more difficult. In these circumstances, some management in the execution of its trusteeship is not likely to give full attention to the interest that the general public has in corporate enterprise. Such public interest as is shown is likely to be incidental to the main interest, namely, the perpetuation of management's welfare.

RECENT TRENDS

Fortunately, in recent years, the expansion of governmental regulation and a more critical public attitude has checked some phases of the growth of management's indifference to interests other than its own. Some companies, notably General Mills and Johns-Manville, have been experimenting successfully with regional shareholders' meetings following the regular annual meeting of the corporation. At these meetings, designed to stimulate shareholder interest, directors encourage questions about corporate problems and seek criticism of their broad business policies. In other instances, company officials have repeatedly stated, as in the case of the American Telephone and Telegraph Company, that they are trustees not only of the shareholders but also of their employees and the general public.[46] To the extent that corporate management seriously accepts the trusteeship of the many varied interests involved in corporate enterprise, great economic progress will have been made. In the rôle of risk-bearers, different classes of shareholders will be fairly treated and sufficiently well compensated so as to be willing to supply more capital when needed. Employees, including salaried managers, will be paid wages commensurate with the value of services rendered and will be assured greater security of employment. And the public will benefit as the recipient of goods and services of the highest quality, and lowest prices attainable under freely competitive conditions. It is obvious, however, that regardless of the type of corporate control ex-

---

[46] The mere fact that managements publicly acknowledge the breadth of their trusteeships is a social gain. Whether they fairly administer them is, of course, quite another matter. There is disagreement, for example, about the sincerity of the management of the American Telephone and Telegraph Company toward its trust. See U. S. Federal Communications Commission, *Telephone Investigation, Proposed Report* (Washington, D. C., U. S. Government Printing Office, 1938), Chap. 17, and N. R. Danielian, *The A. T. & T.: A Story of Industrial Conquest* (New York, The Vanguard Press, 1939), Chaps. 9 and 13.

ercised, the reconciliation of these varied interests is at best a delicate task, subject to varying interpretations. Consequently the equitableness of the results will continue to cause wide differences of opinion. It is equally obvious that only the most socially enlightened groups are going to recognize these mutual self-interests. In these circumstances, therefore, legal protections are necessary, and they must extend beyond the uncertainties of privately initiated lawsuits.

7

The Holding Company

The holding company is a super-corporation. It is the drawstring by means of which other corporations, competing or non-competing, are gathered together through the purchase or exchange of securities. Since the demise of the illegal trustee device in the last decade of the nineteenth century, the holding company has been the most effective method that corporation lawyers have invented to bring the properties of a number of corporations under a single control. The large holding company is represented by such well-known organizations as the American Telephone and Telegraph Company, the United States Steel Corporation, the United Corporation, Sears, Roebuck and Company, the Standard Oil Company of New Jersey, and the National Dairy Products Corporation.

There is no generally accepted definition of the holding company. To call it a corporation which holds stocks in other corporations is too broad a definition, since it would include any industrial or financial institution which holds corporate securities primarily for investment rather than for control. Since the main purpose of a holding company is to exercise control over its subsidiaries, it must be so defined as to recognize the possibilities of a "working" control. Therefore, the holding company shall be defined here as a corporation which, by virtue of its ownership of *voting* stock in one or more other corporations, is *able* to exercise control or material influence over the management of those corporations.[1]

TYPES OF HOLDING COMPANIES

Though the holding companies found in our economic structure are essentially alike, they are variously classified. One method of classification is based on the amount of properties directly owned by the holding company. It is designated a *pure* holding company if it owns outright

---

[1] *Cf.* Guthmann and Dougall, *op. cit.*, p. 606; Bonbright and Means, *op. cit.*, pp. 7–10.

111

little or no property, but exercises its ownership powers over the properties of subsidiaries through its stock ownership. The United States Steel Corporation is representative of this type. In contrast, if it owns large properties directly, as compared with the amount it controls indirectly through voting stock, it is classified as a *property* holding company. The term *parent* holding company is sometimes applied to both of these types. The Securities and Exchange Commission uses the term "parent corporation" to apply to corporations owning 10 per cent or more of the outstanding voting securities of electric, gas, and water corporations.[2] In all other industries, the Commission regards one corporation as a parent of another only if it owns 50 per cent or more of the latter's voting stock.[3]

A second method of classification is based on the type of service the holding company renders to its subsidiaries. The main services are financing, management, engineering, and construction. While holding companies may supply all of these services and perhaps others, the tendency is to classify them in accordance with the most important service. Hence, they may be known as *financing* holding companies, *management* holding companies, and the like.

More recently, greater emphasis has been placed on a structural classification. At the base of the structure are the separate operating companies which own the tangible physical properties. Through the exchange of securities, tiers of holding companies are built up. The holding companies immediately imposed as a first tier or layer on the operating companies are known as *first degree* holding companies; those in the second tier, *second degree;* those in the third tier, *third degree;* and so on. The structural effect is to form a pyramid, at the apex of which is found the *top* or *super* holding company.[4]

Another method of classification, sometimes encountered, is based on the type of business in which the holding company and its subsidiaries are engaged. Thus, they may be railway, utility, financial, or industrial. And these broad categories are often subdivided if necessary.

Since their use has increased, special mention should also be made of the personal or family holding companies. In essence, these corporations are both investment and control devices. Their shares, or trust certificates representing their shares held in trust, are exchanged for the stocks of other corporations held by the members of a family. In this way family income is sustained, and family holdings are maintained and voted as a unit even though, through death or gift, the ownership

---

[2] Public Utility Holding Company Act of 1935, Sections 2a(7) and 2a(8).

[3] *Cf.* Securities and Exchange Commission, *The Distribution of Ownership in the 200 Largest Non-Financial Corporations,* p. 61, note 3.

[4] The actual process of forming the pyramid by exchange of securities will be illustrated later.

interest becomes subdivided.[5] Family holding companies have been found by the Securities and Exchange Commission to be the largest stockholders in a number of outstanding enterprises, such as E. I. du Pont de Nemours and Co., Firestone Tire and Rubber Co., and Pittsburgh Plate Glass Co.[6]

PREVALENCE OF THE HOLDING COMPANY

The use of the holding company is wide-spread in our American economy. In the public utility field it is unquestionably the dominant institution.[7] It is also widely used in the railroad industry.[8] In the industrial field, a study made of the 475 largest corporations as of December 31, 1936, revealed that 39 were pure holding companies; 301 were parent holding companies; 135 were outright operating companies.[9] In other words, about 70 per cent of this group of large industrial corporations were holding companies. In the two hundred largest non-financial corporations studied by the Securities and Exchange Commission, in which the major manufacturing industries, the public utilities, the railroads, and retail distribution and service industries are represented, the holding company is the dominant form. Roughly, 90 per cent of the 200 control one or more other corporations through ownership of stock.

The character of control in the holding companies found among the 200 largest non-financial corporations does not differ greatly from the general picture of control in the entire 200, where 42 corporations were controlled by a majority interest; 97, by a minority interest; 61, by management.[10] Of the 180 companies classified as holding companies in the 200, since they owned controlling stock in one or more other companies, 32 were controlled by a majority interest; 94 by a minority interest; and 54 were management-controlled and were without a dominant stockholding interest.

USES OF THE HOLDING COMPANY

The holding company is used as a means to various ends. In some instances its uses have been legitimate and desirable; in others, illegiti-

---

[5] See *Encyclopaedia of the Social Sciences*, Vol. VII, p. 406. These holding companies are useful also in simplifying tax returns and reducing taxes. These purposes, however, do not concern us here.

[6] Securities and Exchange Commission, *op. cit.*, pp. 77–78.

[7] Federal Trade Commission, *Utility Corporations*, Senate Document 92, Part 72-A, 70th Congress, 1st Session (Washington, D. C.), pp. 34–81.

[8] Bonbright and Means, *op. cit.*, pp. 235–270.

[9] Guthmann and Dougall, *op. cit.*, pp. 618–619.

[10] See Temporary National Economic Committee, *Monograph* No. 29, pp. 1486–1487.

mate, uneconomic, and anti-social. And experience shows that the desirable and undesirable uses have often appeared at the same time.

The holding company may be used to bring together a number of independent operating companies in the same field or related fields. In this way, by horizontal combination or by integration, many economies of larger-scale operation may be effected. Economies may be accomplished through centralized purchasing of materials and credit, through sales promotion, marketing, and the like. Moreover, combination offers opportunities for the better coördination of the production of raw materials, semi-finished, and finished goods to final sale. As a consequence, lower costs of the final products would result. In addition, the parent company, by servicing a number of smaller operating companies, may employ staffs more highly skilled in management, finance, engineering, and other important services.

If the matter is viewed strictly from the financial angle, it will be seen that the holding company serves to accomplish more easily and cheaply the combination of independent corporations. Its use is superior to direct acquisition of properties of one corporation by another, since it avoids the following major legal difficulties: (1) the necessity of obtaining a majority, or, in some cases, unanimous stockholder consent to the fusion; (2) the risk of lawsuits by dissenting stockholders alleging injury to their interests, and (3) the legal difficulties arising from possible interference with the contractual rights of bondholders. Where legal difficulties are not very serious ones there is, however, always the problem of the value of the properties to be acquired. Usually their value increases greatly at the first suggestion that they may be wanted by some other interest. Since stock acquisition can be accomplished quietly, control of properties may be acquired at a lesser cost than ownership by direct purchase. For this reason the control of independent properties through the holding company sometimes is but an intermediate step in complete fusion of properties.

Certain legal conflicts and difficulties confronting an enterprise which owns and operates properties in different states and foreign countries may also be avoided. To simplify tax and accounting problems, for instance, the properties in each state or country are separately incorporated. This arrangement also permits the business to take advantage of special laws of any state or country, and avoids discriminatory measures which might be imposed on non-domestic corporations. At the same time the holding company, acting as a drawstring, keeps the separate companies under the surveillance and control of the top management.

In a federated rather than a fused organization, holding arrangements provide the advantages derived from decentralized administration. Not infrequently boards of directors and principal officers of subsidiaries enjoy some measure of semi-independence. To the extent that this is true, and officials take advantage of it, subsidiary corporations are the proving-ground for the development of directors and executives in the top holding company. It is also possible to pit the performances of the managements of underlying operating and sub-holding companies against each other. In this way the effects of competition may be simulated within the structure of the holding company, with good effects on costs and profits.

Stock control may also allow the less risky activity to be segregated from the more risky by separate incorporation of each branch.[11] By means of this insulation the losses or failure of one subsidiary do not directly affect a more prosperous subsidiary. The holding company itself is affected, of course, but not always seriously, since it is protected by the receipt of income from the securities it holds of the more prosperous subsidiaries, in addition to the income it gets for services rendered to the operating companies.

In the securities markets, the large holding company may acquire capital for its operating subsidiaries more quickly and cheaply than could any one of them attempting to do so alone. It is usually better known in financial circles and can enlist the services of large reputable investment banking houses with wide markets and established marketing services. Smaller operating companies would, with some difficulty, have to seek capital locally or pay the higher rates that accompany the sale of securities in smaller lots.

Unfortunately, the legitimate uses of the holding company device have been weakened by abuses of varying degree. The alleged economies of large-scale production may never be attained, or, if they are, they may not be passed on to the consumer in the form of lower prices and better products. The holding company may serve as an effective monopolistic device to shackle free competition in its field. Even in the case of publicly regulated monopolies, the holding organization may prove to be a fairly effective instrument to confuse and vitiate public control of service charges, financial practices and accounting publicity imposed by law on the operating utilities. To the extent that this prevails, the public pays the penalty of higher prices and misguided investment.

Other advantages may also be lost. Operating companies may not receive management, financial, and engineering services under advantageous terms, but may pay heavily for their place in the structure. Their income may be diverted to serve the interests of the parent corporation, and they may pay fees incommensurate with the services rendered them.

Though it is true that the holding company may provide the benefits of decentralization of management, with attendant opportunities for di-

[11] *Cf.* Kenneth Field, *Corporation Finance* (New York, The Ronald Press Company, 1939), pp. 145–172.

rectors and executives in the subsidiaries to develop themselves for more important positions in the top structure, it does not follow that these good results will be realized. All too frequently many directors resemble honorary colonels.[12] They are unlikely, therefore, to take advantage of the opportunities to improve their directive skills. Consequently their activities on the proving grounds are confined to being occasionally seen and seldom heard, except as they repeat orders and supinely approve policies transmitted from the real control. Moreover, this same condition of director quiescence exists in the top holding companies as well as in the subsidiaries. It is especially prevalent when directors are given qualifying shares by promoters and dominant personalities in the corporate structure. Under such conditions directors are likely to be nothing more than paid "stooges" with far less independence of thought and action than the inimitable Charlie McCarthy is allowed by indulgent Edgar Bergen.[13]

In accomplishing combination easily, the holding company has been used also as an instrument for the issuance of securities the nominal value of which greatly exceeds the value of the underlying operating properties. This was notably true of the United States Steel Corporation at its inception in 1901. It was also true of the Rock Island and the Chicago and Alton Railways.[14] The recent searching inquiry of the Federal Trade Commission into the affairs of the public utility corporations has revealed very considerable capital inflation in that major field.[15] The deception of the public by the issuance of securities which have not been completely described or truthfully represented is an unfortunate practice of long standing, and though not peculiar to holding company finance, it has been accentuated through the issuance of holding company securities, especially during the decade of the 1920's.

An abuse which has often accompanied faulty capitalization has been the failure of the holding company to bargain at arm's length with investment banks which underwrite the issuance of securities. Often the bankers themselves have sponsored the combination of companies or have otherwise been so closely related to the project that competitive bidding for the privilege of disposing of new issues has been precluded. Any advantages which a corporation might gain from a close relationship with an investment banking group familiar with its financial problems is thus lost.

---

[12] Cf. William O. Douglas, Democracy and Finance (New Haven, Yale University Press, 1940), p. 46.

[13] For an excellent discussion of the director problem, see William O. Douglas, "Directors Who Do Not Direct," Harvard Law Review, Vol. XLVII (June, 1934), p. 1305.

[14] Cf. Bonbright and Means, op. cit., p. 17.

[15] Utility Corporations, Senate Document 92, Part 72-A, 70th Congress, 1st Session, pp. 307–322, 845–851.

One of the most important uses of the holding company, and the one most subject to abuse, has been the acquisition and maintenance of control of the underlying corporations with a minimum of investment. Thus the Van Sweringen brothers, with an investment of less than twenty million dollars, controlled railroads with combined assets of over two billion dollars. Similarly, a million-dollar investment by Henry L. Doherty & Co. controlled a billion-dollar utility system. And the investment banking house of H. M. Byllesby & Co. directed a billion-dollar utility system on an investment equal to less than 1 per cent of the consolidated assets. Acquisition of control is accomplished through a judicious issue and exchange of securities, which has become known as pyramiding. The structural result is the corporate pyramid. The financial result is the concentration of control in the hands of a few at the apex of the structure.

THE PROCESS OF PYRAMIDING

Pyramiding can best be understood if we resort to an abstract and somewhat simplified illustration. Let us assume that four independent utility corporations, A, B, C, and D, are operating with identical capital structures. Each company has a property investment of $1,000,000 and securities outstanding according to the following pattern: $500,000 in 4% bonds; $250,000 in 5% non-voting preferred stock; and $250,000 in voting common stock. Two holding companies, X and Y, are now formed. Company X is to bring together operating companies A and B; company Y, operating companies C and D. Each of these first-degree holding companies, therefore, issues the appropriate amounts and types of securities to accomplish its purpose. Company X, for example, issues $260,000 in 6% non-voting preferred stock and $110,000 in voting common stock. Company Y does likewise. X now exchanges its non-voting preferred stock for common stock of A and B. It does this on a share-for-share basis in the following fashion: $130,000 of X 6% preferred for $130,000 A voting common; $130,000 of X 6% preferred for $130,000 B voting common. Holding company X now controls the majority vote in both A and B. The public is induced to buy $50,000 of X common stock and the remaining $60,000 is retained by the promoters of the holding company. The same transactions are carried out to center and maintain control of operating companies C and D in holding company Y. The next step is to establish a second-degree holding company, which we will call Z. This company will draw together X and Y. The capital structure of Z is especially designed for this purpose. It issues $120,000 in non-voting 7% preferred stock and $60,000 in voting common. It exchanges share for share the $120,000 7% preferred for $60,000 of X voting common and for

$60,000 of Y voting common stock. Thus it now controls X and Y, and through them A, B, C, and D. The insiders retain $31,000 in Z's voting common and sell the remainder. This investment of $31,000, through the process of pyramiding a superstructure on four operating companies, controls property values of $4,000,000. And even this small investment can be reduced, if the insiders resort to the use of non-voting common stock or wish to take the risks of minority control.

In actual practice, pyramiding of corporate structures is more pronounced in public utilities and railroads than elsewhere. In both of these fields, there are instances where it has been carried to great extremes. In the Associated Gas and Electric system, for example, there were twelve companies in one line of control from the apex of the pyramid to its base.[16] And the ill-fated Insull system in public utilities and the Van Sweringen system in railroads are other notorious examples.[17]

The greater fluctuation of earnings in industrial corporations prevents extremes of pyramiding in the industrial fields. Industrial operating companies must be careful not to have too many outstanding securities carrying fixed interest or dividend requirements in proportion to their common stock issue. It is obvious that if it is dangerous in this field for operating companies to be faultily capitalized, it is even more so when holding company is piled on holding company. In industrials, therefore, the holding company has been largely used to stifle competition, to gain the benefits of decentralized control, and to profit from any advantages to be derived from legal and accounting autonomy and large-scale operations.

SOME EFFECTS OF EXCESSIVE, UNREGULATED PYRAMIDING

Not only does pyramiding lodge control in the hands of a few with relatively small investment as compared with the property values of the underlying companies, but it may also yield exceptionally high returns at the top. Let us again abstract some of the complicating factors and assume that the management, engineering, and other contracts which the holding companies have with the operating companies exactly cover all holding company expenses, so that the income derived from dividends on the stock of the underlying companies is entirely clear. Let us further assume that our companies, A, B, C, and D, earn 7 per cent on their total capital or $70,000 each per annum. In A, the 4 per cent bonds absorb $20,000 of this amount; the 5 per cent non-voting

---

[16] Federal Trade Commission, No. 72-A, *op. cit.*, p. 159.

[17] For the Insull structure, see *ibid.*, Chart IX, opposite p. 156; for the Van Sweringen system, see Bonbright and Means, *op. cit.*, p. 261.

preferred, $12,500; and $37,500 remains for the common stockholders. This amounts to a 15 per cent return on the common. The same situation prevails in B, C, and D, since their capital structures were assumed to be alike. Since X has exchanged its non-voting preferred to the extent of $260,000 for $260,000, in equal amounts of $130,000 each of A and B common, X will receive as income the dividends on this amount of stock it holds. The income amounts to 26/50ths of $75,000 ($37,500 from A and $37,500 from B) or $39,000. Since X issued $260,000 in 6 per cent preferred stock, it must pay $15,600 in dividends on this amount before it can pay anything to its common stockholders. There remains, therefore, $23,400 to be distributed to the $110,000 in common stock of X. The rate of return on X common is, therefore, about 21.3 per cent. The same situation prevails for holding company Y. But the top holding company, Z, owns $60,000 in X common and a like amount of Y common, hence it will receive 60/110ths of the dividends, or $12,764 from each sub-holding company. This income will be divided as follows: $8,400 or 7 per cent on $120,000 Z preferred stock and $17,128, or slightly in excess of 28.5 per cent, on the $60,000 Z common stock.

An increase above normal earnings in the operating companies will greatly increase the rate of return on the common stock in the superstructure. On the other hand, a shrinkage in earnings in the operating companies will have the opposite effect. Thus, if the earnings of the operating companies in our hypothetical illustration were reduced by one-half, that is, to 3.5 per cent on their total capital investment, they would hardly be able to pay interest on their own bonds and dividends on their preferred stock.[18] Earnings for the superstructure would not be cut in half but would be reduced to nothing. Unless a reserve for such a contingency is accumulated in advance, dividends on the preferred stock in the superstructure would be in arrears and common stock would be worth only its future expectations. And the further removed the holding company is from the operating companies, the worse the predicament in which the holding company shareholders find themselves. Subordinate companies must operate at highly profitable levels if the pyramid is to stand.

Since the top-holding, sub-holding, and operating companies are related to each other not only in the capacity of the owners and the owned, but also as services and serviced, sellers and buyers, creditors and debtors, there are plenty of opportunities for pyramided holding companies to supplement their uncertain dividend income. Contracts are made by

---

[18] A return of 3.5 per cent would amount to $35,000 for each operating company. Bond interest in each instance would absorb $20,000, and preferred stock dividends would take $12,500. Thus only $2,500 would be left for distribution to the common stockholders. It is obvious that the first-degree holding companies would get little income, and second or higher-degree companies, none at all.

the holding companies with their subsidiaries to provide the latter with various services at specified fees. Holding companies purchase properties and re-sell them to the operating companies. Capital funds are borrowed on the presumably better credit rating of the holding companies and are re-loaned to the subsidiary operating companies.

Unfortunately, however, there is no real opportunity for forthright arm's-length bargaining between holding companies and the operating subsidiaries; nor can there be, in a relation which is one of master and servant. Consequently holding companies can supplement their dividend income by mistreatment of their subsidiaries as long as the subordinate companies are able to stand the strain.

An outstanding instance of the failure to bargain for services at arm's length is illustrated by the case of the Associated Gas and Electric Company.[19] The operating subsidiaries were required to pay the holding company a management service fee amounting to $2\frac{1}{2}$ per cent of gross earnings (less inter-company sales). The actual management services for some operating companies were performed, however, by the J. G. White Management Company, which, at that time, was not affiliated with the Associated Company.[20] In the period from January 1, 1925, to July 31, 1927, these operating subsidiaries paid approximately $841,000 for management services. Of this sum, the Associated Gas and Electric Company, though it rendered these subsidiaries no services whatsoever, kept $473,000, while the J. G. White Management Company was paid $368,000. When the Associated Company actually performed the management services for other operating subsidiaries it received the entire $2\frac{1}{2}$ per cent service fee.

A number of similar abuses also appeared where construction services were performed. The Associated Company incorporated special construction companies which it controlled. The construction companies were then allowed to collect a fee or commission amounting to $7\frac{1}{2}$ per cent of the construction costs.[21] The total of management and construction fees collected by the Associated Gas and Electric Company for a part of 1924 and the years 1925–1929 amounted to nearly $10,000,000. Total expenses of about $3,400,000 were incurred to render these services. The net profit on service cost was, therefore, about $6,600,000, or 193 per cent on the cost. In addition to this, the operating companies in this pyramided system were forced to pay excessive service charges for purchasing, merchandising, advertising, and financial services. Numerous insiders personally gained from these arrangements. H. C. Hop-

---

[19] Federal Trade Commission, No. 72-A, pp. 626–632.

[20] The Associated Gas and Electric Company acquired control of the J. G. White Management Company on May 1, 1928; *ibid.*, p. 627.

[21] It should be noted that an arrangement of this sort is no inducement to keep down construction costs in this field.

son, for example, through H. C. Hopson & Company, provided all the financial and auditing services for the Associated system, which he controlled. And Hopson arranged it so that his brother-in-law's company, Daniel Starch and Associates, was awarded the utility system's advertising contracts.

The complicated corporate structure has allowed holding companies to harvest supplementary inter-company profits by the sale and re-sale of properties and securities to subsidiaries at prices hardly established in an independent market.[22] The Federal Trade Commission found numerous instances of this practice in its investigation of the utilities. One of the most flagrant cases involved the W. B. Foshay Company. It transferred properties and securities to its subsidiary, the Public Utilities Consolidated Corporation, receiving in return nearly $2,700,000 in securities of the latter corporation. It then proceeded to re-value these securities upward by $1,614,000. Both the $2,700,000 sale and the $1,-614,000 write-up were treated as income and reported as such to the stockholders and the investing public. Actually the earnings of the operating companies were negligible. The Foshay Company paid dividends, however, from its fictitious income. In time there followed the receivership of the Foshay companies, the dissolution of W. B. Foshay Company, and penitentiary terms for certain of the officials.[23]

Another curious case involved several abuses in a series of complicated and striking transactions. The New England Gas and Electric Association, a Massachusetts trust[24] closely related to the Associated Gas and Electric Company (both controlled by H. C. Hopson and associates), acquired controlling common stock in two New Hampshire utility operating companies, the New Hampshire Gas and Electric Company and the Derry Electric Company. The acquisitions were made in 1924 in the former company, and in 1927 in the latter. The New England Association not only made itself an owner, but it also became a creditor of these companies by lending them money on "open account." With a part of these funds, which cost 8 per cent per annum, the subsidiaries retired bonds bearing a lesser interest rate and preferred stock with a lesser fixed dividend rate. Obviously the arrangement saved the operating subsidiaries no money. In 1929 the New England Association also acquired a $50,000 Derry Electric bond issue, maturing in 1931. As controlling owner of the Derry Electric, the New England Associa-

---

[22] Cf. N. R. Danielian, "From Insull to Inquiry," The Atlantic Monthly, Vol. CLI (April, 1933), pp. 504, 506.

[23] Federal Trade Commission, op. cit., pp. 238–239.

[24] A Massachusetts trust is a business trust, an organization in many ways paralleling the corporation. A trust agreement takes the place of a corporate charter. A board of trustees operates instead of a board of directors. Properties are held in trust for the beneficiaries by the trustees. The trust may issue both bonds and shares, but it remains an unincorporated association.

tion decided to have the Derry Company default on the interest payments on the $50,000 of bonds, even though the books of the latter company showed earnings sufficient to pay the interest charges.[25] As directed from above, the Derry Electric directors waived the ninety-day period of grace to which the company was entitled by contract, and they consented to immediate foreclosure action by the trustee for the bondholder, the New England Association. The trustee foreclosed and sold the property at public auction. Though its directors and stockholders did not vote on the matter, the New Hampshire Gas and Electric Company, obeying the orders of its parent company, the New England Association, bid $547,591 and purchased the Derry properties. Later it voluntarily raised the bid price to $873,950.19 in accordance with a valuation proposed by an Associated Gas and Electric Company engineer.

To make the purchase, the New Hampshire Gas and Electric borrowed the entire amount from the New England Association on "open account" at 8 per cent per annum.[26] Most of the loan proceeds came back to the New England Association, since it was a large creditor of the Derry Company on "open account"; the holder of $50,000 of Derry bonds, and principal stockholder in the Derry Company.

The final result of all these transactions was that the value of the Derry Electric Company was written up 60 per cent; the New Hampshire Gas and Electric Company owned the Derry properties; the New England Gas and Electric Association had a lucrative creditor's "open account" of over $800,000 against the New Hampshire company in place of the former creditor-owner relationship it had with the Derry Electric Company. Moreover, the New England Association controlled the New Hampshire Gas and Electric Company. And by these tortuous financial methods, regulatory control by the New Hampshire Public Service Commission was avoided.[27]

When these various methods of inflating or maintaining income have

[25] 14 New Hampshire Public Service Commission, 82–168 (1931); Federal Trade Commission, *Utility Corporations*, Senate Document 92, No. 48, 70th Congress, 1st Session, Washington, D. C. (1933), pp. 169–247. For a popular account, see also N. R. Danielian, "Gas: A Study in Expansion," *The Atlantic Monthly*, Vol. CLII (July, 1933), pp. 111–123.

[26] The interest on this so-called "downstream" loan was payable monthly. If it was not paid on time it was compounded at the same rate. When the New Hampshire Public Service Commission began to investigate these transactions in 1930 the interest rate was lowered to 6 per cent per annum.

[27] The Commission investigated and issued against the Derry Electric and the New Hampshire Gas and Electric companies orders pertaining to many of their transactions and relationships with each other and with the New England Gas and Electric Association and related companies. These orders were contested, and the case went to the New Hampshire Supreme Court, where it was decided against the Commission as involving matters beyond its control. State of New Hampshire v. New Hampshire Gas and Electric Company and Derry Electric Company, 86 N. H. 16 (1932).

been lacking or insufficient to meet the full requirements of vast pyramided capital structures, pressure has been exerted by control at the apex of the pyramid to manipulate accounting procedure in the companies below. Depreciation charges, for example, have been conveniently reduced to cut operating expenses. By this deceitful practice, the necessary amount of profits has been produced for distribution to shareholders in the superstructure.[28]

The process of extreme pyramiding has not only fostered flagrant inter-company abuses, but at times it has also introduced almost hopeless confusion into the fields of corporation finance and investment. The construction of multi-tier structures has brought into use a bewildering array of security issues, many of them stocks without voting power.[29] This has been true particularly in the railroad and public utility fields. The Associated Gas and Electric Company, for example, at one time had three classes of common stock, six classes of preferred stock, four classes of preference stock,[30] seven issues of bonds and notes, twenty-four classes of debenture bonds (bonds secured only by the general credit of the organization rather than by specific properties or other collateral) many of which were convertible into preferred and common stocks of the holding company or its subsidiary and affiliated companies, and four series of investment certificates. In addition, it also had outstanding at one time or another various options to purchase authorized but non-issued shares.[31] It is obvious that even the ability of an experienced corporation lawyer and a trained financial expert would be severely taxed to understand clearly the status and value of any particular security in such a financial hodge-podge.

From this unfortunate condition two significant problems have arisen, namely: (1) the clash of intra-corporate interests in the pyramided corporate structure, and (2) the increased abuse of the securities markets for new and old issues.

THE CLASH OF INTRA-CORPORATE INTERESTS

Uncontrolled inter-company transactions may injure the interests of particular groups through the sale of assets by one company to another within the holding company structure; the routing of profitable business away from one subsidiary to another; the formulation of inter-company service contracts, property leases, and loans; and the manipulation of accounts to puff profits, conceal losses, or create non-existent deficits.

---

[28] See Graham and Dodd, *op. cit.*, (revised edition), pp. 467–468.

[29] Federal Trade Commission, *op. cit.*, No. 72-A, pp. 136–140.

[30] An issue of stock endowed with certain assurances, preferences, or limitations to distinguish it from other types of preferred stock. See Dewing, *op. cit.*, p. 43.

[31] Federal Trade Commission, *op. cit.*, p. 305.

To suppress protests the perpetrators have relied on human lethargy, the lack of knowledge and organization among the injured shareholders, the prohibitive expense of lawsuits, and the unequal struggle against vast holding company systems.

Where litigation has resulted, the courts have generally held that the burden of proof is on the parent company to show strict regard for its fiduciary position toward all the various companies under its control. Moreover, the parent control must exercise due care and diligence to protect minority interests in the subsidiary companies. Both of these principles were clearly delineated in a case involving a Michigan copper mining company.[32] In this instance the parent company, through its control of the directorate of two subsidiaries in which it exercised a minority "working" control, sought among other things to establish an ore-milling plan which would have been beneficial to itself and to other subsidiaries in which it held a larger stock interest. The plan, however, was considered by the court to be prejudicial to the interests of the two subsidiaries and injurious to their stockholders. The parent corporation, therefore, had not completely maintained the required fiduciary position.

The protection by private legal action, however, has not always been sufficient. The intricate holding company structure has been used sometimes to turn an injured minority stockholder's successful litigation into a hollow victory. A classic instance occurring in the 1890's involved the New York Central and a subsidiary, the New York and Northern Railway.[33] The Central had acquired a majority of the stock of the New York and Northern, but it wished to establish complete ownership. The market prices of the outstanding minority shares, however, were higher than it wished to pay. The Central, therefore, resorted to a circuitous though none the less effective method of property acquisition. Its directors, through their control over the directors of the subsidiary, refused to accept sufficient traffic over the subsidiary road to enable it to obtain enough revenue to meet expenses and pay interest on its outstanding mortgage bonds. Moreover, some of the depleted income was diverted to improper purposes. Meanwhile the directors of the Central had the investment banking house of Drexel, Morgan & Company acquire sufficient of the New York and Northern's second mortgage bonds to exercise foreclosure proceedings as soon as the subsidiary defaulted on its interest payments. The default occurred and the foreclosure followed. This action was opposed by New York and Northern minority stockholders. Defeated in the lower courts, they carried the case to the New York Court of Appeals, where the lower court decree of foreclosure was

---

[32] Hyams v. Calumet and Hecla Mining Company, 221 Fed. 529 (1915).
[33] Berle and Means, op. cit., pp. 240–243; Bonbright and Means, op. cit., pp. 345–347.

reversed. Despite legal defeat, the Central somehow—precisely how has never been revealed—managed a foreclosure sale and took over the property of the New York and Northern.

Since the foreclosure sale caused the value of the New York and Northern stock practically to vanish, an injured stockholder brought suit against the New York Central to recover damages. Holding close to legal technicalities, the court would allow no recovery on the grounds that the action must be taken in the name of the New York and Northern Railway as the injured party. Obviously, however, the subsidiary company would not act to sue its parent, the New York Central, unless compelled by law. Even had the subsidiary taken successful action the Central, as a majority shareholder and major creditor, would have received the lion's share of the recovered damages.[34]

These cases are indicative of the clashes which may and do occur within the holding company structure. The financial network of the holding company structure lends itself particularly to these dangers and abuses. Where the protective element of corporate simplicity is lacking, violations of the fiduciary relations, which the courts impose on control whatever its form may be, can take place with little or no obstruction. Whether the control is by majority or minority ownership or rests in the hands of management alone is unimportant.

THE HOLDING COMPANY AND THE MARKET FOR NEW SECURITIES

The abuses of any market grow out of a combination of low business morals and the ignorance and imperfect knowledge of either buyers or sellers. Where he is dealing with tangible goods the buyer at least has a chance to see them, submit them to tests, and otherwise examine them, but he is still exploited. In buying securities, however, he is purchasing an intangible, representative of underlying values not immediately before his eyes. Or, if he is able to view the tangible properties, they may be arranged on such a vast scale and so inter-related and specialized that their value as a whole is a function of proper organization and operation about which the buyer may know very little. It is imperative, therefore, that the prospective purchaser have all the facts properly presented to him as a first step towards an intelligent evaluation. Otherwise the possibilities of market abuses are very great, and the rewards of shrewd dealing and outright misrepresentation are easily attained.

Where corporate promoters of large-scale industry are forced to submit the full facts concerning new issues to cautious investment bankers

---

[34] See Berle and Means, *op. cit.*, p. 241.

possessed of a strong sense of social responsibility, the public may be well protected. But where the ethics of investment bankers are shady, or where investment bankers are closely related to the promotional aspects of a corporate business, the public is likely to suffer serious losses. In the decade of the 1920's the investor suffered seriously, especially in the public utility field. Public investigation has revealed many unsavory situations.

The public makes its purchases of new securities through various channels. The issuer corporation, or its promoters, may offer and dispose of any new securities to present holders of its outstanding issues on a *pro rata* basis of so many new shares to so many shares of the outstanding issues. The issuer may also attempt to sell its shares directly to customers of its goods or services. It may seek also to sell its securities through the medium of an investment banking house. If the investment bank is unaffiliated with the issuer corporation, its services are obtained only after it has made a careful investigation of the issuer corporation, a close analysis of the proposed new issue, and a general survey of the state of the market. More recently, however, the large holding corporation has turned to investment banking organizations that either control the issuer or are controlled by it. The relations between Halsey, Stuart & Co. and the Insull system, Henry L. Doherty & Co. and the Cities Service Company, and H. L. Byllesby & Co. and the Standard Gas and Electric system are illustrative of this arrangement.

Though all methods of distributing new securities have been subject to abuse, the distribution by controlled or affiliated outlets has been especially conducive to questionable practices, whether selling to old or new investors.[35] In some instances these organizations were in no position to question unsound inter-corporate structural or financial conditions. In other instances they contributed directly to unsound finance. In fact, some investment banks manipulated the market prices of the holding companies' outstanding securities in order to make the new issues appear attractive. Such side-show operations tended to divert the attention of a gullible and somewhat greedy public from the faulty structure of some of the leading utility systems such as the old Insull group.

These unfortunate market activities have encouraged speculation and inflicted heavy financial losses on misled investors. As a result there has developed public demand for some form of Federal regulation of the sale of old and new issues of securities and of the public utility holding company.

In fairness to the public utility holding companies and their subsidiaries, it should be pointed out that, despite the abuses uncovered

---

[35] For an extended summary account of these practices, see Federal Trade Commission, *op. cit.*, No. 72-A, pp. 535–598.

earlier, a subsequent study puts them in a slightly more favorable light.[36] The author concluded that control and operation of the public utilities by holding companies for the period covered—data were largely as of 1939–1940—did not appear to impose a relatively detrimental influence on the consumers of utility services or on investors in operating utilities. Moreover, he found that consumers and investors dependent upon subsidiary companies fare at least as well as like groups under independent operating utilities.[37]

THE HOLDING COMPANY AND THE PROBLEMS OF MONOPOLY

As the Federal Trade Commission has observed, consideration of the holding company cannot neglect the contribution this form of organization has made to monopoly.[38]

In the industrial field the holding company has brought together many formerly independent firms. By horizontal combination it has accomplished in some instances what has amounted to thorough-going monopoly. In other cases, it has quickly brought about vertical integration of properties to produce mammoth business organizations. Although it has by no means always produced monopoly conditions sufficient to warrant legal action under the anti-trust laws, nevertheless it has changed the complexion of competition very definitely. In pricing policies, free and independent action has been superseded by a high degree of market coöperation among giant firms.

Not infrequently, public antipathy to industrial monopoly has been avoided by means of the holding company. The purchase of controlling

---

[36] M. H. Waterman, *Economic Implications of Public Utility Holding Company Operations With Particular Reference to the Reasonableness of the "Death Sentence" Clause of the Public Utility Holding Company Act*, Michigan Business Studies, Vol. IX, No. 5. 1941.

[37] *Ibid.*, pp. 139–140. The funds for this study were furnished by the Engineers Public Service Company owing to its management's desire to determine the facts regarding relative performance of independent and subsidiary companies as a whole. At the time the company was engaged in challenging the reasonableness of Section 11 of the Public Utility Holding Company Act of 1935. Professor Waterman was free to examine the facts, interpret them, and publish the results regardless of their bearing on the case of the Engineers Public Service Company. The sample covered by the study included 182 independent companies and 454 holding company subsidiaries. It is unfortunate, however, that the study depended on data from the years *after* rather than *prior to* the passage of the Public Utility Holding Company Act of 1935. Furthermore, it would seem that holding companies would be inclined to acquire the more efficient operating companies in gaining subsidiaries; hence the real question should be, "Ought not holding company subsidiaries to show a clean-cut superiority over operating independents?"

[38] *Utility Corporations*, Senate Document 92, Part 73-A, 70th Congress, 1st Session (Washington, D. C., U. S. Government Printing Office, 1935), p. 47.

stock in a company formerly recognized by the public as an independent producer has been kept secret to avoid public disapproval. Meanwhile, the bogus independent continued to trade on its past good-will and went through the motions of competition with its former rivals. In this manner patronage which might have switched to other really independent companies was retained by the monopolistically inclined holding company.

In the utilities field two sorts of monopoly have to be kept in mind. On the one hand, there is the local monopoly under public regulation. And on the other hand, there is the holding company which has combined the local monopolies on a regional and often on a national basis. Allegedly established to effect economies not within the reach of the regulated local companies, the holding company system has served frequently to destroy the effectiveness of state regulatory efforts to give the public rates and services equal to or superior to real competition.

Moreover, the holding company has helped to concentrate monopoly profits in the hands of a few individuals. The excess of income over the amount necessary to satisfy docile shareholders can be more easily canalized to the pockets of those who are actually in control. Service charges of a monopolistic nature can be imposed easily on operating subsidiaries. Monopoly gains extracted from an inadequately protected consumer and investor public have served to enhance inequalities in wealth. The personal or family holding companies allow fortunes to be maintained and expanded in industries not especially noted for thorough-going price competition. The most notable single instance of this is the du Pont family control of extensive interests in E. I. du Pont de Nemours & Company and the manifold interests which this company dominates.[39]

CONCLUSION

Since the turn of the century, the holding company has become the dominant species of a dominant genus, the modern corporation. Properly used, as it frequently is, the holding company is a device capable of giving the public the advantages of integrated and coördinated large-scale production. It can be used to avoid complicated legal problems growing out of the fusion of different property interests. It offers the benefits of decentralization of management, while it provides the segregation of risks of business ventures in the same or in related fields. By combining small ventures little known in the major capital markets, it provides the opportunity to reduce the cost of capital acquisition.

[39] For a survey of the du Pont sphere of influence in industry, see the Securities and Exchange Commission, op. cit., pp. 97–100.

Perverted by unscrupulous and reckless individuals or group interests, however, the holding company has been used to accomplish socially undesirable ends. It has been an aid to monopoly. It has drained subsidiaries of their resources. It has provided false prestige and soft berths for inactive and supine directors. It has been used to accomplish faulty capitalization. It has increased the cost of raising capital by its control interests working in harmony with investment bankers. It has contributed both to an unhealthy separation of ownership from control and to the concentration of control in relatively few hands.

The medium by which many of these evil results have been attained and accentuated is excessive and unregulated pyramiding. Aided by lax incorporation laws, pyramiding has allowed individuals to control large property values with a comparatively small investment through the construction of financial hodge-podges with excessive capitalizations. It has facilitated the violation of the rights of one corporate interest by another. It has augmented confusion with respect to the rights of new and old issues of securities, and has encouraged security misrepresentation. In the public utility field, the pyramided holding company has long served to avoid public regulation, and by its relations with operating companies it has vitiated the regulatory work of public service commissions.[40] As a device for the construction of huge business units it has contributed to the more rapid decline of price competition in many fields. And by deceptive practices, as in the case of bogus independents, it has concealed the presence of monopoly at work.

---

[40] Application of the Public Utility Holding Company Act of 1935 by the S. E. C. has shaken down the superstructure of the holding company in this field in recent years.

8

Public Protection for Corporate Investors

In the late nineteenth century and during the first three decades of the twentieth, the great growth of corporate industry sharpened and magnified the possible abuses that might occur in the use of the corporation. Not all people were unaware of the dangers, and protests and warnings were vigorously raised in the public interest.[1] As Commissioner of Corporations, James R. Garfield recognized that corporate affairs needed the healthy sunlight of public scrutiny. In 1904 he advocated a Federal franchise or license for all corporations doing business in interstate commerce. As part of the requirements for obtaining and retaining a license, corporations would have to make such reports and returns as the government desired, and meet all the demands made on them as to organization and management.[2] Presidents Theodore Roosevelt, Taft and Wilson engaged the Federal Government in battle against the growing pressure of monopoly and corporate abuses. Their emphasis, however, was on the elimination of monopoly and unfair competitive practices in commodity and service markets, rather than on the abuses arising from corporate organization. In general, from 1904 to the first administration of Franklin D. Roosevelt, tighter Federal controls for corporate abuses were agitated for in a desultory fashion.[3] The country preferred to leave these matters to the individual states and to private agencies rather than risk the expansion of Federal powers through the requirements of Federal incorporation, Federal license, or more sweeping Federal controls.

---

[1] For example, Louis D. Brandeis, *Other People's Money* (New York, Frederick A. Stokes Company, 1914); Woodrow Wilson, *The New Freedom* (New York and Garden City, Doubleday Page & Company, 1913).

[2] See Federal Trade Commission, *Utility Corporations*, Senate Document 92, Part 69-A, 70th Congress, 1st Session, pp. 4–5.

[3] For a compilation of the proposals and discussions, see Federal Trade Commission, *op. cit.*, pp. 3–135.

EARLY CONTROLS

The individual states sought their own solutions. In 1913, under Governor Woodrow Wilson's leadership, the State of New Jersey reversed its liberal incorporation policy and passed legislation, known as the Seven Sisters Acts, aiming both at the destruction of monopoly and at the prevention of corporate abuses.[4] This forthright action, however, only demonstrated the futility of action by a single state. Incorporators sought charters elsewhere, and New Jersey found it expedient to repeal its restrictive legislation. Other states sought only to curb the most flagrant abuses committed behind the corporate screen. They passed what have become known popularly as "Blue Sky" laws, which were designed to prevent the sale of securities with nothing more tangible behind them than the blue sky.

"Blue Sky" Laws

In Kansas, Bank Commissioner Dolley recognized that the complete laxity of state incorporation laws made it almost impossible to eradicate misrepresentation of security values, and acted to correct the situation. His one-man campaign for protective legislation brought in 1911 a law to prevent the issue of spurious securities. And shortly thereafter other states imitated Kansas.

These early laws were crude and largely unworkable. Moreover, their constitutionality was successfully attacked in the lower Federal courts. The clarifying process of discussion and litigation, however, ironed out the early crudities. Revision or the passage of new laws did much to protect security purchasers from their own ignorance and credulity. In general, an executive of the state was given the power to supervise the sale of securities. The constitutionality of this principle, however, was challenged in litigation that reached the Supreme Court in 1916 in what are now known as the "Blue Sky" cases.[5] But the states were triumphant. Their power to forbid dealing in stocks and other securities within their borders and to subject such business to executive supervision was upheld. Such provisions were not considered arbitrary nor inconsistent with due process of law under the Fourteenth Amendment. The Court further maintained that the laws were not a direct burden on interstate commerce when securities came in from other states and the sellers within the state were required to obtain a license, file information, and submit to state supervision. Thus, state control over the

---

[4] See Seager and Gulick, *op. cit.*, pp. 362–366.

[5] Hall *v.* Geiger-Jones Company, Hall *v.* Coultrap, Hall *et al. v.* Rose *et al.*, 242 U. S. 539 (1917); Caldwell *et al. v.* Sioux Falls Stock Yards Co. *et al.*, 242 U. S. 559 (1917); Merrick *et al. v.* Halsey & Co., *et al.*, 242 U. S. 568 (1917).

issuance of securities, the flotation and sale, and the business of dealing in securities, received the highest judicial approval.

At the present time state "Blue Sky" laws, though they lack uniformity, fall into two broad categories: (1) regulatory acts, and (2) fraud acts.[6]

The regulatory acts include three types of laws. The first provides for the registration of securities with a proper state agency. Sale of unregistered securities, unless exempt under the law, is prohibited, and violation is considered a misdemeanor. Registration does not mean that the state approves the soundness of a security issue. It merely means that the securities are those of an existing and legitimate enterprise. The state supervising agent determines legitimacy and the absence of fraud, from the detailed corporate information which must be supplied. Under the Massachusetts law, for example, the Public Utilities Commission is authorized to investigate the security which is to be sold, and to demand further information if needed to supplement the original data supplied by the applicant at the time of registration.[7]

Teeth were put into these registration laws by providing penalties for violation. Violators are subject to civil or criminal action or both. Fines and jail sentences of varying degrees of severity are imposed by the different states. Under the laws of some states, sales may be voided by the purchaser.[8]

A second type of regulatory law is that which requires dealers to obtain licenses to sell securities within the state. Non-licensed persons are forbidden to sell under penalty of this law. Violation is considered a misdemeanor and is frequently subject to a heavy fine.[9] The protective principle involved is based on dealer reputation. Only reputable persons will be licensed, and it is assumed that they in turn will protect their acknowledged reputation by the sale of issues uncontaminated by fraud. Evidence of good reputation and other information must be filed with the proper state agency by the dealer. The names of the partners

---

[6] See Robert R. Reed, art. " 'Blue Sky' Laws," *Encyclopaedia of the Social Sciences*, Vol. II, pp. 602–604; Emanuel Stein, *Government and the Investor* (New York, Farrar and Rinehart, Inc., 1941), pp. 64–70; Russell A. Smith, "The Relation of Federal and State Security Laws," *Law and Contemporary Problems* (Durham, N. C.). Vol. IV (1937), pp. 241–242.

[7] The Massachusetts law requires that the applicant file the names of the principal officers of the enterprise; the state of incorporation; the general nature of the business; the amount of capital devoted, and proposed to be devoted, to the business in question; the number and classes of securities issued and to be issued; the amount of the secured and unsecured debt, with a brief description of the dates of issue, maturities, and character of such debt, and the character of the security, if any; a description of the respective voting rights, preferences, rights to dividends, profits, and capital of each type or class of security. (*General Laws*, c. 110-A, as amended.) See *U. S. Corporation Manual* (41st edition), pp. 2410–2416.

[8] For example, Illinois Securities Act, Laws of 1919, as amended, Sec. 37.

[9] Illinois Securities Act, as amended, Secs. 29, 30, 31.

or directors and officers in the organization, location of offices, previous business experiences, personal integrity, financial standing of the organization, criminal record, if any, in connection with the sale of securities, are some of the data required by various laws. Some states require the dealer or broker to post a sizable bond as a protection to prospective purchasers, who may sue on the bond in the event they feel they have been defrauded.[10]

A third type of regulatory act provides double protection to the security-buyer, since it not only requires public registration of securities, except for those specifically exempt under the law, but also requires dealers to secure from the proper state official a license to sell. The California law is one of the most complete.[11] And a number of states evaluate and classify the securities. Illinois, for example, grades securities acceptable for sale, as speculative and non-speculative.[12] Class A securities are those which have inherent qualities insuring their sale and disposition without fraud, *e.g.*, securities issued by a government or governmental agency and securities issued by banks, public utilities, and similar enterprises regulated or supervised by a government agency. Securities inferior to Class A then range down to Class D, which must be labeled as such and designated as purely speculative in character.[13] Official attention is levelled particularly at the Class D type.

In a few states, such as New York and New Jersey,[14] the Attorney-General proceeds against the sellers of spurious securities. He may enjoin the sale of fraudulent securities. And he may prosecute the sellers under the criminal laws of the state. The general disadvantage of these fraud laws, however, is that they are not as preventive as they appear at first sight. The tendency is for action to be taken *after* investors have been hurt.

Prohibitions under the Postal Laws

While the states have made their contributions, the United States Criminal Code has long prohibited the use of the mails to schemes and artifices to defraud.[15] The Postmaster-General is empowered to issue

---

[10] See California Securities Act, Laws of 1917, c. 532, as amended, Sec. 6.

[11] Laws of 1917, as amended, c. 532, and Laws of 1937, c. 784. See *U. S. Corporation Manual, op. cit.*, pp. 2235–2249.

[12] Illinois Securities Act, as amended, *U. S. Corporation Manual, op. cit.*, pp. 2310–2332. For a critical evaluation of the early Illinois law, see James W. Angell, "The Illinois Blue Sky Law," *Journal of Political Economy*, Vol. XXVIII (1920), pp. 307–321.

[13] J. W. Angell, *op. cit.*, pp. 309–312.

[14] New Jersey, Revised Statutes of 1937, 49:1–1 to 49:1–29; New York, General Business Law, Articles 23-A and 23-B.

[15] Sections 259 and 732, Title 39, United States Code. These statutes were enacted in their original form by Congress in 1872.

orders to prevent the delivery of mail containing false and misleading representations. These fraud orders also instruct the postmaster at the location of the dishonest enterprise to refuse to cash money orders drawn in favor of the names under which the enterprise is conducted. Every year fraud orders are issued against hundreds of enterprises and individuals in the United States and abroad. Many others, when served with charges of defrauding through use of the mails, voluntarily abandon their enterprises.[16]

Inadequacies of Public Protection Before 1933

Despite the presence of these varied protections, the losses of the American public have been tremendous. During the decade after the First World War, for example, some fifty billions of dollars in new securities were floated. It is estimated that fully twenty-five billions of these proved to be worthless, and many were clearly fraudulent.[17]

Rarely is the public completely protected by the mere presence of laws designed to mete out punishment to wrong-doers or to prevent evil activities. Circumstances invite individuals to violate the laws despite the consequences. Moreover, in the sale of spurious securities, the public itself has encouraged violations. Some investors have failed to report solicitations which appear to be fraudulent. Some have failed to recognize schemes to defraud due to ignorance, credulity, and greed. Some relaxed their vigilance under the false assumption that the "Blue Sky" and postal laws afforded them adequate protection.

Despite their organizational efforts to elevate the ethics of their trade, underwriters and dealers in securities have been responsible in part for great public losses. In the 1920's, for example, they over-stimulated the public appetite for securities by excessive "puffing" of their wares and by high-pressure salesmanship.

The protective "Blue Sky" laws often lacked proper administration. In many states sufficient funds were seldom available for the proper enforcement of the laws. Lack of funds produced two bad results: the employment of inefficient personnel, or the employment of sufficient and qualified personnel which lacked the money to do a thorough job. Even where states did operate efficiently to protect the public, the lack of uniformity among state laws proved to be a serious weakness.[18] In-

---

[16] *Annual Report of the Postmaster-General,* 1940, Washington, D. C., 1941, p. 68.

[17] *Federal Supervision of Traffic in Investment Securities in Interstate Commerce,* H. R. Report No. 85, 73rd Congress, 1st Session, p. 2.

[18] In recognition of this weakness the National Conference of Commissioners on Uniform State Laws in 1930 recommended the adoption of a uniform "Blue Sky"

tentional violators of statutes soon learn to operate where the legal hazards are smallest.

Perhaps the most serious weakness of the state "Blue Sky" laws has been the lack of state power over sales of securities in interstate commerce. Though state officials and the Federal postoffice department have coöperated successfully to some extent, interstate sale has caused the public severe loss. State agencies could not reach it and postoffice policing has not solved the problem.

State legislators have been partially at fault. They have failed to recognize that the problem of state control of security issuance is closely related to the problem of proper incorporation. Broad regulation to protect investors could be better accomplished by including among the requisites for incorporation some regulations which required supervised security issuance, acceptable accounting methods, and adequate reports to investors and to the supervisory agency. The propensity of states to compete for incorporation business has in part prevented action along these lines.

RECENT FEDERAL ACTION

The many wounds left by the frenzied finance of the 1920's, which culminated in the stock market crash of 1929, brought on Federal investigations.[19] Congressional committees and governmental agencies revealed the financial mutilation in all its goriness. Investigations proved conclusively that the public was not shedding crocodile tears nor exaggerating the extent of its financial losses. Consequently, despite some organized opposition, Congress enacted a series of laws designed to offer the public a greater measure of protection from the misuse of the corporate organization and its related institutions. In a span of seven years, 1933–1940, Congress passed the Federal Securities Act of 1933, the Securities and Exchange Act of 1934, the Public Utility Holding Company Act of 1935, the Chandler Act of 1938 amending the national bankruptcy laws, the Trust Indenture Act of 1939, and the Investment Company and Investment Advisers Acts of 1940. In the second of these acts it created the

---

law. The proposed law received the approval of the American Bar Association. Little real progress has been made toward the acceptance of the model law. The difficulties of getting states to adopt uniform laws seem almost insurmountable.

[19] Hearings on the Securities Act before the Committee on Interstate and Foreign Commerce, H. R., 73rd Congress, 1st Session; Hearings before the Committee on Banking and Currency, U. S. Senate, 72nd Congress, 1st Session, on Senate Resolution No. 84, "Stock Exchange Practices"; Report of the Federal Trade Commission to the Senate of the United States pursuant to Senate Resolution No. 83, 70th Congress, 1st Session, "Utility Corporations"; Reports of the Securities & Exchange Commission to Congress pursuant to Section 211 of the Securities and Exchange Act of 1934 and to Section 30 of the Public Utility Holding Company Act of 1935.

Securities and Exchange Commission, which is now largely responsible for the administration of these laws.[20]

The Securities and Exchange Commission

The Securities and Exchange Commission is a body of five men appointed by the President with the advice and consent of the Senate. To prevent complete domination by any political group the law provides that not more than three commissioners may be of the same political party. Appointed for five-year terms at salaries of $10,000 per year, the commissioners are required not to engage in any other business, vocation, or employment. To insure that the commissioners will not be influenced by their personal interests in the administration of the laws under their jurisdiction, no commissioner may directly or indirectly participate in stock market operations or transactions subject to the regulation.

In the fiscal year 1948, the S. E. C. employed 1,149 persons who were engaged for the most part on a permanent basis. The Commission spends annually about $5,600,000, of which approximately 75 per cent goes for salaries. During the course of any fiscal year, however, various fees and other revenue are collected by the Commission. These funds, under the law, are returned to the general fund of the Treasury of the United States. In 1948 the Commission turned over to the Treasury about $946,000 derived from fees for the registration of securities and from fees of registered exchanges. The net public cost of operation of this government agency is, therefore, reduced substantially.

From time to time the Commission has made changes in its organization to provide better coördination and efficiency. At present, in addition to the five commissioners, there are seven main divisions: Corporation Finance; Trading and Exchanges; Public Utilities; Administrative Services; Personnel; Budget and Finance; and Opinion Writing. In addition there are the important offices of the General Counsel; the Chief Accountant; and several advisory offices. The Corporation Finance, Trading and Exchanges, and Public Utility Divisions are concerned largely with *external* operations. The Corporation Finance Division's principal function is the application of the Securities Act of 1933 under which new securities are issued. The Trading and Exchanges Division centers its attention on stock market investigation and enforcement work under the Securities and Exchange Act of 1934. The Public Utilities Division administers and supervises matters falling under the Public

---

[20] The Securities Act was administered by the Federal Trade Commission until jurisdiction was transferred to the newly created S. E. C. in 1934. In the case of the Securities and Exchange Act the S. E. C. shares administrative responsibilities with the Board of Governors of the Federal Reserve System.

Utility Holding Company Act of 1935. *Internal* affairs and planning are handled in their respective fields by the Divisions of Administrative Services, Personnel, and Budget and Finance, as the titles of these divisions indicate. The Division of Opinion Writing, directly responsible to the Commission itself, performs a special and delicate function. It aids the Commission in the preparation of all findings, opinions, and orders promulgated by the Commission under the various laws the latter must administer. Special care is taken to keep members of the Opinion Writing Division from prior participation in proceedings and from contact with members of operating divisions actively participating in proceedings.[21] The General Counsel is the chief legal officer of the organization. And the Chief Accountant not only supplies professional advisory services to the Commissioners but also exercises general supervision over established Commission policy with respect to accounting work coming before the operating divisions of the Commission.

To facilitate further the execution of its wide-spread and increasingly important activities the Commission has divided the country into ten zones, each with a regional field office. These offices and their branches render advisory services, collect information, and enforce the law when the occasion arises.

Congress has equipped the Commission with the necessary powers to administer effectively the laws under its jurisdiction.[22] At the same time, the usual protection against the misconstruction of the laws and the misuse of powers by a public administrative body is provided. The Commission's orders are subject to review in any Circuit Court of Appeals and in the Court of Appeals of the District of Columbia, and may be affirmed, modified, or set aside by the court.

The Federal Securities Act

Chronologically the Federal Securities Act is the first of the series of laws which now fall under the administrative jurisdiction of the S. E. C.

The purpose of this Act is: (a) to provide prospective investors with a full and fair disclosure of the character of new securities to be issued by a business organization, and (b) to prevent misrepresentation and

---

[21] S. E. C., *Fourteenth Annual Report*, Washington, D. C., 1949, p. 114.

[22] The Commission has the power to make the necessary rules and regulations to carry out the provisions of the laws it administers. It is empowered to define technical and trading terms not defined in the laws and prescribe the forms upon which information required under the law shall be set forth. To facilitate investigations the Commission and any of its officers are empowered to administer oaths, subpoena witnesses, take evidence, and require the production of any books, papers, or other documents deemed by the Commission as relevant to any inquiry it makes under its investigatory powers.

fraud with respect to such securities sold through the mails or in interstate commerce.

To accomplish full and fair disclosure the law provides that, save in the case of certain securities exempt under the amended law,[23] an issuing corporation must register the proposed securities with the Commission by filing a registration statement and a prospectus.[24]

The registration statement is a detailed documentary revelation of essential facts about the registrant's financial and business affairs and the security to be offered. In the statement the registrant or issuer corporation must indicate its full business name; the state or sovereign power under which it was organized; the location of its principal office; the general character of the business transacted or to be transacted by it; its capitalization, including authorized and outstanding capital stock, together with the amounts paid up; the types and classes of securities with their various rights, preferences, and options, if any; the amount of the funded debt outstanding or to be created, with a description of the date of maturity and character of such debt, including the rate of interest, method of debt retirement or amortization provisions and the security behind the debt instruments; a detailed balance sheet and profit and loss statement for the latest fiscal year and for each of the two preceding years, or for a shorter period if the registrant has not been in business two years; and all underlying indentures or agreements to any of its securities.

The statement also must reveal pertinent facts concerning the management and principal stockholders of the corporation. Thus, it must include the names and addresses of the corporation's directors, chief executive, financial, and accounting officers, partners if it is a partnership, and

---

[23] The types of exempted issues fall into the following categories: (1) those outside the jurisdiction of the S. E. C., *i.e.*, securities sold intrastate; (2) those issued by Federal or state governments or other political subdivisions or public instrumentalities of the territorial, state, or Federal governments; (3) those the issuance of which, by existing law, is already regulated, namely, the securities of common or contract carriers, securities of state and national banks, and insurance policies and annuity contracts; (4) those under court jurisdiction, namely, certificates being exchanged with existing security-holders after court hearing and approval; (5) those issued by non-profit religious, charitable, educational, and similar institutions; (6) those of coöperative institutions such as building and loan, savings and loan, and farmer coöperative associations; (7) those of a miscellaneous nature, such as short-term obligations of less than nine months' duration, offerings made sixty days prior to or within sixty days of the enactment of the law, and such other classes as the S. E. C. is empowered to exempt by reason of the small amount involved or the lack of public character of the offering, providing such offering does not exceed $300,000.

[24] There are two broad types of registration statements: those of business organizations filed under Schedule A; those of foreign governments or their territorial subdivisions filed under Schedule B. To make registration less onerous under Schedule A, the S. E. C. has devised a series of registration forms to fit the needs of various types of industry.

promoters if it is a business in process of establishment; the amount of stock held by each director or principal officer; aggregate remuneration paid by the issuer to its directors and officers; particular remuneration for services of executive officers, directors, and others having a material relationship with principal stockholders where the compensation exceeds $25,000 per year; full particulars concerning the acquisition of properties from directors and officers; the names and addresses of all stockholders owning more than 10 per cent of any one class of stock or more than 10 per cent of the stock in the aggregate, as of a date twenty days prior to the filing of the registration statement; and full details concerning the acquisition of properties from stockholders owning more than 10 per cent of any one class of stock or 10 per cent of the aggregate total stock.

The connections between the registrant and the underwriter must be shown by providing the following data: the names and addresses of the underwriters; the amount of stock held by them; the details relating to the proceeds of the sale of the issue, the proposed offer price of the security, commissions to the underwriters, and net proceeds to the issuer; and the names and addresses of counsel who passed on the legality of the proposed issue.

The relations of the corporation to other parties important to the conduct of its business are also subject to Commission scrutiny, in that copies of material contracts must be submitted with the registration statement. Furthermore, the registrant must reveal in its statement any threatened or pending legal suits which might affect the value and salability of its securities.

At least one of the three copies of the registration statement submitted to the S. E. C. must be signed by the issuing corporation, its chief executive, financial, and accounting officer or officers and a majority of its directorate or persons performing a similar function. A registrant cannot legally dispose of its securities in interstate commerce until the registration statement becomes effective. The effective date is the twentieth day after the Commission has received the filed statement and the proper registration fee,[25] or such earlier date as the Commission may determine.[26] One purpose of the waiting period after filing is to allow the Commission's staff ample time to examine the data for omissions, inaccuracies, and incomplete disclosure. Where deficiencies appear, the Commission advises the registrant by mail, stating the nature of the deficiencies or inaccuracies in what is known as a "deficiency" letter. Every effort is made to prevent the sale of securities not properly represented. Another purpose of the waiting period is to allow data in the

---

[25] The filing fee is 1/100 of 1 per cent of the maximum aggregate price at which the securities are proposed to be offered, unless this amounts to less than $25.00, in which case the minimum fee is $25.00.

[26] By amendment, Public No. 768, 76th Congress, 1940.

registration statement to become known to the investing public before the securities are offered formally for sale.

At any time after the effective date of registration the Commission may issue an order stopping the sale of a security if it appears that an untrue statement of a material fact has been made or a material fact has been omitted.[27] The registrant must be given proper notice of the stop order, however, and must be accorded a hearing after a stop order has been issued.

The prospectus is compiled from the data in the registration statement. Broadly defined as a "circular, notice, advertisement, letter, or other written or radio communication describing the security offered for sale,"[28] the prospectus is a condensation of the registration statement. It is drawn up in such a form as to enable prospective purchasers to have adequate information about the securities they contemplate buying. The law requires that the prospectus must precede or accompany the sale or delivery of a security through the mails or in interstate commerce.[29]

It is unlawful for any person to sell new securities or transport them in interstate commerce unless the legal requirements as to registration statement and prospectus have been met. To do so subjects the violator to criminal and civil liability.[30] Furthermore, if a registration statement contains an untrue statement of a material fact or the omission of required data, private parties responsible for the registration statement are subject individually or as a group to civil suits.[31] An issuing corporation can never avoid civil liability. Other responsible parties may, however, if they take the proper precautions. They should do all that can be reasonably expected of them to investigate and confirm the validity of statements made in the registration which their corporation has filed with the Commission.[32] In the matter of civil liability the act deals

[27] In J. Edward Jones v. Securities and Exchange Commission, 298 U. S. (1936), the Supreme Court held that a registrant has the unqualified right to withdraw a registration statement before it becomes effective. Justices Cardozo, Brandeis, and Stone dissented from this decision.

[28] Under Section 2, Paragraph 10 of the Act as amended, certain exceptions are made to enable the law to operate practically. Thus, an advertisement which merely describes the security, states its price, indicates by whom orders will be executed, and designates from whom a prospectus may be obtained, is not considered a prospectus under the law.

[29] Sec. 5(b) (2).

[30] Federal Securities Act, as amended, Secs. 5 and 12.

[31] *Ibid.*, Sec. 11(a)(f). The private responsible parties are all those who signed the registration statement. Directors, partners, those who consented to be named in the registration statement as being or about to become directors, partners, or similar functionaries, underwriters, and those accountants, engineers, appraisers, or other persons who consented to the use of their names as having prepared and certified any part of the statement, or who actually prepared and certified any report or valuation made with respect to the statement, are included.

[32] See the Act, Sec. 11(b).

realistically with corporate control. If, by reason of stock ownership or otherwise, a party actually exercises control over someone who is civilly liable under the law, the controlling party likewise becomes liable.[33]

To avoid unfairness and undue litigation under the law, limitations are imposed on litigation, recovery, and damages. In any case, suits must be brought within three years after the security was offered or sold to the public. During this three-year period, suits must be brought within one year of the discovery of the untrue statement or the omission of a material fact. Recovery takes two forms. If the injured party still possesses the securities, he may, upon tender of these, recover the consideration paid for them,[34] plus interest, minus any income derived from the securities. Or, if he has sold the securities, the injured party may recover damages equivalent to the net loss involved, that is, the difference between the price he paid for them and the price he received when he re-sold the securities. Where a defendant can prove that some of the loss is not due to errors or factual inadequacies in the registration statement, but to other causes, such losses are not recoverable. Nuisance suits or defenses without merit are rendered hazardous, since the court may impose on the unsuccessful litigant the reasonable expenses of the party with the meritorious case.

The Commission may estop persons violating or about to violate the law and the Commission's rules and regulations by bringing action in the proper court to enjoin the acts or practices. Where the violation is willful, the violator, upon conviction, may be fined not more than $5,000 or imprisoned not more than five years, or both. Criminal proceedings under the Act are initiated by the Attorney-General at his discretion upon evidence transmitted to him by the S. E. C.

Accomplishments of the S. E. C.

It is difficult to measure accurately the accomplishments of the Commission in its administration of the Securities Act of 1933. Nevertheless, a general statement is presented showing the volume of the Commission's work, and particular instances of public protection are portrayed as samples of its worth to the public.

In the period from July 1933 to July 1948, over 7,500 registration statements have been filed with the S. E. C. and its predecessor, for a brief time, the Federal Trade Commission. During this period slightly more than 6,250 statements were effective. They covered the sale of about 48.8 billion dollars of securities. The annual volume of effective

---

[33] The Act, as amended, Sec. 15.
[34] In no case can more be obtained than the price at which the security was offered to the public.

registrations has varied between a low figure of 123 statements covering issues valued at slightly more than $560,000,000 and a high figure of 880 statements covering issues valued in excess of $4,850,000,000. The following table presents the details.

Table 4

REGISTRATIONS UNDER THE SECURITIES ACT OF 1933

Fiscal year, unless otherwise stated	Number of statements filed	Statements effectively registered		Total amount of securities effectively registered (000 omitted)
		Number	Per cent of total filed	
7/1/33 to 8/31/34 (F. T. C.)	1093	794	72.6	$ 1,245,469
9/1/34 to 6/30/35	440	284	64.5	913,130
1936	781	669	85.7	4,835,049
1937	967	880	91.0	4,851,463
1938	459	412	90.0	2,101,186
1939	375	344	91.7	2,579,193
1940	338	306	90.5	1,786,537
1941	337	313	92.6	2,610,684
1942	235	193	81.9	2,003,421
1943	150	123	82.0	659,480
1944	245	221	90.2	1,759,780
1945	400	340	85.0	3,224,584
1946	752	661	87.9	7,073,280
1947	567	493	86.9	6,732,447
1948	449	435	96.9	6,404,633
Totals	7,588	6,468	85.2 (average)	$48,780,336

Sources: S. E. C., *Annual Reports*, U. S. Government Printing Office, Washington, D. C.

As shown in Table 4, the S. E. C. has examined a great many more statements than those effectively registered.[35] More than eleven hundred have been withdrawn and many of these have had stop or refusal orders issued against them. The actual dollar volume of new issues examined by the Commission, therefore, exceeds by a considerable amount the 48.8 billions effectively registered. It is estimated that the Commission's personnel has scrutinized data concerning about 30 per cent of all the securities actually offered for sale in the United States during this period. A portion of the unscrutinized securities fall into the category, "exempt from registration." They are either issues of governmental

[35] Effective registration does not mean that securities are actually offered for sale; hence there is a discrepancy between the amount of securities effectively registered by the S. E. C. and the amount actually offered for sale.

In recent years many large corporations have avoided registration of their securities by private sales to large insurance companies.

bodies or of banks and common carriers. A few escaped the Commission because their sale took place through intrastate channels.

In addition to the registration statements, the Commission's staff has also examined an equivalent number of prospectuses and numerous supplementary statements and amendments. It has developed scores of criminal cases which were referred to the Department of Justice for action, and has instituted or defended a large number of civil suits under the Act.

While the foregoing data portray the volume of the Commission's work in this field, particular instances serve better to emphasize its protective service to the investing public in forcing truthful disclosure of pertinent facts. A newly organized aircraft company, for example, proposed to offer more than $2,000,000 of securities to the public. In its original prospectus, however, it did not disclose a number of facts of vital interest to prospective buyers: that a substantial bloc of securities was to go to promoters for alleged services; that prospective shareholders were denied preëmptive rights; that almost unlimited dilution of the prospective stockholders' equity might result from the issuance of warrants to underwriters and promoters; and that the underwriters were to control the majority of the board of directors. When the Commission insisted upon full and fair disclosure of this information the company revised its plans substantially. It eliminated the underwriter control and reduced the amount of warrants to be issued and the amount of stock to be utilized for promotional purposes. Publicity obviously had its values.

In another case the Commission uncovered certain hazards of enterprise which the registrant, an automobile manufacturer, preferred not to reveal to the prospective buyers of shares. The prospectus had not mentioned that the issuing corporation might have considerable difficulty in obtaining working capital, and its limited resources would make it unable to conduct an extensive advertising campaign necessary for the successful sale of any new car. The omission of such vital information obviously concealed the highly speculative nature of investment in this venture.

The Commission has also effected numerous downward revisions in the valuation of the properties of issuer corporations. A certain bottling company, for example, included among its assets franchise rights valued at $2,500,000. From other information appearing in the registration statement the Commission concluded that these rights were grossly overvalued. A hearing was conducted and stop-order proceedings were invoked to prevent the issuance of the securities. The registrant thereupon filed with the Commission an amended balance sheet in which the valuation of the franchise rights was reduced to one dollar. In another case where tangible property was involved, a manufacturing corporation arbitrarily placed a value of $700,000 on properties which had cost it $200,000. In this way it was able to create a "surplus" of $500,000. Upon Commission investigation and action the value of the properties was reduced to the original cost figure.

One striking instance of the protection afforded the public by an alert Commission relates to the recent discovery of oil in commercial quantities in the Tinsley Field in Mississippi and the expansion of oil extraction in the Centralia and Sale Fields in Illinois. The Commission's staff noted an unusual movement into these regions by promoters, security salesmen, and "confidence" men, whose operations were being carefully watched elsewhere. Some of these persons had criminal records in security fraud cases. Others had been subjected to disciplinary action of various types on previous occasions. The Commission immediately established a temporary office at Jackson, Mississippi, and a sub-regional office at St. Louis, Missouri. In short order, the more vicious types of corporate promotions were effectively throttled in the oil areas.[36] Final judgments were obtained against several corporations and individuals. And a promotional newspaper was enjoined from continued publication of purported news articles boosting the merits of various questionable oil securities. The salutary effect of the Commission's work was immediately apparent. The "con" men rapidly slunk away. Others with a somewhat higher sense of ethics sought advice from the Commission's attorneys as to methods of procedure in compliance with the statute. But for the speedy action of the Commission, the investing public would unquestionably have suffered severe financial losses from the purchase of unregistered oil securities.

As public policeman of the merchandising of securities in interstate commerce and through the mails, as these specific illustrations indicate, the Commission divides securities into two categories, fraudulent and non-fraudulent. It attempts to prevent the sale of fraudulent securities if such sales fall within its jurisdiction. And it insists that, to be legitimately offered for sale, non-fraudulent securities must be truthfully represented to prospective buyers. The Commission never acts as a public investment counsel. It never passes on the investment merits of non-fraudulent securities.

Criticisms of the Provisions and Operations of the Law

There has been considerable criticism of the provisions and operations of the law. Much of it seems to lack substance and frequently

---

[36] Where fraud is involved in the sale of securities in interstate commerce and through the mails, exemptions under the Act do not apply and the S. E. C. assumes jurisdiction.

amounts to nothing more than thoughtless carping by those who are prone to confuse qualified personal freedom with unrestrained license. Some criticisms are meritorious and deserve consideration.

The common criticisms directed against the law and its operation are as follows: (1) It exempts certain types of securities that should fall under the jurisdiction of the law; (2) the civil liability provisions of the law are unduly burdensome to parties responsible for the issuance and sale of new securities; (3) it is an obstacle to new financing; (4) it is financially too burdensome to issuer and underwriters; (5) it has forced issuers to place security issues directly through private rather than public sale; (6) it has overwhelmed the investor with complicated masses of information, hindering rather than helping to build up a class of informed investors, and (7) the law is too inflexible to allow investment bankers to meet the exigencies of rapidly changing market conditions.

Some institutional investors, such as insurance companies, feel that exemptions of certain types of securities under the law are too broad. In particular, they complain about the continued exemption of state, county, and municipal issues. In this field of finance, deliberate misrepresentations, omissions of material facts, and the presentation of half-truths are not unknown.[37] It is claimed that the framers of the Securities Act erroneously assumed that the public character of the issuers made it unnecessary to subject their issues to the scrutiny of a Federal agency. The law is subject to justifiable criticism in this instance. It is hardly "cricket" to insist that securities issues of private corporations must be scrutinized carefully, while issues of these public bodies may be misrepresented and sold in interstate commerce to an unsuspecting public.

It is also claimed that the law is unduly burdensome in its civil liability provisions. These apply to directors and other responsible parties who sign the registration statement. The claim was possibly valid when applied to the Securities Act as it was originally enacted. Subsequent modifications introduced by amendment have relieved it of much of its force. Experience has shown that cases of civil liability arising under the law have been few.[38] Furthermore, adequate defenses are available to directors who really direct and maintain acceptable standards of prudence in the execution of their duties. To the extent that the liabilities involved decrease the willingness of some men to serve as dummy direc-

---

[37] See C. J. Kuhn, "The Securities Act and the Institutional Investor," *Law and Contemporary Problems*, Vol. IV, No. 1 (January, 1937), p. 86; Shaw Livermore, *Investment Principles and Analysis* (Chicago, Business Publications, Inc., 1938), pp. 514–515.

[38] The S. E. C. reported fewer than two dozen actions under the civil liability provisions of the Securities Act over an eight-year period. See the testimony of Commissioner Ganson Purcell before the Committee on Interstate and Foreign Commerce, H. R., 77th Cong., 1st Session, *Hearings, Proposed Amendments to the Securities Act of 1933 and to the Securities Exchange Act of 1934*, Part I, p. 52.

tors in return for the hollow prestige obtained from the loan of their names, the present civil liability features of the law are a public benefit.

While the presence and operation of the Act may have deterred some new capital financing, it is doubtful whether it has been a very serious deterrent. According to one authority, it is almost unanimously the opinion of those responsible for the investments of our large institutions that other economic factors are responsible.[39] Suggested proof of the soundness of this position is the absence of capital financing in the same period by railroads whose securities are exempt from regulation under this Act. It is also noteworthy that the alleged burdens imposed by the Act have not deterred corporations from refinancing where financial economies are apparent. It follows, therefore, that new capital investment will also not be deterred by the burdens of the Act when the proper economic conditions for new investment are established. This observation appears to be well supported by the very large volume of corporate financing reported since 1945. A substantial share of the total volume was registered with the S. E. C.

Do the requirements of the law impose too great a cost on issuers and underwriters, as some critics claim? It cannot be denied that the issuing corporation does bear substantial new expenses in connection with security registration. A registration statement and a prospectus must be prepared and printed, and a filing fee must be paid to the Federal Government. And there is, perhaps, some additional outlay for the services of legal counsel, accountants, and other experts. The corporation must exercise greater care in the preparation of pertinent financial and business data concerning itself and its securities. The additional cost, however, has not proved to be unduly large when considered in relation to the face value of the securities issued.[40] Moreover, as experience is gained in meeting the demands of the law this expense should decline. And as the corporation learns to prepare its data more carefully, the underwriter has a less costly and less burdensome task in analyzing new security issues. This doubtless has contributed in some measure to the

[39] Kuhn, op. cit., pp. 82–83.
[40] Paul P. Gourrich, formerly head economist of the investment banking house of Kuhn, Loeb & Company, and sometime Director of the Research Division of the S. E. C., estimated that the net increase in expenses, at least for bond issues, has not been more than one-third of 1 per cent of face value. See P. P. Gourrich, "Investment Banking Methods Prior to and Since the Act," Law and Contemporary Problems, Vol. IV, No. 1 (January, 1937), pp. 68–69. Also, see S. E. C., Fourteenth Annual Report, p. 6, which indicates that the cost of flotation of registered securities for primary cash distribution was 6.1% of the aggregate dollar volume of such securities. Commissions and discounts absorbed 5.6%, and the remaining 0.5% covered all other expenses incidental to the flotation of securities, including all costs relative to registration. (Italics are the authors'.) The registration costs represent but a small proportion of "all other expenses."

decreased spread between the selling price of securities to the public and the price paid by the underwriter to the issuing corporation. Spread is based not only on the underwriter's estimate of the present market risks, but also on the known costs of investigation, analysis, and merchandising of securities. Furthermore, prior to the securities legislation, the costs of the issuer and underwriter were lower, perhaps, than they should have been, because they neglected to compile adequate information or failed to disseminate properly the full factual data which they possessed.

In recent years there has been a tendency for large, well-known corporations to sell their new securities directly to large institutional investors, such as insurance companies. This issuer-to-customer merchandising method has hurt the investment bankers who formerly were paid to act as intermediaries. Since such private sales avoid the necessities and liabilities of registration with the S. E. C., the Securities Act has been blamed for the new trend. Undoubtedly the irksomeness, expense, and liabilities attached to registration with the Commission have contributed to the growth of private sales. But the economies of the direct method of placement and the encouragement of the method by the institutional investors must not be overlooked when the situation is being appraised. Entire blame should not be placed on the regulation.

The two most serious arguments that can be marshaled against direct placement of securities without benefit of registration are: (1) that insurance companies buy large issues in private transactions and shortly thereafter resell these non-registered securities; (2) that the large institutional investors, particularly when the volume of new issues is small, purchase the cream of new security offerings, thereby depriving individual investors, eleemosynary institutions, administrators of trust funds, and smaller savings institutions of participation in the higher-class offerings. Both of these arguments carry real weight. The first practice seriously weakens security legislation, since, in effect, the insurance companies are assuming the functions of distribution. The other concerns itself with a result unanticipated in the Securities Act, namely, the dilution of the quality of investments of certain types of investment groups. However, if the insurance companies *do* redistribute new issues directly acquired from the issuers, there is a possibility that small investor groups may acquire these securities from the insurance companies. To the extent that this is so the second argument loses some of its force.

Direct placement should not be prohibited *merely* to protect the vested interests of investment bankers, since such action would be an interference with a more economical means of fund-raising. But if direct placement is likely to weaken seriously the Securities Act or establish *undue* purchasing advantages for the large institutional investors, then private placements should be subject to regulations similar to those imposed on publicly placed offerings.[41]

Beginning in July 1940, the S. E. C. and the investment banking industry through its representative organizations, the Investment Bankers' Association of America, the National Association of Securities Dealers, the New York Stock Exchange, and the New York Curb Exchange, met to consider and formulate proposals for the amendment of the Securities Act and the Securities Exchange Act. In 1941–1942, these proposals were submitted to the appropriate Congressional Committee and hearings were held.[42] In large measure the testimony relating to the Securities Act centered around the following: (1) simplification of registration procedure; (2) the method of offering and selling securities and the dissemination of information prior to and after the effective date of a registration statement; (3) direct sales to institutional investors such as insurance companies; (4) exemption of small issues; and (5) the problem of civil liabilities under the Act.

Out of these deliberations have come some changes. Proceeding cautiously, the S. E. C. has reduced the complications of procedures and forms. In attempting to reduce procedural burdens and costs to issuers and underwriters, however, the Commission has been alert to its primary function under the Securities Act, namely, that it must see that investors are provided with full and truthful disclosure of the relevant, material facts.

In response to the investment bankers' allegations that the law needs to be more flexible so as to allow them legally to meet rapidly changing market conditions, the Commission has permitted the use of the "red herring" prospectus.[43] The use of this type of prospectus, prior to effective registration, permits the dissemination of much information concerning a new issue. The "red herring" prospectus does not contain the finally determined selling price, information about underwriting agreements, and such other data not normally available before the time when the securities are actually offered for sale. The S. E. C. permission to use a preëffective prospectus is admission of the fact that one of the pur-

---

[41] Cf. W. E. Atkins, G. L. Edwards, and H. G. Moulton, *The Regulation of the Security Markets*, (Washington, D. C., The Brookings Institution, 1946) p. 113.

[42] *Proposed Amendments to the Securities Act of 1933 and to the Securities Exchange Act of 1934.* Hearings before the Committee on Interstate and Foreign Commerce, H. R., 77th Cong., 1st and 2nd Sess., Washington, D. C., U. S. Government Printing Office, 1942. These proposals were submitted also to the Senate Committee on Banking and Currency.

[43] The title "red herring" is derived from the practice of printing in red letters diagonally across every page of the prospectus, or along the margins, a very clear legend indicating that the prospectus is not intended as an *offer to sell* the security and calling attention to the Act's prohibitions against any *offers* prior to the date of effective registration. The Commission's General Counsel ruled that the use of such a prospectus was not illegal provided it was for information purposes only.

poses of the waiting period—making available to the general investing public at the offices of the Commission filed information about new issues in advance of offers to sell—had not been realized. The investors prefer to have information made more easily available. Though the "red herring" or preëffective prospectus has been used, the Commission reports that its use has declined in recent years.[44] Nevertheless, the S. E. C. has continued to reformulate its rules in regard to this instrument so as to meet the objections of issuers and underwriters.[45]

Amendment to the Securities Act in 1940[46] has allowed the S. E. C. to adopt the principle of acceleration in regard to effective registration. The registration statement may become effective sooner than twenty days after filing if the S. E. C. approves. This arrangement encourages issuer and underwriter to do a meticulous job in presenting its material and aids underwriters to meet rapidly changing conditions more effectively.

In May 1945 the Congress amended the Securities Act, Section 3 (b),[47] so that issues under $300,000 in total amount might be exempt from registration. The securities industry strove to raise the exemption of small issues to the $500,000 level, whereas the Commission insisted that it not be raised above $300,000. Impressed with the evidence that a very large percentage of securities fraud cases were to be found in the small issues of less than $500,000, the Congress accepted the Commision's viewpoint.[48]

No action has yet been taken by the Congress in regard to direct sale of securities to institutional investors or in regard to the civil liability provisions of the Securities Act.

It has been claimed frequently that the great mass of information that must be spread before the investor through the medium of the prospectus confuses rather than enlightens him and, if this is so, the whole purpose of the Act fails. Possibly the Commission requires too much, but there will never be complete agreement between the regulators and the regulated as to what constitutes adequate information. Many points of disagreement are genuine and are resolved by the development of administrative experience. Since regulation evolves out of neglect of the public interests, a regulatory body such as the S. E. C. must keep constantly to the forefront the factor of public interest. On the Commission rests the responsibility of defining "pertinent information" and obtaining it in the registration statement and the prospectus; hence the S. E. C.

[44] S. E. C., *Thirteenth Annual Report*, Washington, D. C., 1948, p. 24.
[45] S. E. C., *Fourteenth Annual Report*, Washington, D. C., 1949, pp. 18–19.
[46] Public Law No. 768, Title III, 76th Congress.
[47] Public Law No. 55, 78th Congress.
[48] *Proposed Amendments to the Securities Act of 1933 and to the Securities Exchange Act of 1934*, H. R. Hearings, Part II, pp. 660–671.

must be exacting in its demands on the issuing corporation. The job of interpretation is then up to the investor. If he is unable to interpret what he reads, then he should seek advice from competent counsel. While some investors are confused by extensive information, it is an error to say that investors as a group are no better off or are even worse off than they were prior to the regulatory legislation. We might as well argue that the accumulated knowledge of the present day is so confusing that we had better return to gutturals and cave-ways and abandon our present civilization.

9

Public Protection for Corporate Investors
(Continued)

The interests of the great mass of investors are not involved in the sale of new securities, but in the market for securities which have already been issued and sold.

Prior to 1934, the voluntary associations of dealers and brokers, constituting the organized security exchanges, dealt privately with the problem of regulating the market for old securities. They established rules about the release of information to corporate investors. They set up trading rules and regulations and policed the markets. The smaller, unorganized, over-the-counter markets functioned as well as they could within the wide limits of individual ethical standards and the controls of fraud statutes and private legal action. But, at best, self-regulation is biased, and at times it is almost certain to lose sight of the important public functions of the stock market. And fraud laws and private action have proved inadequate. Furthermore, such things as the control of credit used in financing market transactions and protection of the markets from the heavy impact of economic and political disturbances on a large scale exceed the capabilities of private regulation. Misuse of corporate position by individuals and internal corporate abuses were left largely to the restraints of conscience and the probabilities of private legal action. And corporate reorganizations proceeded under a national bankruptcy law outmoded by the growth of corporate enterprise and organization.

The stock market debacle of 1929 furnished the push which initiated Congressional action. An investigation of the securities market was made. The irregularities which were revealed convinced Congress that there was a real need to require full disclosure of legal, financial, and economic facts concerning securities already issued. It also revealed that a poorly informed or misinformed investing public was not only being victimized unfairly by market manipulators, but was being led easily into speculative excesses. The results were bad in any case. Ethical standards were lowered. Distortion of security prices, whether by speculative excesses or by deliberate manipulation, destroyed the value of the market as a guide to investment of new savings and as a measure of the value of bank loan collateral. Moreover, speculative excesses used great quantities of bank credit. A wide-spread belief arose that too much credit had been siphoned into the securities markets, to the detriment of the economic system as a whole. This and other investigations revealed that corporate structures were over-complicated; that corporate officials used their positions of trust for private gain and took advantage of stockholder dispersion and disinterest to misuse the proxy machinery; and that the legal machinery to effect corporate reorganizations quickly and fairly was inadequate for the present needs. Consequently Congress was compelled to pass legislation which would prevent a recurrence of these conditions on any large scale. The Securities Exchange Act of 1934 was one in a series of laws to be enacted.

THE SECURITIES EXCHANGE ACT OF 1934

The purposes of the Act are several. It is designed: (1) To prevent unfair practices on the securities exchanges and markets and to control other practices which might be injurious to the markets; (2) to discourage and control the use of credit to finance speculation in securities; (3) to compel corporations to furnish adequate information about their securities sold in these markets; (4) to prevent corporate officials and insiders from using their advantageous positions unfairly for their own profit, and (5) to establish regulatory machinery to prevent market debacles in event of economic and political emergency.

To attain its objectives, the law created the Securities and Exchange Commission and made it responsible for the administration of the Act, except for the rules and regulations related to the use of credit in the security markets. The Board of Governors of the Federal Reserve System is charged with the latter responsibility.

The law requires that the following be registered with the S. E. C.: (1) Organized exchanges, unless specifically exempted from registration by the Commission; (2) securities listed on the registered exchanges, and (3) brokers and dealers who operate in interstate commerce or through the mails on other than organized exchanges, that is, the over-the-counter operators. Associations of brokers and dealers may also register under the law, although such group registration does not eliminate the necessity of registration by individual brokers or dealers.[1]

---

[1] Public, No. 719 (1938), known as the Maloney Act, amending the Securities Exchange Act. The National Association of Securities Dealers, Inc. (N. A. S. D.) is the only association at present registered with the Commission.

Registration of an exchange is initiated by filing a registration statement with the Commission. The statement must contain fundamental data about the registrant. Some of the more important required data are copies of the articles of incorporation or the constitution, by-laws or rules of procedure, and membership. The registering organization must agree in its statement to supply the S. E. C. with copies of future amendments to its constitution and by-laws. It must agree also to comply, and compel its members to comply, with the rules and regulations developed under the law. The rules of each exchange must, therefore, provide for disciplinary action against members who violate the law.

If a registration statement is being filed by a dealer or broker, it must reveal the name of the registrant, form of business organization, whether he is broker or dealer or both, his manner of doing business with his customers, *i.e*, on margin, as investment counselor, or otherwise, membership on the exchanges, any past misdemeanors connected with the sale or purchase of securities, and other similar important information.[2]

Registration of listed securities requires the issuer to provide the exchange with data similar to those provided the S. E. C. by issuers of new securities under the Federal Securities Act. The exchange then certifies these securities to the Commission.

Ordinarily the registration becomes effective thirty days after the Commission receives either the properly executed application, if the applicant is an exchange or a dealer or broker, or the certification of a registered exchange, if listed securities are being registered. The S. E. C. may shorten this period of waiting if the circumstances seem to warrant such action, or it may prolong it by temporary deferment of action.

Specific practices such as wash sales[3] and matched orders,[4] which create on the exchanges and markets the false appearance of active trading, or by their falsity lead to active trading, are prohibited. Violators are subject to civil and criminal liability. Certain other practices deemed dangerous to the public interest, such as short-selling[5] and price-pegging, are not actually outlawed, but are subject to Commission rules and regulations.

---

[2] Under the law the S. E. C. has the power to segregate and limit the functions of members, dealers, and brokers.

[3] Wash sales are fictitious transactions in which no change in ownership is contemplated or takes place. The parties involved intend to create an artificial price on the stock-tickers to lure the unsuspecting into the market.

[4] In matched orders the trader gives one broker an order to buy and another an order to sell a like amount of a stock, in a manner to raise or depress the market price artificially.

[5] A short sale takes place when one sells stock one does not own but expects to acquire later. Meanwhile one borrows the stock to make delivery. Later the stock is acquired and returned to the lender. The value of the practice of short-selling has been severely questioned.

The curtailment and control of credit resources which might enter speculative channels is accomplished in two ways. Controls are established over margins, that is, the amounts that brokers require their customers to pay down when making speculative purchases of securities, or, to express it differently, the amounts that brokers lend their customers to facilitate stock purchases.[6] And control is established over the amount of borrowing which exchange members, dealers, and brokers may obtain from banks or other sources to carry on their security business. These controls are implemented by confining the sources of stock market credit to member banks of the Federal Reserve System, to non-member banks which agree to abide by the Federal Reserve rules and regulations regarding such credit, or to emergency lenders authorized by the Federal Reserve Board of Governors. The S. E. C. is responsible for the enforcement of the Reserve Board's rules and regulations, violations of which are unlawful.

The law provides several requirements to prevent corporate insiders from utilizing for their own profit information about the affairs of their corporation which, by virtue of their positions, they receive in advance of the ordinary stockholders. Corporate insiders are classified as directors, principal officers, and those who own 10 per cent or more of any one class of registered equity securities (stocks) of a corporation. These insiders are obliged to record their holdings of stock monthly with the Commission. Profits realized from the sale of a corporation's listed securities by a corporate insider are recoverable by the corporation if the insider has not held these securities six months or more.[7] Legal action for recovery must be taken, however, within two years from the occurrence of the profit-taking transaction. Furthermore, corporate insiders are prohibited from making short sales and similar transactions.

The law also deals realistically with the problems related to the perpetuation of control by corporate insiders through the misuse of the proxy machinery. In the case of listed corporations, proxy solicitations are regulated and supervised so as to assure solicited security-holders of adequate information. Proxy material must contain a clear statement of all the important actions to be taken at the corporate meetings; the source of the solicitations, and the interest of the solicitor in the proposed corporate actions. The material must be free of deception.

As a precaution against market disturbances of exceptional propor-

---

[6] Under Regulation T of the Securities Exchange Act the maximum loan by a dealer or broker to a customer is 60 per cent of the current market value of the securities. During the height of speculative activities in the 1920's such loans often ran as high as 90 per cent of the current market value of the securities purchased. The Board of Governors has the power to change the requirements to fit the current situation.

[7] There are certain exemptions under the law. Moreover, stockholders may act to recover the profits for the corporation in event the corporation itself fails to act.

tions or of unusual nature, the Commission is given the power to suspend all trading on any national securities exchange for a period not exceeding ninety days, if the President of the United States approves. It may also suspend trading on any national securities exchange for a period not in excess of ten days.

To put teeth into the Act, violators are subjected to liabilities and penalties. Stock exchanges may have their registrations withdrawn entirely for violations of the Act and its rules and regulations, or for failure to make its members and listed issuers comply. For lesser infractions, registrations may be suspended, though not for more than a twelve-month period. Willful violation by an exchange may subject it to a fine not exceeding $500,000. Members or officers of an exchange are subject either to suspension for a period not exceeding a year, or to expulsion from the exchange, depending on the gravity of their violations. An exchange member, for example, may be suspended for undertaking a transaction for a customer known to be violating the law. He may be expelled from the exchange entirely for undertaking prohibited transactions. And security issues may have their registrations withdrawn entirely, or temporarily suspended, if the issuer corporation fails to conform to the law and the Commission's rules.

Persons who willfully violate the law and the Commission's rules and regulations are criminally liable. Upon conviction, they may be fined as much as $10,000, imprisoned not more than two years, or both. No person, however, is subject to imprisonment if he can prove he had no knowledge of the Commission's rules and regulations. Persons responsible for incomplete, misleading, or false statements filed with the Commission are subject to civil liability.[8] Injured investors, who unwittingly rely on the filed data, may recover actual damages by suit in the proper court.

Other provisions designed to facilitate administration of the law deal with tactics designed either to embarrass the Commission or to trade on the prestige of the S. E. C. or the Federal Reserve Board. The Act declares it unlawful for a corporation's officers, directors, or shareholders to delay or obstruct without just cause the preparation or filing of data required under the law. Furthermore, if an issuer fails to file required data, the Commission may impose and collect a fine of $100 per day for each day's delay, or it may seek to impose the criminal penalties for willful violation.[9] It is also unlawful for anyone to represent to prospective purchasers or sellers of securities that the S. E. C. or the Federal

---

[8] Responsible persons include those who may and do control the actual violator and cause him to interfere directly or indirectly with the operation of the law and its rules and regulations. Such controlling parties are not liable, however, if they can prove that they acted in good faith.

[9] Criminal prosecution is a function of the Attorney-General.

Reserve authority has passed on the merits of, or given approval to, any security or any security transaction.

The Work and Accomplishments of the S. E. C. under the Act

The registration process which the Commission supervises under the Act is a large and continuing task. During the fiscal year 1948, there were registered nineteen national securities exchanges. Five exchanges were granted exemption. Registration requires careful examination of the organization of the exchanges and their rules and regulations. The Commission has handled slightly more than 19,000 effective registrations of brokers and dealers from May 6, 1935, to June 30, 1948.[10] Each year many registrations are withdrawn, cancelled, denied, suspended, or revoked. At the close of the 1948 fiscal year, there were in effect 4,006 registrations.[11] The only registered national securities dealers' association is the National Association of Securities Dealers, Inc. (N. A. S. D.). The N. A. S. D. has a membership of 2,677 dealers and/or brokerage firms whose partners, officers, traders, and salesmen number more than 26,200 individuals. Since the passage of the Act in 1934, thousands of issuers have filed with the Commission thousands of current and annual reports as a part of the requirements of registration of securities on the exchanges. The Commission's annual burden of examination is, therefore, very large. It is the Commission's practice to examine current reports monthly; the work of scrutinizing annual reports is spread over the year.[12]

The Commission also has directly scrutinized data about a great many securities which are admitted to *unlisted* trading privileges on the national exchanges. There are various reasons for trading on an unlisted basis. The security may not yet have wide enough distribution to meet the listing requirements. The corporate management may prefer not to subject the security to the speculative forces of the market. Whatever the reason, there were 491 such stocks and 20 such bonds admitted to unlisted trading on the organized exchanges as of June 30, 1948.[13] Since unlisted securities, usually sponsored by some group of traders and investors, are not under direct jurisdiction of the exchanges, the Commission has assumed the responsibility for their admission to exchange trading privileges.[14]

---

[10] Data compiled from S. E. C., *Annual Reports*, 1–14.

[11] S. E. C., *Fourteenth Annual Report*, Washington, D. C., 1949, p. 43.

[12] The law requires registrants to file their annual reports with the Commission within 120 days of the close of their fiscal year. Since fiscal and calendar years coincide in 78 per cent of the cases, the bulk of the annual reports are filed in April.

[13] S. E. C., *Fourteenth Annual Report*, Table 16, p. 162.

[14] In the case of *listed* securities, the issuer corporation is required to submit detailed financial and business data to the Listing Committee of the registered ex-

Market surveillance constitutes another major section of the Commission's work. In enforcing the provisions of the Act outlawing the manipulation of security prices, the Commission has pursued an administrative policy based on the principle of prevention rather than punishment.[15] Consequently, the Commission systematically observes the market behavior of all securities on all the national exchanges. Stock-tickers are maintained in the Washington and New York offices. Prompt action is taken when market deviations in the price and volume of sales of any stock suggest that the law is being violated. In addition to its own constant check on the market, the Commission receives complaints and reports of suspicious market activities from the public and from the trade.

If the Commission cannot satisfy itself immediately about market movements, it investigates more closely. Through the medium of the "flying quiz," it assembles essential information to complete the market picture. The "quiz" consists of interviews with persons who can throw light on the unusual market behavior. If the Commission's suspicion is sustained, a preliminary trading investigation takes place and a thorough analysis of all transactions is made. Where the results of the preliminary investigation warrant further action, formal proceedings follow.

During the fiscal year 1948, the Commission disposed of 100 "flying quizzes" and had 138 pending at the end of the year. During 1948 it also disposed of 9 formal investigations; initiated 2 new ones; and carried over 34 into the 1949 fiscal year. Where criminal violations are involved, the S. E. C. submits them to the Attorney-General for prosecution. Sixteen such cases were referred to the Department of Justice in the 1948 fiscal year. In certain cases where the S. E. C. uncovers violations of the exchanges' rules and regulations, it refers the cases to the exchanges for corrective and disciplinary action. The remaining cases are handled by the Commission itself.

The value of the S. E. C.'s vigilance over unlawful market manipulation is vividly illustrated by the Commission's expulsion of one market operator and temporary suspension of his two associates. In this case the three operators were members of five different exchanges. The principal operator had bought and sold large blocks of airplane stock on two West Coast exchanges shortly after his two associates had purchased an option on 160,000 shares. The option was exercised in blocks of 20,000 shares within a specified price range. Carrying on his trading in the names of

change. The corporation must also agree to meet other important listing requirements. In this fashion it falls directly under the jurisdiction of the exchanges on which its securities are listed. Since 1910 the New York Stock Exchange has required all securities sold thereon to be listed. For a description of the listing process, requirements, and advantages, see Charles A. Dice and Wilford J. Eiteman, *The Stock Market* (New York and London, McGraw-Hill Book Company, Inc., 1941), Chap. 7.

[15] S. E. C., *Sixth Annual Report*, p. 91.

two impecunious friends, the principal operator sought to stimulate market activity and raise the price of the shares. When the market price rose high enough the option was exercised. The securities obtained under the option were then sold in the artificially stimulated market at a considerable margin of profit per share to the chief manipulator and his associates. The order of expulsion was contested in the courts, but the Circuit Court of Appeals upheld the Commission.[16]

Since 1935, the S. E. C. has proceeded in many cases against issuers of registered securities for failure to comply with rules and regulations under the Act. In the majority of cases registrations were withdrawn, while others were dismissed.

In January, 1940, as a part of its work of market surveillance and control, the Commission adopted rules and regulations relating to security price stabilization and pegging. In certain instances such price controls are necessary and desirable, for example, price-pegging of new security issues pending the complete placement of the securities by the investment underwriters. Were this not done at times, the market prices of the securities already sold might be artificially depressed, and the ability of the underwriters to sell the remaining shares would be impaired. On the other hand, pegging might have bad results for investors. The problem of control is, therefore, a delicate one. The Commission must reconcile investor protection with protection of the investment bankers who underwrite the sale of new issues. Its failure to perform these functions properly will impede the ready flow of capital into industry.[17] During the 1948 fiscal year, 449 registration statements were filed and 199 contained statements of intent to stabilize, if necessary, to facilitate the distribution of offerings. Stabilization was undertaken actually in 71 of these offerings. The S. E. C. in such circumstances was obliged to study carefully all the reports on stabilization so as to determine the lawfulness of the stabilizing activities.[18] The Commission's staff also does much preliminary work in an advisory capacity in connection with stabilization matters.

Of special significance to the process of market supervision was the outbreak of hostilities abroad. The Commission is authorized—if in its opinion the public interest so requires, and if the President approves—to suspend all trading on any national securities exchange for a period not in excess of ninety days. In April, 1938, the Commission established machinery to supply itself with advance market information. When war

---

[16] Wright v. S. E. C., 112 Fed. (2nd), 86–96 (1940). In this case the court also held that the S. E. C. order of expulsion was not a punishment for past offenses but a means of protecting investors.

[17] S. E. C., Sixth Annual Report, p. 99.

[18] Ibid., p. 98. S. E. C., Fourteenth Annual Report, p. 35. Note that these activities of the Commission develop out of the issuance of new securities but involve a practice relating to the resale of securities.

actually broke out in Europe the Commission used and extended its facilities. Studies were made to determine the amount of American securities held by the nationals of each European country, so as to measure the effect of security liquidation on our markets. The United States Treasury, the New York Stock Exchange, and certain firms specializing in foreign dealings coöperated with the S. E. C. to judge the volume and trend of transactions. In May, 1940, when a critical market situation appeared due to the Nazi invasion of the Netherlands and Belgium, the security markets declined considerably. At no time, however, did the market mechanism function in a disorderly fashion. Transactions were always possible, because breaks in the market were kept in most instances to less than a point between transactions.[19] The detailed knowledge which the Commission possessed enabled it to avoid any hasty closing of the security exchanges, yet it stood ready to take drastic measures if the situation warranted it.

As early as 1937 the S. E. C. instituted a program to inspect the activities of over-the-counter brokers and dealers. Inspection has been undertaken annually since that time. In these numerous small private markets the dealer-broker and customer relationship is especially susceptible to abuse. Market inspection by the Commission has had two main objectives: (1) to develop among brokers and dealers a more complete understanding of their obligations under the law, and (2) to check on dealer-broker compliance with the law and the Commission's rules and regulations. Annually the Commission deals with a large number of more or less serious violations of the law. For example, during the 1948 fiscal year, a total of 841 broker-dealer inspection reports were received by the Commission from its regional offices. In 24 inspections, unsatisfactory financial conditions were found which required immediate corrective action or continued surveillance. In 217 inspections, the reports disclosed transactions at prices so different from the prevailing market prices that suspicion was aroused concerning the fair treatment of the customers of the brokerage firms. In 177 inspections, the reports contained data indicating non-compliance with rules and regulations relating to brokers' extension of credit to customers on margin transactions. And in a small number of cases, questions were raised on such matters as improper hypothecation of customers' securities and price misrepresentation. Not infrequently the S. E. C. has found it necessary to deny, revoke, or suspend broker-dealer registrations. Without public supervision the principal-and-agent relation between customer and broker can be exceedingly dangerous for the principal unless he is very experienced and alert. This is illustrated by the actions of the Commonwealth Stock and Bond Company. This company induced some of its elderly customers,

---

[19] See S. E. C., *Sixth Annual Report*, pp. 90–91.

whose savings were invested in certain securities, to execute orders giving the Commonwealth permission to dispose of these securities and replace them with others. Actually the brokerage firm merely substituted securities of lower value and retained for itself, as a secret profit, the difference between the old and the new investments.[20] The S. E. C. uncovered the fraud and revoked the firm's registration. In another instance, the S. E. C. revoked a dealer's registration for a similar violation of customer faith.[21] The dealer, who was also a broker, persuaded his customer to part with certain securities in order to obtain others yielding a better rate of return. Acting as agent, the broker sold his customer's securities and took the proceeds to buy certain bonds for his own account. After a few days, as dealer, he sold these bonds to his customer at a very considerable advance in price. He knew that his customer was ignorant of the true market price of the bonds and unaware of the price mark-up taken by the dealer. These vicious and fraudulent practices occurred not once but several times with customers of this broker-dealer. Obviously, if such violations of trust occur when a Federal agency is present to act in the public interest, there is little doubt that similar and worse violations took place with greater frequency in the absence of public supervision.

In its supervision of brokers and dealers the S. E. C. is given considerable assistance by the self-regulatory efforts of both the organized exchanges and the National Association of Securities Dealers, Inc., (N. A. S. D.). In 1940, for example, the New York Stock Exchange reported several instances of disciplinary action against member firms which had violated margin regulations. And in 1946 five exchanges reported disciplinary action against 39 members. The N. A. S. D. reported to the Commission, in the 1948 fiscal year, the disposition of ten disciplinary cases, in seven of which members were found to have violated the Association's rules of fair practice. Various penalties were imposed consisting of censure, fine and censure, temporary suspension, and revocation of registration, in accordance with the degree of violation.[22] Under the Securities Act (Section 15A (g)) the S. E. C. acts as a board of review if the party charged with the violation applies for relief from the disciplinary action of the Association. Also, where the S. E. C. believes the Association's fair practice rules are being violated, it refers such cases to the Association for action. Thus, under the law, the principle of self-regulation is practiced and coöperation between the S. E. C. and the N. A. S. D. is encouraged. At the same time the S. E. C. is available to

---

[20] S. E. C., *Sixth Annual Report*, p. 111.
[21] In the matter of Duker & Duker, S. E. C., *Decisions and Reports*, Vol. VI, pp. 386–390.
[22] S. E. C., *Fourteenth Annual Report*, p. 47.

supervise N. A. S. D. activities and to protect violators of fair practice rules from arbitrary and unduly severe penalties.[23]

Another phase of market supervision undertaken by the S. E. C. has to do with margin inspections of brokerage firms which, for the most part, are not members of the national securities exchanges. Margin regulations, it will be recalled, are promulgated by the Board of Governors of the Federal Reserve System, but the administration of the rules is vested in the Commission. While the S. E. C. delegates to the exchanges the supervision of their own members, the S. E. C. nevertheless has had much work to do in this field. Some notion of the volume of such work is revealed by the figures which show that during the ten-year period through June 30, 1944, the Commission conducted inspections of the books and records of over 4,000 firms.[24]

In reviewing the work and accomplishments of the Commission under this Act, we should not overlook the influence the Commission has exercised over the reorganization of the nation's two leading stock exchanges, the New York Stock Exchange and the New York Curb Exchange. The insolvency of the firm of Richard Whitney & Company and its suspension from membership in the New York Stock Exchange led the Commission to investigate Whitney's firm in public hearings in the spring of 1938. Revelations of the circumstances of the Whitney failure —personal speculations which involved such widely diverse ventures as the manufacture and sale of applejack, peat humus, and mineral colloids and the misappropriation of customers' securities by Richard Whitney himself—led the Commission and the New York Stock Exchange jointly to reappraise the whole problem of protection of customers' funds and securities.[25] Because Whitney was a brother of a partner in the firm of J. P. Morgan and Company and was a powerful figure[26] on the New York Stock Exchange, this unfortunate case served to strengthen materially the Commission's position in regard to the program of reorganization, reform, and self-regulation which the New York Stock Exchange was

---

[23] *Ibid.*, pp. 48–49.

[24] S. E. C., *Tenth Annual Report*, p. 41.

[25] Richard Whitney & Company had been insolvent for at least three and a half years prior to its collapse. Whitney himself had started his misappropriations as far back as 1926. See S. E. C., *Report on Investigation in the Matter of Richard Whitney et al.*, Washington, D. C., 1938, Vol. I, pp. 1, 13–15, 142–146. Certain losers in the Whitney affair sought to make the New York Stock Exchange financially responsible on the grounds that the Exchange failed to act promptly in this case. The court would not uphold these claims. See Baird *v.* Franklin, 141 Fed. (2nd), 238 (1944).

[26] Since 1912, Richard Whitney had been a member of the New York Stock Exchange. From 1919 until his expulsion in 1938, he was continuously a member of the Exchange's Governing Committee. He served as Vice-President of the Exchange from 1927–1929 and as President from 1930–1935. At one time, 1928–1929, he held the post of Chairman of the Business Conduct Committee.

reluctantly undertaking.[27] The S. E. C. insisted that, in its revised constitution, the Exchange provide for public representation on its governing
board.[28] It was no longer to be considered a private club by its members,
but a public market with important public responsibilities. The Commission also insisted that, under the Exchange's amended constitution, all
general partners of a stock exchange member firm, and not simply those
partners holding seats on the Exchange, become subject to disciplinary
action.

The S. E. C. also considered inadequate the reorganization proposed
by the New York Curb Exchange when it did not provide for representatives of the public on its governing board. Eventually, however, a
satisfactory plan was proposed. The Curb's governing board now includes three non-member governors representing the public.

No examination of the Commission's work would be complete without giving attention to its control of proxy machinery. It will be recalled
that the proxy mechanism has become an important part of the operation of the modern corporation. It has also been subject to considerable
abuse. Pursuant to Section 14 of the Act—and to the appropriate section
of the Public Utility Holding Company Act and the Investment Company
Act of 1940—the Commission has adopted rules and regulations governing the operation of the proxy machinery of all corporations whose
securities are listed on the organized exchanges.[29] Furthermore, stock
exchange members, dealers, and brokers cannot legally give out proxies
on customers' securities in contravention of the rules and regulations of
the S. E. C.

It is fundamental, the Commission maintains, that corporate management and others who solicit proxies, consents, or authorizations from
security-holders should furnish prescribed information in the proxy
statement with respect to all the vital corporate matters upon which
action is to be taken. And this information must be presented in such
a way as to allow the stockholder to vote, or to instruct his proxy to

---

[27] For an interesting account of the battle between the Exchange and the S. E. C.,
see Fred Rodell, "S. E. C. v. Stock Exchange," *Fortune*, Vol. XVII, No. 2 (February, 1938), pp. 64 ff.

[28] The governing board now contains three public representatives. The first three
elected were Carle C. Conway, Robert E. Wood, and Robert M. Hutchins, high
officials in their respective organizations.

[29] Unfortunately the same protections are not available to investors in unregistered
corporations. In June 1946, the Commission forwarded to the Congress a proposed
amendment whereby the Commission would extend to investors in the larger unregistered corporations the same benefits as to financial information, informative
proxy-solicitation materials, and protection against trading by corporate insiders as are
now enjoyed by investors in the securities of registered corporations. The S. E. C.
supported its amendment by a lengthy report containing case histories and other
illustrative materials which revealed that abuses in unregulated securities are in
some respects as great as anything the Securities Exchange Act was designed to
abolish. See S. E. C., *Twelfth Annual Report*, pp. 129–130.

vote, intelligently on each separate matter. At the present time the Commission requires that the material to be used in proxy solicitation be filed with the Commission ten days prior to solicitation. This procedure allows the Commission time to examine the material and detect deficiencies. Accordingly, the embarrassment of sending out supplementary information to correct deficiencies is largely avoided.

As a protection to minority interests, the rules of the Commission provide that such interests shall have the opportunity to present their proposals to the stockholders. Provided the management is given adequate time, it must include in its proxy material the proposals of others. It must also give the stockholders an opportunity to state whether their proxies shall be voted for or against these proposals. Whenever an independent solicitation of proxies is desired, the proxy rules provide that the management group must coöperate in mailing the soliciting literature of the minority or outside interest.[30]

Since the proxy rules of the Commission may be inadvertently or deliberately misinterpreted, the Commission devotes considerable time to conferences with corporate representatives who prepare proxy material. The policy eliminates many difficulties at their inception. Despite this preliminary work, the Commission must examine carefully all the proxy solicitation material that is filed with it. Some idea of the annual volume of work entailed is suggested by the statistical record. The Commission examined more than sixteen hundred separate pieces of proxy material and more than two hundred supplementary pieces in the fiscal year 1948. About 75 per cent of the material is filed annually between the months of March and May, when stockholders' meetings are most common. Since the 1948 experience appears to be typical of the annual pattern, it can be readily seen that the volume of work in this field is not only large but concentrated. Appreciation of its value is suggested by reference to particular instances of protection accorded the investing public.

In one case a company sought to hold a special meeting to amend its by-laws concerning a quorum. It sought common stockholder consent to reduce quorum requirements from 50 per cent to $33\frac{1}{3}$ per cent of the

[30] The extent of coöperation is as follows. Upon written request of the applicant, the issuer shall furnish a statement of the approximate number of recorded holders of any class of securities entitled to proxy solicitation by the issuer or its management, and an estimate of the cost of mailing a specified form of proxy to such holders, and shall mail the properly packaged proxy material with reasonable promptness. The applicant must reimburse the issuer corporation for the reasonable expenses involved or provide a surety bond to cover the expenses. The corporation need not mail the material of the other interests prior to the first day of its own proxy solicitation. A change in rules in late 1947 gives corporate management the option of furnishing a security holder (who wishes to mail solicitation materials) with a reasonably current list of security holders in lieu of mailing his material for him.

stock entitled to vote. No mention was made in the proxy material, however, of the fact that the president of the corporation owned 38 per cent of the common (voting) stock. The S. E. C. insisted that this indispensable information be included in the proxy data to permit intelligent stockholder action. The corporate management agreed, but later abandoned the whole proposal.[31] In another instance the Commission averted grief for stockholders when it insisted that the complete truth be substituted for the partial truth. A corporate management was soliciting stockholder approval of the company's dissolution. The president of the company urged both the preferred and the common stockholders to vote for dissolution. There was nothing in the proxy material, however, that would clearly inform the common stockholders whether or not there would be any funds available for them in the event of dissolution. The president implied that the common stockholders would get something when he stated that he owned six and a half times as many shares of common as he owned of preferred. But he did not tell the shareholders that for each share of preferred stock there were outstanding eight shares of common, and hence his proportionate interest in value terms was greater in the preferred stock than in the common. Obviously his statement as to his own holdings, and the implication as to the effect that dissolution would have on him, were misleading.[32] The Commission compelled a reluctant corporation management to re-state the facts to avoid deception.

One Section (16a) of the Securities Exchange Act—and also a section of the Public Utility Holding Company Act of 1935 and the Investment Company Act of 1940, respectively—require corporate insiders to file reports of certain transactions in and holdings of the securities of their companies. During the past fourteen years 43,243 persons of more than 3,000 issuers have filed 290,241 reports with the Commission. The great bulk of these reports are filed in compliance with the Securities Exchange Act of 1934. To prevent the misuse of advance information the laws permit the issuer corporation, or a stockholder of it acting in the corporation's behalf, to recover from corporate insiders any stock market profits made by short-term trading on the inside information. These corporate insider reports have proved to be very valuable. The Commission reports that substantial amounts, ranging up to several hundred thousand dollars have been recovered under the protective provisions of the law by or on behalf of the issuer corporations. In a number of cases the Commission has been informed of the voluntary payment of such profits to the company by the officer or director.[33] It is very doubtful whether such re-

---

[31] S. E. C., *Fifth Annual Report*, p. 61.
[32] S. E. C., *Fourth Annual Report*, p. 70.
[33] S. E. C., *Fourteenth Annual Report*, pp. 36–37.

coveries and payments would have been made in the absence of protective legislation and the availability of evidence under the law.

The S. E. C. is involved annually in various types of litigation under the Securities Exchange Act. In this field of action we find the Commission engaged in: (1) injunction proceedings in the district courts to restrain broker-dealers and others from violations of the Act and rules and regulations relating thereto; (2) actions in courts of appeal on petitions to review the Commission's orders; and (3) the rôle of *amicus curiae* in actions between private parties.

Criticisms of the Securities Exchange Act and Its Administration

Almost inevitably the Act and its administration have been exposed from time to time to criticism from groups and interests that are affected. Three general claims have been made against the Act: that it is too strict; that it operates unfairly, and that it has deleterious effects on the stock markets.

In the separate reports which the S. E. C. and the representatives of the securities marketing industry[34] submitted to Congress in August, 1941, both groups suggested changes in the law. On many of these proposed changes, largely technical in character, the industry and the Commission are in substantial agreement.[35] For instance, both agreed that it would be desirable to extend the registration of brokers and dealers to partners of firms and to officers and directors of corporations operating in the stock markets. And they both believed that the Commission should proceed against an individual allegedly violating the law without taking action against the entire organization of which he is a part. The injustice of subjecting a whole organization to the unfavorable publicity arising from the misdeeds of one person is to be avoided. The Commission also was not opposed to extension of proxy regulations to companies whose securities are traded over the counter. The New York Stock Exchange favored this proposal, since the existent arrangement did not enhance the popularity of the organized exchanges. Another proposal, in which the industry concurred, would prohibit the withdrawal of broker-dealer registration while a revocation proceeding is in progress. The prohibition would check withdrawals made to avoid full disclosure of the facts.

The industry has often complained, however, about the provisions of the law that require corporate insiders to give their corporation any

---

[34] Chiefly the Investment Bankers Association of America, the National Association of Securities Dealers, the New York Stock Exchange, and the New York Curb Exchange.

[35] *Proposed Amendments to the Securities Act of 1933 and to the Securities Exchange Act of 1934,* pp. 1052, 1066, 1240, 1293–1294.

profits derived from dealings in securities made within six months of the purchase transaction.[36] It is claimed that the provisions are unfair to individuals, work injury on the stock market, and are easily evaded.

The alleged unfairness arises from the fact that insiders are not compensated for losses sustained in market transactions in their company's stock. This argument, however, overlooks the fact that the real purpose of the law is to discourage insiders from speculating in their company's securities. While it may be true that insiders enter the market not to speculate but to thwart others who may be trying to manipulate the price of a corporation's stock, it is doubtful if their action offers the best means to prevent such manipulation. Its control is more properly a function of the police powers of the Commission.

The market injury argument is based on the decline of trading volume. Insiders are unwilling to trade, because their profits belong to their corporation, while they must shoulder the losses. With this loss of volume the market becomes thinner and less continuous. The range between bid and asked quotations is widened, and price spreads from sale to sale are greater. There is no question that the volume of trading has diminished on the securities markets as the new law and its rules and regulations have become effective. But, as one authority suggests, the diminution in trading and the discontinuity of the market cannot be blamed on any single government regulation, but are the results of a long succession of new rules and regulations.[37] Furthermore, a discontinuous market may have come about for other reasons, such as a greater caution on the part of market traders as they gain access to more complete market information.[38] The uncertainty regarding the exact factors which have contributed to the decline in market volume suggests the desirability of a cautious policy in changing the law or its rules and regulations. Meanwhile, the investing public should make up its mind whether it prefers a more discontinuous market, which registers prices relieved of much of the speculative influence, or a more speculative market in which margins between successive transactions are narrower.[39]

The argument that insiders who wish to speculate on the market may easily evade this provision of the law suggests the need for closer Commission supervision, rather than modification of the law. Furthermore, if evasion is wide-spread, as the argument implies, then the recapture of

---

[36] See *The Wall Street Journal*, Vol. CXIII, No. 61 (March 16, 1939), Recommendations of the National Security Exchanges Committee, p. 6; and *The Commercial and Financial Chronicle*, July 13, 1940, pp. 153–154.

[37] James C. Dolley, "Government Regulation of Stock Trading," *American Economic Review*, Vol. XXVIII, No. 1 (March, 1938), p. 24.

[38] Paul M. Sweezy, "The Thinness of the Stock Market," *American Economic Review*, Vol. XXVIII, No. 4 (December, 1938), pp. 747–748.

[39] A discontinuous market is less liquid, that is, the difficulties of selling securities without loss are enhanced by wider price movements.

insider profits has no great effect on the thinness of the market. The industry proponents cannot effectively support both arguments simultaneously.

The Commission's rules and regulations about proxy solicitation have also been criticized. It is claimed that they are too severe and impose an excessive cost on corporations. The complaint is similar to that concerning the registration statement and prospectus under the Securities Act. Does the complaint arise from the stockholders, or is it a complaint of management? If stockholders object to their corporations spending too much money to inform them precisely and fully of proposed actions at annual and special meetings, then the Commission would do well to be less exacting about this phase of the law. On the other hand, if the criticism emanates from management the objection loses much of its force. Experience indicates that the Commission must be exacting if stockholders' interests are to be protected adequately.

Congressional hearings relating to proxy regulations have brought out several interesting aspects on this subject.[40] In the first instance, the proxy regulations do not apply to companies whose securities are not listed on the exchanges. It has been maintained that this has prevented listing in some instances and has encouraged delisting in others. Consequently the exchanges, as stated earlier, favor expansion of proxy regulation to all corporations whose securities are bought and sold in interstate commerce or who engage in interstate trade, provided such corporations exceed a certain size (measured in gross assets) and have more than three hundred stockholders. In the second instance, testimony revealed that many corporation managements have simply failed to solicit proxies. As a consequence the presence of a quorum is prevented at corporate meetings, and in the absence of a quorum for legal action the old directorate continues in office. Management thus becomes self-perpetuating and at the same time escapes proxy regulation.[41] Here is displayed an unfortunate development where regulation inadvertently encourages the self-perpetuation of management and the disfranchisement of widely scattered shareholders who are denied the opportunity of delegating their right of vote by proxy. In the Congressional hearings the S. E. C. went on record in favor of requiring every issuer corporation subject to the proxy regulations of the 1934 Act to submit to its security holders the information specified in the Commission's proxy rules prior to each annual or special meeting regardless of whether or not proxies were actually solicited. On the other hand, the S. E. C. refrained from urging the adoption of changes in the law so that proxy regulations would apply to corporations whose securities were not registered on the

[40] *Proposed Amendments to the Securities Act of 1933 and to the Securities Exchange Act of 1934*, Parts IV and V.
[41] *Ibid.*, Part IV, p. 1240.

organized exchanges. The Commission stated that it did not wish at that
time to urge any expansion of its jurisdiction.[42]

It is interesting to note that few, if any, members of the securities
industry publicly oppose the principle of market regulation. Objections
are directed to particular sections of the law or to the Commission's
rules and regulations. A spokesman for the Investment Bankers Association declared in a joint S. E. C.-industry conference that the area of
agreement between the industry and the Commission far overshadows
the disagreements.[43] Newspaper opinion also has indicated that Wall
Street generally believes that the security and market regulation is fundamentally helpful to the industry.[44]

THE PUBLIC UTILITY HOLDING COMPANY ACT OF 1935[45]

In an earlier chapter the evils of the holding company as they affected
various interests, including the investor, were pointed out. Many of the
abuses, it will be recalled, were facilitated by excessive pyramiding of
the financial structure, particularly in the case of the public utility corporations. After a popular outcry against the abuses, featured in the
Insull, Foshay, and other utility company financial scandals, Congress
passed the Public Utility Holding Company Act of 1935. Appraisal of
the law and its administration will show not only the protections now
afforded investors in the utility field, but also a procedure that might
offer public protection for any of the ordinary fields of industry in which
holding company faults become pronounced.[46]

The broad purpose of the Act is to protect investors and consumers
from the abuses and evils committed behind and within the intricate
structure of the holding company. Since protection of consumers of
utility services falls outside the scope of this study, we shall confine our-
selves to the more important protections afforded investors. In this regard, the Act, through the medium of the Commission, undertakes several related tasks, namely: (1) To supervise and, if necessary, re-vamp
the financial structures of public utility holding companies; (2) to estab-

---

[42] In August 1949, Senator Frear introduced a bill (S. 2408) which, if enacted,
will subject large unregistered companies to proxy and other provisions of the Exchange Act. This bill follows closely S. E. C. recommendations. See Prentice-Hall
Securities Regulation Service, 3rd Edition, Vol. I, Report No. 3, p. 1, dated August
17, 1949.

[43] See *The Christian Science Monitor*, August 8, 1941, p. 19.

[44] *Cf.* B. H. McCormack, *The Wall Street Journal*, January 2, 1940, p. 16.

[45] Title I.

[46] Two well-known authorities on security analysis warn investors and investment
analysts that the ingenious talents of promoters of corporate holding company
superstructures may be directed towards industrials in the future as opportunities
elsewhere are restricted. See Graham and Dodd, *op. cit.*, (revised edition), p. 668.

lish and maintain equitable investor relations within holding company systems, and (3) to maintain equitable business and financial connections between holding companies, their subsidiaries and affiliates.[47]

To accomplish these purposes, the Act requires that, with certain exceptions,[48] all public utility holding companies register with the S. E. C. Proper registration requires the filing with the Commission of detailed information about the holding company, its subsidiaries and affiliates. Among the more important required data are incorporation certificates; by-laws; financial organization; voting trust agreements; terms, rights, and privileges of outstanding securities; arrangements with investment underwriters; and balance sheets and income accounts of the five years preceding registration. In addition, the Commission may require the submittal of all information it considers necessary to protect the public interest. In the event that certain companies refuse to register, they are prohibited from using the mails and other agencies of interstate commerce. This practically means they cannot do public utility business.

Registration is but the first step in the control of the public utility holding company financial structure. Security issuance by registered organizations is also subject to strict supervision. The utility corporation must file and have approved by the S. E. C. a declaration regarding the security to be issued. No declaration can become effective[49] if the security is a preferred stock or an unsecured bond, except in cases where the S. E. C. recognizes the urgent need to use such securities, as in the instances of re-finance or receivership. Financial structures of the future will thus be simpler and of better quality. The S. E. C. may bar a declaration from becoming effective for a variety of important reasons. In general, the proposed securities must not be unsuited to the utility's earning power and existing financial structure. They must not be unduly risky nor likely to be injurious, because of their terms and conditions of sale, to the interests of investors, consumers, and the general public. Efficiently applied, the conditions of rejection should protect the public and utility corporations from unworthy control interests which might

[47] "Affiliate" includes any person or company owning or controlling 5 per cent or more of the voting securities of the company, any officer or director of a specified company or its affiliate, and persons who are so related to the specified company as to interfere with arm's-length bargaining.

[48] If it appears not to be detrimental to investors and consumers, the S. E. C. will exempt from registration any holding company (and its subsidiaries) under the following conditions: where business and income are derived largely from intrastate activity; where the holding company and its subsidiaries are engaged largely in other than public utility business; where a company is a holding company temporarily by reason of securities acquired through a debt, a liquidation process, or an underwriting agreement; and where the public utility company does not extend its operations beyond the state in which it is organized and the states contiguous to it.

[49] The S. E. C. may waive its right to control if a state commission has approved a security issue.

otherwise establish faulty capital structures. And investors are protected not only from the consequences of faulty capitalization, but also from excessive costs in marketing securities and from investment positions unfair to the holders of various classes of securities within the corporation.

With certain exceptions, the law further requires that registered companies obtain S. E. C. approval to acquire the securities or assets of any business. Commission approval is granted if adequate information is submitted to indicate that the acquisitions are economically and financially justified and state laws are not being violated. By such restrictions the future development of utility holding companies is to be controlled.

Reconstruction of holding company systems is also provided under the law. The S. E. C. must investigate the structure of each registered holding company and its subsidiaries. The objectives are several. Financial structures are to be simplified. Stockholder voting rights are to be equitably distributed. Companies are to be restricted to those properties and operations necessary to an "integrated public utility system."[50] Provision is made also for the Commission to allow a registered holding company to control one or more additional integrated systems if, upon investigation, it appears to be uneconomical or contrary to the public interest to do otherwise. In the establishment or maintenance of integrated systems, pyramiding of the corporate structure cannot be too complicated. Holding companies beyond second degree are forbidden, that is, holding companies are not allowed to exist if they are built on a holding company which has a subsidiary which is a holding company. To insure that reconstruction shall proceed under S. E. C. direction, uncontrolled solicitation of stockholder consent by mail or other instrumentalities of interstate commerce is prohibited. The Commission must first have approved the plan or have been its sponsor. Even then solicitation of proxies must proceed according to the law and the S. E. C. rules and regulations.

To force simplification and integration the Commission may request the court to appoint it (or some other party) a trustee to take the necessary steps. And, in the event that reorganization arises from receivership, the receiver or trustee must be either the Commission or some party approved by it. In the latter case, the plans of reorganization must receive Commission approval prior to submittal to the court. Where regis-

---

[50] The Act defines an integrated public utility system to mean one the assets of which are either physically connected or capable of physical connection with one another and which, under normal conditions, may be operated economically as a single, interconnected, coördinated system confined to a single area or region, in one or more states, but not so large as to impair the advantages of local management, efficient operation, and effective regulation. See the Act, Section 2(a) (29)(B).

tered holding company systems proceed voluntarily to simplify and integrate, they, too, must obtain S. E. C. approval of their plans.

It is obvious that these important objectives of the Act can only be met by correct procedure. For example, concepts of proper integration differ. And the process of financial reorganization may eliminate certain inequities among investors only to establish others. Much ill-will and needless expense may be avoided, therefore, if the changes are guided by a competent public administrative body.

Tight controls are established by the law to insure equitable business and financial relations between companies in a utility holding company system. Holding companies cannot borrow from subsidiaries or from holding companies of the same degree, though past loans may lawfully be renewed. Loans by holding companies to subsidiaries, the so-called "downstream loans," must conform to S. E. C. regulations.

The Commission also has the power to establish rules and regulations governing a great array of other important inter-company and intra-company transactions. Thus, it controls dividend payments; acquisition, sale, redemption, and retirement of securities; sale of assets; proxy solicitations; and transactions relating to accounts and costs, reports, maintenance of competition, and so forth, between companies in the same system or affiliates of that system. Service, sales, and construction contracts by means of which holding companies often took advantage of subsidiaries are now definitely under Commission control. Holding companies cannot lawfully make such contracts, and subsidiaries and affiliates may make them only under S. E. C. jurisdiction. In the event that mutual service companies or persons perform such contracts, they must operate under Commission rules and regulations. And a mutual service company must have S. E. C. approval of its ownership, costs, revenues, and the like.

The law also provides for the deflation and control of the political power of the public utilities. Political contributions by any registered company, directly or indirectly, are prohibited. And employed or retained persons, representing registered utility companies before Congress, Congressional committees, or Federal agencies (S. E. C. and Federal Power Commission) cannot legally act in behalf of their employer or client without first registering with the S. E. C. They must reveal to the Commission who employs them and how much they are to be paid, as well as the subject-matter of their lobbying activities. During his employment the lobbyist must render a financial statement to the Commission each month, indicating the amount of expenses incurred and the compensation received for lobbying. In the future a public record of the cost of pressure groups in this field will be available.

Officers and directors of registered holding companies and their subsidiaries must file a record of their security holdings in any of the com-

panies in the system and make monthly reports of their current ownership position. Profits which they derive from purchase or sale of such
securities not held longer than six months may be recovered by the holding company or subsidiary company under the conditions laid down in
the law. The Commission has the power, however, to exempt certain
instances when it is in the public interest.

And finally, the law is made more effective by providing civil and
criminal penalties. These provisions of the law are quite similar to those
found in the Securities and Exchange Act. Willful violations may bring
fine or imprisonment or both to convicted parties, with a maximum
penalty placed at $10,000 and two years in the penitentiary. Holding
companies which engage unlawfully in transactions without registration
are subject to a fine not in excess of $200,000. And in civil suit, parties
who unknowingly relied on false statements may recover actual damages.

The Work and Accomplishments of the Commission under the Act

At the end of the fiscal year 1940, the Commission had registered
144 public utility holding companies with total consolidated assets of
nearly fourteen and a half billion dollars. These holding companies comprised 55 systems and included nearly fifteen hundred holding, sub-
holding, and operating companies.[51] But the Commission was not very
successful in its efforts to encourage holding systems voluntarily to integrate geographically and to simplify their corporate financial structures.[52]
It was necessary to launch formal proceedings to accomplish these objectives. All along the line the great electric and gas utilities gave ground
grudgingly and challenged the S. E. C.'s authority with legal suits,
some of which were carried to the Supreme Court. In the North American and the American Power and Light Company cases,[53] the Supreme
Court upheld the power of the Congress under the commerce clause to
attempt by law to remove the evils of management control through
security holdings by ordering holding companies to divest themselves of
the securities which made such evils possible. Furthermore, the Court
did not find any unconstitutional delegation of legislative power to the
S. E. C. in accomplishing corporate simplification.

With the resistance of the utilities broken by these decisions, the
S. E. C. has made considerable headway with the process of geographi-

---

[51] S. E. C., *Sixth Annual Report*, p. 11.

[52] Only twenty-four applications for the simplification of corporate structures were
filed up to the end of the 1940 fiscal year, and some of these involved but minor
reorganizations. The S. E. C. approved seven of these. See S. E. C., *Sixth Annual
Report*, p. 18.

[53] North American Co. *v.* S. E. C., 327 U. S., 686, 700–711 (1946); American
Power and Light Company *v.* S. E. C., 329 U. S., 90, 103–104, (1946).

cal integration and corporate simplification. Reference to the public utility holding company group in the list of the 200 largest American non-financial corporations will reveal superficially some of the results of the S. E. C. work under the Public Utility Holding Company Act of 1935. More revealing are the data which show that between June 30, 1938, and June 30, 1948, the total number of companies subject to the Act has been reduced from 2,117 to 705. Many have been eliminated by absorption through merger or consolidation; many by sales, dissolution, or other divestment; some by rule or order.[54]

Not infrequently the S. E. C. has ordered the dissolution of unnecessary and improperly financed holding companies. On occasion they have been *top holding* companies and at other times *sub-holding* companies. Where a holding company does not provide some needed economic, financial, or management services for the operating firms below it, the S. E. C. is likely to maintain that it is dispensable. And if the corporate structure of a holding company is unbalanced with too many debt securities, bank loans, and preferred stock in view of its past financial experience, it is likely to be on the receiving end of an S. E. C. dissolution order.[55]

Over the years the Commission has had filed with it a great many applications concerning the acquisition or sale of utility company securities or other assets. Though some of these applications were withdrawn or dismissed for various reasons, the Commission has seldom denied any of these applications.

The S. E. C. has been a participant in the reorganization of numerous registered holding companies which have experienced financial difficulties. One of the most important of the reorganizations under Commission supervision has been that of the Associated Gas & Electric Company, the vast holdings of which were drawn together tenuously by Mr. H. C. Hopson. Its successor company, the General Public Utilities Corporation, has been considerably reduced in size and is a far more integrated organization than its unfortunate predecessor.

Since its creation the S. E. C. has had much work to do in relation to the issuance of new securities by the utility companies. Over a period of fourteen years applications concerning more than twenty billion dollars of such securities have been filed with the S. E. C. About 73 per cent of the total had to do with refinancing, refunding, and reorganization, with the balance representing issues to get new money for the acquisition of property and working capital. The Commission is especially careful to examine proposed new issues in relation to their effects on corporate capitalization. In addition, by careful scrutiny, the rights

---

[54] S. E. C. *Fourteenth Annual Report*, p. 57.

[55] *Cf.* Emory Troxel, *The Economics of Public Utilities* (New York, Rinehart & Co. Inc., 1947), p. 175.

and privileges of investors in the new issues are considered for their fairness in relation to securities outstanding, prospective earning power, and so forth.

In the exercise of its power to supervise dividend policy of utility companies under the Act, the S. E. C. must and does do a very considerable amount of work.[56] This is equally true of its activities to protect the public by supervising the interconnections of investment underwriters and utility corporations issuing securities. Where corporation-banker agreements are not the result of arm's-length bargaining, abuses may develop if careful supervision is lacking. Extension of the practice of competitive bidding for utility securities by investment bankers under S. E. C. rules has redirected the Commission's activities in recent years.

The Commission has received at various times many applications of mutual service and subsidiary companies that wished to enter into service, sales, and construction contracts with operating utilities. In this phase of its activities, the work of the Commission is more extensive and difficult than it appears. The S. E. C. has had to make office and field studies to determine whether these service companies operate at cost and whether the costs are allocated equitably among those receiving the service.

Under the section of the law pertaining to political contributions, various investigations have been made. The most outstanding of these concerned the Union Electric Company of Missouri and other subsidiaries of the North American Company. Prison sentences and fines were imposed on the violators.

The pattern of activity under the Public Utility Holding Company Act of 1935 has been quite varied. In recent years, however, the bulk of the work has been concerned mainly with plans for integration and reorganization and with duties related to the issuance of securities.[57]

Criticisms of the Act and Its Administration

Criticisms of any regulatory law arise from anticipations of its consequences and from the actual results achieved by its application. With respect to anticipated consequences, the public utility industry entertained gloomy notions and had few words of praise for the law. Now that actual integration of holding company systems has been accomplished, critical comment regarding the Commission's skill and judgment can be made. Many will agree that in creating one-area, interconnected electric and natural gas systems throughout the country the S. E. C. has performed a major operation. It has brought company

[56] See, for example, S. E. C., *Sixth Annual Report*, pp. 36–42.
[57] S. E. C., *Thirteenth Annual Report*, p. 67.

management close to the operational scene and to state regulators by scaling down corporate size and striving for localized management. Whether or not it has integrated wisely and well is a more debatable matter. Objective investigators hold that the accomplished integration is imperfect in that the most economical combinations were not prescribed.[58] Even though this may be true, still it cannot be denied that the S. E. C. in its administration of the pertinent sections of the law relating to integration has succeeded in reversing substantially the former uneconomic trend. Moreover, the charge of imperfection of results raises several fundamental questions. Did the Congress intend that the proper function of the Commission in this field should be corrective in nature, or did it intend that the S. E. C. should arbitrarily plan utility structures by edict after long and careful cost studies based on various proposed combinations of properties in attempting to set up optimum-size organizations? Or did the Congress intend that both functions be performed? Since the legislation resulted from the many abuses revealed by elaborate studies made by the Federal Trade Commission and others, it would seem that the *primary* purpose of the law was to enable the S. E. C. to restore the industry to health as quickly as possible by a careful job of pruning. In the process, adjustments to technical and cost conditions should serve as guides in the limitation of holding company control. This is something less than a prescription that the S. E. C., in the process of correction of abuses, lay out a network of perfect utility systems in an industry still in the rapid growth stage. While perfection of results is the *ideal* goal of regulatory bodies, it should not be overlooked that *the best can often be the enemy of the good,* and awaiting *perfect* official plans can defeat or long postpone more attainable, satisfactory results.[59]

In regard to the application of other important sections of the law, the Commission's record looks impressive. Certainly, as a group, the investors in utility securities have received real benefits. And consumers also appear to have benefited. In the incipient stages of the law's administration there may have been some validity to the criticism that the requirements were unduly burdensome. As the Commission has gained administrative experience, however, such claims tend to lose weight. And, in any case, the criticism is hardly fundamental in view of the past

---

[58] *Cf.* Emory Troxel, *op. cit.,* p. 189. See also Robert Blum "S. E. C. Integration of Holding Company Systems," *The Journal of Land and Public Utility Economics,* Vol. 17, No. 4, November 1941, pp. 423–439.

[59] Former Securities Exchange Commissioner Robert K. McConnaughey's *personal* views on Congressional intent in the formulation of the Public Utility Holding Company Act are hereby acknowledged. To him gratitude is also expressed for calling attention to the Supreme Court's expression of the thought that "the best can be the enemy of the good" in Schwabacher *v.* United States of America, 334 U. S. 182 (1948), p. 193.

abuses in the industry and the strong public approval of the broad objectives of the law.

OTHER FEDERAL LEGISLATION VITAL TO INVESTORS

The Congress has passed other important laws vital to investors. Two of these we shall describe and briefly discuss.[60] In chronological order, they are the Chandler Act of 1938[61] and the Trust Indenture Act of 1939.[62]

The Chandler Act of 1938

When a small business reaches that point where it is unable to meet its current obligations and has exhausted its credit, the business will be liquidated. The assets are sold and the proceeds are used to meet debts. Balances, if any, in excess of debts are then distributed in accordance with the recognized rights of shareholders. In most large businesses, however, specialized plant and equipment preclude liquidation. The forced sale of assets, either separately or as a whole, is likely to result in terrific losses. Consequently, in such cases, bankruptcy leads preferably to reorganization. And reorganization involves a readjustment of property rights by a process of scaling down values, meeting *bona fide* claims of creditor groups fairly, and readjusting investor property rights equitably. The complexities of reorganization of a modern large corporation are obvious.

Up to 1934, the reorganization process was conducted through courts of equity.[63] The court appointed a receiver to maintain the corporate properties intact, pending the formulation of an equitable plan of reorganization. The process did not interfere with previously acquired liens or priorities of particular creditors. It was intended that creditors' rights be protected, but the rights and claims of all parties should be considered, even those of the public. While the receiver operated the properties and kept them intact, the various interested parties worked out a readjustment of claims and a reorganization plan which included the acquisition of the assets through a receiver's sale.[64] To facilitate the process,

---

[60] Two others, the Investment Company and Investment Advisers Acts of 1940, fall under the jurisdiction of the Commission and are important to investors, but they lie somewhat outside the scope of our study.

[61] Public, No. 696, June 22, 1938.

[62] Public, No. 253, August 3, 1939.

[63] Much of the material about corporate reorganization is drawn from Norman S. Buchanan, *The Economics of Corporate Enterprise* (New York, Henry Holt and Company, 1940).

[64] Bidders at the receiver's sale are rarely numerous. In fact, the reorganization committee, however designated, is usually the sole bidder.

the court fixed a minimum price below which it would not approve a sale. With this as a guide, reorganization proceedings were pushed through to completion.

Despite the presence of the equity court, abuses crept in and thwarted the intention of the law. Usually, while there were protective committees looking after the interests of the various groups, many security-holders were left without direct representation. And protective committees were often established by those who were more interested in their fees than in their clients. Furthermore, it was not uncommon for the debtor to continue to direct the use of corporate properties, with the result that during reorganization assets were further dissipated.

These faults and the deep distress of the business world in the early thirties called for a new approach to the bankruptcy problem. In 1934 Congress passed the Corporate Reorganization Act (Sections 77A and 77B of the Bankruptcy Act), which it again amended in 1935. In 1938 it passed the Chandler Bill, which is now known as Chapter X of the Bankruptcy Act. In its formulation of the Chandler Law, Congress was much influenced by the exhaustive study which the S. E. C. had made on corporate reorganization and protective committees.[65]

Under the present bankruptcy law providing machinery for corporate reorganization[66] in the Federal Courts, the S. E. C. has the following duties: (1) To participate in reorganization proceedings at the request or the approval of the court in order to render expert assistance to the court and to investors, and (2) to prepare for the courts and investors formal advisory reports on organization matters submitted to it by any Federal Court.

Where the debts of a corporation in reorganization process exceed $3,000,000, the Court must submit to S. E. C. scrutiny any plans of reorganization. And the Court must hold in abeyance its approval of any plan until the Commission makes its report or indicates that it is not to report. When the Court approves a plan and submits it to all the affected parties the Commission's report, if any, must accompany it. If the debts of the corporation are less than $3,000,000 the Court need not consult the S. E. C., but may do so if it desires.

In its advisory capacity, the S. E. C. is a party to numerous proceedings to reorganize financially distressed corporations. In the 1948 fiscal year, for example, the Commission reported that it had participated actively in 84 reorganization proceedings involving indebtedness in excess of $1,130,000,000.[67]

---

[65] Report on the Study and Investigation of the Work, Activities, Personnel and Functions of Protective and Reorganization Committees. The first volume of this report appeared in 1936.

[66] Railroad corporations are not included, since special legislation is provided for them.

[67] S. E. C., *Fourteenth Annual Report*, p. 82.

The law also provides that, except for small corporations,[68] the court may no longer exercise its discretion between appointing a trustee for the properties and continuing the debtor in possession. A trustee must be appointed,[69] and he must be a disinterested party. This precludes creditors, stockholders, officers, directors, and recent underwriters of the securities of the distressed corporation from serving in that capacity.

In short, the present law is based on the principles of full disclosure, unbiased trusteeship, and public representation through the medium of the S. E. C. With these principles there can be little quarrel. The results depend on the competence of the trustees, the soundness of Commission advice, and the alertness of the courts.

The Trust Indenture Act of 1939

A development of interest to holders of corporation bonds, notes, and similar instruments is the passage of the Trust Indenture Act of 1939 as a supplement to the Securities Act of 1933. Usually, when issuing bonds, a corporation makes appropriate arrangements with a trustee to act as representative of the bondholder interests, which are stated in an instrument known as an indenture or agreement. In the event that the corporation defaults on its agreement in any way the trustee, and the trustee only, takes action against the corporation. Bondholders must therefore rely very heavily on the trustee to be independent of the corporation, alert, capable, and willing to act quickly. Investigation, however, has revealed: that indentures have been deficient in disclosure; trustees have not had the necessary qualifications to protect the beneficiaries; and that indentures often have included exculpatory clauses which relieved trustees of their liability for misconduct so that the word "trustee" became virtually meaningless. The Trust Indenture Act is designed, among other things, to eliminate these unfortunate conditions.

Under the Act full and fair disclosure must be made of the essential conditions of trust indentures underlying a corporation's bonds, notes, and so forth, not only at the time of original sale, but thereafter. The procedure to obtain full disclosure follows that of security issuance under the Securities Act of 1933. In fact, the Securities Act is the model followed with respect to exemptions, nature of violations, criminal and civil liabilities, and the like. The Indenture Act also sets up eligibility requirements for trustees, for example, minimum capital requirements and an absence of direct or indirect interest in the debtor company. In addition, it prescribes trustee procedure and relations with bondholders and

---

[68] Those whose debt is less than $250,000.

[69] The Court may appoint some executive of the bankrupt corporation as a trustee to serve under the main, independent trustee. The purpose of this arrangement is to assist the main trustee by providing the skill and services of someone intimate with the properties and the business.

similar creditors. The purpose of all these requirements and specifications is to place trustee behavior on the high standard of the leading trust companies.

The Commission's work in this field has assumed sizable proportions. During the fiscal year 1948, it had had filed with it indentures relating to total offerings of more than two and one half billion dollars. In addition, it had to pass on numerous trustee statements of eligibility and qualification and examine and file trustees' annual reports to security holders. By law trustees are required to deposit such reports with the Commission.

SUMMARY AND CONCLUSION

It is evident that Congress has made a broad and intensive attack on the problems relating to corporation finance and the securities markets. Certainly it can be said without refutation that the public has been provided the machinery with which to forestall or to meet the problems arising from the misuse of important institutions—the modern corporation and the securities system. Under the law the principle of full and fair disclosure of information concerning securities, new and old, sold in interstate commerce and on the organized exchanges has been established. Corporate insiders are no longer capable of taking advantage of their preferred positions either by the misuse of the proxy machinery or by the use of advance information likely to affect the value of their corporation's shares. Transactions between corporations and their directors and officers, including annual compensation, are exposed to public scrutiny. The law and the S. E. C. have improved the operation of the exchanges, impressed them with the magnitude of their public service, "squelched" many of the questionable practices followed within their walls, and provided controls for many phases of their work. They have also offered protection to the public from the abuses of the unorganized markets, and caused operators therein to establish their own organizations for self-regulation under Federal supervision.

In the public utility field, the law has gone even further than elsewhere. Not only have holding companies been required to register under the law, but they are also required to re-vamp their geographic and financial structures when necessary and desirable. Unless the Commission relaxes its vigilance and insistence, excessive pyramiding will disappear. Moreover, the law places utility inter-company transactions, relations with investment bankers, and dividend policy under government scrutiny, and requires utility lobbyists to register with the S. E. C. and account for compensation received in such employment. In addition, holding company officers and directors, as in the case of similar servants of other corporations whose securities are sold in public markets, must turn over stock market profits to their corporations if they have not held their corporation's securities six months or more before trading. Otherwise the corporation may sue to recover the profits.

Corporate reorganization procedure has been improved and the public interest in this financial proceeding has been emphasized. More impartial treatment of all parties to reorganization is assured by the participation of the Securities and Exchange Commission in reorganization procedure, in its capacity of adviser to the courts and protector of the public interest. And finally, legislation has placed eligibility and qualifications of corporate trustees in the hands of the Commission and at the same time it prohibits trustees from escaping blame when derelict in their duties. These arrangements should be most helpful in improving trusteeship.

Whether these changes will meet future problems adequately remains to be seen. Much will depend on the continued intelligent and expeditious administration of the laws by the S. E. C. Much will depend also on the willingness of the better element responsible for corporate affairs and security market operations to keep their houses in order and their less ethical brethren under control. Should it be necessary, the rigid controls of the Public Utility Holding Company Act could be extended to all corporations doing interstate business. Or Congress might accede to public demand for Federal incorporation or Federal license of businesses operating in interstate commerce, and institute more rigid controls through such procedure.

It is obvious that corporate concentration in itself has not been attacked by these controls, except insofar as the reorganization of public utility structures will affect the size of utilities. Possibly better information offered investors may limit the growth of certain companies, but a general reduction in the size of business units is neither the aim nor the probable effect of the regulation. There is no attempt here to solve the basic social problems created by business concentration. It is even possible that the essential corporate problem created by concentration has been avoided. The principle contained in the legislation is still that of ownership control. Owners are to be protected with information and fair conditions, so that they may exercise the planning and directive functions and receive the rewards of property. But will information, unmanipulated markets, proxy controls, and the like, really restore owners to a position of control in our giant corporations? And would the result be desirable, if it could be achieved? The answer to these essential questions should become apparent as time permits an examination of results. It is certainly clear that these controls will not affect importantly the problems created by the disappearance of competition before the advance of monopoly and industrial oligopoly.

PART II

Industrial Monopoly

Introduction

When, in many industries, individual corporations grow to great size and corporate control becomes concentrated in the hands of a few owners or a few management officers, it seems almost inevitable that competition will not everywhere survive. And it has long since become obvious that in a number of industries where public policy has relied on competitive planning, the independence of individual firms has been seriously curtailed. The restraints on competition have ranged from coöperation, in which certain aspects of competition are controlled, to monopoly, in which a single seller controls the sale of a commodity. Where large-scale production is highly developed, the number of firms is reduced, and combinations setting single firms in a position of monopoly become feasible and, at times, peculiarly desirable.

The mere fact that a few companies dominated the cigarette industry in the nineties made it relatively easy for James B. Duke to bring over four-fifths of cigarette production under control of the American Tobacco Company. Any threat of over-capacity in an industry containing a few large firms may make competition very dangerous and the idea of coöperation correspondingly attractive. Where a considerable number of relatively small firms is found in an industry, any over-capacity is corrected without general disturbance. Price reductions merely go far enough to eliminate some of the higher-cost companies. This adjustment is difficult where giant concerns fill the field. No one company is willing to lose sales and probably suffer higher plant costs as its output is curtailed, so price competition may go to extreme lengths. Before any enterprise will surrender its great investment, the health of the whole industry may be threatened. Rather than face a long period of cut-throat competition, the companies may solve their problem by organizing a single firm with control of their combined business.

Whether concentration activity supplies a spur to the formation of monopoly or merely creates conditions favoring combination, it has prepared a background for monopoly in a number of American industries. In some cases it preceded the recognition of certain industries as public monopolies or public utilities, in which public regulation sanctions monopoly or some degree of monopoly. And, wherever a single firm has gained control over the sale of some industrial commodity, concentration has helped it on its way.

American policy has not sanctioned monopoly in the ordinary fields of industry, and its appearance presents a serious problem to a society committed to the competitive system. While the control of supply by a single firm has rarely been complete, sale monopolies have been sufficiently strong to bring results markedly different from the satisfactory output and price policies of competition. Among the products subjected to monopoly at some time or other in the last seventy-five years are aluminum, iron and steel, salt, wall-paper, enamelware, Mazda lamps, asphalt, petroleum products, sugar, tobacco products, shoe machinery, bicycles, gunpowder, cash registers, farm machinery, and ethyl fluid.

Changing business conditions, changes in public taste, and public prosecution have released many of these commodities from the control of a single company. Cash registers, shoe machinery, ethyl fluid, and nickel stand as the important commodities sold on a national scale that appear to be still under such control. Many of those that have escaped did not make their way to real freedom, but have merely exchanged one master for a half-dozen or so. The treatment they receive may still be far from competitive. In the tobacco industry, for instance, where public prosecution ended the rule of the American Tobacco Company, four companies were organized to take over the main part of its business. But competition among these companies, while vigorous in some ways, has shown very little price competition. As will be seen in Part IV, this controlled or partial competition shows many of the effects of monopoly.

In the immediately following chapters a number of representative cases of monopoly are studied. It is apparent that perfect monopoly is about as rare as perfect competition. Only in the case of two products, aluminum and ethyl fluid, has the monopolist had, at least at times, complete control of the supply. And, of course, these products are exposed to the competition of substitutes. In the history of these representative monopolies can be seen the background of concentration and the general conditions that at least offered passive aid to the monopolist. In addition, there appear definite sources of power, such as patents, tariffs, financial strength, and other means, which gave to those firms the specific ability to eliminate competitors and maintain a large control of supply. The effect of monopoly on the efficiency of industry and on its price and output policies can be seen with some definiteness. This suggests reasons for public concern over the disappearance of competition in any private industry. In all these cases, monopoly has been forced to undergo some reorganization. But when the single firm is forced out of its dominant position, satisfactory conditions for competition do not seem to be created. The industry remains so highly concentrated in each of the cases that competitive independence of the individual firms seems very unlikely to develop.

In order to show the general powers and the weaknesses that are found in American anti-monopoly policy, Part III goes on to describe the substance given the Sherman Anti-Trust Act by Congress and by court interpretation. Weaknesses were apparent in both the substance and administration of the Act before 1914, and a general recognition of this fact led to additional legislation in that year. The Federal Trade Commission was set up. Review of its work shows a great deal that is commendable, but still reveals the existence of serious weaknesses in our attack on monopoly.

10

Tobacco

THE BACKGROUND OF MONOPOLY

In the American tobacco industry competition enjoyed a short though not uneventful life. The industry reached appreciable size only after 1860, and fell into the hands of monopolists before the end of the century. By 1840 it had begun a rapid development, but employed only eight or nine thousand men and three and one-half million dollars of capital. Its product was valued at less than six million dollars.[1] Over 40 per cent of the industry was located in Virginia, where it held a place of outstanding importance in the economy of the state.[2] Factories were small, however, and simple hand-tool methods were used. Half the plants in Virginia and North Carolina employed less than twenty workers, and only three employed as many as one hundred.

In the late sixties, tariff protection and a growing national market gave a marked fillip to the industry, which was not suppressed by an increase of nineteen cents a pound in the internal revenue tax.[3] By 1880, ten years before the appearance of the "Tobacco Trust," its capital was ten times greater and its output twenty times greater than in 1840.[4] During these years and up to the turn of the century, markets for various tobacco products did not change materially. Smoking and chewing tobaccos lost a little of their early advantage, doubling their sales while cigar consumption trebled. Applying retail values to census figures, Meyer Jacobstein estimated the annual expenditure on all tobacco products to be somewhere in the neighborhood of five hundred million dollars in

---

[1] *Tenth Census of the United States,* Vol. II, Statistics of Manufacture (1880), p. vii.

[2] Joseph Clarke Roberts, *The Tobacco Kingdom* (Durham, N. C., Duke University Press, 1938), pp. 164, 170.

[3] In the three years 1865 to 1868, when the tax rose from eleven to thirty-three cents, the per capita consumption fell from 1.3 to 1.0 pounds. Cf. Meyer Jacobstein, *The Tobacco Industry in the United States* (New York, Columbia University Press, 1907), p. 49.

[4] *Tenth Census* (1880), Vol. II, pp. 78–79.

1905.[5] Cigars contributed 70 per cent of this sum, and smoking, chewing, and snuff about 27 per cent. The fifteen million dollars spent on cigarettes made up only 3 per cent of the total. Thirty years later the tables were to be completely reversed when cigarettes supplied close to 80 per cent of the value of tobacco products. The years of the trust, however, found cigars and smoking and chewing plug firmly fixed in public favor.[6]

In 1890, monopoly entered the tobacco industry through the avenue of its least important branch, cigarette manufacture. It might seem that J. B. Duke, who was largely responsible for the appearance of the cigarette monopoly, foresaw the coming importance of the field or possessed confidence in his ability to shape its future. It is more reasonable, however, to assume that conditions in the industry at the time account for the course of monopoly developments. The important cigar field possessed characteristics favorable to competition and not monopoly. Machinery had not been developed, and only simple tools in the form of knives, cutting boards, wooden molds and hand presses were required. As a result, a great deal of manufacture was carried on under a household system, and entry into factory production was open to the small enterprises. An experienced workman with a few hundred dollars of capital could set up in business and sell his small output quite successfully in the local market. That this did occur is suggested by census figures. The average enterprise employed only seven workers and about three thousand dollars of capital throughout the eighties.[7] The large number of producers and the ease of entry into the field made monopoly difficult to form and almost impossible to sustain.

In the manufacture of chewing tobacco, snuff, and smoking tobacco, machinery was more important and manufacture in homes was of very slight importance. As a result, in 1880, while the value of these goods fell only 15 per cent below that of cigars, the industry used about 50 per cent less labor. It had only four hundred and seventy-seven establishments, with an average capital of forty thousand dollars, as against the seven thousand with an average capital of three thousand dollars found in the cigar field.[8]

The undoubted organizing genius of J. B. Duke might have turned to suppress competition in this industry, except for the fact that cigarette

[5] Jacobstein, *op. cit.*, p. 46.
[6] Between 1899 and 1923 the physical volume of tobacco and snuff production increased by 40%, while cigars were increasing by 41% and cigarettes by 1710%. *Cf.* Edmund E. Day and Woodlief Thomas, *The Growth of Manufactures, 1899 to 1923*, Census Monographs VIII (1928), p. 54.
[7] Census figures covered establishments turning out five hundred dollars' worth of product of more per year. Of these, 7,145 reported. There was probably an equal number of home producers turning out a few hundred dollars' worth of cigars per year.
[8] *Tenth Census* (1880), Vol. II, pp. 78–79.

production offered easier conquest. For one thing, the smallness of the cigarette industry made conquest relatively simple. After being in the smoking tobacco field with his brothers for seven years, Duke could see no chance that their products would take the lead away from the popular Bull Durham brand, and he is quoted as refusing to play second fiddle to anyone.[9] To escape that rôle he turned to the manufacture of cigarettes.

In addition to its smallness this field held only a few large firms, and thereby supplied a second condition unfavorable to competition. Patented cigarette-making machines, developed and improved in the seventies, reduced the labor cost to one-tenth and fixed large-scale capitalistic methods on the industry. As a result, a market concentration occurred. Over 90 per cent of the industry was found in four cities, namely, New York, Rochester (N. Y.), Durham (N. C.), and Richmond (Va.).[10] In each of these centers one or two factories produced the great bulk of the output. Five large companies controlled nine-tenths of the industry.[11]

Under these conditions, no one firm could ignore the effects of its price and production policy on rival firms. Inevitably, competition would lead to coöperation or to cut-throat practices. Until James Duke appeared in New York in 1884, a gentlemanly sort of competition prevailed. But he had one hundred thousand dollars and his way to make, and the established companies made no move to initiate him into the select circle. On the contrary, they snubbed him.[12] Before the end of the decade he forced his way in. A costly advertising and sales campaign brought his company to the forefront and precipitated a vicious trade war. Peace came with the first of the many combinations that the industry was to see over the course of the next twenty years.

The Cigarette Combine

In the late eighties several projected consolidations came to nothing, but the costly trade war, deliberately precipitated by Duke to force combination, forecast the end of competition.[13] The Duke firm was spending as much as eight hundred thousand dollars a year to create dis-

---

[9] John Wilbur Jenkins, *James B. Duke, Master Builder* (New York, George H. Doran, 1927), p. 65.

[10] *Report of the Commissioner of Corporations on the Tobacco Industry* (1909), Part I, pp. 63–64.

[11] W. Duke and Sons; Allen and Ginter; Goodwin and Co.; Kenney Tobacco Co.; William S. Kimball and Co.

[12] "As late as 1887, when some of the largest manufacturers were preparing for their annual dinner, one of them asked in jest if Duke should be bidden to the feast. 'We don't consider him a manufacturer of cigarettes; he will be broke before the year is out,' was the reply." Jenkins, *op. cit.*, p. 86.

[13] *Ibid.*, Chap. 7.

order in the industry, and threatened to spend materially more if it were needed to bring the last of the independent-minded into line. By 1889, independence seemed a very costly luxury, and the following year saw ten men representing 90 per cent of the industry throw their property together in a newly organized company. The kindly state of New Jersey was chosen for incorporation, and the American Tobacco Company was born. Its incorporators carried on as directors. James B. Duke became its first president.

The Company issued ten million dollars of 8 per cent cumulative preferred and fifteen millions of common stocks. These were exchanged for the tangible and intangible assets of the five combining concerns. The incorporators were not particularly modest gentlemen. By the most kindly interpretation, they did not subscribe more than five million dollars of tangible assets, but they were willing to take twenty millions in stocks for the reputation and good-will they were able to bring to the new firm. Intangible items are valuable in the sale of cigarettes, but not quite that valuable.

After a careful study, the Bureau of Corporations insisted that five millions for intangibles would be a generous allowance.[14] Probably, then, the corporation started with ten millions of assets to back the preferred stock and nothing with which to back the fifteen millions of common stock. It did, however, hold a strategic position in the industry, from which it went on to dominate all lines of tobacco manufacture save that of cigars.

The mere size of the combine spelled serious difficulties for independent cigarette companies. But this was not all. The combining companies were efficient, and all the directors were experienced and able tobacco men. And of even more importance was the fact that the American Tobacco Company gained control of cigarette-making machines. For a short time independents had the use of excellent machines leased for royalty payments by the Bonsack Machine Company. But they lost that important asset when the combine gained exclusive use of them from 1891 to 1895. And they lost the use of other machines as various companies were acquired by the American Tobacco Company. One independent, the National Cigarette and Tobacco Company, managed to hold control over two good machines for a number of years. In 1899, when this company was finally acquired, independents had only a few relatively inferior machines.

The combine also used its financial power to acquire competing companies whenever they would add materially to its control of the market. In particular areas, relatively small producers possessed considerable strength, and it was easier to buy them out, even at high prices, than to

[14] *Report of the Commissioner of Corporations on the Tobacco Industry* (1911), Part II, pp. 94–99.

drive them off the market with price-cutting or advertising campaigns. In its first year the American Tobacco Company spent one million dollars in cash and five millions in stock to eliminate competitors, and the practice continued to be followed throughout the nineties.[15] It culminated in the purchase in 1899 of the tobacco and cigarette business of the Union Tobacco Company. This enterprise had been organized by a syndicate either to fight the combine or to sell its properties at a high "nuisance" value. In any event, the latter occurred. The syndicate sold its six million dollars' worth of assets for twelve and one-half million dollars of the stock of the American Tobacco Company. The combine managed to keep its books balanced by entering an item of nearly seven million dollars for good-will. Since it dropped the brands developed by the Union Company, the actual good-will was probably nothing. In the opinion of the Bureau of Corporations, the seven millions "represented the price which the American Tobacco Company paid to avert a fight."[16]

When opponents were weaker the combine used various methods of ruthless competition, with telling effect. In markets where the cigarettes of small companies were popular, prices were cut below cost. At various times the American Tobacco Company sold cigarettes at $1.47 per thousand in North Carolina and Virginia after paying a tax of $1.50. Losses could be borne by the large company, with its great financial resources and its monopoly profits in other areas. But independents frequently found the burden too great and closed up or sold out to the combine. Mr. Duke's gentle explanation of the price-cutting practice was that "sometimes a brand gets a little weak in a section."[17]

Independents were harassed also by agreements forced on jobbers to handle only the products of the American Tobacco Company. In many cases special discounts were given to wholesalers and jobbers who handled exclusively the brands of the monopoly. In others, the company refused to sell its products to jobbers who thought they had the right to handle whatever brands they wished. Since the jobber could not survive on the small independent tobacco business, he was really given the choice of getting out of the field or conforming.[18] The retailer found it difficult to obtain independent brands and, when he did, frequently hid them under his counter for fear of a visit of inspection from representatives of the combine.

Through the nineties and on until prosecution of the trust in 1911,

---

[15] The authorized capital stock of the American Tobacco Company was increased from 25 to 35 millions in 1891. By 1900 the annual report of the Company showed outstanding stock of 68.5 millions.

[16] *Report of the Commissioner of Corporations on the Tobacco Industry*, Part I, p. 68.

[17] *Report of the Industrial Commission on Trusts and Industrial Combinations* (1901), Vol. XIII, p. 318.

[18] *Ibid.*, pp. 333–337.

the use of these several powers created an effective monopoly of cigarettes. In 1891 the combination produced 88 per cent of the total domestic consumption of cigarettes and little cigars.[19] It lost ground for a few years, but then, as it drove vigorously against independents, its proportion increased to its highest point at 93 per cent in 1899.[20] It was not able to hold this position, and in a few of the years between 1899 and 1911 independents supplied as much as 20 per cent of the market.

Profits also bear witness to the strength of the monopoly control. Earnings of 10 per cent were made in the first year on the fictitious capitalization of twenty-five millions. On the basis of the real tangible and intangible assets this represented earnings of approximately 25 per cent. Through the rest of the nineties earnings were even larger, and the company paid its preferred dividends, built a surplus of eight millions by 1895, and paid common stock dividends of 8 to 12 per cent. When it is remembered that this common stock had no assets behind it, we are forced to admit that Mr. Duke and his *confrères* had the industry thoroughly controlled.

The Spread of Monopoly

With the help of its cigarette profits, and through the use of the same methods that built the cigarette monopoly, the American Tobacco Company rapidly gained control of all other tobacco fields except cigars. In its organization and early development the company had acquired some factories manufacturing plug tobacco. From this start it went on to dominate the plug industry. Between 1894 and 1897, independents struggled against competition in which the combine used several million dollars of cigarette profits. For much of this time, it sold its leading brand, Battle Ax, at a loss, resorted to other unfair methods of competition, and carried on a costly advertising and sales campaign. It acquired one large plug plant and built another to gain 20 per cent of the capacity of the industry.

Continued warfare wearied the independents and brought about the plug combine in 1898. The plug business of the American Tobacco Company and six independents were thrown together in the Continental Tobacco Company. The American subscribed a little over three millions of tangible assets and received over one million dollars in cash and twenty-one millions in the securities of the new company.[21] A few months

---

[19] The combination never controlled less than 90 per cent of the cigarettes exported. Cf. *Report of the Commissioner of Corporations on the Tobacco Industry* (1909), Part I, p. 329, and Tables 38 and 40.

[20] Up to 1898, separate figures are not obtainable for paper cigarettes and all tobacco cigarettes.

[21] Jacobstein, *op. cit.*, p. 107.

later, the Liggett and Myers Tobacco Company, the largest of the independents, was absorbed by exchanging $1,366 of Continental stock for each hundred-dollar par share of its stock. After this transaction the Continental showed seventy million dollars of intangibles among its assets. The Bureau of Corporations concluded that its entire issue of common stock had neither tangible nor intangible values behind it, and even the preferred stock exceeded the fair value of the entire business.[22] Mr. Duke later insisted that he "never bought any business with the idea of eliminating competition."[23]

The Liggett and Myers acquisition was important, for more than a plug business was gained. It brought into the expanding trust very important financiers who first made millions out of the sale of property to the combine and later added importantly to its financial strength.[24] With the entrance of these men the old group of tobacco men, except Duke, dropped out of the center of the picture.

This story of combination is repeated monotonously. A nucleus of snuff manufacture in the American Tobacco Company, a year of cutthroat competition, the purchase of a few important concerns, and then, in 1900, the American Snuff Company was organized. A year later the same process created the American Cigar Company. One relieving variation appeared in this last case. The combine never managed to control over 25 per cent of cigar manufacture.

In 1901, a brief excursion to England yielded fairly satisfactory results. The American combine bought a leading English manufacturer, Ogdens Limited, for five million dollars. It then carried on a mutually destructive trade war with a hastily formed English combination organized in the Imperial Tobacco Company. Inside of a year the usual peace was established to the satisfaction of the large combines. Their home markets were reserved to the domestic companies and the rest of the world was allotted to the British-American Tobacco Company, in which American Tobacco owned two-thirds of the stock and Imperial one-third.

In 1901, the American Tobacco Company and the Continental were united by a holding corporation—the Consolidated Tobacco Company. Two important changes were effected. Firstly, the central financial group bought stock in the new company, and the business thereby acquired thirty millions in cash. Secondly, the stockholders in the two subsidiary companies were persuaded to exchange their stocks for the 4 per cent bonds of the Consolidated. For this purpose, bonds to a par value of $157,000,000 were issued.

---

[22] *Report of the Commissioner of Corporations on the Tobacco Industry* (1911), Part II, p. 99.
[23] Jenkins, *op. cit.*, p. 122.
[24] Thomas F. Ryan, P. A. B. Widener, A. N. Brady, W. C. Whitney, Thomas Dolan.

Continental stockholders received a one-hundred-dollar bond for each hundred-dollar par share, while American Tobacco shareholders were offered two hundred dollars in bonds for each hundred-dollar share. Since the former had never received a dividend and the latter had been getting 6 per cent, the guarantee of 4 per cent to the one and an effective 8 per cent to the other seemed very attractive.

Appearances were deceptive. The transaction left control of the two-hundred-million-dollar corporation in the hands of the small group owning a majority of the forty million dollars of common stock. It gave the old stockholder a bondholder position, but in a very much weakened capital structure. Few, if any, industrial corporations have tried to do business with 80 per cent of their capital liabilities in the form of bonds. And the condition was particularly dangerous in this case, since the combining companies were badly over-capitalized. The value of the actual earning assets fell materially below the value of the outstanding bonds. Any minor adversity would have forced the company to default on its bonds, and bankruptcy could have been avoided only as long as control of the market continued to yield monopoly profits.

In these circumstances, the stockholder would have been as safe to retain his stock equity, and he would have been in a position to get large dividends if earnings were unexpectedly large. The insiders already had seen that a marked increase in profits might result from possible reductions in the internal revenue taxes on tobacco. By kicking the old stockholders upstairs they, as the only surviving stockholders, stood to gain the resultant profits. And if the worst happened they would not suffer more than the bondholders in the collapse of the whole topheavy edifice.[25]

One more reorganization of the trust came in 1904, when the holding company form was given up and the properties were merged in a new American Tobacco Company. It had been believed for some years that the holding company might be immune from Sherman Act prosecution. But, in 1904, the successful prosecution of a railway holding company[26] dispelled this belief. The safest haven from monopoly prosecution seemed to be a complete merger of the complex properties of the combine. In addition, reorganization simplified the structure of the trust and, by a judicious exchange of stocks, and bonds, further increased the powers of the small group in control.[27]

Through these years the combine continued to use its early practices to increase its control in all fields of tobacco manufacture. It developed a retail organization in the American Cigar Stores and made notable gains in the chewing and smoking tobacco industries. Frequently, competing plants were secretly acquired and were run as independents to be

[25] *Report of the Commissioner of Corporations,* Part I, p. 8.
[26] Northern Securities Co. *v.* U. S., 193 U. S. 197 (1904).
[27] Preferred stocks in the subsidiary companies had held voting rights. In the reorganization they were exchanged for bonds.

used for special attacks on genuine competitors. The effect of this expansion on competitive conditions in the various branches of the industry is made very clear in the following table:

Table 5

PROPORTION OF THE ANNUAL OUTPUT PRODUCED BY THE TOBACCO COMBINE[28]

Year	Plug	Smoking	Fine-cut	Snuff	Cigarettes	Little Cigars	Cigars
1902	71.2	66.3	73.7	85.9	84.6	71.8	14.3
1903	76.9	67.1	77.6	89.4	83.9	67.9	16.4
1904	78.2	69.2	80.4	90.6	87.7	79.2	13.9
1905	80.7	68.7	81.7	93.8	84.7	78.3	13.3
1906	81.8	70.6	80.9	96.0	82.5	81.3	14.7
1907	80.5	72.4	81.4	95.7	81.7	90.8	14.5
1908	81.9	73.6	79.2	95.7	81.8	88.7	13.0
1909	83.3	75.3	80.1	96.1	83.6	89.0	13.1
1910	84.9	76.2	79.7	96.5	86.1	91.4	14.4

The table leaves no doubt that the American Tobacco Company held monopoly control over the industry save in the manufacture of cigars. And its power was growing slowly, except in cigarette production, where its large control was merely maintained. Its ability to increase its power further was never tested. In Sherman Act proceedings started in 1908 and completed in 1911, the Department of Justice, at least temporarily, ended the rule of the tobacco barons. The Supreme Court held the company a monopoly in contravention of the Sherman Act, and ordered its dissolution into a number of separate companies.

THE ECONOMIC EFFECTS OF MONOPOLY

The Restriction of Tobacco Manufacture

The common monopoly restriction of output below a normal competitive scale is apparent in the price and profit record of the tobacco combine. An unusual stability in prices and abnormally large profit margins indicated that control prevented supply from growing equally with the expanding market for tobacco products.

In spite of marked changes in cost between 1900 and 1910, the consumer continued to pay the same prices. During 1901 and 1902 the internal revenue tax on manufactured tobacco dropped from twelve to

[28] *Report of the Commissioner of Corporations on the Tobacco Industry* (1915), Part III, p. 2.

six cents a pound without any decline in price.[29] Similar reductions for cigarettes and little cigars also brought no benefit to the consumer. The government merely surrendered some of its revenue to the combine. Conventional prices and standardized packaging cannot explain the stability. In 1898, when taxes had been increased, the combine had maintained conventional prices, but had reduced the size of packages by approximately 15 per cent. Apparently this process would not work the other way when taxes were reduced. At least, it did not.[30]

The only variations in price that did appear during these years benefited the combine at the expense of the distributor. While retail prices stayed the same, the prices paid by tobacco jobbers increased. For example, a leading brand of plug tobacco was maintained at ninety cents a pound, but the price to the jobber increased from approximately fifty-six cents to sixty-two and one-half cents. In part, this reduced margin was a payment collected for increased advertising services performed for the jobber by the combine.[31] In part, however, it merely represented the exercise of monopoly power.

Profit margins increased as control increased. During the struggle to organize the plug industry, when it controlled less than one-quarter of the field, the combine lost three cents on each pound of plug tobacco. In 1900, when it had swallowed up over 60 per cent of the industry, it made almost four cents of profit on each pound. Five years later, control of 80 per cent of the industry yielded profits of nearly eight cents.[32] With cigarettes the story is the same. Only for cigars, where conditions in the industry resisted any growth of monopoly, did margins remain at normal levels.

For their labors the "master builder" and his associates were receiving the comfortable rewards of monopoly. After 1903, the snuff branch of the combine made annual earnings of about 40 per cent on its tangible assets, which was equal to at least 20 per cent on its total assets.[33] On its common stock, which was backed by neither tangible nor intangible values, the American Snuff Company was able to pay dividends of 10 per cent in 1903, and gradually increased them to 27 per cent by 1910. In the cigarette and tobacco fields the yields were as large. Since earnings made their spectacular leap between 1900 and 1903, when taxes were reduced, it is difficult to ascribe the large profits to anything other than

---

[29] Between 1901 and 1903 increases of about one cent per pound in the cost of leaf tobacco for plug and smoking afforded a slight offset.

[30] In 1910, when small increases in taxes appeared, the monopoly passed the tax on to the consumer in the case of some products and absorbed it in other cases.

[31] *Report of the Commissioner of Corporations on the Tobacco Industry*, Part III, pp. 28–31.

[32] *Ibid.*, pp. 2–3.

[33] *Report of the Commissioner of Corporations on the Tobacco Industry*, Part II, pp. 28–31.

monopoly. This conclusion is affirmed by the failure of the combine to earn over 8 per cent in the cigar field, where it had to meet the test of strong competing companies.

The financial group, which had continually improved its control of the common stock of the combination, fared quite well. In eighteen years, investment made in the common stock of the original American Tobacco Company enjoyed cash dividends amounting to 400 per cent, stock dividends of 100 per cent, and an appreciation in value of close to 600 per cent.

The monopoly tribute exacted in each individual purchase of tobacco appears insignificant. If cigarette profits had been reduced to normal levels the price of a package of twenty cigarettes would have been only about a cent and a quarter lower. But the aggregate effects on the consumer, on other consumption goods industries, and on employment and production in the tobacco industry were considerable. By 1910, competitive prices for cigarettes would have saved the smoker a very respectable total—approximately four million dollars annually.[34] For all tobacco products the monopoly "tax" probably approached twenty million dollars.

If the economic effects stopped here, with the consumer piling up his little contributions to Messrs. Duke, Ryan, Whitney and Widener, the harm might not appear to have been very great.[35] Possibly these gentlemen could make better use of the consumer's funds than he could himself.

But implicit in this situation is injury to the tobacco industry and to the general economy of the country. High prices and profits could be realized only through restricting the development of the tobacco industry. If it had been free from control it would have grown to greater size, so that its larger output would have sold at prices that just covered cost, including a normal rate of profit. To obtain monopoly profits the combine had to restrain the growth of the industry so that a restricted output could command abnormally high prices. Some labor and capital had to be held out of the tobacco field, and were thereby forced into less valuable employments in other industries.

In a number of instances during the early years of the cigarette monopoly, plants were closed as they were acquired, and the practice was continued as the combination spread. Between 1900 and 1906, the Continental bought out six firms at a cost of over one and a half million

---

[34] *Ibid.*, Part III, p. 155.

[35] In 1906, 52 per cent of the 402,424 outstanding common shares were distributed as follows: A. N. Brady, 33,334; O. H. Payne, 33,334; P. A. B. Widener, 33,000; Moore and Schley, 31,452; Thos. F. Ryan, 30,000; W. C. Whitney Estate, 29,034; J. B. Duke, 25,000. Cf. *Report of the Commissioner of Corporations on the Tobacco Industry*, Part I, p. 202.

dollars and proceeded at once to close them.[36] When the combine was being prosecuted for monopoly, the Supreme Court commented on "the remarkable fact" that it used "the disbursement of enormous amounts of money to acquire plants, which on being purchased were not utilized but were immediately closed."[37] The court should not have been surprised. A measure of artificial scarcity had to be created to wring monopoly profits out of the buyer.

The Efficiency of Plant Operations

Except for the cigar branch, the tobacco industry required moderately large-scale plants for low-cost production. Skilled management was needed for production and marketing, and it could be supported economically only by a large output. In addition, machine methods created a technique that required large plants for optimum size. And then, efficient operation of these plants at their optimum scale required a considerable output. These conditions were unquestionably conducive to monopoly, but there is no evidence that monopoly made any significant contribution to the growth of an efficient large-scale industry.

It appears that the combine was made up in considerable part of plants that had reached efficient size before they were acquired. In 1898, it possessed five plants turning out over five million pounds of smoking and chewing tobacco, while independents operated seven. Two years later it had ten large plants, and only one independent achieved the five million figure. But the growing monopoly was neither responsible for nor necessary to the development of its large-scale plants. They were bought after they had been built up in competitive circumstances.[38] The cigarette industry did gain larger plants as a result of monopoly. Six factories were acquired in the formation of the American Tobacco Company, and production was gradually concentrated in four of them. Later a larger part of the output came from the two plants located in New York City and Richmond. Even then, a half-dozen independents operated plants that must be classed as large, with annual outputs of over fifty million cigarettes.[39]

Since the combine itself operated two or more plants in every line, it would appear that no branch of tobacco manufacture required a single monopoly-sized plant to achieve large-scale economies. Furthermore, there is no reason to believe that the large independents did not compare favorably. J. B. Duke testified before the Industrial Commission that

---

[36] United States v. American Tobacco Company (1911), 221 U. S. 106, 165.
[37] Ibid., pp. 166–167.
[38] Report of the Commissioner of Corporations on the Tobacco Industry, Part I, p. 355.
[39] Ibid., Part I, Table 42, p. 340.

fixed costs were not "very large" in tobacco manufacture, and therefore concentration in a few plants would reduce costs very little.[40] And independents insisted that any advantages possessed by the plants of the combine were "far more than offset by reason of the expensive way in which they do business and advertise."[41]

Combination Economies

Horizontal expansion in cigarette manufacture and a similar program in other tobacco fields placed an impressive combination in the hands of the Consolidated and, later, the American Tobacco Company. Finally, some vertical integration appeared when the combine organized the United Cigar Stores and acquired plants manufacturing licorice, tinfoil, tobacco bags, and boxes.

Excursions into the supply fields do not seem to have brought any appreciable integration economies. The combine did gain a considerable advantage from monopolizing the manufacture of licorice, which was an important material for plug manufacture.[42] With 95 per cent of the industry controlled, it was able to increase the costs of competing plug producers while taking monopoly profits from the subsidiary.[43] Other supply materials could be obtained as cheaply and satisfactorily in the open market. The combine may have exercised control and possessed advantage, however, in buying leaf tobacco.

The union of marketing and manufacture did bring some economic advantages. Cigars were being made by a large number of producers under a great variety of brands. In order to carry the many brands demanded, the retailer needed a large margin between the manufacturer's price and the retail price to cover his costs. Commonly, for a five-cent cigar the manufacturer received two and one-half cents and the retailer a similar amount. By organizing over four hundred retail stores the combine was able both to reduce the number of brands and to simplify the marketing organization.[44] Real savings were made which, of course, were not shared with the consumer. On the whole, however, integration economies do not seem to have been large. They apparently did not

---

[40] *Report of the Industrial Commission*, p. 328.

[41] *Ibid.*, p. 309, testimony of Mr. Hugh Campbell, President of the United States Tobacco Company.

[42] Licorice made up between 6 and 16 per cent of the factory cost of plug manufacture.

[43] In 1906, New York State successfully prosecuted the leading licorice subsidiary of the combine, MacAndrew, Forbes and Company, as being in restraint of trade, and the price of licorice was subsequently reduced. *Cf.* Jacobstein, *op. cit.*, p. 128.

[44] The United Cigar Stores, capitalized at $4,200,000, was merely the largest of twenty-one subsidiaries in the marketing branch.

impress the organizers of the combine. In 1901, Duke was inclined to claim nothing for his organization on this score.[45]

By its mere size, gained from either vertical or horizontal growth, the American Tobacco Company was able to seize some advantage. It collected an able group of tobacco men in organizing the cigarette trust, and added others as it spread. It is true that, in many cases, when plants were acquired to suppress competitors, the proprietors were bound by contract to stay out of tobacco manufacture for a period of years. But in others, such as the purchase of the R. J. Reynolds Company, the combine was careful to leave Reynolds in charge of its operations. It is possible that only a concern with very large sales could employ costly specialists for the purchasing, producing, and marketing functions. It is worth noting, however, that control of the vast organization slipped out of the hands of the tobacco men who had formed the original combination. By 1898, except for Duke, the dominant figures in the concern were outside financiers such as Oliver E. Payne, who prepared himself for an important rôle in tobacco manufacture by serving in an executive capacity in the Standard Oil monopoly, and William C. Whitney, who gained his training as Secretary of the Navy in Cleveland's cabinet.

The development of the United Cigar Stores casts little credit on the combine's management. George J. Whelan was refused support and almost opposed when he pioneered the development of the retail organization. Only when the stores were an assured success did the American Tobacco Company buy its way into their control and throw its financial strength behind their expansion.[46]

Once embarked in retailing, the combine possessed some advantage over small companies in turning out a complete line of tobacco products. Shipping and handling costs could be somewhat reduced, and some general advertising could be done to push a number of products. Since different tobacco products and different brands were usually produced in specialized plants, savings in freight were not material. Similarly, the general policy of marketing a large number of the brands that had been acquired called for a great deal of specialized advertising and reduced advertising savings.

Size also permitted cheaper buying of some materials in large lots. Although leaf tobacco, supplying most of the raw material cost, was sold to all buyers at auction prices the combine may have possessed some advantage over small concerns.

Finally, it must be noted that it was not the large concern but independent companies that developed the chief by-product of tobacco manufacture. From the scrap and waste product of cigar-making, several

[45] *Report of the Industrial Commission*, pp. 327–329.
[46] Jenkins, *op. cit.*, pp. 117–119.

small independents arose in Ohio and West Virginia to produce a cheap form of chewing tobacco. After 1903, the American Tobacco Company bought its way into the field. It never gained a dominant position, and never enjoyed any particular success, as competing companies kept its earnings down to moderate figures.[47]

The Wastes of Competition

By reducing competitive advertising and the duplication in selling organization typical of competition, the monopoly was able to lower merchandising costs. It should not, however, be given credit for eliminating the huge marketing expenditures made on cut-throat competition before combination appeared. The "cigarette war" of 1889 and the "plug war" of 1894–1897 were very costly, and were ended by the appearance of a monopoly combine. But they were undertaken as a deliberate step to create monopoly, and their huge cost in money and disorder must be charged against the combinations.

Once it had obtained control of the market, the American Tobacco Company made material savings in merchandising. This gain is quite apparent in a comparison of its costs and those of the competing companies that appeared after its dissolution in 1911. The American Snuff Company was broken into three separate parts, while the remaining assets of the combine were largely assigned to four companies. These seven "successor" companies enjoyed as low costs as had the combine in all respects save in selling and advertising.[48] Factory costs were as low in 1912 and 1913 as in 1909 and 1910. Leaf costs were about the same. But, in the latter period, selling expenses increased slightly and advertising expenses markedly. In 1910, the combination spent approximately eleven million dollars on advertising, while its successors spent over twenty-three millions annually. As a result, the ratio of advertising expense to sales income was nearly doubled.

Increases were particularly large in the cigarette field. While manufacturing costs dropped from $1.70 to $1.66 per thousand between 1910 and 1912, the selling cost rose from seventeen to nineteen cents, and advertising costs from sixty to eighty-seven cents.[49] Other products, except flat plug and fine-cut tobacco, showed similar though smaller changes.

In conclusion, it seems that in marketing alone could monopoly claim any advantage over competitive industry. It is impossible to measure the economic loss caused by the restrictive policy that accompanied these

---

[47] *Report of the Commissioner of Corporations on the Tobacco Industry,* Part I, p. 246.

[48] *Ibid.,* Part III, pp. 17–18.

[49] *Ibid.,* Table 127, p. 324.

gains. To make its high monopoly profits, the monopoly restrained the expansion of the industry as demand grew, and profitable opportunity for employment was deliberately denied to labor and capital. It seems that this waste would far outweigh the savings made in marketing. And it must be remembered that these savings are not shared with the consumer. It appears that other large-scale economies, realized by the combine as the market expanded, would have appeared equally well under competitive conditions.

THE STRUCTURE OF THE INDUSTRY SINCE 1911

The Dissolution Decree

In May, 1911, the Supreme Court held the American Tobacco Company a monopoly in violation of the Sherman Act. On the Court devolved the duty of preparing some sort of decree so that "such violation shall be enjoined or otherwise prohibited."[50] An injunction forbidding the company to do business or a forced liquidation would have effected a remedy, but would have injured the property rights of innocent investors and seriously hurt labor and the consumer.

The alternative lay in some plan of reorganization for the American Tobacco Company which would remove monopoly without serious injury to the industry. For the preparation of such a plan the Supreme Court remanded the case to the Circuit Court, where the Department of Justice had won its opening battle with the combine.[51] Somehow this court had to find a plan of dissolution that would eliminate monopoly and still would have, as the Supreme Court directed, "proper regard for the vast interests of private property . . . vested in many persons . . . by way of stock ownership or otherwise."[52]

The task was a difficult one. The company's monopoly rested both in its stockholdings in companies controlling snuff, tinfoil, and licorice manufacture, and in its outright ownership of factories producing cigarettes, little cigars, and various kinds of tobacco products. While separation of the parent and its subsidiaries would have been relatively easy, it would also have been useless. It would have left control of the major products untouched, and probably would have put the stocks controlling the subsidiaries in the hands of the small group controlling the parent company. Successful dissolution obviously required the breakup of the parent concern.

Conferences between representatives of the Court, the company, and

---

[50] The Sherman Act, Section 4.

[51] United States *v.* American Tobacco Company *et al.*, Circuit Court, Southern District of New York, 164 Fed. Rep. 700, November 7, 1908.

[52] United States *v.* American Tobacco Co., *et al.*, 221 U. S. 185.

the Department of Justice brought forth a tentative plan. It was modified slightly after public hearings, and then, in November, 1911, was issued as a formal decree of the Court.[53] It provided, first, for at least two companies in each of the fields dominated by subsidiaries. For example, the American Snuff Company was forced to hand over certain of its plants and brands to two new corporations in return for eight million dollars of their common and preferred stock. This stock was not to be held by the American Snuff Company, but was to be distributed to its stockholders. Secondly, plants of the parent were divided between it and two new corporations—the P. Lorillard Company and the Liggett and Myers Tobacco Company.[54] The capital stocks of the new corporations were given to the American Tobacco Company with the general provision that they be distributed to its stockholders. Thirdly, the American Tobacco Company was required to dispose of its holding in both the British-American Tobacco Company and the Imperial Tobacco Company, and to end its market-sharing agreements with the former. Finally, the decree gave voting rights to the preferred stock of the American Tobacco Company in order to reduce the control possessed by the half-dozen large common stockholders. These various rearrangements were protected by a number of court injunctions which forbade re-conveyance of the properties, any centralization of the control of the separate companies, joint operating arrangements, the use of dummy companies, exclusive dealing, and coöperation between the American and English companies.[55]

Of the fourteen successor companies created by the decree, seven held places of outstanding importance in the industry. Their position in the various branches of tobacco manufacture is apparent from the table on page 203.

It appears that the decree left a very highly concentrated industry. In snuff three successor companies of approximately equal size completely dominated the field. Independents carried on less than 8 per cent of the business. In all other lines, except cigars, the "big four" towered over all competitors. Three of them were represented in the manufacture of cigarettes, and the smallest retained more business than that done by all other companies. Three were left in an outstanding position in plug production. As manufacturers of smoking tobacco, and also fine-cut, one of the four equalled the size of all independents and, except for

---

[53] United States v. American Tobacco Company et al., 191 Fed. Rep. 371.

[54] A seventh large company appeared alongside these when the semi-independent R. J. Reynolds Company was completely separated with the end of stockholding in it by the American.

[55] The several companies and their officers were enjoined for five years by four additional provisions against: (1) interlocking managements or directorates; (2) common purchasing or selling agents; (3) interlocking stock acquisitions; and (4) purchase of the property or the brands of any successor company by another.

Table 6
DIVISION OF THE TOBACCO BUSINESS OF THE UNITED STATES ACCORDING
TO VALUE[56]

	Percentage in Value
Snuff	
American Snuff Co.	35.55
Helme Company	28.95
Weyman & Bruton	27.68
Others never in any way connected with the combination	7.82
Cigarettes	
American Tobacco Co.	33.15
Liggett & Myers	21.03
Lorillard Co.	26.02
Others never in any way connected with the combination	19.80
Plug Tobacco	
American Tobacco Co.	22.98
Liggett & Myers	37.84
Lorillard Co.	4.64
Reynolds Tobacco Co.	15.49
Others never in any way connected with the combination	19.05
Fine-Cut Tobacco	
American Tobacco Co.	13.52
Liggett & Myers	36.26
Lorillard Co.	29.57
Others never in any way connected with the combination	20.65
Smoking Tobacco	
American Tobacco Co.	40.53
Liggett & Myers	16.47
Lorillard Co.	18.88
Reynolds Tobacco Co.	2.73
Others never in any way connected with the combination	21.39

Reynolds, the others outranked the rest of the industry. In addition, two successor companies controlled 90 per cent of the sales of licorice and one, the Conley Foil Company, completely overshadowed all others in the production of tinfoil.

The concentration of business was even greater than the table suggests. In many instances the big companies completely dominated some important grade or class of the various products.[57] The most expensive and the cheapest grades of Turkish cigarettes were almost altogether in the hands of the American Tobacco Company. Lorillard controlled the sale of the middle grade, and Liggett and Myers the sale of cigarettes made from domestic tobacco and blends of domestic and Turkish.[58]

Concentrated ownership also survived. In 1906, seven large holdings controlled 52 per cent of the common shares of the American Tobacco Company. In ordering the distribution of company holdings to individuals, the Court changed the voting rights of some stocks, but not sufficiently to alter the situation. The twenty-five individuals who were

[56] United States v. American Tobacco Co. et al., 191 Fed. Rep. 371, 411 (1911).
[57] Retailing was powerfully influenced by the United Cigar Store organization, which was left intact.
[58] Cf. Stevens, op. cit., pp. 511–512.

defendants in the anti-trust suit held between 28 and 45 per cent of the voting shares in the various successor companies. While the percentage had been reduced, it was still large enough to constitute control of all the companies except in unusual circumstances.[59]

Independent companies argued that an effective cure for monopoly required ownership of the various successor companies by distinct groups of individuals.[60] But the lower Court observed that the Supreme Court had sanctioned common ownership in the dissolution of the Standard Oil Company. It insisted, therefore, that removal of direct monopoly control would meet the requirement of the Sherman Act. It denied that Congress had given the courts "any authority for the proposition that this court may seize the property of private persons who may have offended against the statute and sell it under conditions which would preclude the . . . owner of the equity from bidding at the sale so as to compel the purchaser to pay a reasonable price for it."[61]

Recent Changes

In the past twenty-five years the tobacco industry has been affected by several important changes, but it seems that the more it changes, the more it remains the same. Production methods and consumption habits have been seriously modified, the large firms have moved into new relative positions, and ownership has been materially altered. But both business and control remain concentrated as they were in 1911.

While machine methods have been improved in all branches of the industry, the main technical change has affected cigar production. In 1917 a satisfactory cigar-making machine was patented, with revolutionary effects for the industry.[62] Experienced hand cigar-makers have been displaced or are maintaining a precarious place at very low wages. Small companies have been adversely affected by the great capital needed to acquire machinery and to organize large production and marketing organizations.[63] The number of plants has been cut in half in the last fifteen years, and large plants with annual capacities of over forty mil-

---

[59] *Ibid.*, p. 504.

[60] *Ibid.*, pp. 485–486.

[61] United States *v.* American Tobacco Company *et al.*, 191 Fed. Rep. 371, 383.

[62] National Recovery Administration, *The Tobacco Study* (Washington, D. C., lithographed, 1936), Chap. 5.

[63] Some machines are paid for through a royalty fee, but others have been sold. A machine capable of banding and wrapping over four thousand cigars per hour reputedly sold for $5500 in 1930; a rolling machine sold for $7500, and a machine which "bunched" the cigar filler sold for $1000 to $2200. *Cf.* Reavis Cox, *Competition in the American Tobacco Industry* (New York, Columbia University Press, 1933), pp. 51–53.

lion cigars have trebled.[64] It can be expected that concentration will
develop further as the machine makes inroads into that half of the industry that still uses hand methods. And as this occurs the former individualistic conditions may be seriously modified.

In the cigar machine field, competition will inevitably travel a rocky
road. The International Cigar Machinery Company survived the 1911
dissolution with various patents of the old combine. Recently its machines, manufactured by the American Machine and Foundry Company,
have been responsible for over 40 per cent of the total output of cigars.
It acquired its major competitor, the Universal Tobacco Machine Company, and now faces only one rival in the form of a small branch of a
Swedish company.

Cigar manufacture has not only had to absorb the effects of a technical revolution, but has suffered from a remarkable change in consumption habits. From its favored position of earlier years the cigar has
fallen into relative disfavor. In sharp contrast, cigarette production has
jumped tremendously. It has taken an outstanding lead, possessing a
value far in excess of that of all other tobacco products.[65] The change
in consumers' taste is strikingly shown in the following figures, indicating
the millions of pounds of tobacco leaf used for various tobacco products
in 1905 and 1946:[66]

Year	Cigarettes	Cigars	Tobacco and Snuff	Total
1905	12	124	315	451
1946	1,001	138	168	1,307

While the total use of leaf tobacco has grown threefold, cigar consumption has increased very slightly and tobacco and snuff show a very
considerable decline. Cigarettes have grown in popularity so as to use
three times as much leaf tobacco as all other tobacco products.

While production methods and consumer tastes have been changing
the leading companies have enjoyed varying fortunes. In the important cigarette field, the four successor companies still hold their dominant
position. The importance of individual companies, however, has been
materially altered. Given no cigarette business at all in 1911, the Reynolds Company in recent years has been supplying close to half the
cigarettes smoked in the country. It introduced the Camel brand, along
with some others, shortly after the dissolution of 1911, and by concen-

---

[64] In 1921, 84 per cent of the total cigar production came from plants with
capacities under forty million cigars annually. In 1934, only 45 per cent came from
these small and medium-sized plants. Cf. National Recovery Administration, op.
cit., p. 147.

[65] In 1935 manufacturers' sales stood at the following figures: Cigarettes, $806,003,-
000; cigars, $229,204,000; chewing, smoking and snuff, $170,697,000. Census of Business, Distribution of Manufacturers' Sales, Bureau of Census (1937).

[66] Statistical Abstract of the United States, 1946, p. 856.

trating on it through the twenties moved into first place. Liggett and Myers has stayed in the race with Chesterfields, and the American Tobacco successfully backed Lucky Strike. Only the Lorillard Company, assigned 16 per cent of the total cigarette business, has been unable to hold its place. In 1915, it tried unsuccessfully to popularize the "Tiger" brand, and after 1926 enjoyed only a temporary success with an expensive advertising program for Old Golds.

The competitive position of the "big three" in cigarette production shows an increasing concentration of business and a share of the market for each of them that fluctuates somewhat. The three major brands, Lucky Strikes, Camels, and Chesterfields, supplied 66 per cent of cigarette sales in 1939 and 79 per cent in 1947.[67] Lucky Strikes have led in the years following the close of World War II, but their percentage importance varied considerably—from 29 per cent to 31 per cent. Camels have shown the biggest variation, holding 27 per cent of the market in 1946, 29.5 per cent in 1947, and 27.5 per cent in 1948. Old Golds fell into fifth place below Philip Morris with 8 per cent. The only serious attack on the position of the "big three" was planned by the United Cigar Stores. It managed to organize most of the important independent brands under a subsidiary, the American Products Corporation. This company acquired control of the Falk Company with the Herbert Tareyton Brand, an important minority control of the American interests of Philip Morris, and control of other smaller producers. Unfortunately the parent's independence was short-lived. It disappeared in 1923 when the American Tobacco Company leased the Tareyton and Melachrino Brands for ninety-nine years and acquired the physical assets of the company. A few years later, in gaining control of the Union and United Tobacco Company, the American acquired the brands of the Philip Morris Company and the Continental Tobacco Company and then proceeded to lease them to the Union Tobacco Company.[68]

While dynamic changes have altered the place of individual companies without decreasing the concentration of business, they have also changed the character of control in the three large companies without decreasing its concentration. Each of the three has a large percentage of non-voting stock. The American Tobacco has the least, but only 43 per cent of its stock possesses the voting privilege. And the Reynolds Company has managed to disfranchise nine-tenths of its stockholders.

With this as a base, management control has been built up in each of the big companies. In the Reynolds Company it is effected by stock ownership. Here 35 per cent of the voting stock is held by management officers and directors.[69] In 1935, W. N. Reynolds, serving as director and

---

[67] *Business Week*, April 24, 1948, p. 78; January 29, 1949, p. 67.
[68] *Cf.* Cox, *op. cit.*, Appendix, The United Cigar Store Company.
[69] National Recovery Administration, *op. cit.*, Appendix 3.

as chairman of the executive committee, held 72,300 voting shares, being second only to Bowman Gray, his fellow-director. James A. Gray, who served both as director and as president, had the third largest holding, with 60,000 shares. In the other two companies control is not based on ownership of the strategic voting shares, but is as firmly vested in the management group. Officers and directors owned less than 4 per cent of the voting stock, but the management officers made up the boards of directors. Seventeen officials of the American Tobacco and twelve of the Liggett and Myers Company dominated their boards and thereby controlled their companies. They represented self-perpetuating bodies that were not disturbed by the wishes of the owners. All told, probably a dozen of the dominant men in these three management groups controlled 95 per cent of the tobacco business of the country.

11

Aluminum

An unusual affinity for oxygen hid aluminum from the knowledge of scientists until the nineteenth century. In experiments conducted in 1807 Sir Humphry Davy was unable to prepare pure aluminum, but he was convinced of the presence of a metal in a clay-like material and named it aluminum.[1] Later research revealed the metal in great quantities but never in a pure state. Its various compounds are numerous, ranging from very common aluminum oxides to the more pretentious ruby and sapphire. The commercially important aluminum oxide is found in bauxite, a clay ore which also contains mixtures of iron, titanium, and other materials. The metal clings to its oxygen with such tenacity that even minute quantities of the pure metal were not produced before 1825, and its commercial production on even a moderate scale is a development of the last forty years.

The ordinary smelting process, which uses coke to reduce iron oxides to the pure metal, was useless for the more tenacious aluminum. As a result, early nineteenth-century experiments turned to various chemical attacks on aluminum clays. By 1825, the use of magnesium yielded minute globules of the pure metal. Another quarter of a century saw a production of thirty pounds a year, and the shining metal roused a great deal of interest in the Paris Exposition of 1855. But it still ranked close to the precious metals, with a cost of one hundred dollars a pound. The following thirty years saw no essential change in the young industry. The use of sodium increased the output and reduced costs materially, but commercial use was seriously restricted by the competition of much cheaper metals.

Until 1883 little or no aluminum was produced in the United States. Imports were small, ranging between three hundred and five hundred pounds a year, at prices between eleven and fourteen dollars a pound.[2]

---

[1] J. D. Edwards, F. C. Frary, and Z. Jeffries, *The Aluminum Industry* (New York, McGraw-Hill Book Company, 1930), Chaps. 1 and 2.
[2] Joseph W. Richards, *Aluminum* (Philadelphia, H. C. Baird & Co., 1887), p. 40.

The high costs of the chemical industry and the tremendous advances made in the development of the electric dynamo turned a number of American scientists to the study of electrical processes for the manufacture of aluminum. By 1885, the Cowles Electric Smelting and Aluminum Company of Cleveland was successfully operating an aluminum alloy process. Carbon and the pure aluminum oxide, called alumina, were treated together in an electric furnace at high temperatures to reduce the oxide to pure aluminum. High temperatures, however, made it necessary to collect the volatile aluminum in some more stable metal, usually copper or iron. As a result, only copper or iron alloys could be produced. The most popular of these, aluminum bronze, contained less than 20 per cent of aluminum in alloy with copper, and was even more expensive than pure aluminum.

The high temperature required to keep alumina in a molten state barred the obvious method of obtaining the pure metal through electrolysis. This barrier soon disappeared. A year after he graduated from Oberlin College, Charles Martin Hall found that the chemical cryolite would hold alumina in a liquid state at relatively low temperatures. In a carbon-lined tank it was possible, then, to place a solution of alumina and cryolite and pass an electric current between the lining and carbon rods immersed in the solution. Oxygen was deposited on the latter, and the pure aluminum sank to the bottom of the tank, from which it could be removed.

Hall had difficulty in interesting anyone in his discovery, and the electrolytic process was not immediately developed. The Cowles Company held an option on the process for a year while Hall worked in its Lockport (N. Y.) plant, developing and improving apparatus and materials. The company could not be persuaded to accept the potential fortune that was being offered it, and Hall turned to a small group of engineers in Pittsburgh. A few friends raised twenty thousand dollars and organized the Pittsburgh Reduction Company in 1888.

THE GROWTH OF CONCENTRATION

In its first week of operations the young company produced a hundred pounds of aluminum, which sold for five dollars a pound. The following thirty years saw many changes in American industry, but none more striking than the lusty growth of this infant. By 1907, when its name was changed to the Aluminum Company of America, the twenty thousand dollars of capital had grown to twenty millions, and two decades later, the twenty millions had become two hundred and fifty millions. Meanwhile, production had grown to over three million pounds a week, and the price had dropped to twenty-five cents a pound.

Until 1905 expansion was mainly vertical, as the Pittsburgh Reduction Company entered the various stages of the industry. From its entry into the electrolytic reduction of aluminum in 1888 it expanded backward to develop its own mines, ore refineries, and electric power sites, and forward into the manufacture of semi-finished and finished goods. For several years it bought its raw material, alumina, in Germany, and then from newly-discovered bauxite reserves in Georgia and Alabama. By 1894 it organized the Georgia Bauxite Company and began the purchase of ore reserves. As these acquisitions proved inadequate to meet the growing demand for aluminum, imports of French bauxite were used and the company went on to acquire large holdings in new fields in Arkansas.

Until 1902 the refining of bauxite, to free it of silicon, iron oxide, and other impurities, was done by an independent chemical company. Then, with the construction of a large plant in East St. Louis, this step in the process was undertaken. For electric power in its first reduction plant in Pittsburgh the company generated electricity with steam power. In 1894 it moved to New Kensington, outside Pittsburgh, in order to use cheap supplies of natural gas. A year later a new reduction works was constructed at Niagara Falls, and power was purchased from the Niagara Falls Power Company. By 1897, reduction capacity had been trebled, and the company set out to develop its own power plants. Its first important acquisition was made at Shawinigan Falls on the St. Meurice River in the Province of Quebec.[3]

The company also began to produce finished and semi-finished products. The original plant was expanded to turn out aluminum castings, wire, tubing, sheets, and cooking utensils from the ingot produced in the reduction works. These lines expanded markedly and were organized under two subsidiaries, the United States Aluminum Company and the Aluminum Cooking Utensil Company.

The Advantages of Integration

When the process of integration was finished the company dominated all stages of the industry. Since 1905 it has expanded with the growing industry so as to maintain undisputed leadership. In view of the monopoly charges leveled against the company in recent years, we may find something of value in a study of the motives and forces contributing to its growth. If monopoly exists today, some of the reasons for its existence will be found in these early years. Was it forced by conditions in the industry, or was it created by the controlling group for the comforts and profits it would bring to them?

Patents covering the electrolytic reduction of alumina gave the Pittsburgh Reduction Company a monopoly in the manufacture of aluminum

_____
[3] Operated by a subsidiary, the Northern Aluminum Company of Canada.

ingot for the first nineteen years of its life. At the time Hall was experimenting in the United States, Paul L. T. Héroult was working along similar lines in France. The two men brought their research to successful conclusions at about the same time. Héroult patented the process in various European countries and Hall in the United States.

Hall and his associates were not left in peace to enjoy the patent protection. The Cowles brothers, regretting their refusal to develop the Hall discoveries, acquired certain patents from C. S. Bradley. These gave their owners monopoly over processes using electric current to heat and melt metals for electrolysis. In the Hall process, heat was not needed. However, electricity used to electrolyze the solution of cryolite and alumina inevitably but incidentally generated heat. In 1903 a suit for infringement brought the Cowles brothers three million dollars in damages. As matters stood, the two patents were necessary for the reduction of aluminum. The *impasse* could have been met by a cross-licensing arrangement under which both companies would have the power to produce aluminum ingot. Both were experienced operators, and the presence of two independent manufacturers would have left some semblance of competition in the industry. But the Cowles brothers were willing to surrender the Bradley patents for a good price, and entered an agreement to do so. Thus until 1909 the Pittsburgh Reduction Company continued as the sole producer under the protection of patents.

A number of factors combined to force the company to expand beyond its title rôle. First, there was no market for aluminum ingot when it started operations. The demand of jewelry and novelty manufacturers was small and limited in its possibilities. Neither did the alloy market, quickly captured from the Cowles Company, offer an adequate outlet. While the Pittsburgh Reduction Company was offering aluminum ingot in thousand-pound lots at two dollars a pound, no one was interested in its fabrication. In fact, few people believed it could be produced in such unheard-of quantities. Before the company could realize anything on its patent monopoly, it had to develop sheet mills and foundries and find markets for wire, tubing, castings, and other finished products. Independent companies showed no signs of developing these markets, and the Reduction Company had no recourse but expansion into the semi-finished and finished stages of the industry. As it took the lead in these fields it found outlets for 58,000 pounds of ingot in 1890 and four million pounds in 1900.

In the mining and refining of bauxite there is no reason to believe that independent companies would have failed to keep step with the strides made in the reduction branch. But a second factor, the economies of integration, supplied reasons for vertical growth of the Reduction Company. These economies appeared in a variety of forms. Savings in testing bauxite and alumina were achieved by the integration of the first three stages of the industry. The character of bauxite determines the refining requirements, and the purity of the alumina determines the quality of aluminum ingot. It is probable that independent mining and refining companies would have offered less satisfactory materials for reduction, and more extensive analysis would have been forced on both seller and buyer, with inevitable increases in cost.

Particular advantages seem to have been derived from the integration of power, reduction, and fabrication. The capacity of power and reduction plants could be adjusted so as to assure economical and continuous operation of both. In addition, the knowledge of aluminum markets gained in the fabrication field allowed the company to regularize the use made of its existing reduction capacity and to plan capital expansion with a high degree of safety.

Vertical expansion brought a third advantage in the form of certain savings of large-scale production. In various stages a number of competing companies would have prevented plants from growing to optimum size. For the best use of both equipment and management, large plants were required in the mining, refining, and power stages of the industry. But the small market for aluminum would not support many producers and keep their plants at optimum size. Possibly the reduction company could have bought from one or two large producers in each field, but the vertical expansion assured plants of adequate size.

A fourth factor seems to have been important in the development of power sites by the reduction company. Independent power companies would tend to locate in population and industrial areas in which they could find a varied and assured demand. They would be unwilling to move to isolated locations where they would be wholly dependent on one buyer or might find no buyer. But at out-of-the-way points, site costs are very low. A reduction plant able to take the whole output of power would find a regular and cheap source of energy. Since at least 20 per cent of the cost of the reduction process is for power, this consideration has been important. It made the Pittsburgh Reduction Company willing to move its reduction plants first from Pittsburgh and later from Niagara Falls, and supplied a reason for placing them together with power plants in undeveloped areas.

Finally, only through vertical expansion was it possible in the early years of the industry to build a large combination capable of supporting much-needed research and specialized management. Large sums spent on research were well repaid, but could not have been afforded on the same scale by independents.

Horizontal Expansion Between 1905 and 1940

In detail, the expansion that occurred after 1905 comprises a complicated story. Simply stated, it appears as a horizontal growth in each of the stages of the industry. It is indicated by the capital expansion of the parent company from six to two hundred and fifty millions of dollars and in the appearance of approximately seventy-five subsidiaries.

By 1905, bauxite mining in Georgia, Alabama, and Arkansas was dominated by four companies. The next decade saw the Aluminum Company build up huge ore reserves with the aid of these companies. It acquired controlling shares in the General Bauxite Company, which held the ore properties of the General Chemical Company. By contract the latter was guaranteed adequate bauxite for its chemical industry, and in turn it contracted that none of the ores it purchased would escape into the aluminum industry. Under similar contracts the Aluminum Company acquired the Republic Mining and Manufacturing Company from an abrasive manufacturer and entered a five-year contract to take 37,500 tons of alumina annually from the Pennsylvania Salt Manufacturing Company.[4]

Not content with these acquisitions, the Aluminum Company either leased or bought a large part of the extensive ore resources of British and Dutch Guiana. Purchase of the Bauxites du Midi gave it important holdings in France. Later acquisition of stock in Italian and Jugoslav companies added to its European holdings.

It is not easy to determine the significance of this policy. Possibly it represented nothing more than a desire for protection against an ore shortage. But possibly, since the company's patent monopoly had run out in 1909, it was designed to continue the monopoly through control of the raw material. There is even considerable difficulty in determining the percentage of known ore lands of the United States that is held by the company. At various times the Department of Justice has insisted that it is close to 90 per cent. Company officials have claimed that about half that figure would be correct. It is impossible to determine the commercially available reserves of ore, since its quality and location vary a great deal. As a result, the importance of the holdings of the Aluminum Company cannot be clearly fixed. But unless the company had a strangle-hold on the supply, there would seem to have been no reason for the restrictive agreements it entered into with the General Chemical Company and the Pennsylvania Salt Company. Furthermore, an experienced French company, intending to build and operate a reduction plant in North Carolina in 1912, planned on importing its own ore from France. Any ore lands it could acquire in the United States were too inferior to be worked. Whatever the motives of the Aluminum Company may have been, its purchases seem to have given it a monopoly control over American supplies of its raw material.

---

[4] Donald H. Wallace, *Market Control in the Aluminum Industry* (Cambridge, Mass., Harvard University Press, 1937), p. 104.

In the refining stage the company maintained its one plant at East St. Louis. It grew to huge size as the power and reduction plants placed increasing demands on it. Until 1905 the reduction works were located at Niagara Falls and Massena in New York State and at Shawinigan in Quebec Province. As rising power costs made Niagara Falls a less desirable location, the Massena plant was enlarged, and a million-dollar works was built at Alcoa in Tennessee. In addition, the North Carolina project of the French company was acquired,[5] and a new plant and a new town were built at Arvida on the Saguenay River in Quebec.

As the company added to its reduction capacity it acquired a number of power sites. In Quebec, before 1925, J. B. Duke of tobacco fame and Sir William Price had started the development of an excellent site on the Saguenay River. George Haskell, an important figure in the field of duralumin alloys, was negotiating with them with the intention of building a reduction plant. But the Aluminum Company moved onto the scene and Mr. Haskell was forgotten. It bought the original power company and shortly began generating power for the Arvida works. In a few years the original capacity of one hundred thousand horse-power was jumped to a million by the addition of other sites on the river.

The other major power development has been on the Little Tennessee River. Sites acquired in 1912 received little attention until 1928. Their development in recent years and increase in the capacity of the Massena works have raised the installed horse-power above the half-million mark and given the Company a reduction capacity for over one hundred and thirty thousand tons of metal per year.

All these developments were easily matched by the growth of the Aluminum Company in the manufacture of finished and semi-finished products. Sheet mills were constructed for aluminum and duralumin in New Jersey and Tennessee. An important plant at Massena took over the production of aluminum alloys into structural shapes. The Aluminum Manufacturing Company was organized in 1909 to consolidate four large foundry and casting companies, and by 1940 was doing approximately half the casting business of the country. Its output goes to the United States Aluminum Company, a wholly owned subsidiary of the Aluminum Company. In addition, 40 per cent of its stock is owned by the parent company.

The United States Aluminum Company was developed as the major

---

[5] Various troubles had delayed the construction plans of this French company until 1914, and then the war shut off its financial support in France. Failing to find the needed capital in England or the United States, it was forced to sell its partially constructed plants to the Aluminum Company. In view of the booming war demand for aluminum, it may appear strange that no American capital could have been found outside of the Aluminum Company to take over a very promising development. Or possibly American enterprisers did not feel that a competitor in this field would enjoy good health and a long life.

subsidiary in the production of finished products. It markets the well-known Wearever Brand of utensils through a selling subsidiary, the Aluminum Cooking Utensil Company. Its "competitor," the Aluminum Goods Manufacturing Company, produces the Mirro Brand and represents the consolidation of three of the largest utensil manufacturers. About 30 per cent of its voting stock is owned by the Aluminum Company.[6]

The parent company also extended its control into a number of firms in a variety of fields. It holds 100 per cent of the stock of five small railroad companies, fifteen power and public utility companies, one magnesium company, and one electric carbon company. In addition, it owns smaller percentages of control in other companies in these fields. It also owns about fifteen miscellaneous enterprises ranging from the Union Trust Company of East St. Louis to the Perfection Bake Shoppe, Inc. Finally, the Mellon family ownership of the Aluminum Company gives it extensive financial and business connections in other sections of American industry.

The Economics of Horizontal Expansion

There is no evidence that horizontal expansion brought any advantages similar to those achieved in the early period of integration. It appears that the optimum either for individual plants or for the combination as a whole did not require a size much beyond that enjoyed by the company in 1905. In mining, increase in the scale of operations effected few savings. Generally any increase in the capacity of mines called for proportional increases in equipment. Machinery and equipment are simple and were the same for the small and the large operator. In contrast, the refining stage, producing alumina, is highly mechanized. The treatment of bauxite with caustic soda and the subsequent steps in refining require considerable investment in boilers, vats, and kilns. When a capacity of fifteen to twenty thousand tons is achieved, however, a mere duplication of equipment and labor is required.[7] Plants with one-tenth the output of the East St. Louis refinery would be of optimum size.

The production of ingot aluminum through the electrolytic reduction of alumina is a simple process and requires neither specialized equipment nor management. Growth beyond a very small size merely results in the duplication of the tanks in which reduction takes place. The best scale will be determined by the amount of energy supplied by a power plant of optimum size. Large hydro-electric plants may turn out energy

<hr>

[6] For a description of the inter-corporate relations of the Aluminum Company and its subsidiaries see H. T. Warshow, *Representative Industries in the United States* (New York, Henry Holt and Company, 1928), p. 53.

[7] Wallace, *op. cit.*, p. 193.

more cheaply than small or medium-sized plants. If so, they must find
an outlet for their optimum scale production in large reduction works.
It was in the generation of power that the Aluminum Company came
nearest to finding economic justification for its growth. To utilize sites
with a large head and flow of water and with favorable features for dams
and penstocks the company found it necessary to build large reduction
works. It is conceivable that the whole market for aluminum might be
supplied most cheaply from one gigantic plant. In this case, the economies of scale would require a single firm of monopoly size. Between
1907 and 1912 the Aluminum Company came close to this position. It
acquired sites on the Long Sault section of the St. Lawrence River which
could have been economically developed to supply all the power requirements of the industry for at least a generation. It was not successful,
however, in gaining permission to dam the river. New York State looked
on the project with favor, but the American and Canadian national governments refused the necessary sanction. With that refusal disappeared
any chance of justifying its growth in power and reduction on the basis
of large-scale economies. As the company is now constituted, with a
number of reduction plants at widely separated points, its advantages
could only grow out of the combination of plants.

The same conclusion can be reached for the fabrication and finishing
branches of the industry. In both Europe and America a fairly large
number of such plants has been the rule. It is apparent that the economies accruing to large plants are not sufficient to overcome the advantage of locations near reduction works or near markets.

It seems safe to conclude that any advantages realized by the company must have come from the combination of plants. These might
appear in purchasing, marketing, research, saving cross-freights, and in
plant specialization. Since the company supplies itself with all its materials from ore and chemicals to carbon electrodes, economies in buying by the big combination are negligible. Marketing advantages also
seem to have been unimportant. Certainly, since 1914, independents
would have been able and willing to exploit the market for aluminum
products. While the Aluminum Company has vigorously pushed aluminum into new uses, particularly in the alloy field, its great size and power
restrained independents.

Advertising and sales expenses may have been reduced by the presence of the single firm, but the reduction would be small. In an expanding market with a standardized product, the selling efforts of a number
of independent companies would be almost entirely informative and
not merely competitive. As a result, the selling expense would not be
much greater than that of the horizontal combination.

Specialization in management, production, and marketing, which the
Aluminum Company has sponsored, could not be undertaken by small

firms. Most of the operations in the industry are simple, and a few managers are able to administer large aggregations of capital. In its expansion, however, the company has built beyond the minimum optimum scale, and management costs have grown at least proportionately with output. And since the techniques of the different stages are quite different, the combination has offered no savings in management expenses.

Small enterprises would not be able to specialize in developing new uses for aluminum. Research of this sort would lay destructively heavy costs on their small output. But research advantages do not continue to grow as size increases. The success of specialized firms in Europe and the United States suggests that independents of moderate size are at least as efficient as the big combine in turning out new alloys and new forms of finished aluminum.

Under certain conditions freight costs may be reduced by horizontal combination. Where demand in the market area immediately around a sheet mill, for example, is too small to take the output of optimum scale, the mill will penetrate distant markets where other mills are located. These latter may in turn do the same thing. The industry in the hands of a number of independent companies may use substantially more freight service than would be used by a horizontal combination with fewer plants. The great growth of markets after 1916 has taken most if not all of this saving from the Aluminum Company. In each of the market areas of the United States, demand has been great enough to support several plants at optimum scale.

A last claim concerns advantages in research. In recent years the Aluminum Company has tried to offset the bad publicity of impending anti-trust suits with advertisements pointing out the progressiveness of the company. Beyond any question these claims are justified. But the point at issue lies in another question. Could the same progressiveness have been achieved by a number of independent companies of medium size, or is it directly a product of the horizontal growth of the Aluminum Company? Integration before 1905 did add materially to its research powers. The problems of various stages were studied together and financial resources were assembled. Later growth into each field did not give the company anything more than a proportional increase in these powers. Four or five integrated concerns in the industry together would have been able to do as much. And it is reasonable to presume that competition between them would create greater reasons for progressiveness.

It appears that by 1914 at the latest the aluminum industry was large enough to support a number of independent companies at optimum size. The growth of the single dominant firm does not seem to have been needed for the efficiency of the industry. In other words, the industry was not a "natural" monopoly in the fashion of local telephone and street railway fields. The Aluminum Company grew to monopoly proportions with the first burst of expansion between 1905 and 1914, in which period the patent monopoly over the reduction stage expired. The loss of patent protection and the rapid horizontal growth appear to be associated events. Possibly the management may have been led astray to seek unrealizable economies, but its efficient record weighs against that explanation. More probably it sought to replace the lapsing patent control with overpowering size. Whatever the motives, it did achieve that result.

THE DOMINANCE OF THE SINGLE FIRM

Until 1945, when disposition of war-constructed plants materially altered the structure of the industry, the Aluminum Company dominated, if it did not completely monopolize, the American market for aluminum.[8] The presence of monopoly is never easy to prove, and it is never unqualified by some direct or indirect competition. The formidable size and the price and profit record of the Aluminum Company present evidence of a considerably qualified monopoly control. In the production of primary ingot it stood alone in the United States. No independent producer appeared after the projected French enterprise in North Carolina. Any competition it met came from one of three sources—imported ingot, secondary aluminum ingot re-melted from scrap, and other metals. The first of these showed some strength. At various times before the war imports were sufficiently large to force the Aluminum Company to reduce its price. In 1930, when the tariff was reduced one cent per pound, the domestic price was lowered by a similar amount. Before World War II imports supplied between 12 and 15 per cent of American consumption, and unquestionably provided a check on the national monopoly.

The re-melting of scrap was started in 1914 and has been of growing importance in recent years. Prior to shortages caused by the war it supplied about 35 per cent of the total ingot used in the United States. About 10 per cent of it came back to the Aluminum Company from its own fabricating plants and never got into the open market. In the opinion of Donald H. Wallace, no independent rolling mill could safely rely on the secondary market for supplies of ingot. A material percentage of the re-melt is not satisfactory for rolling, and periodically the supply is inadequate. In 1923, purchases of scrap by the Aluminum Company actually raised its price above primary ingot. At such times the independent fabricator, who had relied on the scrap supply, would be

---

[8] By 1942 scarcity of supplies created by the war brought forth government plans to spend over $350,000,000 in the construction of primary reduction plants. Actually the Federal Government spent $674,000,000 in plant for the expansion of the aluminum industry.

unable to get deliveries from the Aluminum Company. His only recourse would be the use of more expensive imported metal, with probable delays in its delivery. Despite these weaknesses the scrap market did qualify the monopoly. Except in periods of scarcity, it endowed demand for the ingot of the Aluminum Company with an elasticity it would not otherwise have possessed.

In many uses aluminum competes with copper, tin, brass, iron, and zinc. To a considerable extent these metals will be substituted for one another on the basis of their comparative prices. While existing independents who are manufacturing aluminum products may be harassed by this competition, they also receive a measure of protection from it. For if the Aluminum Company desired to expand the sale of ingot to independents, it must consider this competition in setting prices. Unfortunately, the company seems to have preferred to hold ingot prices above cost and expand the demand by developing new uses for aluminum. This was apparent in one of the big markets of the industry. In 1922, automobile manufacturers bought close to twenty thousand tons for use in crank-cases. By 1930, the market had shrunk to one-third. The aluminum industry apparently could find no defenses against the inroads made by the steel industry. Technical advances in steel were largely responsible, but the Aluminum Company, by drastic price reductions, might have retained a larger portion of this market for itself and for independent fabricators. Instead it failed to reduce prices as much as costs were being reduced.

The competition of other metals may not affect the price of aluminum ingot, for another reason. With products such as aluminum cable, which were produced exclusively by the Aluminum Company, prices could be cut without affecting the prices paid by independents for ingot. At times aluminum cable has been sold at prices below that of the metal from which the cable is made. In other words, the parent company can discriminate in favor of its subsidiaries and thereby expand certain markets without lowering ingot prices.

Study of the price and profit records of the company suggests that competitive forces have not been strong enough to create normal competitive conditions. From 1909 to 1935 net annual earnings ranged between −6.7 per cent and 30.6 per cent of total assets.[9] In two normal periods, unaffected by war prosperity or by cyclical depression (1909 to 1914 and 1923 to 1929), average earnings were 17.6 per cent and 10.2 per cent.

The smaller return earned in the second period does not indicate a stronger competition in the American industry. In the first place, investment increased materially, and earnings were small while new plants were being brought into full production. In the second place, reductions

[9] Wallace, *op. cit.*, Appendix C.

in price enjoyed by American consumers can be credited to a considerable extent to foreign and not domestic competition. A cartel of European producers organized in 1925 reduced prices in order to remove a temporary surplus, and the Aluminum Company was forced to follow suit so as to check imports of the metal. The strength of the domestic monopoly is attested by the price changes that occurred when tariff protection was altered. Before 1923 the Aluminum Company held its ingot prices slightly below the price of foreign metal, and thereby enjoyed the full two cents of protection offered by the tariff. When Congress decided that the company needed the protection of an additional three-cent tariff the corporation showed itself to be properly grateful. Its prices were increased by five cents per pound. In 1930, the import duty was reduced from five cents to four cents and prices were reduced one cent.

In regard to aluminum sheet, the company has been accused of lowering prices in order to embarrass competitors. The Baush Machine Tool Company complained that it had been forced to meet unfairly low prices in the sale of aluminum-alloy sheet. In a suit brought against the Aluminum Company it charged that ingot prices were held steady, while the fabricated sheet was sold at prices that did not leave sufficient margin to cover fabrication costs.[10] If the contention were true, the Aluminum Company could use profits from the sale of ingot to cover losses in the sheet business, while independent sheet manufacturers would suffer serious injury. Evidence submitted by the Baush Company was not conclusive, although the Aluminum Company had reduced the margin between ingot and sheet from 9.46 cents to 5.95 cents. It was not possible to show that the reductions were designed to restrain competitors. They might have been made to meet the competition of sheet steel and stainless steel or to expand the general use of aluminum sheet as costs of rolling were reduced.

Economic Effects of Monopoly

Both the presence and the economic injury of monopoly are attested by evidence of typical monopoly effects. Investment in ingot production was carefully restricted so that the output of optimum scale operations could be sold at prices above cost. During the period of patent monopoly, plant expansion lagged behind the growing demand. Then, following a few years of rapid expansion, capacity was again carefully restricted. After 1922 demand grew substantially, and an obviously inadequate investment was continued. Not until 1927 did the company, by plant expansion in the South, recognize the expanding market for its products. In the meantime, it resorted to the importation of some ingot and slow

---

[10] Baush Machine Tool Co. v. Aluminum Co. of America, 72 Fed. (2nd) 236 (1934).

deliveries to buyers. And even after capacity was doubled in the late twenties, the company restricted sales by reducing prices less than the amount of cost reductions. The extent of the restriction in capacity is suggested by the fortunes of the company in the depression. After a huge increase in investment was followed by the collapse of buying in the depression, it still made average earnings of over 3 per cent between 1930 and 1935.

This restrictive policy was inevitably projected into the finishing branches of the industry. Except for the help offered by imported aluminum and re-melted scrap, fabricators were forced to plan their output in view of the ingot situation. They suffered the injurious restriction of monopoly without any compensating benefit. In the short run, the quantity of their products taken by buyers was affected by the cost of ingot. In the long run, they may suffer from real decreases in demand as buyers turn more or less permanently to the use of other metals.

The Aluminum Company and the Law

In the course of its development the Aluminum Company has had a number of skirmishes with the anti-trust laws. Specific acts or practices have been attacked in private suits, proceedings of the Federal Trade Commission, and prosecutions by the Department of Justice. After George D. Haskell, President of the Baush Machine Tool Company, was abandoned by Duke in the Saguenay development in favor of the more powerful Aluminum Company, he sued both the Duke estate and the company under the Sherman Act. In trial of the first suit in the District Court of New Jersey an award of eight millions was rendered against the Duke estate. Haskell never enjoyed the money, however, for the Third Circuit Court of Appeals reversed the decision of the lower court and the Supreme Court refused certiorari.[11] His suit against the Aluminum Company was allowed to lapse.

The setback did not drive the Baush Company from the field. After a lapse of three years, it again sued for damages for alleged injuries attributed to the monopoly of ingot supply and the attempts of the Aluminum Company to monopolize sheet aluminum and various finished products.[12] After losing in the lower court, the complainant won an award of $956,300 in the Court of Appeals.[13] Since the Sherman Act provides for treble damages, the award amounted to nearly three million dollars. But on technical grounds the Aluminum Company obtained an appeal and then won the re-trial.[14] A settlement was finally effected out of court.

---

[11] Haskell v. Perkins et al., 28 Fed. (2nd) 222 (1928); 31 Fed. (2nd) 54 (1929); 279 U. S. 872 (1930).

[12] Baush Machine Tool Co. v. Aluminum Co. of America, 72 Fed. (2nd) 236.

[13] C. C. A. (2nd) 1934; certiorari denied, 293 U. S. 596 (1934).

[14] 79 Fed. (2nd) 217 (C. C. A. 2nd, 1935).

The Federal Trade Commission did not even enjoy this measure of success in either of its two prosecutions. In the first it attempted unsuccessfully to protect the independence of the Cleveland Metal Products Company. This firm, after a considerable experience in the enamelled steel industry, built an aluminum rolling mill as part of its venture in the aluminum utensil field. By 1915, when it was ready for production, it could not get ingot supplies from Europe, and was forced to turn to the Aluminum Company. No harm occurred for several years as the war demand brought it large profits. On the advent of government price-fixing for aluminum finished goods, it was caught in contracts to take ingot from the Aluminum Company in quantities and at prices that were ruinous. It could only escape at the cost of its independence. A new company in which the Aluminum Company owned two-thirds of the stock took over the properties. And here the Federal Trade Commission came onto the scene. It forbade the move as a breach of Section Seven of the Clayton Act, which forbids a corporation to "acquire . . . stock or other share capital of another corporation where the effect of such acquisition may be to substantially lessen competition."[15]

The Commission ordered the Aluminum Company to give up its holdings in the new company, and it was sustained by the Court of Appeals.[16] But the Cleveland company had no place to go except into the arms of the Aluminum Company. It was unable to continue business profitably and owed over five hundred thousand dollars. In a sheriff's sale it was re-acquired by the Aluminum Company. The Federal Trade Commission was not able to prove either that the indebtedness was fictitious or that the company could escape insolvency as an independent.[17] Superficially the Commission's failure can be attributed to war-time economic conditions, but fundamentally it must be laid to the monopoly control of ingot supplies and the financial dominance of the Aluminum Company.

The second action of the Commission grew out of a report to Congress on competitive conditions in the house furnishings industry. From the general investigation the Commission went on to charge the Aluminum Company with unfair practices in the form of "delaying shipment of materials to competitors, forwarding materials known to be defective . . . , discriminating in prices, and hindering competitors from enlarging their operations."[18] Five years later, however, it was forced to admit that the charges could not be sustained by evidence, and dismissed the complaint.[19]

---

[15] 3 F. T. C. 302 (1921).
[16] Aluminum Co. of America v. Federal Trade Commission, 284 Fed. 401 (1922), C. C. A. (3rd) 1922; 261 U. S. 616 (1923).
[17] 299 Fed. 361 (1924).
[18] Federal Trade Commission, *Annual Report*, 1925, p. 88.
[19] Complaint No. 1335.

In 1912, the first action taken by the Department of Justice also concerned trade practices. Unfair methods of competition were charged in the casting and utensil industries, and restrictive contracts concerning bauxite were held to be illegal. In suing, the government did not seek to break up the various combines, but sought only to reach these two evils through court injunction. The Aluminum Company consented to a decree from the court, which meant little.[20] It was forbidden to combine to control the price of aluminum and its products; to harass competitors with price discrimination; to delay, refuse, or threaten to refuse delivery of raw materials.

These prohibitions were almost useless. The Sherman Act already forbade combinations to fix prices, and the Court did nothing to advance the actual application of the prohibition. Price discrimination had already appeared to be very difficult to prove. It was almost impossible to distinguish between delays in deliveries caused by shortage and those designed to harass competitors. And finally, the Aluminum Company enjoyed, as does any private company, the right to refuse to sell to any buyer. Only when the privilege is used to create monopoly or lessen competition materially would the court decree apply. If these conditions could be proved, more stringent measures could be and should be prepared.

Twenty-five years and a number of political administrations passed before the Department of Justice returned to the fray. In April, 1937, Attorney-General Cummings announced the filing of a suit which sought not merely the good behavior of the huge combine, but a reorganization of the property of the parent and twenty-five subsidiary companies. The government petition to the court claimed that these companies manufactured all the virgin aluminum in the United States and sold 90 per cent of the aluminum sheet and about all of the aluminum wire, cable, and tubing. It also claimed that the Aluminum Company had purchased raw materials and plants in Europe in order to keep foreign competitors out of American markets by threatening them with cut-throat competition in their own domestic markets. Testimony in the case occupied some forty thousand pages, along with ten thousand pages of exhibits, and was printed in four hundred and eighty volumes. It took three hundred and sixty-two trial days to present, and when all the testimony was in Judge F. G. Caffey of the District Court, Southern District of New York, ruled against the government on every one of some one hundred and forty points involved in the argument.

The Department of Justice appealed the New York decision to the Supreme Court but ran into somewhat unusual troubles. Four of the Justices disqualified themselves, and no quorum of the Court could be

[20] United States *v.* Aluminum Co. of America, District Court, Western District of Maryland, June 7, 1912.

found. The Aluminum Company, however, was not allowed to enjoy anything more than a delay in the proceedings, as Congress passed legislation permitting the New York Court of Appeals for the Second Circuit to act in place of the Supreme Court. In 1945 the Appeals Court affirmed the decision of the lower court favoring the Company in all save one respect. This respect, however, was a basic one. The Court ruled that the Aluminum Company held monopoly control of ingot production in 1940. The lower court was instructed to reserve final action, however, and not to force the Company to dispose of any plants until disposition was made of government aluminum facilities which were built for war purposes between 1942 and 1945.[21]

In the meantime rather stirring things had been happening in the industry in relation to the disposition of these war-built plants, and the Aluminum Company asked for a ruling to the effect that changed conditions in the industry invalidated the old charge of monopoly. Postwar changes have materially reduced the dominance of the Company in the industry, but the Department of Justice remained unsatisfied and filed civil suit to force it to dispose of certain plants. The Company was given until November 1949 to file an answer. Its defense against disposal of any of its plants is found in the altered structure of the industry after 1945 resulting from the disposition of government plants.

Postwar Reconstruction

Tremendous changes for the aluminum industry came out of the war, but the war period itself showed no signs of reducing the dominance of the Aluminum Company. A primary war requirement was a quick and large expansion of aluminum capacity; and although the government investment of $674,000,000 comprised the major financing, the actual construction and operation of plants was turned over to the experienced operator, the Aluminum Company. In addition, Alcoa nearly doubled its own ingot capacity, increasing its total assets from $251,000,000 in 1939 to $474,000,000 in 1944.[22] Nevertheless, the Reynolds Metals Company[23] entered the primary production of aluminum to become the first domestic company since 1893 to compete in this field. But the Aluminum Company was still left in 1944 owning or operating 96 per cent of alumina capacity, 91 per cent of primary capacity, and between 80 and 90 per cent of important products, such as sheets, rods, bars, and wire.

With the surrender of Japan, the government set out to sell or lease its plants to private companies other than the Aluminum Company. Ap-

[21] Moody's *Industrials 1946*, pp. 355–356.
[22] Report of the Smaller War Plants Corporation, *Economic Concentration and World War II*, Washington, D. C., U. S. Government Printing Office, 1946, p. 106.
[23] Controlled by United States Foil Company, which owns about 54 per cent of Reynolds Metal Company common stock. U. S. Foil Company, in turn, is controlled by 60,000 ($1.00 par value) voting shares.

proach was made to 224 leading metal and metal processing companies, but no one, not even well-fortified companies such as American Smelting and Refining and Kennecott Copper, did more than make inquiries. Patents held by Alcoa on improved processes of extracting alumina from bauxite appeared to be one stumbling block. A second may have been an abiding respect for the general power of Alcoa. An apparent stalemate was broken by Surplus Property Administrator, W. Stuart Symington, who "fired the shot heard round the aluminum world" by accusing the Aluminum Company of blocking the program of surplus plant disposal by its patent control.[24] After anguished and at times angry denials of this claim, Alcoa gave the government free licensing of its patents on alumina extraction. These patents had been "built into" the government-owned plant at Hurricane Creek, Arkansas, and the Reynolds Company lost no time in taking a lease on the plant with an option to buy. In further deals with the government it leased the near-by Jones Mill ingot plant and the ingot plant at Troutdale, Oregon. It paid seven million dollars for the sheet, rod, and bar mill at Listerhill, Alabama, which it had operated during the war and which had cost the government twenty million dollars to build. Reynolds also leased the government sheet mill at McCook, Illinois, and the extrusion plant at Grand Rapids, Michigan.

While Reynolds was busy rounding out an integrated operation, the Kaiser companies entered the industry for the first time by leasing the government alumina plant at Baton Rouge, Louisiana. Kaiser-Cargo, Inc. took a five-year lease on the twenty-two million dollar government plant at Spokane, Washington, and Kaiser-Fraser Corporation took a similar lease on a near-by sheet mill which had cost the government forty-eight million dollars to build. These and other sales or leases of government plants from which the Aluminum Company gained nothing have left control of capacity in the industry in approximately the following condition:

CONTROL OF PLANT CAPACITY IN THE ALUMINUM INDUSTRY, 1947[25]

Production stage	Per cent of total		
	Aluminum Co. of America	Reynolds Metals Co.	Kaiser's companies
Alumina	44	36	20
Ingot	50	30	20
Sheet fabricating	48	30	18[a]

a All others account for 4 per cent.

[24] "Aluminum Reborn," *Fortune*, Vol. 33, No. 5, May 1946, pp. 102–109.
[25] *Business Week*, April 5, 1947, p. 22. No substantial change appears to have taken place in the control of plant capacity since 1947. *Cf.* Standard & Poor's *Industry Surveys*, May 26, 1949.

The effects of this re-shuffling of aluminum facilities will not be seen for some time. A first question for the future is to determine whether the Reynolds and Kaiser interests can be successful competitors of Alcoa. Answering the question will center attention on the relative efficiency of the plants acquired by the two newcomers and the ability of these two interests to find adequate raw material for inexpensive production of alumina. The Reynolds and Kaiser companies have acquired the three ingot plants out of nine built by the government during the war which can produce pig aluminum for fourteen cents or less a pound; any higher cost seems prohibitive. The western plants, however, are handicapped by the need of transporting alumina long distances. Alcoa's plants in the East are reported to incur a cost of 3.2 cents for alumina per pound of ingot. On the West Coast Kaiser obtains alumina from Baton Rouge, Louisiana, and Reynolds from its plant in Arkansas; the reputed cost per pound of aluminum is over five cents. Power costs, a very important cost item in producing ingot, are favorable in the West, where the aluminum producers obtain the bulk of their power from the Bonneville Power Administration. But Alcoa finds very low cost power for its eastern plants by holding favorable power contracts with TVA and at Niagara Falls.

In regard to bauxite or other raw material reserves needed for successful independent operation, Reynolds seems to be in the more promising position. The Company claims to have a lease in Haiti and Jamaica on a hundred years' supply of bauxite. Substitutes for bauxite were vigorously sought during the war, the search being considerably encouraged by twenty million dollars of government funds. Several plants were built which produced alumina from various clays, but their peacetime prospects are not promising. Meanwhile the Aluminum Company has been experimenting on the use of low-grade laterite found in Oregon which contains about equal portions of aluminum and iron. The discovery of economically feasible substitutes in good supply would unquestionably help the competitive situation.

Meanwhile the Department of Justice would like to assist the forces of nature. The skepticism shown by Attorney-General Tom C. Clark in 1945 still persists. The Department maintains:

The best answer to the problem is the elimination of the tremendous advantage of Alcoa, the fruits of its half century of monopoly, by subdividing the company into efficient but competing units. Only in such a climate will the aluminum industry be able to operate on a private-enterprise basis with the efficient and competent operators, new and old, assured of a fair opportunity to live and thrive. Competition would then be self-sustaining with a minimum of Government participation.[26]

---

[26] *Government Document* No. 94, 79th Cong., 1st Sess., p. 32.

The Department of Justice maintains that this program is feasible because plants of the Aluminum Company are not all integrated physically or functionally and could be grouped in clusters so as to retain the advantages of integrated operations.

POSSIBLE PUBLIC POLICIES

It is still apparent that the aluminum industry presents a problem of social control to a society committed to a system of competitive individualism.

The economic characteristics of the aluminum industry show, on the one hand, that monopoly is not a necessary condition and, on the other hand, that classical competition is not feasible. Present demand conditions would support between five and ten large firms at optimum size and optimum scale in the refining, reduction, and power stages. In mining and in the finishing stages a large number of independents would be economically justified. The observed merits of integration and the advantage of large-scale production suggest that five to ten integrated firms of medium size would create a technically efficient industry.

In such circumstances, we would not find the competitive system of Adam Smith. Since the industry would not offer the thousands of small firms necessary for classical competition, public control must choose between the competition of a few relatively large firms and some form of public regulation of the industry which would entail control of prices and output. The choice is not an easy one. At the best, where only a small number of competitors exists, a very qualified independence of decision would be found. Inevitably each company would consider the effect of its price and output decisions on the policies of competitors. At the worst, a thorough-going coöperation would create the monopolistic effects we are trying to avoid.

Decision must be made on the basis of two considerations. Firstly, how do the mal-effects of competition between a few large firms compare with the bad features of public regulation of supply and price? Secondly, what chance is there that even this inadequate competition might give way to complete coöperation? Some answer to the first question is found in studies of imperfect competition and public regulation. The relative merits of the two are not clear, but at least there is no overwhelming case against the competitive control. The answer to the second question will be affected in part by the character of foreign competition. If import duties were eliminated, foreign producers might rush into the American market whenever prices rose to monopoly levels. If this were the case there would be no advantage in monopolistic coöperation between American firms.

Foreign competition could not be relied on unless the present connection between Aluminum, Ltd., of Canada and the American industry were broken. In 1928, this company took over almost all the foreign properties of the Aluminum Company of America. While there is no direct corporate connection between the two, there is a close ownership connection. Controlling shares in both are held by the Mellon family.

In 1936, the Canadian company possessed a capacity equal to one-half that of the Aluminum Company and 25 per cent greater than that of its largest European rival. It came out of the war as the biggest producer in the world, with an ingot capacity of one billion pounds a year, more than twice the capacity of its former parent. It is a powerful company and could harass European producers in a number of markets if it set out to do so. Until the war it was an important member of the European cartel, and it is probable that its coöperation would not be continued if foreign competition became severe in the American market. Even though the Reynolds and Kaiser interests develop successfully, we could not get any help toward creating competition from foreign producers unless the Canadian company were completely divorced from all the American firms.

Tariff protection can be removed, so as to open the reorganized industry to the salutary effects of foreign competition. Europe possesses an efficient aluminum industry, and in peace-time it could be used to check the appearance of monopolistic coöperation and to encourage independence of action in American industry. Almost all the market would be retained by domestic producers unless they raised prices to monopoly levels.

In the past, the Aluminum Company found monopoly power in patents and control of raw materials, and strengthened these with tariff protection and the great force of overwhelming size. Patents are no longer important; a change in Congressional policy could remove tariff protection, and prosecution under the Sherman Act could end the control of raw materials. It is obvious, however, that the effects of the past position of the company cannot easily be removed by a dissolution decree or by the mere appearance of independent companies.

12

Shoes and Shoe Machinery

After 1850 the mechanization of the shoe industry brought new methods to shoe manufacturers and a new field for American enterprise—the production of shoe machinery. The new industry grew with rapidity as inventions created additional machines for the use of the shoe industry. From the first, patented machines assumed a position of unusual importance; later, a single firm, the United Shoe Machinery Company, rose to dominate the manufacture of these machines. Today, to appreciate the monopolistic elements in the shoe machinery industry, we must appreciate the importance of patented machines, the monopoly privileges granted in our patent laws, and the place of the United Shoe Machinery Company.

THE DEVELOPMENT OF SHOE MANUFACTURE
AND SHOE MACHINERY

Shoe manufacture in the United States has followed the usual course of industrial development. Handicraft methods prevailed at first. In Colonial days every farm kitchen was equipped with the requisite hand tools, such as knife, awl, needle, hammer, pincers, and lapstone, with which to perform shoemaking's basic operations of cutting, sewing, and hammering.

About 1750 in Lynn, Massachusetts, a Welsh immigrant, named John Dagys, subdivided the labor of shoemaking so that much of the work could be done in the homes of seafaring families or farmers. This system spread widely with the appearance of good profits. Factors or merchant capitalists supplied the small amounts of capital needed to purchase raw materials. Leather and cloth were cut into the required shapes in the factors' shops. This stock for shoe uppers was then sent to the homes of workers, who stitched it together. Upon completion it was collected and returned to the shops, where skilled workers attached the uppers to the leather soles by hand. For some time this combination of factory and "putting-out" system existed.

In 1845 the first shoemaking machine was adopted.[1] It rolled sole leather stock quickly and soon supplanted the old hand method of hammering sole leather to increase its compactness and firmness. Pegging, skiving,[2] sole-cutting, and stitching machinery appeared shortly thereafter. Soon Elias Howe's sewing machine was adapted to stitching shoe uppers, and shoe workers were brought under a single roof.

The Civil War stimulated other inventions in shoe machinery. The most important were associated with the names of Gordon McKay and Charles Goodyear, Jr. Machines bearing their names are responsible for the production of about 53% of the shoes made in the United States at the present time.[3]

The McKay process is one of sewing waxed linen thread directly through the outer and inner sole of the shoe, so that the thread catches the shoe upper material between the two soles, binding the three parts firmly together. To facilitate this operation the outer sole is made ready by running it through a channeling machine, which cuts a slit around the edge of the sole, folds the leather back to form a lip, and digs a little trench along the inside of the slit. The McKay stitching follows the trenched slit, and the leather lip, which was folded back, covers the stitches on the bottom of the outer sole. This leaves the sole smooth for finishing. The stitches go through the inner sole, however, and are visible inside the shoe. To conceal them and make the shoe more comfortable a lining of leather or imitation leather is used.

The sewing machine for the McKay process was invented by Lyman R. Blake. But its development and manufacture were financed by Colonel Gordon McKay, who purchased the patent rights. The machines and the process have since borne his name.

Just as the Howe sewing machine speeded up the processing of shoe uppers, so, too, the McKay sewing machine facilitated the sewing of soles to uppers, greatly lowering production costs. The McKay machine could process 300 pairs daily, whereas the best a worker could do by hand was 10 pairs a day. This important technological development came

---

[1] The peg-making machine antedated this first shoe machine by a quarter of a century. It turned out pegs for shoemakers. So prolifically did these machines produce pegs that it is said that "city slickers" bought the output to resell as seed oats to gullible New England farmers.

[2] Cutting or shaving down to a thin edge.

[3] In 1937, percentages of total shoe production, according to fundamental process classification, were: Welt, 32.7%; McKay, 20%; stitchdown, 13.2%; cemented, 22.1%; wood or metal fastened, 5.6%; and turned, 6.4%. Cf. Bureau of the Census, Census of Manufactures (1937).

when the Civil War demand for shoes was pressing heavily on shoe manufacturers.

Even though the demand for shoes was increasing, the machines were
not quickly adopted. Masters of the little "ten-footer" shoe shops lacked
the capital necessary to purchase expensive shoe machinery, especially
as it might soon become obsolete. Colonel McKay was forced to find a
more attractive method than outright sale to get his machines into use.
He developed a royalty-leasing system in which the manufacturer paid
a small price for the installation of each leased McKay machine and then
paid a royalty or tax on each pair of shoes made on these machines.
Under these conditions the McKay equipment quickly became a competitive necessity. McKay made his machines more popular by gifts of
stock in his company to large users of his equipment.

The leasing system became so firmly entrenched that shoe manufacturers were reluctant to accept any other arrangement. Later inventions
in shoe machinery had to be introduced under the same system.

In 1862, according to one authority,[4] Auguste Destouy succeeded in
mechanizing the welt process of shoemaking. Destouy's idea was improved upon by Daniel Mills and perfected by Charles Goodyear, Jr.,
who took out patents for a welt-stitching machine in 1871 and 1875.
This long-known process was a very difficult hand method, requiring
extensive training and great skill.

The mechanized process of making welt shoes is carried on in that
part of the factory known as the bottoming or making room. Briefly
stated, the process is as follows.[5] The completed shoe upper, which has
been shaped to the last or shoe form and attached to the insole, is ready
to receive the welt, which is a narrow strip of tough, pliable leather.
The welt is sewed by a Goodyear stitching machine to an inside lip
of the insole, previously prepared by channeling, so that a stout linen
thread passes through the insole lip, the shoe upper, and the welt to unite
all three firmly. The welt protrudes, forming a flange, and to it the heavy
outsole, also channeled, is sewed securely by a Goodyear outsole lock
stitch machine. The shoe then moves on for further processing.

The Goodyear machines turned out welt shoes more exactly made,
more comfortable, and cheaper than those made by hand. Costs were
reduced greatly, and eventually the Goodyear process became a keen
rival of the McKay process.[6] Indeed, the Goodyear method has several
distinct advantages over the McKay process. First, it produces a more

---

[4] Malcolm Keir, *Manufacturing Industries in the United States* (New York, The
Ronald Press Company, 1920), p. 233.

[5] Certain intermediate processes are omitted to avoid confusion.

[6] The ratio of McKay to Goodyear welt shoes fell from 40 pairs to 1 in 1880 to
about 5 pairs to 1 in 1895. The welt shoe is now more popular than the McKay.

comfortable shoe. In the Goodyear welt, the stitches uniting the uppers to the insole and outsole do not appear inside the shoe as they do in the McKay process. Though McKay shoe manufacturers try to eliminate this defect by use of a sock lining, they are not completely successful. McKay shoes are, therefore, sold to customers who cannot afford better ones.[7] Second, the Goodyear welt shoe can be more easily "tapped" or re-soled, consequently it gives more wear than does the McKay type.

The number of Goodyear machines in operation increased from 250 in 1880 to 2500 in 1895. But because the machines were costly and subject to rapid obsolescence, they, too, were leased to shoe manufacturers under the popular royalty system.

Other machines fundamental to shoemaking were introduced after the Civil War. None was as important as the McKay and Goodyear machines, save possibly the lasting machine invented in 1882 by J. E. Matzeliger. Heeling machines also came in after 1870, greatly improving the process of attaching heels to shoes.

Thus it may be safely stated that by 1890, machine development in three of the four basic processes in shoemaking, namely, in the art of stitching the parts of uppers together, in lasting, and in stitching the soles to the uppers, had passed through the difficult initial stages of mechanization. Pattern and last-making had greatly advanced, too, leaving only the process of hand-cutting of linings and leather as the final stronghold in the industry for man's inventive genius to conquer.

Rapid mechanization accounts in large measure for the speedy growth of the American shoe industry after the Civil War. In 1890, thirty-five states reported establishments engaged in shoe manufacture.[8] Two-thirds of the boots and shoes produced in American factories were made in New England, and Eastern Massachusetts was the center of this producing region. Lynn was the leading shoe city. In 1890 its factories numbered 323 and produced shoes valued at $26,000,000.[9] Brockton and Haverhill ranked second and third, respectively. The former city specialized in men's shoes, and had 73 factories producing shoes valued at $16,000,000 in 1890; the latter city had 201 somewhat smaller factories in operation in this same year, turning out footwear valued at $15,000,000. The growth of the industry in the United States was very rapid in the last two decades of the nineteenth century.[10]

---

[7] Cheap, medium, and high-grade shoes are produced by both methods. In general, the McKay process is used on the cheaper grades of women's shoes.

[8] Victor S. Clark, *History of Manufactures in the United States* (New York, McGraw-Hill Book Company, Inc., 1929), Vol. II, p. 471.

[9] Most of the factories in Lynn were moderate in size. The majority did a business varying from $25,000 to $250,000 annually. Very few exceeded annual sales of $1,000,000. *Ibid.*, p. 472.

[10] The rapid growth of the industry is apparent in the following table:

The industry spread out in two ways. In New England, labor troubles drove producers into country regions, particularly into New Hampshire and Maine.[11] In other regions it followed the centers of population, since transport costs of finished goods were more important as a location factor than were the transport costs of raw materials. Furthermore, the style factor was growing in importance, and proximity to the large retail markets was valuable. Consequently cities like Philadelphia and Rochester in the East, and Cincinnati, Milwaukee, and St. Louis in the rapidly developing Middle West, began to claim attention as notable shoe centers.[12] Moreover, mechanization made skilled operatives less indispensable, since machines were readily available everywhere. Though shoe machinery manufacture was centered in Eastern Massachusetts, the service stations of the shoe machinery industry were placed in or near all important shoe centers. Prior to the consolidation of the leading shoe machinery companies in 1899 it was dangerous competitively not to provide shoe manufacturers with first-class service on leased machines.

COMBINATION AND MONOPOLY

In 1898, by a process of direct growth or by combination, several companies dominated the field.[13] The Consolidated and McKay concern produced about 60% of the lasting machines made in the United States; the McKay Shoe Machinery Company manufactured approximately 70%

Census year	1899	1889	1879
Number of establishments..........	1600	2082	1959
Capital invested..................	$101,795,223	$ 95,282,311	$ 42,994,028
Wage earners (average number).....	142,922	133,690	111,152
Wages paid.......................	$ 59,175,883	$ 60,667,145	$ 43,001,438
Miscellaneous expenses............	$ 10,766,402	$ 9,217,519	(a)
Cost of materials used............	$169,604,054	$118,785,831	$102,442,442
Value of product.................	$261,028,580	$220,649,358	$166,050,354
Pairs of shoes produced...........	219,235,419	179,409,388	125,478,511

(a) Not reported.

Sources: Censuses of the United States, particularly the Twelfth Census, Part III, Manufactures, Special Report on Selected Industries.

[11] E. M. Hoover, Jr., *Location Theory and the Shoe and Leather Industries* (Cambridge, Mass., Harvard University Press, 1937), p. 171.

[12] For an interesting and enlightening discussion of the particular reasons for the development of the shoemaking industry in some of these cities, see Hoover, *op. cit.,* Chap. 13.

[13] Testimony of E. P. Howe, United Shoe Machinery Company official, before the Clarke Industrial Commission, House Document No. 183, 57th Congress, 1st Session, 1901–1902 (Washington, D. C.: U. S. Government Printing Office, 1901), Vol. XIV, pp. 482–483.

of the heeling machines and 80% of the metallic fastener machines; and the Goodyear Shoe Machinery Company produced about 80% of the welting and outsole-stitching machines and about 10% of the lasting machines.[14] All of these companies used the rental or royalty system to put their machines into use.

The International Goodyear Shoe Machinery Company handled most of the foreign business in shoe machines, and a sizable portion of its stock was owned by the Goodyear Shoe Machinery Company. There were numerous smaller and relatively unimportant companies operating at this time, such as the Eppler Welt Machine Company, the International Eppler Welt Machine Company, and the Davey Pegging Machine Company.

Some time during the middle 1890's S. W. Winslow of the Consolidated and McKay and E. P. Howe of the Goodyear Company felt that it was high time to combine further. In 1897 formal negotiations were begun.[15] Howe, before the Clarke Industrial Commission, testified that two things in particular motivated further combination: the desire to eliminate the duplication of expense incurred by having branch stations established and manned by each company to service their various machines in the same locality; and the desire to avoid patent difficulties.[16] In regard to the latter, the companies had a tendency to buy up patents which other companies might utilize. Costly litigation might be avoided, too, in instances where one company, such as Goodyear, wished to develop a lasting machine adaptable to its particular line of work, but found the basic patents controlled by the Consolidated and McKay Lasting Machine Company.

A joint agreement was considered in an informal conference, but this method was abandoned because it was thought to be a questionable procedure in view of the statutes of the several states and the Federal Antitrust Law. Complete consolidation seemed less dangerous at the time, since its illegality had not yet been questioned. Howe, one of the prime movers of the combination, told the story to the Industrial Commission as follows:[17]

A plan of consolidation was then considered, and, although the officers of each of the companies knew pretty well about the business and status of the others, all having done business here in Boston for a series of years, still each one was allowed to send its own expert to look over the books and accounts and assets of the other two companies for the purposes of ascertaining whether any plan of consolidation could be devised.

These conferences and negotiations continued for about a year, and finally,

---

[14] United States v. Winslow, 227 U. S. 215 (1913).
[15] Cf. Seager and Gulick, op. cit., p. 281.
[16] House Document No. 183, Vol. XIV, pp. 483ff.
[17] Ibid., pp. 484–485.

without the aid of any so-called promoter or banker or outside influence,[18] a consolidation was agreed upon, taking each company at a price a little lower, quite substantially lower, than its stock was selling for in the market at the time of the consolidation.

The case of the Goodyear Company is illustrative. The capital of the Goodyear Shoe Machinery Company was $3,000,000, its stock being divided into shares of a par value of $25 each. The stock was selling on the market in small lots at $41, $42, and $43 a share, while if there had been any attempt to purchase a block of stock the price would immediately have been enhanced because the stock was not listed and it was difficult to procure it, and any substantial buying would always result in enhancing the price. The Goodyear Company was put into the United Shoe Machinery Company at $40 per share, it being assumed, and I think the assumption was right, that that was as cheap and cheaper than the company could be bought if anybody went out and tried to buy it.

In a similar way the price of the Consolidated and McKay Lasting Machine Company was fixed: that was also about $40 per share. Those two companies got together first. The leading directors and stockholders of the McKay Shoe Machinery Company were disinclined at first to come in. The Goodyear Company consolidated with the Consolidated and McKay Lasting Machine Company and they had got well started when the McKay Shoe Machinery Company decided to come in, and a price of $11 per share was fixed for its stock, the par being $10 per share.

The method of procedure was this: All the directors of the Goodyear Shoe Machinery Company, being large stockholders themselves or else controlling, through their friends, large amounts of stock, sent a circular letter to the stockholders of the company,[19] advising them that the United Shoe Machinery Company had been formed under the laws of the State of New Jersey with an authorized capital of $25,000,000, divided into $12,500,000 preferred and $12,500,000 common stock (par $25), of which it was proposed to issue $8,625,000 of preferred stock and $8,625,000 of common stock for the purchase of all the stock of the companies which I have named—the Goodyear, the Consolidated and McKay Lasting Machinery Company, the McKay Shoe Machinery Company, the Goodyear Shoe Machinery Company of Canada and the International Goodyear Shoe Machinery Company, the Eppler Welt Machine Company, the International Eppler Welt Machine Company, the Davey Pegging Machine Company, and certain minor companies and some outside letters patent. The stockholders were also informed that a syndicate had been formed which would take sufficient common and preferred stock, in equal amounts, at par, to pay the floating debt of the several corporations which I have mentioned and to provide the company with at least a half million dollars in cash as working capital. The stockholders were informed the directors had exchanged their stock on the same terms as were offered to the stockholders and had advised the stockholders to do likewise.

In the case of the Goodyear Company each holder of 100 shares of the Goodyear stock received 80 shares of the preferred stock of the United Shoe Machinery Company and 80 shares of the common stock of the United Shoe Machinery Company, the par of all these stocks being $25. Circulars of the same tenor were sent out by the directors of the Consolidated [and] McKay

---

[18] Italics are added.
[19] This letter was sent out on February 8, 1899.

Lasting Machine Company, the McKay Shoe Machinery Company, and the International Goodyear Shoe Machinery Company.

The process of combination continued, and it was later revealed that over fifty concerns producing shoe machinery or supplies had been brought into the combination within ten years.[20] Furthermore, the United Shoe Machinery Company, by acquisition of the interests of the International Goodyear Shoe Machinery Company and the foreign business of the Consolidated and McKay Lasting Machine and the McKay Shoe Machinery companies, controlled the corporations in Canada and in Great Britain, France, Germany, and Switzerland, and through them practically the whole of the manufacturing territory in Europe.[21]

The corporate history of the United Shoe Machinery Company needs but little further amplification. In 1902 the United Shoe Machinery Company of Maine was organized to function as a selling and leasing organization for the original United Shoe Company in those states which refused to issue a license to foreign corporations of such large capitalization. In 1905 the United Shoe Machinery Corporation, a holding company, was formed. It held practically all the stock of the original company. There seems to be considerable difference of opinion in explaining this corporate development. Company officials declared that it was, in the main, the desire to alter certain charter powers granted to the original company in 1899 that motivated the change. The United States Department of Justice averred, however, that it was undertaken to facilitate the distribution of accumulated profits in the original company and to further monopoly. Twelve years later, in 1917, merger of the original company and the corporation took place and the name, United Shoe Machinery Corporation, was retained.

Owing to the original combination and later acquisitions, the United Shoe Machinery Corporation possessed a complete line of principal and auxiliary machines to be used in the bottoming rooms of shoe factories, that is, machines performing the various operations necessary to attach soles and heels to shoe uppers. The legal monopolies through letters patent which individual companies formerly held on individual machines became, by virtue of the corporate combination, a "pooled" monopoly under the control of a single company.

Statistics prepared by one writer from legal briefs and from judicial opinion show how completely the United Shoe Machinery Corporation dominated the industry in 1911.[22] These data, found in the following table, show that only in outsole stitching was there any semblance of competition in bottoming room machines.

---

[20] U. S. v. United Shoe Machinery Co. of New Jersey et al., 247 U. S. 86 (1918).

[21] See Howe's testimony, House Document, No. 183, Vol. XIV, p. 485.

[22] Eliot Jones, The Trust Problem in the United States (New York, The Macmillan Company, 1928), p. 166. The form of the data is slightly changed, without affecting the content.

Table 7

MACHINES PUT OUT TO SHOE MANUFACTURERS IN THE U. S., MARCH 1, 1911[23]

Type of machine	Put out by United Shoe	Put out by all others	Per cent put out by United Shoe
Clicking	3655	0	100.00
Pulling-over	1632	0	100.00
Lasting	7496	7	99.99
Standard screw	409	0	100.00
Pegging	146	0	100.0C
Tacking	3488	6	99.98
Welt-sewing	2527	142	94.70
Outsole-stitching	2676	758	77.93
Loose-nailing	1835	24	98.70
Heeling	2019	17	99.17
Slugging	1876	23	98.79
McKay sewing	898	8	99.13
	28,657	985	96.56 (average)

In large measure, the corporation maintained this dominant position in the industry by certain unusual business methods. Its machines were placed in two broad categories: general department machines, which might be sold outright to shoe manufacturers without restriction as to use; and special department machines, which were never sold, but were leased under varying types of contracts. In general the contracts took three forms:[24] (1) lease without restrictions as to use; (2) lease with restrictions contained in so-called *tying clauses,* which compelled the lessee to use particular machines only with other special department machines provided by United; and (3) lease without restrictions on payment of a higher royalty charge,[25] and, in some instances, on payment of both a higher royalty charge and an installation charge.[26] Tying clauses which restricted the conditions under which machines could be used were invariably present, however, in the leasing contracts of the most important and indispensable bottoming room machines. For example, the United's "Goodyear department" lease, which was used for over twenty important

[23] Recent data indicate that United still accounts for nearly all the machines put out to shoe manufacturers in the categories shown above in Table 7. In outsole stitching, its output has jumped to 92 per cent of the total machines of that type. See U. S. v. United Shoe Machinery Corporation, Civil No. 7198, in the District Court of the United States for the District of Massachusetts, complaint filed Dec. 15, 1947.
[24] Generalization about these contracts is difficult. There were other contracts which differed somewhat from those listed above.
[25] The higher royalty rate was 10 per cent above the regular rate.
[26] Installation charges ranged from $25 to $1000, with the majority of them in the $200–$500 range.

machines in the bottoming room, contained a section, among others, which stated:[27]

If at any time the lessee shall fail or cease to use *exclusively* welt sewing and outsole stitching machinery held by him under lease from the lessor, in the manufacture of all welted boots, shoes, or other footwear made by or for him, the welts or soles of which are sewed by the aid of machinery, the lessor, although it may have waived or ignored prior instances of such failure or cessation, *may at its option terminate forthwith by notice in writing this lease and license and any other lease and license of machines, machinery, or devices like those or any of them, mentioned in the foregoing "Schedule of Machines," or designed for similar purposes, then existing between the lessor and the lessee,* whether as the result of assignment to the lessor or otherwise, and the possession and full right to and control of all such machines, machinery, or devices held by the lessee under lease or license from the lessor or its assignor shall thereupon revest in the lessor free from all claims and demands whatsoever.[28]

Similar provisions were always to be found in the lease or license of the all-important lasting machines without which shoe manufacturers could not economically produce. Thus the restricted-use clause provided that lasting machines of the United could only be used on welted footwear which had been or was to be welted in whole or in part by the United's welt-sewing or sole-stitching machines; that they could only be used on turned footwear, the soles of which had been or were to be attached to their uppers by United's turn-sewing machines; that they could only be used on footwear which had been or was to be wholly or partially pulled-over, slugged, heel-seat nailed, or otherwise partly made by United's pulling-over or metallic fastener machines. Penalty for failure to observe the restricted use or exclusive use clauses was the invocation of the cancellation-of-all-leases clause, which meant that at its option the United, upon proper notice in writing, could take *all* its machinery out of the shoemaker's factory. Improper observance of the contract provisions could result in quick and complete economic destruction to any shoe manufacturer, regardless of size.

Owing to this sword of Damocles which hung over their heads, competitors of the United Shoe Machinery Company lived only on sufferance of the monopoly. Nor was it easy for potential competitors to enter United's economic kingdom, except by development of a full line of machines technically equal to or better than United's, and with an offer of terms as good as or better than United cared to offer. Yet potential competition did try to enter the field. What happened to it is the story of the "Plant Episode," which follows.

Thomas G. Plant, a well-known shoe manufacturer in Roxbury, Massachusetts, on May 1, 1910, cancelled his leases on a number of United's machines in use in his factory. He replaced them with machines of his

---

[27] A copy of this lease and others is to be found in *House Document*, No. 183, Vol. XIV, pp. 493–497.

[28] Italics in the quoted section are added.

own invention which he had perfected after years of experimentation. Furthermore, he advertised his readiness to supply other shoe manufacturers with his machines. On June 16th United began negotiations for the purchase of his properties. Three weeks later these negotiations were broken off and United filed a series of lawsuits against Plant, alleging breach of contract on the cancelled leases and infringement of patents. Finally, for still undetermined reasons, Plant accepted United's offer.[29] He agreed to sell his entire property, patents, shoe machinery, and shoe business for $6,000,000. United paid $3,000,000 in cash and the balance in its common stock valued at $50 per share, or twice its par value. Plant's decision to sell, made at a very early hour in the morning, seems to support the contentions of Louis D. Brandeis, later Associate Justice of the United States Supreme Court, that the financial influence of the United Shoe Machinery Company had made it extremely embarrassing for Mr. Plant, who was facing debts about to mature and greatly needed bank credit.[30] In short, the transactions had some of the hallmarks of a "forced" sale.

The Supreme Court, by a margin of a single vote, held that the real reason for the Plant purchase was not monopoly, but the effective use of patents of the two companies. Trouble with infringing patents threatened to stop the improvement of machines and, according to the majority of the Justices, supplied a valid reason for absorption of the Plant properties.[31]

What were the reactions of shoe manufacturers to the conditions prevailing in the shoe machinery industry? Generally they favored the leasing system, for it made it unnecessary for them to invest large capital sums in expensive shoe machinery which could lose value quickly through obsolescence. In many instances, mechanization costs were reduced simply to taxes, royalties, and repairs. Overhead on idle machinery and obsolescence costs were borne in the main by the United Shoe Machinery Corporation.[32] And the company gave a desirable and satisfactory servicing to its machines.

---

[29] United Shoe contended, among other things, that Plant had begun the negotiations of sale and agreed to sell when he finally got a satisfactory offer. On the other hand, C. H. Jones, a well-known shoe manufacturer, testified before a Senate Committee in 1911 that he and other shoe manufacturers had been interested in plans to finance Plant's shoe machinery business; that Plant was not trying to force his machines on the United Company; and furthermore that Plant had said that he (Plant) believed the United Company had brought pressure on him to pay a bank debt of $140,000 which was falling due on the very day following the sale of his properties to the United. Cf. Jones, op. cit., pp. 181–183.

[30] Report of the Senate Committee on Control of Corporations, pp. 1188–1190. Cited in Jones, op. cit., pp. 181–182. The United Shoe Machinery Company denied these contentions emphatically.

[31] United States v. United Shoe Machinery Co. of New Jersey et al., 247 U. S. 48–52 (1918).

[32] Ultimately, of course, these costs must be passed on to the shoe manufacturer in royalty rates if the United intends to continue in operation.

Some aspects of the royalty system, however, caused dissatisfaction. Large shoe manufacturers, anxious to receive the benefits of size and large-scale production, were irked by the uniform royalty charges. They preferred royalty rates to be graduated. The little producers, of course, liked the existing system. In addition, some of the large producers were not keenly favorable to a system which made entry into and egress from the shoe business so easy. Small competitors could ever be springing up to peck away at their business.

Though most shoe manufacturers favored the leasing principle, they disliked the tying clauses, and would have preferred to see them stricken out. From time to time associations of shoe manufacturers passed resolutions urging removal of these objectionable features.[33] On one occasion an association entered into negotiations with United Shoe to remove them from the leases.[34] In Massachusetts in 1907 a law was passed, supported by certain shoe manufacturers, which prohibited use of the tying clauses in the state.[35] The efforts came to nothing.

The United Shoe Machinery Company has never admitted the validity of the criticisms directed at the tying clauses. The leasing system, including the tying principle, it inherited from its predecessor companies. The tying arrangements arose out of technical and economic circumstances, and these circumstances still prevailed, according to the United Company. Shoe machines such as theirs must be operated in teams, or else the work done on one machine will hinder work done by a subsequently used machine, or work done by one may be destroyed in part by another. Such technical difficulties would lead to damaged or poorly made shoes, damaged shoe machines, loss of revenue both to the shoe manufacturer and to the United Shoe, and loss of reputation or good will. It can be argued, of course, that United should have let shoe manufacturers have the unhappy experience of using rival machines along with United machines. If its claims were valid, the losses incurred by the shoe manufacturers would have revealed the fact. The revelation would still have been painful and probably would not have enhanced United's good will. At any rate, the company chose not to take the risk.

United Shoe and the Law

But what about the law? Was the combination a violator of the Sherman Act? Previous Supreme Court decisions indicated that the

---

[33] Cf. Jones, op. cit., pp. 176–177.

[34] House Document No. 183, Vol. XIV, Exhibit. Report of the Committee of the New England Shoe and Leather Association on the Modified Form of Lease, pp. 510–512.

[35] Cf. Seager and Gulick, op. cit., p. 295. The bill was introduced by Mr. R. H. Long of Framingham. Mr. Long was at one time or another a manufacturer of shoe machinery, shoes, war supplies, and automobiles.

holding company form was not exempt from the law.[36] Were holders of letters patent subject to conviction of restraint of trade under the Sherman Act? The answers to these questions are to be found in a series of interesting Supreme Court cases relating to the United Shoe Machinery Company and its officials.

The Federal Government instituted a criminal proceeding against S. W. Winslow, President of the United Shoe Machinery Company, and others, charging them with forming a combination in restraint of trade and with conspiracy.[37] The organization of the United Shoe Machinery Company and its acquisition of stocks and business of the various companies were alleged breaches of the Sherman Act. The case concerned the legality of the combination itself. Adjudication of the tying clauses was not involved under the construction placed on the indictments by the United States District Court of Massachusetts.

In 1913 the Supreme Court upheld the legality of the combination. The business of the several companies, prior to combination, was assumed to be legal, and combination was merely an attempt to secure greater efficiency. The machines were patented and were, therefore, separate monopolies. The combining companies manufactured different machines and did not directly compete with each other. One corporation manufacturing 70% of three non-competing groups of patented machines should be as acceptable as three corporations making about the same proportion of each single group of machines. And, finally, the statute did not require the reduction of all business into minute units.

In a civil suit instituted against the United Shoe Machinery Company on December 12, 1911, the government charged a combination of manufacturers of shoe machinery, and specifically attacked certain of the company's leases alleged to restrain competition. Counsel for the United claimed that the company was merely a combination of non-competing businesses and the leases were merely the exercise of legal patent rights. Government attorneys maintained, on the other hand, that the combination itself was illegal and the leases as used extended the illegal control achieved by corporate combination.

From the outset the prosecution faced obvious difficulties. In the first place, the previous case against Winslow had established the legality of the corporate combination. In the second place, earlier patent law decisions, though confused, favored the claims of the United Shoe Machinery Company. Thus, in 1896, the lower Court held in the Button-Fastener Case[38] that a company manufacturing a patented button-fastener ma-

[36] Northern Securities Co. v. United States, 193 U. S. 197 (1904); Standard Oil Company of New Jersey et al. v. United States, 221 U. S. 1 (1911); American Tobacco Co. v. United States, 221 U. S. 106 (1911).

[37] United States v. Winslow, 227 U. S. 202 (1913).

[38] 77 Fed. 288.

chine was within its patent rights when it required the purchaser of the patented machine, as a condition of sale, to buy also its non-patented metallic fasteners for use in the machine. This principle was adhered to by the Supreme Court in 1912 in Henry v. A. B. Dick Company,[39] when the Court upheld the Dick Company's selling arrangements which forced the purchase of its mimeographing materials as a condition under which its patented mimeograph machine had to be purchased. The lower court relied heavily on the precedent established in the Dick case in exonerating the United Shoe.

In 1917, in the Motion Picture Patents case,[40] the Supreme Court overruled the Button-Fastener and Dick decisions. The Court said the Motion Picture Patents Company was not within its patent rights when it attached to its motion picture projecting machines, which it had sold, restrictive conditions regarding the lease of film from a certain company licensed by the Motion Picture Patents Company.[41] This decision brightened the outlook for the prosecution in the United case, and appeal was carried to the Supreme Court.

Nevertheless, the Supreme Court upheld the validity of the United Company's leases.[42] The distinction which it made between the Motion Picture and United Shoe cases turned on whether the machines were sold or leased. In the former case, the machines were sold; in the latter, leased. Since the United retained title to its machines, it was within its legal rights to impose the lease forms then in use. Furthermore, the Court maintained its former position, established in the Winslow case, that the corporate combination, since the units that composed it were non-competing, did not violate the Sherman Act of 1890.

The decision was far from unanimous. Justices McReynolds and Brandeis did not sit on the case. Since both had been involved previously in lawsuits relating to the United Shoe Machinery Company, professional ethics debarred them. The remaining seven justices split 4 to 3.

While the Government's civil suit against United Shoe was under way, Congress had attempted to stop some of the gaps apparent in the Sherman Act by the passage of the Clayton Act in 1914. Section 3 of this Act declared

that it shall be unlawful for any person engaged in commerce, in the course of such commerce, to *lease* or make a sale or contract for sale, goods, wares, merchandise, *machinery*, supplies or other commodities, *whether patented or unpatented*, for use, consumption, or resale within the United States or any Territory thereof or the District of Columbia or any insular possession or other place under the jurisdiction of the United States, . . . where the effect of such lease, sale, or contract for sale or such condition, agreement, or under-

---

[39] 224 U. S. 1.

[40] 243 U. S. 502.

[41] More general restrictive provisions were used in addition to this specific one.

[42] United States v. United Shoe Machinery Co. of New Jersey et al., 247 U. S. 32 (1918).

standing may be to substantially lessen competition or trend to create a monopoly in any line of commerce.[43]

The United States then initiated a case in Missouri, applying for a temporary injunction to prevent the use of the objectionable tying clauses. The injunction was granted November 9, 1915. About eight months later the District Court of Eastern Missouri denied the motion of the United Company to dismiss the case. Eventually it was carried to the Supreme Court, and that body in 1922 affirmed the decision of the lower court by a vote of 7 to 1. The Supreme Court found: That although there was no specific agreement not to use the machinery of a competitor, the practical effect of these restrictive provisions, thus tied together, was to prevent such use and necessarily to lessen competition and tend to create a monopoly in violation of Section 3 of the Clayton Act.[44]

What effect did the 1922 decision have upon the leadership of United Shoe? Writing in the late 1920's, Seager and Gulick in their book, *Trust and Corporation Problems*, maintained that no perceptible change had as yet appeared.[45] Despite the passage of another twenty years, the observations of these two economists have proved uncomfortably accurate. In late 1947 in a suit against United Shoe, the Department of Justice supplied data showing that United Shoe still dominates the industry in most of its phases. In one way or another the corporation has discouraged or absorbed potential direct competitors. At the same time it has developed its position as a supplier of shoe machinery parts and shoe factory supplies. Moreover, it has extended its control into the tanning machinery field by acquisition of most of the capital stock of the Turner Tanning Machinery Company, manufacturer of 75 per cent of the tanning machinery used in tanneries in the United States.[46]

Evidence of Competition

Despite the foregoing facts, events of the last two decades indicate that competition can enter and has entered the field against this economic Goliath. The David in this instance is the Compo Shoe Machinery Corporation, with a leased plant and headquarters in Boston, Massachusetts. It was born in Delaware on January 10, 1929, and manufactures and leases shoe machinery used to cement soles to shoe uppers.[47] Patents

---

[43] Italics are added.

[44] United Shoe Machinery Corporation *et al. v.* United States, 258 U. S. 452 (1922).

[45] Seager and Gulick, *op. cit.*, p. 303.

[46] United States of America *v.* United Shoe Machinery Corporation, Civil No. 7198. See Appendix A, plaintiff's brief, dated Dec. 15, 1947, in the District Court of the United States for the District of Massachusetts.

[47] The cement process of making shoes is by no means new. It preceded the

which protect the company were developed by William H. Bresnahan, one-time employee of the United Shoe Machinery Corporation. He is supposed to have refused United's offer of $55,000 for them, preferring to form an independent company.[48] He succeeded in interesting friends in his project, and soon the Compo Shoe Machinery Corporation was launched, with Mr. Bresnahan as one of its directors and a voting trustee.[49] The newcomer has been very successful. Its growth and prosperity are revealed in the following table:

Table 8

PRODUCTION AND FINANCIAL DEVELOPMENT, COMPO SHOE MACHINERY CORPORATION, 1929–1939, 1945

Year	Compo's machines in service in shoe factories on December 31	Number of shoe factories using Compo equipment	Number of pairs of shoes produced on Compo equipment	Total invested capital in thousands of dollars[a]	Return on average invested capital (per cent)	Dividend record in dollars
1929	(b)	(b)	2,261,254	(b)	(b)	Nil
1930	(b)	(b)	5,100,000	(b)	(b)	Nil
1931	(b)	(b)	10,908,555	(b)	(b)	Nil
1932	(b)	(b)	21,000,000	$ 427	21.60	.25
1933	1778	(b)	27,589,227	556	37.40	.50
1934	2053	(b)	31,041,202	707	32.44	.50
1935	2588	(b)	35,263,524	854	18.82	.50
1936	2707	329	41,023,917	1016	21.60	1.375[c]
1937	2954	342	44,492,251	1035	29.34	2.00[d]
1938	3317	394	47,196,483	1152	22.85	1.00
1939	3137	402	52,240,000	1458	20.07	1.00
1945	(b)	(b)	64,101,468	2198	10.72	.65
1947	(b)	(b)	71,661,136	2560	12.12	.50[e]

a Based on average of invested capital at the beginning and end of the year.
b Data not available.
c $0.75 extra cash dividend.
d $1.00 extra cash dividend.
e Stocks split 2 for 1, October 1946.

Sources: Poor's and Moody's *Industrial Manuals;* Standard and Poor's *Corporation Records.*

The Compo Company has succeeded in placing more and more machines in an increasing number of shoe factories. Concomitant with this

mechanical method of sewing them, but processing difficulties discouraged its use. As better cements were developed, its popularity was revived for a short time in England, and later in Germany as a First World War economy.

[48] For an interesting and informative account of the development of the Compo Shoe Machinery Corporation and the personalities who direct its activities, see *Fortune,* Vol. VIII, No. 3 (September, 1933), pp. 42ff.

[49] Compo has three voting trustees. The voting trust was set up June 30, 1930. This arrangement was to terminate five years later, but extensions allow it to run until March 15, 1956. See Standard and Poor's *Corporation Records,* April–May 1949, p. 3900.

growth has been the steady increase in the number of pairs of shoes produced on Compo equipment. Its capital investment has increased steadily
over the years with a considerable variation in earnings and rates of
return. Its gross income is divided about equally between income from
the sale of cement and solvents and income from rents and royalties.

The United Shoe Machinery Corporation chose at first to ignore the
cement process. The continued success of its rival, however, made it
necessary for Goliath to use David's weapons, so United has developed
machines of its own to make shoes by the adhesive method. Now it shares
the market with Compo and others, with Compo the outstanding competitor in that particular field of shoemaking machinery. The division of
the market and the importance of the adhesive method of shoemaking is
shown approximately in the following table:

Table 9

SHOE PRODUCTION IN THE UNITED STATES BY CENSUS YEARS, 1929–1937,
1945, IN THOUSANDS OF PAIRS

Year	Total number of pairs of boots, shoes, slippers and others	Welted, including Silhouwelts[a]	McKay, including Littleway	Turned	Wood or Metal Fastened	Stitchdown	Cemented	Cemented on Compo Machines	Cemented on machines of all others
1945	483,739[c]	157,699	63,370	25,154	12,093	58,049	123,837	64,101	59,736
1937	424,971	138,962	85,238	27,236	23,651	56,346	93,539	44,492	49,047
1935	388,492	116,923	86,551	25,727	25,997	70,967	59,900	35,263	24,637
1933	349,346	100,744	93,361	32,257	25,984	56,940	40,061	27,589	12,472
1931	316,057	98,204	104,464	38,513	17,956	46,006	10,913	10,918	5
1929	371,519	124,409	126,850	(b)	(b)	(b)	(b)	2,261	......

a The Silhouwelt is a hybrid, being part welt and part a cemented shoe. Welting is sewed to the upper as in
making a regular Goodyear welt shoe, but the outsole is attached to the welt not by stitching but by cementing.
The inclusion of Silhouwelt with welted shoes understates the importance of the adhesive method.
b Not separately given.
c Includes 43,537(000) pairs produced by all other processes not listed.
Sources: U. S. Census of Manufactures and Poor's Industrial Manuals; and Standard and Poor's
Corporation Records.

The statistical data show the rapid rise of cement-processed shoes
since 1929. Moreover, they show that the Compo Shoe Machinery Corporation is meeting with stiffer competition in its field, in the main from
the United Shoe Machinery Corporation.[50] Over the years the demand
for cement-processed shoes has grown. Both Compo and United have
supplied in large measure the machinery to meet this demand. United
has overhauled Compo, it seems, for in 1946 approximately 52 per cent

[50] Hide and Leather and Shoes Blue Book, 1948, lists on p. 341 fifteen companies,
including United and Compo, which manufacture machines for the cement process.
Companies other than Compo and United are unimportant.

of all cement-processed shoes were "bottomed" on machinery of United Shoe manufacture.[51] Since the demand for cement-processed shoes is growing, both companies continue to make rapid strides, with the United tending to overhaul Compo.

The outcome cannot be accurately predicted. It is probable, however, that as competition becomes keener, Compo and United will tacitly pursue the policy of peaceful market-sharing, with its multitude of sins. Both concerns will discover that neither one gains by continued warfare. United is unlikely to try to absorb Compo. Since the concerns are directly competing, it would collide almost certainly with the anti-trust laws. Moreover, the presence of some competition assuages public fear and encourages a more favorable public opinion of the dominant concern.

In addition to Compo, the United Shoe Machinery Corporation has shared the market with a few competitors for a brief period in nearly every line of shoe machinery. For example, in upper-stitching machinery, companies such as Singer Manufacturing and Reece Buttonhole Machinery have challenged the supremacy of United Shoe—Singer through the Hamel Shoe Machinery Company and Reece through the Reece Shoe Machinery Company. But Singer was induced to liquidate the Hamel outfit and transfer Hamel patents to United by license and assignment. Since about 1920 Singer and United have been careful not to engage in the manufacture and distribution of competing lines of machinery. And United hired the chief inventor of the Reece Shoe Machinery Company and then purchased this competitor's assets.[52]

Evidence of Monopoly Profits

The competition which United has faced has not prevented it from gaining abnormal profits. From October, 1905, to the present, preferred stockholders have received their dividend of 6 per cent regularly. Exclusive of extra cash or stock dividends, common stockholders received 8 per cent annually from October, 1905, up to and including April, 1919. In July and October, 1919, they were paid 6 per cent and 4 per cent respectively. In 1920 they received 12 per cent, and in each of the next three years, 8 per cent. After July, 1924, they received 10 per cent annually in spite of the stresses and strains of the 1930's.

In addition, common stockholders have frequently been the recipients of extra dividends of cash and common stock. Since July 15, 1907, United has paid them extra cash dividends eighteen times for a total of 106 per cent. Eight of these cash extras were paid between 1930 and 1939. Dividends in common stock have been paid on seven occasions in the last

---

[51] Brief for the plaintiff, U. S. v. United Shoe Machinery Corporation, p. 27.
[52] See the brief for the plaintiff, U. S. v. United Shoe Machinery Corporation, pp. 19–21.

thirty-three years for a total of 125 per cent. In addition, common stock-holders received on July 15, 1916, 15/1000 of a share of 7% preferred stock of the Thomas G. Plant Company, and on July 5, 1917, 4 per cent in Liberty Loan bonds.

The dividend record does not, of course, portray completely the earnings of the United. Its management has pursued a very liberal dividend policy while maintaining consistently a substantial surplus.[53]

Effects on the Shoe Industry

In view of the fact that the United Shoe Machinery Corporation has made very good earnings and has paid excellent regular dividends and many extras in cash and common stock, despite cyclical fluctuations in general business, the conclusion seems warranted that the corporation might be making some profit which must be labelled monopoly gain.

[53] The data in the following table are derived from the consolidated balance sheets of the United Shoe Machinery Corporation (N. J.) and the United Shoe Machinery Corporation (Me.).

Net Income, Dividend Record, and Surplus Account of the United Shoe Machinery Corporation (N. J.) and the United Shoe Machinery Corporation (Me.),[a] 1929–1939, 1948

Years Ended About Feb. 28	Net Income After Taxes	Preferred Dividend	Common Dividend	Surplus for the Year	Surplus Forward from Previous Year
1948	$ 8,747,246	$382,745	$ 8,079,314	$ 285,187	$15,665,231
1939	9,477,129	414,689	9,172,570	110,130[d]	15,752,298
1938	10,146,153	421,236	9,741,191	16,274[d]	15,349,192
1937	11,349,895	440,908	11,456,886	581,666[d]	15,930,858
1936	10,267,643	446,088	10,308,962	487,407	15,459,487
1935	8,825,515	446,759	10,311,531	1,932,775[d]	16,192,291
1934	9,458,016	456,822	11,543,421	2,452,227[d]	14,519,488
1933	6,023,483	(b)	6,195,012[c]	171,529[d]	14,691,018
1932	7,483,540	(b)	8,787,619[c]	1,304,079[d]	15,995,097
1931	8,351,987	(b)	8,787,474[c]	435,487[d]	16,430,583
1930	9,670,923	(b)	8,787,096[c]	883,827	15,546,756
1929	8,394,082	(b)	8,786,494[c]	392,412[d]	15,939,168

a United Shoe Machinery Corporation of Maine was formally dissolved in 1938.
b Not separately reported.
c Includes both common and preferred dividends.
d Deficit after dividend payments.

Sources: Poor's Industrial Manuals and Standard Statistics Report U-21, revised June 6, 1939; Standard and Poor's Corporation Records, April–May 1949, pp. 3282–3283.

As of February 28, 1949, exclusive of treasury stock held as an asset, the United Shoe Machinery Corporation had outstanding 252,954 preferred shares held by about 1,861 investors, and 2,309,215 common shares scattered among approximately 24,797 holders. On the same date it carried on its balance sheet common stock at $58,239,726; preferred, $10,597,700; reserves, $9,367,425; surplus, $15,665,232.

Therefore, rental and royalty charges on United machines and the prices of its supplies may be greater than they should be. If there were other comparable companies in the field, and if the situation remained the same for United Shoe, the conclusion would have to be—assuming that no collusive action existed—that United was more efficient than its competitors. It would be simply an intra-marginal firm taking advantage of competitive market conditions. In the absence of clean-cut, conspicuous competition, however, it is not possible to reach that conclusion.

Shaving down royalty rates would have no material effect on shoe prices, however, since royalties and such costs are small items in the total cost of a pair of shoes.[54] Therefore, consumers individually are not greatly injured by the lack of vigorous competition in the shoe machinery industry.

In respect to the quality of machines offered the shoe manufacturers, it seems that shoemaking has not suffered. The United Shoe Machinery Corporation is known to have a large staff which spends most of its time improving the present machines and trying to invent new ones. Inventors outside the corporation are free to work on inventions in the field if they wish. There is, to be sure, a serious drawback for those outside. They are faced with the problem of producing and marketing their inventions. In the face of the already firmly established United Shoe Machinery Corporation, this becomes an exceedingly difficult task, unless the inventor brings forth some machine for a bottoming process not already receiving the serious attention of the United Shoe Machinery organization. If the inventor did not wish to build and market his invention, the only alternative would be to sell to the United Shoe. In such circumstances he is likely to have to take whatever the United cares to offer.

It is very probable that the corporation has withheld patents from use. Under present interpretation of the law, however, this is not illegal.[55] It must be borne in mind that a company like the United Shoe has many thousands of dollars invested in machinery in use in shoe factories. Since the directors of the corporation owe direct obligations to the shareholders, machinery in use must first pay for itself before new machinery is introduced to supplant the old. Social gain at the expense of a particular group is not likely to occur if the particular group or its representatives can prevent it. An acceptable remedy is not to be found in attempting

---

[54] Manufacturers' royalty and rental costs per pair of shoes vary with the type of shoe produced. The per pair cost of men's, women's, and children's welt shoes would be higher than the cost per pair of McKay's and turned shoes of identical style and pattern. Figures obtained about 1940 placed the royalty-rental costs per pair of good grade, men's welt shoes at about 9 cents per pair. The cost per pair of women's and children's welts of like grade would be somewhat less, since the number of stitches required is less. On the other hand, fancy stitching, cutouts, and other style features would build up royalty and rental costs on women's and children's shoes.

[55] Continental Paper Bag Co. v. Eastern Paper Bag Co., 210 U. S. 405 (1908).

to force patents into use under our present patent system. In fact, such action might discourage inventions.

Strangely enough, the lack of competition in the shoe machinery industry has maintained strong competition in the shoe industry.[56] Some concentration has taken place in the shoe industry as illustrated by the International Shoe Company, with net sales of $219,000,000 per annum, and Endicott-Johnson Corporation, with net sales of over $148,650,000.[57] Nevertheless, the shoe industry remains keenly competitive, due to the small capital requirements of entrants in the field. This situation was made possible by the policy established long ago by Colonel Gordon McKay, of furnishing machines to shoe manufacturers under leasing arrangements upon payment of royalties. It should not be overlooked, also, that the shoe manufacturer pays the same price per pair, or per 1000 stitches, for the services of these machines, regardless of the number of pairs of shoes he produces in a year. A graduated scale of royalties, desired by some large shoe manufacturers, might create a situation in the shoe industry which would hasten the concentration movement. Strong competition might then disappear, to the detriment of the consumer.

CONCLUSION

In conclusion it can be said that the corporate form of business organization enabled the United Shoe Machinery Corporation to attain its foothold in the industry. Patent monopoly, legal *per se,* was extended beyond its legally intended scope *via* the tying clauses. This enabled the United to make profits on patented and unpatented articles, and prevented competition from easily entering its particular field. Meanwhile, increasing financial power enabled the corporation to retain able legal talent to defend its position, and at the same time allowed it to handle its competitors or potential competitors to its own satisfaction. At present it might be said to be in a preëminent position, so far as certain fundamental lines of machinery are concerned, and could operate in an even more profitable fashion than it now does, should it choose to abuse its position. It seems, however, that United prefers to satisfy most of its trade while it pays its shareholders steadily and well. The shoe industry remains competitive, meanwhile, and more resistant to concentration than many other lines of endeavor.

---

[56] *Cf.* National Recovery Administration, *Report of Survey Committee on the Operation of the Code for the Boot and Shoe Manufacturing Industry* (mimeographed: Washington, D. C., 1935), pp. 12–13.
[57] Standard and Poor's *Corporation Records,* April-May 1949.

13

Petroleum Products

THE OIL REFINING MONOPOLY

It is difficult to imagine modern industry without petroleum oils for lubrication, but the Industrial Revolution was far advanced in England and well under way in the United States while industry still relied on costly and unsatisfactory animal oils. In the early nineteenth century, the efforts to escape this handicap were united by industrial chemistry with the search for better means of illumination. Whale oil and bees-wax and tallow candles were as unsatisfactory for lighting as lard oils for lubrication. In places as far separate as Scotland and New Brunswick various types of bituminous coal were attacked and, by distillation, were forced to yield "coal oil" or "kerosene." By 1854 the New York Kerosene Oil Company was marketing the new fluid, and in a decade kerosene lamps were rapidly displacing older types. Other companies were mixing animal and vegetable oils with kerosene to produce an improved lubricant.

A serious competitor appeared before kerosene had gained an established market for itself. For years salt wells drilled in Kentucky, West Virginia, Ohio, and Pennsylvania had produced small amounts of an evil-smelling oily substance frequently called "rock-oil." As much as two or three barrels a day came from some wells, where it had to be separated from the salt fluid and run off on the ground. In Kentucky and northwestern Pennsylvania this unwelcome by-product was bottled and sold as medicinal oil with avowed properties for the cure of cholera morbus, liver trouble, bronchitis, and consumption.[1] By 1850, some of the oil was being tried on a very small scale as a lubricant, and crudely refined oil was being used in lamps, where it smelled and smoked very badly. But improvements in refining and in lamps soon increased the demand beyond the meagre supplies available, and the price of oil rose sharply.

---

[1] Ida M. Tarbell, *The History of the Standard Oil Company* (New York, McClure Phillips and Co., 1904), Vol. I, p. 5.

At this time Francis Beattie Brewer, an alumnus of Dartmouth College, carried samples of Pennsylvania oil to Doctor Dixi Crosby and Professor O. P. Hubbard of the Dartmouth faculty. Their enthusiasm aroused the interest of another visiting alumnus, George H. Bissell, who played a large part during the next half-dozen years toward exploiting the newly recognized resource. Several years were spent in attempts to enlist financial assistance and several more in stock-jobbing ventures. Eventually, the Seneca Oil Company sent Edwin L. Drake to Titusville in northwestern Pennsylvania to try the drilling technique used for years in the salt industry.[2]

The venture to extract oil out of rock met with a great deal of ridicule until, after drilling seventy feet, Drake struck a pool of oil which with pumping yielded eight to ten barrels a day. Quiet days for Titusville and the surrounding Oil Creek region were gone. A wild rush for leases followed, and by 1860 seventy-four wells were turning out over a thousand barrels a day.[3] Ten years later the region was producing over five million barrels yearly.[4]

The first speculators and operators had no time to worry about what was to happen next. No preparations had been made for local storage or local transportation, the trunk-line railroads possessed neither storage nor car facilities, and refining plants were few in number and crude in method. Whiskey barrels and pits dug in the ground served until better storage was available, and teamsters carried barrelled oil over terrible roads at exorbitant charges until railroad extensions and local pipelines were built and the railroads evolved wooden tank cars.[5]

Many small refineries appeared in the oil region and in or around Pittsburgh, New York, Philadelphia, and Cleveland. The last-named city, however, was destined to become the leading refining center. Situated two hundred miles from the producing region, it was ideally fitted to serve the Western market and enjoyed excellent connections with the East and with the important export market through the New York Central and Erie Railroads and the Erie Canal. Despite the efforts of the Pennsylvania Railroad to maintain Pittsburgh in the lead, Cleveland moved into first place after 1869.[6]

---

[2] Tarbell, *op. cit.*, pp. 7–11.

[3] Paul H. Giddens, *The Birth of the Oil Industry* (New York, The Macmillan Company, 1938), Chaps. 4 and 5.

[4] Today nineteen states combine to produce an annual output of one billion barrels, representing over 60 per cent of the world's supply of petroleum. Pennsylvania reached its peak production in 1891, with 31,424,000 barrels. Its present output of about fifteen million barrels puts it in eighth place, far below the leaders, Texas with 390,000,000 barrels. California with over 200,000,000, and Oklahoma with 185,-000,000. *Cf. Petroleum Facts and Figures*, 1937, p. 62.

[5] *Cf.* Standard Oil Company of New Jersey, *et. al., v.* United States (October, 1909), *Brief for the Appellants*, Vol. II, p. 15.

[6] Tarbell, *op. cit.*, Vol. I, Chap. 2.

In that city a twenty-three-year-old commission merchant, John D. Rockefeller, was making a success in the produce business with his partner, M. B. Clark. They were induced to put four thousand dollars into an oil refining plant started by Samuel Andrews, an able English engineer. By 1865, Rockefeller was willing to transfer his allegiance to the new field, and entered as a partner with Andrews. He brought energy and a remarkable business and financial acumen to the unusual engineering ability of his partner and, although small, the business became one of the most flourishing of the twenty-five refineries in Cleveland. In two years the partnership was enlarged so as to unite the refineries of five firms, and the first step was taken in a long series of combinations.

Organizing for Monopoly

By 1870 the partnership form was found to be too binding, and the business was incorporated in Ohio as the Standard Oil Company. Its million-dollar capitalization, later increased to three and one-half millions, made it one of the largest refining enterprises, possessing about 4 per cent of the refining capacity of the country.

From this time on, competition gave way before succeeding restraints, as various combinations collected around this nucleus. In 1872, the Central Association of Refiners, with Rockefeller as president, brought together the owners of a number of refineries located in Cleveland, Pittsburgh, Philadelphia, and New York. The companies retained their corporate independence, but their owners exchanged the rigors of competition for the ease of coöperation. Others of the better companies were sought out and brought into the same fold, so that by 1874 over 50 per cent of the refining industry was represented in the "Standard Alliance."[7]

This loose confederation lasted until 1882, when a closer union was created. A trust agreement placed the voting stocks of the various companies in the hands of a board of nine trustees. The power of the trust increased as more companies were brought in and as the old members grew in size, until the State of Ohio successfully maintained a suit in which the trust was held to be "against public policy, and accordingly contrary to law."[8] The suit disturbed the combine only momentarily, for in the ensuing reorganizations twenty corporations were left with the business of the participating companies, and the former trustees controlled these corporations. Another alliance then followed, and so things stayed until 1899, when the stock of the twenty corporations was exchanged for the stock of the Standard Oil Company of New Jersey.

---

[7] Standard Oil Company of New Jersey, et al., v. United States (1909), Brief for the Appellants, Vol. II, pp. 39–42.
[8] 49 Ohio 137 (1892).

With its capitalization increased from ten to one hundred and ten million dollars, and with an amended charter, this company looked strangely like the old Standard Oil Trust. Its by-laws were similar to those of the trust agreement, and former trustees made up the majority of its board of directors.[9] And its stock was exchanged for shares of the twenty companies formerly controlled by the trust. It went on from this considerable start to own sixty-five corporations and acquire controlling shares in forty-nine others.

Except in crude oil production, the combination of these companies placed the Standard Oil of New Jersey in a very strong, though unquestionably illegal, position. No act of combining could guarantee that oil would be found when a well was drilled, so the company stayed out of this field. Beyond that stage, however, it completely dominated the industry. In transporting crude oil its pipe-lines reached to most wells in the various producing regions. From storage tanks oil moved into trunk lines stretching from the Kansas and Oklahoma fields through Eastern regions to refineries in the interior and on the Atlantic seaboard. The small percentage of oil which moved by rail used cars of a controlled corporation, the Union Tank Line Company, and export oil was in general carried by vessels owned by subsidiary companies. The Department of Justice claimed with obvious justification that "the Standard had all but a complete monopoly of the pipe-line transportation in the four principal oil fields."[10]

In refining and marketing the New Jersey company managed to maintain itself in an equally comfortable position. It marketed the oil of four large refining companies, such as the Tidewater Oil Company, and its direct subsidiaries operated eighteen refineries to give it control of more than 80 per cent of the market. Its marketing companies were assigned territories in which they generally enjoyed exclusive sales of Standard products. In some areas this was not the case, but nothing more than an imitation competition resulted. In a large territory lying south of Illinois, the Waters-Pierce Oil Company and the Republic Oil Company operated in the area assigned to the Standard of Indiana. Unfortunately for the consumer, the three companies were controlled by the Standard of New Jersey.[11] All told, the government was able to list seventy cases where controlled companies operated in the guise of independents.[12]

If the position of the Standard in the domestic market raised a faint suspicion of monopoly, its price and profit record left little room for doubt. While independents testified that one cent a gallon on refined

[9] United States v. Standard Oil Company of New Jersey, et al., Brief of Facts and Argument for Petitioner, Vol. I, p. 77.
[10] Ibid., Vol. I, p. 159.
[11] Seager and Gulick, op. cit., pp. 351–359.
[12] Brief of Facts and Argument for Petitioner, Vol. II, pp. 150–157.

oil was more than adequate to cover marketing costs and profits, the Standard between 1900 and 1906 was averaging in the neighborhood of three and a half cents. In the Rocky Mountain States the Continental Oil Company managed to struggle along with a mark-up of almost five cents a gallon.[13] And it appears that between 1895 and 1906, while the general price level was increasing 25 per cent, the margin between the cost of crude oil and the price of refined oil increased by 45 per cent.[14]

Profits could not help but be large. Government figures placed the original investment in the holding company at seventy million dollars. On this the combine managed to pay three hundred and twenty-six million dollars in dividends in eight years. And it can hardly be charged with a reckless dividend policy, for its surplus grew to two hundred and sixty-one millions—a sum almost four times greater than the original investment.[15] Some of the companies did a bit better than others. In 1904, the Waters-Pierce Company paid dividends of 600 per cent, and the Standard of Indiana earned over 1000 per cent on its capital stock of one million dollars.[16]

Monopoly Effects

The outstanding effects of the combination were the obvious results to be expected from monopoly. It is quite apparent that the Standard organization was not developed in any spirit of philanthropy. The sale of its products and the general growth of the industry were necessarily held back as high prices restricted the demand. In addition, individual prices varied so as to create considerable discrimination. In 1904, Pittsburgh supported some competing independent companies, and the Standard price for illuminating oil was 8.5 cents, which left a margin for the marketing company of .87 cents a gallon. At the same time in other markets, consumers paid tribute to the combine. Those in Newark, New Jersey, paid a price of 11 cents, which allowed the marketing company a margin of 2.6 cents. The citizens of Albuquerque, New Mexico, were forced to be the most generous. They paid 23 cents, which allowed a margin of 6.48 cents.[17]

The Standard made various claims in attempting to justify its size. It supplied a large market for the producers of crude oil, and its great capital resources allowed it to build storage facilities to smooth out the supplies of crude oil which came irregularly from the wells as new fields were opened. It was able to support research and experimental plants, and had achieved two notable successes along these lines. One of its

---

[13] *Ibid.*, Vol. I, p. 189.
[14] *Ibid.*, Vol. I, pp. 191–206.
[15] *Ibid.*, Vol. I ,Table, p. 168.
[16] *Ibid.*, Vol. I, p. 177.
[17] *Ibid.*, Vol. II, p. 3.

Cleveland plants developed and patented the Frasch process which removed sulphur from the crude oil of the Lima-Indiana field. Similar research mastered the difficulties offered by California crude and allowed the Standard Oil Company of California to exploit hitherto useless resources. The great wealth of the organization also allowed it to carry the heavy capital costs of local and trunk-line pipe systems. As a result, new fields of crude were made available, and large refineries could be located at advantageous points. And finally, the combine claimed that its large volume of business allowed it to set up an efficient marketing system both at home and abroad.[18]

These claims are not without foundation. The Standard organization was unquestionably an efficient one, run by unusually able technicians and financiers. There is, however, no evidence that these same claims could not have been made by any large company under competitive conditions. Monopoly was not needed to support the investment in storage facilities or pipe-lines, and research could have been as well supported by any large company. And certainly, the high profits suggest that the specific effect of the monopoly was not to improve the market for crude oil, but rather to limit it as sales of refined oil were restricted for the sake of monopoly prices. Finally, the location of refineries at strategic points can hardly be claimed as an effect peculiar to monopoly. This is particularly evident in the oil monopoly, where many plants were acquired from independents.

The means which the Standard had to use to get rid of competition suggest that it possessed little if any economic superiority over even relatively small refineries. From the days of the Standard Alliance it was able to demand railroad rebates from the three competing railroads by playing one road against another. It was, however, not efficiency but mere power that allowed it to receive rebates of 25 to 50 per cent on both the freight it shipped and the freight which competitors shipped over the railroads.[19] As a result, many independent refiners dropped out, but their elimination could hardly be credited to the efficiency of the combine.[20]

The pipe-line system of which the Standard boasted was actually started and operated successfully by independents to avoid this railway blockade. In 1874, the Pennsylvania Railroad tried to escape from the clutches of the oil company by building a number of local pipe-lines which would have assured it an independent supply of traffic. The

---

[18] Standard Oil Company of New Jersey *et. al.*, *v.* United States of America, *Brief for Appellants*, Vol. II, pp. 88–98.

[19] Petroleum Industry, 70th Congress, 1st Session, *Senate Document* No. 61 (1927), p. 34.

[20] John Moody, *The Truth About the Trusts* (New York, Moody Publishing Company, 1904), p. 114.

other roads stupidly supported the monopoly, and after a ruinous rate war the Pennsylvania gave up its oil lines to the Standard. Four years later a number of independents organized the Tidewater Pipe Company and built a trunk line from the Pennsylvania fields to a point just outside New York City.[21] Every obstacle was put in the way of the Tidewater, but it began operations in 1879. Again the railroads played Standard's game for it, and rates on a three-hundred-and-ninety-pound barrel moving four hundred miles dropped from $1.15 to ten cents.[22] In addition, the Standard bought up the refineries which the Tidewater served, and someone damaged the Tidewater's pipe-lines. Still the Tidewater Company struggled along until 1883. It finally gave up and passed under the control of the Standard. At the same time more refiners dropped out or were bought out as their position became untenable.

Competitors were also eliminated by various unfair methods of competition. Local price-cutting was not merely used to meet competition, but was actively employed to drive rivals out of the field. Smaller companies were forced to cut prices ruinously, while the Standard could make in one market through monopoly prices what it lost elsewhere in ruthless competition. When it supplied only two-thirds of the Los Angeles market, it sold oil at seven and a half cents, which represented a loss of over three cents a gallon. But in nearby Marysville, where there was no competition, the price was thirteen and a half cents. The practice was sufficiently wide-spread to mark it as a settled policy, not the result of chance circumstances.[23]

Dummy independents not only allowed the combine to avoid the ill-will which it faced in various markets, but permitted it to use them as price-cutters, while the general price on Standard products was maintained. In this fashion price-cutting could be localized where competition needed attention. The attack on independents was aided by the reports which the Company received from the railroads on the movement of all shipments to independent companies.[24]

The Loosening of Monopoly Control

The position of the Standard companies in the industry and the competitive practices they used led the United States Circuit Court in the Eastern District of Missouri to hold them "a combination or conspiracy in restraint of trade."[25] The Court ordered the Standard of New Jersey to cease voting the stock which it held in subsidiary companies and

---

[21] *Senate Document* No. 61, p. 34.

[22] Henry D. Lloyd, *Wealth Against Commonwealth* (New York, Harper and Brothers, 1894), p. 108.

[23] *Brief of Facts and Argument for Petitioner*, Vol. II, pp. 4–146.

[24] *Ibid.*, Vol. II, pp. 358–428.

[25] United States *v.* Standard Oil Co. *et al.*, 173 Fed. Rep. 197–200.

thereafter to receive no dividends from these companies. After the decree was confirmed by the Supreme Court on May 15, 1911, the holding company distributed to its own stockholders the stocks which it held in thirty-three subsidiaries.[26]

This action only altered the superficial appearance of the industry. Common officers and directors for the thirty-four companies were forbidden, but a small group which had formerly controlled the holding company now controlled its separated parts. Independent competition between them could hardly be expected and, in fact, did not appear. Each company stayed in its old market area, which kept it out of competition with other companies.[27]

By loosening the tightly organized control of the holding company, dissolution did leave the way open for change. And a remarkable expansion in both the markets of the industry and the production of crude oil supplied a force that considerably modified the industry. In 1909, fuel oils and illuminating oils were the leading products, with outputs of approximately forty million barrels. Gasoline was a poor third with its thirteen million barrels. By 1925, fuel oil had taken an easy lead with three hundred and fifty million barrels, gasoline was in second place with two hundred and seventy million barrels, and illuminating oil, while its sales had increased 50 per cent, stood at a now insignificant figure of fifty-six millions.[28] As the market for oil was being revolutionized the production of crude oil underwent equally great change with the opening of the mid-continent field and other oil regions in the West.

Expanding opportunities brought new faces on the scene. In 1922, the Royal Dutch Shell enlarged its gigantic international holdings to become an important factor in the American market. Its subsidiary, the Shell Union Oil Company, held nearly two hundred and fifty thousand acres of oil lands in the United States and had large investments in refineries, pipe-lines, tank-cars, and marketing facilities.[29] By 1926 there were nine independent refiners with investments of one hundred million or more. All told, companies never associated with the Standard combine were responsible for 33 per cent of the crude produced, and were almost equalling the old Standard companies in refining capacity.[30]

Coöperation which merely bound the old companies was obviously less valuable. Two developments helped to separate them. Firstly, the direct control of John D. Rockefeller, Jr., was lessened when gifts to various foundations left his personal holdings concentrated in seven

---

[26] Standard Oil Co. of New Jersey *et al. v.* The United States, 221 U. S. 1.
[27] *Senate Document* No. 61, pp. 67–68.
[28] *Ibid.*, Table 19, p. 46.
[29] *Report of the Federal Trade Commission on Foreign Ownership in the Petroleum Industry* (Washington, D. C.: U. S. Government Printing Office, 1923), pp. 2–32.
[30] *Senate Document* No. 61, p. 290.

companies.[31] Secondly, various Standard companies left their old pastures
and wandered into those formerly reserved for other companies.

PRESENT STRUCTURE OF THE INDUSTRY

With the loosening of monopoly controls, the industry failed by a
very large measure to reach conditions needed for the successful operation of the competitive system. A relatively few large refining companies
are now found dominating the sale of gasoline in various sections of the
country, and inevitably their pricing and marketing policies cannot be
those found where a very large number of small sellers exist.

Dominance of the Large Firm

Twenty large refining companies have about 60 per cent of the total
investment in the American petroleum industry. Just prior to World War
II the industry presented the following picture.

Table 10

TOTAL ASSETS AND OIL REFINING CAPACITY OF TWENTY MAJOR OIL
COMPANIES

Company	Total assets Dec. 31, 1939	Per cent of refining capacity (Jan. 1, 1938)
	(Thousands)	
Standard Oil Co. (New Jersey)	$2,034,989	9.9
Cities Service Co.[1]	1,068,578	2.5
Socony-Vacuum Oil Co. Inc.	929,066	8.0
Standard Oil Co. (Indiana)	723,079	6.2
Texas Corporation	661,067	7.5
Standard Oil Co. of California	628,618	5.8
Gulf Oil Corp. of Pa.	523,292	5.0
Shell Union Oil Corp.	401,048	5.8
Consolidated Oil Corp.[1]	357,848	4.8
Phillips Petroleum Co.	223,280	1.5
Tidewater Associated Oil Co.	204,467	3.0
The Atlantic Refining Co.	203,400	2.5
Union Oil Co. of California	187,066	2.2
The Pure Oil Co.	178,567	2.2
Sun Oil Co.	146,431	2.0
The Ohio Oil Co.	133,748	0.6
Continental Oil Co.	127,661	1.0
The Standard Oil Co. (Ohio)	76,072	1.3
Mid-Continent Petroleum Corp.	65,103	0.9
Skelly Oil Co.	62,048	0.5
Twenty Majors	$8,935,428	73.2

[1] Richfield Oil Corp. possessing 2.4 per cent of refining capacity is jointly owned by Cities Service Co. and
Consolidated Oil Corp. and is not included herein.

Source: T. N. E. C., *Monograph No. 39*, Chapter II, Table 2; T. N. E. C. *Hearings*,
Part 14–A, p. 7801.

[31] *Senate Document* No. 61, Table 28, p. 70.

Nine of the listed companies were a part of the old Standard Oil monopoly consisting of those bearing the Standard name and Socony-Vacuum, Tidewater, Atlantic Refining, Ohio Oil, and Continental Oil. The twenty companies controlled about three-quarters of the refining capacity of the country, and they possessed even greater control of plants using the catalytic cracking process, which allows much higher yields of gasoline from crude oil than ordinary refining methods. In this field they held about 85 per cent of the total capacity.[32]

Refinery construction undertaken during World War II added further to the concentration found in the refining industry. Addition of nearly one billion dollars of investment in refineries between 1940 and 1944 increased the capacity of the industry by 20 per cent. Nearly 80 per cent of the addition came under the control of eighteen major companies.[33] Standard Oil Company (New Jersey) enjoyed the largest addition, a capacity valued in excess of ninety million dollars. Standard of Indiana and The Texas Corporation were not far behind with gains of over seventy millions. These gains are all the more important since they largely represent increased capacity in the cracking process. Plants utilizing this process could turn out 122,000 barrels a day in 1940 and over one million barrels by November 1944.[34]

Postwar expansion promises a still further growth in refining capacity and a continuation of the growth of concentration. The outstanding postwar increases in refining capacity are taking place in the East Coast Refinery Zone lying between Bayonne, N. J., and Marcus Hook, Pa. Expenditures on new refineries or on improvement of old plants in this area during 1948 and 1949 are expected to reach 270 million dollars. This will raise the daily refining capacity of the area from 700,000 barrels of crude to around 900,000 barrels and will challenge the refining leadership held by the Houston-Beaumont area on the Gulf Coast.[35]

In various retail gasoline marketing areas the importance of the major companies varies considerably. Some of the companies are found marketing in a fairly restricted area, whereas a few market over almost the whole of the United States. Among the latter are The Texas Corporation, Socony-Vacuum, Standard (Indiana), Gulf, and Consolidated, Standard (Ohio) and Union Oil of California have had the most restricted market areas.

The importance of the major companies varies considerably from state to state. Data for 1938 collected from eighteen of these companies

---

[32] T. N. E. C., *Hearings, Part 14–A*, Table 28c.

[33] Report of the Smaller War Plants Corporation, *Economic Concentration and World War II* (Washington, D. C., U. S. Government Printing Office, 1946), pp. 169ff.

[34] *Ibid.*, p. 170.

[35] See "Refinery Expansion Boosts Capacity 25%," *Business Week*, November 27, 1948, pp. 24–25.

by the Temporary National Economic Committee show virtually all sales in nine states being made by some of the eighteen. In other territories only a slightly smaller concentration is found. For example, in the market area comprised of New York, Maine, New Hampshire, Vermont, Rhode Island, Massachusetts, and Connecticut, seven companies managed to make 80 per cent of the total gasoline sales. The lowest concentration appeared in Nevada, where the five major companies found in the state had sales equal to 46.5 per cent of the total gasoline consumption.[36] Under these conditions a single company will inevitably dominate sales in some of the states. This dominance appeared greatest in Utah, Wyoming, and West Virginia, where the principal company enjoyed between 40 and 60 per cent of the total sales. In the average state the largest single seller supplied between 15 and 25 per cent of the total market.

The transportation of petroleum and gasoline shows much the same pattern of concentration as does the marketing of gasoline. Transportation possesses an unusual importance for the petroleum industry in that its sources of crude oil exist in areas that are quite distant from the major markets. Texas, California, and Oklahoma supply about three-quarters of the total production of crude oil but account for only about one-sixth of the consumption. On the other hand fourteen northeastern states produced 2.51 per cent of the national output of crude oil in 1937 and were responsible for nearly 40 per cent of total gasoline consumption.[37]

At least 70 per cent of the crude oil received at refineries is normally delivered by pipe-line. Tankers or barges account for over 25 per cent, and rail transportation is left with something under 5 per cent. Rail costs are two to three times the cost of movement by pipe-line, while tanker costs are only about half as great as pipe-line costs. However, in the heavy movement of crude oil by tanker from the Gulf Coast to New York and Philadelphia refineries, a prior movement by pipe-line is re- . quired to move oil from the producing fields to Texas and Louisiana ports.

Prior to World War II the twenty major companies owned 72 per cent of crude oil pipe-line mileage, including local gathering lines and long-distance trunk lines. In the latter their control was in excess of 80 per cent and left them in a position to dominate the long-haul land transportation of crude oil.

The large-volume movement of gasoline by long-distance pipe-lines is a relatively recent development. The large refiners moved less than three million barrels in 1929, but ten years later they had built this movement up to nearly ninety million barrels. By this time they owned 6,253 miles of the total mileage of line of 6,510 and were responsible for

---

[36] T. N. E. C., *Hearings, Part 14–A*, Table 38b.
[37] T. N. E. C., *Hearings, Part 14–A*, p. 7719.

the movement of all but an insignificant portion of the total gasoline transported by pipe-line.

In the transportation of petroleum by tanker the major companies repeat the same story of concentration. Before the war fifteen major companies owned 84 per cent of the tankers and 87 per cent of the tonnage, and this situation has not materially changed in the last several years.

In their control of crude oil production the present large companies have departed significantly from the policy followed by the old Standard Oil monopoly. Until 1911 integration was largely limited to marketing, refining, and transportation, but the developments of the last twenty-five years have placed the majors in only a slightly weaker position in the production field than in the other branches of the industry. In 1937, the twenty largest companies owned 23.7 per cent of the producing oil wells and were producing about half of the crude oil output.[38] In proved reserves their position was even stronger. Estimates by the American Petroleum Institute placed proved crude oil reserves in the United States at 17.3 billion barrels, and sixteen major companies reported reserves of 8.9 billion barrels, 51.4 per cent of the total.[39] As the figure for proved reserves climbed to around 24 billion barrels by 1949, the concentration of control also increased.

The Gulf Coast and California tideland areas offer the latest opportunities for opening up large crude oil reserves, and the large capital needed to develop the reserves unquestionably favors the majors. In a strip about 30 miles wide running along the Texas and Louisiana coasts, it is estimated that reserves exist equal to 10 per cent of the presently known reserves of the United States. California underwater oil lands also hold out tremendous promise. Exploration and drilling, however, is an unusually expensive business, and the bigger companies are moving in to dominate the development. Humble Oil, subsidiary of Standard Oil (New Jersey), spent well over a million dollars to build the drilling platform for its derrick eight miles off shore. Magnolia Petroleum Co., owned by Socony Vacuum, spent in the neighborhood of nine million dollars in various offshore explorations. It is evident that there is little scope here for the wildcatter who could once sink a well with a few thousand dollars. And there is little opportunity for the small refining company with resources tremendously greater than the wildcatter but still not equal to the demands of this situation.

Ownership of the tidelands is in dispute, but it is doubtful whether decision one way or another will change the operating and ownership picture. In 1947 the United States Supreme Court held that the Federal

---

[38] T. N. E. C., *Hearings, Part 14—A*, pp. 7780 and 7784.
[39] T. N. E. C., *Monograph No. 39*, p. 10.

Government had "paramount rights in and power over" the tidelands, so that drilling leases obtained from the states by the developing companies were jeopardized. Action by Congress may place the disputed title with the states, but settlement of this issue will merely determine who is landlord. It is very probable that the tenants will be the same in any case.

Foreign reserves of oil are being added to those existing in the United States, and in the development of pipe-lines providing access to these resources only the very largest companies have the financial power required to play for the high stakes that are involved. Well-known names are found behind the several billions of dollars being poured into the development of oil in the Middle East. Behind the Arabian-American Oil Company and its proposed expenditure of two hundred million dollars on pipe-line construction between the Persian Gulf and the eastern Mediterranean are Standard Oil Company of California, The Texas Corporation, Standard Oil Co. (New Jersey), and Socony-Vacuum. In other pipe-line developments in the same general area are found Standard of California, Gulf Oil, and Shell. Control in this distant field may become important to the American market as the United States shows increasing use of foreign crude.[40]

Competition and Monopoly

It is obvious that the structure of the industry has left the independent or non-integrated petroleum refiner in a precarious position in competing with the large companies in the sale of gasoline and other petroleum products. He depends on them for a material portion of his raw material in the form of crude oil. If he operates a straight-run refinery, he must buy from the large, integrated companies the casing-head gasoline required for mixing with his gasoline to increase its volatility. For transportation services he must turn to his larger competitors. Supplying much of the crude oil and selling a large portion of the product, the major companies can go a long way in setting prices for both materials. The independent who must cover his costs and make his profit out of the margin between raw material and finished product is inevitably placed in a vulnerable position. Both his costs and selling price are under control or severe influence of a competitor.

In general the traditional labels of "monopoly" and "competition" fail to describe adequately the market conditions that result from the present organization of the industry. The conditions approach those classified under the term Oligopoly, the results of which are studied at some length in Part IV. However, the industry has not been free of at

---

[40] See "$2–Billion Investment Planned for Middle East," *Business Week*, Sept. 25, 1948, pp. 117–18.

least sporadic returns of monopoly, and in view of its monopoly backgrounds its story can reasonably be completed here.

It is impossible to present fairly in any brief description the varying effects which the present structure of the industry has on the sale of its major product, gasoline. And generalizations from description of market conditions in one section of the country at some one time are very dangerous. However, a description of gasoline marketing in recent years in Ohio probably gives as representative a picture as can be given of the situation frequently found in the various sections of the country.

A considerable measure of competitive pricing is found continuing over relatively long periods in the wholesale and retail gasoline markets of Ohio, but in this market and others this picture has given way at times to outright monopoly coöperation between a few large firms.

The pricing of gasoline in Ohio between 1937 and 1947 shows one company, the Standard Oil Company of Ohio, attempting with only moderate success to set prices that would be followed by other companies.[41] Sohio, as the Company is commonly named, became a partially integrated organization after 1911 in acquiring crude oil sources and both crude oil and product pipe-lines. In its Ohio market the Company encounters about twenty other companies selling gasoline at wholesale or retail, or both. Not all the companies, however, sell in all the counties of the state. Five of the twenty companies are successors or affiliates of the old Standard Oil combine, but the best evidence available indicates that there is no direct management or policy connection between Sohio and these companies.

Standard of Ohio sells gasoline at retail through its own service stations and at wholesale to independent dealers who are quoted a price commonly ranging three to four cents below the retail price.

Between 1911 and 1948 Sohio posted its state-wide price at its offices in Cleveland, undoubtedly with the hope that such publication would influence the price policies of other companies selling in Ohio. For some years the Company followed a high-price policy but could not establish the price leadership it desired. Its sales dropped from 45 per cent of the total in Ohio to as low as 11 per cent as other companies maintained prices below the Sohio level. Somewhere around 1925 Sohio policy changed, although a modified price leadership was still attempted. As prices were reduced below its listed prices by other companies in

---

[41] Edmund P. Learned, "Pricing of Gasoline: A Case Study," *Harvard Business Review*, Vol. XXVI, p. 723–756; an extensive examination of gasoline and crude oil pricing policies was undertaken by the Temporary National Economic Committee, see particularly *Hearings, Parts 14, 15, and 15–A*. For an extremely valuable and comprehensive study of the West Coast market area, see Joe S. Bain, *The Economics of the Pacific Coast Petroleum Industry*, Parts I, II, and III, Berkeley and Los Angeles (University of California Press, 1945). Part II, "Price Behavior and Competition," is especially enlightening. The period studied is from 1929 to 1940.

various sections of the Ohio market, Sohio reduced prices locally to the extent required to stop excessive diversion of its sales to competitive dealers. The over-all effect of its change in policy brought its sales back up to 30 per cent of the Ohio market by 1930. When prices have been reduced in any section of the market, and Sohio has reduced its prices to meet the price-cutting of other sellers, the Company then tries to lead prices back up to its state-wide price by relatively small and experimental increases in price which may or may not be adopted by competitors.

Under competitive conditions it might be expected that gasoline prices would be heavily influenced by crude oil prices, and in the period between 1937 and 1947 the state-wide price of Sohio did reflect changes in crude oil prices. However, the timing and the amount of change in gasoline prices were not tied closely to changes in crude oil prices.

In itself this form of leadership is not harmful and need not lead to price results different from those that would occur under conditions where a very large number of relatively small sellers are present in the market. Under certain conditions the results would be harmful if any large seller used its power with the purpose of keeping smaller local marketers in line. This could be done by introducing severe price cuts in any local area where other sellers cut prices slightly below posted prices. However, in the Ohio market, and rather generally throughout other gasoline market areas, it does not seem that the needed conditions exist to permit this cut-throat competition. Small competitors could be eliminated by very costly price-cutting, but they would almost certainly return soon after higher prices were restored. Ease of entry seems well protected by the varied refinery and geographical origins from which gasoline comes into the Ohio market. As a result, price-cutting to eliminate competitors would probably turn out to be a very costly and useless policy. In the period between 1937 and 1947 there is no evidence to indicate that Sohio did more than follow unwillingly the price reductions instituted by other sellers and on its own initiative moved only to restore higher prices where sporadic cut-throat competition had reduced prices in various localities in the state to uneconomically low levels.

The head office of Sohio was responsible for the setting of the state-wide price until the practice was abandoned in 1948, but departures of local prices from the state-wide price were made on the basis of recommendations from division managers. In general it appears that the Company was satisfied to maintain its prices as much as one and one-half cents above the prices quoted by a fringe of cut-rate outlets. However, evidence presented by division managers that sales were being increasingly diverted in a local market would result in reduction in Sohio prices, although normally these are not cut to the level of the lowest sellers in the market. Elements of non-price competition in the form of convenience of location and quality of service are of considerable importance in normal times. Unquestionably these factors permitted the maintenance of prices above the level set by sellers who depended in larger measure on prices to attract custom.

The foregoing picture indicates a considerable measure of independence between the various marketers, but it is not ever thus. Monopoly was revealed in 1936 when the Department of Justice filed two indictments in the District Court of Wisconsin. In the first, twenty-four oil companies and forty-six individuals were charged with a conspiracy to fix prices for gasoline jobbers. Fourteen of the companies and eleven of the individuals reached an agreement with the Department of Justice whereby they paid fines and costs totaling four hundred thousand dollars.[42]

The second case, also filed in the Wisconsin court, was laid against twenty-four companies, three trade journals, and over fifty individuals.[43] A number of the companies involved were also involved in the first case. It was charged that companies supplying 95 per cent of gasoline in ten middle western states bought up the small amounts of independent gasoline coming into the area and agreed, with the coöperation of the trade journals, to raise prices to monopoly levels. After a jury had found them guilty, the defendants escaped through a unique decision of District Court Justice Stone, which set aside the jury verdict.[44] In a new trial a guilty verdict was again returned against the majority of the defendants, and fines of five thousand dollars were levied against the corporations and one thousand against the individual defendants.

SOURCES OF MONOPOLY AND CONCENTRATION

The history of the old Standard Oil combine shows that a major and early source of the monopoly existed in the willingness of potential competitors to enter into non-competitive alliances. From alliance the steps were easy to reach the trustee agreement and eventually the holding company. As the record shows, railroad rebating, unfair competitive practices, ownership of pipelines, efficiency in production, and the possession of large capitals created other interrelated factors contributing to the growth of monopoly.

[42] United States v. Socony-Vacuum Oil Company, Inc., et al., 23 Fed. Supp. 531.
[43] Among others were the Standard of Indiana, the Socony-Vacuum Company, the Pure Oil Company, The Shell Petroleum Corporation and the Sinclair Refining Company.
[44] The Justice felt that the agreement in the first case had prejudiced the defense of some of the individuals in this case. His dismissal of the jury verdict prevented any appeal to superior courts and left the Department of Justice with the task of re-opening the whole case.

Today most of the same elements are present supporting the dominance of a small number of very large firms. It is interesting to speculate whether or not the present concentration in the industry is a product of the former monopoly. Would it have developed in any event? Nine of the largest twenty companies of today were parts of the pre-1911 combine. They were large firms possessing in varying degrees the advantages of integration. Their preëminence could be challenged successfully by only a few similarly large firms. In this sense the old monopoly condition can be blamed for the structural weakness of competition today.

The control of pipe-lines by the majors is probably the central source of their power. These lines were made common carriers by the passage of the Hepburn Act in 1906 and by virtue of that status must hold themselves out as willing to serve any shipper. But the conditions surrounding service to the independent shipper have made a hard road for the independent. First, in spite of repeated public inquiries, the minimum amount which will be taken from an independent for shipment has been kept very high. Frequently, the small independent does not have the large refining or storage capacity which is required to handle large shipments. Secondly, the rates charged have been high relative to cost of the service. The large refiners must pay the same published rate, but if they handicap their refining operations (and incidentally the refining operations of independents) with high transportation costs, it matters very little. The profits are there, in one pocket or another. A statement presented to the Temporary National Economic Committee on behalf of an independent refiner referred to an article appearing in *Fortune* for June 1939 in which it was stated that a two-million-dollar loss in the retail marketing division of one of the large refiners was balanced by a profit of about equal size made through a 29 per cent ownership interest in Great Lakes Pipe Line Company.[45] And it was maintained that this situation has been a general one lasting over a considerable period of time.

In the retail field the majors have rather consistently attempted to magnify their basic power by exclusive dealing arrangements with service stations and garage operators. These arrangements had the effect of limiting a gasoline station to the sale of the gasoline and oil, and probably the tires, batteries, and accessories, supplied by a single refining company. In June 1948 the U. S. District Court in Los Angeles issued an injunction invalidating the exclusive contracts existing between the Standard Oil Company of California and several thousand dealers. According to the Department of Justice, 99 out of 100 retail gasoline outlets have been tied to a single refining company. It is unlikely, however, that this decision will lead to any great increase in the number of "split stations" which handle several brands of gasoline. It will mean more to inde-

---

[45] T. N. E. C., *Hearings, Part 14*, "Petroleum Industry," pp. 7573–7591.

pendent producers of tires, batteries, and accessories, who have faced serious difficulties in finding retail outlets for their products.

In terms of possible public policies, it is obvious that the problem presented by the oil refining industry has changed in character. The Sherman Act terminated a single firm monopoly. It did not restore the conditions required for independence between firms. It has, however, moved successfully against collusive agreements whose continuance might have restored many of the effects of the old single firm monopoly. More exacting public regulation of pipe-lines specifically designed to improve the position of the independent refiner appears as one definite measure of desirable policy. In large part, however, the present qualified and restrained competition in the industry cannot be explained in terms of specific combinations or agreements. It must be recognized as the product of industrial concentration, directly or indirectly a product of the old monopoly.

14

Ethyl Gasoline, Farm Machinery, Cash Registers, and Nickel

ETHYL GASOLINE

When automobile manufacturers introduced the high compression automobile engine in the early twenties, they solved an old problem and created a new one. The rather high operating cost for fuel was lowered as the power derived from gasoline was materially increased, but, at the same time, a serious "knocking" occurred in the high compression engine. After this knocking had been traced to the gasolines then in use, the General Motors Company set out to find a remedy. Its research organization found that iodine added to gasoline stopped the objectionable noise, but caused corrosion of the engine. Corrosion seemed to be a poor substitute for knocking, and so a trial-and-error search went on. In the course of time tetraethyl lead was found to serve the desired purpose without the disadvantage of iodine. It did, however, deposit lead on the cylinder walls, which was about equally bad. Finally the research forces discovered that ethylene bromide added to the tetraethyl lead would combine with the lead during combustion and the compound would be expelled in the exhaust gases. The addition of a teaspoonful of these two chemicals, known now as ethyl fluid, to a gallon of gasoline produced ethyl gasoline, which today makes up approximately 70 per cent of all gasoline sold in the United States.[1]

Under patents which it acquired, the General Motors Company licensed E. I. du Pont de Nemours and Company to manufacture the fluid, and organized the Ethyl Gasoline Corporation, later named the Ethyl Corporation, to market the new product. The fluid is sold to gasoline refineries, where it is mixed with regular gasolines. The resulting ethyl gasoline is colored for identification and is then marketed mainly through wholesale and retail outlets owned or controlled by the large refining

---

[1] United States *v.* Ethyl Gasoline Corporation, *et al.*, District Court, Southern District of New York, May 19, 1939; 27 Fed. Supp. 959, 961.

companies, or through independent jobbers who re-sell to retail dealers and consumers. There are some twelve thousand independent jobbers, and they handle "a substantial part" of the gasoline sold in the United States.[2]

The General Motors and the Standard Oil of New Jersey, sharing ownership of the Ethyl Company about equally, were not satisfied merely to reap the considerable rewards to be derived from their patent monopoly over an important product for which there was no substitute. Through the Ethyl Company they tied up the whole marketing organization of ethyl gasoline in the United States, so that they were able both to dictate price policies for the industry and to determine who was to be allowed to operate in the distribution of gasoline products. After buying ethyl fluid, the refining companies might have thought that the fluid was theirs to re-sell as they wished in gasoline. But such was not the case. They were required to submit their gasoline price-lists to the approval of the Ethyl Company. Many of the large refiners may have heard of such restraints before, and may not have been irritated by this dictation. But many independent gasoline jobbers were certainly concerned about the restraint that was imposed on them. The refiners were allowed by the Ethyl Company to sell their treated gasoline only to those jobbers who were licensed by it. Each jobber was investigated, and unless his "business ethics" were satisfactory he would not receive the necessary license and would be virtually expelled from the industry. Bad business ethics might deserve such punishment, but it was admitted by the company that in a number of cases it had found the ethics of jobbers unsatisfactory because the jobbers were not maintaining the prices posted for the whole industry by the major oil refining companies.[3] In other words, price competition was unethical.

The company was not very convincing in its attempts to justify its practices.[4] Adulteration was on rare occasions discovered by its field agents, and signs were posted on all pumps warning the consumer that the product contained lead and was to be used for motor fuel only. But these services would have been performed by the large refining companies to protect their own brands, and in any event they do not counterbalance the undesirable effects. The control over prices and the restriction of marketing outlets were sufficient to condemn the scheme. But far more damning was its power to expel any individual distributor from the industry.

The Department of Justice believed that the Ethyl Corporation was restraining interstate commerce illegally, and suit was undertaken under the Sherman Act. In May, 1939, the Federal District Court in the South-

[2] 27 Fed. Supp. 959, 961.
[3] Ibid., 959, 963.
[4] Loc. cit.

ern District of New York held that the company had gone beyond the powers granted by its patent monopoly and beyond its rights as a seller to choose the purchasers to whom it wished to sell. The agreements with refining companies whereby supplies were cut off from "unethical" distributors were condemned. The Court agreed that the Ethyl Company possessed by virtue of its patent monopoly the right to impose any condition of sale and any restriction of supply it desired on the original sale of ethyl fluid, but it did not agree that the company held any legal right either to control the re-sale price or to choose the distributors through whom re-sale was made. As a result, the company was enjoined from continuing its licensing practice for jobbers, and from dictating to the refineries concerning the agents they should use for re-sale of ethyl gasoline. In March, 1940, the decision was affirmed by the Supreme Court.

THE INTERNATIONAL HARVESTER COMPANY

In the nineteenth century expanding markets for American crops, an abundance of land and a relative scarcity of labor brought on marked changes in agricultural methods. In no branch was the change more striking than in the development of harvesting machinery. The early decades of the century saw hay cut with the scythe and grain harvested with the same tool, to the back of which was attached a basket-like frame. In this frame the falling grain was caught and piled in rows to be raked and then tied together in bundles.

Between 1840 and 1890 the cutting, raking, and bundling by hand gave way successively to machine methods, until finally on all but the smallest farms the "binder" drawn by horses and operated by a single worker was doing all three tasks.[5] At the same time the next most important machine, the mower, was being developed for the harvesting of hay. Its use called for less than one-quarter of the labor required by the old hand methods and reduced the cost of harvesting by two-thirds.[6]

Factory production of the early forms of these machines may be said to have started in 1847 with the construction of the plant of Cyrus H. McCormick in Chicago. Others soon followed, but the number of important enterprises was never large. In the early years, companies started with the production of patented machines, and for that reason were not numerous. But before 1900 all the basic patents had expired, and a few large concerns specializing in harvesting machines to the exclusion of other farm machinery continued to dominate the field. Their number was limited somewhat by the large capital required, but mainly by

---

[5] The Official Retrospective Exhibit of the Development of Harvesting Machinery, Prepared by Deering Harvester Co. (1900).

[6] H. W. Quaintance, *The Influence of Farm Machinery on Production and Labor* (New York, The Macmillan Company, 1904), pp. 21–25.

vigorous competition among the existing companies. While competition in price, sales promotion, and service was not as ruinous as the large companies claimed, it was severe enough to deter new firms from entering the industry.

Over nine-tenths of the reapers and mowers manufactured in the United States were being turned out by six companies. Two of these were much larger than the others. The McCormick Harvesting Machine Company had approximately twenty-three million dollars in physical assets, and the Deering Harvester Company seventeen millions,[7] while the other four had only between two and four millions.[8]

In 1902 the International Harvester Company, a newly formed New Jersey corporation, acquired the properties of five of these companies, and a year later it took over the plants of the sixth. Half of its one hundred and twenty million dollar capitalization was used to make these purchases, and to pay J. P. Morgan and Company three million dollars for its service as an intermediary. The other half was used to acquire working capital. Strangely enough, the company actually received assets equal or almost equal to its capitalization, and it stands as one of the few mergers of this period that did not result in great floods of watered stocks.[9]

The consolidation left the new company in control of about 85 per cent of the production of harvesting machines, and the acquisition of competing companies in the following years improved its position.[10] In addition, it gained an important place as a producer of other lines, such as tillage implements, manure spreaders, farm wagons, gasoline engines, tractors, and cream separators.

A number of factors account for its ability to continue to dominate the old lines while becoming the most important single producer in many of the new lines.[11] Firstly, it had the strong financial backing of J. P. Morgan and Company and of John D. Rockefeller, which assisted in the purchase of competing concerns and helped to support an elaborate selling organization in which the ability to offer credit to purchasers was very important. Secondly, its large-scale plants were generally superior, and it enjoyed lower production costs than its smaller competitors and

[7] These values are taken from estimates of the Bureau of Corporations. Cf. Bureau of Corporations, *The International Harvester Co.* (Washington, D. C.: U. S. Government Printing Office, 1913).

[8] These four were: Warder, Bushnell, and Glessner, manufacturing the Champion line of machines in Springfield, Ohio; The Plano Manufacturing Company at West Pullman, Chicago; The Milwaukee Harvester Company at Milwaukee; and D. M. Osborne and Company at Auburn, N. Y.

[9] The Bureau of Corporations estimated that the company had assets of 110 millions. Cf. Report of the Bureau of Corporations (1913), p. 126.

[10] *Ibid.*, p. 10.

[11] The Federal Trade Commission, *Report on the Causes of High Prices of Farm Implements* (Washington, D. C.: U. S. Government Printing Office, 1920), pp. 653–654.

held some advantage in marketing a full line of farm machinery. These advantages allowed it not only to displace competitors, but to do so while its profits were averaging 12 per cent.[12] Finally, it solidified its power by the use of unfair methods. Various dealers in a town were each assigned only one of the five brands of machines turned out by the combine, and the average town, being able to support only a limited number of dealers, found no place for agents of competing companies. At times distributors were forced to deal exclusively in the company's products, and there was some evidence of discrimination in prices to injure competitors.[13] In four or five cases, companies which were acquired by the International Harvester continued to claim independence in order to profit by the anti-trust feeling which existed in certain areas.[14]

Investigations of the International Harvester Company by the Department of Justice led to conferences with the company in which the Department proposed a plan for a consent decree breaking the company into three full-line companies. The International Harvester refused to accept any decree that separated the important McCormick and Deering plants, and the Department filed a petition in the District Court of Minnesota charging a violation of the Sherman Act. In 1914, the Court held the combine to be a monopoly and ordered the defendant to file a dissolution plan which would create "at least three substantially equal, separate, distinct, and independent corporations, with wholly separate owners. . . . "[15]

In the same year, on request of the company, the court amended and seriously weakened this decree so as to require only that the Harvester Company "be divided in such manner and into such number of parts . . . as may be necessary to restore competitive conditions and bring about a new situation in harmony with law. . . . " The results were unfortunate. After argument before the Supreme Court in 1915 and 1918, the Department of Justice and the company reached an agreement which left the McCormick and Deering plants united and required the International Harvester to sell some relatively unimportant plants valued at three million dollars.[16] Of the company's business the brands disposed of represented only 4.9 per cent for grain binders, 10 per cent for mowers, 15 per cent for rakes, and 14.9 per cent for corn binders, and they were all much higher-cost machines than the McCormick and Deering lines.[17] The decree limited the International Harvester to one dealer in

[12] *Report of the Bureau of Corporations* (1913), pp. 23, 26–27.
[13] *Ibid.*, pp. XVIII–XIX.
[14] *Ibid.*, p. 296.
[15] United States v. International Harvester Co., *et al.*, 214 Fed. Rep. 987 (1914).
[16] Consent Decree, District Court, Minnesota, October, 1918.
[17] Federal Trade Commission, *Report on the Agricultural Implement and Machinery Industry* (Washington, D. C.: U. S. Government Printing Office, 1938), p. 158.

each city or town, which opened the door somewhat to the expansion of independent companies.

Table 11

MOWER AND GRAIN BINDER SALES IN THE UNITED STATES[18]

	1911 per cent	1922 per cent	1936 per cent
Grain Binders			
International Harvester	87.2	75.4	56.5
Deere and Co.		12.3	31.7
All others	12.8	12.3	11.8
Mowers			
International Harvester	74.6	66.6	53.4
Deere and Co.		11.2	21.8
All others	25.4	22.0	24.8

In 1923, investigations of the high prices of farm implements made by the Federal Trade Commission and the Department of Justice led to an unsuccessful attempt on the part of the Government to obtain a modification of the consent decree. The changes that have occurred in the industry, as shown in Table 11, above, must be credited largely to business influences, and in a very small degree to efforts of the government.

It appears that the International Harvester is still the outstanding company in the industry.[19] But it has lost ground steadily as Deere and Company has become an important manufacturer of binders and mowers. At the time the International Harvester was organized, the John Deere Plow Company was the leading manufacturer of plows, and had built up an excellent general business in tillage instruments, but had not entered the harvesting field. Just prior to the anti-trust attacks on the Harvester Company, Deere was reorganized and constructed a new factory for the production of binders and mowers. From the sale of its first binders in 1912 it has enjoyed a rapid rise to take an important second place in the industry.[20]

It is probable that recent developments will check any further decline in the relative place held by International Harvester and may actually improve its position. During World War II, tractors and other agricultural machinery were produced in large quantities to meet manpower shortages and maintain food production goals. The war-built plants

[18] *Ibid.*, pp. 161 and 164; Bureau of Corporations, The International Harvester Co. (1913), p. 20.
[19] The International Harvester is particularly weak in some new lines. In 1936, it had under 12 per cent of the sale of combines both to harvest and thresh grain, and these sales were greater than the value of all forms of binders sold in the country.
[20] *Report on the Agricultural Implement and Machinery Industry* (1938), p. 8.

operated by International Harvester cost about forty-eight million dollars, considerably larger additions than were operated by other agricultural machinery companies. Sales in 1945 jumped to $622,000,000 of which $290,000,000 were sales made to the Government. This figure compares with total sales of $212,000,000 in 1939. The war-time plant additions, however, were not large relative to the capital assets of $558,000,000 reported by the Company in 1945 and were by no means devoted wholly to production of agricultural machinery. The larger expansion was contained in a post-war program announced about 1945 which provided for a new plant at Memphis, Tennessee, to produce a mechanical cotton picker; a tractor plant at Wood River, Illinois; a $13,750,000 Diesel engine plant purchased from the Government, and several smaller additions. At present the Company's vigorous expansion in the tractor field has boosted its tractor sales above the value of its farm implement sales.

In most branches of the industry eight companies are responsible for over three-quarters of the sales. They turn out a full line of implements and machinery, and their overwhelming position in the sale of a number of products is clear in the following table.

Table 12

SALES OF EIGHT LARGE COMPANIES AS A PERCENTAGE OF TOTAL SALES IN THE UNITED STATES[21]

Implement	1921		1929		1936	
	No. of Companies	Per cent of Total Sales	No. of Companies	Per Cent of Total Sales	No. of Companies	Per Cent of Total Sales
Grain and rice binders	4	91.3	4	96.9	5	95.4
Combines	2	85.3	6	68.2	7	92.0
Grain threshers	2	28.9	4	64.1	6	72.8
Corn binders	3	95.4	3	96.4	4	100.0
Corn pickers	1	97.5	3	77.9	5	72.8
Mowers	4	81.0	5	92.4	8	91.7
Rakes	4	80.3	5	89.8	7	83.4
Hay loaders	3	76.7	4	84.5	7	76.2
Tractor plows	4	24.6	8	91.1	8	89.5
Disk harrows—horse and tractor	5	53.9[a]	8	80.4	8	80.4
Tractors			7	96.3	7	98.7

[a] Does not include two companies.

When business is concentrated in this fashion real independence is difficult and dangerous. Coöperation in a formal or informal fashion becomes extremely easy to effect.

[21] *Ibid.*, Table 29.

There is no evidence of any formally organized connections between these eight companies in the form of interlocking ownership or interlocking directorates.[22] In the past, trade associations of both manufacturers and retailers have been instrumental in maintaining and increasing prices, but it does not appear that the present Farm Equipment Institute, to which all the large companies belong, has directly reduced price competition.[23] Nevertheless, conditions in the industry are such as almost to preclude thoroughgoing competition, and in the opinion of the Federal Trade Commission an informal coöperation takes the place of competitive independence:

Similarity of policies respecting prices, terms, and competitive practices, tends to result whether the policies are determined by the companies individually and competitively, or by understandings or agreements. For most implements and machines, International Harvester Co. and Deere and Co. generally are regarded by other manufacturers as the "price leaders" of the industry. Announcement of prices by other manufacturers is delayed until the prices of these leaders are published.[24]

THE NATIONAL CASH REGISTER COMPANY

In the 1870's and 1880's, business machines were conspicuously absent from retail shops. Transactions were recorded either in a crude fashion or not at all. Errors were many and losses were large. Petty stealing was widely practiced. Consequently, there existed a rich potential market for a machine to record over-the-counter cash transactions.

Apparently James Ritty, a saloon-keeper of Dayton, Ohio, had experienced pilfering by his bar-keepers. At any rate he conceived the idea of a machine that would record sales.[25] He explained his notion to his brother, a machinist, and between them, in 1879, they invented a cash register which they patented.

The brothers started to manufacture these machines, but the venture was not successful. The business was sold. Then the Rittys' successor failed, and the patent rights and properties were acquired by several Dayton business men who formed the National Manufacturing Company. This organization likewise stumbled down the path of failure, while its owners sought to sell it. In 1884 they found a buyer in John H. Patter-

[22] The eight companies are the International Harvester Co., Deere and Co., J. I. Case Co., Allis-Chalmers Manufacturing Co., Oliver Farm Equipment Co., Minneapolis-Moline Power Implement Co., The Massey Harris Co., and B. F. Avery and Sons Co.
[23] *Report on the Agricultural Implement and Machinery Industry* (1938), pp. 22–26.
[24] *Ibid.*, p. 21.
[25] It is said that Ritty figured out a device while watching the dial which recorded the revolutions of the propeller of a transatlantic steamer on which he was travelling on a vacation voyage to Europe.

son. He bought the controlling interest for $6,500 and re-named the corporation the National Cash Register Company.[26] The real development of the cash register business began when he took over.

Patterson soon discovered that he was confronted with a difficult marketing problem. Retail clerks resented the introduction of the cash register. It either reflected badly on their integrity or forced them into an honesty they found painful. The machines were soon designated "thief catchers." Cash register salesmen, carrying big sample machines, were unwelcome in retail shops, so they found it difficult to reach retail shop-keepers. Regional show-rooms and the practice of sample display in hotel rooms had not yet become popular. The head of the National Cash Register Company had to overcome clerk resistance to develop the potential demand for registers. He devised two methods. Almost simultaneously he launched an unprecedented direct mail advertising campaign among store-keepers, and supplied his sales agents with small models of registers in black leather cases. The latter arrangement, it was hoped, would get salesmen within the front doors of grocery-stores, saloons, and other shops.[27] Both methods brought some success. But clerks still resisted. They tampered with the cash registers and caused them to work improperly. Thereupon Patterson hired Pinkerton detectives to watch his customers' clerks. Evidence was gathered to pin sabotage on the recalcitrant clerks, and gradually their resistance was broken.

Cash registers became accepted not only as an obstacle to dishonesty, but as a protector of the honest clerk's integrity. Latent demand for cash registers became real, effective demand. Meanwhile John H. Patterson had come into complete control of his company. He bought out the company's minority shareholders who were glad to sell because they feared the consequences of Patterson's propensity to spend great sums for advertising and sales promotion. Sales and production expanded, however, and National succeeded.

Other enterprisers recognized the potential profits to be realized in this field. Competing machines were developed and new corporations

---

[26] Patterson had formerly owned a coal business near Dayton. At that time he had been one of the first to use a cash register. He sold this business, and with his brother went West to investigate the opportunities in cattle-ranching and fruit-raising. On the return journey the brothers stopped at Colorado Springs. Here they made the acquaintance of a New England merchant who was on an extended vacation. When asked how he could leave his business for so long, the merchant praised an honest manager and Dayton cash registers. This experience is said to have re-aroused John Patterson's interest in cash registers and led him to buy the Dayton outfit. See Samuel Crowther, *John H. Patterson: Pioneer in Industrial Welfare* (Garden City, New York, Doubleday, Page and Company, 1923), pp. 79–80.

[27] Clerks and bar-tenders soon became suspicious of anyone carrying a small black leather sample case. It is said that salesmen of other products, as a measure of self-protection when approaching the brass rail of a bar, would loudly announce that they were not selling cash registers.

were formed to share a growing and lucrative market. But John Patterson would tolerate no interference. Under his direction the National Cash Register Company became notorious for its predatory methods. According to the company's own statements, the mortality rate among competitors was extremely high. Between 1895 and 1910, one hundred and fifty-eight cash register companies sought to compete with the National. One hundred and fifty-three failed.[28] And well they might, for the Patterson-controlled corporation followed the philosophy that the end justified the means, and the only good competitor was a dead one. Even though the National did 80 per cent of the cash register business in the early years of its life, it went on to destroy competition, and by 1916 acquired a 95 per cent control of the industry.

The methods used by the National were many and vicious. Its salesmen were instructed to gather and report all data pertaining to the business of competitors. These were supplemented by information received from bribed employees of competitors who revealed trade secrets. And transportation employees were paid to disclose the destination of competitors' shipments. This information was used to put pressure on specific competitors to drive them out of business. When it was necessary, bogus "independents" were formed to enlist the confidence of competing corporations.

Salesmen of the National dogged the trail of competitors' sales agents. National cash registers were offered at extremely attractive, below-cost prices to interfere with a competitor's sale or to replace a competitor's machine. The replaced machines were then conspicuously offered on the market at "thirty cents on the dollar" or even labeled as "junk." The National's salesmen were instructed and required to push the sales of National registers, even if they had to make derogatory statements about competitors' products, business character, or ability to meet financial and other obligations. They even had to induce store-keepers to repudiate sales contracts made with competitors. They were taught and encouraged to damage or weaken competitors' machines secretly whenever the opportunity was made available. If these methods failed to prevent competitors' sales, the National was ready to offer a cheaply made machine simulating that of the competitor. This machine became known as a "knocker." The prospective buyer of a cash register was led to believe that this machine was similar to the competitor's machine. By inference the weaknesses of the "knocker" machine were subtly ascribed to the competing machine, and in the end the prospect was induced to buy a regular National cash register.

---

[28] U. S. v. National Cash Register Company, in Equity No. 6802, Circuit Court of the United States, S. D., Ohio, Petition, p. 25. See W. H. S. Stevens, "A Group of Trusts and Combinations," *Quarterly Journal of Economics*, Vol. XXVI (1912), p. 629.

Since cash registers were patented and National possessed two of the basic patents, the Ritty and the Birch, and had acquired improvement patents by purchase, it often used infringement suits to annoy competitors and customers of competitors. In some instances these suits were valid, and were the immediate cause of the disappearance of rivals from the field.[29] In other instances, the claims of infringement were unfounded and were brought not in good faith but to intimidate competitors.[30] And this effect they seemed to have.

The National also devised a unique plan to impress anyone who visited the Dayton plant. A competitors' "graveyard" was maintained in a show-room in the factory. Here the registers of defunct competitors were displayed to customers and to present and potential competitors. Vital statistics revealed the name of the deceased, the date of his departure, the net loss of the unsuccessful venture. This morbid exhibit was strangely enough countenanced by John H. Patterson, who aside from this seemed to take a keen interest in the health and welfare of others.

It would be unfair, however, to maintain that the National attained and maintained its monopoly position solely by questionable means. It undoubtedly enjoyed the services of a capable, hard-driving management which possessed at the outset the advantage of the basic patents in the field.[31] And this combination was buttressed by Patterson's insistence on and confidence in high-pressure salesmanship and advertising.[32] The broadening of its markets by effective sales methods permitted it to reach more quickly the optimum size for technical production and to operate at an optimum scale. The margin of its efficiency, however, was not so great that it willingly allowed the forces of fair competition to drive competitors from the field. Rather it chose to hasten their departure by the adoption of methods that were brutally efficient.

It is not at all surprising that a company which devised and adopted such unethical market practices ran afoul of the anti-trust laws. At an early date after the passage of the Sherman Act, its officers were attacked in a criminal suit.[33] Meanwhile the company whose complaint had brought on the Government suit was absorbed by the National. Either because the Government was rid of a complaining client or because it had lost a valuable witness, it dropped the suit.[34]

---

[29] National Cash Register Co. v. American Cash Register Co., 47 Fed. 212; National Cash Register Co. v. American Cash Register Co., 53 Fed. 367; National Cash Register Co. v. Boston Cash I. & R. Co., 159 U. S. 261.

[30] Patterson et. al. v. United States, 222 Fed. 634 (1915).

[31] Ibid., 222 Fed. 635 (1915).

[32] Crowther, op. cit., pp. 87–167.

[33] U. S. v. Patterson et al., 55 Fed. 605 (1893); 59 Fed. 280 (1894).

[34] Decrees and Judgments in Federal Anti-trust Cases, Vol. I, p. 680. U. S. Attorney Sherman Hoar simply stated that the Government would not prosecute further.

The monopoly continued its practices for nearly twenty years before anti-trust action was again instituted in a criminal and a civil suit. In the former, a Federal Grand Jury charged John H. Patterson and more than a score of the National's other officials with monopoly and the use of reprehensible competitive methods. The lower court convicted all but one officer. President Patterson was sentenced to a year in jail and ordered to pay a fine of $5,000 and costs of the suit.[35] The other officers were similarly penalized. On appeal, however, the Circuit Court reversed the decision of the lower court on technical grounds.[36] The case was remanded to the lower court for a re-trial. Supreme Court review of the case was denied.[37] Meanwhile the company deemed it inadvisable to fight the civil suit. In a consent decree in 1916, it accepted a judgment of violation of the Sherman Act and agreed never again to use a long list of unfair methods of competition. In addition, the company had to pay the costs of the civil suit, and the court retained jurisdiction of the case so as to enforce the decree quickly if its terms should be violated.[38] As a result of the decree the criminal suit was dropped.

So ended for a long while sporadic and unsatisfactory attempts by the Federal Government to bring to justice an organization and its officers who sponsored and insisted on the use of the worst of competitive practices: spying, bribery, intimidation, sabotage of competitors' machines, doing business under false colors, encouragement of contract repudiation among the buyers of competitors' machines, and other intolerable methods. The penalty was merely the payment of costs of suit and the command to be good while they continued to enjoy the fruits of a 95 per cent control of the cash register business!

Nearly ten years elapsed before a Federal agency again clashed with the National. The Federal Trade Commission charged it with the systematic execution of a plan to hinder and restrain competition unduly in the manufacture and sale of cash registers and similar machines.[39] About the same time the Department of Justice alleged that ninety-two National Cash Register sales agents and employees of sales agents were using market tactics in violation of the 1916 consent decree. The proceedings in this instance were not directed against the company itself or against its officers, nor were the company's policies criticized.[40] It was an action against sales employees. In November, 1928, one defendant only was adjudged guilty of contempt of court and fined $1,000 for violating the terms of the 1916 consent decree. In closing the case

---

[35] 201 Fed. 697 (1912); 205 Fed. 292 (1913); *Decrees and Judgments in Federal Anti-trust Cases*, Vol. I, p. 795.

[36] 222 Fed. 599, 650 (1915). Evidence had been erroneously excluded.

[37] 238 U. S. 635 (1915).

[38] *Decrees and Judgments in Federal Anti-trust Cases*, Vol. I, p. 320.

[39] Complaint No. 1328, F. T. C., *Annual Report*, 1926, pp. 144–145.

[40] *The New York Times*, November 3, 1925, pp. 1, 5.

the presiding judge censured the Department of Justice severely for inadequate investigation of the facts and for subjecting the defendant sales employees to groundless prosecution.[41] Shortly thereafter, the Federal Trade Commission dismissed its case against the company.

Precise information about the National's early financial history is not available. It appears, however, that in its infancy the company grew so fast that it was continually short of working capital. President Patterson was forced to borrow heavily from the Dayton banks and to supplement these loans by borrowing from the Banigans of Providence, R. I., wealthy rubber manufacturers.[42] Since the Banigan loans affected the National's capacity to borrow from the banks, Patterson sought advice from A. C. Ratshesky, a Boston banker, who re-vamped the National's financial structure in 1899 and put the company on a firmer financial basis. Thereafter the National found no trouble in getting funds when needed.

It is reasonable to assume that a monopoly position in an expanding market would yield exceptional profits. Doubtless it did, but the company pursued a modest dividend policy in which regularity of payment was stressed, rather than the size of the dividends. Between 1889 and 1926 the company failed but once to pay a cash dividend, and in that year, 1898, it paid a 200 per cent stock dividend. The average dividend from 1906 to 1916 was slightly more than 2 per cent, which is hardly a monopoly return. The explanation of this low return is not to be found in small profits but in these two factors: the Patterson family owned the corporation and John H. Patterson dominated the family. Patterson had strongly established ideas as to how profits should be distributed. Modest dividends, therefore, went to himself and his family, while the remainder of the profits were re-invested in the business. Later Patterson introduced profit-sharing among his employees, and all profits in excess of 6 per cent on the investment were divided equally between the company and the employees as a group.[43] John Patterson was not merely a ruthless competitor, he was also a domineering but benevolent employer. For his paternalism he was dubbed Pioneer of Industrial Welfare by his biographer, Samuel Crowther. From 1917 to 1925, the company's dividend policy became more generous. During these years dividends ranged between 7½ and 9 per cent.

In 1926 the banking firm of Dillon, Read & Company obtained an interest in the Cash Register Company. A new corporation was formed with a Maryland charter, to take over the assets of the Ohio corporation. At the present time New York banking interests represent one-third

---

[41] *Ibid.*, November 13, 1928, p. 51.
[42] Crowther, *op. cit.*, p. 180.
[43] Crowther, *op. cit.*, pp. 260–261.

of the directorate of nine. Over the period 1926–1948, earnings per share have been moderately good.

The National Cash Register Company still commands about 90 per cent of the market. In 1929 it acquired the Ellis Adding-Typewriter Company; in 1931, the assets of the Remington Cash Register Company, once its adversary in a patent suit; and in 1943 it took over the Allen-Wales Adding Machine Corporation. The company now produces around five hundred models, which it sells on the installment plan to a great variety of establishments. Much of its present business is replacement of obsolete machines. While the original patents have long expired, it has a host of improvement patents. Expansion between World Wars I and II was sizable in foreign fields. Nearly fourteen per cent of its assets are now in foreign[44] countries. So strong is the company's hold in the domestic market as well as in the leading industrial nations that it is highly unlikely that strong competition at home can arise against it. Present competition, such as it is, probably acts only as a very moderate brake on the company's pricing policy. The 1916 consent decree doubtless still serves as a considerable restraint on its marketing tactics.

NICKEL

Over 90 per cent of the world's known reserves of nickel are concentrated in enormous ore bodies beneath a few square miles of the Sudbury Basin region lying about 250 miles north of Toronto, Canada. The ore consists of copper and nickel sulphides in combination with significant amounts of platinum, gold, and silver. A ton of ore yields about $16.50 worth of nickel, $8.50 in copper, and $4.00 in platinum, gold, and silver.[45] All the ore bodies are owned by the International Nickel Company of Canada, Ltd. The United States as its major customer has a considerable interest in the monopoly International possesses. In 1948, slightly under 70 per cent of its sales of nickel were paid for in United States dollars. The large part of the remainder of its output goes to English and European consumers. Canada itself uses only about one per cent of the Company's production.[46] Another connection also exists in that about 50 per cent of the ownership of the Corporation lies in the United States. Thus International Nickel derives a large part of its revenue from the United States and returns a considerable portion of its profits to citizens of this country.

Alternative sources of nickel are too small and poor to offer any material competition to International Nickel. The principal reserve exist-

---

[44] Standard and Poor's *Corporation Records*, April–May 1949, pp. 9052–9053.
[45] *Fortune*, Vol. X, No. 2, August 1934, p. 64.
[46] *The Financial Post Corporation Service*, Report of March 2, 1949.

ing outside Canada is in New Caledonia, about 1,000 miles east of Australia. Here a French company operates mines which have ore bodies equal to about two per cent of those in the Sudbury District. In addition to being small the Caledonian properties are costly to work. To meet the tremendous demands of World War II, the United States kept a small Cuban property alive by subsidies; but production ceased when the financial aid lapsed at the close of the war. One Canadian property, owned by Falconbridge Nickel Mines, Ltd., is independent of International Nickel. However, its production is only about five per cent, and its reserves about one or two per cent, of those of its large rival.[47]

Deposits in the Petsamo region of Finland comprise the only major European source, but until recently these were owned by the Mond Nickel Company of England, a wholly owned subsidiary of International Nickel. In 1944, under the terms of the treaty between Russia and Finland, the Petsamo territory was returned to Russia. In this fashion Russia obtained a source of nickel but paid International Nickel ten and one-half million U. S. dollars for its lost assets. It is unlikely that this change in ownership will affect the United States' market in any fashion. Nickel ores have been disclosed in Venezuela, but apparently these will not be allowed to disturb the monopoly. In 1944, International Nickel obtained exploration and mining rights from the Venezuelan government.

The major use of nickel is as an alloy with steel, to which it adds both strength and anti-corrosive qualities. Its use in armament materials has been tremendous, but International Nickel has striven to escape dependence on this widely fluctuating demand by developing a wide variety of industrial uses for nickel. The common nickel-steel alloys containing between two and five per cent of nickel use about one-third of the nickel produced. The automobile industry is the largest single customer using alloy steels where hardness and relative lightness are required, as in transmission gears, drive shafts, roller bearings, and crankshafts. The locomotive industry is also a large user, in steel frames, boilers, and axles. Stainless steel, a steel alloy containing 18 per cent chromium and eight per cent nickel, has been an important competitor of aluminum in the railway supply industry. Its use was pioneered by the Burlington Railroad in its Burlington Zephyr when the railroads were looking for a material for lightweight passenger equipment. Monel metal, named after Colonel Ambrose Monell, first president of International Nickel, has gained a great variety of uses from its anti-corrosive qualities and its considerable strength. Nickel manages to find a great range of markets, even reaching jewelry stores in the form of white gold, a combination of zinc, nickel, and gold.

---

[47] T. N. E. C., *Competition and Monopoly in American Industry,* Monograph No. 21, p. 79.

International Nickel started its corporate existence as a producer of copper. The presence of copper-nickel ores in Ontario had been known since 1848, but development was not undertaken until the Canadian Pacific Railway was built through the Sudbury region in 1883. In 1886 the Canadian Copper Company was organized as a mining enterprise, shipping its ore to the Orford Copper Company in New Jersey for processing. The nickel content of the ore prevented refining by ordinary processes of copper refining, but successful operations were started by uniting the wealth of the Ontario resources with a refining process known to the Orford Company.

In 1902 the International Nickel Company was incorporated in New Jersey with a capitalization of $36,000,000 as a holding company to bring together Canadian Copper, several processing companies in the United States including the Orford Company, and various French and English processing companies. A second and larger combination was effected in 1912, and a second holding company with very slight change in name, International Nickel Company (N. J.) was organized for the purpose.

The company which bears the title role in this present account was organized in 1916 to consolidate and extend the Canadian holdings of the New Jersey Company. The latter held all the stock in the newly formed International Nickel Company of Canada, Ltd. Shortly thereafter the original Canadian company, Canadian Copper, was dissolved. Two important changes were made in 1928. The first separated the American holding company and the Canadian operating company. A new company, International Nickel Company, Inc., was organized in Delaware to hold the properties in the United States, and by exchange of stock the Canadian company ended its corporate connection with the United States companies. The change was one of form more than of substance, since stockholders who formerly owned an interest in the Canadian enterprise through their ownership of stock in the American parent company were left holding shares in the two separate organizations. The Company reported that this change was undertaken because a substantial ownership had developed in Canada and many substantial stockholders desired the separation. *Fortune* Magazine, however, said that the alteration in corporate structure was made "partly to avoid antitrust complications with the U. S. government."[48] The separation left the Canadian company owning an American subsidiary, International Nickel Co., Inc., which owns or controls fabricating plants at Bayonne, N. J., and Huntington, W. Va., and operates various sales offices.

The second change of 1928 solidified the monopoly control over Canadian reserves of nickel in absorbing the Mond Nickel Company into

---

[48] *Fortune*, Vol. X, No. 2, August 1934, p. 102.

the International Nickel Company of Canada by an exchange of International shares for those of the Mond Company. The latter corporation shares with International of Canada the ownership of the Frood mine, the richest in the Sudbury area and in the world. Its merger with International undoubtedly allowed for a more efficient exploitation of the reserves but, at least incidentally, consolidated the position of the combine.

The 1928 reorganization has left International of Canada with a variety of properties owned and operated directly or through subsidiaries. The Mond Nickel Company operates on behalf of International various refining and fabrication plants in England, Scotland, and Wales. In the United States International Nickel, Inc., the Delaware corporation, acts as subsidiary operating a rolling mill, refinery, and extrusion presses at Huntington, W. Va., and a foundry and research laboratory at Bayonne, N. J., on the site of the now-dismantled Orford refinery. Whitehead Metal Products Company of New York manufactures and distributes Monel sinks, range boilers, and water heaters. In Canada, International Nickel in addition to its mining properties operates concentration plants, smelters, refineries, hydro-electric plants, and various by-product operations. In Europe its holdings include an interest in Amalgamated Metals, Ltd., which in its turn is a holding company for various English, German, and Belgian processing companies and a marketing organization for the combined interests in Europe and the Orient.

The outstanding effects of monopoly control have been a remarkable price stability and careful control of the utilization of reserves. The price of nickel in New York varied by only one cent from 1927 to 1931 and remained at a constant price of 35 cents from 1932 to 1948. Precisely the same prices were maintained in Canada and England. This uniformity is remarkable in continuing alike through the booms of the twenties and of the period of World War II and the severe depression of the thirties. In contrast, copper prices have shown a wide fluctuation similar to those of other commodity prices.[49] Selling at 18 cents in 1929, copper fell to a low of seven cents in 1933, climbed to 13 cents in 1937, declined to 10 cents, and after the wartime controlled price of nearly 12 cents rose to 20 cents in 1947.

Production of ore inevitably varied sharply as demand conditions changed and the price of the product remained stable. The greatest variation occurred between 1930, when 2,285,000 tons of ore were treated, and 1932, when only 66,000 tons were processed. Although unsold stock accumulated in 1930 and 1931, the Company did not cut prices but cut output—to the point where it was operating at only 12

---

[49] Copper production of International Nickel is sufficient to allow the Company to rank sixth among world producers.

per cent of capacity. It was content to see its share of the total world sales drop to 60 per cent while sales of its one Canadian competitor rose to 14 per cent and those of its New Caledonian competitor to 17 per cent. In spite of the improved market position of these two companies, the depression position of International Nickel was summarized by the Temporary National Economic Committee as not an altogether alarming one:

> Rather than reduce its price, it chose to wait for business revival to restore its former share. It could well afford to wait. In 1932 when its sales stood at less than 20 percent of its productive capacity, the company met all its expenses, set aside substantial reserves, and paid two-thirds of its interest bill out of its year's earnings. With its break-even point thus established at about 20 percent of capacity, with the only source of nickel capable of satisfying a substantial revival in demand securely in its hands, International was content to sit out the depression. By 1934 it had recaptured 85 percent of the world market. By 1937 its sales were 500 percent above those of 1932, 65 percent above those of 1929.[50]

From the low point in 1932 production has risen by leaps and bounds. Figures are not available for 1940–42, but the total exceeded twelve million tons of ore in 1944, falling to 7,700,000 tons in 1946 but recovering to over ten million tons in 1947.[51]

Profits have been high in most years. A deficit of $135,000 was suffered in 1932, but between 1938 and 1947 the annual net profits have ranged between $32,000,000 and $50,000,000 after taxes, yielding returns of between 15 and 25 per cent of net worth.

It is obvious that the control of nickel enjoyed by the Canadian company has very considerable influence in the United States market, and it should be equally obvious that American anti-trust controls possess no means to reach the monopoly with any serious effect. A civil suit filed in May, 1946, by the Department of Justice alleged that the International Nickel Company, incorporated in Delaware, and its parent the International Nickel Company of Canada have monopolized the business of importing commercial nickel and nickel ores into the United States; have monopolized the manufacture, distribution and sale of nickel and nickel products in this country; and have preserved their monopoly position by cartel agreements with French and German competitors. The Government sought complete separation of the business of the Canadian corporation and its American subsidiary and asked that a plan be formulated by the Court for redistributing the assets of the firms so as to destroy the alleged monopoly.

Nothing much came of the suit. The Government did obtain a consent decree out of the proceedings, but the judgment did not and could not

---

[50] T. N. E. C., Monograph No. 21, p. 80.
[51] *The Financial Post Corporation Service,* Report of March 2, 1949.

affect the fundamentals of the monopoly problem. The decree was confined essentially to two points:

1. Any special or regular forms of nickel rolling material which International Nickel may be supplying to its own rolling mill at Huntington, W. Va., for the production of nonferrous high-nickel rolling mill products are to be supplied also to other United States rolling mills which may desire to make these particular products. Prices are to be as favorable as the company's general prices for nickel sold to the ferrous and other large nickel consuming fields in the United States. The Huntington mill will present to a number of libraries copies of a manual descriptive of rolling mill processes employed by it in using special forms of nickel rolling material.

2. If International Nickel should have occasion to sell nickel rolling material to other foreign producers of such material or of rolling mill products, it will not be a condition of the sale that such producers not import their own production into the United States.[52]

Since the major portion of the company's nickel sold in the United States is used for alloy steels and other related uses which are not affected by the consent decree, it is clear that the successful suit merely touched the fringe of the problem.

Meanwhile the International Nickel Company of Canada continues to consolidate its position. Approximately one million dollars a year is being spent by the Company throughout the world in searching for new nickel ores. In the past fifteen years it has proved some 130 million tons of ore or about 9 million tons per year. This is about the average rate at which the Company has been extracting ore, and today it has as much proved nickel-copper reserves as it had fifteen years ago.

[52] *The Financial Post Corporation Service*, Report of March 2, 1949.

15

The Economics of Monopoly

The preceding chapters have illustrated one type of monopolistic development in American industry. A single firm has held control over a large part of the total supply of some commodity or commodities. The existence of a sale monopoly frequently endowed the companies with a buyer's monopoly also.

In the course of time, most of the companies studied have been forced by public prosecution or by the rise of competitors to share their control with at least a few other firms. And the great merger movement of the Coolidge and Hoover era did not generally push single firms into pre-eminence, but set up a few large companies in the affected industries. Their coöperation, which is studied in Part IV, is probably the outstanding monopolistic problem of the present. Certainly, single-firm monopoly today is an annoyance in a far smaller portion of the American market than was the case between 1890 and 1920. The economic effects of such control, however, still deserve attention. Single firms still control a few national industries and many special products; moreover, their power would grow if public controls were relaxed.

Public policy in the past has attempted to control monopoly by common law and by a variety of state and Federal statutes. The propriety of this policy, or of other treatments for the monopoly held by single firms, rests finally on the effects of such monopoly. And the vigor with which anti-trust laws are administered may depend in part on public appreciation of the economic significance of monopoly.

In an individualistic system the possession of overwhelming economic power by a single company seems in itself to be objectionable. Political democracy is seriously harmed by the presence of concentrated economic power. Economic welfare is injured by the greater inequality of wealth and income created by monopoly and by the arbitrary treatment that may be extended to labor and the consumer. The basic economic objection, however, arises from the inefficiency of monopoly. It influences the production and hence the standard of living of a country by affecting the size of the monopolized industry and the cost of producing goods.

If we think in terms of a number of producers turning out physically similar goods that buyers consider interchangeable, we find under competitive conditions that price and cost considerations fix the size of this industry. Each of these fields of production (smaller units where the products are differentiated) would be allowed by competitive forces to develop only to an ideal size. Each industry would take labor, capital and raw materials in quantities sufficient to yield that output which would be taken off the market at prices covering the lowest possible average cost to the marginal producer. Any other output would be less desirable. For example, if the industry did not develop to this ideal size the lesser product would sell at prices above cost. Since costs are fixed by the value the productive resources have in other fields of industry, this would mean that some resources could move into this industry and would there produce a greater value product. The competitive profit system would tend to bring about this result.

Restriction below the ideal output would not occur under perfect competition. Conditions would permit the movement of labor and capital and no producer could benefit by restricting his sales and raising his prices. Any attempt to do so merely would mean that competitors would undersell him and take away all his business. But under monopoly, restriction is practicable, and offers the means of achieving abnormal profits.

If it is assumed that the monopolist has complete control of supply, has no fear of latent competition or of other interferences, and has a desire to make his total profits as large as possible, he will restrict sales and ask higher prices. The amount of restriction that is most profitable will depend on the character of the demand and the nature of cost conditions.

If the demand is inelastic, that is, if the total of receipts increases as prices are raised and sales curtailed, the reaction of unit costs is of no importance in determining the amount of restriction.[1] The largest monopoly profits would be obtained by cutting production to the smallest output that is feasible from the production point of view. Here the total receipts are at their maximum and total costs would be smaller than for a greater output.

Where the demand is elastic the reaction of total costs to restriction of output becomes immediately important. As output is reduced below the competitive production, the gross income is reduced—buyers are not

---

[1] It is assumed that a restrictive policy does not increase total costs by forcing the producer to give up large-scale methods of production or to assume heavy costs to keep latent competition from becoming active.

offering sufficiently high prices to offset the reduced sales.[2] But total costs will decline, and as long as this decline is greater than the reduction in total receipts, the restriction is worth while. To realize the largest possible total profits the monopolist must cut his production to the point where any further restriction would mean that his total receipts declined more than his total costs. Here it would be apparent that any further reduction would bring higher prices, but would restrict sales too severely, and unit costs would not decline sufficiently to offset the loss in total receipts.

At this point the monopolist would find as large a total of profits as demand and supply conditions would permit. From the point of view of his sales, he would be selling a last unit of goods that increased his revenues by the same amount it increased his costs. If he set his production so as to sell one more unit than this, he would find his total receipts had increased, but by an amount less than the increase in his total costs, and his profits would be smaller.[3]

A restriction of sales as severe as that suggested under inelastic demand conditions is not probable in the ordinary monopolized industry. It is caused by both the inelastic demand for the product and the absolute control of supply. And those conditions are rare. Certainly, few if any single firms have been so favorably placed. In the first place, within the ordinary range of prices very few commodities are so strongly desired by consumers that their use will not expand materially when prices are lowered or contract severely when prices are raised. The business man and the economist know far too little about the elasticity of demand for most products, but in the case of aluminum and ethyl gasoline, for example, substitutes almost certainly make the demand elastic. And furthermore, as in the case of tobacco, where no direct substitute exists, the commodity must struggle for its place in the consumer's limited budget, and high prices will cause a serious shrinkage in consumption.

In the second place, the monopolist must fear the influence of high prices on the amounts buyers will take from him, for he is not commonly in absolute control of the supply. The output of even a few struggling independents would increase significantly as the monopolist attempted to take higher prices from the consumer; for example, if the price of aluminum ingot is low the use of scrap aluminum will stay small, but will grow step by step with increases in price. Hence, the demand the monopolist can count on will be the total amounts taken by

---

[2] Some restriction below the competitive output is assured, since the reduction in sales will place the unit demand price above the total unit cost. This unit cost includes a normal rate of profit on the whole capital invested, so the monopolist will be making the same normal profit and something over.

[3] That is, marginal revenue would be less than marginal cost.

buyers at various prices, minus the supplies that will come from other sources. These supplies will be greater for the higher range of prices and will tend to make the demand for the monopolist's product elastic. Even if the independents are inferior in efficiency and supply only a small part of the market, they place valuable restraints on the restrictive policy of the monopolist. They are frequently protected by the high costs which the monopoly would incur in driving them completely from the field, but public protection for them is easily justified. Public funds spent in protecting them from unfair methods of competition, for example, would pay material dividends in reducing the harmful restriction of production and the high prices resulting from monopoly. Where independents have not survived, public policy might advantageously create competition through the agency of government-owned companies.

The degree of restriction resulting from a monopoly may be influenced also by the manner in which it was formed. If it resulted from a combine organized by former competitors, it must take care of the invested capital of the members of the coöperating group. Inefficient plants would be closed, but their capital costs stand as a charge against those kept in operation. Even if all plants are of comparable efficiency, some might be closed, if marketing and other considerations permitted, in order to allow the survivors to operate near their optimum scale. The burden of the wasted capital will increase the costs of those operating, and restriction may be lessened, as the closing of many plants may seriously increase the costs of the combine. It is apparent, however, that where the monopolist achieves his position by driving competitors out of the field he escapes these costs and his output policy will not reflect their influence. Everything else being equal, the restriction of output will be greater than in the case of the combination.[4]

The Influence of Monopoly on Plant Costs

Many claims of superiority over competitive industry have been made by the large monopoly firms in attempts to justify their position. Some of the claims possess merit, but there is no evidence that monopoly allows companies in the ordinary fields of industry to produce more cheaply than comparable companies in competitive circumstances. The special fields that have come to be designated as public utilities can operate more efficiently in the hands of one company than under competition. The typical monopolies studied in the previous chapters, however, do not show this same phenomenon.

If plant costs are to be held to a minimum the best engineering and

[4] For an abstract analysis of the theoretical points developed in the preceding pages, see the Appendix of this chapter.

management techniques must be used, and the plant must be built to optimum size and operated at optimum scale. Monopoly can only reduce plant costs through its influence on one of these factors.

It is not easy to isolate the effect of monopoly on the technical methods that are developed and used in an industry. Some evidence, however, appears in the cases which were studied. In the manufacture of ethyl fluid, farm machinery, and tobacco products, patents on improved methods and products were important, but were largely developed under competitive conditions. The discovery of ethyl fluid was made by General Motors to improve the operation of their engines. If it had been feasible, that company might very well have been satisfied to keep the fluid for use in their own cars to better their position in the automobile industry. In the case of shoe machinery, various companies had improved the machines used in the bottoming room, and their union made the United Shoe Machinery Company a monopoly. The electrolytic reduction of aluminum was developed by Hall, working alone and without resources. Monopoly was a result of his work, not a cause of it. Before monopoly appeared the tobacco industry made a great contribution in developing machinery for the manufacture of cigarettes and, after the dissolution in 1911, continued to improve its products and its methods. And in the manufacture of shoe machinery, the outstanding contribution of recent years was made by an independent, The Compo Shoe Machinery Corporation.

In the public utility fields the optimum size for a plant is so large, relative to the market, that there is not room for a number of competitive companies of satisfactory capacity. It is clear, however, that this exceptional circumstance does not exist to justify industrial monopolies. In the first place, most of the monopolized companies operate a number of plants. From its earliest days, for example, the tobacco combine was made up of plants that were of optimum size. If they had been competitively operated their size would not have been affected. In the second place, in the rare cases, such as alumina production, where a single plant served the whole industry, economic analysis shows that a number of plants smaller than the giant would be equally efficient.

A number of cost studies have shown that there are limits to the growth of plant size beyond which production becomes more costly. A study made by the Federal Trade Commission shows various cost comparisons for plants of different size in the flour milling industry. In three out of six years the lowest costs are associated with the largest volumes, but, in the other years, plants of medium size enjoyed the lowest costs.[5] In the manufacture of bread the largest plants, turning out over thirty-five million loaves annually, had average costs of 6.85

---

[5] Federal Trade Commission, *Competition and Profits in Bread and Flour* (1928), Table 115, p. 449.

cents, while plants next below them in capacity produced for 6.3 cents. The average cost of the large plant was above the average for the seven hundred and fourteen plants studied.[6] An investigation made for the Temporary National Economic Committee covered eighteen industries producing about one-quarter of American production and showed the same result. Plants were classified as large, medium, or small, and out of fifty-three individual plant-cost tests, the largest plant had the lowest cost in only two tests.[7] A large plant, but not the largest, had the lowest cost in four tests. Medium-sized plants had the lowest cost in twenty-one and small in twenty-six of the cases. On the average, for the whole fifty-three tests, over one-third of the plants in each cost array had lower costs than those of the largest plant.

It appears that largeness is no prerequisite for plant efficiency, and where size is associated with monopoly the resultant restriction of output will probably endanger the scale of plant operations. Unless the number of plants constructed is carefully controlled, as it was in the aluminum industry, or plants are scrapped, a partial and inefficient operation of plants is necessary for the sake of monopoly profits. The evidence suggests that most monopolies resulting from a combination of formerly competing plants fell back on both a scrapping of some plants and a restricted operation of their other factories. Closing some plants completely may improve the scale of operations in others, but still causes an initial waste of capital equipment. In time, monopoly can restore its plants to capacity operation if demand grows as it did in most of the cases studied, and if construction is carefully controlled.

Economies from the Combination of Plants

The various firms that achieved monopoly control almost inevitably developed horizontal and vertical forms of combination. For example, the plants of six companies were brought together so as to make the International Harvester Company a horizontal combination from its inception. The Standard Oil, American Tobacco and the United Shoe had similar origins. Only in the process of its growth did the Aluminum Company spread out to operate a number of plants in various stages of the industry. All these firms, with the exception of the United Shoe Machinery Company, integrated various stages of their industries to form vertical combines. Evidence gathered from the experience of these and other firms, shortly after combination was achieved, can be used to throw some light on the nature and extent of the economies they gained

---

[6] *Ibid.*, p. 295.

[7] Temporary National Economic Committee, Monograph No. 13, *Relative Efficiency of Large, Medium-Sized and Small Business* (Washington, D. C.: U. S. Government Printing Office, 1941), p. 12.

or expected to gain. It will be apparent that monopoly need not be credited with whatever gains they realized unless it was the necessary result of attempts to organize combinations of efficient size.

Eleven of the largest combines of the period were studied by the United States Industrial Commission between 1898 and 1900. In the hearings, representatives of the giant concerns claimed that horizontal combination gave them certain advantages over single plants. Where they operated a number of plants, those that were inefficient or badly located could be closed and operations concentrated in the better plants. In addition, when business was slack, certain plants could be shut down and the remainder operated at optimum scale. H. O. Havemeyer, president of the giant American Sugar Refining Company, claimed important savings for his company on both these scores.[8] Yet it is doubtful if monopoly organizations would be any more effective in weeding out inefficient firms than would competition. However, the handling of fluctuations in demand so as to keep plants at capacity could be done only by a large combine.

It was claimed also that the operation of a number of plants in the same stage of the industry allowed material savings in freight costs. Plants might be located at favorable points and customers served from nearby factories. As Mr. Havemeyer admitted, the closing of plants to concentrate production in a few not only precluded any gain on this score, but actually entailed an increase in freight costs. The sugar combine concentrated the production of twenty-four plants into five large refineries located at New Orleans, Boston, and New York, and shipping distances were generally greater than before combination. It is probable that the Aluminum Corporation, the United Shoe Machinery, and the American Tobacco made gains in plant size only to lose some of them in freight costs greater than a competitive industry would have faced.

Another advantage was realized when combination allowed competing brands and conflicting patents to be brought under one control. The International Silver Company, which produced about 50 per cent of the country's supplies of silver-plated and sterling silver table-ware, allowed a number of its acquired brands to decline while it pushed the sale of certain brands bearing the name of Rogers Brothers.[9] Similarly, the American Steel and Wire Combine and others found at times that patents were acquired with absorbed firms, and possible conflict was avoided by using some patents and dropping others.[10] It is possible that some economic gains were made by putting competing patents and brands "to sleep," but it is obvious that the practice was more closely

---

[8] H. R. No. 476, 56th Congress, 1st Session, *Preliminary Report on Trusts and Industrial Combinations* (1900), pp. 109–110.

[9] *Ibid.*, p. 1072.

[10] *Ibid.*, p. 1028.

bound up with the elimination of competition than it was with the reduction of competitive wastes.

Advantage in acquiring specialized business ability was also claimed by the large combines. J. B. Duke gave this as the important virtue of the tobacco trust. Different types of skill and experience could be brought together and a high degree of managerial specialization might result. But the advantage contains its own limiting features. Specialized management must be coördinated. And coördination becomes increasingly costly as a business grows in size and entails the delegation of important matters of superintendence to subordinates. It may be significant to note that Mr. Duke allowed all the important management positions in the American Tobacco to fall into the hands of a narrowly specialized group of financiers.

The personal concern of an owner-operator plays a smaller and smaller part as a hierarchy of employed managers is built up. And there is no assurance that specialized skill is an adequate offset for the loss of direct control by owner groups. Certainly, in the pre-combination days in the shoe machinery industry, in tobacco manufacture, and in oil refining there were plentiful signs of alert and able managements.

It is a rather striking fact that in all the testimony presented to the Industrial Commission, the defenders of combination made no claims for any economies of integration. The reason is implicit in the nature of the combines. The Aluminum Corporation, for instance, made gains from coördinating the various stages of the industry, but the expansion that swept it into a monopoly position was a horizontal growth that added nothing to the integration of the company. Similarly, in 1901 the great United States Steel Corporation combined iron ore mines, railroads, lake ore carriers, coal coking plants, and various works producing a variety of finished steel products. But it gained nothing in the way of integration that had not been achieved earlier by constituent companies such as the Carnegie Steel.[11] And among the large companies, integration did not seem to guarantee high profits. From 1915 to 1918 earnings among the steel companies varied inversely with the degree of integration. Companies operating only rolling and finishing mills made average returns of over 36 per cent on their investment, while those that produced their own ore, coke, and pig iron made returns of 22 per cent.[12]

The mere size of these giant combines did bring them certain economies. Some of the trusts were inclined to argue that their size was attractive to customers in that it brought an assurance of steady and adequate supplies of the product. The general public attitude toward

---

[11] Commissioner of Corporations, *Report on the Steel Industry* (1911), Part I, p. 108.

[12] Federal Trade Commission, *War-Time Profits and Costs of the Steel Industry* (1925), p. 32.

the trusts hardly seemed to offer any general support to such claims. And it does not seem that the large combines put much stock in their own claims, for they frequently hid their identity behind dummy independents.

The large control held by the American Steel and Wire Company was used to tighten credit conditions for customers and to deny their claims for damages and short deliveries. While the exercise of this power might reduce costs for the company, it probably effected no real economic gain and hardly endeared the company to its customers.[13]

When size is gained through absorbing independent companies, it may bring savings by eliminating highly paid management officers and by curtailing the office organization of the constituents. In this fashion the overhead cost laid on each unit of the product may be lessened. It is not possible to measure these gains nor the offsetting costs that may follow them. There is likely to be little decrease in salary cost if the important officers of the combine take very large salaries and bonuses. And the enlarged central office required to coördinate the policies of the subordinate companies may eat up a considerable portion of the overhead economies. Finally, if inflated values are paid for the acquired properties, and if promoters take large profits, as was the case in the tobacco, steel, oil and most other combines of the early trust period, operations start under a severe handicap.

It has been a popular belief that a large company can purchase materials and credit more advantageously than a small business. Some advantage does exist on this score. For example, the Federal Trade Commission found that the large meat-packers were able to get commercial credit at lower rates than small distributors and jobbers.[14] And it is true that as an industry grows it tends to gain so-called external economies that come from a better organization of the supply industries as their market expands. But the growth of single firms to monopoly proportions is not needed for the growth of an industry. Quite the reverse, it will usually restrict the size of an industry as the firm seeks monopoly profits. In 1901, Charles R. Flint, associated as organizer and management officer through the nineties with a half-dozen different combines, said that generally a large business found no advantage in buying staple supplies and in some cases suffered because of the large amounts it had to obtain.[15] He intimated that advantage would only come when a firm was the sole or nearly sole buyer. Then, of course, its advantage arises from its monopoly position and constitutes no economic gain.

---

[13] *Preliminary Report on Trusts and Industrial Combinations*, p. 1032.

[14] Federal Trade Commission, *The Meat Packing Industry* (1919), p. 31.

[15] Report of the Industrial Commission, *Trusts and Industrial Combinations* (1901), Vol. XIII, p. 36.

The Earning Record of Large and Small Companies

Earnings are influenced by too many factors for them to be used as an index of efficiency, but the ability of small corporations to make relatively good records at least minimizes the claims made for largeness. The Temporary National Economic Committee found that in eighty-four tests the largest company had the best rate of return on invested capital in only twelve instances. Corporations of medium size enjoyed the largest rate in fifty-seven cases, and companies classified as small in thirteen.[16]

A more comprehensive study made by William Leonard Crum throws a somewhat more favorable light on the earning power of the larger concerns.[17] On the basis of their total assets, companies were divided into ten size-classes. The smallest class included corporations with assets between zero and $50,000 and the largest, corporations with assets of one hundred million or more. Data on earnings and assets were obtained from reports of the United States Treasury for the years 1931–1936. In 1932, at the depth of the depression, the zero to $50,000 class showed a rate of return of –28.09%, the next larger class –12.97, and so on with smaller and smaller deficits until the fifty to one hundred million class was reached and positive earnings of .30% were recorded.[18] For 1936, the best of the six years, the smallest class is the only one showing a deficit, and earnings increase steadily until the fifty to one hundred million group is reached. Then, for companies over that size, earnings appear that are slightly below the average for all sizes. With that one exception the profit rate increased in all the six years as the size-class increased.[19]

While the general record of the larger companies is impressive, a further break-down of the figures shows that smallness does not preclude the chance of large profits. An important section of the enterprises in the small groups has a better record than large companies. When attention is directed to the corporations reporting some positive income, and corporations having deficits are ignored, the relation between size and rates of return is reversed. In 1932 the smallest of such companies show earnings of 8.88%, and the rate declines steadily for each larger class until the one to five million dollar group is reached. These companies earned 5.60% and those in the next two larger groups 5.91%. Cor-

[16] T. N. E. C., op. cit., p. 13.

[17] William Leonard Crum, Corporate Size and Earning Power (Cambridge, Mass., Harvard University Press, 1939).

[18] The rate of profits expresses the earnings before tax deductions as a percentage of the book value of the owners' equity. Size is measured by the total assets as reported on balance sheets accompanying corporate income tax returns.

[19] Crum, op. cit., Table II, p. 31.

porations over the fifty million dollar mark reëstablished the trend with earnings of 5.34%. In 1936 the same relationship is observed. The five smallest classes have average earnings of 11.04% and the five largest only 8.15%.[20]

It is apparent that small companies in the deficit class were very numerous and their losses were serious. The number of small and medium-sized companies in the income category is great enough, however, to suggest that largeness is not required for favorable earnings. In the manufacturing division the companies reporting an income showed approximately the same relation between size and earnings as that for all corporations, and the number of companies in the smallest group was not negligible. For 1932 they held about 15 per cent of the total assets of all manufacturing corporations of that size class. In 1936 they made up 44 per cent.[21]

Scattered studies by the Federal Trade Commission also indicate favorable opportunities for the small company. In its study of profits in the manufacture of bread and flour the Commission found that even where the largest plants had the lowest plant costs they still did not enjoy the best rate of profits. The smaller companies were financially more successful, either because they had markedly lower investment costs or because they were able to get better selling prices.

A study of pig iron companies in 1918 shows the same condition. The group of companies with the best rate of profits were small in size and had relatively high plant costs. It appeared to the Commission that their low capital costs more than balanced their relatively high operating costs, so as to leave them in a comparatively favorable condition.[22] In the manufacture of beehive coke, used in smelting iron, companies with average investments under one million dollars earned markedly larger returns than those with capitals over five million dollars.[23] In a report on one hundred and forty-three Southern Pine lumber companies, the Federal Trade Commission found companies of medium size with the best record, and the smaller companies inferior to both medium and large

---

[20] Many production and market factors undoubtedly combine to explain the relative success of different classes of companies, but small corporations generally possess a financial feature that may be of significance. They borrow more of their total capital than do large corporations. As a result, if they were making the same rate of return on their total capital as their large rivals, and if the rate of interest was below this return, there would be left a residue for the small owner's equity which would yield a rate above that realized by the owner in the large company. At the same time, of course, the risk would be greater. For the distribution of total capitalization and of borrowed capital by asset classes see Twentieth Century Fund, Inc., *How Profitable Is Big Business* (New York, 1937), Table 15, p. 60.

[21] Crum, *op. cit.*, Table VIII, p. 60.

[22] Federal Trade Commission, *War-Time Profits and Costs of the Steel Industry* (1925), p. 13.

[23] *Ibid.*, p. 42.

companies.[24] In all the regions studied, large companies but not the largest produced at the lowest costs.[25]

The Earnings of Monopoly Combinations

When a company reaches monopoly size, its earnings may be favorably influenced by its market control or by its ability to reduce some of the costs of competition. The early trusts apparently found considerable economies in the reduction of their sales forces as competing companies were absorbed. The Whiskey Trust that sold 85 per cent of the liquor products of the country in 1901 claimed that the disappearance of competition in Kentucky alone saved a million dollars a year in sales expenditures.[26] And selling costs increased in the tobacco industry after the dissolution of the American Tobacco Company. Large sums spent annually for advertising, style competition, and various forms of sales promotion are unquestionably a cost imposed on producers by the competitive system. While some of the effort is informative and would probably be continued by monopoly industries, much of it arises from the inevitable duplication of competitive enterprise.

The gains realized by the large combines were apparently lost or offset somewhere in their operations, for their financial record was not very good. In spite of the large hopes of investors and the even larger promises of promoters, profits from the combination movement of the eighties and nineties were small. A statistical study of thirty-five large industrial combines picked at random from companies organized before 1904 compares their records after combination with the previous records of the constituent companies.[27] And the consolidated companies show up badly. First, they earned little more than half the profits promised by promoters and bankers responsible for their formation. Only in five cases out of the thirty-five did the actual earnings come up to the forecasts. And more than an extravagance of claims is indicated. The earnings of the separate companies before combination were nearly a fifth larger than the earnings in the first year after combination. And, in case that appears to be too early a test, time did not improve the record materially. During their first ten years, when they had at least normally good business conditions, the combines made average returns at least 10 per cent below what the constituents had made as separate companies. For example, the companies thrown together to make the United States

---

[24] Federal Trade Commission, *War-Time Costs and Profits of Southern Pine Lumber Companies* (1922), pp. xiv and 84–85.

[25] *Ibid.*, p. 59.

[26] Report of the Industrial Commission, *Trusts and Industrial Combinations* (1901), Vol. XIII, p. 829.

[27] A. S. Dewing, "A Statistical Test of the Success of Consolidations," *Quarterly Journal of Economics,* Vol. XXXVI (1921–1922), pp. 84ff.

Steel had earned annually approximately one hundred and eight million dollars before the consolidation. And the Steel Company, in its first ten years, had average annual earnings of only ninety-two millions. The combination seemed to work no miracle for the companies that formed the American Beet Sugar Company and the American Window Glass Company. In each of these cases, the combines earned about one-quarter the previous earnings of the separate companies.

Still another test compared the earnings of the giant concerns in their first and tenth years. It showed profits in the tenth year to be about 7 per cent less than in the first. As A. S. Dewing, the author, concluded:[28]

After sufficient time had elapsed to permit the consolidation to perfect its organization, to reconstruct its plants and to effect all the anticipated economies of combination and large-scale production, and after considerable sums of new money had been invested in betterments and new plants, the earnings gradually diminished until they were no more, perhaps a little less, than during the first year of consolidation. And the first year's earnings . . . were less than the earnings of the separate plants before consolidation.

From this record it would seem probable that a number of the combines organized before 1900 must be regarded as definite failures. One authority, Eliot Jones, puts the following trusts in that category: asphalt, bicycle, cordage, cotton duck, cotton yarn, glucose, linseed oil, malt, newsprint paper, paper bag, salt, shears and scissors, silverware, sole leather, starch, upper leather, wall-paper, whiskey, and writing-paper.

Failures suggest that the mere act of combination and the mere possession of size do not assure efficient and profitable operations. And success, if achieved through certain means, may indicate the same thing. The qualified success of the United States Steel and other big combines seems to rest in an important degree on the tolerant coöperation of supposed competitors. Unfair methods of competition were used to build the tobacco monopoly and the oil refining monopoly. The use of great financial resources played an important part in building up the American Tobacco, the United Shoe Machinery Company, the Standard Oil, and many other combines. Patents and tariffs offered protections to many. And the possession of almost exclusive control of raw materials protected the Aluminum Corporation from the attacks of domestic competitors. Success has depended on too many other advantages for it to indicate efficiency. In fact, the use of other powers may, in some cases at least, suggest the possible presence of inefficiency.

Conclusion

Monopoly seems to offer no production gains to offset its essential fault. A certain amount of the labor and other productive resources of

[28] *Ibid.*, p. 94.

the country are kept out of the monopolized field and are forced into other employments. And they produce a smaller value product than they otherwise would. This loss does not seem to be offset by any marketing or production advantages of monopoly.

Many related evils grow out of the faulty control of production. In a number of instances substantial control of the market has brought injury to the consumer in the form of high prices; and it always leaves the consumer with inadequate defenses against deterioration in the quality of goods. Labor may be forced to sell its services without the presence of the competitive bidding needed to protect wages and conditions of employment. The small enterpriser is robbed of an opportunity or is placed in a vulnerable position if he pits his little strength against the power of the monopolist. By pouring large incomes into a few hands monopoly generally decreases the economic satisfactions derived from the national income. The concentration of ownership present in the large corporation means that monopoly profits increase an already excessive inequality in the distribution of income.

In addition to creating a continuing economic waste in the restriction of production, the single firm adds seriously to the instability of industrial production. When economic conditions change in various phases of the business cycle the prices of monopolized goods remain much more stable than other prices. The rigidity not only increases the impact of depression and prosperity changes in the monopoly industries, but distorts the connection between monopolistic and competitive fields. Particularly in recession periods may such maladjustments create serious injury. An unnecessary amount of unemployment is created in the monopolized fields and an injurious rigidity of costs is laid on any industry using the monopolized products.[29]

A society finding varied benefits and satisfactions in a system of economic and political individualism must find monopoly objectionable from many points of view. Not the least of these is the threat that monopoly develops against political individualism. When control of economic affairs is concentrated in a few hands, democracy becomes a meaningless form. And even the form will not survive. The entrenched economic group will attempt to control the political organization of the country to protect its economic position, and injured interests will attempt to organize so as to improve their position. Political individualism will give way as the political unit becomes the group instead of the individual. Democracy will be succeeded by the forms and principles of authoritarianism.

---

[29] The influence of price rigidity on the business cycle is analyzed in Part IV, Chap. 29.

APPENDIX

In the following table an abstract illustration suggests how the inter-action of supply and demand under competitive conditions would fix the size of the industry and how that size would be affected by the appearance of monopoly. It is assumed that the first unit of product comes from the lowest-cost firm and each increase of one unit comes from the successive entry of added firms, while the superior firms do not increase their production.[30] The first two rows in the table show an imaginary

Table 13

1. The range of demand prices........................	$50	$22	$14	$10	$7	$5
2. Amount taken at these prices......................	1	2	3	4	5	6
3. Additions to total revenue yielded by one added sale.	$50	-$6	-$2	-$2	-$5	-$5
4. The range of costs................................	$3	$4	$5	$6	$7	$10
5. Amount supplied at these cost prices..............	1	2	3	4	5	6
6. Additions to cost incurred to produce one added unit.	$3	$4	$5	$6	$7	$10

demand condition—the amounts buyers will take at various prices. The fourth and fifth rows show the supply condition. Competition would bring five firms into the field and the production would be five units. The selling price would be seven dollars, and the fifth or marginal firm would have an average cost of seven dollars, while the better producers would enjoy the profits of their superiority.

If it were assumed that all five firms are brought into one combination, and if no new firms appeared, the size of the industry would be considerably altered. The monopolist would aim at the largest possible profits, and would set his sales at the output where his total revenue, less his cost of production, is greatest. The third line in the table shows how much one added sale increases the total revenue. The figures are derived from the previous two rows. For example, the sale of one unit brings in a revenue of fifty dollars and the sale of two a revenue of two times twenty-two dollars. The total, forty-four dollars, is six less than the previous total, so the added revenue when two units are sold instead of one would be minus six dollars. The sixth row shows how much one added sale increases the cost. In order to make his profits as great as possible, the monopolist would stop his production just short of the point where another unit would add less to his revenue than it added to his costs.

In the above illustration monopoly profits would be greatest when one unit is produced.

----

[30] It would be reasonable to assume that superior firms would increase their production until their marginal cost reached the level of the average cost of the marginal producer, but the above assumption allows a simpler illustration and does no injury to the argument.

The sale of a single unit yields a revenue of fifty dollars for a cost of three. A second unit would actually decrease the total revenue without bringing any comparable reduction in costs. The monopolist, if his control were perfect, would not produce beyond one unit. The price of the commodity would be set at fifty dollars; the monopolist would make large profits and output would be seriously restricted. Probably only one of the five plants would be operated.

If the best firm in the industry seized monopoly control by driving others out of business, its profits would be forty-seven dollars. All this would not be monopoly profit; under competitive conditions the firm would make intra-marginal profits of four dollars. If the monopoly resulted from a combination of the formerly competing plants, the cost of producing in the one surviving plant would have to bear the fixed expenses of the plants that were held idle. Or if several of the plants were kept in operation, costs would be higher, since inferior plants would be kept in use and all the plants would be operated at less than their optimum rate. In either case the monopoly profits would be reduced.

If we assume that the first five firms are brought under one control but the sixth firm comes in as a competitor, we will find the position of the monopoly materially changed. This sixth firm is able to produce one unit for a cost of ten dollars, and we may assume that it would push its production past the least cost point, so as to produce two units if the price were as high as fifty dollars. For prices between twenty-two dollars and ten it would produce one unit. Below ten dollars it would sooner or later be forced to drop out. In the following table, the first two rows show the demand condition used in the previous illustration, while the third row shows the supply position of this competitor.

For the figures in the fourth row the amounts that would be supplied by the independent are subtracted from the amounts demanded at various prices. These remainders constitute the amounts the buyers would take from the monopoly at the several prices, or in other words, the demand for the product of the monopolist.

Table 14

1. The range of demand prices.................... $50	$22	$14	$10	$7	$5
2. Amount taken at these prices................... 1	2	3	4	5	6
3. Amount supplied by the competitor at these prices 2	1	1	1	0	0
4. Amount buyers would take from monopolist at these prices................................... ?	1	2	3	5	6

Now, while the demand for the product as a whole is still inelastic, the demand for the goods of the monopoly has become elastic except at the lower range of price: that is, at a price of twenty-two dollars buyers would expend just twenty-two dollars on the monopoly goods, while at a price of fourteen dollars they would spend twenty-eight dollars, and so on.

With this elastic demand the limited monopoly would realize the largest possible profits from a less severe restriction of output than was the case when no competition existed. More than one unit would be sold. At the price of fifty dollars buyers would take one unit and at least three would be put on the market. The monopoly could not be sure of even one sale at that price. To make maximum profits it would increase its output to the point where the added revenue from the sale of an additional unit would just equal the cost of that unit. To stop short of this point would be to sacrifice some of its profits in missing sales that would bring in more than they added to costs. To go beyond this point would similarly mean an injury to the total profits in selling a unit that added more to the cost than it brought in added revenue. In terms of the figures used in the previous tables this may be illustrated as follows:

Table 15

1. The range of demand prices	$22	$14	$10	$7	$5
2. Amount buyers take from the monopoly at these prices	1	2	3	5	6
3. Addition to total revenue of the monopoly from an added sale	$22	$6	$2	$5	−$5
4. Addition to cost incurred to produce one added unit	$3	$4	$5	$6	$7

When the monopoly produces two units, the second unit adds four dollars to the cost and six dollars to the revenue, so its production would be profitable. Any greater output, however, would reduce the monopoly profits. A third unit would add five dollars to the cost and only two dollars to the total revenue. Two units would be produced and sold for a total revenue of twenty-eight dollars. The total cost is seven, so profits would be twenty-one dollars. The combine would keep two plants in operation and the independent would operate one.

The independent firm is an inferior one and supplies only a small part of the market, yet it sets valuable restraints on monopoly power. In the illustration, a competitive industry would have sold five units at a price of seven dollars and would have operated five plants. With no check on its control, a monopoly would set a price of fifty dollars and restrict production to one plant—20 per cent of the competitive output. But, restricted by some competition, it would set a price of fourteen dollars and operate two plants. The independent would be operating one, so the industry would be brought up to 60 per cent of the ideal competitive size. It is obvious, however, that, even when some competitive supply is present, public policy needs to be concerned with the under-production fostered by monopoly. And that concern must be very great in case patents or other devices grant the monopolist an unqualified control.[31]

---

[31] This conclusion attracts the attention to the considerable injury done by the tariff that excludes some foreign competition from fields under domestic monopoly control. It also suggests the value that may in special cases be found in government-sponsored competition.

PART III

Public Regulation of Monopoly and
Competitive Practices

16

Common Law Background and State Anti-Trust Action

Long in advance of the trust movement in the United States, a fairly definite public attitude toward monopoly was manifested in the doctrines of the law. For centuries it had been observed that unified control of the supply of a commodity was injurious both to fellow-traders and to the consuming public. The antipathy to monopoly was reflected in the doctrines of monopolizing and restraint of trade which originated in the English common law. This body of traditional law, developed through precedent and to be found in the reported judicial decisions, has had an important bearing upon the formulation and interpretation of anti-trust statutes in the United States. These statutes are of relatively recent date. The earliest ones were enacted by the states in the late 1880's, and Congress entered the field with the Sherman Act in 1890. Prior to these formal expressions of policy, the meagre protection afforded the public against the concentration of economic power emanated almost entirely from the common law as interpreted and applied by American judges. Even today statutory provisions are being interpreted in the light of the doctrines of this judge-made law as they stood in the late nineteenth century.

Since the Sherman Act of 1890 stands as the most important expression of American public policy relating to industrial monopoly, it will be treated more comprehensively than other monopoly legislation in this discussion of public regulation. To provide a necessary historical background, however, consideration will first be given to the experience under the common law and the attempts of the individual states to meet the problem.

COMMON LAW BACKGROUND

There are several developments in the English common law which impinge upon the problem of preserving free competition.[1] The most im-

---

[1] For detailed and authoritative accounts of the common law relating to monopoly, see J. A. McLaughlin, *Cases on the Federal Anti-Trust Laws* (New York, The Ad

portant of the doctrines which emerged was that termed "restraint of trade." Since this phrase appears most prominently in the Sherman Act, it is deserving of particular attention. Its meaning in the common law has had a great influence upon the interpretation of the Federal anti-trust statute. Other common law rules or doctrines may be subsumed under the general heading of "monopoly" or "monopolizing." Although some of the offenses may have been of passing significance in the changing English economy, nevertheless they were indicative of the attitude of the traditional law toward interferences with competition, and have supplied working precepts for the modern attack upon monopolistic practices.

Monopoly or Monopolizing

It has often been pointed out that at common law there was never an offense known as "monopoly."[2] Any attack upon the exclusive control of a product has always been undertaken by declaring unlawful the means used to accomplish the objective. What might be regarded as an apparent exception to this statement was the express annulment of private monopoly patents granted by the Crown in the famous Case of Monopolies in 1602.[3] The court decided that the exclusive grant of power to make playing cards in England was a void monopoly at common law. This decision was confirmed by the anti-monopoly Act of 1623 and subsequent statutes. But it should be noted that this revolt was directed at the abuses associated with the exercise of the royal prerogative. It did not outlaw the granting of monopolistic privileges by Parliament nor the exercise of restrictive powers by guilds and towns. Nevertheless, the evils of monopoly were recognized and the future course of public sentiment and judicial opinion was suggested.

The earliest offenses at common law were forestalling, regrating, and engrossing. These practices, which were punishable as crimes, were of particular moment in the many small medieval communities that depended on local sources of supply for food and other necessities of life. To control local supplies and thereby enhance prices was not over-difficult, and it was of prime importance that free competitive markets be maintained. As codified in the statute of 1552,[4] the gist of each offense

---

Press, Ltd., 1930), Introduction; Edward A. Adler, "Monopolizing at Common Law," *Harvard Law Review*, Vol. XXXI (1917), p. 246; Bruce Wyman, *Control of the Market* (New York, Moffat, Yard and Company, 1911), Chap. 6; M. W. Watkins, *Industrial Combinations and Public Policy* (Boston, Houghton Mifflin Company, 1927), Chap. 11; National Industrial Conference Board, *Mergers and the Law* (New York, National Industrial Conference Board, Inc., 1929), Chap. 1.

  [2] Adler, *op. cit.*, p. 258; Watkins, *op. cit.*, p. 236.
  [3] Darcy *v.* Allen, 11 Coke 84 (1602).
  [4] 5 and 6 Edw. VI. c. 14.

may be defined as follows: forestalling was the buying of goods on their way to market or in any way preventing their entrance to the market; regrating was the buying of foodstuffs in any market with the intent of re-selling them in the same market or within four miles of the place; and engrossing was the acquisition of large quantities of a product by buying or contracting for growing crops with the purpose of selling the product at enhanced prices. The common feature of these offenses, it will be observed, was monopolizing or the deliberate manipulation of prices by interfering with the supply of goods.

As a national economy evolved, with less dependence upon local sources of supply, and as middlemen came to be recognized as legitimate economic functionaries, these offenses became obsolete. By 1772, the influence of the *laissez-faire* policy, then gaining general acceptance, brought about repeal of the law of 1552. Despite the formal repeal of the statute, however, the common law origin of the offenses enabled judges who were so inclined to punish individuals who enhanced prices by engrossing or "cornering the market."[5] It was not until the Act of 1844,[6] which prohibited prosecutions at common law, that complete freedom of action was accorded all traders. Since 1844, strangely enough, there seems to have been nothing illegal in an individual attempting to absorb the market supply of a commodity for the purpose of charging extortionate prices.[7]

Joint action on the part of traders with the intent to control the market was also regarded as a public offense at common law. Such confederacies were indictable under the doctrine of conspiracy. Originally applied to laborers who combined for the purpose of raising wages or bettering hours of work,[8] it was only logical that this doctrine should be extended to so-called "conspiracies to monopolize."[9] Whether it was due to the rarity of such concerted efforts on the part of business men, or simply to the failure to detect and prosecute them, it is certain that the number of such cases in the courts was not great. And during the course of the nineteenth century, the conspiracy doctrine seems to have met the same fate as the offenses of forestalling and engrossing. It is not now illegal in England to combine for the purpose of dividing business, restricting output, or fixing prices.[10]

The authorities do not agree as to whether or not the English doctrine

---

[5] King *v.* Waddington, 1 East 143 (1800); King *v.* Rusby, 2 Peake 189 (1800).

[6] 7 and 8 Victoria, c. 24.

[7] Watkins, *op. cit.*, p. 241.

[8] N. I. C. B., *Mergers and the Law*, pp. 11 ff.

[9] Anonymous, 12 Mod. 248 (1699), plate-button makers agreeing not to sell below a set price; King *v.* Norris, 3 Kenyon 300 (1758), all producers in Droitwich fixing the price of salt; King *v.* De Berenger, 3 M. & S. 67 (1814), conspiracy to enhance price of government bonds by false rumors of Napoleon's death.

[10] See N. I. C. B., *Mergers and the Law*, p. 15, and authorities there cited.

of monopolizing ever became a part of the American common law. For a time the colony of Virginia did proclaim and enforce the English statutes against forestalling and engrossing, and there were numerous colonial statutes which either forbade these or similar practices, or fixed prices to prevent their evil effects.[11] But it is doubtful whether American courts have ever recognized them as criminal offenses.[12] It is also true that industrial combinations were never prosecuted as criminal "conspiracies to monopolize."[13] The phrase was often used to condemn combinations that were attacked on some other ground, but it did not constitute a recognized criminal offense. It was not until anti-monopoly statutes were enacted by the state and Federal governments in the latter part of the nineteenth century that these old common law doctrines were revived and definitely incorporated into American law.

Restraint of Trade

Contracts in "restraint of trade," or what might otherwise be termed contracts not to compete, had a definite technical meaning as originally used in the common law. The concept embraced contracts in which an individual agrees not to engage in a given business or occupation. Such restrictive covenants are usually ancillary to the main contract of sale of a business or of employment. The purpose is to protect the good will purchased with the physical property of a business or to protect an employer from the competition of employees or apprentices at the expiration of their terms of service or training. Such covenants were originally held to be void and unenforceable at common law. In the earliest English case, decided in 1415, a dyer agreed for a consideration to refrain from practising his trade in a town for six months. The judge denounced the arrangement with some vehemence, saying: "By God, if the plaintiff were here, he should go to prison until he paid a fine to the King."[14] The reason for the unqualified condemnation of such contracts was not the preservation of competition, but the fear that individuals would be deprived of their means of livelihood and become public charges—a matter of real concern in a rigidly organized feudal society. Incidentally, of course, such restrictive arrangements deprived the economy of the services of a useful person and did restrict competition to some extent.

The emergence of a more flexible economic society and the trend toward greater freedom of contract led to a relaxation of the rule that

---

[11] Franklin D. Jones, "Law of Business Competition," *Yale Law Journal*, Vol. XXXVI (1926), pp. 42–55.

[12] Watkins, *op cit.*, pp. 241–242. But see Adler, *op. cit.*, for the view that the courts of certain states did recognize engrossing and forestalling as offenses and that Section 2 of the Sherman Act includes them.

[13] McLaughlin, *op. cit.*, p. 21.

[14] Dyer's Case, Y. B. 2 Hen. V. fol. 5, pl. 26 (1415).

all restrictive covenants were against public policy and void. Exceptions to the general rule were made as early as 1613,[15] and by the time the leading case of Mitchel v. Reynolds[16] was decided in 1711, covenants were upheld for which adequate consideration had been given and which were limited in time and space. General restraints, such as might cover moved any time limitation on the operation of covenants.[17] The validity the courts discarded the test of adequacy of the consideration and removed any time limitation on the operation of covenants.[17] The validity of partial restraints of trade was judged in terms of their reasonableness.[18] A restraint was reasonable and lawful if it was adapted to the main purpose of the contract, that is, the sale of good will, and if it did not go beyond that which was necessary to protect the legitimate interests of the party in whose favor it was imposed. A restraint which exceeded the necessities of the particular case would be oppressive to the party bound by it and an undue interference with competition, and therefore unreasonable and void.[19] Important in the determination of reasonableness were such factors as the purpose of the restraint, the nature and extent of the business, and the effect upon the public.[20] But the final development in the law was the validation of general restraints. It was recognized that in the case of businesses operating in a large market the reasonable needs of the buyer of an enterprise might require a covenant unrestricted as to space. For example, in 1894 an English court upheld a covenant involving the sale to a competitor of a business having a world market. It applied to the whole world for a period of twenty-five years.[21] American courts have upheld restraints which covered virtually

[15] Rogers v. Parrey, 2 Bulst. 136 (1613); Jollyfe v. Broad, Cro. Jac. 596 (1620).
[16] 1. P. Wms. 181 (1711).
[17] Hitchcock v. Coker, 6 Ad. & El. 438 (1837).
[18] In holding a covenant void in Horner v. Graves, 7 Bing. 735 (1831), Chief Justice Tindal said: "We do not see how a better test can be applied to the question whether this is or not a reasonable restraint of trade than by considering whether the restraint is such only as to afford a fair protection to the interests of the party in favour of whom it is given, and not so large as to interfere with the interests of the public. Whatever restraint is larger than the necessary protection of the party requires can be of no benefit to either. It can only be oppressive. It is, in the eye of the law, unreasonable. Whatever is injurious to the interests of the public is void on the ground of public policy."
[19] Judge William H. Taft summarized the common law of trade restraints as interpreted in the United States in his very scholarly opinion in U. S. v. Addyston Pipe & Steel Co., 85 Fed. 271 (1898).
[20] The modern rule as stated by an American court was put as follows in Hubbard v. Miller, 27 Mich. 15 (1873): "If, considered with reference to the situation, business and objects of the parties, and in the light of all the surrounding circumstances, . . . the restraint contracted for appears to have been for a just and honest purpose, for the protection of the legitimate interests of the party in whose favor it is imposed, reasonable as between them, and not specially injurious to the public, the restraint will be held valid."
[21] Nordenfeldt v. Maxim Nordenfeldt Co., A. C. 535 (1894).

the whole country.[22] The sole test of the validity of any restrictive covenant, whether partial or general, seems now to be one of reasonableness.

Since the now famous "rule of reason" originated in connection with these technical restraints and developed in response to changed economic conditions and doctrines, these restraints have deserved some attention. But it is manifest that the monopoly problem in the United States is much broader than that suggested by restrictions upon the economic activities of parties who sell their enterprises. Companies such as the American Tobacco Company have strengthened their market control by the purchase of several competing firms accompanied by contracts not to compete.[23] The chief instruments, however, have been contracts, understandings, and combinations entered into by competitors for the prime purpose of controlling or suppressing competition. When these arrangements were brought to the attention of the courts in the latter half of the nineteenth century, it is interesting to note, the technical term "restraint of trade" was applied to them. They were essentially agreements not to compete, albeit involving obligations on the part not of one but of several parties, so the use of the old phrase to describe them is understandable. It is in this new or derived sense that "restraint of trade" is significant in American anti-trust policy.

Agreements between competitors to fix prices, restrict output, divide territory, or pool earnings were regarded by the great majority of American courts as being against public policy. They were held to be contrary to the public policy of free competition. These contracts were not illegal in the sense that it was a criminal offense to participate in such arrangements. The courts simply held them to be void and therefore unenforceable. In this respect their legal status was the same as the original technical "restraints of trade."

Two illustrative cases will indicate the attitude of the courts. One of the first cases in the records is India Bagging Association v. Kock,[24] decided in 1859. Eight firms holding a large amount of cotton bagging in New Orleans agreed for three months not to sell any bagging without the consent of the majority. The association sought to recover the stipulated money penalty from a member who violated the agreement. The suit was dismissed. The court declared that the contract was "palpably and unequivocally a combination in restraint of trade, and to enhance the price in the market of an article of primary necessity to cotton planters. Such combinations are contrary to public order, and cannot be enforced in a court of justice." The second case, Salt Co. v. Guthrie (1880),[25]

---

[22] Diamond Match Co. v. Roeber, 106 N. Y. 473 (1887); Trenton Potteries Co. v. Oliphant, 58 N. J. Eq. 507 (1899).

[23] See American Tobacco Co. v. U. S., 221 U. S. 106 (1911); and Diamond Match Co. in Richardson v. Buhl, 77 Mich. 632 (1889).

[24] 14 La. Ann. 168 (1859).

[25] 35 Ohio St. 666 (1880).

involved an agreement between practically all the salt producers of a large territory in Ohio to sell their product at prices fixed by a committee. In an action against a recalcitrant member, the contract was held in restraint of trade and void. The court said: "The clear tendency of such an agreement is to establish a monopoly, and to destroy competition in trade, and for that reason, on the ground of public policy, courts will not aid in its enforcement. It is no answer to say that competition in the salt trade was not in fact destroyed, or that the price of the commodity was not unreasonably advanced. Courts will not stop to inquire as to the degree of injury inflicted upon the public. It is enough to know that the inevitable tendency of such contracts is injurious to the public."

In adjudging the validity of agreements whose sole purpose was to restrain competition, most courts in the United States were not disposed to apply the so-called "rule of reason."[26] This attitude was assumed because of the absence of any main contract, as in the case of restrictive covenants, whereby the reasonableness of the restraint might be tested. Since the only purpose and effect of such direct agreements were to reduce competition, there could be no circumstances to "justify or excuse" the restraint. These courts insisted that public policy was to foster competition. They would not give judicial support to direct interferences even when the amount of injury to the public was small.

Some courts, however, were inclined to be more compromising. They did inquire into the reasonableness of restraining agreements. If it were shown that the combination did not include all the producers supplying a product or did not seek to restrict entry into the field, the court would uphold the arrangement.[27] In Skrainka v. Scharringhausen,[28] for example, a Missouri court had before it an agreement among twenty-four operators of stone quarries in St. Louis. They agreed for a period of six months to operate through an exclusive agent who apportioned output and sold at fixed prices. The court upheld the agreement because it did not embrace all quarrymen in the area and was limited as to time and place. It said: "There is no evidence that it works any public mischief, and the contract is not of such a nature that it is apparent from its terms that it tends to deprive men of employment, unduly raise prices, cause a monopoly, or put an end to competition." This case and a few others decided by

---

[26] Watkins, op. cit., pp. 228–232. Some of the leading cases in addition to the India Bagging and Ohio Salt cases above cited are: People v. Sheldon, 139 N. Y. 251 (1893), involving a combination of all coal dealers in Lockport, N. Y.; Morris Run Coal Co. v. Barclay, 68 Pa. St. 173 (1871), an association of five coal companies controlling the bituminous coal trade in Northern Pennsylvania; Craft v. McConough, 79 Ill. 346 (1875), grain dealers agreed secretly to fix prices and divide profits; Vulcan Powder Co. v. Hercules Powder Co., 96 Cal. 510 (1892), four powder companies agreed to sell at fixed prices and divide sales.

[27] N. I C. B., Mergers and the Law, pp. 18–19.

[28] 8 Mo. App. 522 (1880).

American courts suggest that unless an actual monopoly was created an agreement would be enforced.[29]

A similar view seems to have prevailed in the English courts. Unless the provisions of contracts to control prices and output or to divide markets are found to be unduly oppressive to outsiders or the public, they are upheld as reasonable restraints of trade.[30] The English courts appear to be particularly generous in giving their support to price-fixing arrangements and their enforcement.[31] A definite trend toward artificial controls by industry groups seems to have taken place since about 1930, with ultimate effects which may be injurious to the whole English economy.[32]

---

[29] Leslie v. Lorillard, 110 N. Y. 519 (1888); Herrimen v. Menzies, 115 Cal. 16 (1896); Dolph v. Troy Laundry Machinery Co., 28 Fed. 553 (1886).

[30] N. I. C. B., p. 16. Some of the leading cases are Wickens v. Evans, 3 Younge & J. 318 (1829); Collins v. Locke, 4 A. C. 674 (1879); Cady v. Daly, I. R. Ch. 306 (1910).

[31] Professor Ben W. Lewis, in his authoritative and interesting pamphlet entitled *Price and Production Control in British Industry* (Chicago, University of Chicago Press, 1937), states (p. 3): "Britain's attitude toward 'restraint of trade' has for decades been conspicuously different from our own. The British people are completely unaware of a 'trust' problem. England has no antitrust law, and agreements between producers to control prices and output and to divide markets are believed enforceable in the English courts under the ordinary laws of contract." He cites a recent English case (Thorne v. Motor Trade Association, House of Lords, 1937), in which a trade association was sustained in its attempt to collect a money penalty from a trader (whether or not a member) as the price of not placing him on the "stop list" for disregarding association-fixed prices.

The enactment of the Monopolies and Restrictive Practices (Inquiry and Control) Act, 1948 (11 & 12 Geo. 6, Ch. 66) gives evidence of some British concern over trade restraints since World War II. The purpose of the Act is "to make provision for inquiry into the existence and effects of, and for dealing with mischiefs resulting from . . . any conditions of monopoly or restriction . . . prevailing as respects the supply of . . . goods, buildings or structures, or as respects exports." A Commission is established to investigate and report on matters referred to it by the Board of Trade. If the Commission finds conditions or arrangements which "operate against the public interest," it may recommend appropriate action by the government or by the parties themselves. But discretionary power lies with a competent authority, such as the Board of Trade or the Minister of Supply, whose orders declaring anything unlawful must be approved by Parliament.

[32] Professor Lewis says (*Ibid.*, pp. 29–32): " . . . While there may be differences of informed opinion as to the exact extent and effectiveness of price and output control in England, it cannot reasonably be denied that control is widely present to such a degree as substantially to alter the whole character of the 'market' and to make prices emanating therefrom quite unreliable as indices of underlying economic conditions. . . . One cannot avoid the feeling that in strengthening the lines of control, planlessly, within each industry, the British are trading long-run development for immediate prosperity in particular industries; that industrial progress is being sacrificed to the protection of existing interests; and that domestic markets are being saved for British producers at the expense of the great export industries which, bewildered, are themselves turning to control devices which can scarcely be effective in an international economy. It is difficult to avoid the conclusion that Britain is seeking to control competition by eliminating its essential elements."

But while the English and some American common law courts did permit some relaxation in the general rule against the validity of agreements to restrain trade, the most authoritative view of the American judiciary seemed to be that restrictions on competition were bad in all circumstances. Judge William H. Taft, later Chief Justice of the Supreme Court, reviewed the common law in his famous opinion in the Addyston Pipe case.[33] He concluded: "Upon this review of the law and the authorities, we can have no doubt that the association of the defendants, however reasonable the prices they fixed, however great the competition they had to encounter, and however great the necessity for curbing themselves by joint agreement from committing financial suicide by ill-advised competition, was void at common law, because in restraint of trade, and tending to a monopoly."[34] Without unduly anticipating the discussion which is to follow, it may be suggested here that the view that concerted action on the part of competitors to control the market is invariably an unreasonable restraint of trade has prevailed in the interpretation and application of the Sherman Law.

Thus far consideration has been given to the judicial attitude toward loose combinations designed to suppress competition. Such combinations embraced a number of individual firms which, except for the price or other subject-matter of contract, were independently controlled and operated. Since the courts declined to enforce agreements not to compete, such arrangements were not altogether satisfactory instruments for maintaining market control. Forms of union were required which would yield more secure legal and economic control of the operations and policies of the constituent producing units. As revealed in the case histories already studied, loose pooling or price-fixing arrangements were supplanted by close forms of combination in some industries. The forms commonly employed were the technical trust and the corporation.

In some measure at least, the law kept pace with these developments. Public opposition to the trust device was particularly strong because of the secrecy with which the trust could be organized and operated, the great power exercised by a small group of men, and the obvious intent to monopolize. Responding to public sentiment, the authorities of several states moved against the more notorious of the trusts. Louisiana attacked the cotton oil trust, New York the sugar trust, Ohio the Standard Oil trust, and Nebraska the whiskey trust.[35] The underlying reason for these actions was the monopolistic character of the combinations. But

---

[33] U. S. v. Addyston Pipe & Steel Co., 85 Fed. 271 (1898).

[34] *Ibid.*, p. 291.

[35] People v. North River Sugar Refining Co., 121 N. Y. 582 (1890): State v. Standard Oil Co., 49 Ohio St. 137 (1892); State v. Nebraska Distilling Co., 29 Neb. 700 (1890).

the most feasible method was to seek the revocation of the charters of the corporations that had entered the trust arrangement. The chief ground upon which the courts upheld the state authorities was that the constituent corporations had exceeded their charter powers in conveying control of their enterprises to a board of trustees. But it was also emphasized that the restraints of trade effected by these combinations were against public policy and therefore unlawful. This appears to have been the ground upon which the Ohio court ordered the Standard Oil Company of Ohio to forfeit its charter. In holding that the Standard Oil trust was organized for an unlawful purpose, the Court said: "Its object was to establish a virtual monopoly of the business of producing petroleum, and of manufacturing, refining and dealing in it and all its products, throughout the entire country, and by which it might not merely control the production, but the price at its pleasure. All such associations are contrary to the policy of our state and void."[36]

Corporate combinations were also attacked without the aid of legislative enactment. The holding company was not available as a means of combining competitive enterprises. American courts adhered to the common law view that corporations could not legally acquire and hold the shares of other companies for purposes of control.[37] Corporations that acquired the actual assets of competing concerns were not debarred from so doing by any general principle of corporation law. On several occasions, however, the courts interfered when the plain purpose was to obtain a monopoly. In a private action over a contract relating to the purchase of one of the numerous companies acquired by the Diamond Match Company, a Michigan court raised the question of public policy on its own motion.[38] It found that the company was seeking to establish a monopoly in friction matches, and held the contract void because it was in furtherance of the unlawful purpose of the combination. A more striking case was that in which the state of Illinois succeeded in revoking the charter of the Distilling and Cattle Feeding Company.[39] This Illinois corporation was a successor of the whiskey trust and owned nearly all the distilleries in the United States. The court found that the original trust had intended to and actually did achieve a monopoly of the industry and was undoubtedly in unlawful restraint of trade. The mere fact that it had changed its form did not render it a lawful combination. Its corporate charter gave it authority to acquire property but not to suppress competition in contravention of established public policy.

---

[36] State v. Standard Oil Co., 49 Ohio St. 137 (1892).

[37] De La Vergne Refrigerating Machine Co. v. German Savings Institution, 175 U. S. 40 (1899). New Jersey legalized the holding company for the first time by statutory enactment in 1888.

[38] Richardson v. Buhl, 77 Mich. 632 (1889).

[39] Distilling Co. v. People, 156 Ill. 448 (1895).

Appraisal of Common Law

The doctrines of the common law obviously favored the preservation of competition. They reflected the public policy to which the great majority of American people subscribed. In England, however, there appears to have been a gradual relaxation of the common law rules. A considerable measure of protection against monopolizing was probably afforded by England's nineteenth-century policy of free trade and the foreign competition which it encouraged. But in American courts a stronger position seems to have been maintained. The criminal offenses of engrossing and forestalling, and conspiracy to monopolize, were never prosecuted by public authorities and did not find a place in the body of traditional American law. During the early days of the combination movement, however, the ancient doctrine of restraint of trade was given a new meaning and applied to contracts and combinations entered into by rival firms for the sole purpose of restricting competition. The more authoritative view was that such agreements could not be justified and upheld on the ground of reasonableness. A similar view seems to have obtained with respect to trusts and corporate combinations that were attacked under the convenient doctrine of limited charter powers.

While the substance of the law conformed to sound public policy, its attack upon monopoly was definitely weak. The weakness lay in the want of an aggressive public prosecution and adequate penalties. Apart from the few public prosecutions of the trust device, the cases which came to the attention of the courts were civil suits by private parties. Such actions were brought against firms that violated their agreements not to compete. When an alleged breach of contract was brought before it, the court could inquire into the lawfulness of the contract. But the court could go no further than to declare the contract void and unenforceable if it restrained trade. It had no authority to inflict punishment on the contracting parties. This legal status was undoubtedly a factor of some importance in protecting the public, since parties to such contracts were always tempted to seek greater profits by shading prices or enlarging output. The fact that price and pooling agreements have persisted to the present time, however, suggests that their unenforceability in the courts has not been a decisive factor in compelling their abandonment.

STATE ACTION

The combination movement which appeared after the Civil War exposed the inadequacies of the common law. Great agitation for corrective legislation arose. Popular opposition to monopolistic combinations became particularly violent during the eighties. It was directed at both the railroads and the industrial combinations. Some success had been attained against the railroads by the enactment of the Granger legislation in the early seventies, but it was not until Congress passed the Interstate Commerce Act in 1887 that the campaign against railroad abuses really began to bear fruit. Shortly thereafter numerous laws were placed on the statute books which prohibited trusts, pools, and similar devices designed to restrict competition in the fields of manufacturing and trade. The first anti-trust legislation was enacted by the states, notably Kansas, Michigan, Maine, Missouri, and Texas. At least thirteen states had acted when Congress passed the Sherman Anti-trust Act on July 2, 1890.[40] But long before the states passed statutes, some of them had condemned monopoly in their constitutions. The Maryland Constitution contains the declaration, originally framed in 1776, that monopolies are "odious, contrary to the spirit of a free government and the principles of commerce, and ought not to be suffered."[41] Fourteen states or territories had such constitutional provisions by 1890.[42] It is probable that the early constitutional provisions were designed to prevent legislatures from creating state monopolies or conferring monopolistic privileges upon private groups, but their generality made it an easy matter to interpret them to embrace the modern phenomenon of private industrial monopoly.

The wave of state anti-trust legislation continued after 1890 in response to the strong feeling against the wide-spread combination movement. About two-thirds of the states had taken some action by 1900.[43] By 1941, all but eight states had prohibited monopolies and restraints of trade either in their constitutions or statutes, or both. The eight states which have no constitutional provision and no general anti-trust statute are Colorado, Delaware, Nevada, New Jersey, Oregon, Pennsylvania, Rhode Island and West Virginia. These states have a miscellany of statutory provisions relating to conspiracy, discrimination, and certain special matters, but the common law must be relied upon for any general attack on monopoly.[44]

---

[40] Seager and Gulick, op. cit., pp. 341–343.

[41] Constitution of 1867, Art. 41.

[42] Seager and Gulick, op. cit., pp. 341–342. Six of the fourteen states having constitutional provisions also had statutes.

[43] Ibid., p. 343.

[44] A very valuable compilation of the constitutional provisions, statutes, and applicable court decisions of the forty-eight states in the anti-trust field has recently been published by the Marketing Laws Survey of the Works Progress Administration. It is entitled State Antitrust Laws (Washington, D. C., U. S. Government Printing Office, 1940).

It may be noted here that the anti-trust law of Colorado was held to be unconstitutional by the Supreme Court in Cline v. Frink Dairy Co., 274 U. S. 445 (1927); and that New Jersey enacted anti-trust laws in 1913, the so-called Seven Sister Acts, which had been repealed by 1920.

Constitutional and Statutory Provisions

The state constitutions and statutes present a great variety of form and expression. Constitutional provisions are sweeping and general. "Perpetuities and monopolies are contrary to the genius of a free government and shall never be allowed," is the phrasing adopted substantially by several states.[45] Somewhat more explicit is the provision in the New Hampshire Constitution which declares: "Free and fair competition in the trades and industries is an inherent and essential right of the people and should be protected against all monopolies and conspiracies which tend to hinder or destroy it." The legislature is granted the authority to enact laws "to prevent the operations within the state of all persons and associations, and all trusts and corporations, foreign or domestic, and the officers thereof, who endeavor to raise the price of any article of commerce or to destroy free and fair competition in the trades and industries through combination, conspiracy, monopoly, or any other unfair means. . . . "[46]

These general declarations are indicative of the policy of the states. To be effective, however, it is clear that they must be supported by legislative action. Supplementary legislation must define the legal offenses, provide machinery for enforcing the law, and set adequate penalties for violations.

Although the details of the various state laws vary greatly, the central idea of all of them is to prevent agreements or combinations which preclude the competitive determination of output and prices. The contracts and combinations which were unenforceable at common law because they restrained trade are made positively illegal. The more comprehensive of the laws prohibit combinations of capital, skill, or acts by two or more persons or firms for the purpose of creating restrictions in trade, preventing or lessening competition in the manufacture or sale of commodities, regulating or limiting the production of any commodity, or fixing the selling price of commodities.[47] Trusts, pools, and monopolies, usually defined in the foregoing terms, are often expressly forbidden.[48] Certain competitive practices which are conducive to monop-

---

[45] The Constitutions of Arkansas, Oklahoma, Tennessee, North Carolina, Texas and Wyoming.

[46] Constitution (of 1784 as amended in 1903), Part II, Article 83.

[47] Anti-trust statutes of California, North Dakota and Texas. See Joseph E. Davies, *Trust Laws and Unfair Competition* (Washington, D. C.: U. S. Government Printing Office, 1916), Chap. 4, for an analysis of the important provisions of state anti-trust laws.

[48] Agricultural coöperatives and labor unions are commonly exempted from the anti-trust acts, but the laws are generally interpreted not to condone unduly oppressive action on the part of labor unions. See *State Antitrust Laws*, pp. LI–LII.

oly control, such as exclusive dealing arrangements and local price discrimination, are also prohibited in some of the state laws.[49]

Administration of the laws is commonly entrusted to the Attorney-
General of the state, although in many states county or district attorneys
are also charged with the duty. Enforcement may likewise be obtained
through legal action by private parties. Persons who are injured by
violations of the law are usually authorized to bring suit for double or
treble damages. They may also bring injunction suits to prevent violations.

There is little uniformity in the penalties for violations. In most of
the states violations of the law are criminal offenses punishable by fines
and imprisonment. Persons who violate the law individually or as officers
of corporations or combinations are subject to fines ranging from a few
dollars to several thousand dollars and to maximum prison terms ranging
from 6 months to 10 years. Corporations can only be fined, of course, but
the fines can be quite large if, as in Texas, the maximum of $1,500 is
imposed for each day's violation. Another common remedy is the forfeiture of the charters of domestic corporations and the revocation of the
rights of foreign corporations to do business in the state. Many of the
states expressly provide that all contracts or agreements which violate
the anti-trust laws are void and unenforceable. Finally, damages may
be assessed or injunctions issued in the private suits by injured parties.

Effectiveness of State Regulation

It goes without saying that the mere enactment of state laws, however competent their draftsmanship and however salutary their purpose,
will not remove the evil at which they are directed. Their effectiveness
depends upon the vigor with which they are enforced and the scope
which they possess.

Since some of the states never did enact anti-trust laws, it is apparent
that there could be no concerted attack upon monopoly. But more important is the fact that the great majority of the states having adequate
laws made no serious effort to enforce them. The greatest inactivity
seems to have prevailed in the Eastern and the Western states. Due
perhaps to their large agrarian population, the states in the central part
of the country, both North and South, were more aggressive. The most
active was Texas, with perhaps Missouri and Illinois taking second and
third honors.[50]

A number of factors probably account for the inactivity of so many
states. Sheer inertia on the part of prosecuting agencies because of

---

[49] Davies, *op. cit.*, pp. 184–195. The recent wave of state anti-discrimination
laws, directed largely at the chain store, will be considered in a later section.

[50] *State Antitrust Laws*, p. LVI.

inadequate resources, lack of independence, and preoccupation with the multitude of other legal matters was probably an important factor. The task of gathering and presenting evidence of monopoly to a court in the case of powerful concerns operating on a regional or national basis is truly a formidable one, and can be undertaken only by an experienced and well-financed legal staff. Furthermore, the limited jurisdiction of the states made prosecution of large concerns seem useless. The prosecution of large industrial combinations was bound to raise the question of interstate commerce, over which the states have no authority. Moreover, there was a definite feeling on the part of some states that it just didn't pay to gain the ill will of business by subjecting it to close inspection and vexatious litigation. The better policy was to encourage business enterprise so as to build up the industry of the state. Some states, particularly New Jersey, had found the chartering of corporations a lucrative source of revenue, and they were disposed not to destroy it by stringent incorporation and trust laws. New Jersey repealed her laws of 1913 after a short and fruitless experience, and Delaware has never tempted the fates by enacting a general anti-monopoly law. Other states were impressed with the futility of trying alone to do anything about the trust problem, and adopted the apathetic attitude of their sister states.

Even those that made a real attempt to enforce their laws met with indifferent success. Texas had a protracted skirmish with the Standard Oil trust. The Waters-Pierce Oil Company, a Missouri corporation, was found to be a member of the oil combination and its permit to do business in the state was revoked in 1898.[51] The cancellation of the privilege necessarily applied only to domestic commerce, but the company was dissolved. It was merely a formal dissolution, however, for a new Waters-Pierce Company was created and accorded the right to do business in Texas in 1900. The new subsidiary of the Standard pursued the same policies of monopolization, operation of bogus independents, and exclusion of competitors by unfair means. A second suit was brought by the state, which resulted in the assessment of a fine and the revocation of the permit to do business.[52] Upon appeal to the Supreme Court of the United States, the decision was upheld and the fine of over $1,600,000 found not to be excessive for a company owning over $40,000,000 of assets and paying huge dividends. The fine was paid, but it appears that the company was permitted to continue to operate in Texas. The oil trust was not dealt a serious blow.

The results of Missouri's efforts were similar. The oil trust also figured in its outstanding case. Three subsidiaries of the Standard Oil

---

[51] Waters-Pierce Oil Co. *v.* Texas, 44 S. W. 936 (1898); 177 U. S. 28 (1900). For a fairly detailed account of the anti-trust activity of Texas and Missouri, see Seager and Gulick, *op. cit.*, pp. 348–366.

[52] Waters-Pierce Oil Co. *v.* State, 106 S. W. 918 (1907); 212 U. S. 86 (1909).

Company of New Jersey, the Standard of Indiana, Waters-Pierce Oil Company, and Republic Oil Company, controlled more than 85 per cent of the oil business in Missouri. Standard of Indiana and Waters-Pierce divided the state and operated only in their allotted territories, while Republic posed as an independent and sold oil products throughout the state. Practices typical of the oil trust were used to eliminate competitors and to obtain monopoly gains. These companies were held to have violated the state laws and a judgment was entered fining each of them $50,000 and ousting them from the state.[53] But the only company that was absolutely ousted was the Republic Oil Company, the bogus independent. The ouster of the Waters-Pierce Company, a domestic corporation, was suspended upon proof of compliance with the court's order, and the Standard of Indiana succeeded in having its ouster suspended on a promise to mend its ways.[54] Other proceedings against such defendants as the International Harvester Company,[55] members of the Yellow Pine Manufacturers' Association,[56] and the meat packers,[57] had about the same result. Fines ranging from $1,000 to $50,000 were levied against each of the defendants, and suspended ousters were decreed. The courts appeared to be very reluctant actually to force offending firms from the state for fear that it would work economic injury upon its citizens. The threat of ouster was always present and served possibly as a deterrent to continued unlawful activity, but the only penalties really inflicted were modest fines.

State experience indicates clearly that more was needed than the independent and usually hesitant action of forty-eight separate jurisdictions to meet the problem of monopoly. State legislation, adequate in its substance and properly enforced, can serve a real purpose in eliminating agreements and combinations that restrain local trade. But state action can be of little aid in coping with a trust problem which is interstate or national in character. Concentration of economic power in the hands of combinations that reach far beyond the confines of any single state or group of states must be dealt with by the national government. This was recognized, fortunately, even when state action was in its infancy. Almost simultaneously with the enactment of the first state laws, Congress passed the Sherman Anti-trust Act of 1890.

---

[53] State v. Standard Oil Co. et al., 116 S. W. 902 (1909); 224 U. S. 270 (1912).

[54] 158 S. W. 601 (1913).

[55] State v. International Harvester Co. of America, 141 S. W. 672 (1911); 234 U. S. 199 (1914).

[56] State v. Arkansas Lumber Co. et. al., 169 S. W. 145 (1914).

[57] State v. Armour Packing Co. et. al., 73 S. W. 645 (1903).

17

The Sherman Act and Its Interpretation

The same economic and social forces which impelled the states to act against industrial monopoly induced the Federal Government to enter the field of trust regulation. The strong public sentiment against monopolies was acknowledged in the platforms of all of the political parties in the presidential campaign of 1888. Republicans declared their opposition "to all combinations of capital, organized in trusts or otherwise, to control arbitrarily the condition of trade among our citizens," and recommended Congressional legislation.[1] The Democratic platform proclaimed: "Judged by Democratic principles, the interests of the people are betrayed when, by unnecessary taxation, trusts and combinations are permitted to exist, which, while unduly enriching the few that combine, rob the body of our citizens by depriving them of the benefits of natural competition."[2] Judging by these declarations, Congressional action was certain to be taken, irrespective of which party won the election.

In his first message President Harrison, true to the Republican pledge, urged Congress to give "earnest attention" to the trust problem. He evidenced a healthy respect for the dangers inherent in monopolistic combinations: "When organized, as they often are, to crush out all healthy competition and to monopolize the production or sale of an article of commerce and general necessity, they are dangerous conspiracies against the public good, and should be made the subject of prohibitory and even penal legislation."[3]

During 1888 and 1889 numerous anti-trust bills were introduced in both houses of Congress. Senator Sherman introduced bills on two occasions, the second on December 4, 1889, and took a leading part in the consideration of the proposed legislation. The subject of the trusts was debated at length in committees and on the floor of the Senate. The

---

[1] T. H. McKee, *National Conventions and Platforms* (Baltimore, The Friedenwald Company, 1906), p. 241.

[2] *Ibid.*, p. 235.

[3] J. D. Richardson, *Messages and Papers of the Presidents* (New York, Bureau of National Literature, Inc., 1897), Vol. XII, p. 5478.

debate centered around questions of scope, terminology, and remedies, since there was very general agreement that legislative action was necessary.[4] A bill, drafted by the Senate Judiciary Committee and reflecting the numerous amendments which had been offered to the original Sherman bill, was passed by the Senate with only one dissenting vote on April 8, 1890. The House, after considerable debate and conference with the Senate on proposed amendments, approved the Senate measure without dissent. When signed by President Harrison on July 2, 1890, the law carried the title, "An act to protect trade and commerce against unlawful restraints and monopolies."[5] Commonly it has been called the Sherman Anti-trust Act, even though the final draft was written by others and bears little resemblance to the original bill proposed by Senator Sherman.

PROVISIONS OF THE SHERMAN ACT

The Sherman Act is comparatively brief, consisting of eight short sections. Its substantive provisions—the definition of what is legal and what is illegal—are to be found in the first three sections and the last section. Provisions relating to procedure and penalties are scattered through almost all sections of the statute.

The definitions of illegal action are in terms of the familiar common law. Section 1 declares that "every contract, combination in the form of trust or otherwise, or conspiracy, in restraint of trade or commerce" is illegal. This provision is directed at joint action on the part of producers or traders and covers all combined action irrespective of the manner in which it is effected. In conformity with the constitutional powers delegated to the Federal Government, it is expressly stated that the trade or commerce restrained must be that among the several states or with foreign nations.

Section 2 states that "every person who shall monopolize, or attempt to monopolize, or combine or conspire with any other person or persons, to monopolize, any part" of interstate or international commerce is committing a criminal offense. This prohibition is designed to curb individual as well as joint action which has monopolization as its purpose or effect. It would appear to be a strong and useful provision, since it embraces both actual and attempted market control and applies to the monopolizing of "any part" of commerce. In practice, however, it has not figured prominently in anti-trust proceedings until recently.

Section 3 applies the prohibition of trade restraints to the commerce

---

[4] For an interesting account of the legislative history of the Sherman Act, see A. H. Walker, *History of the Sherman Law* (New York, The Equity Press, 1910), pp. 1–46.

[5] Act of July 2, 1890, c. 647, 26 Stat. 209.

of the District of Columbia and the territories of the United States. Section 8 defines "person" or "persons" to include corporations and associations.

On the remedial side, the Sherman Act goes much beyond the common law. Procedures and remedies are provided which enable both public authorities and private parties to act against injurious combinations. The Federal district courts (until 1911 the circuit courts) are given jurisdiction over proceedings to enforce the law. Public action is made the responsibility of the several Federal district attorneys under the direction of the Attorney-General. Today the real source of enforcement is found in the Anti-trust Division under the control of the Attorney-General. Private actions must, of course, be brought by injured parties under the usual civil processes of the courts.

The Government may proceed against violations of the law by means of a criminal action, a civil suit, or an action to seize and condemn property owned by a combination which is moving in interstate or foreign commerce. Since the penal process of forfeiture of goods has remained a dead letter in the administration of the law, it will require no comment. Criminal actions are brought under the established criminal procedure of grand jury investigation, indictment, and jury trial. Persons violating the law are guilty of misdemeanors and may be punished by a fine not exceeding $5,000, or imprisonment of not more than a year, or both.[6] According to subsequent amendment, the officers or directors who are responsible for the corporate acts are subject to the prescribed penalties when corporations violate the law.[7] And it was expected that criminal penalties would serve as strong deterrents to wrongdoing.

Civil suits may be brought by the Attorney-General "to prevent and restrain" violations. These proceedings in equity are designed not to punish offenders but to restrain existing violations and to restore competitive conditions. Courts of equity have a broad discretion in the choice of remedies and have given relief in various ways. The only one mentioned expressly in the statute is the injunction whereby a court order may be used to prohibit certain acts. Violation then may be punished by fine and imprisonment in contempt proceedings. Another is the dissolution decree. This consists in a court decree requiring the defendant combination to be dissolved and the component elements so reorganized as to restore competition. The court undertakes to formulate a plan which in its judgment will create conditions that are in harmony with the law. Notable examples are the dissolution decrees in the Stand-

---

[6] It is interesting to compare these criminal penalties with those included in the Sherman Bill of 1889 and with the amendment of Senator Reagan, which was provisionally adopted by the Senate in 1890. These provided fines not exceeding $10,000, or imprisonment not exceeding five years, or both.

[7] Clayton Act, 38 Stat. 730 (1914), Sec. 14.

ard Oil[8] and American Tobacco[9] cases. Disintegration of these combinations along prescribed lines was ordered as a means of preventing future transgression of the law.

A third remedy is the consent decree. In this case the defendants agree to accept the court order without having been tried and found guilty of violating the law. This has become increasingly important as a means of enforcing the law. The content of such a decree is usually decided upon by negotiation between the Attorney-General and the defendant, and this eliminates the need for long and costly court proceedings. A classic example is the consent decree of the Meat Packers, entered February 27, 1920.[10] Curiously enough, the packers asserted "their innocence of any violation of law in fact or intent," and assented to the decree because they desired "to avoid every appearance of placing themselves in a position of antagonism to the Government." The decree contained a comprehensive injunction against monopolizing or restraining trade, and required such affirmative action as the divestiture of interests in public stock-yards, market newspapers, and the business of producing and selling various grocery products. Consent decrees, however comprehensive their terms and even though they contain errors of law, are a valid exercise of judicial power and binding upon the parties.[11] They are enforceable, like injunctions and dissolution decrees, through contempt proceedings.

Private action against illegal combinations embraces suits for damages and injunctive relief. Any person whose business or property is injured by reason of anything which is unlawful under the act, is accorded the right to recover threefold damages and costs. Moreover, pursuant to Section 5 of the Clayton Act of 1914, final judgments or decrees, other than consent decrees, in criminal or civil prosecutions brought by the Government are *prima facie* evidence against defendants in private suits. This makes it easier, presumably, for injured parties to establish grounds for recovery. The risk undertaken by a wrongdoer is thereby enhanced. Under the original Sherman Act, a private person could not sue for

---

[8] U. S. *v.* Standard Oil Co. (1911), *Decrees and Judgments in Federal Anti-trust Cases* (1918), p. 136. Speaking of remedies in the Standard Oil case (221 U. S. 1, 1911), the Supreme Court said: "It may be conceded that ordinarily where it was found that acts had been done in violation of the statute, adequate measure of relief would result from restraining the doing of such acts in the future. . . . But in a case like this, where the condition which has been brought about in violation of the statute, in and of itself, is not only a continued attempt to monopolize, but also a monopolization, the duty to enforce the statute requires the application of broader and more controlling remedies." Twofold remedies were applied, namely, forbidding the unlawful acts in the future and dissolving the combination.

[9] U. S. *v.* American Tobacco Co. (1911), *Decrees and Judgments in Anti-trust Cases* (1918), p. 165.

[10] U. S. *v.* Swift and Co. *et. al.*, *Consent Decree in the Supreme Court of the District of Columbia*, February 27, 1920.

[11] Swift & Co. *v.* U. S., 276 U. S. 311 (1928).

injunctive relief.[12] Only the Government could maintain such a suit. But Section 16 of the Clayton Act now gives private parties the definite right to obtain injunctions against threatened loss or damage by the violation of the anti-trust laws.[13]

Individual protection is not altogether confined to such actions as may be initiated by injured parties. An established violation of the Sherman Act may also be used as a defense by a party who, for example, breaks a contract with the illegal combination.[14] But it is a good defense only if the contract sued upon is an essential part of an illegal scheme.[15] Contracts which are in themselves lawful and not intimately related to the maintenance of the illegal combination will not be invalidated by the monopolistic character of the plaintiff. This is an important limitation. The Sherman Act seems to go no further than the common law in rendering contracts which restrain trade unenforceable.

In various respects the Sherman Act advanced beyond the common law. On the substantive side, however, its contribution was slight. It defined illegal action in the common law terms of "restraint of trade" and "monopolizing." But despite the various interpretations placed upon it in the common law, the ambiguous phrase "restraint of trade" was not defined. Did it refer to restrictive covenants ancillary to the sale of a business or to the more modern notion of restrictive agreements between trade competitors? If to the latter, were all collusive arrangements bad, or simply those that "unreasonably" restrained trade? The law condemned both actual and attempted monopolizing, and embraced both individual and joint efforts to monopolize. What constitutes monopolizing was not explained, and nothing indicated the distinction, if Congress recognized any, between monopolizing and restraint of trade. The law did express a policy with respect to interstate commerce. The common law policy, formerly applied only by the state courts, was adopted for application to national commerce by the Federal courts. The exact nature of that policy had to await judicial interpretation of the statute.

A much greater contribution was made with respect to procedures and remedies. The basis for aggressive action against combinations was laid in arranging for government proceedings. A type of prosecution could be chosen which would fit the needs of each situation. Equity court jurisdiction over anti-trust proceedings was particularly valuable in that it made available the remedies of injunction and dissolution. These have not been effectual in all instances, but they have been more useful than the punishment afforded by the criminal courts. The special

---

[12] Paine Lumber Co. v. Neal, 244 U. S. 459 (1917).
[13] Lord v. Radio Corporation of America, 24 Fed. (2nd) 565 (1928).
[14] Continental Wall Paper Co. v. Louis Voight & Sons Co., 212 U. S. 227 (1909).
[15] Connolly v. Union Sewer Pipe Company, 184 U. S. 540 (1902); D. R. Wilder Manufacturing Co. v. Corn Products Refining Co., 236 U. S. 165 (1915).

suit for treble damages by injured parties was a desirable innovation supplementing public action. Private damage suits as well as the more recently provided injunctive proceedings have yielded some good results, but what success the Sherman Act has had has come largely from government proceedings.[16]

ADMINISTRATION AND INTERPRETATION

A study of the decisions of the courts is necessary to gain an understanding of the meaning of the Sherman Act. It has already been suggested that while the general intent of Congress may have been clear, terms were used which had no single and precise meaning in the common law. The Supreme Court, in the final analysis, had to determine the exact scope and content of the law. And the interpretation placed upon the language used by Congress has had much more than an academic significance. The effectiveness of the anti-trust policy declared by Con-

---

[16] It should be noted here that certain minor legislation supplementing the Sherman Act was passed prior to the major legislation of 1914. These acts are as follows:

Wilson Tariff Act, 28 Stat. 570 (1894), amended 37 Stat. 667 (1913). Every combination or agreement involving importers is declared contrary to public policy and illegal if it is intended to operate in restraint of free competition or trade, or to increase the prices of imported articles or manufactures into which they enter. Provision is made for criminal punishment, injunction, forfeiture of property, and private suit for threefold damages, in language substantially similar to that of the Sherman Act. These anti-trust provisions were not applied in court until 1927. See U. S. v. Sisal Sales Corporation, 274 U. S. 268 (1927).

Expediting Act, 32 Stat. 823 (1903), amended 36 Stat. 854 (1910). The purpose of this act was to expedite the hearing and decision of suits brought by the United States under the anti-trust laws and the Interstate Commerce Act. Suits in equity in the district courts are to be given precedence over others and expedited in every way, when the Attorney-General shall certify that they are of "general public importance." It is also provided that appeals from final decrees of district courts in such cases must be taken directly to the Supreme Court, within sixty days.

Immunity Rights, 32 Stat. 854, 903 (1903), amended 34 Stat. 798 (1906). The immunity provision of 1903 granted freedom from prosecution to persons with respect to matters about which they had given testimony or produced evidence in anti-trust proceedings. In the famous "immunity bath" decision, the meat packers were sustained in their contention that they were entitled to immunity from criminal prosecution because of testimony rendered in an investigation by the Bureau of Corporations (U. S. v. Armour & Co., 142 Fed. 808 (1906)). As a result Congress, in 1906, limited the right of immunity to natural persons who give testimony or produce evidence under oath in obedience to a subpoena.

Act Creating Bureau of Corporations, 32 Stat. 827 (1903). The Bureau of Corporations, headed by a Commissioner of Corporations, was established in the Department of Commerce and Labor. Its duties were to investigate the organization and conduct of industrial corporations engaged in interstate commerce and to gather data which would enable the President to recommend regulatory legislation. The President was to determine what information should be made public. The Bureau could compel the testimony of witnesses and the production of documentary evidence.

gress in 1890 has been conditioned in large measure by the judicial construction of the law.

Court interpretation will be considered under four general topics: (1) Federal Jurisdiction; (2) Scope; (3) Forms of Organization; and (4) Degree of Restraint. Within each topic the cases will be treated chronologically in order that the evolution of doctrine and its impact upon the industrial scene may be noted.

(1) Federal Jurisdiction

The jurisdiction of the Federal Government under our dual system of government is confined by the terms of the Constitution to commerce among the several states and with foreign nations. Commerce within each state remains subject to the control of the state government. While this jurisdictional rule is simple and readily understood, its application to specific situations has caused endless controversy and litigation. In this respect the application of the Sherman Act to monopolistic arrangements has not been exceptional.

The first case to come before the Supreme Court under the Sherman Act involved the question of Federal power. It was the case of United States v. E. C. Knight Company,[17] decided January 21, 1895. The American Sugar Refining Company, already in control of 65 per cent of the sugar refined in the United States, acquired in 1892 the stock of the E. C. Knight Company and three other independent refining companies located in Philadelphia. These four firms produced about a third of the sugar refined domestically, so the combination obtained virtually complete control of the industry. The only remaining independent firm was the Revere Company of Boston, a small company which refined about 2 per cent of the domestic output. The government did not seek to restore competition by breaking down the combination into a substantial number of independent concerns. Its object was less ambitious than that. What it charged was that the agreements under which the purchase of the stock of the Philadelphia companies was accomplished were combinations restraining trade in violation of the Sherman Act. The relief sought embraced a cancellation of the contracts, the return of the stock which had been transferred, and an injunction against further violations of the law.

The Supreme Court, in upholding the decisions of the lower courts,[18] held against the government. This strange result in a case relating to a well-nigh perfect monopoly was reached because of an extremely narrow view of the scope of Federal authority. It was conceded that a

---

[17] 156 U. S. 1 (1895).
[18] 60 Fed. 306 (1894); 60 Fed. 934 (1894).

monopoly in the manufacturing of sugar existed, but this was insufficient to establish Federal jurisdiction. The contracts and acts of the defendants were held to relate to the sugar refining business in Pennsylvania and bore no direct relationship to interstate commerce. "Commerce succeeds to manufacture," declared the Court, "and is not a part of it." Failure of the government to prove its allegation that the combination intended to put a restraint upon commerce was emphasized by the Court. Yet, as Justice Harlan pointed out in his strong dissenting opinion, the lower court had stated that the object of the acquisitions was "to obtain a greater influence or more perfect control over the business of refining and selling sugar in this country."[19] Perhaps the government was at fault in not presenting the case properly to the courts, but it would seem to have been too obvious for elaborate proof that the companies were engaged in selling their product throughout the nation and that their sole purpose was to monopolize that interstate trade.[20] One might agree with the statement that manufacturing is not commerce, and still find the court's conclusion to be nonsensical. Surely exclusive control of the supply of sugar was more than indirectly related to interstate trade.

The decision did irreparable damage to the cause of maintaining competitive conditions. Both official and popular opinion was that Congress was impotent to deal with monopolistic combinations in the fields of manufacturing and mining. Recourse was to be had only to action by the states, and they were admittedly incapable of effectual attacks upon the trusts. Industrial promoters and business men were quick to take advantage of the apparent helplessness of the government. With the upturn in business conditions in the late nineties an unprecedented merger movement took place. During the period 1897 to 1903, over 225 combinations were organized.[21] Many of them controlled large percentages of the productive capacity in their fields, and some have to this day dominated their industries. A number of circumstances favored this great orgy of combination, but it is generally acknowledged that the abortive decision of the Supreme Court in the Knight case was a significant factor.

---

[19] 60 Fed. 306, 308.

[20] In commenting on the Knight case, William H. Taft said (*The Anti-trust Act and the Supreme Court*, New York, Harper & Brothers, 1914, p. 59): " . . . The case for the Government was not well prepared at the circuit. No direct evidence that the sales of sugar across State lines, and the control of the business of such sales and of prices, were the chief object of the combination was submitted to the court. Nor was this chief feature of the Government's real case sufficiently set forth in the bill of complaint. And yet these facts must have been easily capable of proof. Especially noteworthy was the failure of the bill to pray for specific action by the court to enjoin the continuance of the combination."

[21] See Seager and Gulick, *op. cit.*, pp. 60–67, for a brief account of this period in the American trust movement.

The decision has never been formally overruled. As a practical matter, however, subsequent decisions of the Supreme Court have rendered it of little current importance. The first assault on it as a troublesome precedent was the case of the Addyston Pipe & Steel Co. v. United States.[22] Six producers of cast-iron pipe with plants located mainly in the South entered a pooling and price-fixing arrangement. Competition between the contracting parties was eliminated in a market area embracing some thirty-six states. While they were subjected to some competition from other firms, their market control in the area was sufficient to enable them to maintain unreasonably high prices. In upholding the decree of the lower court perpetually enjoining the defendants from maintaining the combination, the Supreme Court rejected the contentions of the defendants that the commerce power did not embrace interference with private contracts and that the restraint was a reasonable one directed at preventing ruinous competition.[23] On the dominant issue of Federal power, Mr. Justice Peckham observed that the combination related to the sale and delivery of pipe across state lines. Since the direct effect of the combination was to regulate interstate commerce and not simply the manufacture of a product, the Court held that the case was not covered by the Knight decision. An agreement to restrict competition between sellers, albeit they were manufacturing concerns, was acknowledged to be a direct restraint of interstate commerce.

The Addyston Pipe decision established the authority of the Federal Government over collusive marketing arrangements of industrial concerns. But since it involved a loose combination of firms, it had little effect in stemming the merger movement of the late nineties. The question whether or not there had been any change in attitude with respect to close combinations had to await further pronouncements of the Supreme Court. Definite indications of a broad interpretation of interstate commerce appeared in several cases which were decided shortly after 1900.[24] But the constitutional issue as regards industrial mergers was finally resolved in the famous Standard Oil and American Tobacco cases of 1911.[25]

It was perhaps not difficult to distinguish the Knight and Standard Oil cases, since the oil monopoly was engaged in refining, selling, and the actual transport of oil products in interstate commerce. In fact, the

---

[22] 175 U. S. 211 (1899).

[23] U. S. v. Addyston Pipe & Steel Co., 85 Fed. 271 (1898). The Circuit Court of Appeals, in an opinion by Judge Taft, reversed the decision of the Circuit Court dismissing the government's petition on the ground that the challenged agreements were not directly related to interstate commerce (78 Fed. 712, 1897).

[24] Northern Securities Co. v. U. S., 193 U. S. 197 (1904); Swift & Co. v. U. S., 196 U. S. 375 (1905).

[25] Standard Oil Co. v. U. S., 221 U. S. 1 (1911); U. S. v. American Tobacco Co., 221 U. S. 106 (1911).

Court indicated a certain amount of impatience with the argument that the act could not be applied. It said:[26]

> But all the structure upon which this argument proceeds is based upon the decision in United States v. E. C. Knight Co. . . . . The view, however, which the argument takes of that case and the arguments based upon that view have been so repeatedly pressed upon this court in connection with the interpretation and enforcement of the Anti-trust Act, and have been so necessarily and expressly decided to be unsound as to cause the contentions to be plainly foreclosed and to require no express notice.

The opinion holding the American Tobacco Company to be a restraint of trade and a monopolization of commerce took even less notice of the question of Federal power. Here the merger of tobacco firms was engaged purely in the manufacture and sale of tobacco products. The combination was essentially the same as that involved in the Knight case. Yet the Court found no difficulty in finding the restraining combination to be directly and substantially related to interstate commerce.

The broad interpretation of the concept of interstate commerce finally adopted by the Supreme Court saved the Sherman Act from being a complete failure. It is still true that the litigants must show a direct and substantial connection between interstate commerce and the contracts or combinations alleged to be unlawful. This requires adequate proof and makes more difficult the prosecution of trade restraints. The difficulty is inevitable in a dual system of government.

(2) Scope

It is undoubtedly a fact that the Sherman Act was directed primarily at the suppression of industrial monopoly. But the terms of the law denouncing restraints of trade are exceedingly broad. It will be recalled that "every" contract or combination in restraint of trade is declared unlawful and "every" person attempting to monopolize or conspiring with others to monopolize is guilty of illegal conduct. In view of the primary objective of the law its all-inclusive language afforded ground for considerable controversy as to whether or not all combinations were subject to the act. Combinations which were particularly concerned were those relating to labor, railways, and agricultural associations. Not only was it necessary for the Supreme Court to decide what Congress had intended as regards these organizations, but the whole question of sound public policy was raised time after time. Both Congress and the courts have had a hand in formulating policy since the first anti-trust statute was passed over a half-century ago. The extent to which the anti-trust laws have been and may now be applied to the combinations mentioned above, as well as to those engaged in foreign trade, is an im-

---

[26] 221 U. S. 1, 68–69.

portant element of national trust policy. The question of scope will be considered under the following four headings: (a) Railways; (b) Labor; (c) Agricultural Associations; (d) Foreign Trade; and (e) Insurance.

(a) Railways

Whether or not railway combinations were subject to the Sherman Act was decided in the case of United States v. Trans-Missouri Freight Association in 1897.[27] This was an association of railroads created for the purpose of establishing rates and regulations on freight traffic. Much of the traffic within the large area west of the Mississippi and Missouri Rivers was included. Representatives of the carriers held meetings periodically to determine rates and regulations on competitive traffic and to consider proposed changes. Fines were imposed upon members who reduced the rates fixed by the association, unless due notice had been given or the reductions were made in good faith to meet the competition of non-member lines. The sole objective of the plan was alleged to be the prevention of ruinous competition. Since the pooling of traffic or income had been made illegal by the Interstate Commerce Act of 1887, the carriers used direct agreements on rates as a curb on competition. They maintained that the rates fixed were no more than reasonable.

The legality of the agreement was defended on two grounds, first, that the Sherman Act did not apply to common carriers by railroad, and second, that even if it did, the agreement was a reasonable restraint of trade and not in violation of the law. The Supreme Court, in reversing the decisions of the lower courts,[28] held against the railroads on both contentions by a vote of five to four.[29] In support of the proposition that railroads were excepted from the law, it had been pointed out that Congress, in passing the Interstate Commerce Act, had recognized the peculiar economic and legal features of the carriers. Railways were to be treated as natural monopolies, and a special administrative agency was established to regulate the all-important matter of rates and charges. Since common carriers had been provided for in special legislation, it was reasonable to assume that a general statute directed at the evils of industrial trusts was not intended by Congress to apply to them. But the Supreme Court declined to accept this reasoning. Since the Interstate Commerce Act neither authorized nor prohibited the agreement in question, there was no inconsistency in applying the anti-trust law. And a literal interpretation of the statute presented no other alternative. *Every* contract or combination restraining trade was outlawed, so there

---

[27] 166 U. S. 290 (1897).
[28] United States v. Trans-Missouri Freight Association, 53 Fed. 440 (1892); 58 Fed. 58 (1893).
[29] *Ibid.*, 166 U. S. 290 (1897).

could be no exclusion of an agreement between competing railroads en-- gaged in interstate commerce from the scope of the act.

Although the Supreme Court has steadfastly maintained its original position, with respect both to loose combinations[30] and to combinations effected by stock ownership or lease,[31] the wisdom of the policy of enforcing competition between railroads may be questioned. The danger of cut-throat competition, with its consequences of highly unstable rates, discrimination, and impairment of financial strength and service, is very real in an industry characterized by large overhead costs and a chronic condition of unused capacity. During the period prior to 1906, when Federal regulation was weak and unable to render effective protection to the public against the exercise of monopoly power, there was some merit in insisting upon competition. Even during this "doldrums" period, however, compelling economic forces led to an informal coöperation between the railways which destroyed the effectiveness of the pronouncements of the Supreme Court.[32] When Federal control was strong enough to cope with the monopoly power of the carriers, there was good reason to acknowledge the advantages of combination and coöperation.

By 1920 Congress was ready to make further concessions to the idea that railroads had best be treated as monopolistic enterprises. The Transportation Act of 1920 legalized pooling agreements when approved by the Interstate Commerce Commission and provided for the consolidation of the railroads into a limited number of systems.[33] In carrying out any arrangement duly approved by the Commission, the railroads were relieved from the operation of both state and Federal anti-trust laws. But it should be emphasized that there was no complete reversal of policy. Pooling agreements were to be authorized by the Commisssion only if they did not "unduly restrain competition," and competition was to be preserved "as fully as possible" in the consolidation plan.

The Transportation Act of 1940 eliminated the requirement of a predetermined consolidation plan and permits the Commission to approve mergers and consolidations if they are consistent with the public interest. With the extension of Federal control to highway and water carriers, a like policy respecting combination has been adopted.[34] The

---

[30] United States v. Joint Traffic Assocation, 171 U. S. 505 (1898). This Association included most of the railroads operating between Chicago and the Atlantic coast, and was formed to establish reasonable rates, prevent unjust discrimination, and effect economies in freight and passenger operations.

[31] Northern Securities Co. v. U. S., 193 U. S. 197 (1904); U. S. v. Union Pacific Railroad Co., 226 U. S. 61 (1912); U. S. v. Southern Pacific Co., 259 U. S. 214 (1922).

[32] The Interstate Commerce Commission stated in 1901 that the decisions in the Trans-Missouri and Joint Traffic Association cases had "produced no practical effect upon the railway operations of the country." Annual Report, 1901, p. 16.

[33] The Interstate Commerce Act, Section 5.

[34] Motor Carrier Act, 1935; Transportation Act of 1940.

same pooling and consolidation rules are applicable to rail, motor, and water carriers, and any transactions approved by the Interstate Commerce Commission are exempted from the Sherman Act.

A further exemption from the anti-trust laws was accorded carriers by the enactment of the Reed-Bulwinkle Bill, over a presidential veto, in June 1948.[35] It has been a long-standing practice in the transportation industry for the carriers operating in a region or area to associate themselves in bureaus or conferences for the purpose of consultation and the determination of rates and related matters of service. The rates agreed upon by the conference, often after public hearings in which interested shippers and carriers have presented their views with respect to proposed changes, are published and filed by the carriers with the Interstate Commerce Commission and are subject to its control. Such coöperative machinery and procedures have been defended by the railroads as a practical means, impossible of attainment through independent action alone, of achieving a rate structure which does not discriminate against particular localities and regions and which permits the free flow of traffic between connecting carriers by the establishment of through routes and joint rates. Those familiar with the process of rate-making, including the Interstate Commerce Commission, the state regulatory bodies, and many shippers and their organizations, have been fully aware of the operation of rate bureaus and associations and have approved of them. It was not until the Department of Justice instituted a civil suit against the western railroads and others in 1944[36] and in the same year appeared as *amicus curiae* in the original suit brought by the State of Georgia in the Supreme Court against numerous railroads[37] that the question of the legality of railroad rate associations and other types of joint action was raised under the Sherman Act. No final decisions have been rendered on the main issues in these cases. In its decision allowing Georgia to file its complaint charging the railroads with a conspiracy to use coercion in the fixing of joint through rates and to discriminate against Georgia in the rates which are fixed, the Supreme Court held, however, that rate-fixing combinations by carriers "have no immunity from the anti-trust laws."[38] The Interstate Commerce Commission, while exercising broad regulatory powers over the carriers, was found not to have authority to attack, to approve, or to supervise rate-fixing combinations or their activities.

The recently enacted amendment to the Interstate Commerce Act[39] clarifies the legal status of rate-making conferences or bureaus as regards

---

[35] Interstate Commerce Act, Part I, Section 5a. (Public Law 662, Law without approval, June 17, 1948).

[36] United States *v.* Association of American Railroads et al., U. S. District Court for Nebraska, Sept. 27, 1945. Civil Case No. 246.

[37] Georgia *v.* Pennsylvania Railroad Co., 324 U. S. 439 (1945).

[38] Georgia *v.* Pennsylvania Railroad Co., 324 U. S. 439, 457 (1945).

[39] Section 5a.

common carriers by railroad, motor vehicle, water, or pipe-line, and freight forwarders. Agreements among carriers relating to rates and charges or rules pertaining thereto, or procedures for the joint consideration of these matters, must be approved by the Interstate Commerce Commission. Before its approval is given, interested parties must be afforded a reasonable opportunity for a hearing, and the Commission must find, among other things, that the agreement furthers the national transportation policy laid down by Congress. All agreements providing a procedure for the joint consideration of rates must accord to each party the "free and unrestrained right to take independent action either before or after any determination" has been arrived at through the procedure. Moreover, every bureau or conference established under an approved agreement must maintain accounts and records that are open to the inspection of the Commission and must submit such reports as the Commission may require. These are safeguards against the use of coercion upon individual carriers in the fixing of rates and collusion on the part of a group of railroads in the formulation of rate policies that are detrimental to a particular region or to the nation as a whole. Joint action by the carriers, which appears to be necessary for the maintenance of an orderly and non-discriminatory rate structure, is thereby relieved from the operation of the anti-trust laws and placed under the strict control of the Interstate Commerce Commission.

Coöperative action by transport agencies which is not covered by the provisions of the Interstate Commerce Act can still be prosecuted under the anti-trust laws. It would appear, for example, that agreements having the effect of restricting competition in service are illegal. In the suit brought against the western railroads in 1944 it was alleged, among other things, that certain roads agreed to retard the shipment of perishable products to eastern destinations in order to equalize their service with carriers capable only of less expeditious service. The railroads were said to have agreed, also, to prevent the installation of air-cooling equipment on passenger trains and the provision of such recreational facilities as radios and motion pictures. Agreements of this character, which may be justified in some instances on the ground that they curb competition in service which is wasteful, have not as yet been exempted from the Sherman Law.

(b) Labor

Although the relation of labor to the Sherman Act constitutes a significant chapter in American economic and legal history, only the main outlines of that story can be treated here. Labor unions had long been recognized as legitimate organizations for collective bargaining. Their nature and purpose were such as to distinguish them clearly from combinations of capital. Yet Congress had not specifically excepted them or their activities from the operation of the statute. Despite the failure so to do, it was contended from the beginning that the intent of Congress was to confine the anti-trust law to industrial combinations. When the courts declined to accede to this view, Congress was induced to re-state public policy relating to labor activities. But it did not amend the law so as to exclude the acts of labor unions. In certain circumstances the Sherman Act may still be applied.

One of the first injunctions against a labor union issued under the anti-trust law was in the famous Debs case of 1894. The American Railway Union, of which Eugene V. Debs was president, declared a boycott against the Pullman Company to force arbitration of a labor dispute which had caused a strike of Pullman employees. Members of the union refused to operate trains which included Pullman cars. Resistance on the part of the carriers led to strikes and violence which interfered seriously with the operations of railroads entering Chicago. The government obtained an injunction against Debs and others on the ground that they were conspiring to obstruct the mails and restrain interstate commerce. In upholding the injunction in subsequent contempt proceedings, the Federal Circuit Court construed the Sherman Act to include not only combinations of capital but combinations of any character restraining trade.[40]

The injunction, instrumental along with the employment of military force in breaking the strike, was sanctioned by the Supreme Court.[41] The court did not reach this decision, however, on the strength of the Sherman Law. Ample ground for enjoining the acts of the union and its officers was found in Federal power over the mails and interstate commerce. Justice Brewer concluded his opinion by saying: "We enter into no examination of the act of July 2, 1890, . . . upon which the Circuit Court relied mainly to sustain its jurisdiction. It must not be understood from this that we dissent from the conclusions of that court in reference to the scope of the act, but simply that we prefer to rest our judgment on the broader ground which has been discussed in this opinion. . . ."[42]

In 1908 the Supreme Court had occasion to rule definitely that labor unions were within the scope of the anti-trust law in Loewe v. Lawlor.[43] This case, often referred to as the Danbury Hatters' case, involved a suit for treble damages by a hat manufacturer against the members of the Danbury local union and officers of United Hatters of North America. In order to force the firm to employ union members only, a strike had been called and a boycott declared upon the hats made by the plaintiff.

---

[40] U. S. v. Debs et. al., 64 Fed. 724 (1894).
[41] In re Debs, 158 U. S. 564 (1895).
[42] Ibid., p. 600.
[43] 208 U. S. 274 (1908).

The boycott was enforced throughout the nation with the aid not only of United Hatters but of the American Federation of Labor, with which it was affiliated. So effective were the strike and boycott that large losses were sustained by the Loewe Company. When suit for damages was brought, the Circuit Court of Connecticut dismissed the complaint because interstate commerce was not involved.[44] The Supreme Court reversed this judgment and held that combinations composed of laborers were included within the term "every" contract or combination restraining trade.[45] It also declared that a secondary boycott of goods in interstate commerce is an unlawful restraint of trade and that recovery for injuries sustained therefrom may be had. When the case was finally settled after further litigation, the union was obliged to pay a judgment of $310,000, including interest.

The decisions applying the Sherman Act to labor were a serious threat to trade-union activity. Labor organizations sought strenuously to obtain relief from injunctions and damage suits. When the Clayton Act of 1914 was passed, Congress acquiesced in the demand for limitations upon the activities of the Federal Courts in the labor sphere. Section 6 of the Clayton Act declares "that the labor of a human being is not a commodity or article of commerce," and provides that labor organizations or their members shall not be construed "to be illegal combinations or conspiracies in restraint of trade, under the anti-trust laws." Section 20 forbids the issuance of an injunction in a labor dispute "unless necessary to prevent irreparable injury to property or to a property right" for which there is no adequate remedy at law. Injunctions may not be issued against strikes, peaceful picketing, payment of strike benefits, boycotts, or any act which would be lawful in the absence of an industrial dispute.

These provisions were hailed as a great victory for the cause of labor. It was believed that unions had been expressly liberated from the scope of the oppressive anti-trust laws. But labor was due for a great disappointment. The ambiguous language of the Clayton Act was construed by the courts in such fashion as to render little change in the law of labor. In considering the language relating to picketing, for example, the Supreme Court stated that it "introduces no new principle" into equity jurisprudence and "is merely declaratory of what was the best practice always."[46] And in the Duplex Printing case of 1921 it was clear that the law with respect to secondary boycotts remained unchanged.[47] The International Association of Machinists endeavored to compel the Duplex

---

[44] Loewe v. Lawlor, 148 Fed. 924 (1906).

[45] Loewe v. Lawlor, 208 U. S. 274 (1908).

[46] American Steel Foundries v. Tri-City Trades Council, 257 U. S. 184, 203 (1921).

[47] Duplex Printing Press Co. v. Deering, 254 U. S. 443 (1921).

Printing Press Company, a manufacturer of printing presses in Michigan, to accept the closed shop and other union terms. A direct strike having been unsuccessful, a secondary boycott against the sale and use of the firm's products was instituted. The machinists, with the aid of others, threatened customers in New York City with sympathetic strikes, boycotts, and other interferences if Duplex machines were installed or operated. The Duplex Company, availing itself of the right conferred on private parties by the Clayton Act to get injunctive relief, sought an injunction against the acts of the union in New York. The district court refused to enjoin the defendants, and was upheld by the Circuit Court of Appeals on the ground that the Clayton Act legalized secondary boycotts in cases between employer and employees.[48] But the Supreme Court, with Justices Brandeis, Holmes, and Clarke dissenting, declined to sanction this view.[49] It maintained that the anti-injunction provisions of the Clayton Act were applicable only to disputes between an employer and his immediate employees. Since the offending boycotters were not employees of the complainant and not directly engaged in a dispute about the terms of their own employment, they were not immune. To protect the Duplex Company against irreparable damage from the obstruction to its trade imposed by the illegal conspiracy, an injunction was held to be justified.[50]

A further attempt to limit the injunctive powers of the courts was made in the Norris-La Guardia Act of 1932.[51] The broad aim of the law was to restore to labor the rights which Congress had intended in passing the Clayton Act. Among other things, the restrictions on the issuance of injunctions are made applicable to labor disputes involving employees in an industry having "direct or indirect" interests in the

---

[48] Ibid., 247 Fed. 192 (1917); 252 Fed. 722 (1918).

[49] Ibid., 254 U. S. 443 (1921).

[50] Under the interpretation of Section 20 of the Clayton Act adopted in the Duplex case, the Supreme Court decided adversely to the union in Bedford Cut Stone Co. v. Journeymen Stone Cutters' Association of North America, 274 U. S. 37 (1927). In retaliation for the refusal of operators of limestone quarries in Indiana to renew their trade agreement with the stonecutters' union, the union ordered its members not to work upon or place stone which had been shipped from these anti-union quarries. Since the strikes of union members coerced builders not to purchase the stone of the complainants and thereby curtailed their interstate sales, the combination was found to be in undue and unreasonable restraint of trade.

Justice Brandeis, in a dissent in which Justice Holmes concurred, remarked: "If, on the undisputed facts of this case, refusal to work can be enjoined, Congress created by the Sherman Law and the Clayton Act an instrument for imposing restraints upon labor which reminds of involuntary servitude." He emphasized that the court had permitted the United States Steel Corporation and the United Shoe Machinery Company to dominate their respective industries under the celebrated "rule of reason," and that it could not have been the intent of Congress to apply a more rigorous rule to labor organizations. He held that the union conduct, since it was not tainted with fraud, intimidation, or violence, was a reasonable restraint of trade.

[51] Act of March 23, 1932, 47 Stat. 70.

dispute, and irrespective of whether or not they are employees of the recalcitrant employer. No mention of the secondary boycott is made, perhaps because of the general disapproval of this labor weapon, but the ground for the decision in the Duplex case is definitely removed.

The Supreme Court now appears to be willing to give full force and effect to the labor policy set down by Congress.[52] In United States v. Hutcheson,[53] for example, the Court had before it a criminal prosecution under the Sherman Act growing out of a jurisdictional dispute between two rival unions. A long-standing controversy between the carpenters' and machinists' unions in regard to the erection and dismantling of machinery culminated in a strike by the carpenters against Anheuser-Busch, Inc., and certain construction companies in St. Louis, when the disputed jobs were given to the machinists. Anheuser-Busch was picketed and the union requested its members and their friends not to purchase the company's beer. In holding that the union activities could not be criminally prosecuted, the Court reviewed the effects of the Clayton and Norris-La Guardia Acts upon the anti-trust law. It was concluded that the conduct complained of was allowable under these acts and that an injunction could not have been issued against it. This being true, it was held that Congress could not have intended that the labor union was criminally liable for its acts punishable with imprisonment and heavy fines. Picketing and boycotting activities are lawful under the anti-trust laws so long as a "union acts in its self-interest and does not combine with non-labor groups."

But even apart from the modifying statutes, a recent clarification of the Sherman Act seems to have restricted its application to labor union activities. In Apex Hosiery Co. v. Leader,[54] the Supreme Court, with Chief Justice Hughes and Justices Roberts and McReynolds dissenting, declined to sustain a trebled judgment of $711,932.55 for damages inflicted by a "sit-down" strike. The strike was called by the hosiery union, then having only 8 of the 2500 employees in the Philadelphia factory as members, in order to compel the operation of a closed shop. The plant was forcibly seized and occupied for a month and a half, during which time the sit-down strikers wrecked machinery and other property and prevented the shipment of $800,000 worth of finished hosiery. Some 80 per cent of the hosiery was to be shipped in interstate commerce.

The majority of the Court, in an opinion written by Justice Stone, held that the Sherman Act does apply to labor unions, that the strikers committed illegal acts punishable under the laws of Pennsylvania, and that there was an intentional obstruction of interstate commerce. Yet

---

[52] Milk Wagon Drivers' Union v. Lake Valley Farm Products, Inc., 311 U. S. 91 (1940); United States v. Hutcheson, 312 U. S. 219 (1941).

[53] 312 U. S. 219 (1941).

[54] 310 U. S. 469 (1940).

the conduct of the union did not constitute a violation of the Sherman Law. The ground for this ruling was that the restraint in question was not of the character proscribed by the anti-trust law. It was held that the particular type of restraint to which the law applies is one which involves the "market control of a commodity, such as to 'monopolize the supply, control its price, or discriminate between its would-be purchasers.'" The purpose of the statute was not to police interstate commerce, but to prevent interferences with market or price competition. Since the intent and effect of the union's activities in the instant case were not to affect hosiery prices or to suppress competition in the hosiery market, the Sherman Act was not violated. The fact that the restraint was effected by violence and not peaceful means was held not to alter the conclusion.

While the activities of labor unions are still subject to the anti-trust laws, it is apparent from the court decisions that the use of injunctions and damage suits is definitely circumscribed. The test of legality is to be whether or not the given conduct is intended directly to suppress commercial competition. The same rule is to be applied to labor activities as to combinations of capital. It is not enough to show that a strike, for example, interferes with interstate commerce and prevents employers from competing in the market. The restraint must have or be intended to have an effect upon market prices. Where the monopolistic effect is attained by coöperation between labor groups and others, it is clear that the law may be invoked. Such coöperation between manufacturers, building contractors, and union carpenters, which prevented non-union-made millwork from entering the Chicago market and thereby increased the price of buildings, was condemned in United States v. Brims.[55] A similar conspiracy of marketmen and union members to monopolize and control prices in the poultry market of the New York metropolitan area was enjoined in Local 167 v. United States.[56] And in Allen Bradley Co. v. Local Union No. 3 (325 U. S. 797), decided in 1945, the Supreme Court condemned the coöperation of electrical workers with electrical equipment manufacturers and contractors in closing the New York market to equipment produced elsewhere. Said the Court: "Our holding means that the same labor union activities may or may not be in violation of the Sherman Act, dependent upon whether the union acts alone or in combination with business groups. This, it is argued, brings about a wholly undesirable result—one which leaves labor unions free to engage in conduct which restrains trade. But the desirability of such an exemption of labor unions is a question for the determination of Congress."

Moreover, it should be noted that, quite apart from the anti-trust laws, the remedy of injunction against the activities of labor unions is

---

[55] 272 U. S. 549 (1926).
[56] 291 U. S. 293 (1934).

still available to the Federal Government in certain circumstances. In the celebrated case of United States *v*. United Mine Workers,[57] a restraining order and a temporary injunction preventing a union and its officers from precipitating a nation-wide strike in the bituminous coal mines were upheld by the Supreme Court. The mines had previously been seized under the authority of the War Labor Disputes Act in order to prevent labor disturbances from disrupting the coal industry and the national economy during the transition from war to peace. The restraints on the union were imposed pending judicial interpretation of the provisions of a labor contract between the Government and the union, the union having asserted its right to terminate the agreement. In upholding the Government, the Supreme Court held that the proscriptions on injunctions found in the Norris-LaGuardia and the Clayton Acts did not apply to disputes between the Government and its employees. Since there was no express reference to the United States and no indication in the legislative history of the statutes that Congress intended to include the United States in the general term "employer," the Government could not be found to have given up remedies otherwise available to it. The restraints imposed on injunctions are applicable only to labor disputes between private employers and their employees.

The Labor-Management Relations Act of 1947,[58] otherwise known as the Taft-Hartley Act, goes even further in restoring the injunction as an instrument in dealing with labor disputes. Whenever the President believes that a strike or lock-out, actual or threatened, affecting an entire industry or a substantial part of it, will imperil the "national health or safety," he may appoint a board of inquiry to investigate the issues involved in the dispute. When the board of inquiry has reported, the President may direct the Attorney-General to obtain an injunction preventing the strike or lock-out from taking place or continuing. The district court is to issue the restraining order only if it finds that the strike affects a substantial part of an interstate industry and will imperil the "health or safety" of the nation. If an injunction is issued, the parties, with the assistance of the Mediation Service, must make every effort to reach a settlement. The same board of inquiry that reported previously is reconvened, and if the dispute is unsettled after 60 days, it will report the status to the President. Within the next 15 days, the National Labor Relations Board is required to conduct a secret ballot of employees to determine whether they wish to accept the final offer of settlement of the employer. The result of the balloting is to be certified to the Attorney-General within 5 days and at that time, or sooner if a settlement is reached, he is to have the injunction discharged. If the dispute has not

---

[57] United States *v*. United Mine Workers, 330 U. S. 258 (1947).

[58] Public Law 101, 80th Congress, 1st Session. Passed by Congress over the President's veto on June 23, 1947. See Prentice-Hall, Inc., *Labor Relations*, pars. 20,011, *et seq.*; 36,400 *et seq.*

been resolved, the President must then report on the whole matter to Congress "with such recommendations as he may see fit to make for consideration and appropriate action." From the foregoing it is clear that the injunction is to be used in national emergencies as a means of instituting a cooling-off period, which may run as long as 80 days, during which the parties to the dispute are to attempt to work out a settlement. Strikes and lock-outs are illegal during this period.

Among other things, the Labor-Management Relations Act also declares secondary boycotts and jurisdictional strikes to be unfair labor practices. The preliminary investigation of charges of these unlawful practices is to be given priority over other cases by the National Labor Relations Board. And where there are grounds for believing the charges to be true, the Board is obliged to obtain a restraining order pending the final adjudication of the matter. Such a restraining order, which is limited to 5 days, may be had if it is alleged that the employer will suffer "substantial and irreparable injury." Moreover, an employer who is injured by unlawful secondary boycotts and jurisdictional strikes may sue the union responsible for them for damages sustained.

With the recently enacted labor legislation on the statute books, it is apparent that public policy has turned the full cycle. Labor activities that were once successfully attacked under the Sherman Act as illegal restraints of trade, then sanctioned by the courts under the Clayton and Norris-LaGuardia Acts, have been definitely outlawed. And the remedy of injunction, against which labor has fought strenuously for many years, continues to be available, not to private employers it is true, but to the Government. The Sherman Act has been supplanted by other legislation with respect to the broad range of labor union activities and continues to be a factor only where monopolistic ends are attained through collusion between labor organizations and other parties.

(c) Agricultural Associations

Although prior to 1914 no decision concerning agricultural associations was ever rendered by the Supreme Court, it may be safely assumed that the broad language of the Sherman Act would have been held to include combinations of farmers that restrained interstate trade. Lower Federal courts had held the law applicable to monopolistic practices of agricultural combinations,[59] and the Supreme Court stated in the Danbury Hatters' case that "organizations of farmers and laborers" were not exempted.[60] Since the latter case did not involve a farmers' combination, the declaration must be regarded as an *obiter dictum*.

[59] Steers v. United States, 192 Fed. 1 (1911); United States v. King, 250 Fed. 908 (1916).
[60] Loewe v. Lawlor, 208 U. S. 274 (1908).

Beginning in 1914, however, Congress enacted a series of statutes favoring the development of agricultural marketing associations and protecting them from the anti-trust laws. Apparently Congress has desired to further the interests of the large number of scattered producers by allowing a coöperation which promised improved farm products and substantial marketing economies. The Clayton Act of 1914 authorized the existence and operation of agricultural organizations not having capital stock or conducted for profit, and provided that the anti-trust laws should not be construed to make them illegal or to forbid their members from carrying out their legitimate objectives.[61] The Capper-Volstead Act of 1922 extended and broadened these exemptions, and provided a special procedure for action by the Secretary of Agriculture if he believes that an association "monopolizes" or restrains trade "to such an extent that the price of any agricultural product is unduly enhanced."[62] The Agricultural Marketing Agreement Act of 1937, a re-enactment and amendment of the Agricultural Adjustment Act of 1933, seeks to establish orderly marketing and parity prices on farm products by authorizing the Secretary of Agriculture to enter into marketing agreements with producers or others handling agricultural commodities.[63] Any such agreement is lawful under the anti-trust laws.

Despite the immunity conferred upon them, farmers' associations are not at liberty to do anything they please. A secondary boycott used by a Maine potato association to coerce outsiders was held not to be lawful conduct in attaining legitimate objectives under the Clayton Act.[64] And in the case of United States v. Borden Company,[65] the Supreme Court held the Sherman Act applicable to a price-fixing conspiracy in which one of the participants was an association of milk producers. The milk producers' association had joined with distributors, labor officials, municipal officials, and others, to control the supply of fluid milk entering the Chicago market and to fix both the prices paid to producers and the prices charged consumers. No marketing agreement or other arrangement with the Secretary of Agriculture had been effected. In the absence of such official sanction, the court held that the Marketing Agreement Act of 1937 did not divest commerce in farm products of the protection afforded by the Sherman Law. Furthermore, it was held that neither the terms of the Clayton Act nor those of the Capper-Volstead Act authorized the type of conspiracy between farmers and others which was being prosecuted. Agricultural producers are extended special privileges

---

[61] Section 6.
[62] 42 Stat. 388 (1922). It appears that the Department of Agriculture has never taken any action with respect to coöperatively determined prices under this law.
[63] 50 Stat. 246 (1937).
[64] United States v. King, 250 Fed. 908 (1916).
[65] 308 U. S. 188 (1939).

as regards union for marketing purposes, but they may not combine with others with the intent of monopolizing a market.

(d) Foreign Trade

It was the intention of Congress to promote a policy of free competition both in domestic interstate commerce and in foreign trade. Monopolizing and restraint of trade or commerce "among the several States, or with foreign nations," are proscribed by the terms of the Sherman Law. Only a few cases were adjudicated in the courts relative to foreign trade until recent years. The early cases concerned actions of ocean shipping companies or commercial importers. Although it was undoubtedly covered by the anti-trust act, monopoly in export trade gave rise to no litigation. Very significant modifications in anti-trust policy regarding at least two phases of foreign trade provide a large part of the reason.

Several decisions relating to coöperation between steamship companies and the use of unfair competitive methods were rendered by lower Federal Courts prior to the First World War.[66] Because most of these arrangements were discontinued with the outbreak of war, the Supreme Court declined to review the questions on their merits, on the ground that they had become moot.[67] In Thomsen v. Cayser,[68] however, the Supreme Court held that a combination of foreign-owned common carriers operating between New York and South African ports violated the Sherman Act. The carriers had entered a so-called "conference" or agreement not to compete amongst themselves, and had utilized "deferred rebates" and "fighting ships" to suppress outside competition. The combination was found to restrain unreasonably the foreign commerce of the United States. It could not be excused, said the Court, on the ground that it was beneficial and "was induced by good motives or produced good results."

Impressed with the usefulness of conference agreements as means of curbing excessive competition and maintaining stable rates and satisfactory service, Congress, after due investigation, modified the traditional policy with respect to them.[69] Such conference agreements were legalized under the anti-trust laws, but at the same time were brought within governmental control in the Shipping Act of 1916.[70] Agreements between common carriers engaged in foreign commerce resulting in the fixing of rates, pooling of earnings, or the regulation of traffic must be

---

[66] U. S. v. Hamburg-American Steamship Co., 200 Fed. 806 (1911); Same, 216 Fed. 971 (1914); U. S. v. Prince Line, 220 Fed. 230 (1915).

[67] 239 U. S. 466 (1916); 242 U. S. 537 (1917).

[68] 243 U. S. 66 (1917).

[69] Report on Steamship Agreements and Affiliations in the American Foreign & Domestic Trade, 63rd Congress, 2nd Session, House Document No. 805 (1914).

[70] 39 Stat. 728 (1916).

filed with and approved by the United States Maritime Commission. Numerous unfair or discriminatory practices are also outlawed. In cases where practices violate the anti-trust laws but are covered by the Shipping Act, individuals must seek relief from the Commission in the first instance.[71]

But even more significant to the American economy is the modification of traditional anti-trust policy with respect to export trade. Prompted by the mercantilist notion that export trade should be given encouragement, despite its restrictive policy upon the importation of foreign goods and services, Congress enacted the Webb-Pomerene Act in 1918.[72] Business interests engaged in foreign trade advocated the legalization of export associations as a means of better meeting the strong competition encountered in foreign markets. And the Federal Trade Commission gave them support. It found the explanation for the greater competitive strength of British and German traders not in the fundamental principle of comparative advantage but in the "superior facilities and more effective organizations" maintained in foreign countries.[73] Legal restrictions prevented the development by American firms of "equally effective organizations for overseas business." The Commission recommended that with appropriate safeguards for domestic consumers and competing producers, legislation be enacted to permit coöperative action by firms engaged in export trade.

The heart of the Webb-Pomerene Act is the provision that nothing in the Sherman Law is to be construed as declaring illegal "an association entered into for the sole purpose of engaging in export trade and actually engaged solely in such export trade, or an agreement made or act done in the course of export trade by such association, provided such association, agreement, or act is not in restraint of trade within the United States, and is not in restraint of the export trade of any domestic competitor of such association."

General supervision over export associations with an eye toward preventing an abuse of their privileges was vested in the Federal Trade Commission. Every association is required to file organizational papers with the Commission and to supply annually such information respecting its organization and business as the Commission may require. The Commission may proceed against unfair methods used against competitors in export trade, even though the practices are carried on "without the territorial jurisdiction of the United States." And it is directed to investigate the conduct of export combinations which may be suspected of restraining the export trade of domestic competitors or "which artificially

---

[71] U. S. Navigation Co., Inc., v. Cunard Steamship Co., 284 U. S. 474 (1932).

[72] Export Trade Act, 40 Stat. 516 (April 10, 1918).

[73] Federal Trade Commission, *Report on Coöperation in American Export Trade.* Part I, p. 3 (1916).

or intentionally enhances or depresses prices . . . or which substantially lessens competition within the United States." If a violation of the law is established, the Commission may only recommend that the association readjust its organization or conduct. In the event that the recommendations are ignored, the matter is to be referred to the Attorney-General for such action as he may deem proper.

Not a great many industries have taken advantage of the provisions of the law. The number of associations has varied from a low of forty-three in 1920 and in 1935 to a high of fifty-seven between 1929 and 1931. There were fifty-one associations registered with the Commission on June 30, 1948.[74] In the peak year of 1929, the total exports of the combines amounted to $724,100,000, or slightly less than 14 per cent of the total merchandise exports of the United States. The products exported by the associations include a considerable variety of raw materials and manufactured goods, but by far the greatest concentration is in metals and metal products and in the products of wells and mines.

The striking fact about the operation of the Webb-Pomerene Act, however, is the relatively small amount of supervision which has been exercised over the affairs of the export associations. Up to 1944, the Commission expended an insignificant portion of its efforts and budget in the administration of the law.[75] It confined its surveillance to the routine tasks of registering the associations, accepting periodic reports, and publishing summaries of trade statistics and of the advantages allegedly accruing to participating firms. No careful analysis of the effects of their operations upon output or prices in domestic trade was ever made. Yet this was regarded as of vital importance by legislators when the policy was debated in Congress, and the Commission was given full responsibility for protecting domestic interests.[76] During the first twenty-five years that the law was in effect, the Commission brought only one formal action against an export association. It recommended some readjustment of the business of a plywood association in order to eliminate restraint upon the export trade of other American firms.[77] Apart from possible informal action, the only other proceedings under the law related to unfair methods of competition. A handful of complaints were brought by the Commission, chiefly against misrepresentation, but most of them were dismissed without any reasons given.[78]

---

[74] *Annual Report*, 1948, p. 67.

[75] The cost of administering export trade was reported as $4921 of total costs of $1,152,542 in 1929, and in 1940 the cost was $9252, as compared with total costs of $2,252,989. F. T. C., *Annual Reports*, 1929, p. 141; 1940, pp. 150–151.

[76] See Leslie T. Fournier, "The Purposes and Results of the Webb-Pomerene Law," *American Economic Review*, Vol. XXII (March, 1932), pp. 18–33.

[77] Pacific Forest Industries, January 27, 1940, F. T. C., *Annual Report*, 1940, pp. 129–130.

[78] For a collection of these complaints, see Commerce Clearing House, Inc., *Trade Regulation Service* (ninth edition), Vol. I, pp. 741–743.

Exemplary conduct on the part of export combinations might supply reason for the meagre regulatory action. But the evidence which has come to light would seem to deny any such optimistic explanation. In taking advantage of the extremely liberal ruling by the Commission as to what might be done under the terms of the law, exporters have pursued policies injurious to domestic markets. In 1924, after inquiry from a group of silver producers, the Commission ruled, among other things, that (1) an association might enter into coöperative arrangements with foreign companies for the sole purpose of operation in foreign markets, and (2) that associations need not engage in actual selling but could confine their activities to allotting export orders among their members or fixing prices at which products were to be sold.[79] The Commission overlooked the fact that the original purpose of the law was to enable exporters to obtain the economies inherent in joint selling agencies.[80] Under its rulings this limited objective was obscured, and emphasis was placed upon the purpose of controlling price and output policies in world markets. And if we had no conscience where foreign markets were concerned, we should have had the intelligence to recognize that monopoly in the world market would mean monopoly in our domestic market.

The interrelation of markets is clearly evident in the operations of Copper Exporters, Inc. Organized in 1926 by the leading American copper producers, it associated itself by agreement with practically all of the important copper producers and dealers in the world.[81] The resulting international cartel fixed prices and allocated sales on a world basis. The domestic price moved upward along with world prices, and was pegged at eighteen cents per pound for a whole year beginning April 15, 1929. This was accomplished in the face of a declining demand and an increase in stocks, and gave clear evidence of concerted action by domestic suppliers. When the world depression and the accumulated stocks of copper made it impossible to maintain the artificially fixed price, both the London and the New York prices fell precipitously. In 1930 and 1931 producers agreed to curtail world production, but they did not prevent the American price from falling to five cents per pound. Since 1933, Copper Exporters has been inactive, and most of its members have withdrawn.[82]

Since 1944, a marked change has occurred in the policy toward export associations. Both the Federal Trade Commission and the Department of Justice have launched campaigns against associations that have

[79] Letter of Federal Trade Commission to Silver Producers' Committee, dated July 31, 1924; reproduced in T. N. E. C., *Monograph* No. 6, pp. 125–128.

[80] Fournier, *op. cit.*, pp. 21–22.

[81] For accounts of the activities of Copper Exporters, Inc., see Fournier, *op. cit.*, and T. N. E. C., *Hearings on Cartels*, Part 25, (1940), pp. 13089–13301.

[82] Another illustration of the operation of the Webb-Pomerene Law is found in the workings of the Sulphur Export Corporation described in Chap. 28.

participated in international cartel arrangements with adverse effects upon competition in domestic and foreign trade. The Commission has reviewed the practices of many of the associations registered with it and has discovered that fifteen associations have had agreements at one time or another with foreign producers. In several instances a study of the effects of these agreements allocating foreign markets and governing terms of sale has demonstrated that independent American exporters have been injured and that there has been a substantial lessening of competition in domestic trade. Among the associations for which the Commission has made recommendations for the adjustment of their business are Phosphate Export Association, Sulphur Export Corporation, Export Screw Association, and General Milk Company.[83] No penalties are involved in the procedure available to the Commission, but if the associations do not comply with the recommendations they may be prosecuted under the Sherman Act by the Department of Justice.

Acting independently of the Commission and as part of its drive against international cartels, the Department of Justice has succeeded in its suits against the United States Alkali Export Association,[84] and Electrical Apparatus Export Association.[85] Each association was found to have entered cartel agreements that restrained trade. A noteworthy holding in the Alkali case is that the Department of Justice need not wait for the Commission to investigate and make recommendations before it may bring action under the Sherman Act. The Electrical Apparatus Association, sponsored by Westinghouse and General Electric, was dissolved by consent decree in 1947. The legal theory underlying this action is that any agreement with non-members which restrains export trade is unlawful and not permitted under the Webb-Pomerene Act. This interpretation is at variance with the view of the Commission that cartel agreements are bad only if domestic trade or the trade of competing exporters is restrained, but it is one which is more in keeping with the Act's original purpose of promoting foreign trade.

American experience under the Export Trade Act suggests the folly of encouraging producers to combine for trade purposes. The policy is quite contrary to our traditional attitude toward combinations in domestic trade, yet official sanction is given to the creation of combines to exploit the consuming public of foreign countries.[86] If the relative ef-

---

[83] *Annual Reports*, 1946, pp. 68–70; 1947, pp. 82–84; 1948, pp. 69–70. For the details of the recommendation concerning the Sulphur Export Corporation, see Chap. 28.

[84] United States Alkali Export Association *v.* United States, 325 U. S. 196 (1945).

[85] U. S. *v.* Electrical Apparatus Export Association, Southern District of New York, Consent Decree, March 12, 1947.

[86] It is interesting to note that in 1919 the Federal Trade Commission stated that some fear had been expressed in South American countries that the consuming public would be harmed by strengthening the hands of American trusts and monopolies. T. N. E. C., *Monograph* No. 6, p. 245.

ficiency of various branches of American industry makes for participation in foreign commerce, there would seem to be no need to eliminate competition. And it is inconceivable that producers who act in collusion with respect to foreign sales and prices will not be tempted to follow like procedures in domestic markets. Whether or not they do so consciously, the very fact that the source of supply is common to both markets makes it inevitable that output and price policies will be intimately related. In such circumstances it is an arduous task to prove a conspiracy which "artificially or intentionally" enhances prices within the United States. Certainly the generosity of the Federal Trade Commission in construing the law and its belated vigilance in protecting the domestic economy suggest that the departure from traditional policy has gone too far. A reconsideration is called for on grounds both of principle and experience.

The only phase of international trade not subjected to a change of anti-trust policy has been importing. Despite a confirmed disposition to exclude foreign competition by means of the tariff, Congress has never been willing to allow combines to control goods entering the country. The Sherman and Wilson Tariff Acts[87] stand on the statute books as manifestations of this policy, while the Tariff Act of 1930 condemns unfair methods of competition in the import trade.[88]

Until the recent drive against international cartels, little has been done against combinations affecting import trade. The leading case of United States v. Sisal Sales Corporation,[89] decided in 1927, involved the importation of sisal from Mexico, a fibre from which more than 80 per cent of the binder twine used in the United States is manufactured. Sisal Sales Corporation, with the aid of American banking firms and others, had become the exclusive selling agent in the world market for the sole Mexican enterprise buying sisal from producers. Being the only American importer, it was able to fix arbitrarily high prices. The Supreme Court found the combination to be in violation of both the Sherman Act and the Wilson Tariff Act. Since the conspiracy was entered into by parties within the United States and effected by acts within its borders, the Court was able to distinguish it from an earlier case in which the action had taken place in a foreign country.[90] Subsequent cases against

---

[87] 28 Stat. 570 (1894), amended 37 Stat. 667 (1913). The provisions of the act have been outlined earlier in this chapter.

[88] 46 Stat. 703 (1930). Administered by the United States Tariff Commission, the cases of unfair competition consist chiefly of alleged patent infringement and the copying of domestic articles by importers. The Tariff Commission has recommended that patent cases be transferred to the Federal Courts exclusively and that other unfair competition cases be handled entirely by the Federal Trade Commission. See *Annual Report*, 1936, pp. 45–47.

[89] 274 U. S. 268 (1927).

[90] American Banana Co. v. United Fruit Co., 213 U. S. 359 (1909).

the quinine and potash monopolies were settled by consent decrees.[91] The foreign monopolies were enjoined from fixing re-sale prices, discriminating between purchasers, and other practices within the United States, but acts and agreements entirely completed without the United States were exempted from the law.

An attempt was made in the late 1920's to revise the Webb-Pomerene Act in such fashion as to permit combines for importation of crude rubber, potash, sisal, and such other raw materials as might be certified by the Secretary of Commerce. The purpose was to combat, by the creation of bargaining monopolies, certain foreign monopolies in raw commodities. The Newton Bill contained various safeguards against withholding stocks, raising prices, and other possible abuses within the domestic market.[92] They were to be administered by the Federal Trade Commission. Although supported by Secretary of Commerce Hoover, the Department of Justice, and numerous trade organizations, the bill failed of enactment. One of the main arguments in favor of this bill was removed in 1928 when the British announced the discontinuance of their restrictions on rubber. It was fortunate that the proposed plan did not materialize. Collective action might have increased the bargaining strength of American buyers, but the creation of a buyers' monopoly to match the sale monopoly seems a poor way to create competition. Much more effective means to assure supplies of essential products at fair prices can be found in the development of substitutes and alternate sources of supply. There is a real danger to the domestic economy in placing control of essential raw materials in the hands of import associations. Adequate safeguards strictly enforced would meet the situation. But experience with export associations suggests that existing regulatory machinery cannot be relied upon to deal effectively with legalized monopoly.

(e) Insurance

For a period of 75 years prior to 1944, the Supreme Court had consistently held that state regulation of the insurance business, including tax laws, did not violate the commerce clause of the Constitution. As early as 1866, the state of Virginia, among others, had sought to correct the widespread abuses which prevailed in the insurance business by passing regulatory legislation. In sustaining the Virginia statute, which regulated foreign insurance companies, the Supreme Court in 1869 held

---

[91] U. S. v. N. V. Amsterdamsche Chininefabriek *et al.*, D. C. N. Y. 1928 (Dutch Quinine Monopoly); U. S. v. Deutsches Kalisyndikat Gesellschaft *et al.*, D. C. N. Y. 1929 (Franco-German Potash Cartel).

[92] H. R. 8927, 70th Congress, 1st Session (1928).

that it did not transgress Congressional authority over interstate commerce because "issuing a policy of insurance is not a transaction of commerce."[93] This holding was reaffirmed in subsequent cases. In 1895, the Court made the flat statement, "The business of insurance is not commerce."[94] And in a case decided in 1913, in which the New York Life Insurance Company protested against a Montana tax on the ground that its business was so conducted as to be in interstate commerce, the Court remarked that "contracts of insurance are not commerce at all, neither state nor interstate."[95] It was in this legal environment, then, that the insurance business had grown up. The Federal Government had never asserted any control in this sphere and the states were upheld in their individual efforts to enforce satisfactory business conduct. This situation prevailed despite the nationwide character of the business of most insurance companies and the communication of information and the movement of persons, money, and papers across state lines in the negotiation and execution of policy contracts.

In the case of United States v. South-Eastern Underwriters Association,[96] decided in 1944, the Supreme Court had before it for the first time the question of whether or not a Federal statute, the Sherman Act in this instance, could be applied to insurance transactions which stretch across state lines. The South-Eastern Underwriters Association and its membership of nearly 200 private stock fire insurance companies, operating in Alabama, Florida, Georgia, North Carolina, South Carolina, and Virginia, were charged with conspiracies in violation of the Sherman Act. The member companies, which controlled 90 per cent of the fire insurance and "allied lines" sold by stock fire insurance companies in the six states, not only fixed and maintained arbitrary and non-competitive premium rates and agents' commissions but employed boycotts and other types of coercion and intimidation to force non-members into the conspiracies and to compel persons who needed insurance to buy from them on their terms. Non-members of the Underwriters Association, for example, were cut off from the valuable opportunity to reinsure their larger risks. And members refused to have any dealings with persons needing insurance who patronized outsiders. These policies and practices were effectively policed by state inspection and rating bureaus and local boards of insurance agents in certain cities.

The Supreme Court upheld the United States in a 4 to 3 decision. The Court's majority held that the nationwide insurance business, involving the transmission of great quantities of documents, communications,

---

[93] Paul v. Virginia, 8 Wall. 168, 183 (1869).
[94] Hooper v. California, 155 U. S. 648, 654–655 (1895).
[95] New York Life Insurance Co. v. Deer Lodge County, 231 U. S. 495, 503–504, 510 (1913).
[96] United States v. South-Eastern Underwriters Association, 322 U. S. 533 (1944).

and money across state lines, was "commerce among the several states." It is not deprived of its interstate character "merely because it is built upon sales contracts which are local in nature."[97] Since many similar enterprises and transactions had been held by the Court to be within the commerce power, it was both unrealistic and inconsistent to hold to the doctrine that the insurance business as now conducted did not constitute interstate commerce. It was held also that the Sherman Act was intended to prohibit conduct which restrains or monopolizes the interstate fire insurance business. Nothing in the legislative history or the language of the Act was found to support the contention that Congress intended to exempt insurance companies. Finally, the Court expressed the view that the argument that application of the Sherman Act necessarily invalidated many state laws regulating insurance was exaggerated. Said the Court, "No states authorize combinations of insurance companies to coerce, intimidate, and boycott competitors and consumers in the manner here alleged, and it cannot be that any companies have acquired a vested right to engage in such destructive business practices."[98]

Although the insurance decision appears to be logical and realistic, the reversal of a long-standing legal doctrine created confusion and consternation in the insurance field and in some governmental quarters. There was great agitation on the part of those concerned to maintain and strengthen the edifice of state regulation that had covered the insurance business. Responding to these appeals, early in 1945 Congress enacted legislation, amended in 1947, which created a so-called "moratorium period" extending to June 30, 1948.[99] The law declares that the continued regulation and taxation of the insurance business by the states is in the public interest. In order to give the states an opportunity to revise their laws and thus to assure more adequate state regulation, the application of the anti-trust laws with respect to rate-fixing by insurance companies was suspended until June 30, 1948. After this date, the anti-trust laws are to "be applicable to the business of insurance to the extent that such business is not regulated by state law." The moratorium, it should be noted, was applicable only to the rate-fixing feature of the South-Eastern Underwriters decision. At no time was the Sherman Act made inapplicable to agreements or acts pertaining to boycotts, coercion, or intimidation.

By June 30, 1948, the great majority of states had passed rate regulatory laws that were patterned after proposed legislation approved by the National Association of Insurance Commissioners and applicable

---

[97] 322 U. S. 533, 547 (1944).
[98] 322 U. S. 522, 562 (1944).
[99] Public Law No. 15, 79th Congress, 1st Session, approved March 9, 1945, amended by Public Law No. 238, 80th Congress, 1st Session, approved July 25, 1947.

to all the important fields of insurance except life insurance.[100] The essential features of rate control include a filing of all premium schedules with a state insurance commissioner who has the authority to disapprove any schedule if he finds that the rates are "excessive, inadequate, or unfairly discriminatory." Rate schedules are open to public inspection, and any person may study not only the rates charged but the statistics and computations on which they are based. Rating bureaus must register with state officials, and their services must be made available to all insurance companies that wish to use them in determining their premium rates. Under this nationwide system of state control, patrons of insurance companies will be given some assurance that the premium rates charged bear a reasonable relation to the costs of rendering the service. And competitive pressures may be enhanced to some extent, since opening the accumulated statistics and knowledge of the rating bureaus to all firms may induce new companies, particularly mutual insurance companies, to enter the field.

The continued application of the anti-trust laws will prevent agreements among insurance companies in which companies agree not to file lower rates than their competitors. Moreover, boycotting is proscribed. This is important with respect to reinsurance, since this service will now be open to all companies. And applicants for insurance will not be artificially restrained from dealing with any available insurance firm. The combination of state regulation and the restraining influence of the anti-trust laws should be conducive to the attainment of conditions in the insurance field that best serve the interests of the consuming public.

(3) Forms of Organization

There is no ambiguity in the language of the Sherman Act with respect to the various organizational forms which a restraint of trade or monopoly may take. "Every contract, combination in the form of trust or otherwise," is made illegal in the first section. This phrasing seems to leave little room for doubt as to the inclusion of all forms of business organization. Yet there could be no certainty until the courts had passed upon specific cases.

The cases decided by the Supreme Court have confirmed the view that the Act means what it says. Loose-knit combinations effected by simple price agreements were condemned in the Trans-Missouri and Joint Traffic cases,[101] and price-fixing and pooling were involved in the suc-

---

[100] See George K. Gardner, "Insurance and the Anti-Trust Laws—A Problem in Synthesis," 61 *Harvard Law Review* 246 (January, 1948); Pat McCarran, "Insurance as Commerce—After Four Years," 23 *Notre Dame Lawyer* 299 (March, 1948).

[101] 166 U. S. 290 (1897); 171 U. S. 505 (1898).

cessful Addyston Pipe case.[102] Some doubt as to the inclusion of corporate combinations might have arisen from the Knight case,[103] but it could not be serious in view of the emphasis placed upon the intrastate character of the sugar trust's business. The only real attempt to challenge the all-embracing nature of the law was with respect to the holding company. But in the classic Northern Securities Company v. United States the Supreme Court found no ground for an exemption.[104]

The Northern Securities Company, a New Jersey corporation created in 1901, controlled most of the stock of the Northern Pacific and Great Northern Railways. These two railways, the first dominated by J. P. Morgan and the second by James J. Hill, were parallel and competing roads extending from Duluth and St. Paul to the Pacific Coast. Despite the inability of an earlier attempt at consolidation to circumvent a Minnesota law, the combination was effected.[105] It came as a compromise after a dramatic financial struggle between the Hill-Morgan interests and those of E. H. Harriman. When the Northern roads acquired a controlling interest in the Chicago, Burlington & Quincy in order to give them a connection with Chicago, Harriman, who controlled the Union Pacific, was much concerned, and in self-defense acquired vast holdings of the stock of the Northern Pacific. Since there was considerable legal doubt as to who would win actual control over the Northern Pacific, the fight was compromised by the exchange of the stock of the Northern Securities Company for the shares of both the Northern Pacific and the Great Northern. Competition between the two railroads was thereby eliminated, although there still existed a rivalry for traffic between them and other trans-continental roads.

The Government brought suit to dissolve the combination and to compel the holding company to divest itself of the stocks of the competing roads. A decree of a lower court requiring the dissolution of the combination was upheld by the Supreme Court by a vote of 5 to 4. Justice Harlan, speaking for the majority, ruled in general that (1) railroad carriers are embraced by the act; (2) all direct restraints of trade are unlawful, and not only those unreasonable in their nature; and (3) that a combination need not be shown to result in a complete suppression of trade, if it can be shown that by its natural operation it tends to create monopoly and to deprive the public of the advantages of competition.

The defendants had contended that the Northern Securities Company was chartered by New Jersey and authorized to acquire stocks of other companies, and hence an enforcement of the Sherman Act would amount to unauthorized interference with the internal commerce of the

---

[102] 175 U. S. 211 (1899).
[103] 156 U. S. 1 (1895).
[104] 193 U. S. 197 (1904).
[105] Pearsall v. Great Northern Railway Co., 161 U. S. 646 (1896).

states. The Court was not impressed. It was admitted that the power of state corporations to acquire and hold stocks is largely a matter of state regulation and not within the sphere of interstate commerce. But, said Justice Harlan, "No State can, by merely creating a corporation, or in any other mode, project its authority into other States, and across the continent, so as to prevent Congress from exerting the power it possesses under the Constitution over interstate and international commerce, or so as to exempt its corporation engaged in interstate commerce from obedience to any rule lawfully established by Congress for such commerce." Since it was the national policy to eliminate combinations whose purpose and effect were to suppress competition, the powers of state corporations could not be permitted to stand in the way of achieving the objective.[106]

While the economic results of the dissolution of the Northern Securities Company were of little account because of the community of interest which followed, the case was tremendously important to the administration of anti-trust policy.[107] It was the first victory in the Supreme Court for the Government in a case involving a close-knit combination. Moreover, it dispelled any illusion on the part of business men that the convenient holding company device could be used safely to create monopoly. It encouraged the Government to attack combinations that used the device, and discouraged promoters. The tobacco combination, for example, in 1904 shifted its organization from the holding company form to an asset-owning corporation, allegedly because of the Supreme Court decision. This decision may have been of considerable significance as a factor explaining the end of the great combination movement started in the late nineties.

Subsequent decisions and pronouncements have reinforced the con-

---

[106] Justice Holmes, in his dissenting opinion, argued that the holding form of combination was not covered by the language of the statute, since it simply ended competition between the parties to the community of interest. He said: " . . . In my opinion there is no attempt to monopolize and what . . . amounts to the same thing, . . . there is no combination in restraint of trade, until something is done with the intent to exclude strangers to the combination from competing with it. . . . " Since the case involved a fusion of competitors and there was no evidence of intent to exclude others, he held there could be no unlawful combination.

[107] The shares of the railroad companies were distributed ratably to the shareholders of the Northern Securities Company. Harriman objected to being made a minority shareholder in each road, but was overruled in Harriman v. Northern Securities Co., 197 U. S. 244 (1905). The Hill-Morgan group held majority control in each railroad, so there was little chance for the restoration of competition.

The economic desirability of combining the two properties was recognized by the Interstate Commerce Commission in 1929. A "final plan" of consolidation, promulgated on December 9, 1929, placed the Northern Pacific and the Great Northern in System No. 12 (159 I. C. C. 522). A petition for stock control and lease by a holding company was actually approved by the Commission in 1930 (162 I. C. C. 37), but the application was later withdrawn, and nothing has been done to effect a consolidation.

clusion that the form of the combination is no bar to the application of the law. In the American Tobacco case the Court stated that the policy of the law cannot be frustrated "by resorting to any disguise or subterfuge of form."[108] The company owned and operated physical properties which had been combined by consolidation, and also owned stock in some subsidiaries. And later a minority stockholding was recognized as a means by which violations of the law might be organized.[109] Even the loosely organized and conventional trade association was brought within the orbit of the statute when it was used as an instrument for the suppression of competition.[110]

(4) Degree of Restraint

How far may a combination go in restricting competition or in controlling a market before it runs afoul of the anti-trust law? The question presents the most controversial as well as the most difficult issue which has arisen in the interpretation and administration of the law. The key words of the statute, "restraint of trade" and "monopolize," were familiar terms in the common law, but they were given no precise definition by Congress. It was up to the courts to determine their meaning and to apply them to the modern industrial world. The general objective of the law was to maintain competition, but when virtually every business situation or arrangement presented an admixture of competitive and monopolistic elements, it was no easy task to distinguish the lawful from the unlawful. Yet the success or failure of the anti-trust policy depended in great measure on the ability of the courts to establish standards which could be helpful in detecting and suppressing the monopolistic elements which were adverse to the public interest.

It was in connection with this question of the degree of restraint that the "rule of reason" was injected into the interpretation of the Sherman Act. Since the notion of reasonableness has played such a large part in testing the legality of trade restraints, the origin and nature of the rule will first be considered. Certain of the more important decisions applying the rule of reason will be analyzed in the following chapter.

When the Supreme Court was first importuned to adopt the rule of reason, it rejected the suggestion by a vote of 5 to 4. This was in the Trans-Missouri Freight Association case[111] of 1897, the facts of which have already been outlined. The carriers contended that Congress intended only to outlaw those trade restraints which were "unreasonable" and therefore unlawful at common law. It was urged that, since the

---

[108] 221 U. S. 106 (1911).
[109] U. S. v. Union Pacific Railroad Co., 226 U. S. 61 (1912).
[110] American Column & Lumber Co. v. U. S., 257 U. S. 377 (1921).
[111] 166 U. S. 290 (1897).

freight association merely sought to prevent ruinous competition and
to maintain reasonable rates, the restriction of competition was reasonable and lawful. But the Court declined to accept this view, because of
the unqualified condemnation of "every" trade restraint. The all-inclusive language of the statute left no room for the legal standards of the
common law, even assuming that the railroad agreement not to compete
might have been upheld under that law. Any exceptions would have to
be written into the law by Congress and could not be inserted "by a
process of judicial legislation wholly unjustifiable."

Despite the uncompromising attitude which the majority of the Court
seemed to have assumed, it cannot be said that its members were willing
to go to the extreme of condemning all restraints or limitations on competition. Justice Peckham conceded, for example, that the restrictive
covenant which was ancillary to the sale of a business was not within
the scope of the law. This type of contract, it will be recalled, was the
first to be judged in restraint of trade under the common law, and in
connection with which the rule of reason later originated. And in the
Joint Traffic Association case[112] of 1898, Justice Peckham mentioned the
formation of a corporation, a partnership, or a common selling agency
by two persons engaged in the same business as not necessarily violating
the law. These contracts were necessary for the promotion of legitimate
business and restrained interstate commerce only in "some remote and
indirect degree," and hence could not be regarded as true restraints of
trade.

It is fruitless to speculate on the precise meaning of the Sherman Act
as interpreted by the Court. That could only be ascertained by decisions
in cases presenting a variety of business situations, and these were never
presented to the Court. The most that can be said is that the majority
inclined toward a more literal and severe construction than did Justice
White and the dissenting minority. For this reason promoters and business men had more to fear from the operation of the anti-trust law. Any
combination of considerable power or size was suspect under the law,
irrespective of its purpose or ability to control the market. But it should
be recognized that, despite anything said by Justice Peckham regarding
the lack of Congressional intent to codify the common law, the actual
decisions on the facts presented in the Freight Association cases were
not inconsistent with the common law. While there was some disposition
on the part of certain American courts to apply the test of reasonableness to horizontal agreements between competitors, the weight of
American legal authority was to the effect that all agreements restricting
competition between members of the same industry were unlawful.[113]

---

[112] 171 U. S. 505 (1898).

[113] See the section on the development of the common law, especially the views
of Judge Taft as set forth in the Addyston Pipe Case. For a confirmation of the

They were void, regardless of good motives or reasonableness of the prices fixed. There was not the sharp break with the common law that might be inferred from the contentions of the railroads and the disagreement between the members of the Court.

Fourteen years after its pronouncements in the Traffic cases, the Supreme Court was prepared to re-state its position with respect to the degree of trade restraint permitted under the Sherman Law. This was done by way of *obiter dictum* in the classic Standard Oil[114] and American Tobacco[115] cases of 1911. The facts of these cases have been set forth in detail in previous chapters, so it is unnecessary to review them here. Suffice it to say that in the organization and competitive behavior of these companies the Court found unmistakable evidence of an intent to monopolize their respective industries and to protect their monopolies by the exclusion of competitors. The combinations were found to be illegal, and their dissolution was ordered.

Chief Justice White, who had also written the minority opinion in the Trans-Missouri Traffic case, expounded the "rule of reason" at great length in his majority opinion in the Standard Oil case. His basic notion was that the terms of the statute had well-known meanings in the common law and that they were employed by Congress in their common law sense. What were the meanings of "restraint of trade" and "monopolize" in the common law? Since there were divergent views as to the definition of restraint of trade in the common-law precedents, it was necessary for Chief Justice White to choose between them. His examination of the precedents led him to the conclusion that all agreements restricting competition were tested by the rule of reason and that only those which restrained trade unreasonably were unlawful. In this he was following the English precedents and a minority of American courts. Those contracts were unreasonable which tended to produce the effects of monopoly, such as restrictions on the freedom of traders, curtailment of output, and undue enhancement of prices. Thus viewed, monopoly and restraint of trade were synonymous terms, and were to be so treated in applying the Sherman Act. When the phrase "restraint of trade" was used in the first section of the law, it was the equivalent of undue restraint or "monopolize," and the effect of the section was to outlaw "all means of monopolizing trade." The purpose of the second section of the law was to reënforce the first section by forbidding all "attempts" to monopolize trade or to restrain it unduly by any means whatsoever. The two sections of the law were read together and harmonized in this

---

general views expressed above see T. N. E. C., *A Study of the Construction and Enforcement of the Federal Anti-trust Laws*, Monograph No. 38 (1941). This excellent study, written by Professor Milton Handler, is highly recommended.

[114] 221 U. S. 1 (1911).
[115] 221 U. S. 106 (1911).

fashion. Their legal meaning was the condemnation of "unreasonable restraints of trade" *or* "monopoly."

Since the Supreme Court had explicitly rejected the "rule of reason" in the Traffic Association cases, over the strenuous objection of Justice White and his dissenting minority, one might justifiably conclude that the Court reversed itself in 1911. Curiously enough, this was not admitted. An effort was made to reconcile the decisions on the ground that the earlier cases had distinguished between restraints having direct and immediate effects upon interstate commerce and those only remotely affecting commerce. It is doubtful whether this distinction, which seems to emphasize the jurisdictional aspect of interstate commerce, could be interpreted to mean the rule of reason. Chief Justice White did not believe so in 1897, and he was not too sure of his new position in 1911. He stated: "And in order not in the slightest degree to be wanting in frankness, we say that in so far, however, as . . . the language referred to conflicts with the construction which we give the statute, they (Traffic Association cases) are necessarily now limited and qualified."[116] But Justice Harlan, who concurred in the dissolution of the oil and tobacco trusts and dissented from the enunciation of the rule of reason, was strongly of the opinion that the Court had reversed itself.[117] He cited language from numerous decisions of the Court showing the acceptance of the doctrine that "every" restraint, reasonable or unreasonable, was illegal. Concern was expressed over the indefiniteness of the new legal standard and the difficulties inherent in its application. His main criticism, however, was that the Court was here usurping a legislative function in reading new words into the statute and thereby modifying what was to some a harsh public policy. He feared the effects of such "judicial legislation" upon our traditional institutions.

It was more or less inevitable, irrespective of the wanderings of the courts in the realm of legal rationalization, that a "reasonable" interpretation of the Sherman Act would be reached eventually. A literal construction of the rhetorical phraseology of the statute would have been impracticable and virtually impossible of strict enforcement. Economic forces were at work which made for larger and larger production units. There were economies to be had from large-scale production, such as specialization of labor and machinery, the use of mechanical power, and quantity buying of materials. A public policy which prevented the attainment of greater efficiency in production and trade would have been most unwise. There would have been no challenge to firms that attained greater size and efficiency through a process of growth and capital expansion. Yet a combination of competing firms that sought the same management and production economies would have been suspect and

---

[116] Standard Oil Co. *v.* United States, 221 U. S. 1, 67–68 (1911).
[117] *Ibid.*, pp. 82–106.

probably prosecuted under a strict interpretation of the law. Under a more liberal interpretation, however, where combinations were created not for the purpose of economical operation but for the control or suppression of competition, the law could take hold. The rule of reason made the law more flexible, but it was still directed at the evil of monopoly. Monopolistic combinations were not to be tolerated even under the more liberal construction. No business arrangement or combination that was inconsistent with the purpose of maintaining a competitive economy was to be condoned. So interpreted, the rule of reason was in harmony with the original intent of Congress.

Despite the elaborate re-statement of the law, numerous questions of vital importance were left unanswered. How was monopoly to be defined? What objective tests were to be applied to ascertain the existence of monopoly? Did overwhelming size and the power to control prices and output constitute monopoly? Or was it necessary to show an assertion of that power? These and other issues were to be decided on the facts presented in subsequent cases.

18

Application of the Sherman Law after the
Rule of Reason

The classification of cases decided by the Supreme Court into those involving close-knit combinations and those relating to loose combinations will be followed in the consideration of Sherman Act interpretation after 1911. In the present chapter, however, the discussion will be confined to the close combinations. Agreements and other forms of coöperation between competing firms will be considered in a subsequent chapter. The legality of such arrangements will be taken up at the conclusion of a study of their nature and prevalence in American industry.

It should be pointed out at this juncture, however, that the enunciation of a rule of reason has had little if any effect upon the legality of coöperative arrangements between competitors. Courts have been disposed, with the possible exception of the Appalachian Coals[1] case of 1933, to find illegal any contract for division of territory, control of supply, fixing of prices, or other restriction on competition. The very fact of an agreement not to compete has been accepted as evidence of restraint of trade and an attempt to monopolize. There has been no insistence upon a showing of wrongful intent on the part of the contracting parties, and good motives have not been permitted to justify collusive action. No inquiry has been made into the degree of market control enjoyed by the parties and the existence of actual monopoly power. The restriction upon competition itself has been regarded as an injurious element in the economy and therefore unlawful. The only perceptible change worked by the rule of reason is that restrictive agreements are now termed "unreasonable restraints of trade."

The standard of reason has been far more important in the merger or consolidation cases. Since firms combined for a variety of reasons, it could not be assumed that the restriction of competition resulting from

---

[1] Appalachian Coals, Inc., v. United States, 288 U. S. 344 (1933). But cf. United States v. Socony-Vacuum Oil Co., 310 U. S. 150 (1940).

a merger was conclusive evidence of monopoly or an attempt to monopolize. It was necessary to make a careful investigation of the facts in each case before judgment was rendered. One of the most important elements to establish was the intent of the parties. If it were shown that the intention was to create a monopoly, there could not be much doubt as to the probable consequences of a consolidation of firms. As suggested in the Standard Oil and American Tobacco decisions, intent was to be inferred from the history of the combination, methods used to obtain control, the extent of market control, and the manner in which control was exercised and maintained against outside competitors. The companies had actually succeeded in gaining over 85 per cent control of their respective industries, frequently using predatory methods to stamp out competitors, so there was little difficulty in finding wrongful intent and illegal combination. Even good intentions could not have condoned these trusts if the law were to be taken at all seriously. If the general approach of the courts was to be fruitful, it could be so only in cases where there was real doubt as to the existence of monopoly. But even in these cases, it is questionable whether moral considerations are satisfactory data upon which to base a determination of the economic fact of monopoly power.

It is noteworthy that the close combinations condemned by Supreme Court decisions since 1911 have involved chiefly common carriers alone or railroads in relation to the anthracite coal industry. The first of these was the St. Louis Terminal case.[2] Here was presented a monopoly of railroad terminal facilities which was significant because of the peculiar geographical position of St. Louis. The city is located on a group of hills hugging the west bank of the Mississippi River. Although twenty-four railroads converged at St. Louis, not one of them passed through the city or had its own direct physical connections with the others. The limited space available and the prohibitive cost of constructing tunnels, bridges, and rail connections precluded individual action in supplying the necessary facilities. The Terminal Association, organized by some of the railroads in 1889, gradually acquired all of the independent terminal companies that owned ferries, bridges, and other facilities in the area, and operated them as a single system. Only fourteen of the twenty-four interested carriers were proprietary members of the association. Other railroads could be admitted to the joint use of the terminal system, but only with the unanimous consent of the fourteen member companies. The power thus retained had not been abused, however, since the terminal company paid no dividends and had permitted non-member roads to use the facilities at the same rates charged the proprietary companies.

---

[2] United States v. Terminal Railroad Association of St. Louis, 224 U. S. 383 (1912).

The only practices warranting condemnation were certain discriminations against some traffic moving over the terminal facilities.

The Supreme Court conceded that in ordinary circumstances the unification and exclusive use of terminal properties would not be unlawful. An intent to monopolize was inferred in this particular case from the extent of the control over facilities which all carriers were under compulsion to use. Although it had not been exercised, the proprietary roads had the clearly stated authority to exclude others. The Court emphasized the fact that this was of great importance, because of the physical and economic impracticability of constructing new and competing terminal facilities. Since non-member carriers were compelled to use the unified system, the mere existence of the power of exclusion made the combination illegal.

The remedy decreed by the Court was based on the point that the terminal association was not an "impartial agent" of all the railroads. The petition of the government to dissolve the association and apportion its business among three companies was not granted. It is at this point that the standard of reason could be said to come into full play. The Court was impressed with the economic advantages of unification and wished to preserve them. Hence, the parties were permitted to file a plan modifying the administrative features of the associations. Provision was to be made for the admission of any existing or future railroad to joint ownership on reasonable terms, and for the use of the combined facilities at equitable rates by those carriers electing not to become joint owners. The discriminatory practices against certain traffic were to be abolished, but nothing was to interfere with the exercises of the regulatory powers conferred by statute upon the Interstate Commerce Commission. Such a reorganization, in the opinion of the Court, would preserve the efficiencies of terminal unification and place the carriers on such a basis of equality as to avoid the harmful consequences of monopoly.

Involved in the other two purely railroad cases were the Union Pacific, the Southern Pacific, and the Central Pacific.[3] These carriers are important elements in the trans-continental system. The Union Pacific operates from Omaha, Nebraska to Ogden, Utah, where it joins the main line of the Central Pacific extending to San Francisco. A branch line of the Union Pacific reaches from Ogden to Portland, Oregon, from which Pacific port a steamship line is operated to San Francisco. The Union Pacific has, therefore, no direct rail connection with San Francisco, although it was provided in the Pacific Railroad Acts of 1862 and 1864 that the Central Pacific and Union Pacific should be operated as a con-

---

[3] United States v. Union Pacific Railroad Co., 226 U. S. 61 (1912); United States v. Southern Pacific Co., 259 U. S. 214 (1922).

tinuous line. The rail line of the Southern Pacific extends from New Orleans to Los Angeles, and up the Pacific Coast to San Francisco and Portland. The inter-corporate connection between these companies dates from 1885, when the Southern Pacific obtained a ninety-nine-year lease of the Central Pacific. A controlling interest in the stock of the Central Pacific was also acquired in 1899. The Union Pacific, dominated by Harriman, whose ambition was to obtain control of the western railroads, entered the picture shortly thereafter. It succeeded in acquiring a 46 per cent stock interest in the Southern Pacific in 1901. These were the combinations which the government sought to break up.

On the strength of the Northern Securities decision and other railway cases, the Supreme Court dissolved the Union Pacific-Southern Pacific combination in 1912[4] and the Southern Pacific-Central Pacific combination in 1922.[5] The basis for the decisions was simply that the combination of competing firms eliminated existing competition. Such a consolidation, said the Court in the Union Pacific case, destroyed or greatly abridged the "free operation of competition theretofore existing," and tended to bring about higher rates and less activity in furnishing prompt and efficient railway service. The Court concluded: "Nor does it make any difference that rates for the time being may not be raised and much money be spent in improvements after the combination is effected. It is the scope of such combinations and their power to suppress or stifle competition or create monopoly which determines the applicability of the act."[6] In the Southern Pacific case, ten years later, the Court said: "These cases, collectively, establish that one system of railroad transportation cannot acquire another, nor a substantial and vital part thereof, when the effect of such acquisition is to suppress or materially reduce the free and normal flow of competition in the channels of interstate trade."[7]

These cases are noteworthy applications of the Sherman Act, in view both of earlier and later decisions. As with the situation in the Northern Securities case, the carriers involved were still subject to the competition of other trans-continental systems such as the Santa Fe and the Milwaukee. But they were not parallel lines and did not have the same eastern termini. It could not be urged seriously that a monopoly of transcontinental rail service had been attained. Each railroad had the inevitable regional monopoly on local traffic in the area served, but the relatively small percentage of their total traffic for which they had competed was still subject to the competition of other carriers. Significant also is the fact that there were no unfair practices or an attempt to exclude com-

---

[4] 226 U. S. 61 (1912).
[5] 259 U. S. 214 (1922).
[6] 226 U. S. 61, 88 (1912).
[7] 259 U. S. 214, 230 (1922).

petitors or interfere with their operations. Rates had not been increased; indeed, the Interstate Commerce Commission had full authority to prevent any such exercise of monopoly power. It was clearly not an abuse of power which the Courts fastened upon in these cases; rather, it was suppression of competition resulting from the union of powerful firms in a field occupied by relatively few sellers.[8]

Although coöperation and competition in the anthracite coal industry will be considered at some length in a subsequent chapter, brief notice must here be given to two Supreme Court decisions relating to mergers of railroad and coal companies.[9] Practically all the anthracite coal in the United States is found in a relatively small area in northeastern Pennsylvania. At an early date the railroads serving this area began to acquire extensive holdings of coal lands. By 1912, six railroad companies and their coal-mining affiliates had acquired about 90 per cent of the unmined anthracite deposits, and were producing about 75 per cent of the annual output of anthracite. The Reading Company, a holding corporation, owned all the stock of the Reading Railway Company and the Reading Coal and Iron Company. It also owned a controlling interest in the Central Railroad of New Jersey, which in turn controlled a large coal company. Over 33 per cent of the annual production of anthracite was controlled by the Reading combination. The Lehigh Valley Railroad, through its coal company subsidiary, had followed a similar policy of acquiring competing coal companies and had concentrated under its control about 20 per cent of the anthracite business. Both of these combinations were condemned as monopolies. They were also found to violate the Commodities Clause of the Interstate Commerce Act, which prohibits a railroad from carrying a commodity produced or owned by it, or in which it has any interest.

An intent to monopolize was inferred from the history of the combinations and their energetic conduct in acquiring independent coal properties. The Court found that the Lehigh Valley, because of the extent of its control in the restricted anthracite area, had attained "a practical monopoly . . . of the transportation and sale of anthracite coal derived from such lands."[10] In the Reading case, the Court held that the creation of the holding company in 1896 violated the law. The combine controlled about 20 per cent of the total output, which, in the opinion of the Court, gave it the power "to increase or decrease the output of coal from very extensive mines, the supply of it in the market, and the cost of it to the consumer; to increase or lower the charge for transporting such coal to

---

[8] For a penetrating analysis of these and other cases discussed in this section, see T. N. E. C., *Monograph* No. 38, *op. cit.*

[9] United States *v.* Reading Company, 253 U. S. 26 (1920); United States *v.* Lehigh Valley Railroad Co., 254 U. S. 255 (1920).

[10] 254 U. S. 255, 270 (1920).

market; and to regulate car supply and other shipping conveniences, and thereby to help or hinder the operations of independent miners and shippers of coal."[11] The acquisition of the Central Railroad of New Jersey and its coal subsidiary in 1901 enhanced this power, for it increased the combination's share of the total business to 33 per cent. "This acquisition," said the Court, "placed the Holding Company in a position of dominating control not only over two great competing interstate railroad carriers but also over two great competing coal companies. . . . Again, and obviously, this dominating power was not obtained by normal expansion to meet the demands of a business growing as a result of superior and enterprising management, but by deliberate, calculated purchase for control. That such a power, so obtained, *regardless of the use made of it,* constitutes a menace to and an undue restraint upon interstate commerce within the meaning of the Anti-Trust Act, has been frequently held by this court."[12]

The Court was undoubtedly right in its general appraisal of the competitive situation in the anthracite industry. Nothing approaching pure competition was possible with such a heavy concentration of coal lands and production in the hands of so few powerful companies. Actual collusion between them and domination over independent firms had been demonstrated and condemned in earlier court proceedings.[13] The striking fact is that the individual combinations, controlling about 33 and 20 per cent of the total output respectively, were held to have attempted and actually achieved monopoly power. Significant, also, was the assertion that it is the existence of a combination and its inherent power that violates the law, "regardless of the use made of it." In emphasizing the existence of monopoly power rather than its exercise in the determination of legality, the Court was following the Northern Securities and Union Pacific line of decisions. These expressions are of particular interest in the light of the decisions and judicial utterances in another group of monopoly cases that are now to be considered.

Several outstanding consolidation cases involving manufacturing enterprises were decided by the Supreme Court within about the same period as those already discussed. They were the United Shoe Machinery cases,[14] the United States Steel Corporation case,[15] and the International Harvester case.[16] The facts concerning these combinations, with the exception of the Steel Corporation, were developed in the chapters on in-

---

[11] 253 U. S. 26, 48 (1920).

[12] *Ibid.,* p. 57 (italics added). Chief Justice White and Justices Holmes and Van Devanter dissented.

[13] United States *v.* Reading Company, 226 U. S. 324 (1912).

[14] United States *v.* Winslow, 227 U. S. 202 (1913); United States *v.* United Shoe Machinery Co., 247 U. S. 32 (1918).

[15] United States *v.* United States Steel Corp., 251 U. S. 417 (1920).

[16] United States *v.* International Harvester Co., 274 U. S. 693 (1927).

dustrial monopoly. Brief reference must be made, however, to the court decisions and their significance in the interpretation of the Sherman Act.

The United Shoe Machinery Company was notably successful in defending itself in two anti-trust suits that reached the Supreme Court. The issue determined in United States v. Winslow,[17] a criminal proceeding, was that the original merger of the three important manufacturing firms, "taken by itself," was lawful. Justice Holmes, speaking for a unanimous Court, asserted that "on the face of it the combination was simply an effort after greater efficiency."[18] The dominance of the combining units in their respective branches of the shoe machinery industry was said to have been based on the ownership of superior patents, and it was assumed that there had been no illegality in this situation. It was affirmed, moreover, that the companies did not compete with each other. In view of these findings, the Court held that there was no legal objection to further concentration in the field. No notice was taken of the fact that the companies were at least partially competitive and that greater competition between them might have developed had they remained independent.

In the second Shoe Machinery case,[19] a dissolution suit decided in 1918, questions were raised as to the legality of the combination and the tying leases. Both were upheld by a 4 to 3 decision. Any doubts raised by the conflicting evidence as to intent were resolved in favor of the combination.[20] The firms united in the original consolidation were again found to have been complementary and not competing, and the 57 subsequent acquisitions were said to have "added nothing of obnoxious power to the United Company nor in any practical or large sense removed competition."[21] The extent of the combination's control in the industry and its great power to monopolize did not receive the same emphasis as in other cases. Illegal dominance was found not to exist, despite production of about 95 per cent of the shoe machinery used in the United States. Justice McKenna said: "The company, indeed, has magnitude, but it is at once the result and cause of efficiency, and the charge that it has been oppressively used is not sustained."[22] The tying agreements imposed on lessees of shoe machinery were not regarded as oppressive either to customers or to potential competitors. They were viewed simply as a legitimate exercise of the monopoly power inherent in patents. The Court seemed to have little appreciation of the tremen-

---

[17] 227 U. S. 202 (1913).

[18] Ibid., p. 217.

[19] U. S. v. United Shoe Machinery Co., 247 U. S. 32 (1918).

[20] For a careful review of the evidence pointing to an intent to monopolize and the actual achievement of monopoly, see the dissenting opinion of Justice Clarke, with which Justices Day and Pitney concurred. Ibid., pp. 75–91.

[21] Ibid., p. 54.

[22] Ibid., p. 56.

dous power to exclude competition which the tying agreements placed in the hands of a concern that had already succeeded in concentrating control of virtually all essential patents.

The presence of the individual patent monopolies and the difficulty of unscrambling the long-established patent pool explain partly why the Court was reluctant to dissolve the combination. It was also impressed with the efficiency of the concern and the desirability of composing patent difficulties. But despite these factors, its failure to find illegal monopoly is difficult to explain. While no inquiry was made into the behavior of prices and profits, there could be no denying the power to control output and prices and to exclude outside competition. The effect of the tying clauses was clearly to prevent new entries into the field.

Since the Court would admit neither an intent to monopolize nor the exclusion of competition by oppressive tactics, the Shoe Machinery cases stand for the proposition that there is nothing illegal in attaining by combination of partially competing firms a predominance approaching 95 per cent of an industry's output. Such a doctrine, if generally applied, would give enterprises unlimited scope for expansion and reduce competition to the point of complete extinction. Firms of the size and strength of United Shoe Machinery, whether or not they exercise their power, are quite incompatible with anything resembling pure competition.

The next opportunity afforded the Supreme Court to state its views respecting the lawfulness of corporate consolidations was in the United States Steel Corporation case of 1920.[23] Two justices did not participate in the consideration of the case, and the remaining justices voted 4 to 3 against dissolution.[24] In so doing, they validated the largest industrial merger ever to have been created in the United States.

In its organization as a New Jersey holding company the United States Steel Corporation acquired the stock of twelve operating companies to combine the three dominant groups controlled by Morgan, Carnegie, and Moore. Each group was composed of companies which had earlier been independent, so the final consolidation represented a union of approximately 180 firms. All stages of the industrial process, from the mining of ore to the fabrication of finished iron and steel products, were brought under the control of the holding company. It controlled in the neighborhood of 70 per cent of the total output of steel products. By the time the government brought suit in 1911, however, the percentage of control had dropped to about 50.

---

[23] United States v. United States Steel Corporation, 251 U. S. 417 (1920).
[24] The members of the Court divided just as they had done in the Shoe Machinery case. Justices McKenna, Holmes, Van Devanter and Chief Justice White constituted the majority; Justices Day, Pitney, and Clarke were the minority; and Justices Brandeis and McReynolds did not participate.

Further acquisitions of ore and steel properties were made after the original consolidation. The most important of these was the purchase of the Tennessee Coal and Iron Company in 1907. This valuable acquisition was made under panic conditions, and was said by the Court to have had the approval of President Roosevelt. Relations with independent firms were maintained on a coöperative rather than a competitive basis. Price and market agreements kept competition in check for the years immediately after 1901. During and after 1907, price understandings were reached under the leadership of the Steel Corporation at the famous Gary dinners. Coöperation was also maintained under the Pittsburgh Plus system of quoting prices, but this pricing scheme and the opportunity for leadership afforded by it were not considered by the Court. In general, the Corporation followed a policy of "live and let live." It did not resort to predatory tactics designed to crush competitors.

In arriving at its decision, the majority of the Supreme Court first considered the element of intent. The government had urged that the clear purpose of the organizers of the Corporation had been to acquire a monopoly, and that they had succeeded in attaining their objective. The lower court, which had unanimously dismissed the charges against the defendant, had been divided on the question of illegal purpose. But the Supreme Court conceded that the original concentration of competing firms and subsequent acquisitions, although motivated in part by the desire for integration and increased efficiency, were evidence of wrongful intent. This finding, it might have been supposed, would have scored heavily against the company. It did not, however, because the Court found that the illegal purpose had never been realized. A monopoly was not achieved. The statute, said Justice McKenna, is directed "not against an expectation of it (monopoly), but against its realization." This, it would seem, was an unduly narrow interpretation of a law which prohibits not only monopolizing but even an "attempt to monopolize."

The majority, in considering the element of monopoly, acknowledged that the power attained was much greater than that of any single competitor. But it was no greater than that of all of them combined. Considerable importance was attached to the decline in the dominant position of the Corporation, and the testimony of both customers and competitors that genuine and vigorous competition prevailed in the steel industry. Further evidence of the presence of competition and the failure to achieve monopoly was found, strangely enough, in the necessity for persuading independents to coöperate through pools, associations, trade meetings, and the Gary dinners. These practices were declared to be illegal, certainly, but their weight in sustaining guilt was minimized by the assertion that they were "transient in their purpose and effect." They had been abandoned just before the suit was begun, not because of the fear of prosecution, but because of their futility. There was no evidence of an intention to resume the illegal practices, concluded the Court, hence no corrective action was sought by the government nor actually required.

There was still the element of great size to be considered. As to this, the Court said: "The Corporation is undoubtedly of impressive size and it takes an effort of resolution not to be affected by it or to exaggerate its influence. But we must adhere to the law and the law does not make mere size an offense or the existence of unexerted power an offense. It, we repeat, requires overt acts and trusts to its prohibition of them and its power to repress or punish them. It does not compel competition nor require all that is possible."[25] The test of legality was not size or power, but the exercise of power. United States Steel had not, in the opinion of the Court, exerted the power inherent in great size by fixing monopoly prices or excluding outside competitors. Of great importance was the fact that the Corporation had a clean record as regards the use of practices designed to destroy competitors. None of the unfair practices utilized by the Standard Oil and American Tobacco trusts characterized its competitive conduct, a point of which much was made in distinguishing the case from these earlier decisions.

Finally, a factor which seemed to have considerable bearing on the outcome of the case was the possible effect of the corporation's dissolution upon industry. Fear was expressed that the public interest would be injured, primarily because of the disturbance to foreign trade.

Probably the best commentary on the decision of the Court is the dissenting opinion of Justice Day. He agreed that mere size, if obtained by natural growth, was not unlawful. But he insisted that the combination of competing firms with intent to obtain monopoly gains and the continued exercise of power to fix prices through coöperation with independent firms did constitute unlawful conduct. The steel combination, with its vast resources and capital, had the power to dominate the industry and to restrain competition in any way it saw fit. He cited earlier decisions of the Court, especially the railway cases, as authority for condemning power so derived from combination and conspiracy. "That the exercise of the power may be withheld, or exerted with forbearing benevolence, does not place such combinations beyond the authority of the statute which was intended to prohibit their formation, and when formed to deprive them of the power unlawfully attained."[26] And he made a most significant observation when he said that the statute was not "intended to merely suppress unfair practices." In emphasizing the exemplary conduct of the steel combination, its failure to harass or destroy competitors particularly, the majority of the Court did reduce the law pretty much to a prohibition of predatory conduct.

[25] 251 U. S. 417, 451 (1920).
[26] *Ibid.*, pp. 464–465.

Finally, Justice Day found no merit in the view that the dissolution of a corporation which had long been in existence should be denied on the ground that it would inconvenience investors and disturb trade. Such a procedure was not only inconsistent with earlier judgments, but had the effect of sanctioning combinations that violated the more fundamental policy of maintaining competition.

One further comment on the Steel decision is pertinent. The prosecution failed, apparently, to impress upon the Court the nature of the Pittsburgh Plus system of pricing and its true economic significance. Under this basing point system, steel products were sold at all points in the United States at the Pittsburgh price plus freight from Pittsburgh to point of destination. All firms, regardless of their location, sold steel at these uniform prices. The system was firmly supported by the Steel Corporation and was operated successfully because of the close coöperation of its "competitors." This artificial pricing arrangement was obviously not a competitive phenomenon. Had the Court been informed of its true nature, it could not have escaped the conclusion that coöperation was not abandoned before suit. It would also have viewed differently the willingness of competitors to testify to the vigorous competition in steel. It is true that the Court spoke tolerantly of price imitation by competitors of United States Steel. Nevertheless, the Court would have had difficulty in condoning a monopolistic price arrangement that operated even more effectively than an outright agreement.

The tolerant attitude toward large aggregations of capital manifested in the Steel and Shoe Machinery cases had the effect of discouraging prosecutions against consolidations in industry. Not only did the government dismiss appeals to the Supreme Court in a number of cases,[27] but few prosecutions were undertaken thereafter. The only subsequent case involving a large manufacturing combination that the Supreme Court had an opportunity to review was that relating to the International Harvester Company.[28] And here the Court reaffirmed the position taken in the Steel case.

The International Harvester case arose in an attempt on the part of the government to obtain a modification of the consent decree entered in 1918. Among other things, the company had agreed to dispose of three of its branded harvester lines. Its control of agricultural machinery production was thereby reduced from about 85 to 64 per cent. The government, however, had reserved the right to seek further relief in the event that the consent decree did not effect a restoration of competitive

---

[27] U. S. v. Quaker Oats Company, 232 Fed. 499 (1916), 253 U. S. 499 (1920); U. S. v. American Can Company, 230 Fed. 859 (1916), 234 Fed. 1019 (1916), 256 U. S. 706 (1921); U. S. v. Keystone Watch Case Co., 218 Fed. 502 (1915), 257 U. S. 664 (1921).

[28] U. S. v. International Harvester Co., 274 U. S. 693 (1927).

conditions and a "situation in harmony with law." Acting upon this reservation, the government urged that the International Company was still a monopoly, and sought to have its business and assets divided between three separate companies. The government relied in large part on a study of prices and competitive conditions in the farm implement business, made by the Federal Trade Commission.

Upon appeal from the lower court decision upholding the defendant, the Supreme Court held that competitive conditions were established through compliance with the consent decree of 1918. Here, as in the Steel case, the Court was much concerned with the business practices of the combination and the possible abuse of power. It found that its resources, while much larger than those of any single competitor (but not much larger than those of all combined), had not been used to restrain trade. Prices had not been reduced below cost for the purpose of driving out competitors, nor had they been regulated for the industry. Citing the Steel decision, the Court said: "The law, however, does not make the mere size of a corporation, however impressive, or the existence of unexerted power on its part, an offense, when unaccompanied by unlawful conduct in the exercise of its power."[29] It was conceded that the independent firms were in the habit of selling their implements at the approximate prices charged by International, but it was done "independently and as a matter of business expediency." There was nothing illegal in this price leadership. Justice Sanford said: "And the fact that competitors may see proper, in the exercise of their own judgment, to follow the prices of another manufacturer, does not establish any suppression of competition or show any sinister domination."[30]

It is interesting to note, finally, the attitude of the Court toward the report and findings of the Federal Trade Commission as regards competitive conditions in the industry. This report had been made at the request of the Senate and pursuant to the investigatory powers delegated to it. Data had been obtained largely from the manufacturers themselves. The report was introduced in evidence over the objection of the International Company. The Court appraised the evidence as follows: "It is entirely plain that to treat the statements in this report—based upon an *ex parte* investigation and formulated in the manner hereinabove set forth—as constituting in themselves substantive evidence upon the questions of fact here involved, violates the fundamental rules of evidence entitling the parties to a trial of issues of fact, not upon hearsay, but upon the testimony of persons having first-hand knowledge of the facts, who are produced as witnesses and are subject to the test of cross-examination."[31] This unwillingness to accept economic and statistical

---

[29] *Ibid.*, p. 708.
[30] *Ibid.*, pp. 708–709.
[31] *Ibid.*, p. 703.

analysis in proof of monopoly, even when submitted by an impartial and experienced government body, suggests the difficulty of enforcing economic policy through the traditional legal processes.

The cases reviewed speak for themselves. No broad generalization can be drawn from the evidence as to the degree of restraint permissible under the law. The introduction of the rule of reason, while undoubtedly a factor making for leniency in application, has not contributed a concrete standard by which the legality of mergers may be tested. Each case has been decided on its specific facts, and any legal doctrines enunciated have been regarded as limited largely to the particular case under review. The law is still directed at monopoly, but what constitutes unlawful monopoly is for the Supreme Court to say. Several criteria are mentioned in the cases, such as intent to monopolize, a lessening of existing competition, the extent of market control, and the abuse of power. But the weight accorded to any one of the factors varies with the specific case, thus making results inconsistent and most unpredictable.

The most severe applications of the law were in the railway and anthracite coal cases. Here the creation of the combinations themselves and the suppression of existing competition were found to be unlawful. At least in the railway cases, there was no abuse of power, such as the exclusion of competitors by unfair means. No evidence appears as to the extent of market control in the railway cases, but in the coal cases it was about 20 per cent for the Lehigh Valley and 33 per cent for the Reading Company. Perhaps the regional character of the monopolies and the small probability of new competition arising were important factors in these decisions. But there was less public need for drastic action in the railway cases than in those involving other industrial enterprises. Not only might the mergers afford economies in operation, but the authority of regulatory bodies over rates and service was available to prevent abuses of monopoly power.

The Supreme Court, unfortunately, looked upon powerful combinations in the field of manufacturing with much greater complacency. Apart from the dissolutions of the Standard Oil and American Tobacco trusts, actions which could hardly be avoided, there was a marked unwillingness to find industrial mergers in violation of the law. In sharp contrast to the degrees of market control found unlawful in the coal cases, the Court found no legal objection to 50 per cent control in the Steel case, 64 per cent in the Harvester case, and 95 per cent in the case of Shoe Machinery. Emphasis in this line of decisions was not upon the existence of power, but upon intent to monopolize and the exercise of power. These considerations were permitted to becloud the central issue of whether or not there existed economic control of the market. The motives of the parties to a combination are not only difficult to determine, but can shed little light on the actual power of a concern to affect output and price in an industry. The futility of this attack is well illustrated by the Steel case, where despite the admission of illegal intent it was found to have been abandoned, and therefore of no legal consequence. In giving great weight to the failure to exercise monopoly power through the fixing of prices or the exclusion of competitors by predatory means, the Supreme Court placed its blessing on vast concentrations of economic power. There can be little doubt that firms controlling 50 per cent of an industry have it within their power to exercise considerable control over production and price policies. Independent firms are quite unwilling to risk the grave consequences of non-coöperation with the dominant concern. It is futile to look to the oppression of competitors as the test of legality in these circumstances. The heart of the evil is in the very existence of such dominant concerns. They present a danger both to the competitive economy and to the democratic system itself. Their conduct may be "reasonable" today, but in the absence of continuous administrative supervision there is no assurance of enduring behavior which will yield the best economic and social results.

Recognizing the weakness in the judicial attack upon industrial firms of overwhelming size, Judge Learned Hand raised some hope for improvement in his opinion in the Aluminum case of 1945.[32] A Circuit Court of Appeals held that the Aluminum Company of America monopolized interstate commerce in virgin aluminum ingot in violation of Section 2 of the Sherman Act. In reaching its decision, the Court found that Alcoa manufactured over 90 per cent of the virgin aluminum ingot sold in the United States, which percentage control of the market was "enough to constitute a monopoly."[33] Within the limitations set by the existence of substitute commodities, potential imports, and scrap or secondary aluminum, Alcoa had the power to fix prices. And the power had been exercised, in the opinion of the Court, despite the admission that Alcoa had not abused its power by extracting from consumers an extortionate profit. Whenever Alcoa sold its aluminum ingot, it must necessarily sell at some price, and the only price at which it could sell was one that it had itself fixed. Any distinction between the existence of monopoly power and its exercise is "purely formal," for when a monopo-

---

[32] United States v. Aluminum Company of America, 148 Fed. (2nd) 416 (1945). The Circuit Court of Appeals reversed the decision of the District Court, 44 Fed. Supp. 97 (1941), in which Judge Caffey had held that the evidence was insufficient to sustain the charges of monopolizing and conspiracy to restrain trade.

The Supreme Court was unable to entertain the appeal for lack of a quorum of six justices qualified to hear the case, since several justices had been officials of the Department of Justice when the case was in process. Hence, under an amendment to the United States Code enacted by Congress in 1944, the Supreme Court referred the appeal to the special court of last resort headed by Judge Learned Hand.

[33] 148 Fed. (2nd) 416, 424 (1945).

list enters the market "the power and its exercise *must needs coalesce*."[34] Having recognized that the existence and exercise of power cannot be disassociated, the Court pointed out that all contracts fixing prices are unconditionally prohibited under the Sherman Act. "Indeed it would be absurd," said the Court, "to condemn such contracts unconditionally, and not to extend the condemnation to monopolies; for the contracts are only steps toward that entire control which monopoly confers: they are really partial monopolies."[35] A concern of sufficient size to dominate a market inevitably fixes prices and, in the opinion of the Court, has the same illegal status as a price-fixing arrangement amongst a group of rival firms.

One of the purposes of the anti-trust laws, said the Court, "was to perpetuate and preserve, for its own sake and in spite of possible cost, an organization of industry in small units which can effectively compete with each other."[36] Only where a monopoly "may have been thrust upon" a firm through the automatic operation of economic forces could an exception be made. But the Court could find no evidence in the history of Alcoa that monopoly was inevitable and that it could not have avoided control of the market. "It insists that it never excluded competitors," wrote Judge Hand, "but we can think of no more effective exclusion than progressively to embrace each new opportunity as it opened, and to face every newcomer with new capacity already geared into a great organization, having the advantage of experience, trade connections and the elite of personnel. Only in case we interpret 'exclusion' as limited to manoeuvres not honestly industrial, but actuated solely by a desire to prevent competition, can such a course, indefatigably pursued, be deemed not 'exclusionary.' "[37] There need not be shown, in other words, that predatory tactics or unlawful competitive practices have been utilized. As a matter of fact, the Court did find unlawful the price squeeze on aluminum sheet. The price of aluminum ingot had been held at such a high level in relation to the price of aluminum sheet that competing sheet rollers had been unable to make a living profit. But the Court was careful to point out that it was holding Alcoa to have monopolized the ingot market "regardless of such practices."[38] And no specific evidence of "intent" to monopolize is necessary, for a monopolist must be assumed to know what he is doing. In order to fall within section 2 of the Sherman Act, concluded the Court, "the monopolist must have both the power to monopolize, and the intent to monopolize. To read the passage as demanding any 'specific,' intent, makes nonsense of it,

---

[34] *Ibid.*, p. 428.
[35] *Ibid.*, p. 428.
[36] *Ibid.*, p. 429.
[37] *Ibid.*, p. 431.
[38] *Ibid.*, p. 432.

for no monopolist monopolizes unconscious of what he is doing. So here, 'Alcoa' meant to keep, and did keep, that complete and exclusive hold upon the ingot market with which it started. That was to 'monopolize' that market, however innocently it otherwise proceeded."[39]

It is apparent that the doctrine expressed in this case marks a distinct advance over the decisions in the earlier cases involving manufacturing combinations and goes a long way in reconciling the economic and legal definitions of monopoly. The practical significance of the case in dealing with large combinations is limited, however, owing to the large percentage of control there found to exist. While 90 per cent of the supply was found to be enough to constitute a monopoly, the Court stated that "it is doubtful whether sixty or sixty-four per cent would be enough; and certainly thirty-three per cent is not."[40] Only a handful of industries would be affected if the 90 per cent rule were to be adhered to rigidly, and many dominant firms would escape prosecution even if the courts receded to the doubtful point of 60 or 64 per cent control of an industry. Of the manufacturing combinations attacked in the past, only the United Shoe Machinery Corporation would clearly fall within the prescribed limits.

A further qualification on the importance of the Aluminum decision is the fact that the case was decided by a special lower court. Not all that was held or said in the opinion may be accepted as good law by the Supreme Court. But there is fairly good assurance that the Supreme Court will approve, for in the Tobacco case of 1946[41] the Court took occasion to endorse specifically much that had been said.

The Tobacco case involved a criminal action against the three leading cigarette producers, namely, American, Liggett & Myers, and Reynolds, in which they were convicted of restraining trade and monopolizing in a substantial degree the purchase of leaf tobacco and the sale of cigarettes. Defendant companies produced about two-thirds of the domestic output of all cigarettes and over 80 per cent of the standard-price cigarettes, and purchased from 50 to 80 per cent of the flue-cured, burley, and Maryland tobaccos. The only question before the Supreme Court was whether or not the crime of monopolization under Section 2 of the Sherman Act required a showing of actual exclusion of competitors. And this was answered to the effect that actual exclusion was unnecessary. The defendants were "found to have conspired to establish a monopoly and also to have the power and intent to establish and maintain the monopoly."[42] As in the Aluminum case, the emphasis was upon the possession of power and not upon the exercise of that power in a

---

[39] *Ibid.*, p. 432.
[40] *Ibid.*, p. 424.
[41] American Tobacco Co. v. United States, 328 U. S. 781 (1946).
[42] *Ibid.*, pp. 814–815.

harmful manner. Said the Court, "The authorities support the view that the material consideration in determining whether a monopoly exists is not that prices are raised and that competition actually is excluded but that power exists to raise prices or to exclude competition when it is desired to do so."[43] This view is a decided contrast to the holding in the Steel and Harvester cases that "the existence of unexerted power" is not an offense, and quite in line with the decisions in the railway and anthracite coal cases that the existence of power is a menace "regardless of the use made of it."

In referring to the Aluminum case, Justice Burton stated that the issue there decided "closely approached" that in the instant case and was decided "under unique circumstances which add to its weight as a precedent."[44] Welcoming the opportunity to endorse certain of the statements, the Court quoted at length from the opinion. Among other things, approval was given to the holding that monopoly power can not be disassociated from its exercise in the fixing of prices, that the use of unlawful trade practices need not be shown to establish exclusion of competitors, that a showing of any "specific" intent to monopolize is unnecessary, and that the law is directed at the prevention of prospective competition as well as the elimination of existing competition.[45] The Supreme Court did not expressly approve the holding that 90 per cent control of a field constituted illegal monopoly per se, but it did endorse the statement that "to have combined ninety per cent of the producers of ingot would have been to 'monopolize' the ingot market."[46]

Perhaps the most significant aspect of the Aluminum and Tobacco cases is the clarification of the legal meaning of Section 2 of the Sherman Act and its restoration as an instrument for attacking monopoly power. The big advantage of proceeding under Section 2 rather than Section 1 is that it affords a direct attack on a dominant firm without having to establish collusion. Since "every person who shall monopolize, or attempt to monopolize," as well as one who conspires with others to monopolize, commits an offense, antitrust proceedings need not be confined to cases where there is evidence of combination or conspiracy to monopolize or restrain trade. The potentialities of Section 2, long neglected in the administration of antitrust policy, may yet be realized. If applied in the manner suggested in the Aluminum case, the Sherman Act becomes more than a proscription of predatory trade practices as regards dominant manufacturing concerns. With the emphasis upon the existence of monopoly power as the important factor in determining legality and the recognition of the economic fact that a monopolist cannot help but exer-

---

[43] *Ibid.*, p. 811.
[44] *Ibid.*, p. 811.
[45] *Ibid.*, pp. 813–814.
[46] *Ibid.*, p. 814.

cise his power whenever he engages in trade, the law takes a realistic view of the problem of corporate concentration and opens up some promising possibilities.

Valuable opportunities to apply the new doctrines of the law have been presented, but with mixed results. The most noteworthy are United States v. Paramount Pictures, Inc.,[47] and companion cases[48] involving the motion picture industry, and United States v. Columbia Steel Co.[49]

The Paramount case was an equity proceeding against the five major motion picture companies, namely, Paramount Pictures, Inc., Loew's, Inc., Radio-Keith-Orpheum Corporation, Warner Bros. Pictures, Inc., and Twentieth Century-Fox Film Corporation; and three lesser companies, Columbia Pictures Corporation, Universal Corporation, and United Artists Corporation. These companies produce nearly all the domestic output of films. The five major film concerns are great integrated companies that make, distribute, and exhibit motion pictures. Unlike the minor producers, they own or control theaters throughout the United States. In 1945 they had interests in about 17 per cent of the theaters, but such was the strategic importance of these theaters that they paid 45 per cent of the total film rental collected by the eight defendant companies. In the 92 cities of the country having populations over 100,000, at least 70 per cent of the first-run theaters are affiliated with one or more of the five majors. In 38 of these cities there are no independent first-run theaters. In the cities of 25,000 to 100,000 population, the majors have interests in about 60 per cent of the first-run theaters. In some 300 smaller towns they control all the theaters. And they have interests in many theaters that are privileged to show pictures only on the second, third, fourth, or later run.

Owing to their great size and power in both production and exhibition, the major companies have been able to impose upon the industry a series of trade practices designed to exploit their dominant position and to restrict opportunities for independents in nearly every part of the business. A basic practice is that of leasing rather than selling films, which, of course, are copyrighted. They are licensed to be shown for a limited number of years and, with rare exceptions, seem to disappear from the market long before copyrights expire. Competition is thereby restricted to the current output. The licensing agreement is the vehicle used for a variety of restrictions. For example, periods of time known as "clearances" are stipulated between the successive runs of a feature within a particular area or in specified theaters. These are designed to

---

[47] 334 U. S. 131 (1948).

[48] Schine Chain Theatres, Inc., v. United States, 334 U. S. 110 (1948); United States v. Griffith, 334 U. S. 100 (1948).

[49] 334 U. S. 495 (1948).

protect the large downtown theaters that enjoy first-run privileges and get the cream of the business. A second-run theater may show a picture only after an extended period of time has elapsed after the first showing and then only for a limited period. Subsequent runs are subject to similar restrictions. Coupled with clearance provisions is the fixing of minimum admission prices. These minimum prices have been substantially uniform in the contracts of the producers and have been fixed at a level in the second-run theaters, for example, which will permit the better houses safely to charge higher admission prices. Block-booking is also a practice of long standing. Feature pictures have been offered for license on the condition that other films to be released during a given period also be taken. Exhibitors are then prevented from bidding for single features on their individual merits.

Favoritism has also been shown toward the large theater circuits that have been built up in various sections of the country. These large firms, independently owned, have combined as many as 148 theaters located in 76 towns in a single chain.[50] By combining the buying power of all its theaters, both those located in towns where it controlled all the theaters and those in towns where competition existed, a circuit has been able to obtain advantages not enjoyed by competitors. The master agreements with the large circuits have made it impossible for the small competitor to obtain the choice first runs and have contained such other preferences as unreasonably long clearances, concessions on admission prices, and large privileges in the selection and elimination of films.

The Supreme Court upheld the lower court in its finding that the restrictive practices mentioned above as well as a host of others were illegal. Only in the case of clearances was some justification found, although the burden of proving their reasonableness was placed upon the defendants. But the Supreme Court declined to go along with the lower court in the further remedy it decreed to restore competition. The "root of the difficulties," in the opinion of the lower court, lay not in the ownership of theaters by the major producers but in the maze of vicious and unlawful practices that had been fastened upon the industry. Hence, it ordered that films be licensed on the basis of competitive bidding. It chose not to require the divestiture of theater holdings, because it would be damaging to the majors and the public. The substitution of open bidding for the private deals that had favored the big exhibitors was thought to be of great advantage to the small independent operator. The Supreme Court believed, however, that the structure of the industry precluded effective competition and that the necessary supervision of a

---

[50] Schine Chain Theatres, Inc. v. United States, 334 U. S. 110 (1948); United States v. Griffith, 334 U. S. 100 (1948); United States v. Crescent Amusement Co., 323 U. S. 173 (1944).

system of competitive bidding represented an impossible task for the courts.

Not only did the Supreme Court find the remedy of competitive bidding inadequate and impracticable, but it expressed disapproval of the lower court's examination and findings with respect to the results of the defendants' admitted conspiracy to obtain a monopoly in the exhibition of motion pictures. There had been no finding, for example, as to the presence or absence of monopoly on the part of the five majors in the all-important first-run field for the entire country, in the 92 largest cities of the country, or in separate localities. Unless such matters were explored, said Justice Douglas, remedies could not be devised which would effectively deny to the majors the retention of the fruits of their conspiracy. In the companion Griffith and Schine cases,[51] which in-volved large independent theater circuits, it had been declared that the ownership of theaters is vulnerable to attack where they have been acquired or their strategic position maintained by means of practices that are unreasonable restraints of trade. Parity of treatment of the big independent circuits and the circuits affiliated with the five majors required that the monopoly status of both be determined in order that the exhibition field be pried open to competition in the future.

A majority of the Supreme Court was unwilling to hold that vertical integration of producing, distributing, and exhibiting motion pictures is illegal *per se*. If this conclusion had been reached, as the Department of Justice had urged, a divestiture of theaters could have been ordered forthwith. The legality of vertical integration, like other combinations of business units, turns on whether the purpose is "to gain control over an appreciable segment of the market and to restrain or suppress competition, rather than an expansion to meet legitimate business needs."[52] Or, if power to exclude competition, though unexercised, is created by the integrated enterprise, and an intent to use that power is shown, a violation of the Sherman Act occurs. Said the Court, "Size is itself an earmark of monopoly power. For size carries with it an opportunity for abuse. And the fact that the power created by size was utilized in the past to crush or prevent competition is potent evidence that the requisite purpose or intent attends the presence of monopoly power."[53] The nature of the market to be served by the vertical integration and the leverage on that market which it makes possible are factors in determining the existence of monopoly power.

---

[51] 334 U. S. 100 (1948); 334 U. S. 110 (1948).

[52] 334 U. S. 131, 174 (1948).

[53] *Ibid.*, p. 174. Justice Cardozo had enunciated this doctrine in the Swift case, when he said that "size carries with it an opportunity for abuse that is not to be ignored when the opportunity is proved to have been utilized in the past," and suggested further that mere size might be illegal if "magnified to the point at which it amounts to a monopoly." United States *v.* Swift & Co., 286 U. S. 106, 116 (1932).

In remanding the Motion Picture cases to the lower courts for further findings as regards the existence of monopoly, the Court made possible the remedy of divestiture of theater holdings. Such a course of action is the only effective way of restoring competition and is strongly suggested in the Court's opinions.

The Columbia Steel case,[54] in contrast to the Motion Picture cases, produced nothing in the way of concrete results and little by way of principle or theory. In this litigation, the Government sought to prevent the acquisition by Columbia Steel Company, a wholly-owned western subsidiary of the United States Steel Corporation, of the assets of the Consolidated Steel Corporation. Consolidated was the largest independent steel fabricator on the West Coast. It fabricates and sells in its natural market area of eleven western states two types of products: structural steel, which includes building frameworks and bridges, and plate products, which consists largely of tanks, boilers, and welded pipe. The materials used for these products are chiefly rolled steel shapes and plates, types of rolled steel products which have been made from ingots by means of rolling mills. Indeed, it was for the purposes of assuring a more adequate market for its rolled steel products that United States Steel accepted the offer of Consolidated to sell its fabrication properties in 1946. The ingot and rolled steel capacity of United States Steel in the West had been greatly augmented a few months previously by the purchase of the steel plant located at Geneva, Utah, from the United States Government. The Geneva plant, erected to meet the urgent wartime demand for steel at a cost of nearly $200,000,000, was acquired at a price of $47,500,000 and the promise to spend nearly a like amount in the construction of additional facilities at Geneva and at California points. Western steel companies had submitted five other bids, but they were less advantageous. Independent western enterprise was either unable or unwilling to assemble and to risk the large amount of required capital, with the inevitable results of further concentration in the hands of the technically skilled and financially strong United States Steel Corporation.

The Attorney-General, in accordance with the procedure laid down in the Surplus Property Act of 1944, was given the opportunity to render an opinion concerning the legality of the Geneva acquisition. Attorney-General Clark, apparently in the face of a contrary opinion by his Anti-Trust Division,[55] advised that the sale of the Geneva property

---

[54] United States v. Columbia Steel Co., 334 U. S. 495 (1948). For discussions of this case, see Sergei S. Zlinkoff and Robert C. Barnard, "Mergers and the Anti-Trust Laws: The Columbia Steel Case," *University of Pennsylvania Law Review*, Vol. 97 (1948), pp. 151–179; "United States Steel's Westward March: A Chain Reaction of Concentration," *Stanford Law Review*, Vol. 1 (1948), pp. 108–125.

[55] Zlinkoff and Barnard, *op. cit.*, note 30, p. 159.

as such did not constitute a violation of the anti-trust laws. He noted that the ingot capacity of United States Steel had declined from 35.3 per cent of the total national capacity in 1939 to 31.4 per cent in 1946, and that the Geneva acquisition would increase the percentage to 32.7 per cent as contrasted with the 50.1 per cent of national capacity held in 1901. Considering the Pacific Coast and Mountain states alone, United States Steel's percentage would be increased from 17.3 per cent to 39 per cent of ingot capacity in the area (51 per cent if Colorado were excluded) if the Geneva plant were acquired. These figures were interpreted in the light of the dictum in the Aluminum case. There, it will be recalled, Judge Hand voiced the opinion that to constitute monopoly "it is doubtful whether sixty or sixty-four per cent would be enough; and certainly thirty-three per cent is not."[56] On this basis, the proposed sale was not legally objectionable. The subsequent purchase of Consolidated by United States Steel, however, was challenged immediately upon its consummation.

It was charged that the acquisition was an unlawful restraint because: first, it would eliminate competition in the sale of fabricated steel products between Consolidated and the fabricating subsidiaries of United States Steel; second, it would eliminate competition in the sale of rolled steel products between United States Steel and rival producers, for Consolidated would buy all its rolled steel from its parent concern. It was further charged that the purchase indicated an effort on the part of United States Steel to attempt to monopolize the production and sale of fabricated steel products in the Consolidated market in violation of Section 2 of the Sherman Act.

By a 5 to 4 decision, the Supreme Court refused to uphold the prosecution. In reaching its conclusion, the Court analyzed the nature and extent of competition on the basis of the facts presented to it. Except for the sale of pipe, where the national market was the competitive area, the Court adopted the eleven-state Consolidated market as the region to be considered in determining the legality of the merger.

The legality of the merger as a case of vertical integration was first considered. Basing its contention on the Yellow Cab case,[57] in which it

---

[56] 148 Fed. (2nd) 416, 424 (1945).

[57] United States v. Yellow Cab Co., 332 U. S. 218 (1947). It was charged that the Checker Cab Manufacturing Corporation, a manufacturer of taxicabs at Kalamazoo, Michigan, acquired control of companies operating taxicabs in several large cities and insisted that they buy their cabs exclusively from CCM and at prices above the market. Other manufacturers of taxicabs were thereby excluded from 86 per cent of the Chicago market, 15 per cent of the New York market, 100 per cent of the Pittsburgh market, and 58 per cent of the Minneapolis market. The defendant companies sought to justify the arrangement on the ground that they constituted an integrated enterprise and there could be no conspiracy among affiliated concerns in a single business unit. The Court held that the common ownership and control of the companies did not liberate the alleged illegal restraint from the im-

was held that corporate integration of companies conspiring to exclude competitors did not excuse the offense, the Government urged that the vertical integration and accompanying exclusion of rival firms from the sale of rolled steel to Consolidated was illegal *per se*. Adhering to the views expressed in the Paramount case, the Court held that the legality of vertical integration and exclusive dealing depended upon such criteria as the nature of the market to be served, the effect on the opportunities of competing producers, and the purpose or intent of the combination. Applying these standards, it was found that the merger "does not unreasonably restrict the opportunities of the competitor producers of rolled steel to market their product."[58] Over a ten-year period Consolidated had purchased only 3 per cent of the rolled steel sold in the eleven-state area. The Government had emphasized the fact that nearly 13 per cent of the plates and shapes, as distinguished from all rolled steel products, had been bought, but the Court accepted the 3 per cent as representing the true picture and ventured to predict that the proportionate future share would be smaller if the western steel industry developed as anticipated.

Like tests were applied in determining the legality of the horizontal combination. There was inadequate evidence with respect to the extent of actual or potential competition in the sale of pipe. On the basis of that available the Court found that the competition between Consolidated and United States Steel was not so substantial that its elimination would in the circumstances constitute an unreasonable restraint. Sufficiently specific evidence as regards actual competition among the 90 firms selling structural steel products was available to enable the Court to assume that United States Steel could be expected in the future to sell about 13 per cent and Consolidated about 11 per cent of structural steel products in the area. The Court disavowed any attempt "to pre-

---

pact of the law. It held also that the amount of interstate commerce involved was not a material factor since the law makes illegal the monopolizing of "any part" of interstate commerce.

This decision dealt only with the question of the sufficiency of the complaint to allege a violation of the Sherman Act. No evidence had been taken. The question of intent, for example, had not been determined. When, in subsequent proceedings before the District Court, evidence to support the allegations had been presented, the Court held that the proof showed that the stock relationships of the defendants did not arise as a result of a "deliberate, calculated purchase for control" of the sales of taxicabs; hence there was no violation of the law. Nor were cabs purchased under compulsion, in the opinion of the Court, except for a limited time prior to 1935 when exclusive dealing contracts were in effect. CCM was the only manufacturer continuously engaged in the production of purpose-built cabs in the period 1928 to 1942. The vehicles supplied by the large automobile manufacturers for use as taxicabs were converted pleasure cars. It was within the area of business judgment, held the Court, for the defendant operating companies to decide which cabs best suited their large city needs and there should be no disturbance of their decision to buy CCM purpose-built taxicabs. 80 Fed. Supp. 936 (1948).

[58] 334 U. S. 495, 527 (1948).

scribe any set of percentage figures by which to measure the reasonableness of a corporation's enlargement of its activities by the purchase of the assets of a competitor. The relative effect of percentage command of a market varies with the setting in which that factor is placed."[59] And the Court agreed that the elimination of potential competition in the manufacture and sale of steel products other than those presently produced was a factor to be considered. Taking these considerations into account, however, the conclusion was reached that it had not been proved that combining 24 per cent of the structural fabricating facilities in the trade area was an unreasonable restraint. But notice was served on United States Steel that "to hold this does not imply that additional acquisitions of fabricating facilities for structural steel would not become monopolistic."[60] If taken seriously this statement may prevent the further growth of concentration by the acquisition of independent enterprises, but the damage to competition in the western market has already been done and with impunity may be aggravated by expansion through investment of new capital.

The charge that United States Steel was attempting to monopolize the western market in violation of Section 2 of the Sherman Act was hastily dismissed. Little importance seems to have been attached to this charge by the Government despite the significance of Section 2 in recent cases. In ascertaining specific intent, the Court expressed a willingness to consider not only the 180 acquisitions consummated prior to 1920, but also the 8 acquisitions between 1924 and 1943 and the acquisition of Geneva in 1946. The Geneva acquisition was thought to be "of significance in ascertaining the intent of United States Steel in acquiring Consolidated."[61] An assured outlet for rolled steel was obtained, and this reflected a "normal business purpose" rather than an intent to circumvent the law. Since the Attorney-General had approved the Geneva acquisition, little weight was given to this or earlier acquisitions as evidence of intent to monopolize.

It is interesting to speculate whether or not the Government would have accepted the bid of United States Steel for Geneva, had it known that the company would acquire some competing fabricating facilities rather than promote competition in the area by constructing its own. Having accepted the bid, a chain reaction of concentration was started which could not be stopped by legal proceedings. Perhaps this was the only way that an unsubsidized steel industry could be brought to the West, but the price in terms of competitive individualism may come high.

In continuing to emphasize the extent and consequences of market

---

[59] *Ibid.*, pp. 527–528.
[60] *Ibid.*, p. 529.
[61] *Ibid.*, p. 532.

control, without at the same time abandoning the consideration of abuse of power, the Court followed the general approach and doctrines of the Aluminum, Tobacco, and Motion Picture cases.[62] The degree of market control and its effects were explored on the basis of the available evidence, but found not to be sufficiently substantial to warrant condemnation. Had substantial power been found to exist in the market area, good business intentions or failure to show the actual exclusion of competitors would presumably not have saved the combination. Nevertheless, the Columbia Steel decision emphasizes sharply the difficulty of curbing by legal means the growth of economic power through the gradual acquisition of the assets of small rival firms. A majority of the Supreme Court, while willing to consider size and its impact on the market as significant factors in the appraisal of lawful conduct, is not sufficiently impressed with size and the market control which goes with it to take a firm stand against its enhancement by acquisition and merger.

From the standpoint of remedies, recent experience has not uncovered any outstanding innovations, although some modest results have been achieved. The question of remedy to be applied in the Aluminum case was deferred until the effect of the Government's disposal of its war surplus aluminum plants could be observed.[63] Competitive conditions have not been created in the aluminum industry, in the opinion of the Department of Justice, and in 1948 it petitioned for a dissolution of the Aluminum Company.[64] In the Tobacco case, the Big Three and their officials were fined a mere $255,000 and the companies left in possession of whatever monopoly power they had previously enjoyed.[65] In the Pull-

[62] That abuse of power is still a major factor in some instances is well illustrated by the current A & P case. In upholding the decision of the lower court, the Circuit Court stated: "The Government insists that this case is not an attack upon A & P because of its size or integration and the power that may rightly go with such size and integration, but it is an attack upon the abuse of that power." United States v. The New York Great Atlantic & Pacific Tea Co., 173 Fed. (2nd) 79, 82 (1940). Among other things, A & P was found to have succeeded in its buying policy of establishing a two-price level, the lower for A & P and the higher for its competitors. Its large buying power was used to coerce suppliers to sell to it at preferential prices and terms by threatening boycotts, blacklists, and entry into manufacturing and processing. The quantity discounts and other concessions were rarely related to any demonstrable cost savings from the purchase of large quantities. It was found, moreover, that A & P had pressured local grocers, even to the extent of selling below cost, and forced some of them out of business. The Court found ample evidence to sustain the finding that A & P was guilty of abusing its great accumulation of power.
[63] 148 Fed. (2nd) 414, 446 (1945).
[64] News Release, Department of Justice, September 24, 1948. Much was made in the subsequent trial in 1949 of the approval of the War Assets Administrator of a deal to sell to Alcoa the Government's $19 million aluminum reduction plant at Massena, N. Y., for $5,000,000. As a part of the bargain, Alcoa agreed to let the rest of the industry use its alloy patents and several of its most important fabricating patents without charge. The Department of Justice opposed the transaction and obtained a deferment of the actual transfer of the property until the Court ruled on the anti-trust action.
[65] American Tobacco Co. v. United States, 328 U. S. 781, 783 (1946).

man case, the separation of the manufacture of Pullman cars from their operation was achieved, and the stock of the Pullman Company, the firm rendering sleeping-car service, was acquired by a group of railroads.[66] While the conduct of the dining and sleeping-car service by the railroads themselves may or may not result in better and more efficient service, the separation of car manufacture from operation will unquestionably inject a valuable competition into the manufacture and sale of passenger equipment. In the National Lead case,[67] however, the Supreme Court refused to order divestiture of plants of National Lead and du Pont so as to increase the number of competitors in the titanium market to a larger number than four. In the Motion Picture cases, two of the major producers anticipated probable drastic court action and have consented to divorce their exhibition business. RKO and Paramount have agreed to transfer their theaters to new companies which will be independently owned and controlled, and to dispose of their interest in most of the theaters that are jointly owned with local operators.[68] In the case of Paramount, the present circuit of 1,450 theaters will be reduced to between 400 and 650 theaters, depending on the number of partially owned theaters converted to full ownership, and independent competition will be restored in substantially all communities where Paramount controls more than one theater. The new theater companies may make future acquisitions of theaters only with the approval of the courts, and the new producing companies are forbidden from discriminating in the licensing of feature films to any theater or any run. These decrees appear to effect a complete separation of the theater business from production and distribution of pictures and to curtail materially the control of the theater circuits.

The Pullman and Motion Picture decrees do indicate a willingness on the part of the courts to effect some basic changes in the structure of the industries involved which may promote competition. Only such reorganizations strike at the fundamentals of the monopoly problem. Consumers are thereby rendered a wider market in which to exercise choice. But the number of independent firms emanating from the typical disso-

---

[66] United States v. Pullman Co., 50 Fed. Supp. 123 (1943); 53 Fed. Supp. 908 (1944); 55 Fed. Supp. 985 (1944); 64 Fed. Supp. 108 (1946); 330 U. S. 806 (1947); 331 U. S. 865 (1947).

A similar result is being sought in United States v. Western Electric Co., and American Telephone and Telegraph Co. On the ground that Western Electric manufactures and sells more than 90 per cent of all telephone equipment in the United States and sells at higher prices than would prevail if effective competition existed, the Government seeks a separation of Western Electric, a wholly owned subsidiary, from American Telephone and Telegraph and the dissolution of Western Electric into three competing manufacturing concerns.

[67] United States v. National Lead Co., 332 U. S. 319 (1947).

[68] United States v. Paramount Pictures, U. S. District Court, New York, Consent Decrees, Equity No. 87-273, November 8, 1948, and March 3, 1949.

lution is likely not to be large. In such circumstances, unless there is some variation in the business policies of the competing companies, the consumer still has no real alternative. There is a chance, however, that, in the absence of collusion, economic pressures and the uncertainty of the reactions of rivals to price cuts may yield distinctive behavior approaching effective competition.

19

The Federal Trade Commission and Control
of the Competitive System

HISTORICAL BACKGROUND OF THE 1914 LEGISLATION

The 1914 legislation, comprising the Federal Trade Commission Act[1]
and the Clayton Act,[2] was enacted in the attempt to provide a remedy
for the apparent shortcomings of the Sherman Act policy. Critics of the
anti-trust law and its interpretation saw various weaknesses. Certain industrial interests were critical of the vagueness of the law. They urged
that they did not know and could not find out what business organizations and methods were wholly legitimate under the statute.[3] In their
opinion, government policy offered insufficient protection to industrial
combinations and practices which were designed to enhance the efficiency of the economic system. They suggested that some administrative
body be created which would have the authority to advise business interests concerning the legality of contemplated undertakings.[4] Not only

---

[1] Public No. 203 (63rd Congress), approved September 26, 1914.
[2] Public No. 212 (63rd Congress), approved October 15, 1914.
[3] That the complaint of vagueness and uncertainty had not been dissipated many
years later is manifest from the following expression by Thurman Arnold, former
Assistant Attorney-General in Charge of the Anti-Trust Division of the Department
of Justice: " . . . There is a complaint that the anti-trust laws are not clear and
that business men do not know how they apply to the particular problem of the industries in which they are engaged. What is the reason for this and what is the
remedy? Is it a failure in the skill of the legislative draftsmen or the legal scholars
to define their terms, and is the remedy to be sought by further abstract definitions?
I do not think so. I have no faith in blanket amendments. . . .
"The clarification of the anti-trust laws depends upon applying them to particular
cases. . . . At present we are faced with forty years of non-enforcement. Therefore in scarcely any of our present industrial situations is the application of the
law clear. The boundaries of the application of the law to every industry are yet
to be determined. It can only be determined by bringing the cases; pushing the
frontiers of the anti-trust law to whatever extent the courts deem that their logic
will carry them." Address entitled, "The Policies of the Anti-Trust Division," September 3, 1938.
[4] Mr. George W. Perkins and Judge Elbert H. Gary, among others, advocated
that a Federal commission be created which would have the power to license inter-

was advance advice to be obtained from this commission, in order to eliminate uncertainty and litigation, but it was hoped that it would follow a policy which would be more tolerant of large enterprise.

Other critics, perhaps the great majority, inveighed not against the seeming harshness of the Sherman Act policy, but largely against its inadequacy and impotence. They were critical not only of the substance of the law as it had been revealed in the course of judicial interpretation, but of the manner in which it had been administered.

A number of considerations were involved in the critique of the substantive aspects of the law. First, many believed that the enunciation of the "rule of reason" in the Standard Oil and Tobacco cases in 1911 had greatly weakened the law. It would enable the courts to confer immunity upon combinations which were illegal under the terms of the statute as enacted by Congress in 1890. The Supreme Court, it was charged, had grasped the authority to decide what combinations were in its opinion economically justified. The judiciary would therefore exercise legislative power. Even the Senate Committee on Interstate Commerce, whose majority held moderate views, stated that it had full confidence in the intelligence, integrity, and patriotism of the Supreme Court, but found itself "unwilling to repose in that court, or any other court, the vast and undefined power which it must exercise in the administration of the statute under the rule which it has promulgated."[5] It was not appreciated by these critics, apparently, that the sweeping and inclusive language of the Sherman Act, adopted probably for its rhetorical and political value rather than its precise legal meaning, required definition and elucidation to make the policy workable. The "rule of reason" still permitted effective action against combinations and agreements which were monopolistic in purpose and effect. This, undoubtedly, was the real intent of Congress when it enacted the law. It is unlikely that Congress intended to condemn business arrangements which, without materially restricting competition, sought to promote economies and greater efficiency in manufacturing and marketing. The Supreme Court may have exercised a legislative function in declaring the policy in this field, but there appears to have been ample economic justification for the interpretation.

---

state corporations and to render advance judgments on their proposed actions or policies submitted for its examination. Policies or actions were to be approved only if, in the opinion of the Federal body, they did not "unreasonably restrain trade." *Hearings before the Committee on Interstate Commerce*, U. S. Senate, 62nd Congress (1912), Vol. I, pp. 1089 ff.; Vol. II, pp. 2407–2411. In general, these proposals embodied the idea of President Theodore Roosevelt that a distinction would be drawn between combinations which had been developed by unfair means and those which had been built up through efficiency and natural economic growth. The latter were not to be destroyed, but licensed and regulated in the public interest by a competent Federal agency.

[5] *Senate Report*, No. 1326, 62nd Congress, 3rd Session (1913).

Second, irrespective of legal interpretation, the Sherman Act was weak in that it was only directed at industrial combinations which had attained a status threatening the complete disappearance of competition. The force of the law could come into play only in the effort to suppress a concern which dominated some industry. But once such a state of . affairs had been reached, experience had shown that it was virtually impossible to restore competitive conditions by means of criminal penalties or dissolution decrees. Moreover, the threat of criminal and civil penalties had not deterred promoters from combining competitive concerns so as to dominate markets and achieve monopoly gains. Since it was impossible to restore competitive conditions with the instruments at hand, it had become apparent that a satisfactory trust policy required the fashioning of implements which could be used to prevent the formation of monopolistic concerns. There could be little doubt that prevention was a necessary adjunct to any remedial policy. What preventive measures were available and worthy of adoption comprised the essential question.

The problem of prevention led to the final criticism of the Sherman Act, namely, its ineffectiveness in dealing with unfair competitive practices. The view was quite generally held that many of the trusts attained their dominant position, not by superior productive and selling efficiency, but by the exercise of unfair methods of competition.[6] Our review of the trust movement has indicated the wide-spread use of unfair methods by industrial combinations, and shown how very effective these competitive weapons were in the hands of the large combinations. Any policy of prevention, it seemed, would have to include an attack on the methods which had been utilized to destroy the one-time competitors of the trusts.

Both the Sherman Act and the common law, the latter to be considered subsequently, were of some aid in meeting the problem of unethical and uneconomic business practices. But their effectiveness was extremely limited. The Sherman Act provided an indirect control of competitive practices, at least so far as industrial combinations were concerned. No specific prohibition of unfair practices was embodied in the statute, but under the "rule of reason" the business practices of

---

[6] Note the following from William H. S. Stevens, *Unfair Competition* (Chicago, The University of Chicago Press, 1917), pp. 219–220; " . . . The belief may be expressed that this study has demonstrated that it is most fallacious to assume that business in the United States has been conducted upon a basis of fair competition. If anything, the contrary has been the case in a large proportion of instances. . . . In many cases competition has not had the opportunity to operate freely in industries in which such organizations exist, and the frequent prevalence of unfair methods in these industries suggests such practices as one of the important causes of the development and continuance of monopolistic concerns. In numerous individual instances the more extensive the development or the employment of these methods the more comprehensive and absolute the monopoly."

combinations were of great importance as evidence of illegal intent and abuse of power.[7] The courts recognized the connection between the use of aggressive competitive methods and the achievement of a monopoly status. They undertook, therefore, to enjoin the use of particular unfair practices. In a number of important cases that came before the courts during and after 1911, competitive conduct was relied upon by the government as proof of monopolistic intent and was subjected to examination and judgment. The student is already familiar with the methods used to suppress competition in the classic Standard Oil and American Tobacco cases. They included espionage, the use of bogus independents, preferential railway rates, local price-cutting, the use of fighting brands, and exclusive dealing arrangements. Numerous practices were also restrained in the consent decrees entered into by defendant companies charged with violation of the Sherman Act. Among these were tying contracts,[8] price discrimination,[9] predatory price-cutting,[10] inducement of breach of contract,[11] and intimidation in various guises.[12] Likewise, some unfair practices were enjoined in private actions brought under Section 7 of the Sherman Law, although here again the practices were actionable only when they were part of a scheme to monopolize or to restrain trade.[13]

As a factor in improving the general standards of competitive conduct, however, the indirect attack made by the Sherman Act was quite weak and ineffectual. Neither the decrees in the litigated cases nor the consent decrees were conclusive as to the legality of the individual practices which were curbed by the courts. As one authority has put it: "One can only speculate as to the factors that condition their validity. It seems reasonably clear that, save for the more brutal practices, most of these methods violate the Sherman Act only when they are part of a

---

[7] In the American Tobacco Company case, the Supreme Court stated: "We think the conclusion of wrongful purpose and illegal combination is overwhelmingly established by the following considerations: a. By the fact that the very first organization or combination was impelled by a previously existing fierce trade war, evidently inspired by one or more of the minds which brought about and became parties to that combination. b. Because, immediately after that combination and the increase of capital which followed, the acts which ensued justify the inference that the intention existed to use the power of the combination as a vantage ground to further monopolize the trade in tobacco by means of trade conflicts designed to injure others, either by driving competitors out of the business or compelling them to become parties to a combination." 221 U. S. 106, 182.

[8] U. S. v. General Electric Co. (1911), *Decrees and Judgments in Anti-Trust Cases* (Washington, D. C., U. S. Government Printing Office, 1918), p. 267.

[9] *Loc. cit.*

[10] U. S. v. du Pont de Nemours and Co. (1912), *ibid.*, p. 193; U. S. v. American Thread Co. (1914), *ibid.*, p. 449.

[11] U. S. v. Burroughs Adding Machine Co. (1913), *ibid.*, p. 457.

[12] U. S. v. National Cash Register Co. (1916), *ibid.*, p. 315.

[13] See Milton Handler, "Unfair Competition," *Iowa Law Review*, Vol. XXI (1936), pp. 175, 218–219.

scheme to stifle competition and to obtain control of an industry."[14] Hence, without proof of a general policy designed to eliminate competition, an isolated attack upon a particular unfair practice would not be sustained in the courts. Thus, tying contracts, exclusive dealer arrangements, and similar practices were held not to be illegal in and of themselves, and courts would not entertain suits alleging injury from them. Moreover, the Sherman Act attack was weak because it could not begin to function at all until a firm or combination of firms had obtained or manifested an intent to obtain dominant control of an industry. This precluded any governmental attempt to curb unfair practices instrumental in building up the initial control. A small firm that was operating independently could utilize questionable methods with impunity, yet both competitors and consumers might suffer injury therefrom. The common law did supplement the Sherman Act attack upon unfair practices, particularly as regards specific methods and smaller firms. Before considering its scope and content, however, it will be well to point out the administrative weaknesses of the Sherman Law which were also important factors in the enactment of the 1914 legislation.

From the standpoint of administration, experience had revealed a number of serious deficiencies. These were, first, the relatively infrequent and often inexpert prosecutions of the trusts by the Department of Justice. Political considerations seemed to determine the extent to which enforcement of the statute was undertaken. Little or nothing was done when the political party in power found itself obligated to the business interests. In some instances, such as the United States Steel case, the prosecution was not skillful, and in others the charge was not pressed vigorously. Aberrations in policy and consequent failure to maintain an adequate staff of experienced prosecutors in the anti-trust division of the Department of Justice were responsible. Second, dissolution decrees were inadequate to restore competitive conditions in the industries concerned. Communities of interest effected through the common ownership of the stock of the successor companies spelled continued coöperation in the industry. The fewness of the companies emanating from the dissolution produced a like condition resulting in a restrained or monopolistic sort of competition. Third, administration of the law was both slow and costly. An inordinate length of time was often required to prosecute and to obtain a definitive decision by the courts. Cases such as those involving the meat packers, the International Harvester Company, and the General Electric Company consumed many years, and even then the results obtained were not altogether satisfactory. Finally, the shortcomings of the administrative record disclosed the need for an expert agency to administer anti-trust policy. Such an administrative tribunal would

---

[14] *Ibid.*, p. 216.

take over and integrate some of the functions performed by the courts, the Department of Justice, and the Bureau of Corporations. It would, therefore, combine investigatory, advisory, executive, and judicial functions. Such a Federal agency, it was believed, would make for a more sustained as well as a more enlightened attack upon the problem of maintaining competition.

The Common Law and Unfair Methods of Competition

It has already been noted that the common law as well as the Sherman Act provided some restrictions upon business enterprise in the choice of competitive methods. Virtually all branches of the common law affected the organization and conduct of business in some measure, but the judicial doctrines of unfair competition which evolved in the course of the nineteenth century related specifically to competitive behavior. Just as the common law gave no comfort to monopolistic enterprise, so also it moved, however haltingly, to establish a plane of fair competition. The doctrines of unfair competition were not developed as a result of deliberate planning or conscious endeavor to construct a set of competitive rules which might be enforced by the state. On the contrary, they were formulated by the method of trial and error, namely, in the process of adjudicating the civil rights of private parties in private suits. They originated, moreover, in an economy of small-scale enterprise. Firms were numerous and of about equal size and bargaining power, and operated within restricted markets. Where the essential conditions for competition were thus present in a substantial degree, it was not necessary for the law to go a long way in protecting traders against over-aggressive action on the part of competitors. The extent to which the common law of unfair competition did supply standards of business conduct and was effective in meeting the problems of an economy featured by large industrial units will be treated briefly.[15]

It gave some measure of protection to business interests from several more or less distinctive types of injury. They were, first, diversion of patronage by deceitful means; second, the misappropriation of competitors' confidential information; third, interference with business relations of competitors. A short consideration of each will follow.

The original meaning of "unfair competition" was confined to the diversion of patronage by means of simulating trade-marks and trade-names. Imitating the mark or name of a rival's product gave the public the misleading impression that the spurious goods were produced by

---

[15] For excellent discussions of the common law doctrines of unfair competition, their origin, scope, and limitations, see Handler, *op. cit.*, pp. 179–213; National Industrial Conference Board, *Public Regulation of Competitive Practices* (New York, National Industrial Conference Board, Inc., 1929), pp. 29–41.

the owner of the mark or name, and enabled the infringer to "pass off" his wares as such. Such practices were condemned by the courts, and the condemnation extended not only to trade-names but to the deceitful imitation of labels, packages, dress, form and appearance of articles. Two purposes were accomplished. The originator of the name or distinctive feature of a product was safeguarded from having his good-will exploited, and the consuming public was protected from the confusion emanating from the deception practiced by the imitator. The owner of the trade-name, obviously, was most interested in protecting his own property, but usually judicial relief depended upon the dual finding of probable deception of the public and diversion of his patronage.

But the remedy afforded a plaintiff was not always satisfactory. A court decree against the infringement of a trade-mark prohibited any use of the mark, but a decree against the deceitful use of a trade-name was usually restricted to the elimination of the deceit. In other words, the trade-name could be used if precautions were taken to avoid confusing the public. Thus, in the classic Waterman pen case,[16] the L. E. Waterman Company, manufacturer of the well-known "Waterman's Ideal" pens, obtained a decree against a firm that branded its pens with the name A. A. Waterman. Relief was limited, however, to the requirement that the defendant indicate on its pens that it had no connection with the L. E. Waterman Company. Manifestly, this sort of decree would not remove confusion in the minds of purchasers, for unless the initials of the maker of the original pen were recalled by a buyer he might regard the imitation as the original. The reason for the limited injunction in these cases seems to have been the fear that if the infringing use were totally banned, it would confer a monopoly of the common words of the language upon the first user. Whatever the merit of this contention, it is apparent that the efforts of firms to create markets for their products by means of misrepresentation and misappropriation were not curbed effectively.

The misappropriation of the confidential information of rivals, the second type of injury, was subject to injunction by courts of equity. Relief was first extended to secret formulae and novel manufacturing processes, but was later widened to include confidential information relating to commercial operations. Certain requirements had to be fulfilled to obtain judicial relief. The information had to be unique and outside the fund of common trade knowledge, ordinary precautions had to be taken to prevent disclosure, and the information must not have been obtained by lawful means. The typical case involved either the exploitation of trade secrets by former employees of the originator, or the competitive use of confidential information obtained from employees of a

---

[16] Waterman Co. v. Modern Pen Co., 235 U. S. 88 (1914).

rival. This protection against the dishonest taking of secret information was predicated upon the desirability of encouraging and rewarding originality and inventiveness. But it is noteworthy that the law's philosophy did not go so far as to afford protection against outright imitation and copying in the absence of misrepresentation. The courts permitted the copying of ideas, advertising schemes, designs, styles, and the physical appearance of articles of trade, where there was no deception as regards origin. This was allowed on the theory that imitation is inherent in the competitive process. To outlaw design and style piracy, the modern name for the practice, was to set up exclusive rights which would impair competition and work to the disadvantage of the consumer.

The third species of unfair trade practice which was actionable at common law was interference with the business relations of competitors. These interferences were essentially attacks upon competitors designed to damage their business and thus indirectly to further the interests of the aggressor. A variety of weapons was utilized. Among these were: (1) molestation and physical interference, (2) defamation and disparagement, and (3) inducing breach of contract.

Physical interference and deliberate molestation were competitive weapons which the courts had no difficulty in curbing as unfair trade practices, even though they often involved assaults upon customers and other third parties. Such crude practices as shooting at a competitor's customers, threatening them with personal injury, shadowing a rival's salesmen, arranging for the arrest of competitors' employees on false charges, blocking and obstructing the entrance to a rival place of business, and inducing competitors' employees to commit sabotage were litigated in the courts.[17]

Misrepresenting or "knocking" the products of a competitor is known as disparagement in the law. Customers are here sought not by proclaiming the merits of a given product, but by making false statements about the quality or value of a rival's products. Legal action was based on the law of personal defamation, although a disparagement is a derogatory criticism of a competitor's product and not of his character. Where the criticism of goods also reflects upon the reputation of the producer or dealer, it may be a defamation as well as a disparagement. The essential features of the wrong are a false statement which has been willfully published or uttered and which causes special damage. Although disparagement was actionable, it was exceedingly difficult to prove special damages, because it had to be shown that specific sales were lost as a result of the disparagement. Consequently, the cases in which damages were recovered were extremely rare. Moreover, courts of equity were reluctant to grant injunctions against the practice, on the questionable

---

[17] Handler, *op. cit.*, pp. 201–202.

ground that this would impair the constitutional rights of free speech and trial by jury. The ineffectiveness of the remedy, therefore, thwarted the elimination of a selling method which had no conceivable justification. Other practices which were closely related to the tort of disparagement and which were actionable were the circulation of untruths regarding a firm's credit or continuance in business, and groundless threats of patent or trade-mark litigation.

Inducing breach of contract was a further method of harassing competitors which came to the attention of the courts. The action grew out of the ancient doctrine prohibiting the enticement of employees, which, incidentally, was in itself a valuable protection to competitive firms. Beginning with Lumley v. Gye,[18] in which the malicious inducement of a breach of a contract between a theatrical producer and an opera singer was held to be actionable, the tort was developed until it embraced every type of contract. The prohibition was extended to include not only the intentional inducement of breach, but interference with or prevention of the performance of a competitor's contracts. In some states, liability for procuring a breach of an existing contract was limited to cases in which it had been accomplished by such wrongful means as deceit or duress. These jurisdictions, however, have begun to remove this requirement.[19] There was also some uncertainty as to what circumstances constituted justification for interference in contract relations between others. But it had become settled that competition did not justify interference with existing contractual arrangements, such, for example, as between a business rival and a customer. Thus, the common law afforded remedies against the invasion of a private right, and at the same time furthered the public interest by insuring the integrity of contracts.

The foregoing sketch of the common law has suggested its scope and in some measure its limitations in coping with competitive abuses. That the common law made some contribution to the creation of a plane of fair competition is clear. But its shortcomings were even more apparent. Professor Milton Handler has appraised the common law of unfair competition as follows:

The ideas which are common to the competitive torts are . . . extremely simple. Misrepresentation, misappropriation, diversion of trade, interference with trade relations, attacks upon competitors—these are the stuff out of which the law of unfair competition was built. The common law reached only the crudest competitive excesses. It left untouched many abuses which it was equipped to handle. It had reached its maturity without developing any principle or procedure whereby the hosts of abuses that annoyed and hampered the honest and efficient tradesman might be eliminated. Judicial regulation of unfair competition has been and still is hopelessly incomplete and superficial and

---

[18] 2 E. & B. 216 (Q. B. 1853).
[19] Handler, op. cit., p. 211.

there is no hope that the inadequacies of common law doctrines and methods can ever be overcome by the courts, unaided by legislation.[20]

A number of the inadequacies on the substantive side may be pointed out. Many trade methods were outside the scope of the law because they were of such a character that it was difficult to prove the special injury essential for a private action in the courts. A large number of the newer modes of destructive competition, particularly those utilized by the trusts, came within this category. Thus, such practices as the operation of bogus independents, the use of fighting brands, local price-cutting, tying contracts, and exclusive dealing arrangements afforded no ground for legal action. They were competitive methods which were directed not so much at individual competitors as at the reduction of competition from all sources. It was virtually impossible, therefore, to sustain a plea of special damage.[21] And even though special injury might have been apparent, such accepted doctrines as the boycott, or the absolute right of a single seller to refuse to deal with any person, and the right to dispose of property at any price one is able to obtain, would have proved to be insurmountable obstacles to judicial relief. Except in cases of collusion between firms, it was not apparent to the courts that such matters as competitive pricing and boycotting could be subject to abuse in the hands of powerful single corporations. The legal concept of unfairness in the competitive system had not developed to the point where methods which enabled producers to obtain patronage on some basis other than efficiency of operation and quality of product were proscribed.

Practices which were not directly associated with the combination movement were also sacrosanct under the law. Espionage, apart from the rule against misappropriation of confidential information, appears not to have been unlawful. While "passing off" and disparagement were unlawful, it has been seen that the ineffectiveness of the remedies afforded by the courts militated against the complete suppression of these practices. Moreover, false advertising and misbranding could not be curbed under the common law, notwithstanding the unethical and uneconomic nature of these competitive methods. The honest producer was at the mercy of those who practiced these frauds upon the public. The false claims of unscrupulous producers caused losses to honest competitors by diverting patronage which they would normally enjoy, by forcing them to reduce prices to meet the competition of inferior goods falsely described, or by destroying the confidence of the public in the product of an entire industry. Yet despite these unfortunate results, the injured competitor could not bring action in the courts. The classic

---

[20] *Ibid.*, pp. 212–213.
[21] National Industrial Conference Board, *op. cit.*, pp. 37–38.

Washboard case[22] indicates the typical attitude of the courts. A court composed of Judges Taft, Lurton, and Day, all of whom later became members of the Supreme Court, refused to enjoin the misbranding of zinc washboards as aluminum upon the complaint of the sole producer of aluminum washboards. There was no claim that the defendant sought to make the public believe that its goods were those of the complainant. The burden of the complaint was that the misbranding caused injury to the complainant because purchasers who really wanted the genuine article were induced to buy the spurious washboard. The court held, however, that a competitor could not bring suit to prevent such deception of the consuming public. It was the court's opinion that the traditional doctrine of passing off could not be extended to requiring all producers "to deal solely in goods that are exactly what they are represented to be."

The procedural weakness of the common law was no less serious than the inadequacy of its content. The rules which had evolved with respect to unfair competition in trade could be administered only by the courts. And courts could act only if private parties brought their grievances to them for adjudication. They could not undertake to police the field of industry and trade in order to detect and eliminate abuses. Neither could private parties be relied upon to bring the necessary actions, because lawsuits were costly and their outcome uncertain. Moreover, sheer inertia and absence of a compelling interest in higher standards of business conduct militated against liberal use of the right to sue in the courts. In special cases a small enterpriser would not dare to sue a large producer on whom he depended for certain services or for sale of his product. These factors pointed to the need for the assumption of greater responsibility on the part of the government itself if competition were to be relied upon as the instrument for economic control. The most promising method was the establishment of administrative control of business practices.

Political and Legislative Background

Political recognition of the weaknesses of the Sherman Act and the inadequacies of the common law led to the enactment of the 1914 legislation. Anti-trust policy was an important issue in the presidential campaign of 1912.[23] The Republican party promised supplementary legislation to outlaw specific acts which "uniformly mark attempts to restrain and to monopolize trade," and to create a Federal trade commission

---

[22] American Washboard Co. v. Saginaw Mfg. Co., 103 Fed. 281 (1900). See also Mosler Safe Co. v. Ely-Norris Safe Co., 273 U. S. 132 (1927).

[23] For a detailed account of the political and legislative history of the 1914 legislation, see Gerard C. Henderson, *The Federal Trade Commission* (New Haven, Yale University Press, 1924), Chap. 1.

which would take over functions exercised by the courts and thereby "promote promptness in the administration of the law and avoid delays and technicalities incident to court procedure."[24] The new Progressive party, whose candidate was Theodore Roosevelt, favored strengthening the Sherman Law by prohibiting sharing the market, local price-cutting, exclusive dealing and other unfair practices. It also emphasized the need for an administrative agency to license and supervise the trusts.[25] The Democrats expressed dissatisfaction with the manner in which the Sherman Act had been enforced, and regret that the law had been weakened by judicial construction. They favored the "prevention of holding companies, of interlocking directors, of stock watering, of discrimination in price and the control by any one corporation of so large a proportion of any industry as to make it a menace to competitive conditions."[26] But their candidate, Woodrow Wilson, roundly criticized the proposal of Roosevelt to create a Federal Commission to license and supervise the trusts as an "avowed partnership between the government and the trusts."[27]

The concrete form of the administrative program for trust legislation was contained in President Wilson's message to Congress on January 20, 1914.[28] So far as substantive changes were concerned, his program was an elaboration of the ideas presented in the campaign. But as regards method, it is interesting to note, he advocated the establishment of a commission. His recommendation was qualified, however, by his opposition to any Federal agency that would make terms with monopoly or assume any control which would make the government responsible. It was conceived as an instrument for investigation and publicity, and for the effective enforcement of a policy of maintaining competitive conditions.

A number of bills were introduced in both Houses of Congress to give effect to the administration program.[29] There was much difference of opinion both with respect to general policy and to the detailed provisions of the contemplated statutes. Among the controversial questions which arose were: first, whether specific practices to be forbidden should be individually defined or simply included under a blanket prohibition of all "unfair methods of competition"; second, whether, in addition to investigatory and advisory functions, the commission should be given

[24] *Republican Campaign Text-Book*, Philadelphia, Dunlap Printing Company, 1912, pp. 272–273.
[25] Progressive National Committee, *Platform of the Progressive Party* (New York, Stoddard-Sutherland Press, 1912), pp. 6–7.
[26] *Republican Campaign Text-Book*, 1912, p. 279.
[27] Woodrow Wilson, *The New Freedom* (New York, Doubleday, Page & Company, 1913), p. 202.
[28] *Congressional Record*, 63rd Congress, 2nd Session, pp. 1962–1964.
[29] See Henderson, *op. cit.*, pp. 24–27.

regulatory powers and the authority to render advance opinions on the legality of business practices; third, the necessity for judicial review of the cease and desist orders of the commission if it were given regulatory powers; fourth, the efficacy of criminal penalties for violations of the law. These highly controversial matters were finally settled and the results embodied in two separate but related statutes, namely, the Federal Trade Commission Act and the Clayton Act.

IMPORTANT PROVISIONS OF THE 1914 LEGISLATION

Substantive Provisions

There were five new principles of substantive law embodied in the 1914 legislation relating to trade competition and industrial monopoly.[30] Four of these were included in the Clayton Act and one in the Federal Trade Commission Act.

The most important single section in the 1914 legislation, on the substantive side, was Section 5 of the Federal Trade Commission Act. In this section "unfair methods of competition" were "declared unlawful." This was a general and all-inclusive condemnation of unethical and uneconomic trade practices. It was sufficiently broad to cover a wide range of unfair practices, and did not attempt to apply inflexible definitions of an extensive list of proscribed practices to a variety of dissimilar circumstances and industries. It also looked to the future, since it could be interpreted to embrace new unfair methods which were likely to be developed in a constantly changing economic world. As Senator Cummins stated, the Congressional purpose was to permit the words "unfair competition" to "grow and broaden and mold themselves to meet circumstances as they arise."[31]

But the generality and vagueness of the language which Congress employed were not an undiluted blessing. The phrase "unfair methods of competition" could be given content and meaning only in terms of specific practices. This could be accomplished only through the process of administrative and judicial action. And the phrase itself could not be of great assistance in guiding those responsible for its construction. It had been used in a great variety of senses by those who supported the law. The intention was, apparently, that it should include not only practices which were deceptive and fraudulent, such as misrepresentation and simulation of trade-names, but practices which tended to destroy com-

---

[30] The Clayton Act, a catch-all piece of legislation, also contained provisions relating to banks and common carriers, to labor organizations and the issuance of injunctions in trade disputes, and to other matters which are beyond the scope of this study.

[31] *Congressional Record*, Vol. LI (1914), p. 14,003.

petition and establish monopoly. Doctrines which had evolved in the regulation of "unfair competition" under the common law, and the principles which had emerged in the enforcement of the Sherman Act, were to be drawn upon in defining the scope and content of Section 5. But even with the aid of the Congressional debates, the common law, and the Sherman Act, it was to be anticipated that the commission and the courts would find it a long and laborious process. The diverse and shifting views of the courts and the contribution to the law of unfair competition which the courts have permitted the Federal Trade Commission to make will be considered in a later section.

Two of the legal principles included in the Clayton Act relate specifically to methods of competition. Two types of trade practice were singled out for special treatment. Section 2 dealt with price discrimination and Section 3 was concerned with tying and exclusive dealing arrangements.

Section 2 prohibits discrimination in price between different purchasers of commodities where the effect "may be to substantially lessen competition or tend to create a monopoly in any line of commerce."[32] Price differences based upon differences in grade, quality, quantity, or costs of selling or transportation were not prohibited, since obviously they are not discriminatory or unfair. Moreover, discrimination made in good faith to meet competition was declared to be lawful, and the right of sellers to select their own customers was specifically safeguarded. This section, it should be emphasized, did not outlaw discrimination as such; it came into play only if the price discrimination lessened competition substantially or tended toward monopoly. It was directed at two types of price discrimination: first, the local price-cutting which the powerful combinations had used either to drive competitors out of business or to bring them to terms; second, the price discrimination which, though it did not impair competition with the seller's rivals, favored particular buyers and gave them an unfair competitive advantage over distributors that paid higher prices. The wisdom of treating both local and personal discrimination in a single section was dubious. Prohibiting local price-cutting was intended primarily to preserve rather than to regulate competition. Personal discrimination may work a very real injury on those customers that are required to pay the higher prices, and yet may not result in a substantial lessening of competition. Hence, the prohibition fell short of complete protection against all unfair discrimination. It may also be observed that in prohibiting discrimination, Congress was venturing more or less into a new policy as regards monopoly. By implication, at any rate, Congress here recognized the futility of attempting to maintain pure competition and accepted the inevitability of monopolis-

---

[32] It is interesting to speculate whether the split infinitive merely represented Congressional grammatical standards of 1914 or an attempt to emphasize the word "substantial."

tic power. This follows from the fact that price discrimination commonly springs from conditions of monopoly. In outlawing discrimination an attempt was being made to force industrial concerns to behave as they would if competition prevailed. The burden of the seemingly new policy was to prevent quasi-monopolies from further extending their control over the market (local price-cutting), and to prevent them from pursuing price practices which had the effect of impairing competition between their customers (personal discrimination).

Section 3 prohibits the use of tying and exclusive dealing contracts. It forbids any person to lease, sell, or contract to sell patented or un-patented goods, or to fix a special price on condition that the lessee or purchaser do not use or deal in the goods of a competitor of the seller or lessor, where the effect of such an arrangement may be to lessen competi-tion substantially or tend to create a monopoly. This section was also designed to cover two types of practice. It was intended primarily to meet the tying practice upheld in the Dick case,[33] where the manufac-turers of a patented mimeographing machine required purchasers to use with the machine only the paper and ink supplied by them. Similar practices on the part of the United Shoe Machinery Corporation had been the cause of serious complaint and had been found not to violate the Sherman Act.[34] The second practice covered by the section was that of a manufacturer who required his wholesale and retail distributors to agree not to handle the products of his competitors. Such exclusive dealing arrangements, it will be recalled, were not unlawful either under the Sherman Law or the common law. But again it must be emphasized that the law did not condemn all tying or exclusive dealing arrangements, only those which lessened competition substantially or tended toward monopoly. This langauge more or less frustrated the purpose of the law so far as the regulation of competition is concerned, since it could be applied only to large concerns that dominated a particular industry. It would be virtually impossible to show a substantial lessening of com-petition flowing from exclusive dealing contracts, for example, if sellers were numerous and thus no single seller was able to close any substantial number of distributive outlets to competitors. Yet tying up dealers for a long period of time, especially if they are the most desirable distribu-tors, may constitute a real obstacle to anything approaching the opera-tion of pure competition. Section 3, in other words, was designed not to maintain a plane of fair competition but to preserve competition, the objective of the Sherman Act.

The two remaining principles of law set forth in the Clayton Act relate not to the regulation of competitive methods but to the regulation

[33] Henry v. A. B. Dick Co., 224 U. S. 1 (1912).
[34] United States v. United Shoe Machinery Co., 247 U. S. 32 (1918).

of methods of combination. Sections 7 and 8 dealt with intercorporate stockholding and interlocking directorates, respectively.

Section 7 forbids the acquisition of the stock of one corporation by another, or the combination of two or more corporations by stock acquisition, where the effect may be to lessen competition substantially between the corporations involved, to restrain commerce in any community, or tend to create a monopoly. The regulation was not to apply to purchases of stock solely for investment nor to the creation of legitimate subsidiary corporations. This section was directed at the use of the holding company as a means for creating unlawful combinations and was clearly supplementary to the Sherman Act. But the test of illegality which it applied appears to be more drastic than that contained in the Sherman Act. There is no requirement as to the nature or degree of competition which must have prevailed between the companies prior to combination. A lessening, or prospect of lessening, of competition between the combining corporations is sufficient, and it is not excused by possible production economies or by the presence of competition in the rest of the industry. However, despite this drastic control of corporate interrelationships, there was doubt whether the section could contribute a great deal to the prevention of industrial concentration. The acquisition of a controlling stock interest of a competing company is illegal under the act, but there is nothing to preclude the same result being reached through the acquisition of the assets of a competing concern. Since the law only outlaws one method, albeit the simplest and most feasible in actual practice, it could not be regarded as having far-reaching importance.

Section 8 of the Clayton Act, among other things, imposed limitations upon interlocking directorates as between industrial concerns. Any person is prohibited from being a director in two or more corporations, any one of which has a capital and surplus of more than a million dollars, if the business and location of the corporations are such that "the elimination of competition by agreement between them would constitute a violation of any of the provisions of any of the anti-trust laws." The test of legality adopted here was that of the Sherman Act, yet this test was so vague and indefinite that it could not be applied with ease. The courts had not made it clear whether, under the rule of reason, all agreements which eliminated competition were bad, or whether those that only partially restrained trade and left the whole market relatively free would be upheld. It is quite incomprehensible that a test of this character should be used in a statute that was intended to clarify and make more definite the provisions of the Sherman Act. But apart from this ambiguity, the section held little prospect of effectiveness in protecting against monopoly, since it did nothing to disturb the common ownership of the stocks of two competing corporations by a single person. As long as a person can exercise voting rights, he can act through a trusted representative on the board of directors of a competing corporation and obtain the same result as he would if he were a member of both boards.

Administrative and Procedural Provisions

The main administrative and procedural provisions in the 1914 legislation are to be found in the Federal Trade Commission Act. It provided for the creation of the Federal Trade Commission and outlined its powers and duties.

The Commission was to consist of five members.[35] They were to be appointed by the President, with the advice and consent of the Senate, for terms of seven years and at salaries of $10,000 per year. Not more than three of the Commissioners could be members of the same political party, and they could engage in no other business or employment. Any Commissioner could be removed by the President for "inefficiency, neglect of duty, or malfeasance in office." The Commission was authorized to employ such attorneys, special experts, examiners, and other employees as it should find necessary for the performance of its duties.

The powers and duties delegated to the Commission could be divided into three categories as follows: First, duties of investigation and inquiry concerning business organization, practices and related matters; second, duties of an advisory nature in connection with the administration of the anti-trust laws; third, the duty of enforcing the substantive provisions of the 1914 legislation.

Broad powers of investigation were delegated to the Commission.[36] It was authorized to "gather and compile information" concerning the "organization, business, conduct, practices, and management" of any corporation engaged in interstate commerce and its relation to other business firms or individuals. It could require corporations to file annual or special reports furnishing information relating to the matters of organization and practices. Upon the direction of the President or either House of Congress, it was authorized to investigate and report the facts concerning any alleged violation of the anti-trust laws. And it could investigate trade conditions in foreign countries where combinations or the practices of traders might affect the foreign trade of the United States. In order to insure that the Commission would obtain the information which it deemed necessary in these inquiries, it was to "have access to . . . any documentary evidence of any corporation being investigated."[37] And it could "require by subpoena the attendance and testimony of witnesses and the production of such documentary evidence

---

[35] Sections 1 and 2 deal with the Commission's structure.
[36] Section 6. Banks and railways were excluded.
[37] Section 9.

relating to any matter under investigation."[38] These powers were similar to those of the old Bureau of Corporations, which had been a fact-finding agency and whose functions and staff were to be taken over by the new organization. It was hoped that the discovery and public disclosure of business practices would arouse public opinion and thus serve to check the use of improper methods. The facts obtained were also to be used as the basis for recommendations to Congress for additional legislation.

The advisory powers which were conferred upon the Commission related primarily to the enforcement of the anti-trust laws. Recommendations to Congress for further legislation are an exception, of course, since that advice relates to broad matters of policy as well as to the administration of existing laws. As regards enforcement of the anti-trust laws, the Commission was authorized, upon the application of the Attorney-General, to investigate and make recommendations for the readjustment of the organization and business of corporations alleged to be violating the anti-trust acts.[39] Further aid was to be rendered the Attorney-General through the investigation of the manner in which court decrees in anti-trust suits were being carried out. The findings in these investigations, which could be undertaken upon its own initiative or upon the request of the Attorney-General, were to be transmitted to the Department of Justice together with recommendations for future action. In addition to serving the legislative and executive branches of the government in an advisory capacity, the Commission was to render assistance to the judiciary in anti-trust suits brought by the Attorney-General. It was provided that a court, if it believed that the government was entitled to relief, could refer the suit to the Commission "as a master in chancery" to ascertain and report an appropriate form of decree.[40] The report was to be purely advisory, however, since the court was authorized to adopt or reject it, in whole or in part, and to enter any decree which it saw fit.

The regulatory functions of the Commission, the third category of powers and duties referred to above, relate to the enforcement of the substantive provisions of the 1914 legislation. These included Section 5 of the Federal Trade Commission Act and Sections 2, 3, 7 and 8 of the Clayton Act. The jurisdiction of the Commission was made exclusive with respect to the prevention of the trade practices condemned in Section 5. As regards the enforcement of the substantive provisions of the Clayton Act, however, it was given coördinate jurisdiction with the Department of Justice. The Clayton Act, by express provision, was made a part of the anti-trust laws,[41] and the Attorney-General was made re-

---

[38] Loc. cit. Penalties of fine and imprisonment for failure to obey subpoenas or other lawful requirements of the Commission, to be assessed through court action, are provided for in Section 10.

[39] Section 6.

[40] Section 7.

[41] Clayton Act, Section 1.

sponsible for the institution of proceedings in the district courts to prevent and restrain its violation.[42] Actions by private parties under the anti-
trust laws were also authorized. Private actions could take the form
either of a suit for treble damages for injuries sustained[43] (an action
already possible under the Sherman Law), or a suit for injunctive relief
against threatened loss or damage.[44] But it should be noted that the
Federal Trade Commission was delegated no authority to enforce the
provisions of the Sherman Act, despite the rather general opinion that
their effective enforcement required administrative action. That it did
have jurisdiction over some of the monopolistic practices encompassed
by the Sherman Act and that it was so intended by Congress will be
made clear in the later discussion.

The administrative procedure for carrying out the regulatory function
was outlined in the legislation.[45] Whenever it should "have reason to
believe" that any unfair method of competition was being used, and if
it should appear that a proceeding "would be to the interest of the
public," the Commission was authorized to issue a complaint against the
offender. The complaint was to contain the charges and a notice of
hearing on a day at least thirty days after the service of the complaint.
The testimony offered at the public hearing by the Commission, the
offender, or any other party that had been permitted to intervene, was to
be reduced to writing and filed with the Commission. If the Commission
concluded that the facts found from the record supported the charges,
it was required to make a report of its findings of fact and issue an order
demanding the respondent to cease and desist from using the unlawful
method of competition.

If a respondent failed to obey the cease and desist order, the Commission was empowered to apply to a Circuit Court of Appeals for enforcement. A transcript of the record in the proceeding, including the
testimony and the report and order, was to be filed with the court. The
court was authorized to enter a decree affirming, modifying, or setting
aside the Commission's order. Should the party against whom the order
was issued wish to take the initiative, he was at liberty to petition a
Circuit Court to have the order set aside, and the same process of judicial
review was set in motion. In reviewing an order of the Commission, the
courts were to limit themselves to a consideration of the legal issues.
It was clearly provided that "the findings of the commission as to the
facts, if supported by testimony, shall be conclusive." Once a Circuit

---

[42] *Ibid.*, Section 15.

[43] *Ibid.*, Section 4.

[44] *Ibid.*, Section 16. Another innovation worthy of mention was the making of
final judgments or decrees (except consent decrees) in suits brought by the United
States under the anti-trust laws *prima facie* evidence against the defendants in proceedings brought by any other party (Section 5).

[45] Federal Trade Commission Act, Section 5; Clayton Act, Section 11.

Court of Appeals had issued an appropriate decree, it was to be final, except that it was subject to review by the Supreme Court upon certiorari. A respondent that disobeyed a final decree upholding an order of the Commission could, of course, be punished for contempt of court.

The foregoing review of the 1914 legislation indicates that the basic policy of Congress was still that of preserving competition. This had been the policy embodied in the Sherman Law. Only the emphasis had been changed. That statute had confined itself largely to the suppression of combinations that actually controlled the market. The new legislation sought to eliminate business methods which operated to stifle competition and which might lead to monopoly. For this purpose it condemned such practices as price discrimination and tying arrangements in circumstances where the effect might be to lessen competition substantially or create monopoly. While supplementary to the Sherman Act policy of maintaining competition, these provisions of the Clayton Act were designed to prevent monopoly by attacking it in its incipient state. This was likewise true of the declaration that "unfair methods of competition" were unlawful, since it was intended to embrace monopolistic practices. But in this phrase, which differed but slightly from the "unfair competition" of the common law, Congress manifested a new intention. Practices which had no direct relation to monopolizing, but which were unfair on both ethical and economic grounds, were to be suppressed. In short, the Federal Trade Commission was directed both to preserve competition and to maintain a proper plane of competitive behavior.

Perhaps the most nearly unique contribution of the 1914 legislation was its method for enforcing these policies. While the old procedures were retained and actually strengthened, exclusive reliance was no longer placed upon the courts. A public agency was made available to those engaged in interstate commerce who were threatened with injury by the unfair tactics of competitors. Since the Commission was to exercise a combination of investigatory, advisory, and regulatory functions, there was the prospect that it would develop into a truly expert administrative body. So far as regulation was concerned, distinct advantages were to be seen in lodging functions of an executive, legislative, and judicial character in the same tribunal. With such a definite responsibility and wide discretionary authority, it was anticipated that the Federal Trade Commission would contribute materially to the maintenance of the competitive system.

20

Organization and Procedure of the Federal
Trade Commission

Some study of the organization of the Federal Trade Commission is needed before the legal interpretation of the 1914 legislation and the accomplishments of the Commission can be presented. Matters of procedure have a definite bearing upon the efficiency of the administrative process. And the latter must be an important consideration in any evaluation of the whole public policy.

ORGANIZATION OF THE COMMISSION

The Commission, which is composed of five Commissioners, is the body which is directly responsible for the performance of the tasks delegated to it by Congress. It must act as a unit upon the numerous matters which come within its jurisdiction. For example, in formal cases involving violations of the law, the Commissioners hear the final arguments, deliberate upon the evidence and argument before them, and render their decisions. There is no permanent chairman of the tribunal. The chairmanship rotates, each Commissioner serving in that capacity for at least one year during his term of seven years. It is the function of the chairman to preside at the meetings of the Commission, to supervise its activities, and to sign the more important official reports at the direction of the Commission. The permanent executive officer of the Commission is the Secretary.

It is obvious that the Commissioners could not alone carry the administrative burden which has been imposed upon the Commission. Congress has provided appropriations for building a staff of substantial proportions. During the fiscal year ending June 30, 1948, the Commission expended $2,954,498.[1] On June 30, 1948, the staff numbered 600 officials and employees. It included attorneys, economists, accountants, and administrative personnel engaged in Washington and in the five branch offices.[2] The Commissioners direct the work of this staff, each Commissioner being in charge of a segment of the whole task.

Although it has a staff organization of ten operating bureaus or units, the work of the Commission is organized under three general categories: administrative, economic, and legal. This organization conforms closely to the division of functions set forth in the statute, namely, investigation and regulation. The advisory function can be performed by both the economic and legal bureaus, depending upon the nature of the information and advice sought. But here, as in other matters, the formal separation into bureaus does not preclude coöperation among them in performing specific tasks.

The administrative management of the Commission is the responsibility of the secretary, who heads the executive office. The bureau of administration provides administrative services to the operating bureaus and comprises such units as budget and planning, personnel, legal and economic records, legal research, services and supplies, and library.

The bureau of industrial economics conducts the general investigations of the Commission that are primarily of an economic nature. It is under the direction of the Chief Economist, and has an expert staff of economists, analytical accountants, and statisticians. General inquiries, undertaken by the direction of the President or Congress or upon the initiative of the Commission, are to be distinguished from the investigations of specific acts or practices of particular concerns over which the Commission has regulatory authority. They are usually undertaken to determine remedies for faulty conditions that may develop in a particular industry and for the purpose of reporting on general economic conditions that may be of aid in developing an anti-monopoly program. The method of inquiry is less formal than in regulatory proceedings, and the investigation is often carried on in coöperation with the industry. Since the Commission was organized in 1915, it has made more than one

---

[1] *Annual Report,* 1948, p. 78. The following table gives the expenditures and personnel for every third year since the Commission became a working organization:

Year	Expenditures	Personnel	Year	Expenditures	Personnel
1915	$ 99,946		1933	$1,398,973	427
1918	1,423,394		1936	1,821,726	571
1921	880,174		1939	2,197,174	687
1924	979,440		1942	2,338,921	684
1927	960,882		1945	1,997,547	451
1930	1,465,448	450	1948	2,954,498	600

[2] *Ibid.,* p. 9. Branch offices are maintained in New York, Chicago, San Francisco, Seattle, and New Orleans. They are staffed chiefly by attorneys who investigate cases that originate in the vicinity of these offices.

hundred important investigations and reports.[3] Some of these, such as the investigations of the meat-packing industry, American export trade, electric and gas utilities, and chain stores, were significant factors in the enactment of legislation by Congress. Not all of the general investigations have been carried on exclusively by the economic division. Some of them have been conducted in coöperation with the legal division, an example being the very comprehensive inquiry into the electric and gas utility industry which resulted in the publication of ninety-five volumes of data, testimony, summaries, and recommendations.

As a part of its routine the economics division provides assistance in the handling of legal cases and evaluates pricing policies and distribution practices as they relate to the legal issues of monopoly controls. Since 1947, in coöperation with the Securities and Exchange Commission, it has gathered data and published quarterly reports relating to the financial characteristics and operating results of manufacturing companies. When the preparation of annual reports can be undertaken, it is hoped that they will provide data for the construction of an "index of concentration" for each of the major manufacturing industries.[4]

The legal division is charged with the regulatory work of the Commission. It investigates the unfair methods of competition which are condemned in the statutes, and conducts the trial of cases before the Commission and the courts. From the point of view of expenditures and personnel it is by far the largest and most important of the Commission's divisions. It in turn is made up of a number of separate agencies, which are called bureaus. These are as follows: the office of the general counsel, the bureau of litigation, the bureau of legal investigation, the bureau of stipulations, the bureau of trade practice conferences and Wool Act administration, and the bureau of trial examiners. The general legal staff is subdivided in this fashion both for convenience in procedure and for fairness to the parties who are proceeded against by the Commission. Since the Commission is both a prosecuting and a judicial agency, some separation of function must be maintained in the stages of the procedure prior to final decision by the Commission. Each of the bureaus named above is independent and responsible only to the Commission. Contact with the whole Commission is maintained through the individual Commissioners who have supervisory charge of one or more of the bureaus.

The functions of these legal units will be made clear in the discussion of the regulatory procedure. It may be pointed out, however, that the general counsel acts as legal adviser to the Commission, has charge of all proceedings in the courts, and prepares applications for the cancellation of registered trade-marks that violate the Lanham Trade-Mark Act

---

[3] For descriptions of the general inquiries conducted by the Commission, including titles of published reports, see *Annual Report,* 1948, pp. 118–136.

[4] *Annual Report,* 1948, pp. 27–28.

of 1946. The bureau of legal investigation, through its division of field investigation and division of radio and periodical advertising, is responsible for investigations preliminary to the issuance of formal complaints and industry-wide investigations when simultaneous action against all members of an industry is undertaken. The bureau of litigation performs the task of prosecuting complaints before the Commission. Attorneys who do this work have the same status as those who represent the defendants and must confine their efforts to influence the final decision in a particular case to public proceedings. Members of the bureau of trial examiners, as the name suggests, preside at the trial of formal complaints. They rule on the admissibility of evidence and conduct hearings in accordance with the Administrative Procedure Act of 1946. After the record is closed in a case, they make a recommended decision. The bureau of stipulations handles the negotiation of voluntary agreements of parties to cease unlawful practices, while the bureau of trade practice conferences deals with the formulation and administration of rules of fair competition for various industry groups and administers the Wool Products Labeling Act.

THE COMMISSION'S PROCEDURE IN REGULATING COMPETITION

The regular procedure of the Commission is based upon the provisions of the Federal Trade Commission Act. Its essential features are preliminary inquiry, issuance of a complaint, hearing, oral argument, and issuance of a cease and desist order. The cease and desist order may then be enforced with the aid of the courts. But, in addition to this regular administrative procedure, the Commission has developed two other methods which are less formal in character. These have been instituted under the general authority conferred upon the Commission "to make rules and regulations for the purpose of carrying out the provisions of this Act."[5] The informal procedures, which will be explained below, are the "trade practice conference" and "stipulation." They are strictly supplementary to the regular administrative procedure, however, since no regulation or policy embodied in trade practice rules or stipulations can be enforced in the courts. It is only through the regular procedure of complaint, hearing, and cease and desist order, that a ruling of the Commission can be placed before the courts and enforcement obtained. The methods of the Commission will be considered in the following order: regular administrative procedure, stipulation, and trade practice conference.

---

[5] Section 6 (g).

Regular Administrative Procedure

A case before the Commission may originate in one of several ways. The most common origin is through a complaint on the part of a competitor, a consumer, or from some other public source. Such an application may be made without formality, but it must contain a brief statement of the facts and must be signed by the complainant. Another way in which a case may start is upon the Commission's own motion. In the field of false and misleading advertising, many of the cases arise as a result of the work of the radio and periodical advertising division. This division surveys and scrutinizes the advertising matter published in newspapers and magazines and broadcast over the radio or by television.[6] If an advertisement appears on its face to be misleading, an inquiry is undertaken by this specialized division.

The formal procedure of the Commission does not start until a complaint has been issued. Before this takes place, much work of an informal nature must be done. In the first step, after an apparent violation of the law has come to its attention, the Commission considers the matter of its jurisdiction. There are three elements which must be satisfied. First, the practice complained of must be carried on in interstate commerce. Second, it must be prohibited by some provision in the statutes administered by the Commission. For instance, to proceed under the general prohibition of unfair methods in Section 5 of the Federal Trade Commission Act, it must be apparent that the practice is actually unfair.[7] Third, if the proceeding is under Section 5, it must be found that the prosecution of a complaint "would be to the interest of the public." This requires that the abuse be of sufficient importance in the competitive system to warrant the attention of a public agency. If it is purely a private controversy which can be settled by private litigation in the courts, there is little need for the intervention of the Commission.

When the Commission, through its bureau of legal investigation, has determined that it has jurisdiction, the matter is docketed for investiga-

---

[6] During the fiscal year ended June 30, 1948, the Commission reported that it examined 308,544 advertisements appearing in newspapers, magazines, and farm and trade journals; 12,903 pages of mail-order catalogs, and 643,604 commercial radio broadcast continuities. Of these, 11,119 advertisements in newspapers and magazines, 325 advertisements in mail-order catalogs, and 8,819 advertising broadcast statements were marked as containing representations which might be false or misleading. Of the 332 new investigations initiated during the year relative to false and misleading advertising, 140 originated through the Commission's continuing survey of advertising. Early in 1948 the Commission initiated coverage of television advertising. (*Annual Report,* 1948, pp. 37–40.)

[7] Before the amendment of Section 5, by the Wheeler-Lea Act of March 21, 1938, it was also necessary to show the presence of competition, inasmuch as "unfair methods of competition" were proscribed. Since the statute now reads "unfair methods of competition . . . and unfair or deceptive acts or practices," the showing of competition is not essential for jurisdiction.

tion. If it does not concern advertising, a preliminary investigation is then undertaken by the field investigation division of the bureau of legal investigation. The chief of the division assigns the investigation to an attorney or a branch office. Without disclosing the identity of the complainant, the attorney interviews the party complained against, advises him of the charges and requests evidence in defense or in explanation of the practice. The attorney may also find it desirable to interview consumers or competitors of the respondent in order to ascertain the competitive effect of the practice and the interest of the public in the proceeding. All facts pertaining to the matter are obtained. The attorney then summarizes the evidence, reviews the law in the case, and recommends what action should be taken.

In advertising cases the procedure of the radio and periodical advertising division is more specialized. A questionnaire is mailed to the suspected party. This requests him to furnish both a sample or quantitative formula of the advertised product, and the advertising material used. These are then referred to the Commission's bureau of medical opinions or through it to an appropriate technical agency of the government for a scientific opinion.[8] The advertising is carefully scrutinized in the light of the scientific opinion, and any portions which appear to require substantiation or explanation are noted. Questionable advertising statements and the scientific opinion are brought to the attention of the advertiser, and he is given the privilege of submitting evidence to substantiate or explain his representations. This may be done by correspondence or by personal conference. Further action in a case depends on the ability of the advertiser to substantiate his claims to the satisfaction of the division.

Before a case goes to the Commission, it is reviewed by the top officials in the bureau of legal investigation. They may recommend one of three things: (1) that the case be closed for lack of evidence or for the reason that the practice is not unlawful; (2) that the case be closed upon the signing by the respondent of a stipulation of the facts and an agreement to cease and desist from the objectionable practice, or (3) that a formal complaint be issued. The recommendation and all the facts in the case are then considered by the Commissioners. If they decide that a complaint should be issued, the matter is turned over to the bureau of litigation, which prepares the formal complaint and handles the trial of the case. If they decide to permit the respondent to sign an agreed statement of the facts and to promise voluntarily to cease the

---

[8] The government agencies to which the Commission may refer a matter for scientific opinion are the Bureau of Standards, the Public Health Service, the Food and Drug Administration, the Bureau of Home Economics, and the Bureau of Animal Husbandry of the Department of Agriculture. The Bureau of Standards has tested and rendered opinions about a long list of commodities, including artificial teeth and limbs, batteries, caskets, golf-balls, coal, razors, and watches.

practice, the bureau of stipulations is called upon to negotiate the stipulation.

The formal procedure begins with the issuance of the complaint. All proceedings up to this point have been informal and strictly confidential. But publicity is given to the contents of the complaint, and the whole formal proceeding is a public record. The complaint, it should be noted, is issued in the name of the Commission. This is done on the ground that the Commission is a public agency having a mandate to protect the public from obnoxious competitive methods. Since it was not created to settle controversies between parties, the original complainant is not a party to the case. His identity is never disclosed. If it were, many individuals would refrain from making complaints for fear of retaliation by the respondent. The practice may encourage ill-founded charges against competitors for the purpose of harassing them, but, on the whole, is a desirable one.

After the complaint has been served upon the respondent, he may, within twenty days, file an answer denying or admitting the allegations of fact. If no answer is filed, the Commission is at liberty to make its findings and issue an order. In the event of a denial, the statute provides for a hearing. This takes place before a trial examiner thirty days or more after the respondent has been served with the complaint. Both the Commission and the accused are represented by counsel, and each presents his oral and documentary evidence for the formal record upon which the case is decided. The hearing is not unlike a court trial, although the technical rules of evidence are not adhered to rigidly. When the taking of testimony has been concluded, the trial examiner prepares a recommended decision supported by findings of fact and conclusions of law to which either side may file exceptions. Briefs are then filed and the case comes up for oral argument before the full Commission. The final argument is the only opportunity afforded counsel for the Commission and the respondent to present their contentions directly to those who make the decision. It is a valuable part of the procedure.

The Commission may reach a decision either sustaining the complaint or dismissing it because of insufficient proof, an intervening court decision, or some other reason. If the charges are sustained, the Commission makes its findings of fact, states its conclusion that the law has been violated, and issues an order requiring the respondent to cease and desist from the unlawful practice. Within sixty days of being served with the order, the respondent is required to make a written report stating the manner in which he has complied.

If respondents fail to obey orders to cease and desist, the powers of the courts must be invoked to obtain compliance. Under the terms of the original legislation of 1914, the Commission was required to apply to a circuit court of appeals for review and enforcement. In order to obtain a decree of enforcement, it was necessary for the Commission to prove not only that its order was valid, but that it had actually been violated.[9] Punishment could be inflicted for a violation of the law only if it were shown at a later date that the offender was in contempt for violating the decree of the court. This enforcement procedure was unsatisfactory, for it was cumbersome and expensive. It impaired the effectiveness of the Commission's remedial action and its prestige as an administrative body.

A very important change in the enforcement procedure for orders issued under the Federal Trade Commission Act was made in the amendments embodied in the Wheeler-Lea Act of 1938.[10] Congress, for no apparent reason, failed to amend the corresponding provisions of the Clayton Act, so the old method must be used with respect to the enforcement of Clayton Act orders.[11] The Trade Commission Act, amended in accordance with the repeated recommendations of the Commission,[12] provides that an order shall become final sixty days after issuance, unless a petition is filed by the respondent in a Circuit Court of Appeals praying that the order be set aside.[13] If a petition for a court review is filed, the date when the order becomes binding is extended and depends, of course, upon the extent of the subsequent court proceedings. To the extent that an order is affirmed, the court is required to issue its own order commanding obedience to its terms. Furthermore, any respondent who violates an order of the Commission after it has become final is subject to a civil penalty of not more than $5,000 for each violation.

The advantages of these modifications are clear. By making its orders final and conclusive, contingent upon appeal by the respondents, the Commission is relieved of the responsibility of having to initiate enforcement proceedings. The heavy civil penalties attaching to a violation of a final order will force companies either to obey the order or to bring court action to set it aside. It will still be necessary for the Commission to exercise vigilance as regards the continued observance of orders which have become final, either through failure to act within the prescribed time or through a court decree, but it is unlikely that formal action will have to be taken in many cases. This has been the experience of the Interstate Commerce Commission, whose orders have enjoyed a similar legal status since 1906. Not only will enforcement be much more effec-

---

[9] F. T. C. v. Standard Education Society, 14 Fed. (2nd) 947 (1926); F. T. C. v. Balme, 23 Fed. (2nd) 615 (1928).

[10] Public No. 447 (75th Congress), approved March 21, 1938.

[11] For the past several years the Commission has been recommending that Congress amend the Clayton Act so that orders thereunder will have the same status as to finality and penalties for violation as those under the Trade Commission Act. Annual Reports, 1946, p. 12; 1948, p. 12.

[12] See Annual Reports, 1935, p. 15; 1936, p. 17; 1937, p. 15.

[13] Section 5.

tual, but it will be accomplished more expeditiously and with less effort on the part of the Commission.

It should also be noted at this point that special provisions for the prevention of the dissemination of false advertisements relating to food, drugs, medical devices, and cosmetics were added to the law by the Wheeler-Lea Act.[14] Because of the vital connection between the false advertising of these products and the public health, injunction and criminal action are provided to supplement the regular formal procedure. The Commission, if it is in the public interest, may obtain an injunction in a Federal district court against the dissemination of a false advertisement, pending the outcome of regular proceedings. Hence, deceptive advertising which may have injurious consequences for the consuming public can be suppressed immediately. Furthermore, criminal penalties of fine and imprisonment may be assessed for the more serious violations. Criminal action can be brought where the use of the product deceptively advertised may be injurious to health or where the false advertisement is published with intent to defraud or mislead. Since the Commission does not have the power of a court to levy penalties, the facts relating to criminal violations are to be certified to the Attorney-General, and it is his duty to take appropriate action in the courts.

Stipulation

A stipulation, in the sense here used, is a signed statement of fact and an agreement to discontinue an unlawful business practice. It has already been noted that the Commission permits respondents to make such formal promises after the completion of the preliminary investigation. If the stipulation is satisfactory to the Commission, the case is closed.[15] No immediate penalty attaches to its violation. If such violation is discovered, a cease and desist order is issued forthwith, and enforced through the regular court procedure.

The stipulation procedure was inaugurated in March, 1925, when the Commission announced a change of administrative policy. Crowded dockets and the slow disposition of cases demanded some remedial action.[16] The stipulation device offered attractive possibilities. Unfair

[14] Sections 12 to 16, inclusive.

[15] Prior to February, 1934, the Commission published the facts agreed to by the respondent, but did not disclose the name of the party. This was not a desirable practice, for it tended to destroy the preventive function of the Commission. If a guilty party could escape without even having the public informed of his conduct, there was little incentive for him to conduct his enterprise in a manner beyond reproach. The Commission now follows the more acceptable practice of publishing the name of the respondent together with the summary of the facts.

Several authorities have criticized the Commission because of its inability to function expeditiously. See Henderson, *op. cit.*, pp. 87–91; National Industrial Conference Board, *Public Regulation of Competitive Practices*, p. 253.

methods could be prevented in this manner just as well as through the more elaborate formal procedure. Moreover, this could be done without the heavy expense and the considerable delay that the latter procedure entailed. It was also believed that the opportunity afforded unintentional offenders to avoid the expense and embarrassment of prosecution would supply an incentive to abandon their questionable practices.

Although the Commission does not permit stipulation in all cases, particularly in those involving fraud or parties whose word cannot be relied upon, its use has grown in importance. During the fiscal year ending June 30, 1948, for example, 263 applications for complaints were referred to the bureau of stipulations, as compared with 70 that resulted in the issuance of complaints.[17] It is true, of course, that many of the stipulations related to advertising cases, some of which involved issues of minor importance. Nevertheless, the expedient has a significant place in the Commission's operations, and has resulted in a notable improvement in efficiency.[18]

Trade Practice Conference

The trade practice conference is the second method devised by the Commission to meet the deficiencies of its regular administrative procedure. It began in 1919 under the title of trade practice submittals. Members of an industry were invited to attend a conference and to formulate a code of trade practice rules for the approval of the Commission. The object was to enlist the coöperation of industry groups in the task of eliminating trade abuses. It was more practicable to have an industry agree to abstain from competitive methods which were widespread and distasteful to all, than to proceed against each individual. When an industry group formulated rules applicable to its particular problems, the Commission hoped that individual members would report violations and thereby assist in the necessary policing to obtain general compliance. The method was conceived, therefore, both as an attempt at "self-regulation" of business and as a means of lightening the administrative burden of the Commission.

From 1919 to 1926, some 17 trade practice submittals were held. To meet the growing demand for these submittals, the Commission created in 1926 the Trade Practice Conference Division to handle this work. It arranges for the conferences, aids the industry in the formulation of rules, holds public hearings on proposed rules, and participates

---

[17] *Annual Report,* 1948, pp. 41, 54.

[18] It has been estimated by the Commission that the average cost of handling a case under the formal procedure is $2,500, while the cost of settling a case by stipulation is less than $500. *Annual Report,* 1928, p. 22.

in the administration and enforcement of the rules which the Commission has approved. Prior to the National Industrial Recovery Act some 143 conferences had been held, although codes of fair practices acceptable to the Commission did not result from all of them. During the period of the N. R. A., the regulation of unfair practices was taken over by N. R. A. codes. The conference procedure was revived after 1935 and, by 1948, about 160 industries were covered by trade practice rules. Since 1946, the Commission has undertaken to call trade practice conferences on its own motion rather than waiting for industries to take the initiative. This is part of a general program to eliminate unfair trade practices simultaneously throughout an industry by industry-wide investigations and coöperative means.[19]

The Commission divides the rules into two groups. Group I rules cover practices which have been condemned as "unfair methods" by the Commission or the courts. These rulings are enforced by the Commission. Group II rules embrace practices which the industry regards as unsound or unethical, but which are not unlawful. These rules are to be enforced by the industry. They cover a wide range of business conduct and reflect the peculiar problems that beset the industry. The Group I rules are no more than codifications of the Commission's decisions, phrased so as to be made applicable to the particular industry. This constitutes, perhaps, the chief virtue of the trade practice conference. It acquaints the members of an industry with the requirements of the law as regards business conduct and thus enables them better to observe it. So far as the enforcement of the law is concerned, it is doubtful whether the conference has contributed a great deal. It is too much to hope that the mere formulation of a conference agreement "leads to the wholesale elimination and abandonment of unfair and illegal methods of competition."[20] Perhaps the following conclusion is nearer the truth: "The trade practice conferences, at best, constituted an inexpert codification of the common law and Commission rulings on unfair competition, coupled with the vague aspirations of industry regarding the elimination of annoying and irritating trade practices. The gap between the written prohibition and enforced observance was never bridged."[21]

This discussion of organization and procedure shows that the Commission has been able to develop a mechanism fairly well adapted to the

---

[19] See *Annual Reports*, 1946, pp. 2–3; 1947, pp. 2–3; 1948, pp. 3–4. Commissioner Mason in his minority recommendations, has urged frequently that Congress give the trade practice conference procedure a more specific statutory foundation than that implied in the Trade Commission Act. He would enlist the coöperation of the Departments of Commerce and Justice in the promulgation and administration of conference rules. The objectives would be to effect a "reign of law in commerce" and greater coöperation between businessmen and government. See *Annual Reports*, 1947, p. 13: 1948, p. 14.

[20] *Annual Report*, 1938, p. 107.

[21] Handler, *op. cit.*, p. 255.

performance of its basic functions. It has evolved through a trial-and-error process. The present separation into administrative, economic, and legal divisions is both logical and practicable. Advantages of specialization are obtained, yet coöperation is had wherever it can be of value to the whole organization. The legal division, divided into separate bureaus, seems to have succeeded in creating a structure which separates the prosecuting and judicial functions. It is extremely important that those who perform the judicial function maintain an attitude of strict impartiality. Yet this is difficult to achieve in an organization where personal friendships are bound to arise and where a feeling of group loyalty prevails. Impartiality is encouraged by the present organization of the legal division, but how far it is achieved in practice is difficult to ascertain.

The regular administrative procedure of preliminary investigation, complaint, hearing, oral argument, and deliberation by the Commission appears to fulfill every requirement of due process. A party is afforded ample opportunity to state his defense and to have the case considered on its merits. But the procedure is not adapted to obtaining a quick decision and a prompt remedy. It is cumbersome and inefficient. Its limitations have been overcome in some measure by the supplementary methods of stipulation and trade practice conference. The former has made a real contribution to the effectiveness of the Commission's work. What the trade practice conference has contributed is more difficult to estimate. In either case the regular machinery of the Commission has to be depended upon for enforcement.

21

Interpretation and Administration of the 1914 Legislation

In considering the administrative regulation of business methods under the 1914 legislation, it will be desirable to divide the field according to the nature of the practices dealt with by the Federal Trade Commission. They may be conveniently classified into two groups: first, those which are essentially unethical because they involve an element of fraud or dishonesty; secondly, those practices which are condemned not because they are dishonest, but solely because they have a tendency to suppress competition or to create a monopoly. This classification conforms to the dual purpose that Congress had in mind in creating the legislation of 1914, and was the classification recognized implicitly by the Supreme Court in the first important case relating to the jurisdiction of the Federal Trade Commission.[1] It was the intent of Congress that the Commission should endeavor both to maintain a proper ethical plane of competitive behavior and to preserve competition by eliminating monopolistic elements. The practices which fall in the first category are attacked exclusively under Section 5 of the Federal Trade Commission Act, which prohibits all "unfair methods of competition" in interstate commerce. Cases which fall in the second category arise under either this section or the various sections of the Clayton Act relating to monopolistic combinations or practices. In the following discussion, consideration will first be given to the policy of maintaining competition.

---

[1] Federal Trade Commission v. Gratz, 253 U. S. 421, 427 (1920). Note the following from the majority opinion of Justice McReynolds: "The words 'unfair methods of competition' are not defined by the statute and their exact meaning is in dispute. . . . They are clearly inapplicable to practices never heretofore regarded as opposed to good morals because characterized by deception, bad faith, fraud or oppression, or as against public policy because of their dangerous tendency unduly to hinder competition or create monopoly."

THE POLICY OF MAINTAINING COMPETITION

In its attempt to maintain competitive conditions, the Federal Trade Commission has attacked a variety of forms and practices which are conducive to monopoly. These range from simple agreements between competitors for uniform prices to practices which are directed at competitors in order to retard their growth or eliminate them completely. They will be discussed under the following heads: (1) Corporate combinations; (2) agreements and understandings between competitors; (3) re-sale price maintenance; (4) price discrimination; (5) tying and exclusive dealing arrangements. The first two involve combination or collusion between two or more firms for the purpose of fixing prices, maintaining the existing channels of trade, or eliminating practices which are regarded by the participants as detrimental to their best interests. The third, re-sale price maintenance, is undertaken by a single firm selling a differentiated product, but it tends to be monopolistic in that it eliminates price competition between distributors who are bound by the re-sale arrangements. Price discrimination and tying and exclusive dealing arrangements are also practices engaged in by single firms, albeit large and quasi-monopolistic enterprises, which are directed at competitors in the effort to extend their control over the market.

(1) Corporate Combinations

The provisions of Sections 7 and 8 of the Clayton Act, making intercorporate stockholding and interlocking directorates unlawful in certain circumstances, are directed at the combination and coöperative action of competing corporations. It was the intent of Congress to supplement the more general provisions of the Sherman Act by outlawing particular methods which were being employed to concentrate economic power and destroy competition. But the record of the Federal Trade Commission as regards the administration of these provisions shows clearly that they have been quite ineffectual in achieving their purpose.

The prohibition of interlocking directorates where any one of the corporations exceeds a certain capitalization, and where competition would be eliminated, has been of no practical significance whatever. The Commission has issued several complaints charging violation of Section 8, only to dismiss them finally. Hence the courts have had no opportunity to construe the provision. The most favorable judicial construction, however, would not make the section a potent factor in removing collusion between competing firms; it could in no way disturb the ownership by a single person of the voting stocks of two competing corporations. A person may be disqualified from acting as a director in both corporations, but as long as he has the votes he can elect a trusted representative and act through him to harmonize the policies of the nominally independent and competing companies. The requirements of the statute can be avoided with little difficulty, therefore, and the desired result attained through the employment of dummy directors.

Section 7 forbids the acquisition of the whole or any part of the stock of one corporation by another, or the acquisition of the stock of two or more corporations by a holding company, where the effect may be to lessen competition substantially between the corporations involved, to restrain commerce in any community, or tend to create a monopoly. Two important questions have been considered by the courts in the interpretation of this provision, and in each instance the construction placed upon the terms of the law has worked against its effectiveness. The first relates to the power of the Commission to force a company to give up assets purchased through the voting of stock illegally acquired in competing corporations. The second relates to the necessary amount of preëxisting competition between the combining firms before there can be a substantial lessening of competition.

The first problem arises from the defective draftsmanship of the law, for the prohibition relates only to the acquisition of stock and does not apply to physical assets. It has been possible for companies to evade the law with impunity by using their stock control to effect a purchase of the assets of other firms. The first order of the Commission under Section 7, for example, was made in 1921 and was directed against the Aluminum Company of America.[2] It was upheld in the courts,[3] but "the practical effect of the judgment was destroyed"[4] by a subsequent court ruling which permitted the Aluminum Company to buy at a sheriff's sale the properties of the company whose stock had been acquired.[5] Orders were also issued against the Western Meat Company, Swift and Company, and Thatcher Manufacturing Company, requiring them to restore the competitive conditions existing prior to the illegal acquisition of stock in rival companies. The latter two companies, before the date of the issuance of formal complaints by the Commission, had dissolved the competing corporations of which they had acquired control, and obtained possession of their physical assets. The Western Meat Company had not done so prior to the institution of formal proceedings, but admitted its intention and urged its lawful right so to do. In deciding all three

---

[2] 3 F. T. C. 302 (1921).

[3] 284 Fed. 401 (1922); sustained 261 U. S. 616 (1923).

[4] F. T. C., *Annual Report*, 1927, p. 13.

[5] F. T. C. *v.* Aluminum Company of America, 299 Fed. 261 (1924). It was charged by the Commission that the alleged debt to the Aluminum Company which forced the sheriff's sale was entirely fictitious. The final result was that the Aluminum Company of America obtained possession of the physical properties of the only important competitor in the manufacture of sheet aluminum in the United States.

cases in a consolidated proceeding,[6] the Supreme Court fastened on this point of distinction. It was held that when the stock of a competitor was still held by the respondent when proceedings were formally instituted, as in the Western Meat case, the order requiring the divestiture of the illegally-held stock could include a prohibition against the use of the stock to effect a transfer of the assets from the acquired company to the respondent.[7] But at the same time the Court held that the Commission had no authority to compel the divestiture of property actually obtained prior to the issuance of the complaint. "The act," it was stated, "has no application to ownership of a competitor's property and business obtained prior to any action by the Commission, even though this was brought about through stock unlawfully held."[8] This was the ruling of the majority of the Court. It ignored the language of Section 11 of the statute, which, as emphasized in the dissenting opinion of Mr. Justice Brandeis and three of his associates, gives the Commission the power to act when it has "reason to believe any person is violating *or has violated*" any of the provisions of the law.[9]

In its most recent case the Supreme Court[10] appears to have gone even further in destroying the authority of the Commission to restore the competition suppressed by the acquisition of stock. A holding company was created and exchanged its stock for the common stock of two competing companies engaged in the manufacture of electric wiring devices. Upon the issuance of a complaint by the Commission, but before an order had been issued, the holding company assigned its acquired stocks to two newly-created holding companies, and by corporate action it was then dissolved. The stockholders of the two new holding companies then joined with the preferred stockholders of the subsidiary manufacturing companies in approving a merger agreement whereby a new corporation was formed which took over in its own right all of the assets formerly belonging to the manufacturing companies. Thus, through a cleverly conceived scheme of erecting corporate dummies and transferring stocks and physical assets, the interested persons effected a merger of competing enterprises in a new corporation having more com-

---

[6] F. T. C. *v.* Western Meat Co., Thatcher Mfg., Co. *v.* F. T. C., Swift & Co. *v.* F. T. C., 272 U. S. 554 (1926).

[7] For subsequent proceedings in the Western Meat case, see Western Meat Co. *v.* F. T. C., 33 Fed. (2nd) 824 (1929), and F. T. C., *Annual Report*, 1930, pp. 89–91. The meat company bought the physical assets of the acquired corporation at a sale to satisfy a judgment taken by default for an alleged debt owed the meat company, a transaction similar to and probably inspired by the successful one undertaken by the Aluminum Company, but later disposed of them when the Commission brought the case to the Supreme Court a second time.

[8] 272 U. S. 554, 561.

[9] 272 U. S. 554, 564. Italics in the opinion.

[10] Arrow-Hart & Hegeman Electric Co. *v.* F. T. C., 291 U. S. 587 (1934).

plete control than the original offender in the case. This evasion of the Commission's authority was upheld by the Supreme Court in a five to four decision, on the grounds that the merged corporation was not in existence when the Commission initiated its action against the dissolved holding company, had never held any stock contrary to the terms of the statute, and could not be compelled to divest itself of physical assets. In other words, if the offenders can perpetrate their adroit manipulations with sufficient celerity they can escape. If the Commission is to accomplish anything under the present statute it must act with like speed, a factor which may encourage hasty and ill-considered action, and which should play little part in proceedings where both the letter and the spirit of the law have been clearly violated.

The second problem mentioned above, it will be recalled, involved the question of what constitutes a substantial lessening of competition. The statute does not require "substantial competition" between the companies involved as a necessary condition. It is conceivable, therefore, that the law could be given a literal interpretation and the elimination of even an "unsubstantial competition" held to be a substantial lessening of competition. This point was squarely presented in the proceeding against the International Shoe Company.[11] The respondent company had purchased the stock and later the assets of the McElwain Company, a shoe manufacturer that was threatened with financial failure as a result of the trade depression of 1921. In vacating the order of the Commission, the Supreme Court held that there had been no substantial competition between the two companies prior to their merger, and hence there could be no "substantial lessening of competition" within the terms of the statute. The majority of the Court found that the shoes produced by each company were in the main of different grades and were sold in separate markets, there being no competition in respect of 95 per cent of the business. In the opinion of Justices Stone, Holmes, and Brandeis, however, the Commission's finding of substantial competition was supported by the testimony in the record. There was ample evidence to show that the rival products appealed to the same buying public and so were competitive.

The decision places some curb on the authority of the Commission and makes for considerable uncertainty with respect to the application of the statute. There can be little criticism of the general rule laid down by the Court, since if competition is in truth slight between two firms there can be no great injury to the competitive economy in their combination. But as this case well illustrates, there may be a wide variance of opinion as to what facts prove the existence of competition and a

---

[11] International Shoe Co. v. F. T. C., 280 U. S. 291 (1930).

substantial amount of it. This is particularly true when there are numerous classes, grades, and styles of commodities which are capable of satisfying the same want. It is fortunate that in the great majority of combinations substantial competition between the merged units is obvious.[12] That being the case, the Court's decision cannot operate as a drastic curb upon the Commission's power.

In view of the adverse court decisions rendered under Section 7, it is to be expected that changes in the law would have been recommended to Congress. The Federal Trade Commission and the Temporary National Economic Committee have made such recommendations. The most important suggestion, first made by the Commission in December, 1934, is that Section 7 be amended to prohibit the acquisition or consolidation of physical assets in the same circumstances as those in which stock acquisitions and consolidations are prohibited.[13] This would include both the indirect acquisition of assets through the use of stock unlawfully acquired, and the direct acquisition of physical properties. Since the merging of physical assets appears to be the method of consolidation most frequently employed at the present time, some such amendment is essential if the section is to accomplish the general purpose of preventing the growth of monopoly. Between 1929 and 1935 preliminary investigations of 547 mergers by the Commission revealed that 54 per cent of them involved the merging of assets. The proportion increased from year to year during this period, and the trend has continued since 1935 to the point where nearly all combinations are now effected by the merging of assets.[14]

Two recommendations of somewhat lesser importance should be noted.[15] The first is that the law should be amended to forbid the acquisition of the stock of *one* or more corporations by a holding company, instead of *two* or more as in the present law. This would cover the situation where a holding company acquires control of a firm which is a competitor of one of its subsidiaries, a combination which would be just as destructive of competition as the control of two competing companies. The second recommendation would amend the law to allow a company that is bankrupt or on the verge of bankruptcy to sell its assets to a competitor, since this may be the only available market. It would not be permitted, however, where the financial difficulties were brought about by collusion with the competing company for the purpose of evading the law.

---

[12] National Industrial Conference Board, *Public Regulation of Competitive Practices*, p. 223.

[13] F. T. C., *Annual Report*, 1935, p. 48.

[14] F. T. C., *Annual Report*, 1948, pp. 16–22.

[15] *Ibid.*, pp. 15–16. The Commission here reprints excerpts relating to the amendment of Section 7 from a preliminary report of the Temporary National Economic Committee to the United States Senate.

Finally, as a result of its investigation of the agricultural implement and machinery industry the Commission made an interesting recommendation in 1938.[16] It was found that prior to the enactment of the Clayton Act most of the high degree of concentration in the farm machinery industry was created by the acquisition of either the capital stock or assets of competing companies. Since then it has come from the acquisition of the actual assets of competitors rather than their capital stock. The Commission recommended that the acquisition of the stock or assets of a competing corporation be prohibited where the aggregate output of the corporations involved was 10 per cent or more of the total output of any industry or branch thereof in the United States, or of the sale of the product as to which the corporations are in competition. If less than 10 per cent of the output were controlled the prohibition would apply only on definite evidence of a restraint of competition or monopoly.

This amendment, it was pointed out by the Commission, would have the advantage of establishing a positive legislative standard.[17] It would define the limit of corporate size and power which could be achieved by acquisitions of other firms, and would prevent the development of conditions which are conducive to monopoly and monopolistic competition. So far as the whole problem of concentration of economic power is concerned, however, the value of such a restriction on corporate size would be distinctly limited, because it is applicable to only one method of growth. Berle and Means estimated that 81.5 per cent of the growth in the assets of the two hundred largest corporations in the six-year period from 1922 to 1927, inclusive, resulted from new capital obtained from the sale of securities and the reinvestment of earnings.[18] The remaining 18.5 per cent of the growth of these companies was attributed to additions through consolidation or merger. But even though this manner of growth is the least significant statistically, it is of peculiar importance because it directly reduces the number of competing firms in the market, and hence destroys an essential condition for pure competition. It may, nevertheless, be a mistake to fix an exact percentage of corporate control applicable to all industries. Whether or not a 10 per cent control would endanger competition depends upon the specific circumstances. The characteristics of industries vary widely, and any attempt to apply a blanket rule would likely make for the inclusion of combinations which are not serious threats to competition and which might contribute materially to productive efficiency. It was this consideration, apparently, that led the Commission to omit this specific recommenda-

[16] *Report on the Agricultural Implement and Machinery Industry*, House Document No. 702, 75th Congress, 3rd Session, p. 1038.
[17] F. T. C., *Annual Report*, 1938, p. 19.
[18] Berle and Means, *op. cit.*, p. 43.

tion from a subsequent discussion of suggested amendments of Section 7.[19] The Commission said:

The permissible percentage of corporate control over an industry should be elastic. A given percentage in one industry might be wholly harmless to the public interest, while the same or even a smaller percentage in another industry might be gravely prejudicial. The minimum percentage necessary to effective corporate control of an industry is quite analogous to the minimum percentage of stock ownership necessary to control a corporation. In both cases it varies widely according to circumstances.[20]

The most pressing need is that Section 7 be amended to include the acquisition of assets. Effective action can then be taken to prevent combinations which are really a menace to free competition.

(2) Agreements or Understandings Between Competitors

The Federal Trade Commission has also attacked loose combinations effected by agreements or tacit understandings between firms which are ostensibly independent and competitive. Such conspiracies to restrain trade are unlawful under both the common law and the Sherman Act, whether they obstruct the business operations of outside producers or stifle competition through price-fixing or the allotment of market territories. While the Commission has been delegated no specific power, it has assumed jurisdiction over such cases by viewing them as unfair methods of competition.[21] Strictly speaking, however, a combination of traders to fix prices, for example, is not a method of competition. The offense in such a case is not in the manner in which the traders compete, but rather in their failure or refusal to compete. To the extent that advertising or some other form of non-price competition still exists it might be said that the method of competition has been changed, but the fact remains that the most important phase of the competitive process is held in abeyance when prices are fixed by agreement. The principle of law embodied in the Sherman Act is being enforced by the Commission under a statute which is not an anti-trust law, but it is being done with the apparent assent of Congress and with the definite approval of the Supreme Court.

The Commission has been upheld by the courts in all cases in which its orders relating to restraints of trade have been challenged. The leading case, which involved the Pacific States Paper Trade Association,[22] falls within the group of cases where orders were directed pri-

---

[19] F. T. C., *Annual Report*, 1939, pp. 14–16. See also *Annual Report*, 1948, pp. 11–12.

[20] *Annual Report*, 1939, p. 16.

[21] See, for example, Association of Flag Manufacturers, 1 F. T. C. 55 (1918); and Botsford Lumber Co. *et al.*, 1 F. T. C. 60 (1918).

[22] F. T. C. *v.* Pacific States Paper Trade Assn., 273 U. S. 52 (1927).

marily against price-fixing.[23] Wholesale dealers, doing 75 per cent of the business in paper and paper products exclusive of roll newspaper, were members of local and general trade associations. Uniform prices were fixed and diligently enforced by the local associations as regards intrastate sales. The same price-lists were habitually used by salesmen in making sales beyond the states in which the dealers were located and in making local sales which were filled by direct shipments from outside mills. There appeared to be no evidence of an outright price agreement with respect to interstate trade. The Commission had inferred, however, that the use of the established price-lists lessened competition and fixed prices in interstate commerce. In this conclusion, the Supreme Court agreed. It stated: "An understanding, express or tacit, that the agreed prices will be followed is enough to constitute a transgression of the law. No provision to compel adherence is necessary. It would appear difficult for these jobbers to maintain a uniform price-list in the State while making sales across the line at different and competing prices."[24] The issue of whether or not the Commission had the delegated authority to suppress such a restraint upon interstate commerce was not considered by the Court. It appears to be settled definitely, therefore, that the Commission has jurisdiction over collusive agreements, express or tacit, in restraint of trade.

A second group of cases involves concerted action on the part of distributors to maintain the "regular" or "legitimate" channels of trade. Numerous orders against conspiracies to prevent the development of newer methods of distributing products have been issued by the Commission and in many cases have been subjected to court review. They have been upheld by the courts without exception.[25] A typical case is that relating to the efforts of the Arkansas Wholesale Grocers' Association to maintain the old-line channel of trade in the grocery business.[26] The Association, which included two-thirds of the wholesale grocers in Arkansas, threatened to boycott, and its members did withdraw patronage from manufacturers that sold directly to chain stores, coöperatives,

---

[23] Some of the cases involving conspiracies of this type are: Association of Flag Manufacturers, 1 F. T. C. 55 (1918); Music Publishers Association, 5 F. T. C. 465 (1923); Washington Cereal Association, Oregon Cereal & Feed Assn., 11 F. T. C. 396 (1927); Mercerizers Assn. of America, 15 F. T. C. 1 (1931); Viscose Company et al., 25 F. T. C. 421 (1937). Orders directed at these price-fixing combinations are rarely appealed to the courts, for it is settled that they are unconditionally illegal.

[24] 273 U. S. 52, 62. It is noteworthy that ten years after the Commission's order was upheld, the respondents were proved by the Commission to be violating the court decree and fined $10,000 for contempt of court. 88 Fed. (2nd) 1009 (1937).

[25] See, for example, National Harness Mfrs. Assn. v. F. T. C., 268 Fed. 705 (1920); Western Sugar Refinery Co. v. F. T. C., 275 Fed. 725 (1921); Southern Hardware Jobbers Assn. v. F. T. C., 290 Fed. 773 (1923); F. T. C. v. Wallace, 75 Fed. (2nd) 733 (1935).

[26] Arkansas Wholesale Grocers Assn. v. F. T. C., 18 Fed. 866 (1927).

or retailers and allowed them prices lower than those they could get from "legitimate" wholesale grocers. It was the Commission's judgment, affirmed later by the court, that this was a conspiracy which threatened to exclude competitors from the market and was therefore an unlawful restraint. The outlawing of such tactics has a firm economic basis, for to allow established distributors to interfere with the development of more efficient methods of marketing can only impair economic progress and welfare.

Finally, the Commission has condemned collective action directed at the attainment of such diverse objectives as the open shop,[27] a guarantee against price decline,[28] the elimination of the business of collecting and selling back-number magazines in competition with current issues,[29] and the prevention of style piracy.[30] Attempts to eliminate style piracy are worthy of further consideration. Original designs and styles, usually created by the manufacturers of high-priced products, are often copied by other producers as soon as they appear in public and are sold at prices below those charged by the originators. The practice appears to be general and particularly annoying in the clothing industry. It may be important, however, in any field where style changes are frequent and of great commercial value. In order to combat the practice, a substantial number of manufacturers of women's high-priced hats and dresses organized guilds in their respective industries. The members registered their so-called original designs and styles with the guilds and agreed among themselves not to sell any hats or dresses to retailers who purchased goods which the guilds found to embody copies of their designs. Means were employed which forced a large number of retailers throughout the nation to coöperate with the guilds.

The Commission issued cease and desist orders against the "unfair methods of competition" of the guilds and their members, and these were unanimously upheld by the Supreme Court. The reasons for finding their conduct unlawful were carefully stated by Justice Black in the Fashion Originators' Guild case.[31] Defendants admitted that their "original creations" could not be patented or copyrighted and that there was no legislation preventing the copying of these designs. They urged, however, that the sale of copied designs was economically bad, an unfair practice, and a tortious invasion of rights, all of which justified combined action to destroy such competition. But the Court refused to find any justification for a combination which ran counter to the public policies laid down in both the Clayton and Sherman Acts. Since members of the

---

[27] Cigar Manufacturers Assn. of Tampa, Florida, 5 F. T. C. 1 (1922).

[28] St. Louis Wholesale Grocers Assn., 7 F. T. C. Decisions 1 (1923).

[29] Butterick Publishing Co. v. F. T. C., 85 Fed. (2nd) 522 (1936).

[30] Fashion Originators' Guild v. F. T. C., 312 U. S. 457 (1941); Millinery Creator's Guild v. F. T. C., 312 U. S. 469 (1941).

[31] 312 U. S. 457 (1941).

Guild could sell to retailers only on the condition that they would not deal in the garments manufactured by "style pirates," there was a violation of the exclusive dealing section of the Clayton Act. And the plan was held to conflict with the principles of the Sherman Act in a number of respects. It narrowed the outlets for garment manufacturers and the sources of supply for retailers; subjected those refusing to conform to the Guild's policies to an organized boycott; suppressed competition from the sale of unregistered textiles and copied designs; and interfered with the exercise of governmental power in attempting to make and enforce rules regulating commerce.

The fact that the combination had not achieved a complete monopoly was immaterial in view of its clear purpose and tendency. Justice Black said: "It was . . . one of the hopes of those who sponsored the Federal Trade Commission Act that its effect might be prophylactic and that through it attempts to bring about complete monopolization of an industry might be stopped in their incipiency."[32] Finally, the Court pointed out that it was not essential for a combination to have fixed prices or limited output, or to reduce the quality of its product, in order to be declared unlawful. The Commission had found a sufficient degree of control over the industry to warrant suppression of the combination before these or other undesirable practices were undertaken.[33]

The legal doctrine expressed in these cases finds support on economic grounds. To forbid the copying of styles and designs would be to suppress a significant part of the competitive process. It is largely through the imitation of new productive methods that general efficiency in production is increased. Likewise, the imitation of new styles and designs of products makes for a more rapid and wide-spread distribution of them and increases the satisfactions obtained by the great mass of consumers. One can be sympathetic with those who wish to encourage originality by rewarding it more highly, but the price would seem to be too high if it meant the impairment of competition and the loss of consumer satisfactions.

While the Commission has not prosecuted a large number of cases involving combination and restraint of trade, it has been very successful in this field. It owes its success probably to the fact that the law was well settled by cases adjudicated under the Sherman Act. Since the substantive law is the same in both cases, the question may be raised as to whether or not it is desirable for the Department of Justice and the Federal Trade Commission to have concurrent jurisdiction in this province of regulation. It has been argued that these cases should be prose-

---

[32] *Ibid.*, p. 466.

[33] The Millinery Creator's Guild case (312 U. S. 469) was decided the same day on the authority of this decision. In the Millinery case, there was a finding by the Commission of interference with normal price competition.

cuted under the Sherman Act. It might be conducive to greater administrative efficiency if the responsibility for enforcing the anti-monopoly policy were concentrated in the Department of Justice.[34] And furthermore, since the Sherman Act is a criminal statute, its use might be a more effective deterrent. It is true that the Federal Trade Commission Act is essentially a remedial statute, but it does not follow that it is an ineffective instrument in removing trade restraints. Any violation of a court decree affirming an order of the Commission may be punished for contempt of court, and the Wheeler-Lea Act of 1938 provides for substantial fines for the violation of an order of the Commission, irrespective of whether or not it has been affirmed by a court. And it is doubtful if more effective enforcement would be obtained if the field were left entirely to the Department of Justice. The Department of Justice has not always had the disposition nor the resources to pursue a rigorous antitrust policy. The Federal Trade Commission, although not entirely free from politics, does have a trained staff, experience, and information concerning trade and industry, which are valuable in detecting violations of the law and in prosecuting them. Since the disadvantages of joint responsibility are not apparent, the public will be best served if each agency retains jurisdiction and makes a diligent effort to enforce the law in this highly important field.

(3) Re-sale Price Maintenance

Re-sale price maintenance is an attempt on the part of a manufacturer to control the price at which dealers may re-sell his products to consumers. No business policy with which legislative bodies, the courts, and the Federal Trade Commission have had to deal has given rise to greater and more heated controversy than re-sale price maintenance. The controversy has been reflected in the unsettled state of public policy with respect to the practice during the course of the last half-century. But before considering and appraising its legal status, one should notice its economic features.

Re-sale price maintenance is the outgrowth of mass production and the national advertising of consumers' goods which are identified by brand or trade-mark. Manufacturers have built up a preference for their particular products by means of great advertising campaigns. It is possible to do this, of course, only if the products are branded so that their source can be ascertained easily. Imperfect competition between manufacturers is thus created. The market is divided into a series of sub-markets, each occupied by a manufacturer who has created a prefer-

---

[34] National Industrial Conference Board, *Public Regulation of Competitive Practices*, pp. 211–215.

ence in the minds of buyers for his product over those of other producers. Within the limits imposed on any monopolist, the producer is in a position to control the supply and price of his differentiated product. Brand identification also aids his control over the price at which the retailer sells. The advantage of handling products with established reputation and clientele will induce many dealers to accept the terms of re-sale prescribed by the producer. In the absence of differentiation it is immaterial to dealers and consumers from whom they buy, and sellers are powerless to exact a standard re-sale price.

Not only are manufacturers of distinctive products in a position to insist on re-sale price maintenance, but many believe it desirable to do so. They regard price-cutting as counter to their best interests. It is contended that the best results from a sustained program of advertising can be obtained if the advertised article has not only a uniform appearance and a standard quality but a standard price. A variable price destroys the single complex which has been created in the consumer's mind and impairs the value of producer advertising. But the main objection centers about the use of nationally advertised brands as "loss leaders." Producers are irked by the fact that chain stores and other large-scale distributors find it profitable to reduce the prices of well-known brands to cost or less in order to attract customers. It appears to be a more effective way to gain a reputation for economical selling than the reduction of prices on all or a great number of products. And it secures direct benefits for consumers without incurring the costs of most advertising. Like a great deal of advertising, however, it may be deceptive—consumers may be given the false impression that the retailer is offering exceptional values in all the goods he sells. But whatever the merits of "loss leaders," it is contended that the retailer is appropriating and destroying the good-will created by the expenditure of large sums for advertising. Manufacturers are convinced that this type of price-cutting reduces total sales and profits. This paradoxical result is reached because the price-cutters have no intention of making a sustained effort to push the sale of a product on which they obtain no profit or suffer a loss. Moreover, those merchants who maintain the standard price find it difficult to counteract the feeling on the part of consumers that their prices are exorbitant, and they are discouraged from handling the product. If they meet the price competition, they are apt to bring pressure on the manufacturer to reduce his price to them, and his profit margin may be cut below a reasonable level if he acquiesces in their demands.

The vast majority of independent retailers also favor price maintenance. They appear in many cases to be more insistent upon the practice than manufacturers, for the latter cannot be too sure that their best interests always lie in furthering a policy which tends to keep their products out of the hands of large-scale distributors. Independent merchants, however, are engaged in a bitter struggle for survival with the more progressive and efficient chain and department stores. They denounce all forms of price-cutting, and they would be happy to remove the chief competitive weapon used by the large-scale distributors. It is natural, therefore, that small-scale retailers and their suppliers should seek the coöperation of producers to curtail competition so as to maintain prices that will give them a satisfactory profit. They appear to be quite willing to give up their individualism and independence as a cost of insuring their survival. And many manufacturers favor the retention of a large number of small retail outlets, even though this comprises an inefficient marketing system, because they fear the great bargaining power inherent in a few large distributors.

On the other side of the issue lie the interests of large-scale distributors and the consuming public. The big distributors prefer to determine their own sales policies, particularly in the matter of pricing. It is only through price reductions that they can obtain the large volume which enables them to obtain the economies of large-scale operation. Moreover, because they usually operate on the cash-and-carry basis, their actual costs are less than those of the independent retailer who often gives an elaborate delivery and credit service. These cost factors, plus varying freight costs, should be reflected in the prices charged. To do otherwise is to discriminate against the great mass of consumers who are anxious to obtain merchandise at the lowest possible prices. The manufacturer may set what prices he likes in selling to the distributor or retailer, but beyond that he has no legitimate right to control the marketing process. The policy of maintaining uniform re-sale prices tends to discriminate against the efficient retailer, introduces rigidities into a marketing system which is in need of reorganization, and prevents the consumer from getting the very real benefits of low-cost distribution.

Prior to the activity of the Federal Trade Commission, the courts had passed upon the legality of re-sale price maintenance on a number of occasions. The first case was decided by the Supreme Court in 1889, and a re-sale price contract was upheld as a reasonable restraint of trade.[35] This view prevails under the common law in England.[36] Under the Sherman Act of 1890, however, such contracts did not fare so well. In the leading case of Dr. Miles Medical Co. v. Park & Sons Co.,[37] a manufacturer of a patent medicine sought to prevent a large distributor in the drug trade from obtaining his product and selling it at cut prices in violation of re-sale price contracts entered into with all of his recog-

---

[35] Fowle v. Park, 131 U. S. 88 (1889).
[36] Ware v. Motor Trade Association et al. (1912) 3KB40. 19 A. L. B. 893.
[37] 220 U. S. 373 (1911).

nized distributors. In denying the relief sought, the Supreme Court held that re-sale price contracts are in restraint of trade because they destroy competition between distributors. There could be no distinction between a manufacturer binding a large number of retailers to sell at a uniform price and the dealers themselves agreeing to sell goods at a fixed price.[38] But means other than contracts yielding the same result were upheld in subsequent cases. In United States v. Colgate & Co.,[39] for example, the company urged dealers to adhere to uniform prices, requested and often received information concerning price-cutters, and denied supplies to those who failed to respect promises to maintain the re-sale price. The case originated as an indictment under the criminal section of the Sherman Act and was complicated by procedural technicalities, but the decision upheld the company on the ground that it possessed, as does any seller, an unqualified privilege to choose its customers and to refuse to sell whenever it wished.[40] In other words, a trader may choose his customers on any condition which he sees fit to establish. Thus, as one critic has put it, "the questionable doctrine stands that one may exercise his privilege of refusal to sell in order to promote the anti-social practice of eliminating competition between distributors."[41] A second device which has withstood legal attack is the agency arrangement. Agency has been upheld on the ground that title to the goods is retained by the manufacturer, and therefore he has legal control over all elements of sale, including the price.[42]

The very considerable activity of the Federal Trade Commission in the field of re-sale price maintenance has been confined largely to cases involving coöperative effort on the part of a manufacturer and his dis-

---

[38] It was decided in Bauer & Cie. v. O'Donnell, 229 U. S. 1 (1913), that even a patentee could not control the re-sale price of a patented article. The attempt was here made to designate the sale of the product as a "license to use," but the Court declared this to be a "mere play upon words." It based its decision on the rule that once a patented article is sold, the patentee loses any rights flowing from the patent monopoly.

[39] 250 U. S. 300 (1919).

[40] Professor James A. McLaughlin has commented as follows: "United States v. Colgate & Co. is a caricature illustrating the unreality that can be achieved through an accumulation of procedural technicalities. . . . Out of the strange procedural wilderness . . . emerged the uncouth doctrine of a supposed unqualified privilege of refusal to sell.

"The case inevitably caused trouble to the district courts. Apparently no judge and no counsel having occasion to litigate re-sale price maintenance cases realized how remote from the facts the Supreme Court's decision was from the facts of the Colgate Company's program. The decision merely stood for an unsound abstraction based upon the Supreme Court's questionable construction of the district court's ambiguous misconstruction of the district attorney's technical reconstruction of the facts." J. A. McLaughlin, "Fair Trade Acts," University of Pennsylvania Law Review, Vol. LXXXVI (June, 1938), pp. 808–810.

[41] McLaughlin, op. cit., p. 812.

[42] U. S. v. General Electric Co., 272 U. S. 476 (1926).

tributors.[43] The leading case concerned the Beech-Nut Packing Co.,[44] which adopted a policy of price maintenance to be enforced by exercising its right to refuse to sell to price-cutters. It employed an elaborate system for detecting price-cutting, including the use of serial numbers on its products, reports from salesmen, and information solicited from wholesalers and retailers. Detailed records were kept concerning the behavior of its dealers, and those found to be non-coöperative were denied supplies. The Commission issued an order against this set-up, on the ground that it was an unfair method of competition within the terms of Section 5. In reviewing the order, the lower court found the Beech-Nut system to be substantially the same as that presented in the Colgate case and reversed the order.[45] Upon appeal, however, the Supreme Court announced that its decision in the Colgate case had been "misapprehended" and upheld the Commission.[46] It found that the Beech-Nut system went far beyond the simple refusal to sell goods to obnoxious dealers. In the opinion of the Court, the active coöperation between the manufacturer and his distributors in enforcing the policy of standard re-sale prices constituted a conspiracy to suppress competition among retail distributors. The methods used were quite as effective as contracts would have been in accomplishing the same purpose. Apparently, if the company had acted only upon information coming to it through the ordinary course of business, it would have been upheld.[47] But in going out of its way to procure information, especially soliciting and obtaining the aid of other customers, the Beech-Nut Company overstepped the bounds of legality.

The Commission had insisted that a policy of re-sale price maintenance was absolutely illegal under Section 5, irrespective of the method used. This was a logical position. If the vice of re-sale price maintenance is the suppression of competition between retailers, as clearly held in the Dr. Miles case, it would appear to be immaterial what method was used to achieve the restraint. To hold that illegality depends on how information about price-cutting is obtained is to avoid the main issue and to lay down a rule which is difficult of enforcement. The Supreme Court, however, would not accept the Commission's lead, and required it to modify its order to conform to the principle that there had to be some element of coöperation to bring the price policy under the ban of the law.

[43] In addition to more than 200 cases which were disposed of in their initial stages, the Commission had docketed 154 complaints involving re-sale price maintenance prior to June 30, 1928. Of these complaints, 105 were dismissed, 2 were settled by stipulation, 43 orders to cease and desist were issued, and 4 cases were still pending on June 30, 1928. House Document No. 546, 70th Congress, 2nd Session, F. T. C., *Report on Re-sale Price Maintenance* (1929), Part I, p. 109.

[44] F. T. C. v. Beech-Nut Packing Co., 257 U. S. 441 (1922).

[45] Beech-Nut Packing Co. v. F. T. C., 264 Fed. 885 (1920).

[46] 257 U. S. 441 (1922).

[47] Cream of Wheat Co. v. F. T. C., 14 Fed. (2nd) 40, 50 (1926).

Despite the confusion and uncertainty which characterized the law in this field, the powers of the Commission were "invoked with a frequency and with a degree of success which constituted a constant source of irritation to those who think of price-cutters as anti-social characters."[48] Of the orders challenged in the courts, the great majority were affirmed.[49] Orders have been overruled in several cases where it was not demonstrated that coöperation existed between the manufacturer and his dealers.[50]

The loophole created by agency arrangements and the privilege of refusal to sell did not satisfy the proponents of the policy. For many years there was concerted action by interested groups to legalize re-sale price contracts.[51] It finally bore fruit first in the state legislatures and later in Congress. California enacted a so-called Fair Trade Law in 1931,[52] which legalized re-sale price contracts on any commodity which bears the trade-mark, brand, or name of the producer and which is in "fair and open competition with commodities of the same general class produced by others." This law was greatly strengthened in 1933 by an amendment which makes such contracts enforceable against any dealer who sells below the established price regardless of whether or not he is a party to them. The Act provides that "wilfully and knowingly advertising, offering for sale or selling any commodity at less than the price stipulated" in any contract entered into pursuant to the law "is unfair competition and is actionable at the suit of any person damaged thereby."[53] It is immaterial whether the person advertising or selling is or is not a party to such contract. This far-reaching statute enhanced the popularity of re-sale price contracts and was made the basis for a phenomenal campaign throughout the states. Retail druggists and their associations were potent forces in promoting the legislation and their suggested draft of the law was faithfully followed.[54] Little opposition appears to have been encountered. By the end of 1936, at least 15

---

[48] McLaughlin, *op. cit.*, p. 811.

[49] See L. S. Lyon, M. W. Watkins, and V. Abramson, *Government and Economic Life* (Washington, The Brookings Institution, 1939), Vol. I, p. 292, for the citations of ten court decisions upholding orders of the Commission. Among others were Cream of Wheat Co. v. F. T. C., 14 Fed. (2nd) 40 (1926); and Armand Co. v. F. T. C., 78 Fed. (2nd) 707 (1935), certiorari twice denied, 299 U. S. 597, 623 (1936).

[50] American Tobacco Co. v. F. T. C., 9 Fed. (2nd) 570 (1925), affirmed, 274 U. S. 543 (1927); and Harriet Hubbard Ayer, Inc., v. F. T. C., 15 Fed. (2nd) 274 (1926), certiorari denied, 273 U. S. 759 (1927).

[51] An active campaign to secure the enactment of Federal legislation sanctioning re-sale price maintenance was conducted for many years by an organization called the American Fair Trade League. Among the numerous bills introduced to this end were the Stevens Bill, H. R. 13,305, 63rd Congress, 2nd Session (1915), and the Capper-Kelly Bill, S. 97, 72nd Congres, 1st Session (1932).

[52] Cal. Stat. 1931, Chap. 278.

[53] Cal. Stat. 1933, Chap. 260.

[54] McLauglin, *op. cit.*, pp. 815–818.

states had approved Fair Trade Laws.[55] There was some doubt as to
their constitutionality when different state courts of appeal rendered
conflicting decisions.[56] But the matter was cleared up when the Supreme
Court approved the virtually identical California and Illinois statutes in
December, 1936.[57] The decision was based on the asserted fact that a
distributor owns the commodity, but does not own the brand or trade-
mark and the good-will which it symbolizes. A dealer is free to sell the
product at any price he sees fit, providing he removes the identifying
brand or mark and does not utilize the good-will of the producer to
achieve the sale. The Court recognized that the question of whether
price-cutting is injurious to the good-will and business of the producer
and to the general public "may be regarded as fairly open to differences
of opinion."[58] Since the legislature had decided that good-will was damaged, however, it was free to protect the property, and the means employed were perfectly legitimate.[59] With this sweeping victory in the
courts, most of the remaining state legislatures climbed on the band-
wagon. At the present time 45 states have legalized re-sale price contracts.[60] The only territory outside the fold comprises the states of Missouri, Texas, and Vermont, and the District of Columbia.[61]

The final step in the almost complete reversal of public policy in this
sphere was the enactment by Congress of the Miller-Tydings Act in
1937.[62] Re-sale price maintenance contracts which are lawful in the

---

[55] Commerce Clearing House, *Trade Regulation Service* (eighth edition), pp.
10,002–10,003.

[56] The highest courts of California and Illinois upheld their respective acts. Max
Factor & Co. *v.* Kunsman, 55 Pac. (2) 177 (1936); Pyroil Sales Co. *v.* The Pep Boys,
55 Pac. (2) 194 (1936); Seagram-Distillers Corp. *v.* Old Dearborn Distributing Co.,
2 N. E. (2) 940 (1936). The New York Court of Appeals held the state act viola-
tive of both state and Federal constitutions as applied to non-contracting retailers.
Doubleday, Doran & Co. *v.* Macy & Co., 199 N. E. 409 (1935). This decision was
subsequently reversed in Bourjois Sales Corp. *v.* Dorfman, 7 N. E. (2) 30 (1937).

[57] Old Dearborn Distributing Co. *v.* Seagram-Distillers Corp., 299 U. S. 183
(1936); Pep Boys *v.* Pyroil Sales Co., 299 U. S. 198 (1936).

[58] 299 U. S. 183, pp. 195–196.

[59] In reply to the allegation that the dealer had been deprived of the constitutional
right to dispose of his property on his own terms, the Court said: "We find nothing
in this situation to justify the contention that there is an unlawful delegation of
power to private persons to control the disposition of the property of others. . . .
The restriction, already imposed with the knowledge of appellants, ran with the
acquisition and conditioned it." *Ibid.,* p. 194.

[60] Commerce Clearing House, *Trade Regulation Service* (ninth edition), pp. 7501–
8996. Prentice-Hall, Inc., *Labor Guide,* Trade Regulation Edition, par. 22,011.

[61] *Ibid.* There is no statutory prohibition in Vermont, hence re-sale price contracts might be upheld except as to non-contracting parties. They are absolutely
illegal in the other three jurisdictions. The Florida Fair Trade Law was declared
by the Florida Supreme Court to be price-fixing statute and an unconstitutional
exercise of the state's police power in 1949. Liquor Stores, Inc. *v.* Continental Distilling Corp., Fla. Sup. Ct., 1949. However, the Florida legislature promptly reënacted
a new law effective June 1, 1949. (Prentice-Hall, Inc., *Labor Guide,* Trade Regulation Edition, par. 22,021.)

[62] Public No. 314 (75th Congress), approved August 17, 1937. The Act was passed
in the form of an amendment to Section 1 of the Sherman Act.

state in which the re-sale is to be made are exempt from the provisions of the Sherman Act and the Federal Trade Commission Act. Opposed by the President and the Federal Trade Commission on the ground that it would damage consumers through increased prices, the exemption was enacted as an unrelated "rider" clause to a bill providing revenue for the District of Columbia. The President signed it reluctantly. Like the state Fair Trade Acts, contracts are confined to branded or trade-marked goods which are in free and open competition with products of the same general class. Also, as in the state laws, horizontal price agreements between manufacturers, or wholesalers, or retailers are prohibited. Since all of the state laws make re-sale price contracts enforceable not only against those who sign them but against all other dealers as well, the same may be true of contracts in interstate commerce.

What is the economic significance of this shift in policy? It is obvious that the "fair trade" legislation goes far beyond the elimination of the "loss leader." No attempt is made to distinguish good from bad price-cutting. The legislation precludes all types, and therefore protects the independent retailers and their suppliers in their competitive struggle with the more efficient large-scale distributor. Manufacturers are encouraged to build up good-will through advertising. Price competition is supplanted by sales promotion and other types of non-price competition. Producers are given greater control over the market, and may seek to maintain a large number of small outlets at the expense of the development of low-cost marketing. They are aided in this by the pressure of small retailers to initiate re-sale price programs. Concerted action on the part of distributors to force manufacturers to place products under re-sale price maintenance at prices which will yield satisfactory margins to them seems not to be uncommon, despite the illegality of such collusion.[63]

Reporting in 1945 on its study of the operation and effects of re-sale price maintenance, the Federal Trade Commission disclosed that the system had been adopted most extensively in such lines as drugs, toilet goods, cosmetics, liquor, and sporting goods. Many manufacturers of branded goods, particularly food and other staples, had refused to fix minimum re-sale prices, and others had done so reluctantly as a result of pressure from organized groups of retail dealers. Prices of chain stores, department stores, and certain independent merchants were increased when re-sale contracts were put into effect. In voicing its opposition to the legalization of the practice, the Commission said, in part: "Resale price maintenance, legalized to correct abuses of extreme price competition, is subject to use as a means of effecting enhancement of prices by secret agreements and restraint of competition by coercive action on the

---

[63] *Report of the Federal Trade Commission on Resale Price Maintenance*, (Washington, D. C., U. S. Government Printing Office, 1945), pp. LVI–LXI.

part of interested coöperating trade groups of manufacturers, wholesalers, and retailers in such ways and to such an extent as to make it economically unsound and undesirable in a competitive economy. . . . The Commission believes that the consumer is not only entitled to competition between rival products but to competition between dealers handling the same branded product."[64]

(4) Price Discrimination

It will be recalled that price discrimination was specifically dealt with in the 1914 legislation. Section 2 of the Clayton Act forbids discrimination in price between different purchasers of commodities, where the effect of such discrimination "may be to substantially lessen competition or tend to create a monopoly in any line of commerce." Certain provisos further limited the scope of the prohibition. It did not apply to differences in price based on a dissimilarity in grade, quality, or quantity, or differences that made only due allowance for variation in the cost of selling or transportation. Such price differentials are obviously not discriminatory or unfair. Moreover, discrimination made in good faith to meet competition was not proscribed, and the right of sellers to select their own customers was preserved.

The Clayton Act was designed to meet two types of discriminatory practice, namely, geographical and personal discrimination. Most important in the eyes of the legislators, perhaps, was local price-cutting. In order to eliminate a competitor, a powerful firm or combination might temporarily cut prices in a particular area, with the intent of increasing them to a profitable level when the local competitor had been forced out of business or had joined the combination through agreement or merger. Local discrimination was clearly an unfair method of competition, for it was instrumental in extending the market control of monopolistic enterprise. It had been used to great advantage by the Standard Oil and American Tobacco companies, a factor which materially influenced the Supreme Court in its finding that these concerns had deliberately sought monopoly power in their respective fields.[65]

Also included in the prohibition was price discrimination which places certain enterprises or groups of enterprises at a competitive disadvantage because they are forced to pay higher prices than their competitors. Unfairness of this sort had long been a matter of public concern in the

[64] *Ibid.*, p. LXIV.

[65] Standard Oil Co. v. U. S., 221 U. S. 1 (1911); U. S. v. American Tobacco Co., 221 U. S. 106 (1911). The Report of the Judiciary Committee of the House stated: "We are not dealing with an imaginary evil or against ancient practices long since abandoned, but are attempting to deal with a real, existing, wide-spread, unfair and unjust trade practice." *House Report*, Vol. II, No. 627, 63rd Congress, 2nd Session (1914), p. 8.

case of railways and other so-called natural monopolies, and had been outlawed in the Interstate Commerce Act and the numerous state statutes applicable to railways and public utilities. The Clayton Act generalized the policy so as to include protection for customers of all monopolistic concerns. As will be revealed shortly, there was some doubt in the minds of the courts whether or not the language of Section 2 did apply to the prices which an individual seller offered his customers. There is reason to believe, however, that Congress intended to write a law sufficiently broad in scope to embrace personal as well as geographical discrimination.[66]

(a) Personal Discrimination

Personal discrimination will first be considered. The type which has generated the greatest controversy as regards the interpretation of the Clayton Act has been discrimination based upon trade status.[67] This has been a long-established price policy. Manufacturers have very commonly sold identical products at different prices according to whether the purchaser is a jobber, wholesaler, retailer, or final consumer. The classifica-

---

[66] The original bill before the House prohibited price discrimination "with the purpose or intent to thereby destroy or wrongfully injure the business of a competitor of either such purchaser or seller." The House Report, cited above, stated that this section "expressly forbids discrimination in price . . . when such discrimination is made with the purpose or intent to thereby destroy or wrongfully injure the business of a competitor either of such dealer or seller." This phraseology was discarded in conference, and the substitute phrase, "where the effect of such discrimination may be to substantially lessen competition or tend to create a monopoly in any line of commerce," was adopted. Congressman Webb, in presenting the Conference Report to the House, stated: "We felt that that would tend to give the section more elasticity and breadth." *Congressional Record*, Vol. LI, p. 16,273.

[67] Another type of discrimination is that based upon the use to which the product is to be put. This is a familiar practice in the public utility field, where water, gas, and electricity are commonly sold at higher rates to domestic consumers than to commercial and industrial users. It is to be found in markets for agricultural and industrial products also where the essential conditions prevail, namely, an element of monopoly on the selling side of the market, varying elasticities of demand for the different uses, and the inability of buyers to divert low-priced units to the more valuable uses. Examples include milk of identical quality which is sold by coöperative associations of dairy farmers at a variety of prices depending upon whether it is to be used for fluid consumption, cream, butter or cheese-making, or canning as condensed or evaporated milk. Plate glass per square foot is sold at considerably higher prices in large pieces than in small ones, although the small pieces are as costly to produce as the large ones. Demand for large pieces is relatively inelastic, whereas the smaller pieces must be sold in competition with window glass, and hence the demand is relatively elastic. Likewise, prices of aluminum have varied according to whether it was to be used for one purpose or another. Aluminum cable, although costly to fabricate, has been sold at lower prices per pound than aluminum ingots, because the former comes into competition with copper cable for transmission purposes. (A. R. Burns, *The Decline of Competition* [New York, McGraw-Hill Book Company, 1936], pp. 274–277). The Commission seems not to have handled any cases involving discrimination of this type, although it is clearly a manifestation of monopoly power.

tion of buyers is based upon the nature and scale of their operations. Jobbers and wholesalers perform the function of carrying inventories and distributing goods to the numerous small retail outlets. They have in the past, at any rate, purchased in considerably larger quantities than retailers. But with the integration of the services of wholesaling and re-tailing in the modern chain store, department store, and coöperative buying association of retailers, the volume of purchases no longer corre-sponded closely to the trade status of the purchaser. The large-scale retailing organizations, since they also purchased in large quantities, have demanded the same trade discounts accorded wholesalers. Some manu-facturers refused, and their price policies were alleged to be discrim-inatory. They are discriminatory, of course, if the differences in price do not conform to the differences in the total cost of doing business with each class, *i.e.,* where the net yield on sales is not uniform.

The Mennen Company, in the marketing of its toilet preparations, refused to grant "wholesaler" discounts to a coöperative organization of retail druggists which ordered goods in wholesale quantities. This was done on the ground that the members of the "buying clubs" were the real purchasers, and since they sold directly to consumers they could not qualify for the wholesale price concessions. The Federal Trade Com-mission found this to be illegal price discrimination and issued an order against it.[68] Upon court review the order was reversed, certiorari being denied by the Supreme Court.[69] The Circuit Court of Appeals found nothing repugnant in the price policy, saying: "There is nothing unfair in declining to sell to retailers on the same scale of prices that it sold to wholesalers, even though the retailers bought or sought to buy the same quantity the wholesalers bought."[70] If the economic criterion of dis-crimination is held to be a variation in the net yield to the seller on different sales, this assertion is palpably false. But the court did not base its decision wholly on this ground. It was ruled that competition between the Mennen Company and other manufacturers could not be lessened by the price policy in question, and therefore it was not unlaw-ful. The basis for this conclusion was its interpretation of the provision of the law that discrimination was illegal if its effect was to lessen com-petition "in any line of commerce." The phrase "in any line of com-merce" was construed to mean that prejudice to the interests of Mennen's competitors had to be proved, an unlikely result of the price policy in question. Thus, even though the favored buyers were given an undue advantage over other purchasers and competition between them was im-

---

[68] 4 F. T. C. 258 (1922).

[69] The Mennen Co. *v.* F. T. C., 288 Fed. 774 (1923); certiorari denied, 262 U. S. 759 (1923).

[70] 288 Fed. 774, 783.

paired, the statutory prohibition did not apply. The court asserted that Congress had intended only to suppress local price-cutting directed at a competitor of the seller, and had not sought to protect the competition between purchasers of a single seller. As indicated earlier, both the broad language of the law and its legislative history fail to support this interpretation.[71]

While the Commission was unsuccessful in preventing discrimination between buyers, the ruling of the Supreme Court in a private suit, strangely enough, constituted the exact interpretation of the Clayton Act unsuccessfully sought by the Commission. In Van Camp Co. v. American Can Co.,[72] it was alleged by George Van Camp and Sons Company that the American Can Company was unlawfully discriminating against it and in favor of its competitor, the Van Camp Packing Company, in the sale of tin cans. It was charged that the American Can Company sold cans to the plaintiff company at its publicly announced standard prices, whereas the Van Camp Packing Company was able to purchase its requirements at 20 per cent below these prices. A further allegation, among others, was that the American Can Company furnished sealing machines to both packers, but charged the plaintiff a fixed rental, while furnishing them free of charge to the Van Camp Packing Company. Pending the determination of the issue of illegal discrimination, the Circuit Court of Appeals certified two questions to the Supreme Court relating to the interpretation of Section 2 of the Clayton Act. The purport

---

[71] Although the issue in the cases involving the National Biscuit and Loose-Wiles Biscuit companies (7 F. T. C., 206 and 218, 1924) was not quite the same as in the Mennen case, the result in the courts was quite as unsatisfactory to the Commission. These companies had adopted a system of graduated quantity discounts which gave to the newer large-scale distributing organizations a much better "break" than discounts based on trade status. The chain stores were allowed to combine the purchases of all the separate units in calculating the discounts, even though each unit placed its orders and was served individually. They refused, however, to grant like discounts on the aggregate of pooled orders of independent retailers purchasing through coöperative agencies. The cost of selling to the units of a chain system was found to be the same as the costs incurred in dealing with a like number of independent stores. The Commission found that this price policy gave the chains an undue competitive advantage.

The Circuit Court of Appeals revoked the order of the Commission, National Biscuit Co. v. F. T. C., 299 Fed. 733 (1924); certiorari denied, 266 U. S. 613 (1924), and affirmed the non-discriminatory character of the discount policy on the flimsy ground that the units of the chain store could not be regarded as separate purchasers, despite the fact that they were solicited and deliveries made to each individually. The basic philosophy underlying the decision appears to have been that sellers have unlimited freedom to conduct their business affairs; they may select their own customers and sell to them on whatever terms they choose. It may be questioned, however, whether the privilege extends to a firm that solicits orders and actually sells to its various customers at prices which disregard relative cost. Under conditions of pure competition no such price policy could prevail.

[72] 278 U. S. 245 (1929).

of these questions was whether or not Section 2 was applicable to price discrimination which might substantially lessen competition "not in the line of commerce wherein the discriminator is engaged, but in the line of commerce in which the vendee of the discriminator is engaged."[73] The Supreme Court answered the queries to the effect that the phrase "in any line of commerce" must be taken in its literal meaning. Thus, any price policy which prejudices the interests of certain purchasers or types of distributors may be attacked under the Clayton Act. The Court rejected the reasoning and the conclusion reached in the Mennen case. As a result, the statutory prohibition took on new vitality and appeared to be of some practical significance.[74] Before the Commission was able to test its own strength under the new interpretation of the law,[75] however,

---

[73] *Ibid.*, pp. 249–250.

[74] See Ladoga Can Co. *v.* American Can Co., 44 Fed. (2) 763 (1930); certiorari denied, 282 U. S. 899 (1931), in which the plaintiff company was awarded triple damages on the ground of serious price discrimination. The contention was rejected that the discrimination was made in good faith and to meet competition because the manufacturer feared that a buyer would make his own cans.

[75] The Commission did issue its complaint against the Goodyear Tire & Rubber Co., charging that the terms of its contract for supplying Sears, Roebuck & Co. with tires were unlawfully discriminatory, on September 13, 1933, and issued its order on March 5, 1936. (F. T. C., *Annual Report*, 1936, pp. 63–64.) But it was not until February 16, 1939, due largely to litigation as to whether the issue had become moot as a result of the enactment of the Robinson-Patman Act, that the order was considered on its merits and then set aside [Goodyear Tire & Rubber Co. *v.* F. T. C., 101 Fed. (2nd) 620 (1939) certiorari denied, 308 U. S. 557 (1939)]. The Commission found that Goodyear had entered a contract in 1926, renewed in 1928 and 1931, to supply all of the tire requirements of Sears, Roebuck & Co. on a cost-plus 6 per cent profit basis. The great bulk of its tires had been distributed through approximately 25,000 retail dealers. It was found that under the terms of these contracts the "net average sales price discrimination as between Sears, Roebuck & Co. and other dealers, over the entire period, varied from 29 per cent to 40 per cent on eight sizes of tires, or an aggregate of $41,000,000 on all sizes." (F. T. C., *Annual Report*, 1936, p. 64.) It appears also that Goodyear had given to Sears, Roebuck a large bloc of its common stock and $800,000 in cash with which to buy more stock, as a consideration for renewing the contract in 1931 without opening it to competition. These discriminatory prices, the Commission found, enabled the mail-order house to undersell, at a profit, other retail dealers at prices 20 to 25 per cent lower than the general re-sale price on tires of comparable grade and quality. This was a factor in driving retail tire dealers and small manufacturers who supplied them out of business. Since the great price differential accorded Sears, Roebuck could not be justified on the grounds of quantity, quality, differences in cost of selling or transportation, or competition, the Commission ordered Goodyear to fix net realized prices which "take into account and make due allowance, and only due allowance, for differences in the cost of transportation and selling tires to individual tire dealers on the one hand and Sears, Roebuck & Co. on the other."

The Circuit Court of Appeals set aside the Commission's order on the ground that it had no authority to prevent price differentials "reasonably based on quantity." It held that the proviso in Section 2 exempting quantity discounts was not qualified by the second proviso exempting price differentials "that make only due allowance for differences in the cost of selling or transportation." According to this interpretation, any difference in quantity justified any amount of discrimination. Had the Section not been amended by the Robinson-Patman Act, this ruling would have permitted wholesale evasion.

Section 2 was immeasurably strengthened by the amendments embodied in the Robinson-Patman Act of June 19, 1936.[76]

Perhaps the most important factor accounting for the passage of the Robinson-Patman Act was the growing importance of the mass distributor, notably the chain store. With their survival in the competitive struggle threatened, independent wholesalers and retailers were particularly interested in curbing price practices that they regarded as unfairly advantageous to the large-scale buyers and distributors.[77] Their political power was shown to be no less strong here than in their fight to legalize re-sale price maintenance. But it is noteworthy that a very extensive investigation of chain stores by the Commission yielded conclusions favorable to the independent wholesalers and retailers.[78] The Commission found that chain store merchandising had economic advantages flowing from the integration of production and marketing, from savings involved in avoiding credit and delivery service, and from benefits realized from large-scale advertising. Any program to eliminate them, said the Commission, "would involve radical interference with the rights of private ownership and initiative, virtual abandonment of the competitive principle, and destruction of the public advantage represented by lower prices and lower cost of living."[79] But the Commission did conclude that the special buying advantages which the chains had secured should be checked. The large chains with their superior bargaining power had been able to force concessions of various kinds from manufacturers. The preferential treatment granted chains embraced volume allowances, promotional allowances, allowances in lieu of brokerage, freight allowances, and guarantees against price decline.[80] This discrimination in prices and terms by producers against independents and in favor of chains, concluded the Commission, accounted "for a most substantial part of the chains' ability to undersell independents." That it was real discrimination was indicated by the Commission's judgment that "many of

---

[76] Public Act No. 692, 74th Congress, approved June 19, 1936.

[77] The act is frequently referred to as the "Anti-Chain Store" Act. The bill introduced in Congress by Senator Robinson and Representative Patman was drafted by counsel for the United States Wholesale Grocers' Association. This organization actively sponsored the measure and played a very important part in obtaining its enactment into law. For a detailed discussion of the legislative background and content of this law, see B. A. Zorn and G. J. Feldman, *Business under the New Price Laws* (New York, Prentice-Hall, Inc., 1937); and W. Patman, *The Robinson-Patman Act* (New York, Ronald Press Company, 1938).

[78] See F. T. C., *Final Report on the Chain Store Investigation*, Senate Document No. 4, 74th Congress, 1st Session (1934). The inquiry was both exhaustive and protracted, since it was started under a Senate Resolution passed in 1928 and cost over a million dollars. Thirty-three individual reports on various phases of the industry were submitted in addition to the final report of December 14, 1934.

[79] F. T. C., *Annual Report*, 1935, p. 32.

[80] For a summary of the kinds of preferential treatment granted to chain stores by manufacturers, see F. T. C., *Final Report on the Chain Store Investigation*, pp. 59–63.

the low buying prices of the chains had little, if any, relation to differences in quantity or cost of selling."[81]

The Commission acknowledged the difficulties and uncertainties of enforcing Section 2 of the Clayton Act under the various provisos limiting the scope of the prohibition. It recommended that these be eliminated and that there be substituted a broad prohibition of unfair and unjust discrimination.[82] The principle would be applied by the Commission, subject to review by the courts, to particular cases and situations, thus making it a judicial rather than a legislative matter. If the proviso permitting discrimination based on "quantity" were retained, it was suggested that it be made clear that "only due allowance" therefor could be made in fixing price differentials or discounts.[83] Otherwise any quantity difference could be made to justify any amount of difference in price, and the law could be evaded in wholesale fashion. This recommendation anticipated the adverse court decision the Commission was soon to receive in the case involving the exceptional prices accorded Sears, Roebuck & Co. by the Goodyear Tire & Rubber Co. in the sale of tires.[84]

As amended by the Robinson-Patman Act, Section 2 of the Clayton Act now provides that price discrimination between purchasers is unlawful if it substantially lessens competition or tends to create a monopoly in any line of commerce (the old language), or where the effect may be "to injure, destroy, or prevent competition with any person who either grants or knowingly receives the benefit of such discrimination, or with customers of either of them." This new language makes it absolutely clear that it is the intended policy of Congress to protect more than the competition between producers and manufacturers. The amended law goes beyond the old Clayton Act, in that it is not necessary to show that the discrimination lessens competition in a whole "line of commerce." It is enough to show that competition with certain persons, namely, with the discriminator or with the favored buyers, is injured, destroyed, or prevented. The precise meaning of this language will be made clear only through decisions of the Commission and the courts. If it is interpreted to mean that a discrimination which injures any competitor or competitors—for example, independent grocers—is unlawful, it will be a potent factor in eliminating the evils at which the act is directed.

Differentials in prices are to be permitted, of course, if it can be dem-

[81] F. T. C., *Annual Report*, 1935, p. 33.
[82] F. T. C., *Final Report on Chain Store Investigation*, pp. 96–97.
[83] *Ibid.*, p. 97; and F. T. C., *Annual Report*, 1935, p. 15.
[84] Goodyear Tire & Rubber Co. v. F. T. C., 101 Fed. (2nd) 620 (1939); certiorari denied, 308 U. S. 557 (1939). See note 75 of this chapter for a full statement of this case.

onstrated that there are differences in the cost of manufacturing, selling, or delivery "resulting from the differing methods or quantities" in which a commodity is sold or delivered. A seller may, however, make only "due allowance" for these differences in cost in fixing prices. Quantity discounts must be definitely related to differences in cost, a fact which will compel sellers to study costs of manufacturing and distribution and to adduce cost evidence in justification of their schedules of quantity discounts.[85] A host of theoretical and practical problems will arise in the ascertainment of relative costs and their reflection in price schedules, but the principle is sound and the Commission and the courts can probably be relied upon to make it workable by being satisfied with a reasonable or approximate relationship between cost and price. There is one feature of the provision which deserves notice, however, and that is the apparent right of sellers to refuse to give discounts to quantity buyers where there are demonstrable savings in cost. To the extent that sellers avail themselves of this right there will exist real discrimination against large buyers and a departure from the results of competition. Perhaps the great bargaining power of large firms will be sufficient to prevent any impairment of their economic advantage in mass purchasing. Nevertheless, so long as such discrimination is not unlawful, the policy contained in the Robinson-Patman Act cannot be defended wholly on the ground that it seeks to simulate the competitive process.[86]

A further control of price differentials arising from the quantity purchased suggests a more positive protection of competition. The Commission is authorized, upon due investigation and hearing of all interested parties, to "fix and establish quantity limits, and revise the same as it finds necessary," as to particular commodities or classes of commodities, "where it finds that available purchasers in greater quantities are so few as to render differentials on account thereof unjustly discriminatory or promotive of monopoly in any line of commerce." This is significant in that it constitutes a shift toward direct price control for industry in general. But perhaps more significant is the fact that Congress is here attempting to place limits on the advantages of size, even where size results in superior efficiency. Up to this time the anti-trust laws had been construed as not making "mere size an offense,"[87] and had condemned concentrations of control only when unfair means were used to achieve them or when their power had been abused. But the Commission may here restrict the size of distributing firms by withdrawing from them the

---

[85] If proof of discrimination is made, the burden of rebutting the *prima facie* case by showing justification rests on the respondent. A seller may rebut the case by showing that his lower price or the furnishing of services or facilities to purchasers was made in good faith to meet competition; Sec. 2 (b).

[86] See A. R. Burns, "The Anti-Trust Laws and the Regulation of Price Competition," *Law and Contemporary Problems*, Vol. IV (June, 1937), p. 313.

[87] U. S. v. U. S. Steel Corp., 251 U. S. 417, 451 (1920).

advantage of quantity discounts which may be perfectly justifiable on the basis of cost.[88] The test of whether price differentials are "unjustly discriminatory" or "promotive of monopoly" is not that of differences in cost, but whether the number of purchasers able to take advantage of the larger discounts is small. It is apparent that Congress was impressed with the contention that there was a prospect of the retail market being dominated by a few large concerns, with a corresponding restriction of opportunities for small independent enterprises. And to retain the large number of units essential for competition, it was willing to sacrifice the efficiency of the large firm. Whether this is too heavy a cost or not is debatable, but it might seem that Congress was unduly alarmed over the probability of monopoly in the field of retail distribution. In view of the size of the market, the great variety of services sought by consumers, the small investment required, and the ease of entry, it is doubtful whether a few firms will ever achieve domination. At present it does not seem the part of wisdom to curb the marked growth in efficiency and the price competition stimulated by the large-scale firm in the retailing field.

In addition to discrimination in price, the Robinson-Patman Act attempts to deal with other matters which have the same discriminatory effect. Large-scale distributors were shown to have benefited from brokerage payments from sellers where purchases were actually negotiated directly and without the aid of brokers.[89] Such "false" brokerage payments or any other compensation paid by a seller to a buyer or his agent were prohibited.[90] Some ambiguity in the provision was introduced by the inclusion of the phrase "except for services rendered" in connection with the sale or purchase of goods. Despite this language, Congress interpreted the provision as a flat prohibition of all payments of brokerage either to buyers or sellers, or to their agents.[91] No effect upon com-

---

[88] The quantity limitation provision was supported on the analogy of the Interstate Commerce Commission's traditional policy of refusing to permit railroads to quote lower freight rates on trainloads than on carloads. Admitting the lower cost of shipment by trainload, the Commission has nevertheless held against special rates on the ground that they would give an undue preference to the few large shippers able to take advantage of them, and would facilitate the further concentration of business in their hands. It is interesting to note, however, that in the so-called Blackstrap case (Molasses from New Orleans, La., to Peoria and Pekin, Ill., 235 I. C. C. 485), decided December 4, 1939, the Commission allowed the establishment of rates on a quantity larger than a carload. Special circumstances were held to justify the departure from the long-established rule. Shippers of molasses were able to move their product over the water route from New Orleans to Peoria in multiple-bargeload quantities at a very low cost, and the trainload rates were simply "designed to meet competition from other modes of transport whose unit of transportation is not limited to single carloads."

[89] F. T. C., *Final Report on the Chain Store Investigation*, pp. 27–28.

[90] Sec. 2 (c).

[91] It appears that the phrase "except for services rendered" was inserted at the request of representatives of voluntary coöperative organizations owned by retailers

petition need be shown. The effect of this provision will be to prevent large firms from receiving any part of the economies of direct and quantity buying in the form of "fictional" and perhaps secret brokerage payments. They may receive them only in the form of price differentials which meet the requirements laid down by Congress.

Devices for secret price discrimination, as advertising allowances, promotional allowances of various types, and services or facilities furnished by sellers, are also controlled. But they are not prohibited entirely. And excessive allowances for the selling services performed by retailers are not forbidden. It is required, however, that all services rendered by the seller, or any payments passing to the buyer in consideration of services rendered by him, shall be available to all purchasers on "proportionally equal terms."[92] The latter phrase is the heart of the provision, yet it is most ambiguous. It fails to indicate any element or standard for the calculation of proportionality.

Since the enlargement of the Commission's authority over price discrimination,[93] it has been very active in this field. During the period of nearly twelve years ending January 1, 1948, the Commission instituted several hundred cases and entered 186 cease and desist orders against violators of the amended Section 2 of the Act.[94] The great majority of the orders, 104 in number, have been based on the brokerage section of the Act. Of the remaining orders, 55 have derived force from the provisions relating to direct price discrimination and 27 from the provisions dealing with promotional allowances, the furnishing of services and

---

or wholesalers because they felt that their organizations rendered a true brokerage service. The various Congressional committees handling the legislation disregarded the phrase in interpreting the statute as an unconditional prohibition of brokerage payments to buyers. See Zorn and Feldman, *op. cit.*, pp. 204–211.

[92] Sec. 2 (d) and (e).

[93] The enforcement provisions of the law respecting discrimination were also strengthened by the Robinson-Patman Act. A receiver of a price discrimination, one who knowingly induces or receives such preferential treatment, is made liable (Sec. 2(f)). Moreover, criminal penalties are made available for local and personal discrimination (Sec. 3). No prosecutions have yet been instituted by the Department of Justice under Section 3, and there is considerable doubt as to the wisdom of providing criminal penalties in addition to the civil remedies available under Section 2.

It should be noted that there is a definite trend toward state legislation of the Robinson-Patman type. The laws are called usually "Unfair Practices Acts" or "Unfair Sales Acts," and prohibit either price discrimination or sales below cost or both. About 37 states have laws of one sort or another, 19 of them having laws forbidding both price discrimination and sales below cost. To meet constitutional requirements, the laws must be construed to forbid the price practices only where there is an intent to injure competitors or to destroy competition. In contrast to the "Fair Trade Laws" legalizing re-sale price maintenance, which are civil statutes with minor exceptions, these laws provide criminal penalties for violations. See Commerce Clearing House, *Trade Regulation Service* (ninth edition), pp. 7501–8996.

[94] Commerce Clearing House, *Robinson-Patman Act Symposium* (1948 edition), p. 118.

facilities by sellers, and the inducing or receiving of discriminations in price.

The scope and meaning of the brokerage section of the amended law have been clearly established through favorable court review of a considerable number of the Commission's orders. In enforcing the law against price concessions in the form of brokerage payments or similar allowances under Section 2(c), the Commission has proceeded not only against the chain store organizations but against independent purchasing agencies and coöperative buying agencies utilized by many small manufacturing and mercantile firms. A collective purchasing agency which acts for buyers, or which is controlled in any degree by the buyers, may not receive brokerage from sellers and transmit the sums to or use them for the benefit of purchasers.[95] This flat prohibition to receive or pay brokerage, based on the idea that the intermediary is acting and can only act exclusively for the buyer, applies even where services of genuine value are actually rendered to the seller. In other words, the phrase "except for services rendered" has no significance in these circumstances and is interpreted to mean merely that brokerage may be paid by a seller to his own agent or broker for actual services rendered. Where there is direct dealing between seller and buyer, which has been the situation in most of the cases handled by the Commission, the prohibition is no less absolute. The issue raised in these proceedings, as illustrated by the leading case against the Great Atlantic and Pacific Tea Company,[96] is whether the saving resulting from not using a broker may be considered to be a saving in selling cost which will justify a lower price under the price discrimination provisions of Section 2(a). The A & P, after the enactment of the Robinson-Patman Act, had directed its field buyers to accept from suppliers the amounts formerly received

---

[95] The leading cases are Biddle Purchasing Co. v. F. T. C., 96 Fed. (2nd) 687 (1938), certiorari denied 305 U. S. 634 (1938); Oliver Bros. v. F. T. C., 102 Fed. (2nd) 763 (1939); Quality Bakers of America v. F. T. C., 114 Fed. (2nd) 393 (1940); Modern Marketing Service v. F. T. C., 149 Fed. (2nd) 970 (1945). In the Biddle case, it was shown that the purchasing company provided a market information and purchasing service to a large number of wholesalers and jobbers and sold the products of many manufacturers, canners, and packers. The Oliver firm rendered a similar service to over 300 wholesalers of automobile, electrical, plumbing, and hardware supplies. The Quality Bakers case involved coöperative purchasing of flour, supplies, and baking equipment by some 70 wholesale baking concerns. Modern Marketing Service was an agency performing purchasing and other services for the wholesale grocers and affiliated retail food stores of the Red and White organization. Brokerage fees had been collected from such firms as Diamond Match, Morton Salt, Quaker Oats, Ralston Purina, and Procter and Gamble, and returned to the buyers as advertising allowances.

[96] Great Atlantic & Pacific Tea Co. v. F. T. C., 106 Fed. (2nd) 667 (1939), certiorari denied 308 U. S. 625 (1940). See also Southgate Brokerage Co. v. F. T. C., 150 Fed. (2nd) 607 (1945), in which it was held that a brokerage firm which bought goods for its own account as part of its operations could not accept brokerage commissions on such direct purchases.

as brokerage in the form either of lower invoice prices or quantity discounts. But the Commission held, and was fully sustained by the courts, that the brokerage section is to be applied independently of other sections of the act and that any saving in selling expense effected through eliminating a broker can not be used to justify a lower price. Also, the effect upon competition need not be considered in applying the specific rule against brokerage payments.

The effect of the Commission's strict interpretation of the brokerage rule, which appears to be quite in harmony with the intent of Congress, has undoubtedly been to curb the abuses at which the law was directed. In so doing, however, there may be by-products from the disturbance in the marketing sphere which are not altogether good. If large-scale distributors elect to buy only from suppliers who make no sales through brokers or to engage in their own manufacturing operations, brokers who would otherwise perform valuable services for small buyers may be forced out of business. Hardship may also be imposed upon small business by thwarting efforts to attain more economical purchasing through coöperative buying arrangements. These are consequences that are inconsistent with the maintenance of fair competition among distributors, and suggest the desirability of an approach to the problem that recognizes the validity of payments to intermediaries in the marketing system for genuine services rendered to either party, buyer or seller.

Discrimination in the area of non-price competition, it will be recalled, is governed by rules saying that sellers may furnish or pay for facilities or services used in promoting sales only if they are made available to all buyers on "proportionally equal terms." Coöperative merchandising is largely confined to trade-marked products and often takes the form of some kind of advertising or the furnishing of sales personnel. Two illustrations suggest the nature of the problem here dealt with. The Corn Products Refining Company during the years 1936 to 1939 spent over $750,000 in advertising the candy of the Curtiss Candy Company as being "rich in dextrose."[97] Since advertising services were not furnished to its other customers on like terms, the Corn Products Company was found by the Supreme Court to have violated the statute. In the Elizabeth Arden cases,[98] the respondent's system of rendering demonstrator service to its retail customers in the sale of cosmetics was

---

[97] Corn Products Refining Co. v. F. T. C., 324 U. S. 726 (1945).

[98] Elizabeth Arden Sales Corp. v. Gus Blass Co., 150 Fed. (2d) 988 (1945), certiorari denied 326 U. S. 793 (1945); Elizabeth Arden, Inc. v. F. T. C., 156 Fed. (2d) 132 (1946), certiorari denied 331 U. S. 806 (1947). In the Blass case, the operator of a department store in Little Rock, Arkansas, recovered triple damages from Arden for discriminating against it in the furnishing of demonstrator service. Its competitor had obtained such services on more favorable terms. Arden sought to defend itself by showing that payments for service were based upon the volume of purchases of each competitor, but the Court found that actually no such basis had been used.

under attack. The terms for furnishing the service and the payments to dealers were based on the volume of purchases, the size and character of the store, and the services and facilities offered by the store. The result of applying these terms was that Arden furnished demonstrator service to about 10 per cent of its customers, the remaining 90 per cent being automatically excluded. This was not rendering service or payments on "proportionally equal terms," in the judgment of the Commission and the courts, rather it was providing coöperative merchandising service on no standard other than "the seller's discretion or favor." The only appropriate basis is one which can be proportionalized, and this appears to be, in the light of the decisions, a standard based on the volume of purchases. In such circumstances, no competing customer will be excluded from participation in a plan for coöperative merchandising if he so desires. The effect of applying such a rule will be greater equality of treatment of customers, with the larger buyers obtaining quite legitimately the larger benefits. There may be considerable curtailment in the expenditures of manufacturers for joint advertising programs, however, if they are compelled to spread their limited advertising budgets over all their retail outlets so thinly.

In administering the amended section of the Clayton Act relating to direct price discrimination, the Commission has encountered a variety of price differentials existing under varying competitive conditions. It has been its task to determine whether these are economically justifiable or are price discriminations which adversely affect competition. The validity of some types of discounts has been upheld in most instances. Discounts allowed for the payment of bills within a designated time are usually open to all customers and therefore lawful. Functional discounts or those offered to jobbers, wholesalers, and retailers according to the distributive function which they perform are not regarded as discriminatory nor are they required. Where purchasers perform both wholesaling and retailing functions, discounts may be given only on that part of the purchaser's business that is actually done under the function for which the discount is allowed. In the leading Standard Oil case,[99] for example, the respondent sold gasoline to four "jobbers" in Detroit at one and one-half cents less than the price to some 358 retail service stations in the area. One of these dealers used all of his purchases to supply his own retail gasoline stations, whereas the other three sold some to retailers and used the rest in their own stations. The Commission found that the discrimination was not justified on the basis of cost savings and that a substantial competitive advantage was enjoyed by these dealers which diverted business from other retailers. Standard Oil was ordered to cease granting discounts on gasoline sold at retail by the "jobbers."

---

[99] Standard Oil Co. v. F. T. C., 173 Fed. (2d) 210 (1949).

Quantity discounts of various kinds have been given a great deal of attention. There are two principal types. One is "unit delivery" discounts, which are those based on quantities delivered at a given time and place. The other is "volume" or cumulative discounts, those which are granted on the basis of aggregate purchases over a period of time. "Unit delivery" discounts, since they are based on the size of individual orders, can ordinarily be justified on the basis of cost savings and have been upheld.[100] If the quantity limits are too large and many buyers cannot take advantage of them, however, the Commission is disposed to question them. Cumulative or "volume" discounts, on the other hand, have been consistently held to be discriminatory.[101] This type of discount is usually available only to large buyers and is unjustifiable from the cost standpoint because the periodic purchases ordinarily embrace a large number of relatively small orders and delivery at the separate plants of the purchaser. In line with this reasoning, quantity discount arrangements have been condemned in cases where separate purchasers combined purchases or bought through coöperative buying agencies in order to qualify for discounts, and where chain organizations received discounts on aggregate purchases of the separate units of the chain.[102] Price concessions to large buyers on merchandise to be sold under their own private brands have also been condemned.[103]

The Morton Salt case,[104] decided by the Supreme Court in 1948, gave judicial approval to the Commission's approach to the elimination of discriminatory quantity discounts. Morton Salt Company maintained on its best grade of salt a schedule of prices available to all purchasers as follows: $1.60 per case of salt in less-than-carload purchases, $1.50 in carload purchases, $1.40 in 5,000-case purchases in any consecutive twelve months, and $1.35 in 50,000-case purchases in any consecutive twelve months. Both the carload-lot and the quota discounts were attacked as tending to injure competition, the fact being that only five large chains had ever bought enough to obtain the $1.35 per case price. On the other hand, the carload-lot discount was obtained by all except a fraction of one per cent of Morton's customers. It was not proved that the discounts were based on actual savings in cost. The Commission did allow, however, "price differences of less than five cents per case which do not tend to lessen, injure, or destroy competition." Except for the qualification on the allowable differential of five cents per case, which

---

[100] Kraft-Phenix Cheese Corp., 25 F. T. C. 537 (1937); American Optical Co., 28 F. T. C. 169 (1939).

[101] H. C. Brill Co., 26 F. T. C. 666 (1938); Standard Brands, Inc., 30 F. T. C. 117 (1940).

[102] Simmons Co., 29 F. T. C. 727 (1939); Sherwin-Williams Co., 36 F. T. C. 25 (1943).

[103] U. S. Rubber Co., 28 F. T. C. 1489 (1939).

[104] F. T. C. v. Morton Salt Co., 334 U. S. 37 (1948).

the Court believed had the undesirable effect of shifting to the courts the task of trying issues of possible injury to competition, the Commission was fully upheld. The most noteworthy feature of the Court's decision was the holding with respect to the effect of a price discrimination upon competition. The Court held that the Commission need not find that discriminations in fact have harmed competition, "but only that there is a reasonable possibility that they 'may' have such an effect." If the Commission found that the discounts offered competing buyers were sufficient to influence the re-sale price of salt, it would be enough to support the conclusion of injury to competition. But this view was not unanimous. Mr. Justice Jackson contended that the record should show a "reasonable probability" rather than a "reasonable possibility" that the discounts harmed competition. Said he, "The Court uses overtones of hostility to all quantity discounts, which I do not find in the Act, but they are translated into a rule which is fatal to any discount the Commission sees fit to attack."[105]

While the Commission has exercised its authority over quantity discounts in a far-reaching manner and has been upheld by the courts in the main essentials of its policy, no attempt has as yet been made to fix quantity limits beyond which differences in price justified by cost shall not be permitted. Requests have been made by representatives of several industries to invoke this power, and an investigation of the rubber tire industry has been undertaken,[106] but the Commission is moving slowly and rightly so in this precarious sphere.

(b) Geographical Discrimination

In the Congressional debates over the original Clayton Act, there was great emphasis placed upon local price-cutting as a nefarious competitive device. It is interesting to note, however, that there has been a dearth of cases relating to this practice. The Commission has raised the question on several occasions, but has ordered companies to cease from lowering prices in certain markets for the purpose of eliminating competitors in only a few cases.[107] A private suit supplied the outstanding case. In it the American Tobacco Company was held to have reduced the price for Lucky Strike cigarettes in Puerto Rico below that in the United States for the purpose of destroying the business of a local producer.[108] Lack of

---

[105] 334 U. S. 37, 58 (1948).

[106] Commerce Clearing House, *Robinson-Patman Act Symposium* (1948 edition), pp. 23–25.

[107] Pittsburgh Coal Company of Wisconsin, 8 F. T. C. 480 (1925). More recent cases are Metz Bros. Baking Co., 30 F. T. C. 268 (1939); E. B. Muller & Co. *v.* F. T. C., 142 Fed. (2d) 511 (1944); Samuel H. Moss, Inc. *v.* F. T. C., 148 Fed. (2d) 378 (1945), 155 Fed. (2d) 1016 (1946).

[108] Porto Rican American Tobacco Co. *v.* American Tobacco Co., 30 Fed. (2d) 234 (1929), certiorari denied, 279 U. S. 858 (1929).

extensive use of the section may indicate that the practice has actually been abandoned by businessmen to a large extent, or that the statutory exemption of price-cutting "to meet competition" has nullified the effective application of the prohibition. Price-cutting is usually sporadic and temporary in character, and it is hard to prove that it is not used to meet competitive situations. It may be, however, that the practice is on the wane because of the statutory prohibition, or because modern market conditions make it impracticable to maintain such price policies. Market information is widely disseminated these days, and producers may incur the ill-will of the great mass of their customers if they give to some buyers a more favorable price.[109] The possibility that a local price war may spread rapidly to other regions and the growing conviction on the part of businessmen that price competition of any sort is disadvantageous may be further deterrents to local price discrimination.

While various types of geographical discrimination received some attention under the original provisions of the Clayton Act, discrimination emanating from zone systems of pricing appears not to have been attacked. No case was prosecuted where sellers charge delivered prices that are uniform for all points in a large territory. Yet the degree of discrimination may be substantial when transportation costs are not uniform and are a considerable part of the final price. The legality of uniform delivered pricing on a zone basis by competing firms is being considered by the Commission under the revised law in the National Lead case,[110] but no authoritative economic or legal analysis of the problem has as yet appeared.

The Commission did concern itself, however, with pricing under basing-point systems.[111] The outstanding case was the order against the so-called "Pittsburgh Plus" system of quoting prices for rolled steel products.[112] It was found to be discriminatory in violation of the Clayton Act, as well as an unfair method of competition.[113] The United States Steel Corporation, without appeal to the courts, consented to comply with the terms of the Commission's order "in so far as it is practicable to do so." The elimination of this monopolistic pricing policy, although

---

[109] See National Industrial Conference Board, *op. cit.*, pp. 69–71, for a discussion of reasons for the apparent discontinuance of the policy of local price-cutting.

[110] In the matter of National Lead Co., F. T. C. Docket No. 5253, Complaint issued April 12, 1946.

[111] F. T. C., *Price Bases Inquiry* (1932), p. 13.

[112] In the matter of United States Steel Corp., 8 F. T. C. 1 (1924).

[113] Purchasers of steel products from manufacturing points other than Pittsburgh were obliged to pay prices which yielded the producers varying net amounts depending upon the differences between the transportation cost from the basing-point and from the actual point of production. Users of rolled steel products in the Chicago area, for example, though purchasing from a Chicago mill, had to pay a higher price than Pittsburgh competitors by the amount of the freight rate between the two points, thus placing them at a considerable competitive disadvantage.

it left untouched the power to enforce discriminatory prices, represented an important achievement of the Commission. With the enactment of the Wheeler-Lea Act in 1938, Congress provided that all orders of the Commission issued prior to its enactment were to become final sixty days thereafter. The Steel Corporation petitioned a circuit court of appeals to review and set aside the order of July 21, 1924. The Company feared, apparently, that current practices in the pricing of rolled steel products might be found to have been proscribed by the broad terms of that order. But on October 5, 1948, after having publicly announced a method of pricing steel products that does not conflict with the order, the Steel Corporation consented to the entry of a court decree affirming the Commission's order.[114]

After the enactment of the Robinson-Patman Act, the Commission renewed its assault upon the basing-point system of pricing and won several notable victories in the courts. Both the single and multiple basing-point systems were attacked when used in connection with the sale of products where transportation charges are of major importance. In the Corn Products[115] and Staley[116] cases, the Commission found delivered prices calculated on a single basing-point to be discriminatory, and in this it was upheld by the Supreme Court. The Corn Products Refining Company, a large producer of corn derivatives, had plants in both Chicago and Kansas City from which deliveries of glucose were made to a large number of candy manufacturers. Sales were made at delivered prices computed by adding to a base price at Chicago the freight rate from Chicago to destination, irrespective of whether the corn syrup was shipped from Chicago or Kansas City. The result was that on shipments from Kansas City to destinations where the freight was less than from Chicago, the delivered price contained more than the actual cost of freight or so-called "phantom freight." Freight was "absorbed" on shipments from Kansas City to points where the actual freight was in excess of that from Chicago. Factory net returns, delivered prices less actual freight costs, varied at Kansas City according to the destination of the glucose. The consequence of this pricing system, found the Commission, was to favor candy manufacturers in the Chicago area and to discriminate against and among competing candy producers located at a distance from Chicago and served from the Kansas City plant. In upholding the Commission, the Supreme Court noted that basing-point price systems are not illegal *per se*. They are unlawful only if they have an adverse effect upon competition. And it was observed by the Court that Section

---

[114] U. S. Steel Corp., *v.* F. T. C., C. C. A. 3rd, No. 6796, October 5, 1948.

[115] Corn Products Refining Co. *v.* F. T. C., 324 U. S. 726 (1945), affirming 34 F. T. C. 850 (1942).

[116] F. T. C. *v.* A. E. Staley Mfg. Co., 324 U. S. 746 (1945), affirming 34 F. T. C. 1362 (1942).

2(a) of the Clayton Act does not require a finding that competition has in fact been adversely affected. "The statute is designed to reach such discriminations 'in their incipiency,' before the harm to competition is effected. It is enough that they 'may' have the prescribed effect."[117] Since glucose is a principal ingredient of low-priced candy and small differences in the sales price of such candy are enough to divert patronage from one firm to another, the Commission had inferred a "reasonable probability" that the discriminations may substantially lessen competition. It was for the Commission to determine the weight to be given to the established facts and the inferences to be drawn from them, hence the Court accepted the Commission's judgment.

The Staley company was a competitor of the Corn Products company and had its plant at Decatur, Illinois. Instead of selling its products f.o.b. Decatur, the Staley company adopted the basing-point system of the rival Corn Products company. With Chicago as the basing-point, buyers next to the plant in Decatur paid more than Chicago purchasers by the amount of the freight from Chicago to Decatur. Discrimination among buyers was effected by the charging of unearned freight and freight absorption; in this, as in the Corn Products case, there was found to be a lessening of competition. The Supreme Court upheld the Commission in rejecting the defense, allowed under the statute, that the price discriminations were made in "good faith" to meet the low prices of a competitor. The firm had never attempted to establish its own non-discriminatory price system, but had followed "slavishly" a competitor's system that resulted in systematic discriminations. Since artificially high prices had been established in markets where the Staley company had a freight advantage over Chicago through the inclusion of "phantom" freight, there could be said to have been no attempt to reduce prices to meet those of rival firms. As regards freight absorption, such as occurred in the selling of Staley's glucose in the Chicago market, the Court was not so firm in its condemnation. Chief Justice Stone said: "It does not follow that respondents may never absorb freight when their factory price plus actual freight is higher than their competitors' price, or that sellers, by so doing, may not maintain a uniform delivered price at all points of delivery, for in that event there is no discrimination in price."[118] A definition of discrimination in terms of varying "mill net" returns is obviously incompatible with the latter assertion, which makes it clear that the Court was basing its condemnation of single basing-point systems largely upon differences in delivered prices which could not be justified by sellers.

---

[117] 324 U. S. 726, 738 (1945).
[118] 324 U. S. 746, 757 (1945).

In the Cement[119] and Rigid Steel Conduit[120] cases, the Commission's orders directed against the use of multiple basing-point methods of pricing were upheld by the Supreme Court. The Cement case was a proceeding against the Cement Institute and its 74 members that produced about 98 per cent of the cement in the nation. This industry-wide investigation required three years for the hearing of evidence alone and resulted in the accumulation of a record of unprecedented size. Imbued with the idea that price competition is wholly unsuited to it because of the standardized nature of the product, overhead costs, and fluctuating demand, the industry had for years controlled competition through various coöperative practices.[121] Of substantial aid in effecting coöperation was the marked concentration in the industry. When the case was instituted in 1937, five firms controlled over 39 per cent of the productive capacity, the largest of these being Universal Atlas Cement Company, a subsidiary of the United States Steel Corporation. Cement was sold from the 165 plants in operation in 1937 only at delivered prices computed by adding rail freight to the base price at the basing-point designated for a particular territory. Less than one-half of the mills were located at approximately 70 basing-points, there being 79 basing-point mills and 86 non-basing-point mills in 1937.

The Supreme Court sustained the Commission on both counts in its complaint. Under the first count, the Commission had found that competition in the cement industry was restrained through agreements and understandings to employ a multiple basing-point system of pricing. The collective maintenance of this pricing system constituted an unfair method of competition in violation of Section 5 of the Federal Trade Commission Act. In support of its decision the Commission disclosed such collective practices as distributing freight rate books for use in calculating identical prices, discouraging the shipment of cement by truck or barge, opposing the erection of new plants, concealing quality differences in the product, and punishing firms that deviated from the system by cutting prices in their territories. Under the second count, the Commission found unlawful price discrimination among purchasers consisting in the varying mill net prices received from customers in different localities. The effect of this systematic discrimination was to lessen competition substantially among the cement producers. The Court found no merit in the contention that the discrimination inherent in systematic freight absorption, as distinguished from the collection of

---

[119] F. T. C. v. Cement Institute, 333 U. S. 683 (1948), affirming 37 F. T. C. 87 (1943).

[120] Clayton Mark & Co. v. F. T. C., 336 U. S. 956 (1949), affirming Triangle Conduit & Cable Co. v. F. T. C., 168 Fed. (2d) 175 (1948).

[121] For a description of the economic and legal background of the basing-point cases in steel, cement, and corn products, see Fritz Machlup, *The Basing-point System* (Philadelphia, The Blakiston Company, 1949), Chap. 3.

phantom freight, is justified as a price reduction made in "good faith" to meet competitors' lower prices. Such a defense, ruled the Court, is applicable only to "individual competitive situations" and not to a general system of competition. In other words, sellers may in individual and isolated instances market products in a competitor's territory by matching his lower prices and thereby absorbing freight, but may not do so where its systematic character suggests that a formula is being utilized for collusive purposes and results in identical prices.

In the Rigid Steel Conduit case, the 14 manufacturers controlling 93 per cent of the production of coated steel pipe used to encase electrical wiring in building construction were found to be using unlawfully a pricing formula with Pittsburgh and Chicago as basing-points. A price-fixing conspiracy was found to exist which was effectuated by the collective adoption and use of the multiple basing-point system. But even in the absence of an agreement or a conspiracy, "the individual use of the basing-point method, with knowledge that other sellers use it," was held to be an unfair method of competition.[122] Such individual use of the system was regarded as comparable to collective use, since the effect was for all firms to sell at identical prices in all markets, and therefore unlawful. The Supreme Court, by a 4 to 4 decision and without opinion, upheld the lower court's decision affirming the order of the Commission.

Although the Commission had attacked only those delivered price arrangements that were manifestly injurious to competition, the outlawing of collusive discrimination raised a storm of protest of which Congress took immediate notice.[123] Deprived of their traditional pricing systems, the steel and cement industries adopted the f.o.b. mill method of pricing in the summer of 1948. The change was accompanied by price increases, widespread speculation as to possible adverse effects upon the location of industry and small business, and apprehension lest local monopolies would be fostered. Some of the agitation was founded upon a sincere belief that the absorption of freight associated with delivered price systems independently maintained by sellers had an uncertain legal status.

In an attempt to clarify the law, amendments to the Federal Trade Commission and Clayton Acts were considered in 1949.[124] The proposed

---

[122] 168 Fed. (2d) 175, 180 (1948).

[123] On June 12, 1948, by Senate Resolution 241, a Subcommittee on Trade Policies of the Senate Committee on Interstate and Foreign Commerce was established to study the effects of the discontinuance of the basing-point system and to make such recommendations for legislation as it deemed advisable. Senator Capehart, chairman of the Committee, appointed an advisory council of forty members to aid in the investigation. Some idea of the views of this group is gained from the comment that it "includes at least seven executives of companies who have lost to the FTC in price-fixing cases in which identical delivered prices figured heavily in the evidence." *Engineering and Mining Journal,* Vol. 149 (September, 1948), p. 101.

[124] Commerce Clearing House, *Trade Regulation Service* (Ninth edition).

amendments allow a seller, acting independently, to quote or sell at delivered prices and to absorb freight. Seemingly appropriate safeguards are included. No collusive agreement or monopolistic practice is to be carried out or to be involved in the use of these sales methods. Any discrimination involved in selling at delivered prices or in absorbing freight to meet the prices of a competitor is unlawful only if it substantially lessens competition. These amendments have the approval of both the Federal Trade Commission and the Department of Justice and are apparently consistent with the policies already pursued by these enforcing agencies. There may be no serious objection to a clarification of the law which allows the mild and harmless discrimination inherent in delivered pricing and freight absorption practiced independently by sellers and based solely on business convenience and competitive need. But the change in the law will be unfortunate indeed if it means the reintroduction of basing-point systems that have been used so effectively in the past to restrain price competition and to distort natural market structures.

(5) Tying Contracts and Exclusive Dealer Arrangements

Large enterprisers have usually undertaken tying contracts or exclusive dealer arrangements in order to acquire or maintain patronage in that part of the market where some competition was encountered. By their use the efforts of actual or potential competitors to extend their market were thwarted and the arrangements tended to suppress competition. Despite this, the courts found that under the prevailing law of 1914 they could not condemn the development. To meet the situation, particularly the tying contracts uncovered in the Dick[125] and United Shoe Machinery[126] cases, Congress enacted Section 3 of the Clayton Act. Section 3 forbids the sale or lease of either patented or unpatented articles if the purchaser or lessee is required *not to use or deal in* the goods of a competitor of the producer, and if the effect of such an arrangement may be "to substantially lessen competition or tend to create a monopoly in any line of commerce."

The efficacy of this prohibition is not limited to the activities of the Federal Trade Commission. A number of the outstanding cases have arisen through suits of private parties and prosecutions by the Department of Justice. While these cases do not provide evidence relating to the value of the administrative regulation of business practices, they do provide precedents for the judicial review of the Commission's orders, and serve to indicate the general effectiveness of the law.

It is clear from the language of Section 3 that Congress did not intend to condemn all tying contracts. Only those tying restrictions are unlaw-

---

[125] Henry v. A. B. Dick Co., 224 U. S. 1 (1912).
[126] United States v. United Shoe Machinery Co., 247 U. S. 32 (1918).

ful which lessen competition substantially or tend to create a monopoly. This qualification has caused the greatest difficulty and controversy in the interpretation and application of the statute. The relative size and position of the producer in his industry has been important in determining the degree to which competition has been lessened. In the leading case involving the United Shoe Machinery Corporation,[127] the Supreme Court emphasized the fact that the defendant controlled 95 per cent of the shoe machinery production. It said: "When it is considered that the United Company occupies a dominating position in supplying shoe machinery of the classes involved, these covenants signed by the lessee and binding upon him effectually prevent him from acquiring the machinery of a competitor of the lessor except at the risk of forfeiting the right to use the machines furnished by the United Company which may be absolutely essential to the prosecution and success of his business."[128] A similar consideration led the courts to condemn the restrictive clause in the agreements of the Radio Corporation of America licensing the manufacture of radio sets. The Radio Corporation, owner of numerous patents on radio apparatus, required its licensees to use only its tubes (upon which the basic patent had expired) in the original equipment of radio sets. Since the Radio Corporation and its licensees controlled about 70 per cent of the receiving set business, and the Corporation 62 per cent of the entire tube field, there was found to be a substantial lessening of competition in the manufacture and sale of radio tubes.[129] The factor of dominating position was also significant in the invalidation of the tying clause contained in the leasing contracts for the patented tabulating machines of the International Business Machines Corporation.[130] In this instance a clause provided that if cards not purchased from the owner of the machines were used, the contract of lease would be terminated. Its only competitor in the field, Remington Rand, Inc., used the same type of lease.[131] And they had agreed not to try to sell tabulating cards to each other's customers. The Court stated that International Business Machines sold 81 per cent of the total output of tabulating cards and derived one-third of its gross receipts from this source. And it appeared that others could manufacture cards suitable for use in the machines. These facts led the Court to the conclusion that the tying clause eliminated competition in the sale of tabulating cards and "has in fact been an important and effective step in the creation of monopoly."

---

[127] United Shoe Machinery Corp. v. United States, 258 U. S. 451 (1922).
[128] Ibid., pp. 457–458.
[129] Lord v. Radio Corp. of America, 24 Fed. (2nd) 505 (1928); certiorari denied, 278 U. S. 648 (1928).
[130] International Business Machines Corp. v. United States, 298 U. S. 131 (1936).
[131] Remington Rand, Inc., agreed to abide by the decision in the above case.

The Federal Trade Commission issued a considerable number of orders against tying contracts in the years immediately following its organization. In several early cases it was found that firms were attempting to utilize patent rights for the extension of control over articles which were unpatented.[132] These orders, which included one against the A. B. Dick mimeograph concern, were accepted without appeal to the courts. The Commission did not meet with the same success, however, with respect to the 27 orders issued in the so-called "tank-and-pump" cases.[133] These orders were directed against a practice of oil companies whereby tanks and pumps were leased to dealers at a nominal rental on condition that they confine the use of this equipment to the storage and sale of gasoline purchased from the lessor. There was no stipulation that a dealer could not also lease the equipment of a competitor and sell his gasoline, but, since a single set of equipment was sufficient to handle the business of many filling stations, the contracts had the effect of confining the purchases of a dealer to the products of one company. Small independent refiners felt that the tying practice was disadvantageous to them because they would also have to supply tanks and pumps in order to obtain market outlets for their gasoline. It was a desire to protect the competitive interests of this group against the large refiners that prompted the Commission to attack the restrictive leases. But the orders were promptly vacated by the courts on the ground that no substantial lessening of competition had been demonstrated. Justice McReynolds, in the course of his opinion in a consolidated case, said: "Neither the findings nor the evidence show circumstances similar to those surrounding the 'tying' covenants of the Shoe Machinery Company. Many competitors seek to sell excellent brands of gasoline. . . . The contract, open and fair upon its face, provides an unconstrained recipient with free receptacle and pump for storing, dispensing, advertising and protecting the lessor's brand. . . . No purpose or power to acquire unlawful monopoly has been disclosed, and the record does not show that the probable effect of the practice will be unduly to lessen competition. Upon the contrary, it appears to have promoted the public convenience by inducing many small dealers to enter the business and put gasoline on sale at the crossroads."[134] After this thumping reversal, there was no further judicial test of the Commission's power to suppress tying contracts for a number of years. But more recently a number of orders have been issued against firms who have leased machinery on the condition that only supplies furnished by

---

[132] A. B. Dick Co., 1 F. T. C. 20 (1917); National Binding Machine Co., 1 F. T. C. 44 (1917); Chamberlain Cartridge & Target Co., 2 F. T. C. 357 (1920).

[133] Two of the cases were: Sinclair Refining Co., 2 F. T. C. 127 (1919); and Standard Oil Company of Indiana, 2 F. T. C. 26 and 46 (1920).

[134] F. T. C. v. Sinclair Refining Co., 261 U. S. 463, 474–475 (1923).

the lessor be used in the machines. These have met with the approval of the courts, since the firms involved occupied influential positions in their fields.[135]

The unlawfulness of the closely related practice of exclusive dealing also hinges on the question of whether or not competition is substantially lessened. Here again the size and strength of the firm appears to be the guiding consideration. In the leading case, Standard Fashion Co. v. Magrane-Houston Co.,[136] the Supreme Court grounded its decision, voiding an exclusive dealer contract, on the dominating position of the manufacturer of dress patterns in the pattern field. It was shown that the Standard Fashion Company together with two allied firms controlled two-fifths of the 52,000 pattern agencies in the United States. Since there was no provision for exclusive representation, that is, tying up only one dealer in a town in exchange for the promise to handle no patterns of other manufacturers, the arrangement had the effect of excluding competitors from a large share of the market. There was a clear monopoly in small communities and a substantial threat of one even in the larger centers where the best stores were likely to be tied up. A similar situation was presented in the Q. R. S. Music Company case, prosecuted by the Commission.[137] The respondent was found to control over 50 per cent of the business in music-rolls for player-pianos, and had entered into exclusive dealing agreements with several hundred of the largest dealers in musical instruments. The dominant position of the firm and the decided restriction imposed upon the opportunities of competitors by the exclusive dealing arrangements were important factors in the issuance of an order by the Commission and its approval in the courts.[138] A like order was issued and upheld against the Carter Carburetor Corporation, one of the largest manufacturers of automobile carburetors. The company was restrained from carrying out a policy of charging higher prices or refusing to sell to service stations and other dealers who used or dealt in the products of its competitors.[139]

The reversal of the Commission's order against the Pearsall Butter Company[140] is a further indication of the importance of size. In the

---

[135] Signode Steel Strapping Co. v. F. T. C., 132 Fed. (2d) 48 (1942); Thomson Mfg. Co. v. F. T. C., 150 Fed. (2d) 952 (1945), certiorari denied 326 U. S. 776 (1945).

[136] 258 U. S. 346 (1922). A proceeding attacking substantially identical contracts was undertaken by the Commission against the Butterick Company, which controlled the Standard Fashion Company and several other pattern concerns. The Commission's order was upheld fully in Butterick Co. v. F. T. C., 4 Fed. (2nd) 910 (1925); certiorari denied, 267 U. S. 602 (1925).

[137] 7 F. T. C. 412 (1924).

[138] F. T. C. v. Q. R. S. Music Co., 12 Fed. (2nd) 730 (1926).

[139] Carter Caburetor Corp. v. F. T. C., 112 Fed. (2d) 722 (1940).

[140] B. S. Pearsall Butter Co., 5 F. T. C. 127 (1922); B. S. Pearsall Butter Co. v. F. T. C., 292 Fed. 720 (1923).

Commission's opinion the respondent was restraining competition in the sale of oleomargarine through its practice of refusing to sell to wholesalers except on an exclusive dealing basis. The Commission's findings revealed that there were numerous competitors in the respondent's territory, some of whom also used exclusive dealing contracts. Upon judicial review the order was vacated because there was a "mere possibility" of undesirable consequences. The court emphasized the fact that since the company did only about 1 per cent of the total business of the country, it held no dominant position in the industry. Moreover, exclusive representation accompanied the exclusive dealing arrangement, and no effort was made to impose restrictions on retail dealers. In these circumstances, there could be no finding of a substantial lessening of competition.

It should be noted, also, that exclusive dealing restrictions on agents of the seller have been sustained. This was the outcome of a proceeding in which the Commission attacked the Curtis Publishing Company's practice of requiring wholesale distributors of its magazines not to handle the periodicals of other publishers. The Commission held that the company sold its products to magazine dealers and suppressed competition through exclusive dealer arrangements which hampered other publishers in obtaining distributing facilities.[141] The company contended that its dealers did not buy its publications, but handled them as agents for the company. It went on to argue that a statute applicable solely to sales or leases could not properly interfere with it. In upholding this contention and vacating the Commission's order, the Supreme Court declared: "Judged by its terms, we think this contract (between respondent and its distributors) is one of agency, not of sale upon condition, and the record reveals no surrounding circumstances sufficient to give it a different character. This, of course, disposes of the charges under the Clayton Act. The engagement of competent agents obligated to devote their time and attention to developing the principal's business, to the exclusion of all others, where nothing else appears, has long been recognized as proper and unobjectionable practice."[142]

As an analysis of the cases shows, the practices of tying and exclusive dealing are not unfair competition as such and hence are not unlawful in all circumstances. Users or dealers in differentiated products are not insured complete liberty of choice as to the other products which they must use or might choose to handle. A manufacturer of a distinctive product may interfere in some measure with the trading opportunities of competitors. He has been precluded from doing so, however, where a

---

[141] Curtis Publishing Co., 2 F. T. C. 20 (1919).
[142] F. T. C. v. Curtis Publishing Co., 260 U. S. 568, 581–582 (1923).

dominating position in the field has already been acquired by means of patents or combination. Attempts on the part of the Commission to go beyond this have been frustrated by the courts.

There is some indication on the basis of two recent decisions of the Supreme Court that the Commission may find it somewhat easier to attack objectionable tying and exclusive dealing arrangements. In the International Salt case of 1947,[143] the Court had before it the company's practice of leasing its patented salt machines on condition that lessees buy salt for use in the machines exclusively from it. It was true that the defendant was the country's largest producer of salt for industrial uses, but there was no evidence of the proportion of the business of supplying salt machines controlled by International, nor was there a showing of the actual effect of the tying clauses upon competition. The crux of the matter was that the company had closed this particular market for salt against competition, and, according to Justice Jackson, "Not only is price-fixing unreasonable *per se*, . . . but also it is unreasonable, *per se*, to foreclose competitors from any substantial market."[144] The volume of business involved ($500,000 in 1944) could not be regarded as "insignificant or insubstantial," and the obvious tendency of the arrangement, in the opinion of the Court, was in the direction of monopoly.

A similar line of reasoning in Standard Oil Co. of California v. United States,[145] led the Court to find unlawful exclusive dealing arrangements between Standard and independent service stations. Exclusive supply contracts had been entered into with 5,937 independent dealers who undertook to buy all their requirements of petroleum products from Standard and in some instances tires, tubes, and batteries, as well. These dealers purchased about $58,000,000 worth of gasoline, comprising 6.7 per cent of the total in the area, and about $8,000,000 of other products from Standard in 1947. The defendant was the largest seller of gasoline in the area, having sold 23 per cent of the total in 1946, but was found as a matter of law not to occupy a dominant position. The Court held that actual diminishing of competition need not be shown and that it is sufficient to prove that "competition has been foreclosed in a substantial share of the line of commerce affected." In conclusion, it was stated: "It cannot be gainsaid that observance by a dealer of his requirements contract with Standard does effectively foreclose whatever opportunity there might be for competing suppliers to attract his patronage, and it is clear that the affected proportion of retail sales of petroleum products is substantial."[146]

---

[143] International Salt Co. v. United States, 332 U. S. 392 (1947).
[144] *Ibid.*, p. 396.
[145] 337 U. S. 293 (1949).
[146] *Ibid.*

With less emphasis upon the degree of market control and more upon the actual business which is affected by restrictive practices, the way should be opened to the elimination of many restraints on competition that serve no legitimate economic need. It is still true that not all tying and exclusive dealing arrangements are illegal, but their use by incipient monopolies may be prevented more easily.

22

Maintaining Standards of Fair Competition

Thus far, the discussion of the 1914 legislation has centered around the attempt to protect the existence of competition in the economic system. It is now the purpose to consider activities of the Federal Trade Commission relating to the maintenance of standards of fair competition. Practices which fall within this sphere of activity are those which are essentially dishonest and unethical, but which do not necessarily suppress competition or create monopoly. They are the type of unfair practice with which the common law attempted to deal, and include such things as the deceitful diversion of patronage, misappropriation of confidential information, and disparagement. While practices of this sort are fraudulent and therefore deserving of extermination, they are also uneconomic in character. Their elimination is grounded on the notion that economic welfare will be enhanced only if competitors are permitted to survive on the basis of their efficiency in production and their ability to meet the effective demands of consumers. Competitors who utilize unethical means to obtain patronage injure their more scrupulous and efficient rivals and reduce the total satisfactions of consumers. The very survival of the competitive system, like democracy itself, requires individual honesty and fair dealing.

In endeavoring to establish certain ethical standards of competitive conduct, the Commission has operated exclusively under Section 5 of the Federal Trade Commission Act, which outlaws "unfair methods of competition" in interstate commerce. Under this broad authority the Commission has endeavored to suppress a great variety of competitive practices, and many orders have been issued. In fact, at least three-fourths of the Commission's orders have pertained to practices involving elements of deception or fraud. A large measure of success has attended the efforts of the Commission here, especially as regards misrepresentation and deceptive advertising. Before looking at the nature and scope of its proceedings, however, it will be desirable to analyze the limitations upon its jurisdiction as interpreted by the Supreme Court.

I. JURISDICTION OF THE COMMISSION

In reviewing the practices attacked by the Commission as "unfair methods of competition" under Section 5, the Supreme Court in a number of cases has established certain requirements which must be met if an order is to be upheld. The significant tests are: First, is the practice carried on in *interstate commerce;* second, is it actually *unfair;* third, is it a *competitive* practice; fourth, is the proceeding to the *"interest of the public"?* Strictly speaking, these were the tests which were applied prior to the Wheeler-Lea Act of 1938.[1] The 1938 amendment of Section 5 did materially affect the requirement of competition, however, and the change will be considered in the following discussion of the basic requirements.

(I) Interstate Commerce

Since all exercise of Federal power over trade and commerce is governed by constitutional law, it is obvious that the jurisdiction of the Commission could extend only to practices in interstate commerce. On several occasions the courts have upset orders of the Commission on the ground that their subject-matter was intrastate commerce and therefore beyond Federal power.[2] Only one case will be considered, namely, Federal Trade Commission *v.* Bunte Brothers, Inc.[3] This decision by the Supreme Court is significant because it confines the jurisdiction of the Federal Trade Commission to more narrow limits than that of Federal administrative agencies regulating railroads and labor relations.

The order reviewed by the Supreme Court forbade the use of lotteries in the sale of candy, a practice which is clearly unlawful. The respondent was Bunte Brothers, a candy manufacturer in Illinois, who sold so-called "break and take" packages to traders within the state. This was clearly intrastate commerce. But the Commission forbade such intrastate sales because the respondent was able thereby to compete unfairly with manufacturers outside of Illinois who were definitely precluded from selling chance assortments of candy in the Illinois market. The Supreme Court, with Justices Douglas, Black, and Reed dissenting, refused to assent to this application of the classic Shreveport doctrine—a court holding which gave the Interstate Commerce Commission authority over intrastate railway rates which discriminated against and thereby injuri-

---

[1] Public No. 447 (75th Congress), approved March 21, 1938.

[2] Winslow *v.* Commission, 277 Fed. 206 (1921); Canfield Oil Co. *v.* Commission, 274 Fed. 571 (1921); Utah-Idaho Sugar Co. *v.* Commission, 22 Fed. (2nd) 122 (1927); California Rice Industry *v.* F. T. C., 102 Fed. (2nd) 716 (1939).

[3] 312 U. S. 349 (1941).

ously affected interstate traffic.[4] It was held that the Federal Trade Commission Act prohibits unfair practices *in* interstate commerce and does not extend to those which in any way affect interstate commerce. Mr. Justice Frankfurter stated: "The construction of section 5 urged by the Commission would thus give a federal agency pervasive control over myriads of local businesses in matters heretofore traditionally left to local custom or local law. Such control bears no resemblance to the strictly confined authority growing out of railroad rate discrimination. An inroad upon local conditions and local standards of such far-reaching import as is involved here, ought to await a clearer mandate from Congress."[5] Until Congress undertakes to give the Commission express power to protect interstate commerce against unfair practices carried on in local business, the Commission must confine itself to the statutory jurisdiction of practices *in* interstate commerce.

(2) Unfairness

Since the beginning there have been wide differences of opinion as to what specific practices should be included in the rather vague and general category of "unfair." Some believed that the language covered only those practices which were proscribed by the common law as "unfair competition." Others believed that the phrase applied to all practices deemed by the Commission to be against the public interest.[6] Senator Cummins, for example, stated that the intent of Congress was to allow the words "unfair competition" to "grow and broaden and mold themselves to meet circumstances as they arise."[7] This at any rate suggested that the concept was to be an elastic one, but it did not specify the new conditions to be covered by the law.

The first case involving Section 5 to come before the Supreme Court was Federal Trade Commission *v.* Gratz.[8] The Gratz Company had refused to sell steel ties for baling cotton unless a certain amount of jute bagging was also purchased. The Commission had condemned this practice of combination selling or full-line-forcing as monopolistic in the circumstances presented. But the Court reversed the Commission on the technical ground that the complaint failed to allege, although the findings were substantiated by the record, that there was a substantial lessening of competition. In the course of its opinion, the Court made a most significant and often-quoted declaration. It said: "The words 'unfair method of competition' are not defined by the statute and their

---

[4] Houston & Texas Ry. *v.* U. S., 234 U. S. 342 (1914).

[5] F. T. C. *v.* Bunte Brothers, Inc., 312 U. S. 349, 354–355 (1941).

[6] For a concise statement of the numerous and conflicting definitions of the terms "unfair methods of competition," see Handler, *op. cit.*, pp. 237–240.

[7] 51 *Congressional Record* 14,003 (1914).

[8] 253 U. S. 421 (1920).

exact meaning is in dispute. It is for the courts, not the commission, ultimately to determine as matter of law, what they include. They are clearly inapplicable to practices never heretofore regarded as opposed to good morals because characterized by deception, bad faith, fraud or oppression, or as against public policy because of their dangerous tendency unduly to hinder competition or create monopoly."[9]

This was a very narrow and restrictive interpretation. The clear statement that the courts were to have the final word as to what practices are unfair was not surprising. Since unfairness involves statutory interpretation, a question of law, it could not be otherwise. But the small content given to the phrase "unfair methods of competition" seems unfortunate. The inclusion of monopolistic practices was quite in line with the intention of Congress and, as shown earlier in this discussion, has served a useful purpose. It was also logical to include practices of a deceptive, fraudulent or oppressive nature. But the significant fact is that the law was to be applied only to those deceptive practices *which up to that time* had been regarded as "opposed to good morals." Since the courts reserved the right to make the ultimate decision as to unfairness, it was to be implied that the statute covered only those practices condemned under the common law and the Sherman Act. Such a conception was unduly rigid and would have left little or no room for the growth which Congress contemplated when delegating authority to the Commission in general and comprehensive terms.

Fortunately, the view expressed in the Gratz case has not prevailed. But for a long time it was quoted with approval, and was a significant factor in impeding the attempts of the Commission to build up a law of unfair competition. The first break came in the Winsted Hosiery case,[10] when the Supreme Court upheld an order against a practice which was not actionable at common law or under the Sherman Act. Action had been taken against the respondent on the ground that it misbranded and falsely advertised its products. It labelled and advertised its products as "cashmere," "gray wool," and "worsted," when in truth they were composed largely of cotton. The Commission found that a substantial part of the consuming public was deceived by this misrepresentation and purchased these goods when they actually wanted all-woolen garments. Consequently, trade was diverted from producers of genuine woolen garments and other direct competitors who branded their products truthfully. The company contended that misbranding was so common in the industry that its faulty labelling deceived no manufacturers or dealers. The lower court of appeal reversed the Commission's order on the ground that there was no monopoly, deception, or injury to other manufactur-

---

[9] *Ibid.*, p. 427.
[10] F. T. C. *v.* Winsted Hosiery Co., 258 U. S. 483 (1922).

ers.[11] This decision, however, was reversed by the Supreme Court and the order fully sustained. The Court repudiated the contention of the company and held that consumers were misled by the misbranding, and, hence the business of honest competitors was necessarily affected. The Commission was justified, therefore, in finding it an unfair method of competition.

It was not until 1934, however, that the Supreme Court reviewed the whole subject and stated a concept of unfair competition quite at variance with the original definition. In Federal Trade Commission v. R. F. Keppel & Bro., Inc.,[12] the Court sustained an order prohibiting the use of lotteries or gaming devices in the sale of penny candies. Apparently, there was no element of monopoly or deception in the sales method used. It was deemed unfair because other sellers would lose patronage unless they stooped to a practice which they were "under a powerful moral compulsion not to adopt."

Mr. Justice Stone, speaking for a unanimous court, discussed the meaning and scope of Section 5 as follows:

. . . We cannot say that the Commission's jurisdiction extends only to those types of practices which happen to have been litigated before this Court. Neither the language nor the history of the Act suggests that Congress intended to confine the forbidden methods to fixed and unyielding categories. . . . While this Court has declared that it is for the courts to determine what practices or methods of competition are to be deemed unfair, Federal Trade Commission v. Gratz, *supra,* in passing on that question the determination of the Commission is of weight. . . . New or different practices must be considered as they arise in the light of the circumstances in which they are employed.[13]

A decided change in attitude on the part of the Court is indicated. Some twenty years after the enactment of the law the original intent of Congress appears to have been formally recognized. The Court still reserves the right to say what practices are unfair, a situation which probably must obtain until Congress enumerates the specific practices which are unlawful. The Commission, however, is conceded the right to extend its jurisdiction to "new or different" practices, and its determinations are to have "weight." The category of unfair practices is not closed, it is subject to expansion and growth. The precise boundaries of this new sphere of operations are not defined, but it seems clear that the Commission is to be given greater freedom to achieve a higher plane of competitive conduct.

(3) Competition

Since the law is phrased in terms of "unfair methods of competition," it would be expected that the Commission's jurisdiction depended on a

---

[11] 272 Fed. 957 (1921).
[12] 291 U. S. 304 (1934).
[13] *Ibid.,* pp. 309–314.

showing that competitors existed and were adversely affected by the unfair methods in question. This issue was involved in the important
Raladam case.[14] The Raladam Company sold a thyroid obesity cure
which it advertised as a safe, effective, and dependable remedy. The
Supreme Court, in reviewing the order of the Commission, agreed that
the preparation could not "be used generally with safety to physical
health except under medical direction and advice."[15] But it was not
enough to show that the advertisements were "dangerously misleading."
The order was vacated because the Court found in the record no proof
of the existence of competitors or that they had been injured. The Commission had rested its decision on the presumptions that the interests of
the medical profession were injured and that trade was diverted from
other manufacturers of similar preparations. But the Court declared
that physicians were engaged in a profession and not a trade, and were
not in competition with the respondent. Also, there was no proof as to
the existence of legitimate producers of "anti-obesity remedies" who
were injured and deserved protection against the dishonesty of the
respondent. The Court emphasized that the existence of either present
or potential competition satisfied the requirement of the statute, but
could not find even potential competition when applying its rule to the
facts in the case.

This decision has been criticized severely for leaving the Commission
without power to attack practices which injured consumers rather than
competitors. It seemed, unfortunately, to allow the escape of unfair
methods injurious to consumers, where the competing producers in an
industry are not injured because they all use the faulty practice. If
enough producers are guilty, no one is guilty.

It was primarily in reaction against this situation that Congress, in
1938, amended Section 5 through the enactment of the Wheeler-Lea
Act.[16] The amended statute makes "unfair or deceptive acts or practices in commerce" unlawful in addition to "unfair methods of competition." It does not require proof of the existence of competition and
injury to competitors. The Commission, thereby, extends its jurisdiction
to all unfair and deceptive business practices. Explicit recognition is
given to the need for protection to consumers as well as competitors.
It is true, of course, that consumers were given a large measure of protection even under the original statute. But now the elimination of deceptive and unfair practices, which interfere with the choices of consumers and tend thus to reduce their total satisfactions, is regarded as

---

[14] F. T. C. v. Raladam Co., 283 U. S. 643 (1931); affirming 42 Fed. (2nd) 430
(1930).
[15] 283 U. S. 643, 646.
[16] Public No. 447 (75th Congress), approved March 21, 1938.

an end coördinate with that of maintaining a plane of fair competition.[17]

While it is not related to the question of competition, one other observation should be made with respect to the new language. The insertion of the term "acts" has significance from the point of view of the commission's authority. It will enable the Commission to proceed against the sporadic use of questionable means or single acts which might develop into an established unfair method or practice. The courts have held conflicting views as to when an unfair act or acts became a "method" within the meaning of the statute.[18] Under the new provision the Commission should be able to perform the function of *preventing* the growth of unfair trade and monopoly much more advantageously.

(4) Public Interest

It will be recalled that Section 5 of the Federal Trade Commission Act provides that the Commission shall issue a complaint against any person using an unfair method of competition, "if it shall appear to the Commission that a proceeding . . . would be to the interest of the public." Considerable discussion has taken place regarding the meaning and effect of this so-called public interest clause. Former Commissioner Rublee, who claimed to have suggested the clause, stated that the purpose was simply to give the Commission some discretion in deciding whether a complaint should be issued even where jurisdiction was clear.[19] It was a measure to prevent the Commission from being overburdened with cases which had no great public significance.

But in the important Klesner case,[20] the Supreme Court decided that it was within the province of the courts and not the Commission to determine finally whether proceedings were in the public interest. The case involved a controversy between two merchants in the city of Washington over the right to use the name "The Shade Shop." The Commission undertook to settle the quarrel and issued an order in the case. The Supreme Court held that the Commission was not justified in assuming jurisdiction, since there was no "specific and substantial" public interest in the case. The Court found the controversy to be essentially private in character, and declared that "the mere fact that it is to the interest of the community that private rights shall be respected is not enough to support a finding of public interest."[21]

---

[17] For a discussion of the nature and significance of the 1938 amendments, see Martin L. Lindahl, "The Federal Trade Commission Act as Amended in 1938," *The Journal of Political Economy*, Vol. XLVII (August, 1939), pp. 497–525.

[18] *Ibid.*, p. 509.

[19] George Rublee, "The Original Plan and Early History of the Federal Trade Commission," *Proceedings of the Academy of Political Science*, Vol. XI, No. 4 (1926), pp. 117–118.

[20] F. T. C. *v.* Klesner, 280 U. S. 19 (1929).

[21] *Ibid.*, p. 28.

The decision has the merit perhaps of restraining the Commission from the prosecution of petty squabbles between competitors that can be settled satisfactorily through private actions in the courts. The Commission is advised to employ its resources in eliminating practices which threaten the existence of competition, or which adversely affect the interests of a substantial number of consumers or competitors.[22] These are the consequential matters for which the expenditure of public funds is justified. It must be recognized, nevertheless, that the administrative discretion of the Commission has been curbed by the courts beyond the intent of Congress. No harm will be done if the courts confine their interdictions to cases which are insignificant or for which there are adequate remedies in the courts. But there is the danger that over-zealous courts will substitute their judgment for that of the Commission in really important cases. Having been charged with the broad mandate to eliminate unfair competition, and being in close contact with trade and industry, it would seem that the Commission should be privileged to decide what proceedings will be in the interests of the public.

II. NATURE AND SCOPE OF THE COMMISSION'S ACTIVITIES

The proceedings which fall within the category of those designed to maintain decent standards of business conduct cover a wide range of competitive practices. The great bulk of them are unfair methods used in the promotion of sales. They have the dual effect of misleading consumers in their effort to spend their incomes most wisely and of destroying the opportunity of producers to sell their goods and services on the basis of merit. The proper functioning of the economic system is thereby impaired.

In considering the administrative record of the Commission in this sphere, the practices which have been dealt with may be classified as follows: (1) Misrepresentation or deception; (2) lotteries; (3) commercial bribery; (4) disparagement and miscellaneous interferences with competitors. This classification is necessarily arbitrary. It can be maintained, for example, that the use of lotteries as a sales device involves such an element of deception as to merit no separate treatment. It might also be urged that disparagement and other harassing tactics should be treated as monopolistic practices, since they do involve attacks upon individual competitors and are obstructive in character. The threat to the maintenance of competition in most instances is so slight, however, that they might better be treated simply as unfair competition.

---

[22] At least one of the tests of public interest was suggested by Justice Brandeis in the Winsted Hosiery case, when he said: "As a substantial part of the public was still misled by the use of the labels which the Winsted Company employed, the public had an interest in stopping the practice as wrongful." 258 U. S. 483, 494.

That the Commission has operated with some vigor in attempting to stamp out dishonest trade practices is evidenced by the statistics of complaints and orders issued by it. The vast majority of the 5,573 formal complaints issued up to June 30, 1948, have related to these business practices. And of the 2,149 orders to cease and desist that the Commission issued prior to June 30, 1938, it has been calculated that approximately 88 per cent dealt with the methods of competition here considered.[23] It is probably true, also, that this type of practice is the subject matter of nearly all of the cases which have been settled by stipulation. So far as the number of proceedings is concerned, therefore, it is apparent that the Commission's activity in maintaining fair competitive standards has assumed first place in its regulatory work.

(I) Misrepresentation

Misrepresentation in the sale of products has been the subject of more complaints and orders of the Commission than any other single unfair practice.[24] There are a great number of methods that may be utilized to effect misrepresentation. The most common are the inaccurate labelling and marking of products and the making of false and misleading statements in the advertising of commodities and services. But the important consideration is not the method used; it is rather whether or not false information has actually been disseminated. Administrative control will be analyzed, therefore, on the basis of the facts which have been misrepresented. It will include misrepresentation as to: (a) Character of products, (b) quality, (c) origin, (d) value.

(a) Character of Products

Encouraged by its sweeping victory in the Winsted Hosiery case,[25] the Commission has proceeded vigorously against the practice of falsely describing the composition of goods offered for sale. It will be recalled that the practice of mislabelling textile fabrics had become so common in the trade that manufacturers and dealers were fully aware of the inaccuracies of the labels and were not deceived by them. This fact, how-

---

[23] National Industrial Conference Board, *Public Regulation of Competitive Practices in Business Enterprise* (New York, 1940), p. 299. Appendix A of this work contains a complete statistical summary of the Commission's proceedings from 1916 to 1938. For a less comprehensive summary see L. S. Lyon, M. W. Watkins, and Victor Abramson, *Government and Economic Life* (Washington, D. C.: The Brookings Institution, 1939), Appendix B.
[24] Misrepresentation, including trade-mark simulation and the use of bogus independents, was the subject-matter of 1,436 of the total number of 2,149 orders issued by the Commission through June 30, 1938. National Industrial Conference Board. *Public Regulation of Competitive Practices in Business Enterprise*, p. 299.
[25] F. T. C. v. Winsted Hosiery Co., 258 U. S. 483 (1922).

ever, was held not to justify the practice. So long as the consuming public was deceived by the inaccurate labels, and consumers were induced to buy materials which they did not intend to purchase, the trade practice was clearly unfair. Moreover, injury was suffered by competitors who produced the genuine article or marked their substitutes truthfully.

Numerous industries have been subjected to the Commission's regulation. In the paint and varnish industry a large number of orders have been issued against respondents who falsely represented their products as containing the standard amount of white lead, or pure ingredients such as linseed oil and shellac.[26] Manufacturers of fur products,[27] jewelry,[28] leather goods,[29] metal products,[30] stationery,[31] and toilet articles[32] have been enjoined from misrepresenting the character of their products on a great many occasions. Similarly, sellers of hats, typewriters, and tires, who failed to disclose that the products offered for sale were renovated or rebuilt and not new, have been attacked by the Commission,[33] as has the issuance of old films under new titles without indicating that the pictures were reissues.[34]

But it is in the textile field that the Commission has probably been most active in suppressing the fraud of promoting sales by the inaccurate description of products. The prevalence of misbranding is due in part to the inability of the average purchaser to ascertain the fibre content of

---

[26] Specimen cases are Louis Leavitt v. F. T. C., 16 Fed. (2nd) 1019 (1926), affirming order in Louis Leavitt, 9 F. T. C. 221 (1925); and F. T. C. v. Cassoff, 38 Fed. (2nd) 790 (1930), modifying and affirming order in L. F. Cassoff, compl. 1062 (1924). In the Leavitt case the decree of the court was violated on two occasions, the court imposing a fine of $500 in 1929 and a fine of $1,000 in 1935 (*Annual Report*, 1936, pp. 81–82).
For citations and summaries of the hundreds of orders and stipulations issued by the Commission in proceedings involving misrepresentation see Commerce Clearing House, *Trade Regulation Service* (ninth edition), pp. 6525–6813; 12,011–15,500.
[27] Golden Fur Dyeing Co., 14 F. T. C. 377 (1931), and Hugh Wallace Co., 20 F. T. C. 46 (1934), are illustrative cases.
[28] Bradley-Boston, Inc., 15 F. T. C. 20 (1931); Bulova Watch Co., 16 F. T. C. 529 (1932).
[29] Masland Duraleather Co. v. F. T. C., 34 Fed. (2nd) 733 (1929), upholding order in Masland Duraleather Co., 12 F. T. C. 351 (1929); and Ohio Leather Co. v. F. T. C., 45 Fed. (2nd) 39 (1930), vacating and later modifying the order in Ohio Leather Co., 12 F. T. C. 323 (1929).
[30] National Silver Co. v. F. T. C., 88 Fed. (2nd) 425 (1937), affirming order in National Silver Co., 22 F. T. C. 730 (1936); National Silver Co., 24 F. T. C. 722 (1937), modified 27 F. T. C. 558 (1938).
[31] Turner & Porter, 7 F. T. C. 100 (1923); Process Engraving Co., 30 F. T. C. 720 (1940).
[32] Palais Royal, 4 F. T. C. 305 (1922); Jean Vivadou Co., 24 F. T. C. 124 (1936).
[33] Typewriter Emporium, 1 F. T. C. 105 (1918); Ironclad Tire Co., 1 F. T. C. 380 (1919); Gilman Hat Co., 17 F. T. C. 352 (1933).
[34] Fox Film Corp. v. F. T. C., 296 Fed. 353 (1924), affirming order in Fox Film Corp., 6 F. T. C. 191 (1923).

textile fabrics. The coming of rayon and its struggle to attain its present strong position among the older textile fibres has also contributed to the need for extensive regulatory action. It has not been the Commission's purpose to interfere with the development and use of this synthetic product. Here, as elsewhere, it has been recognized that imitation and substitute products may be as serviceable as the originals, and that the public will gain from the introduction of cheaper products to serve old uses. It has insisted, however, that prospective purchasers be duly informed of the nature of the substitute commodities, and that consumer acceptance be obtained on the merits of substitutes, rather than on the established reputation of the genuine product. In line with this policy the Commission at an early date recognized the term "rayon" as properly designating artificial silk products made from cellulose.[35] It has issued numerous orders and stipulations against representing fabrics composed wholly or partly of rayon as "silk," "pongee," "satin" or "taffeta."[36] Trade practices in the older branches of the textile industry, as evidenced by the Winsted case, were not beyond reproach, and they also have been subjected to repeated action by the Commission.[37]

Perhaps the most notable feature of the attempt to eliminate misrepresentation in the textile industry has been the establishment of positive obligations upon producers to label their products truthfully. This has been accomplished by the Commission through the trade practice conference. For the wool industry Congress took a hand and enacted the Wool Products Labelling Act of 1939.[38] The first rules were those promulgated for the rayon industry.[39] They not only condemn the misbranding of rayon fibre, but declare it to be an unfair trade practice to conceal or fail to make disclosure of the fibre content of fabrics containing more than one fibre. Such disclosure is to be made by designating each constituent fibre in the order of its predominance by weight. It is further recommended as a Group II rule, one of those rules which are not legally binding, that sellers disclose the actual proportions or percentages of the constituents of mixed fabrics. Similar fibre identification rules

---

[35] See official resolution of the Commission published October 31, 1925, Commerce Clearing House, *op. cit.*, p. 20, 275.

[36] Puritan Silk Corp., 8 F. T. C. 361 (1925); Bernard-Hewitt & Co., 12 F. T. C. 291 (1928); Kemper Silk Co., 14 F. T. C. 326 (1931).

[37] Illustrative cases are Nashua Mfg. Co., 8 F. T. C. 407 (1925) (labelling cotton blankets as "Woolnap"); Sea Island Thread Co., 11 F. T. C. 97 (1927) (selling cotton sewing thread as "Satin Silk"); Louis Fabrikant, 23 F. T. C. 610 (1936) (using name "Camel Suede" on fabric not made of camel wool).

Very few cases have been appealed to the courts. The Commission's order was fully upheld in Sea Island Thread Co. *v.* F. T. C., 22 Fed. (2nd) 1019 (1927). In N. Fluegelman & Co. *v.* F. T. C., 37 Fed. (2nd) 59 (1930), the order was modified to permit the respondent to mark goods "Satinmaid" if it were shown equally conspicuously that they were cotton fabrics.

[38] Public No. 850, approved October 14, 1940, effective July 14, 1941.

[39] Trade Practice Rules for the Rayon Industry, October 26, 1937.

appear in the trade practice rules of the silk industry.[40] The silk rules also govern the weighting of silk products, and require not only the disclosure of metallic weighting, but the proportion or percentage thereof in any silk product. These rules, drawn up with the coöperation of the industries themselves, manifest real progress in giving concrete meaning to unfair competition in particular fields.

Whether the courts will uphold the Commission in its attempt to fix positive requirements for the branding of merchandise has not been established. It may be significant that the part of an order requiring a respondent to use words describing each constituent fibre in the order of its predominance by weight and to state the percentage of any fibre not present in substantial amount was found by a court to be too burdensome, and was modified.[41] However, no trade practice rule such as this governed the trade in woolens,[42] and it does not follow that the courts will withhold their approval from a development which offers so much promise for the textile and other industries.

Because it was doubtful whether the Commission had the authority to compel manufacturers and others to affix labels to their products and to require certain specified information on these labels, Congress enacted the Wool Products Labelling Act. It was conceded that any dishonest disclosure on labels could be attacked, but it was not certain that full disclosure of pertinent facts could be required.[43] The peculiar circumstance in the woolen trade which seemed to warrant a special law was not so much the failure to disclose the presence of substitutes in alleged wool products as the failure to reveal the amount of shoddy or reclaimed wool contained in woolen fabrics.[44] The amount of reclaimed wool used by wool-textile manufacturers was estimated to be about one-half of the virgin or new wool used in the country, yet rarely was the presence of reclaimed wool ever disclosed to the buying public.[45] Considerable divergence of opinion existed as to whether such disclosure was necessary to

---

[40] Trade Practice Rules for the Silk Industry, November 4, 1938.

[41] Gimbel Bros. v. F. T. C., 116 Fed. (2nd) 578 (1941).

[42] Other circumstances in the case were probably of importance. The dress fabrics advertised as woolens were a job-lot of "mill ends." The complaint was that Gimbel Bros. represented mixed goods as all-wool, and the court stated that the order requiring the identification of fibres in the order of their predominance went beyond the complaint. The court did insist that the respondent designate the constituent fibres other than wool, if wool were mentioned, and that the quantity of wool be not exaggerated.

[43] Proposed trade practice rules for the wool industry were published by the Commission on November 26, 1938, and public hearings were held December 14–15, 1938, but the rules were never adopted. They provided for the disclosure of virgin and reclaimed wool and other fibres in "woolen" fabrics.

[44] For a legislative history and explanatory summary of the law see F. J. C., Annual Report, 1941, pp. 7–8.

[45] Report of W. T. Kelley, Chief Counsel, Federal Trade Commission, on Wool Fabric Labelling, Hearings on H. R. 944, before Sub-committee of House, Interstate and Foreign Commerce Commission, 76th Congress 1st Session (1939), p. 6.

protect the consumer, and whether it could actually be enforced.[46] The quality of woolen fabrics does not always depend on the amount of new wool used, for there are many grades of virgin wool, the lowest of which are inferior to the better grades of reclaimed wool. Moreover, it is not established that the presence of reworked or reused wool in a fabric can be detected by laboratory tests. It was urged, therefore, that a prejudice against fabrics using reworked wool would be built up by requiring a disclosure which could not be defended on the basis of merit.

In order to protect manufacturers, distributors, and consumers from the unrevealed presence of substitutes and mixtures in woolen products, the statute provides that the misbranding of woolen products moving in interstate commerce is an unfair method of competition and an unfair and deceptive act or practice under the Federal Trade Commission Act.[47] A product is misbranded if it is falsely identified or does not have a label which shows the precentage by weight of (a) wool, (b) reprocessed wool, (c) reused wool, (d) each fibre other than wool if 5 per cent or more, and (e) the aggregate of all other fibers.[48] The name or registered identification number of the manufacturer or a dealer must be included.[49] Both reprocessed and reused wool are fibers obtained from woven or felted wool products, the distinction being that reused wool is that obtained from products which have been used in any way by ultimate consumers. Presumably the fibre reclaimed from fabrics which have been used is inferior to other types of reclaimed fibre.

General authority to administer the law is vested in the Federal Trade Commission. It is authorized to make rules and regulations pertaining to the manner of disclosing information required by the statute and other matters, and to enforce the law under its regular procedure. The Commission, by itself or in coöperation with other agencies, is authorized to make any necessary tests and examinations of wool products, but it is unlikely that this procedure will be of great value in enforcing the law. It is doubtful whether laboratory tests are adequate to detect reprocessed or reused fibre in wool products. Chief reliance will have to be placed upon the records customarily kept by manufacturers showing the nature and quality of fibres in their products. Under penalty of fine,

---

[46] It is of more than passing significance that the bill was strongly supported by the wool-growers, the hope being that the demand for virgin wool would be increased. Wyoming attempted to enforce such disclosure.

[47] Certain wool products are exempted, namely, carpets, rugs, mats, or upholsteries. Also, exports are excluded if they are branded in accordance with the specifications of the purchaser and the laws of the foreign country. Imported woolen products, of course, are subject to the provisions of the law.

[48] Wool Products Labelling Act, Section 4, and regulations thereunder.

[49] *Idem.* Other requirements are that the percentage of non-fibrous loading or adulterating matter must be revealed and, in the case of wool products represented as wool or containing other fibres, the percentage of wool must be shown in words and figures plainly legible.

manufacturers are now required to keep such records of fibre content, and to preserve them for at least three years.[50] Inspection of these records, it is believed, will afford evidence as to the adequacy and truthfulness of the information contained on labels. In addition to its usual process of administration, the Commission is authorized to bring in the courts seizure and condemnation proceedings against misbranded goods and to obtain injunctions against violations. Willful violations of the law are subject to criminal penalties.[51]

The new law marks a great advance in consumer protection. Its positive requirements will make it difficult for manufacturers to delude purchasers into the buying of goods that they do not want. Unfortunately, however, the requirements regarding reclaimed wool may not work out as anticipated. Quality woolens often contain a considerable amount of reclaimed wool, and it would be unfortunate indeed if for that reason buyers were now to reject these products. Enforcement of the law has required continuous surveillance of the labelling practices of specific concerns. During the fiscal year 1948, the Commission reported that field inspections had been made of 8,966 manufacturers and dealers in wool products which covered more than 23 million articles.[52] Correction of improper labelling practices has been achieved largely through voluntary action, although some formal proceedings have been necessary. The Commission has found it unnecessary to invoke the more drastic remedies available against deliberate violations of the law.

Another difficult and controversial issue which has arisen in the Commission and in the courts with respect to misrepresenting the character of products has related to the use of descriptive names and terms which have lost their original meaning and have acquired in popular usage different or secondary meanings. The question has been whether or not these ambiguous terms actually deceive the consuming public and warrant administrative action. A few outstanding cases will illustrate the point in question and suggest the effectiveness with which the Commission and the courts have handled the matter.

One of the most interesting cases involved the attempt of the Commission to prohibit the use of the name "castile" to describe soap not made exclusively from olive oil.[53] The Commission conceded that the name was no longer understood to mean soap manufactured in the province of Castile, Spain, but found that by custom and usage any soap whose oily ingredient is derived from olives is known as castile soap. Evidence was adduced to show that a pure olive oil soap has distinctive qualities which are desired by many consumers as well as by members of the medical

---

[50] *Ibid.*, Section 6 (b).
[51] *Ibid.*, Sections 7 and 10.
[52] *Annual Report*, 1948, pp. 63–65.
[53] James S. Kirk & Co., 12 F. T. C. 272 (1928).

profession, and that these purchasers were deceived when buying imitation castile soap. Upon review by a Circuit Court of Appeals, however, the Commission's order was set aside.[54] The court accepted the contention of the producer that the term "castile" had lost its secondary meaning and was currently understood to mean any unscented toilet or household soap. Its decision was predicated largely upon a definition published by the Bureau of Standards which indicated that "castile" soap might be made from oily ingredients other than olive oil. The Supreme Court refused to review the case.[55]

The Commission also failed in its effort to eliminate the practice of labelling or describing furniture as "walnut" or "mahogany" when in fact it was composed of an inferior wood with a veneered surface. Despite a trade practice conference rule of retail furniture dealers condemning the practice,[56] certain manufacturers failed to disclose the true nature of their veneered products. But a Circuit Court of Appeals refused to uphold orders to cease and desist.[57] The court found that dealers were not deceived, and rested its decision on this fact. The main consideration, however, was whether or not the ultimate purchaser was misled by the faulty labelling. The Commission had found as a fact that retailers usually marked their merchandise in the same manner as the manufacturers, and that these markings induced purchasers to buy furniture which they believed was made of the solid wood named on the tag. This finding of fact was simply denied by the court, although with the admission that it might tend to deceive the "grossly uninformed of the public." The Commission, unfortunately, did not appeal the case to the Supreme Court. Not only had the lower court disregarded the Commission's finding that ultimate consumers were deceived, but it had rested its decision on a point that had been held to be immaterial in the Winsted case.[58]

Somewhat greater success attended the efforts of the Commission to restrain importers of a certain hardwood from the Philippines from describing and selling the product as "Philippine mahogany." It was found that the Philippine hardwood did not have the qualities and virtues of genuine mahogany, and that describing it as "Philippine mahogany" deceived the consuming public and injured honest competitors. In upholding the Commission's order, the Circuit Court of Appeals denied the contention that the term "Philippine mahogany" had acquired a sec-

[54] James S. Kirk & Co. v. F. T. C., 59 Fed. (2nd) 179 (1932).

[55] 287 U. S. 663 (1932).

[56] See F. T. C., *Trade Practice Conferences*, "Retail Furniture Dealers of New York City" (March 15, 1928), p. 57.

[57] Berkey & Gay Furniture Co. v. F. T. C., 42 Fed. (2nd) 427 (1930).

[58] For a sharp criticism of the court's decision and of the Commission for accepting it without appeal, see National Industrial Conference Board, *Public Regulation of Competitive Practices in Business Enterprise* (New York, 1940), pp. 132–134.

ondary meaning in the trade and was understood to designate a wood *resembling* genuine mahogany.[59] Many manufacturers and dealers as well as the general public believed the product to be true mahogany. The Supreme Court refused to review the decree of the lower court.[60] But despite the judicial approval of its position, the Commission did not pursue its chartered course. In a proceeding concluded not long thereafter, it reversed itself in permitting the use of the word "mahogany" to describe the wood if properly modified by the term "Philippine."[61] No explanation of this shift in policy was made, but it is perhaps significant that the adopted view conformed to that vigorously expressed by Commissioner Humphrey in a dissenting opinion in the original case.[62] At any rate the net result of all this painstaking investigation and litigation was the same as that in the Castile and Veneer cases. Manufacturers and final consumers, although admittedly under the impression that they were purchasing genuine mahogany grown in the Philippines, were not to obtain the protection which they undoubtedly deserved.

An issue similar to the one presented in the Mahogany cases was raised in the so-called White Pine cases. In these, however, the Commission sought its goal with clear purpose and vigor. A Supreme Court decision of great importance to the whole regulatory process was the culmination of its effort. The attack was upon the practice of some fifty lumber manufacturers in western states who were selling a species of yellow pine, botanically known as *Pinus ponderosa*, under the name of "California white pine." While found to resemble the true white pines in several of its "immediately obvious qualities and in several of its utilities," the Western yellow pine belongs to a different botanical species and is inferior to white pine with respect to such qualities as durability under exposure, proportion of heartwood to sapwood content, softness of texture, lightness, and ease of working. The Commission found great confusion and abuses emanating from the use of the false name, especially in the Eastern and Middle Western markets, where the Western lumber competed with the highly regarded white pine lumber indigenous to these regions. Not only were consumers and architects misled, but retail dealers could not easily distinguish the false from the genuine white pine products. In such circumstances, retail lumber dealers, honestly or unscrupulously, often supplied buyers with the inferior Western product when they actually wanted true white pine. These facts prompted the

[59] Indiana Quartered Oak Co. *v.* F. T. C., 26 Fed. (2nd) 340 (1928).
[60] *Ibid.*, 278 U. S. 623 (1928).
[61] Gillespie Furniture Co., 15 F. T. C. 439 (1931). Commissioners McCulloch and Hunt dissented, the former filing a strong dissenting opinion. The court's order of affirmance in the Indiana Quartered Oak case was modified, upon petition of the company, to conform to the Commission's altered position in the matter (58 Fed. (2nd) 182, 1932).
[62] Indiana Quartered Oak Co., 10 F. T. C. 300, 313–319 (1926).

Commission to conclude that there was an unfair diversion of trade from those dealing in true white pine products and those marking ponderosa products truthfully. Thirty-nine firms were ordered, therefore, to cease using the word "white" in describing their products.[63]

Most of the firms agreed to abide by the Commission's orders, but fourteen of them petitioned a Circuit Court of Appeals for review. The court set aside the orders on the ground that the testimony was insufficient to support the Commission's findings of an unfair method of competition or that the prevention of the practice was in the public interest.[64] In upsetting the order, emphasis was placed upon the fact that recommendations of the Bureau of Standards for the simplification of commercial practice specified "California white pine" as the commercial equivalent of *Pinus ponderosa*. It was also stressed that some doubt existed as to the marked superiority of white pine over the yellow species, that savings accrued to the users of the cheaper pine, and that conservation of the limited supply of white pine would be effected by a larger consumption of the Western variety.

When the case was appealed to the Supreme Court, however, a unanimous decision was rendered which overruled the holding of the lower court and sustained the Commission on every point.[65] Justice Cardozo wrote an excellent opinion which goes far in clarifying and defining the nature of unfair methods of competition. In the first place, he rendered a sharp criticism of the lower court for disregarding the Commission's findings of fact. After quoting the statute to the effect that findings of fact shall be conclusive if supported by testimony, Justice Cardozo said: "The Court of Appeals, though professing adherence to this mandate, honored it, we think, with lip service only. In form the court determined that the finding of unfair competition had no support whatever. In fact what the court did was to make its own appraisal of the testimony, picking and choosing for itself among uncertain and conflicting inferences. Statute and decision forbid that exercise of power."[66]

In considering the merits of the case, the opinion was no less forceful. The recommendation of the Bureau of Standards as regards uniformity of nomenclature was held not to be binding upon a regulatory agency whose function is to make competition fair. It was held that there was ample evidence to sustain the conclusion that the genuine white pine is materially superior to the Western yellow pine. That the two woods are similar in some respects makes substitution easier and is actually conducive to misrepresentation and confusion. There was ample evidence to show confusion and its undesirable consequences. To the argument that

[63] Long-Bell Lumber Co., 15 F. T. C., 139, 168 (1931).
[64] Algoma Lumber Co. *v.* F. T. C., 64 Fed. (2nd) 618 (1933).
[65] F. T. C. *v.* Algoma Lumber Co., 291 U. S. 67 (1934).
[66] *Ibid.*, p. 73.

there was no great injury to consumers, since a cheaper price was obtained for the slightly inferior product, the Court replied: "But saving to the consumer, though it be made out, does not obliterate the prejudice. Fair competition is not attained by balancing a gain in money against a misrepresentation of the thing supplied. The courts must set their faces against a conception of business standards so corrupting in its tendency. The consumer is prejudiced if upon giving an order for one thing, he is supplied with something else."[67] A like answer was given to the contention that the practice tended to conserve forest resources. This was admitted to be an important objective, "but the end will have to be attained by methods other than a license to do business unfairly."[68]

An important issue was whether or not the misapplied name had attained such general acceptance as to give it a secondary meaning which removed the possibility of deception. It was pointed out that it had been adopted without fraudulent design some thirty years before, and its use had not been challenged. The Court conceded that confusion might have been slight in local markets in the West, but in other areas this was not the case. Justice Cardozo said:

> The evidence here falls short of establishing two meanings with equal titles to legitimacy by force of common acceptation. On the contrary, revolt against the pretender, far from diminishing, has become increasingly acute. With the spread of business eastward, the lumber dealers . . . were involved in keen competition with dealers in lumber from the pines of the east and middle west. In the wake of competition came confusion and deception. . . . Then, if not before, misbranding of the pines was something more than a venial wrong. . . . They were not at liberty to enlarge the area of their business without adjusting their methods to the needs of new conditions.[69]

In other words, to establish secondary meanings for terms used to brand substitute products it must be shown that they are generally accepted and understood by both consumers and dealers throughout the whole market area.

The full support given by the Supreme Court to the findings and decision of the Commission in this case have had a marked influence upon its authority and prestige. After the admonition of the Court, lower courts have not cast aside lightly the inferences drawn from the evidence gathered by the Commission. The opinion, moreover, strengthens the power of the Commission to remove misrepresentations effected by misnaming imitation or substitute products. Not only has the Commission succeeded in several close cases,[70] but it has opened for reconsideration

---

[67] Ibid., p. 78.

[68] Ibid., p. 81.

[69] Ibid., pp. 80–81.

[70] See F. T. C. v. Maisel Trading Post, Inc., 77 Fed. (2nd) 246 (1935), 79 Fed. (2nd) 127 (1935), and 84 Fed. (2nd) 768 (1936), involving use of terms "Indian" and "Indian-Made" to describe jewelry made in part with machinery; and F. T. C.

its ill-advised action in the cases involving the misbranding of "Philippine mahogany."[71]

(b) Quality of Products

Closely related to the misrepresentation of the character and composition of commodities is deception relating to the quality, condition, or effects of products. Exaggerated and misleading advertising claims are no less injurious to the consuming public and to honest competitors than the false marking of goods. Such claims range from downright falsehoods to "puffing" or excess praise of goods offered for sale. In the absence of definite standards available in determining the composition of products, it is somewhat more difficult to ascertain that a given advertising practice actually deceives consumers and therefore induces them to purchase something which they would not otherwise have bought. Even though the Commission may not have insisted upon absolute truthfulness in advertising, its performance suggests that this is a fertile field for operations.

Prior to 1929 the Commission did not entertain a great many proceedings relating to quality misrepresentation. An occasional order was issued, such as that directed at falsely representing that a certain breed of hogs was more resistant to disease than others.[72] Some related to representations that a certain battery would last forever,[73] or that a relatively weak preparation was a powerful disinfectant.[74] One order is especially noteworthy, however, for upon appeal the court set it aside and laid down a doctrine which is still of importance. The Commission found that a label containing a pictorial representation of an open-ended mattress greatly exaggerated the resiliency of the cotton filling so as to deceive and mislead a substantial number of purchasers.[75] The reviewing court held that the illustrations, admittedly exaggerations, were merely fanciful and not intended as actual descriptions.[76] It could see no basis for finding that purchasers relied on the exaggerated pictures and were deceived as to the qualities of the product. After referring to the dissenting opinion of Commissioner Humphrey[77] with approval, the court said: "The statu-

---

v. Hires Turner Glass Co., 81 Fed. (2nd) 362, 364 (1935), relating to the use of the term "copper-back mirror" to describe mirrors which did not have the copper backing electrolytically applied.

[71] National Industrial Conference Board, op. cit., p. 135.

[72] L. B. Silver Co. v. F. T. C., 289 Fed. 985 (1923).

[73] Universal Battery Service Co., 2 F. T. C. 95 (1919).

[74] Ginso Chemical Co., 4 F. T. C. 155 (1921).

[75] Ostermoor & Co., 10 F. T. C. 45 (1926).

[76] Ostermoor & Co., Inc., v. F. T. C., 16 Fed. (2nd) 962 (1927).

[77] Commissioner Humphrey emphasized the magnitude of the administrative task of enforcing exact truth in advertising and the dire effect of such a policy upon the advertising business. He said, in part: "The order is an attempt to compel exact

tory power to prohibit unfair methods of competition cannot be stretched to this extent; the slightest pictorial exaggeration of the qualities of an article cannot be deemed to be either a misrepresentation or an unfair method of competition. The time-honored custom of at least merely slight puffing, unlike the clear misrepresentation of the character of goods, . . . has not come under a legal ban."[78] The court was careful to confine its tolerance of puffing to that which was "merely slight," but in the opinion of the Commission it was more than that in this case. It is apparent that, once one departs from the policy of insisting upon truthfulness in the description and advertising of products, it is most difficult to fix the frontier of "illegal" prevarication.

When the Commission established the Special Board of Investigation in 1929, later reconstituted as the Division of Radio and Periodical Advertising, a real drive on misrepresentation of quality and effects was started. This administrative unit examines newspaper, magazine, and radio advertising for false and misleading representations, and recommends to the Commission appropriate action against violators of the law.[79] A large proportion of the proceedings have dealt with exaggerated claims regarding the qualities or therapeutic effects of such products as food, medicines, medical devices, and cosmetics. The Raladam case was one of the first of these. In this case, it will be recalled, the Commission met defeat at the hands of the Supreme Court because it was not shown that trade competitors existed and were actually injured.[80] But even before this jurisdictional requirement was removed by the enactment of the Wheeler-Lea amendment in 1938, the Commission continued its vigorous campaign against deceptive advertising. A substantial number of cases were appealed to the courts, but the Commission was sustained in practically all instances. Illustrative of these were orders which forbade representing a bath salts as a remedy for obesity,[81] a hair dye to be

---

truth in advertising. It will be noticed that the order allows no room whatever for exaggeration. It eliminates the thrilling and time-sacred art of 'puffing.' . . . If the Commission is going to attempt to enforce *exact truthfulness* in advertising, it seems to me that we should realize the magnitude of the undertaking. The respondent is forbidden by the thickness of a cotton fibre to misrepresent the thickness to which the layer of an opened-up mattress will expand. . . . If this order is sustained and the policy therein announced enforced, it will destroy one-half of all the magazine advertising in America." 10 F. T. C. 45, 57–58.

[78] 16 Fed. (2nd) 962, 963.

[79] See Chapter 20, Organization and Procedure of the Commission, for a description of the functions and operation of the Division of Radio and Periodical Advertising.

[80] F. T. C. v. Raladam Co., 283 U. S. 643 (1931). The Commission was unanimously upheld by the Supreme Court in a second action against Raladam started in 1935. F. T. C. v. Raladam, 316 U. S. 149 (1942).

[81] E. Griffith Hughes, Inc., v. F. T. C., 77 Fed. (2nd) 886 (1935); certiorari denied, 296 U. S. 617 (1935).

safe, non-toxic or non-poisonous,[82] and a bunion remedy to be a permanent and effective cure.[83]

The Wheeler-Lea Amendment of 1938 has materially strengthened the hand of the Commission. Since "unfair or deceptive acts or practices in commerce" are now unlawful in addition to "unfair methods of competition," the Commission must no longer take pains to show injury to competitors when it attacks unfounded and exaggerated claims concerning the virtues of products. It has jurisdiction even if every producer in the industry is a knave and defrauding the public. But also important is the fact that the false advertising of food, drugs, medical devices, and cosmetics is specifically outlawed. The law is not as stringent as it might be, since only advertisements which are misleading in a "material respect" are proscribed.[84] This phrasing leaves room for a certain amount of "puffing," a practice which can hardly be condoned in the case of medicinal preparations and curative devices. There is a real danger to public health when people are induced to rely upon impotent, albeit harmless, curatives for afflictions which require prompt and expert medical attention. It is noteworthy, however, that an advertisement is to be tested not only on the basis of the representations positively suggested but also on the basis of material facts which it *fails to reveal*.[85] Following the precedent of fixing positive requirements for the labelling of textile products, the Commission may here find statutory authority for setting up requirements as to what must be disclosed in the advertising of food and drug products. A step in this direction is the trend of Commission rulings not only to prohibit false representations but to require warnings of any possible danger to health involved in using medicinal preparations or devices.[86]

Injunction and criminal penalties, provided to supplement the Commission's regular procedure in attacking false advertising of food, drugs, and cosmetics,[87] seem to have been found very useful. Within about two years of the enactment of the law, the Commission obtained twenty-three injunctions restraining the dissemination of false advertisements

---

[82] F. T. C. v. Inecto, Inc. (1935), F. T. C., *Statutes and Decisions*, Vol. II, p. 288.

[83] Fairyfoot Products Co. v. F. T. C., 80 Fed. (2nd) 684 (1935). It was urged by the offender in this case that any exaggeration in its advertising was in the nature of legitimate "puffing." To this the Court replied (p. 686); "Just where lies the line between 'puffing,' which is not unlawful and unwarranted, and misleading representations in advertising, is often very difficult of ascertainment. But in our judgment this case does not present such embarrassment, since the advertising here condemned is well beyond any 'puffing' indulgence."

[84] Federal Trade Commission Act, Sec. 15 (a).

[85] *Ibid.*

[86] American Medicinal Products, Inc. v. F. T. C., 136 Fed. (2nd) 426 (1943); Earl Aronberg v. F. T. C., 132 Fed., (2nd) 165 (1942); Dearborn Supply Co. v. F. T. C., 146 Fed. (2nd) 5 (1944). See, also, Commerce Clearing House, *Trade Regulation Service* (ninth edition), pp. 6701–6719.

[87] *Ibid.*, Sections 13 and 14.

until the completion of regular proceedings against the advertisers.[88] The great majority of these cases related to drug products and devices which were dangerous and injurious to health when used under customary or prescribed conditions.[89] Two of the cases involved no injury to health but irreparable pecuniary damage. False representations were being made about the awarding of prizes in contests involving the sale of cosmetics. One successful criminal prosecution was brought by the Attorney-General against the false advertisement of a dangerous drug, resulting in the conviction and fining of the defendant.[90]

The Commission has continued to obtain the support of the courts.[91] They now appear to observe scrupulously the mandate to accept the findings of the Commission when supported by evidence. The findings have often been based upon the testimony of medical experts who based their opinions upon general medical and pharmacological knowledge.[92] Such testimony has been accepted as substantiating the facts in the face of conflicting testimony on the part of other experts and doctors who had actually administered the alleged remedies.

In concluding this discussion of misrepresentation of the quality and effectiveness of products, attention should be directed to the device of falsely claiming that a product is endorsed or used by some governmental agency, or by a quasi-public body such as the American Medical Association. The obvious purpose is to convey the impression that such endorsement signifies a product of superior quality. There is little difficulty in attacking the practice where direct claims of approval are shown to be false.[93] Where it is done by means of trade names or corporate names, thus implying some official use or connection, it is not as easy to prove deception. But even here the Commission has been sustained in

[88] F. T. C., *Annual Report*, 1940, p. 95.

[89] These products included electrolysis machines for the removal of superfluous hair, abortifacients, emmenagogues, aphrodisiacs, and cures for obesity and dipsomania. Some of the principal ingredients were dinitrophenol, various hydrochlorides, desiccated thyroid, ergot, and black hellebore. The Commission now maintains a medical advisory service to aid it in determining the validity of advertising claims of food, drugs, devices, and cosmetics.

[90] F. T. C., *Annual Report*, 1940, pp. 99–101.

[91] See, for example, Justin Haynes & Co., Inc., v. F. T. C., 105 Fed. (2nd) 988 (1939), certiorari denied, 308 U. S. 616 (1939), misrepresenting the curative properties of Aspirub, which contained a small amount of aspirin; Dr. W. B. Caldwell, Inc., v. F. T. C., 111 Fed. (2nd) 889 (1940), falsely representing that the pepsin content of its medicine had therapeutic value; and Neff v. F. T. C., 117 Fed. (2nd) 495 (1941), alleging effectiveness of Glantex in curing a variety of serious diseases.

[92] See the cases cited next above, especially the Neff Case.

[93] See Guarantee Veterinary Co. v. F. T. C., 285 Fed. 853 (1922), affirming the Commission's order against falsely advertising that the Government had adopted the respondent's salt blocks and had purchased its entire southern output; and Allied Golf Co., 7 F. T. C. 250 (1924), in which golf balls were labelled "official" and represented as standard and official as required by the United States Golf Association and the Royal & Ancient Club of St. Andrews, Scotland.

its attempt to prevent traders from taking unfair advantage of their competitors.[94]

Advertising by means of endorsements or testimonials by private individuals has also received the attention of the Commission. An order against the use of testimonials not obtained from the person whose name was used, and the garbling of those actually obtained, so as to make them substantially untrue, was sustained in the courts.[95] In its attempt to require the disclosure of payment for testimonials, however, the Commission has not been successful. The particular case involved the very common practice of paying substantial amounts to prominent people for the use of their signed testimonials.[96] The statements relating to "Cutex" manicure preparations were admitted by the Commission to be truthful expressions of opinion. In reversing the order, the circuit court said:

> It is doubtful if the public is gullible enough to believe that such testimonials are given without compensation. But if they are paid for, providing they are truthful, no one is deceived. . . . Because a prominent person ventures an opinion without being requested to do so is no guaranty either of veracity or good judgment. If the testimonials involved here represent honest beliefs of the indorsers, there is no misrepresentation concerning the product, and no unfair competition is created. We have no right to presume that indorsers of commercial products falsify their statements because they have received compensation.[97]

Unfortunately, the Solicitor-General declined the Commission's request to appeal the case to the Supreme Court.[98] Despite the firm assurance of the reviewing court that no one is foolish enough to believe that testimonials are voluntary and free and that opinions are not colored by the substantial remuneration received, an authoritative decision is to be desired. It certainly is a great temptation for endorsers to vouch for the honesty of statements which are prepared and submitted to them by the advertisers if a handsome reward is to be obtained. Perhaps mere "puffing" is not serious, but administrative control is justified when unfounded claims as to the effectiveness of products are declared to be "honest" opinions by those seeking to capitalize on current prominence

---

[94] See F. T. C. v. Civil Service Training Bureau, Inc., 79 Fed. (2nd) 113 (1935), in which the Commission was upheld in requiring the company to cease using "civil service" or "bureau" in its name; and F. T. C. v. Army and Navy Trading Co., 88 Fed. (2nd) 776 (1937), forbidding the use of the words "Army and Navy" in the respondent's trade name, but permitting their use in connection with goods actually made for the Army or Navy Departments and acquired by it.

[95] F. T. C. v. Standard Education Society et al., 86 Fed. (2nd) 692 (1936); 302 U. S. 112 (1937).

[96] Northam Warren Corp. v. F. T. C., 59 Fed. (2nd) 196 (1932).

[97] Ibid., pp. 197–198.

[98] F. T. C., Annual Report, 1932, p. 105.

or popularity.[99] The whole practice of testimonial advertising would be difficult to justify as a good use of productive resources.

One final proceeding pertaining to endorsements deserves comment. For years *Good Housekeeping Magazine,* a wholly owned subsidiary of Hearst Magazines, Inc., has maintained organizations for testing various products. Seals of approval have been issued on products tested, and these seals have been used on the merchandise and in various types of advertising. Numerous forms of shields and emblems have also been issued to advertisers, one of them reading "Guaranteed as advertised in *Good Housekeeping,*" which have been used in general sales promotion. After due investigation the Commission issued an order against Hearst Magazines, Inc.[100] It found, among other things, that the respondent's tests were generally inadequate to assure the fulfillment of the claims made for such products, and that its representations caused readers to believe that its so-called guaranty of products advertised in *Good Housekeeping* was a genuine and unlimited guaranty. Moreover, it was found that the respondent represented, directly and by inference, that claims made for products and services advertised in its periodicals were true. Many of the advertisements, it was revealed, actually contained false and misleading statements concerning the therapeutic value of medicines, the properties of cosmetics, the quality and fibre content of fabrics, and other matters. The result of these findings was an order requiring the company to discontinue its unlawful practices. It is significant in that it strikes not at the producers themselves but at the advertising medium which, for a price, has aided them in disseminating their spurious claims. There is little doubt that *Good Housekeeping,* through its manifold devices, succeeded in building up a reputation for itself as a *bona fide* testing agency, and in turn for the products which it endorsed. To dispel a costly illusion of many consumers was a real public service.

(c) Origin of Products

A third general type of misrepresentation which the Commission has attempted to suppress has been that which falsifies the origin of commodities. The term "origin" is here used broadly to include the actual firm which produces the goods, the scope or nature of the firm's business activity, or the place or region of production. The objective is virtually the same in all cases. It is to take advantage of certain public preferences

---

[99] In suggesting that the Commission's jurisdiction over the use of paid testimonials might now be sustained by the courts, one commentator stated: "One cannot be dogmatic in prediction, but the practice is so outrageous that wishful thinking can be pardoned. The tone of this decision (Northam Warren) is as unfortunate as the Gratz case." Handler, *op. cit.,* p. 249, note 320.

[100] 32 F. T. C. 1440 (1941).

or to avoid the disadvantages of prejudices held by the public. Preferences have usually been built up on the basis of quality or price considerations, and may apply to single firms or to the output of a whole region. Popular prejudices may be due to poor quality of product in some areas, dislike of certain countries or peoples for political reasons, or dislike of certain firms because of their monopolistic position or anti-social business policies.

Commercial origin may be said to include deception concerning the identity and the nature of the firm supplying a particular good. Devices which have been directed at this end are trade-name or trade-mark simulation, bogus independents, and misrepresentation of trade status. Geographical origin, on the other hand, pertains to deception relating to the place, locality, or region from which goods originate.

Perhaps the most venerable trade practice designed to misrepresent the commercial origin of goods is the simulation of trade-marks or trade-names. The practice of "passing off" a firm's products for those of an established and reputable concern, it will be recalled, was one of the first offenses to be recognized as unfair competition under the common law. Despite the remedy of private action, the Commission has attacked the practice. Its jurisdiction in the field is limited, however, since the Supreme Court held in the Klesner case[101] that the controversy over the use of the trade-name "Shade Shop" was essentially a private dispute and lacking in "public interest." But where the public is clearly deceived by the use of a mark or name which has been deliberately stolen from an established concern, the Commission has not been prevented from exercising its authority. Illustrative of recent orders which have been sustained are those prohibiting the use of "Duraleather" to designate an imitation leather because of its similarity to the word "Duro" used by a producer of genuine leather,[102] the use of the word "Champion" on spark plug cable sets and automotive specialties,[103] and the use of the name "Remington" on radios.[104] Despite the fact that the concerns affected could use their own resources to obtain relief in court actions, there would seem to be sufficient public interest in eliminating deception of the public and the theft of good-will to warrant proceedings by the Commission.

---

[101] F. T. C. v. Klesner, 280 U. S. 19 (1929), discussed in considering jurisdictional requirements for Commission action.

[102] Masland Duraleather Co. et al. v. F. T. C., 34 Fed. (2nd) 733 (1929).

[103] F. T. C. v. Real Products Corp. et al., 90 Fed. (2nd) 617 (1937). Judge Manton commented as follows on the matter of public interest: "The existence of a public interest here may rest either on the deception suffered by the public or the prejudice occasioned to competitors. On either ground the public is entitled to be protected against unfair practices and its interest in such protection is specific and substantial. Nor is it necessary that the product misrepresented be inferior or harmful to the public. The deceptive misrepresentation suffices."

[104] Pep Boys—Manny, Moe and Jack, Inc., v. F. T. C., 122 Fed. (2nd) 158 (1941).

As a result of the enactment of the Lanham Trade-Mark Act of 1946,[105] the Commission's authority over unfair competition stemming from the use of trade-marks has been extended materially. The law requires the patent office, for the first time, to maintain an official register of trade-marks. It is the duty of the Commission to study these registrations to ascertain whether the trade-marks have been lawfully procured and are being properly used. The Commission is empowered to apply for the cancellation of a trade-mark when it was obtained fraudulently or when the mark has become a common descriptive name with the expiration of the patent—for example, the use of the words "aspirin," "shredded wheat," or "cola," which have assumed general meanings. Trade-marks consisting of immoral or scandalous matter, flags or insignia of any government, or names of living persons without their consent are subject to cancellation. The use of a trade-mark after registration is to be investigated also, and may be canceled if used deceptively to misrepresent the nature or source of the goods or services to which it is attached. The Commission has instituted work in connection with this statute which should bear fruit in greater protection to both producers and consumers.

The operation of bogus independents for the purpose of destroying the competition of real independents was a very common practice amongst the early trusts. They were employed not only to wage price wars against independents, but to obtain confidential information regarding their rivals' operations. But the Commission has issued very few orders relating to the practice, perhaps partly because it is no longer extensively employed, and they have not been reviewed by the courts. The only order against a firm using trade tactics characteristic of the trust era was that against a company manufacturing labels and devices for marking textiles.[106] The firm already controlled about two-thirds of the business in the field, and was using the bogus independent for price-cutting and other purposes in an attempt further to limit competition. In the other proceedings the objective of employing the bogus independents was not to obtain monopoly control so much as to acquire or hold business which they could not do directly.[107] In one instance at least, the prejudice of buyers was due to the inferior grade of product purveyed by the firm.[108] It has been argued that failure to disclose ownership of subsidiaries in

[105] Public Law 489, 79th Congress (1946).
[106] Kaumagraph Co., 20 F. T. C. 1 (1934).
[107] Fleischmann Co., 1 F. T. C. 119 (1918); A. A. Berry Seed Co., 2 F. T. C. 427 (1920); St. Louis Lightning Rod Co., 3 F. T. C. 327 (1921); Dixie Hatcheries, 26 F. T. C. 953 (1938). In Armour & Co., 1 F. T. C. 430 (1919), the respondent sold fertilizer products through an acquired subsidiary whose name included the words "Farmers' Coöperative," although prior to the issuance of the order it voluntarily divulged that it was "Armour-owned."
[108] A. A. Berry Seed Co., 2 F. T. C. 427 (1920).

such circumstances as these is "not deceit but ordinary privacy."[109] It may be admitted that the situation is not as serious as in cases where the bogus independent is being used to perpetrate monopoly by unfair practices, but nevertheless such a view runs counter to the basic proposition that the functioning of competition is dependent upon full knowledge of market conditions. If buyers are misled and actually purchase goods from firms which they have reason to repudiate, and if competitors are not only unaware of the true identity of some of their rivals, but lose business because of the practice, there would seem to be both economic and legal justification for its condemnation. It is no more difficult to choose methods which reveal than it is to select those which conceal, and this might well be insisted upon where concealment interferes with the efficient operation of the competitive system.

Judging by the number of cases which have been handled by the Commission, the most important misrepresentation relating to the commercial origin of products is that of trade status. Falsely claiming to be a manufacturer, a miller, or a producer of some sort is for the purpose of taking advantage of the public's preference for such concerns. It is generally believed that goods obtained directly from a producer are apt to be of superior quality and certainly cheaper in price than those purchased from retailers or wholesalers. While the elimination of the middleman may or may not yield a more economical product, the Commission has insisted that sellers adhere scrupulously to the truth in representing the nature of their marketing or producing function. In this it has been fully sustained by the courts.

The leading decision is that in the Royal Milling Company case.[110] This firm, together with several others, used trade names containing the words "milling company," "mill," or "manufacturer of flour," when in fact they were engaged in mixing and blending flour which had been purchased from concerns who ground wheat into flour. The Commission found that their practices prejudiced their competitors and the public, and ordered them to remove the misleading words from their tradenames and to cease any other misrepresentation. Upon review, the lower court set aside the orders on the ground that there was insufficient public interest in the proceedings.[111] But the Supreme Court reversed the lower court. In dealing with the main question of public interest Justice Sutherland said:

If consumers or dealers prefer to purchase a given article because it was made by a particular manufacturer or class of manufacturers, they have a right to do so, and this right cannot be satisfied by imposing upon them an exactly similar article, or one equally as good, but having a different origin. . . . A

---

[109] National Industrial Conference Board, *op. cit.*, pp. 207–209.
[110] F. T. C. *v.* Royal Milling Co., 288 U. S. 212 (1933).
[111] Royal Milling Co. *v.* F. T. C., 58 Fed. (2nd) 581 (1932).

large number of buyers, comprising consumers and dealers, believe that the price or quality or both are affected to their advantage by the fact that the article is prepared by the original grinder of the grain. The result of respondents' acts is that such purchasers are deceived into purchasing an article which they do not wish or intend to buy, and which they might or might not buy if correctly informed as to its origin. We are of opinion that the purchasing public is entitled to be protected against that species of deception, and that its interest in such protection is specific and substantial.[112]

It is abundantly clear from the foregoing statement that, irrespective of the relative quality of the article sold or any question of financial loss a seller may not deceive purchasers as to the origin of goods. The Court, however, did not go so far as the Commission in prescribing a remedy. It allowed the firms to retain their corporate names, since they had acquired considerable trade value, on the condition that qualifying terms were used to indicate their true business status.[113] On the strength of this decision the Commission has proceeded against a large number of companies. Many of the proceedings have related to rectifiers or blenders of liquor who represented themselves as distillers, to dealers in drugs and toilet articles who allegedly owned laboratories and manufacturing establishments, to clothing producers who asserted that they were weavers of cloth, and to furniture dealers who represented themselves as manufacturers.[114] Orders have also been issued prohibiting correspondence schools from using the words "college" or "university" in their corporate names.[115]

Geographical origin of some products is of prime importance to the purchasing public. Apart from the prestige value attached to certain products of foreign manufacture, there are in many instances real qualitative differences flowing from the natural resources and workmanship of foreign countries or regions. It goes without saying that English woolens, French wines and cosmetics, Havana cigars, and Panama hats have sales appeals not enjoyed by domestic products. The products of other countries, on the other hand, may be in disrepute because of quality considerations or even because we dislike a nation's political or foreign policies.[116] Similarly, within the United States, the words "Tampa" in connection with cigars, "Barre" in connection with granite, and

---

[112] 288 U. S. 212, pp. 216–217.

[113] For other cases permitting the use of qualifying words to cure the deception in the trade name, see F. T. C. v. Mid-West Mills, Inc., 90 Fed. (2nd) 723 (1937); and Bear Mill Mfg. Co., Inc., v. F. T. C., 98 Fed. (2nd) 67 (1938).

[114] The citations of these cases and many more in other fields may be found in Commerce Clearing House, *Trade Regulation Service* (ninth edition), pp. 6801–6808.

[115] American College et al., 27 F. T. C. 699 (1938); McKinley-Roosevelt College of Arts and Sciences, 30 F. T. C. 1052 (1940).

[116] Orders have been issued against the sale of toys made in Japan and marketed in containers marked "Made in U. S. A." (American Toy Works, 25 F. T. C. 647, [1937]); and against concealing the words "Made in Japan" on bicycle frames by placing the respondent's name plate over them (K. & K. Supply Co., Inc., 28 F. T. C. 1195, [1939]). It may be noted that the Tariff Act of 1930 requires that all imported products be marked clearly so as to indicate the country of origin.

"Grand Rapids" in connection with furniture, are suggestive of particular qualities which consumers desire.

The Commission has issued a great many orders and stipulations against the misrepresentation of geographical origin on the solid ground that consumers and honest competitors are damaged by the practice. Trades in which this practice seems to have been most prevalent are beverages, clothing, food, tobacco, and toilet articles.[117] Although the Supreme Court has not rendered an opinion, the U. S. courts of appeal have approved the Commission's policy.[118] Attempts have been made to obtain acceptance of qualifying words to correct the deception. By the very nature of the practice, however, false geographic names can be contradicted but not qualified. As the Court said in a case in which the user of the name "Havana Smokers" wished to indicate that the cigars were made in the United States of domestic tobacco: "The difficulty of petitioner's position lies in the fact that the implication of the word 'Havana' is totally false. The purchaser can be guided by either label or legend, but not by both. . . . We doubt if petitioner would accede to a true qualification—'Fake Havana Smokers.' "[119]

(d) Value of Products

Another type of misrepresentation which has been subjected to administrative control is that relating to the value of products. The deception of the consuming public is achieved in a variety of ways, but the purpose is always the same. It is to create the false impression that the prospective buyer is getting an unusually good bargain. Such appeals may be made, among other ways, by offering "free" goods which actually are not free, or by marking fictitious prices on goods offered for sale. These methods have been the subject of the greatest controversy.

For some years it appeared that the Commission was powerless to eliminate the practice. Numerous orders were issued,[120] but where any of them were appealed the courts found the sales method to be quite legitimate.[121] But when the Supreme Court had occasion to review the

---

[117] See Commerce Clearing House, *Trade Regulation Service* (ninth edition), pp. 6751–6773.

[118] See, for example, F. T. C. *v.* Bradley, 31 Fed. (2nd) 569 (1929), designating a domestic soap "English Tub Soap"; F. T. C. *v.* Walker's New River Mining Co., 79 Fed. (2nd) 457 (1935), use of "New River" in corporate name and in selling coal not mined in the "New River district" in West Virginia, an area famous for quality coal; Heusner & Son *v.* F. T. C., 106 Fed. (2nd) 596 (1939); El Moro Cigar Co. *v.* F. T. C., 107 Fed. (2nd) 429 (1939), relating to the use of "Havana" on domestic cigars.

[119] Heusner & Son *v.* F. T. C., 106 Fed. (2nd) 596 (1939).

[120] See Commerce Clearing House, *Trade Regulation Service* (ninth edition), pp. 6560–6569.

[121] Orders were set aside by Circuit Courts of Appeals in Chicago Portrait Co. *v.* F. T. C., 4 Fed. (2nd) 759 (1924), certiorari denied, 269 U. S. 556 (1925), and John C. Winston Co. *v.* F. T. C., 3 Fed. (2nd) 961 (1925), certiorari denied, 269 U. S.

whole question in connection with the sales methods employed by the Standard Education Society, it left no doubt as to the unlawfulness of misrepresenting the value or price of goods offered for sale.[122] Among other things, the book company represented that it was giving away a set of encyclopedias to specially selected people for advertising purposes and that they were paying only for the loose-leaf extension service. The regular price of the combination offer was represented to be $150, whereas the special price of $69.50 was alleged merely to be the customary price for the loose-leaf supplement. The Commission found that the ordinary price of the books and the service was $69.50, and ordered the firm to discontinue its fictitious pricing.

The Circuit Court of Appeals, again manifesting the captious attitude which has so definitely restrained the Commission's progress, reversed that part of the order relating to the misrepresentation of price. The court said: "We cannot take seriously the suggestion that a man who is buying a set of books and a ten years' 'extension service' will be fatuous enough to be misled by the mere statement that the first are given away, and that he is paying only for the second. Nor can we conceive how he could be damaged were he to suppose that that was true. Such trivial niceties are too impalpable for practical affairs, they are will-o'-the-wisps, which divert attention from substantial evils."[123] But the Supreme Court disagreed thoroughly with this reasoning. Justice Black, speaking for a unanimous court, replied:

> The fact that a false statement may be obviously false to those who are trained and experienced does not change its character, nor take away its power to deceive others less experienced. There is no duty resting upon a citizen to suspect the honesty of those with whom he transacts business. Laws are made to protect the trusting as well as the suspicious. The best element of business has long since decided that honesty should govern competitive enterprises, and that the rule of *caveat emptor* should not be relied upon to reward fraud and deception.[124]

After rebuking the lower court for not accepting the findings of fact

---

555 (1925). In the former case the respondent was ordered to cease representing falsely that reproductions of family portraits were being offered at prices lower than those customarily charged. The Winston case involved the sale of cumulative loose-leaf encyclopedias under special terms which suggested that the price charged was for the loose-leaf service and that the ten-volume encyclopedia was free.

But in a later proceeding relating to the same practice of falsely representing that the encyclopedia was free to certain influential persons in a combination offer of an encyclopedia and an extension service, the Circuit Court upheld the Commission's order and the Supreme Court denied certiorari. Consolidated Book Publishers. Inc., v. F. T. C., 53 Fed. (2nd) 942 (1931); 286 U. S. 553 (1932).

[122] F. T. C. v. Standard Education Society, 302 U. S. 112 (1937).

[123] F. T. C. v. Standard Education Society, 86 Fed. (2nd) 692 (1936), pp. 695-696.

[124] 302 U. S. 112, p. 116.

which were amply supported by the testimony before the Commission, the Court upheld the Commission in full.

The decision, like that in the Royal Milling Company case, goes a long way in supporting the Commission's policy of wiping out deception in sales methods. Even though the actual quality of goods may measure up to representations made, sellers are not at liberty to delude customers into thinking that they are obtaining exceptional values. Moreover, the language of Mr. Justice Black suggests that the standard of conduct imposed upon traders is such as not to deceive the unwary and inexperienced as well as the more skeptical and astute. This should not be an onerous burden on competitive enterprise, and is certainly in harmony with sound public policy.

The courts have continued to uphold recent orders of the Commission relating to pricing, without exception.[125] Of particular interest is the drive against the advertising of the automobile manufacturers and their financing companies with respect to finance charges on installment purchases of automobiles. The orders against General Motors and Ford prohibited them from using the words "six per cent" or the symbol "6%" in connection with the cost of their deferred-payment plans.[126] It was found that purchasers were misled into the erroneous belief that the "6%" plan contemplated a simple interest charge of 6% per year on the unpaid balance as reduced by monthly payments. The 6% was actually applied to the original balance and the finance charge thus computed really amounted to an interest of about 11½% per year on the deferred installments. Prospective users of the plan might easily believe that they were obtaining the convenience of financing through the agency from which they purchased cars at rates of interest as good as those to be obtained on money borrowed from banks. In upholding the Commission's order against General Motors, the court said: "It may be that there was no intention to mislead and that only the careless or the incompetent could be misled. But if the Commission, having discretion to deal with these matters, thinks it best to insist upon a form of advertising clear enough so that, in the words of the prophet Isaiah, 'wayfaring men, though fools, shall not err therein,' it is not for the courts to revise their judgment."[127] The Supreme Court refused to review the order.[128]

[125] In Thomas v. F. T. C., 116 Fed. (2nd) 347 (1940), an order was sustained which prohibited the respondent from misrepresenting that his feather quilts were being offered at one-half the regular price as part of his direct selling methods.

[126] Most of the automobile companies and three financing companies, including Chrysler, Packard, Graham-Paige, Hudson, and Reo, entered stipulations agreeing to discontinue the practice, and the complaints were dismissed. 24 F. T. C. 1397 (1937).

[127] General Motors Corp. v. F. T. C., 114 Fed. (2nd) 33 (1940). See also Ford Motor Company v. F. T. C., 120 Fed. (2nd) 175 (1941), certiorari denied, 314 U. S. 668 (1941).

[128] General Motors Corp. v. F. T. C., certiorari denied, 312 U. S. 682 (1941).

(2) Lotteries

The traditional American attitude, as evidenced by the postal laws and state statutes, has been that lotteries are opposed to the public good. Cognizant of this public policy, the Commission has persistently sought to eliminate sales methods embracing an element of chance or lottery. Some of the early cases involved the use of prizes which were distributed by chance in connection with the sale of tea and coffee.[129] Since about 1930, however, the number of cases has become much more numerous, and the commodities involved have been chiefly confections and novelty merchandise.[130] The candy trade seems to have been peculiarly susceptible to the use of sales schemes involving chance. Candy firms have not only been subjected to many cease and desist orders, but they have fought most vigorously to defend their practices.

The outstanding issues involving lotteries arose in the Keppel case.[131] The broad implications of the opinion of Mr. Justice Stone in this case with respect to the content and definition of unfair methods of competition have already been considered. The respondent and some forty others sold penny candies in assortments known as "break and take" packages in competition with manufacturers of so-called "straight goods" packages. One variety of the break and take package contained a few pieces within the wrapper of which was concealed a single penny. The pieces of candy in these packages were either smaller than those sold by competing firms or of inferior quality. The candy was sold largely to school children. It was argued before the Court that the Commission was in error in condemning the practice, since there was no deception to the consuming public, and no injury to competitors, because they were free to adopt the same sales methods.[132] The Court admitted that there was no deception, but seemed to retract this judgment when it pointed out that school children could not intelligently judge a transaction in which they were offered an inferior product. It was also conceded that competitors were free to adopt the lottery method to maintain their competitive position, but it was forcing them to descend to a practice which they were "under a powerful moral compulsion not to adopt." This was eminently unfair. Mr. Justice Stone declared that the statute does not "authorize regulation which has no purpose other than that of relieving merchants from troublesome competition or of censoring the morals of business men." He continued:

---

[129] See, for example, Buddha Tea Co., 1 F. T. C. 159, 163 (1918).

[130] During the period June 30, 1930, to June 30, 1940, the Commission issued approximately 388 complaints and 312 orders with respect to lotteries.

[131] F. T. C. v. R. F. Keppel & Bro., Inc., 291 U. S. 304 (1934).

[132] It was on these grounds that the lower court had reversed the Commission's order in 63 Fed. (2nd) 81 (1933).

But here the competitive method is shown to exploit consumers, children, who are unable to protect themselves. . . . Such devices have met with condemnation throughout the community. . . . It is clear that the practice is of the sort which the common law and criminal statutes have long deemed contrary to public policy. For these reasons a large share of the industry holds out against the device, despite ensuing loss in trade, or bows reluctantly to what it brands unscrupulous. It would seem a gross perversion of the normal meaning of the word, which is the first criterion of statutory construction, to hold that the method is not "unfair."[133]

Strange as it may seem, over a score of cases involving lotteries have been considered by the Circuit Courts of Appeals since the affirmation of the Commission's order in the Keppel case. The condemnation of such practices has been extended to situations where the product was not of inferior quality,[134] and where it was not sold to children.[135] Even in the complete absence of deception and where buyers evidenced a preference for the merchandise sold under the lottery schemes, the practice has been pronounced unethical and against public policy, and therefore unfair. Apart from some modification of the language of orders,[136] the Commission has met defeat in only one instance.[137] And this was because of its attempt to proscribe the practice in intrastate commerce.

(3) Commercial Bribery

Another sales method which is designed to obtain patronage on a basis other than the merits of the product is commercial bribery. Commercial bribery may be defined as the giving of gifts to employees or agents of a customer or prospective buyer, without the knowledge of the customer, for the purpose of inducing sales. The vice of the practice is, of course, that the purchasing agent is induced to sacrifice the interests

---

[133] 291 U. S. 304, p. 313.

[134] Minter v. F. T. C., 102 Fed. (2nd) 69 (1939). In the course of his opinion Circuit Judge Clark said: "This case seems to us a futile continuation of earlier litigation. The trade practices of these petitioners have already been expressly condemned in a unanimous opinion of the United States Supreme Court (Keppel case). . . . The petitioners and the other practitioners of this type of merchandising have followed that ancient precept of the sea, 'women and children first,' except that they pervert instead of protect weakness. Taking candy from children has never been highly regarded. Forcing it upon them through their possession of an instinct that the adult world recognizes and has always recognized as at the bottom of many of its troubles, seems to us shameful."

[135] Hofeller v. F. T. C., 82 Fed. (2nd) 647 (1936); certiorari denied, 299 U. S. 557 (1936), involving the prize package candy usually sold in burlesque theatres and at carnivals; and Chicago Silk Co. v. F. T. C., 90 Fed. (2nd) 689 (1937), relating to the sale of ladies' silk hosiery.

[136] See, for example, Sweets Company of America, Inc., v. F. T. C., 109 Fed. (2nd) 296 (1940), in which, over the dissent of Judge Clark, the court modified the order prohibiting the packaging of candies whose sales "may be made" by means of lottery, to read "are likely to be made."

[137] F. T. C. v. Bunte Brothers, Inc., 312 U. S. 349 (1941).

of his employer. His purchases are conditioned not upon the relative quality or price of the goods offered by competing sellers, but upon the amount of personal gain. The economic cost is reflected in the survival of firms that might be forced to withdraw if manufacturing and selling efficiency were the sole standard to be met. If all firms in an industry adopt the practice in self-defense, perhaps no firm suffers a competitive disadvantage, but the additional selling costs are a burden upon the consuming public and expansion of the industry is curtailed.

During its early years the Commission made a concerted drive upon commercial bribery and issued a great many orders. Certain industries, notably paint and varnish, dye and chemical, and ship chandlery, were particularly addicted to the practice.[138] Little resistance seems to have been encountered as regards the worst forms of bribery, such as the giving of secret money bribes with the obvious purpose of corrupting the employees of buyers.[139] It would have been difficult to defend such as fair means of competition.

The Commission, however, has been restricted by the courts in its campaign against all forms of bribery. An order against the practice of entertaining employees of customers by furnishing them cigars, liquor, meals, and theatre tickets was vacated.[140] The record indicated that the company spent about as much for entertainment in one year as it paid to branch managers and salesmen, and expended amounts ranging from $5 to $125 on a single occasion. But the court found the practice not to be unfair, since such entertainment has been an "incident of business from time immemorial" and the expenses involved are allowable deductions in determining Federal income taxes. It was also suggested that even the payment of money or the giving of valuable presents, while admittedly a fraud actionable between individuals, was not a practice so affecting the public as to be within the jurisdiction of the Commission. This undoubtedly would not be the view of the courts today. But the main point in the case does illustrate the extremely difficult question of distinguishing between ordinary business courtesy and commercial bribery. It would be absurd to attempt to suppress all hospitality, however trivial and unconcealed its character. But where it is so lavish as to have no other purpose or effect than to influence agents in placing their orders, it would appear to be both unethical and uneconomical competition. A public policy which sanctions all "entertainment" would seem to be as bad as one which attempts to eliminate every business courtesy.

---

[138] See Commerce Clearing House, *Trade Regulation Service* (ninth edition), pp. 6301–6302.

[139] An enforcement order was granted with the respondent's consent in F. T. C. *v.* Grand Rapids Varnish Co., 41 Fed. (2nd) 996 (1929).

[140] New Jersey Asbestos Co. *v.* F. T. C., 264 Fed. 509 (1920).

The Commission has also been frustrated in its endeavor to suppress gifts to salesmen of retailers designed to induce them to push the sale of the producer's goods. In the leading case, premiums such as necktie sets, watches, and diamonds were given to salesmen with the knowledge and consent of the retailers but without disclosure to prospective customers.[141] The court of appeals found the practice not to be unfair. It declared that "the public, if it has an interest in competition has such interest only in the competition between different merchants," and that "there can be nothing in the contention that some special interest in a clerk which is undisclosed to the buying public represents an unfair method of competition, because of an incentive and opportunity of the clerk to deceive the public."[142] Both the conclusion and the reasoning of the court are of doubtful validity. It certainly is of importance for a prospective buyer to know whether a clerk stands to gain personally when offering his advice as to the relative merits of competing goods which he handles. And it is obviously unfair to competitors who are quite helpless to protect themselves unless they stoop to the same questionable and costly sales method. If economic activity is to be effectively regulated, fair competition between producers must extend to the point where the goods are placed in the hands of the consumer. In the eyes of the Commission, the court's decision does not prevent it from prohibiting the payment of "push money" in all circumstances. A subsequent order was issued, but limited to those payments which were made "without the knowledge or consent of the employers."[143]

The Commission, as early as 1918, recognized that treating commercial bribery as an unfair method of competition was not the best method of attack, and recommended that Congress make it a criminal offense.[144] It can deal only with the giver of the bribe, and it was suggested that the recipient, who is equally guilty of the crime, should also be punished. Despite general disapproval of the practice on the part of business men as well as others, Congress has not acted.[145] In the meantime, the Commission has issued occasional orders and has approved a great many trade practice conference rules prohibiting the giving of "money or anything of value" to representatives of customers "without the knowledge" of such customers.[146]

---

[141] Kinney-Rome Co. v. F. T. C., 275 Fed. 665 (1921).

[142] Ibid., p. 669.

[143] Twinplex Sales Co., 11 F. T. C. 57 (1927).

[144] Special Report Dealing with Commercial Bribery, 66th Congress, 2nd Session, Senate Document No. 258 (1920), which also contains the report submitted in 1918.

[145] It is noteworthy that the Federal Alcohol Administration Act of 1935 prohibits commercial bribery.

[146] For trade practice conference rules, see Commerce Clearing House, Trade Regulation Service, (ninth edition), pp. 20,001–20,518.

(4) Disparagement and Miscellaneous Interferences with Competitors

The Commission has attacked a number of practices which tend primarily to injure competitors rather than the consuming public. These include, among others, disparagement, espionage, threats of harassing litigation, and inducing breach of contract. Most of these oppressive trade tactics, it will be recalled, were recognized as unlawful under the common law, although the remedies afforded were not always adequate. And it is a significant fact that relatively few cases involving conflicts between competitors have been handled by the Commission. The number of cease and desist orders is quite insignificant as compared with the number of orders involving misrepresentation. This may be due in part to a general rise in the standards of business ethics. More important, perhaps, is the fact that the courts have not permitted the Commission to make any real contribution to the law of unfair competition in this sphere. They have either insisted upon the elements essential to action under the common law, or have found some such defect as an absence of public interest in the proceedings.

Of the practices here considered, disparagement of a competitor or his product has been most frequently enjoined. That the practice of making false representations about a trade rival for the purpose of injuring him richly deserves condemnation cannot be denied. Illustrative actions are those enjoining butter manufacturers from urging falsely that oleomargarine is made from cocoanut oil which is foul and unfit for human consumption,[147] a producer of surgical dressings from falsely alleging that products of competitors not widely known were not safe or sanitary,[148] a producer of aspirin from falsely representing that it only had the right to use the word "aspirin" and that competitors' products were counterfeit,[149] and a newspaper publisher from making false statements regarding the financial condition of competitors.[150] The authority of the Commission to prevent the making of such statements as these could not be seriously questioned. The Commission has been upheld by the courts, even where the false propaganda was allegedly used in defense against similar means employed by the competitor.[151] But where

---

[147] National Dairy Union, 16 F. T. C. 101 (1932); Crescent Creamery Co., 16 F. T. C. 142 (1932).

[148] Johnson & Johnson, 26 F. T. C. 134 (1937).

[149] Bayer Co., 19 F. T. C. 229 (1934).

[150] Blackwell Journal Publishing Co., 23 F. T. C. 413 (1936).

[151] Chamber of Commerce of Minneapolis v. F. T. C., 13 Fed. (2nd) 673 (1926). In Perma-Maid Co., Inc., v. F. T. C., 121 Fed. (2nd) 282 (1941), the court affirmed an order forbidding a distributor of stainless steel cooking utensils to represent that the preparation of food in aluminum utensils causes the formation of poisons and that such food is dangerous to health, notwithstanding the discontinuation of the practice.

the Commission sought to protect a misbranded antiseptic product of varying composition, as in the case of John Bene & Sons, a court found the proceeding not to be in the public interest.[152] The statements were based on competent analyses of the product but were exaggerated and perhaps misleading. In a subsequent case, an order was vacated because of insufficient evidence.[153] Proof of a dozen instances of disparagement by 600 salesmen over several years was inadequate to demonstrate an unfair method of competition.

It would be unfortunate indeed if these reversals were interpreted to curb the Commission's authority to proceed against actual disparagement. The 1938 amendment of Section 5, which extends the Commission's jurisdiction to unfair "acts" or "practices," will probably overcome the difficulty of inadequate evidence. More serious is the holding in the Bene case. There would seem to be no objection to the view that disparaging statements must be in fact false. Appropriate economic action can only be taken on the basis of full knowledge of conditions, and the dissemination of true information, even about a competitor, would further rather than hinder the achievement of this end. The difficulty lies in the fact that the public interest requirement, mentioned as the legal basis for the holding, might be used to preclude action in this type of case, where often the controversy is between two competitors. Private actions in the courts are not satisfactory, since special damage must be proved in order to recover, and injunctions can rarely be obtained. The Commission is not compelled to make findings of special damage. The issuance of cease and desist orders, which really operate as injunctions, seems to be the best method of attack upon this annoying and grossly unfair practice.

Proceeding on the general assumption that spying on competitors to obtain confidential business information was not in harmony with an acceptable standard of commercial ethics, the Commission issued a number of orders against the practice.[154] No effort was made to confine the orders to the acquisition of any particular type of information, nor was consideration given to the use to which the information was to be put. Any secretive method was proscribed as commercial espionage. But in the only case to come before the courts, the Commission's order was vacated on the ground that there was not substantial evidence to show that the "information was unlawfully used to hinder or stifle competition."[155] It was suggested also, although not definitely held, that espionage consisted in the obtaining of information relating to a secret process

---

[152] John Bene & Sons, Inc., v. F. T. C., 299 Fed. 468 (1924).
[153] Philip Carey Mfg. Co. v. F. T. C., 29 Fed. (2nd) 49 (1928).
[154] Botsford Lumber Co., 1 F. T. C. 60 (1918); The Oakes Co., 3 F. T. C. 36 (1920).
[155] Philip Carey Mfg. Co., 29 Fed. (2nd) 49 (1928).

or formula. This appears to be in line with the common law doctrine, which confines espionage to the acquisition of trade secrets. The use of underhanded methods to obtain information about competitors' facilities, extent of operations, costs of operation, or even lists of customers in some jurisdictions cannot be prevented. The Commission has issued no orders relating to espionage since this court decision in 1928.

To threaten competitors and perhaps their customers with litigation when there is no intention of actually bringing suit is a practice which can have no other objective than that of injuring competitors. The practice has been used to advantage by firms seeking a monopoly position. Most of the cases, it appears, have related to groundless threats to sue for patent or trade-mark infringement. Of the two orders of the Commission which have been challenged in the courts, neither has been upheld.[156] On the advice of reputable attorneys, the respondents in both cases circularized a few customers of a competitor, warning that suits for patent infringement were to be brought. No action had been taken prior to the issuance of the Commission's complaints. The fatal defect in each case was that the Commission had failed to prove bad faith in making the threats. It was also held, in the more recent decision, that the controversy was of a private character. The court remarked: "It was never intended that the Commission should act the part of a petty traffic officer in the great highways of commerce."[157] This jurisdictional point would seem to bar Commission proceedings. Fortunately, as Professor Handler has pointed out, the private remedy is adequate and Commission intervention is really unnecessary.[158]

It should be noted, in conclusion, that the Commission has also issued a number of orders relating to inducing breach of contract and the related practice of enticing competitors' employees. These practices have been condemned in circumstances indicating clearly that the purpose was to injure the competitor rather than to further directly the competitive interests of the aggressor.[159] At common law these practices were unlawful. The courts have had no occasion to consider the lawfulness of any order of the Commission, so it is not clear whether the Commission's authority is greater or less than that under the common law. If, perchance, the public interest requirement is found to preclude jurisdiction over these methods, it is probable that the courts can give adequate protection to damaged parties.[160]

----

[156] Heuser v. F. T. C., 4 Fed. (2nd) 632 (1925); Flynn & Emrich Co. v. F. T. C., 52 Fed. (2nd) 836 (1931).

[157] 52 Fed. (2nd) 836, p. 838.

[158] Handler, op. cit., p. 250.

[159] For brief summaries of the Commission's proceedings relating to these practices, see Commerce Clearing House, Trade Regulation Service (ninth edition), p. 6411.

[160] A novel and ingenious practice akin to the type here considered, in that the

Summary and Evaluation

For over thirty-five years the Federal Trade Commission has functioned as an investigatory and regulatory agency designed to improve the operation of the economic system. Having reviewed its efforts to preserve competition and to elevate the standard of competitive behavior, certain conclusions may now be drawn concerning the effectiveness of those efforts. In such an appraisal, attention may be directed both to the contribution which has been made to the substance of the law of unfair competition and to the general efficiency of the Commission's administrative process.

On the whole, the Commission has not been a potent force in directly protecting competition. Monopoly cases have constituted a relatively small percentage of its total proceedings. Though it was organized primarily as an agency to attack intercorporate relationships and trade practices which were conducive to monopoly, it is a singular fact that so little has been accomplished in this sphere. Price-fixing combinations and other trade restraints have been subsumed under unfair methods of competition with judicial approval. Re-sale price maintenance was attacked with some vigor until the shift in state and national policy legalized the practice in no uncertain terms. One factor which appears to be responsible for the dearth of monopoly proceedings is the costly nature of these investigations. They cover wide areas and numerous producers, and require the services of experienced attorneys to make the difficult showing that concert of action directed at fixing prices or restricting production does exist.[161] An encouraging feature of the Commission's performance is the increase in the number of proceedings relating to restraint of trade in the last ten years.[162]

The provisions of the Clayton Act, designed to eliminate intercorporate connections and trade practices which might eventually flower into monopoly, have been of little aid. Defective draftsmanship on the part of Congress and an apparent unwillingness on the part of the courts

---

purpose is to harass and cause financial loss to competitors, is the making of spurious requests for catalogues and estimates of mail-order houses. Firms handling building materials have encouraged employees and others to do this. See, for example, Botsford Lumber Co., 1 F. T. C. 60 (1918). In one instance a civic organization endeavored to protect local traders by ridding the community of mail-order catalogues by such means as offering prizes for them and arranging for their acceptance in lieu of admission charges to theatres. Chamber of Commerce of Missoula, 5 F. T. C. 451 (1923).

[161] Statements of James A. Horton, Chief Examiner, and W. T. Kelley, Chief Counsel, Federal Trade Commission, before the Temporary National Economic Committee, *Final Report and Recommendations*, Senate Document No. 35 (1941), pp. 299–311.

[162] Corwin D. Edwards, *Maintaining Competition* (New York, McGraw-Hill Book Company, Inc., 1949), pp. 296–297.

to interpret the laws in such fashion as to give them real force have been largely responsible. Section 7 was designed to prevent the merging of competing corporations by the acquisition by one corporation of the voting stock of other corporations. But this preventive instrument has been rendered impotent by the holding that the Commission has no power to force the divestiture of physical assets, even though such assets have been acquired through a purchase of stock made in violation of the law. Until Congress amends the section to embrace acquisitions of physical assets, as recommended strongly by both the Commission and the Temporary National Economic Committee, the prevailing trend toward fewer competing firms in many sections of industry cannot be arrested. Another abortive attempt to prevent monopolistic market structures was the prohibition of interlocking directorates in certain circumstances. Since there is no limitation on the ownership of voting stock in competing firms by a single person or interest, the use of dummy directors is a legitimate device for effecting coöperative action.

Even the prohibitions of such monopolistic practices as tying and exclusive dealing, and price discrimination, have not been fully effectual. Insufficient recognition has been given both by Congress and the courts to the fact that these practices can be carried on only by concerns which have some measure of monopoly power. The courts, until recently, have so construed the qualifying language which restricts unlawfulness to situations where the effect "may be to substantially lessen competition or tend to create a monopoly" that the Commission may successfully attack tying contracts and exclusive dealing arrangements only when they are utilized by concerns that are already dominant in their respective fields. The limitation has made it virtually impossible for the Commission to check these obstructive practices in the early stages of monopoly growth, and hence the Commission's preventive function has been defeated. The attack upon price discrimination, notwithstanding the classic order against Pittsburgh Plus, was for long restrained by the unfortunate ruling that the prohibition did not apply to discrimination which injured customers of a discriminating seller. Under the clarification and strengthening afforded by the Robinson-Patman Act, however, the Commission has been able to proceed apace not only against discriminatory basing-point systems and price discounts, but against such discriminatory practices as fictitious brokerage and advertising allowances.

Much greater success has attended the efforts of the Commission in the realm of unethical practices which impair the quality of competitive behavior. Misbranding and fraudulent advertising have been vigorously dealt with since the Commission was first upheld in the classic Winsted case. The fact that the Commission suffered repeated reversals in early cases relating to other activities perhaps accounts for its concentration in this field. With a decided difference in the general tone of its opinions from that expressed in the Gratz case, the Supreme Court has proceeded in recent years to place its stamp of approval upon the Commission's condemnation of lotteries, misrepresentation of trade status, and fictitious pricing.[163] Under this new dispensation it is likely that the Supreme Court will permit the Commission to go considerably further in building up a law of fair competition. The change in the attitude of the courts as well as the Wheeler-Lea Amendments of 1938 should enable the Commission, in the field of trade regulation, to attain the authority and prestige so long enjoyed by the Interstate Commerce Commission in transport matters.

There is little doubt that the substantive law of trade practices is superior to the common law. The chief merit is the relief from the requirement that special injury to the complaining parties be shown. It is sufficient to show that a given practice has a tendency to deceive consumers or to injure competitors. The public interest requirement places a definite limitation upon the scope of the Commission's performance, but if interpreted only to bar proceedings in private controversies for which there are adequate remedies in the courts, it will not constitute a serious deterrent to the attainment of the public good.

The economic effect of the elimination of misrepresentation and kindred practices is to insure more fully that competitors will survive on the basis of efficiency. Consumers are able to ascertain the true qualities of products more easily, especially under the current trend toward full disclosure of content, as in the textile field, and will spend their incomes more wisely. Those firms which have relied upon deception to build up

---

[163] After having talked about court reversals and affirmations throughout this discussion of the Commission's performance, it may be interesting to set down the statistics concerning the fate of cease and desist orders in the courts. Of the 382 orders which were appealed to the Circuit Courts of Appeals up to June 30, 1948, 68 petitions had been withdrawn, 2 had been remanded to the Commission, and 303 had been decided as of that date. Of the 303 decisions, 200 were in favor of the Commission and 103 for other parties. Many of the 103 orders reversed were in consolidated proceedings (furniture veneer and tank and pump cases), so if actual cases are counted the number of reversals would be 52. Some 60 petitions for enforcement of orders were also passed upon by the lower courts, and the Commission was sustained in 56 of these cases.

Petitions for review of the decisions of lower courts were filed in the Supreme Court in 105 cases. The Commission was sustained in 79 of these cases, either by formal decision or by a denial of certiorari to respondents. Of the remaining cases, 24 were decided in favor of respondents and 2 were withdrawn by the Commission.

The foregoing statistics, while in terms of orders rather than cases involving a given trade practice, indicate that the record of the Commission in the courts has not been good. It is significant, however, that since the Raladam decision in 1931 the Commission has been reversed by the Supreme Court in only 4 cases and has been denied certiorari in 2 others. It is extremely important to note also that the Commission had issued 3,964 orders to cease and desist prior to June 30, 1948. When the 103 orders reversed by the lower courts and the 24 orders reversed by the Supreme Court are related to this figure of 3,964, it puts the Commission's record in a much better light. F. T. C., *Annual Report*, 1948, pp. 50–51.

consumer preference will lose this advantage, and the demand for their products will revert more closely to the perfect elasticity which characterizes pure competition. With the dissipation of this monopolistic element, predicated upon inadequate and false consumer knowledge, competition will be improved, patronage will be diverted to those firms supplying the most acceptable products in terms of quality and cost, and greater satisfactions will be obtained from productive resources. Maximum satisfaction can be obtained, however, only if all elements of monopoly are removed. The Commission must move against monopolistic market structures and practices more vigorously. It is also apparent, as the Commission has vigorously pointed out, that the restrictions placed upon price competition by state "fair trade" and "unfair practices" acts and the Miller-Tydings Enabling Act are counter to the basic tenets of a competitive economy. The Temporary National Economic Committee has recognized the uneconomic character of re-sale price maintenance and has recommended that the Miller-Tydings Act be repealed.[164]

An evaluation of the general efficiency of the Commission's administrative process raises a number of issues. In the first place, there is little question that the administrative control of trade practices is far superior to that under the common law. There is some assurance that action will be taken against the dishonest and predatory element in business. It is no longer necessary to rely upon court action by private parties, suits which were infrequently brought because of the cost and the uncertainty of result. The Commission, an expert body supported by public funds and under a mandate to act in the public interest, assumes the initiative and carries the proceedings through to a conclusion.

But have all the advantages of administrative control been realized? It is safe to say that they have not been. For one thing, the Commission's procedure has been cumbersome and slow.[165] Unless fairly expeditious action is taken, parties are uncertain as to whether given practices are unfair, injured parties are not given prompt relief, and the preventive function is impaired. Numerous factors probably account for the lack of expedition in handling cases. Inadequate appropriations and in-

---

[164] T. N. E. C., *Senate Document* No. 35, p. 33.

[165] National Industrial Conference Board, *Regulation of Competitive Practices* (New York, 1929), pp. 252–253; Henderson, *op. cit.*, p. 89. In this connection, note the following from the *Task Force Report on Regulatory Commissions* (1949) prepared for the Commission on Organization of the Executive Branch of the Government: " . . . The Federal Trade Commission has fallen far short. As the years have progressed, the Commission has become immersed in a multitude of petty problems; it has not probed into new areas of anticompetitive practices; it has become increasingly bogged down with cumbersome procedures and inordinate delays in disposition of cases. Its economic work—instead of being the backbone of its activities—has been allowed to dwindle almost to none. The Commission has largely become a passive judicial agency, waiting for cases to come up on the docket, under routinized procedures, without active responsibility for achieving the statutory objectives." Appendix N, p. 125.

sufficient personnel are perhaps the most important. Increases in appropriations and personnel have taken place over the years, but they have
not kept pace with the growing volume of proceedings due in part to
new legislation. Another factor is the cumbersome and time-consuming
character of its procedure. The numerous steps in the procedure, while
perhaps necessary to insure due process of law, afford great opportunity
for delay. The stipulation procedure, the trade practice conference,
industry-wide investigations, and the new enforcement procedure in the
courts have undoubtedly contributed to more efficient administration,
but it appears that they are not enough. Perhaps the answer lies in the
introduction of methods of approach which will make enforcement of the
law somewhat more automatic than at present. The Commission must
now proceed against a great many individual firms that indulge in an
unlawful practice. A codification of clearly unfair practices, either by the
Commission under a definite delegation of authority from Congress or by
Congress itself, and the attachment of a substantial money penalty for
engaging in these practices might be undertaken.[166] A clear and definite
statement of proscribed practices, with adequate provision for additions
thereto as circumstances require, would give fair warning to business
men, and the prospect of money penalties would serve as a deterrent to
unlawful action. Detection of violators and the imposition of penalties
would be entrusted to the Commission. Under such an arrangement it is
likely that the number of cases would be brought within manageable
proportions.

Another question is whether or not the Commission has actually been
an expert body devoted to the vigorous enforcement of the national policy
of maintaining free and fair competition. Effectiveness of administration depends in great measure upon the quality of the personnel. In this
respect the Federal Trade Commission has not been as fortunate as the
Interstate Commerce Commission. The latter agency, from the very beginning, has been noted for the ability and public vision of its members.
But the same statesmanlike qualities have not characterized the Trade
Commission throughout its career.[167] The early Commission, while it
suffered from a very rapid turnover in membership as well as in staff,
did make a real effort to give new content to the meaning of unfair competition and to assert its authority. Its effort, however, received little
sympathetic treatment at the hands of the courts. A part of the difficulty

---

[166] For a discussion of constructive proposals for codifying and defining unlawful
trade practices, see Handler, *op. cit.*, pp. 259–262; Nelson B. Gaskill, *The Regulation
of Competition* (New York, Harper & Brothers, 1936), pp. 138–175.

[167] For an appraisal of the Commission's personnel and policies, see E. Pendleton
Herring, *Public Administration and the Public Interest* (New York, McGraw-Hill
Book Co., 1936), Chaps. 7 and 8; and Carl McFarland, *Judicial Control of the
Federal Trade Commission and the Interstate Commerce Commission, 1920–1930*
(Cambridge, Mass., Harvard University Press, 1933), Chap. 5.

was the failure of the Commission to render informative opinions which analyzed the evidence and the argument presented, and gave full and convincing explanations of the reasons for its decisions.[168] Formal statements of findings of fact and conclusions, without reasons, are unsatisfactory both to the parties concerned and to the reviewing courts. The courts are unable to determine whether expert judgments have actually been rendered in a particular case, and are tempted to substitute their own appraisal of the evidence. This condition is being corrected in the Commission as well as in all regulatory agencies by the requirements of the Administrative Procedure Act of 1946. All decisions must include a statement of findings and conclusions upon the material issues of fact, law, or discretion as well as the "reasons or basis" upon which they are founded.

Under the leadership of the Commissioners appointed by the Republican administrations in the early 1920's, however, there was a decided shift in the policies of the Commission. These conservative appointees were more friendly to the business interests, and readily acceded to the views of the courts that the Commission was not intended to be a resourceful and energetic pioneer in the realm of trade regulation. The announced objective was to coöperate with business rather than to subject it to penetrating economic investigation and perhaps embarrassing publicity and painful litigation.[169] Among other things, economic investigations were not given the proper encouragement, no publicity was given to the names of respondents who entered stipulations to discontinue unlawful practices, and the trade practice conference procedure was liberalized and its use greatly expanded.[170] The Commission went so far in its trade practice conference activities as to raise the suspicion that the industry conferences and rules were being used for price-fixing and other illegal purposes. An informal protest was registered by the Department of Justice. A modification in policy ensued, when, without any official explanation for its action, a general revision of trade practice rules was ordered by the Commission in 1930.[171]

With the inauguration of a Democratic administration in 1933, the

---

[168] Henderson, *op. cit.*, pp. 333–337.

[169] Commissioner William E. Humphrey, appointed to the Commission by President Coolidge in 1925, remarked as follows concerning the policy of the Commission as it functioned under the Wilson Administration: "Under the old policy of litigation it became an instrument of oppression and disturbance and injury instead of a help to business. It harassed and annoyed business instead of assisting it. Business soon regarded the commission with distrust and fear and suspicion—as an enemy. There was no coöperation between the commission and business. Business wanted the commission abolished and the commission regarded business as generally dishonest." Address of January 6, 1931, quoted by Herring, *op. cit.*, p. 125.

[170] See Herring, *op. cit.*, pp. 125–138, for an interesting and informative review of the change in policy.

[171] Gaskill, *op. cit.*, pp. 106–124; Herring, *op. cit.*, pp. 129–133.

pressure of politics was once again felt by this supposedly independent and expert administrative body. But at this point forces were set in motion to guide the veering craft back to the course originally charted in 1914. One of the first steps taken by President Roosevelt was the removal from office of Commissioner Humphrey,[172] who for over eight years had championed the policy of leniency in regulation and coöperation with the industry. Commissioners were appointed whose social and economic philosophies were more acceptable. But apart from the administration of the new Federal Securities Law of 1933, the Commission found itself far in the background as a regulator of business practices. The violent aberration in trust policy instituted by the National Industrial Recovery Act of 1933 left little room for the exercise of its delegated authority. With the passing of this abortive experiment in 1935, however, the Commission was able once more to assert itself as an agency dedicated to the task of preserving free and fair competition. Such factors as a more harmonious and socially-minded membership, increased Congressional support and appropriations, much-needed supplementary legislation, and a more sympathetic attitude on the part of the courts,[173] have greatly strengthened the Commission. There is some prospect now that the rôle envisioned for the Commission in the American economic scene by its founders in 1914 will be realized.

---

[172] Commissioner Humphrey was asked to resign on August 31, 1933. President Roosevelt stated in his letter: "I do not feel that your mind and my mind go along together on either the policies or the administration of the Federal Trade Commission, and, frankly, I think it is best for the people of this country that I should have a full confidence." Commissioner Humphrey refused to resign and on October 7, 1933, was removed from office. Humphrey's executor, the former Commissioner having died on February 14, 1934, challenged the power of the President to remove a member of an administrative commission from office and sought to recover back salary due him. Upon appeal to the Supreme Court, it was held that the President has no authority to dismiss a member of a commission performing quasi-judicial and quasi-legislative functions except for the reasons of inefficiency, neglect of duty, or malfeasance in office prescribed in the statute. Humphrey's Executor v. U. S., 295 U. S. 602 (1935).

[173] Judicial hostility has been replaced by judicial approval to such an extent that we have the strange situation of a member of the Commission recommending that Congress curtail the authority of the Commission. As an introduction to his minority recommendations in 1948, Commissioner Lowell B. Mason said: "In the greatest and most complex economy in the world it is necessary that we have a capable and efficient quasi-judicial agency to prevent unfair practices in commerce. But administrative agencies diminish their effectiveness when they claim powers in excess of those that can be justified under a democratic form of Government. In a manner of speaking, they price themselves out of the market. This overzealousness puts ammunition in the hands of those who would destroy administrative law." Among other things, he recommended that the scope of judicial review of Commission orders be extended to findings of fact as well as of law. See F. T. C., Annual Report, 1948, pp. 12–13.

PART IV
Oligopoly and Industrial Coöperation

Introduction

In altering the internal pattern of the modern corporation and in providing a favorable ground for the growth of monopoly, corporate concentration has created two serious difficulties for the competitive system. Unfortunately it presents another closely related problem. Industry after industry shows two or three or a dozen firms producing almost the whole output which, to the consumer, constitutes the supply of a commodity. Yet competitive concepts are based on the assumption that the number of competitive companies is so large that each can and must make its price and output plans independently.

A number of products are produced by industries in which as few as eight companies are responsible for 90 per cent of the output. Among these products are typewriters, chewing-gum, ammunition, cigarettes, linseed oil, motor vehicles (except motorcycles), safes and vaults, linoleum, rubber tires and inner tubes, sewing-machines, rayon, writing-ink, and matches. In a dozen industries a single company possesses only a few small rivals.[1] In others, concentration has advanced nearly as far, leaving two or three large concerns to account for over 70 per cent of the production of such articles as electric motors, milk-bottles, locomotives, biscuits, fruit-jars, and cast-iron enamelware.

In over 10 per cent of the industries covered by the Census of Manufactures a single producer accounts for something between 50 and 75 per cent of the total production; in approximately 20 per cent the four largest are responsible for 65 to 90 per cent of the supply, and the eight largest for 75 to 100 per cent. Even these figures do not indicate the full extent to which the market is dominated by a few sellers. An "industry" may produce a variety of articles, and a company concentrating on the production of a few of them will have a greater importance than the general figures indicate. Similarly, the plants of a company may be concentrated

[1] Among these companies are The American Can Co., The American Car and Foundry Co., The American Smelting and Refining Co., The American Sugar Refining Co., The International Match Co., The Koppers Co., The National Biscuit Co., The National Lead Co., The Procter and Gamble Co., The Singer Manufacturing Co., and The Union Carbide and Carbon Corporation. *Cf.* T. N. E. C., Monograph No. 21, *Competition and Monopoly in American Industry* (1940), pp. 113–121.

in one area of the country, and in that area it may possess an importance
not adequately represented by national figures.

CONCENTRATION AND INTERDEPENDENCE

When as a result of concentration the number of firms producing a
physically similar product is reduced to a small figure, one important
condition for complete competition will almost certainly be missing.
The general picture presented by economic theory is one in which the
conceptual supply unit is the industry. The size of the unit is adjusted
through the influence of supply and demand changes affecting costs and
prices so as to direct the entry or exit of firms at the margin. To make
his profits as large as possible, the individual seller is described as adjusting his production to the point where his marginal cost is equal to
the ruling price for the industry product. This general explanation is
not reasonable if it cannot be assumed that there is sufficiently free
entry into the industry and a sufficiently large number of producers to
prevent any individual firm from possessing the power to change the
ruling price for the industry as a whole by some change in its production
policy.

If any producer is sufficiently large to change the level of prices for
the industry, the competitive process will not function. First, the firm
may possibly increase its profits by restricting production below the ideal
envisaged in competitive theory. If it restricts, it will lose some sales to
other companies, but the rise in the going price for the products of the
industry may be sufficient to increase its total profits. Second, the competitive independence of the several companies in the industry can no
longer be maintained. It becomes obvious that any important change in
the business policy of one giant concern both affects and is affected by
the policy of others. The producer cannot simply adjust his production to
fit the existing price, but must give major attention to the influences
which the present production and price policies of other companies will
have on his business and the manner in which their reactions, induced
by changes in his business policy, will affect the operation of any new
policy.

The influence which one firm will exercise on the cost level of others
also creates a considerable interdependence. Where few buyers are
present, the prices paid for labor and materials can be importantly affected by the policy of any one company. No company can plan to
expand its production without considering the effects which other company plans would have on its costs and profits. The three large tobacco
concerns together make nearly half the total purchases of leaf tobacco,
and are even more important buyers of certain types of cured tobacco.

The size of the purchases, and the prices paid by any one of them, are of very direct concern to the others. With the four large meat-packers buying between 50 and 80 per cent of the various supplies of livestock, this same interdependence inevitably exists. The packers commonly determine the prices they will offer by deducting their processing costs and an allowance for profits from current prices for meat. Obviously any unusual buying by any one of the packers would affect the profits of the others, and his own profits would be influenced by the reaction of the others. The packers, of course, have taken steps to forestall any competitive disturbance, but whether they do or not, the fact of a very close interdependence would remain. Competitive independence must give way before an interdependence which is allowed no place in competitive theory.

While concentration will force the dropping of competitive concepts, it will not develop relations in an industry that can be contained in simple monopoly concepts. If the several companies were symmetrical in all respects, it would be possible to find a monopoly price which would be suitable for all. But differences in the demand enjoyed by the interdependent firms and difference in their supply situation would mean that the ideal monopoly price for one seller might serve another very poorly. And even more important in invalidating traditional monopoly generalizations is the fact that the interdependence in itself does not entail the complete unity necessary for monopoly.

As one seller raised his price materially above competitive levels, it might or might not serve the interest of others to follow him. Depending on the amount of their sales increase and its effect on their production costs, the others, or some of the others, might make larger profits by no increase in price, or even by reductions. And, of course, the wisdom of the price increase of the first seller would have to be reconsidered in the light of the price policies pursued by the others. The elasticity of the demand for his products is important in determining the level of price which will give him the largest monopoly profits, but this elasticity may be importantly affected by the price policies followed by the manufacturers of goods that are in direct competition. If their price policies are similar to his, the shape of the demand curve for his products will not change. If they follow only part way in increasing prices, his demand will become more elastic, and probably some part of the original increase in price would have to be abandoned as he suffered severe reductions in the volume of sales.

When the output of different sellers is not differentiated by the influence of such things as advertising or style differences, and if competition comes only from physically similar products, it is possible that each seller would find that there was a perfectly elastic demand for his product at the price level maintained by others—that is, under conditions of perfect competition any price increase on his part would reduce his sales to zero. However, the competition faced by most goods comes in considerable part from other commodities that are physically dissimilar. Meat competes for a place in the consumer's budget not only with a great variety of foods, but with clothing, housing and a hundred other goods and services. All these affect the elasticity of demand for meat and, in most cases, if meat prices are raised while the prices of these "substitutes" remain the same, the quantity of meat demanded will decrease, but not to zero. In other words, perfect elasticity of demand does not exist. And to the extent that the seller has been able to persuade the buyer that his product possesses distinctive qualities not possessed by physically similar commodities, he can be independent of the price level set by direct competitors. But even in this case one seller may feel his product is so firmly differentiated that he need not fear the effect that high prices might have in attracting new competitors into existence. However, another may wish to avoid the price that is best for short-run monopoly profits, in order to minimize the risk he may face from the appearance of new enterprises.

Certain supply considerations may also prevent the several companies from agreeing on a single price. If their unit costs are at different levels or react differently as output is restricted, there will be no one price which will yield the maximum profits for all. When fixed costs are very important in the production of one company, it gains less as prices are raised and output reduced than does a firm with a larger proportion of variable costs. And finally, restriction may reduce raw material or labor costs for one and not for another manufacturer. It is obvious that United States Steel, owning extensive ore properties, could not benefit from a restriction in steel output that reduced the demand for ore. But others, buying ore supplies on the open market, would probably find that their ore costs were reduced as the demand for ore declined.

The study of a number of representative cases undertaken in this part shows that this interdependence frequently spells the end of competitive independence. Competition is replaced by coöperative action organized in various forms. A leading firm may set prices that are accepted by the others in the industry. The small group may work through some plan whereby the market is divided between the individual companies without the appearance of competition. Or finally, some form of association may be maintained by conventional arrangements or by formal organization which allows the producers to plan collectively their price and output policies. Unfortunately, the coöperation may bring effects that are little if any better than those associated with monopoly. The cases studied do suggest that conditions do not permit the coöperating producers to achieve as profitable and socially injurious results as those created by monopoly.

In various ways this collusion is more serious than monopoly. For one thing, it is tremendously more common. As the following chapters suggest, it is an actual or a threatening condition in the majority of our large industries and in many small markets. For another, it is more difficult to attack than monopoly. In the ordinary fields of industry there is something artificial in the domination of a single firm. The study of monopoly showed the large monopoly threatened frequently by its own inefficiency, and by the recurring appearance of independents that had to be bought off or eliminated by costly cut-throat competition. Although industrial coöperation is strengthened frequently by patents, unfair competition and other devices, it rests directly on a business condition that is very common—the growth of large corporate units and the resulting concentration of business.

23

The Iron and Steel Industry

While the materials used in iron and steel-making and the main production steps have remained essentially unchanged over a long period of time, the structure of business organization and the competitive aspects of the American iron and steel industry have altered considerably. As late as 1890 it showed little evidence of either horizontal or vertical combination, and appeared to be highly competitive. Gentlemen's agreements and pools were not uncommon, but their temporary nature indicates that they did not seriously limit competition.[1] Their frequent recurrence, however, suggests that leaders in the industry had no great enthusiasm for competition and suffered it only because pools failed to curtail it. More thorough-going combination offered both an escape from this situation and the possibility of large-scale economies. At the same time, developments along this line were being encouraged by financiers seeking promotion profits, and were being made easy by the availability of the holding company.

THE ORGANIZATION OF THE INDUSTRY

Combination first appeared as individual companies expended horizontally in various stages of the industry. There was at first very little of it in the production of iron ore. Although the mines were concentrated in Minnesota, Wisconsin, Michigan, and in the district around Birmingham, Alabama, the mine companies were generally small. But in the heavy steel section of the industry a number of large companies appeared. They were engaged in the smelting of ore with coke to produce pig iron and in the treatment of pig iron in open-hearth or Bessemer

---

[1] Quarrels over tonnage allotments, the failure to include all producers, and the entry of new competitors broke up pools among producers of wire nails, steel rails, billets, and ore; cf. *The Report of the Commissioner of Corporations on the Steel Industry* (Washington, D. C., U. S. Government Printing Office, 1911), Part I, p. 2.

furnaces to produce steel ingots.[2] The finished steel companies, fabricating a number of products from the slabs and blooms obtained from heavy steel producers, remained small. And there was generally very little integration between the three stages of the industry. The one outstanding exception to this rule, the Carnegie Steel Company, operated in the heavy and semi-finished branches of the industry, and through the Frick Coke Company and the Oliver Iron Mining Company held deposits of coking coal and iron ore.

In the short space of three years this whole situation was changed. A remarkable combination movement started in 1898 and left almost the whole industry by the end of 1900 in the hands of a few companies. The rapidity of the movement and the size of the various companies is apparent from the following table:

Table 16

LEADING COMBINATIONS IN THE IRON AND STEEL INDUSTRY, 1898–1900

Year of Incorporation	Name of Organization	Authorized Capital
1898	American Steel & Wire Co. of Illinois	$ 24,000,000
	American Tin Plate Co.	50,273,000
	American Car & Foundry Co.	60,000,000
	American Iron & Steel Mfg. Co.	20,000,000
	Empire Steel & Iron Co.	10,000,000
	Federal Steel Co.	230,217,179
	National Enameling & Stamping Co.	30,600,000
	Pressed Steel Car Co.	25,000,000
	Republic Iron & Steel Co.	55,000,000
	Sloss-Sheffield Steel & Iron Co.	23,835,000
	U. S. Cast Iron Pipe & Foundry Co.	30,000,000
	Virginia Iron, Coal & Coke Co.	20,000,000
1899	American Steel & Wire Co. of N. J.	70,156,000
	American Steel Hoop Co.	33,000,000
	National Steel Co.	61,561,000
	National Tube Co.	80,000,000
1900	American Bridge Co.	70,156,000
	American Sheet Steel Co.	54,000,000
	Carnegie Company of N. J.	345,081,813
	Crucible Steel Co. of America	50,000,000
	Shelby Steel Tube Co.	15,000,000

A number of these large companies were under the influence of three great industrial and financial personalities: Andrew Carnegie, a canny Scot and top-ranking steel man; J. P. Morgan, Sr., a powerful and able financier; and Judge W. H. Moore, astute lawyer, promoter, and finan-

---

[2] The Bessemer process has been displaced to a considerable extent by the open-hearth method. Since impurities can be disposed of more readily in the latter, it is able to use pig iron of widely varying chemical analysis.

cier, whose stardom was dimmed somewhat by the lustre of the other two.

Carnegie's company, Carnegie Steel, was largely independent of the other steel companies, except at one point where it was highly vulnerable. It produced crude and semi-finished steel which it sold to companies manufacturing finished steel products. Some of these companies, such as National Tube, were under Morgan control, and some, like the American Steel and Wire Company, a partially integrated concern, were under the aegis of John W. ("Betcha-million") Gates. Carnegie could be economically embarrassed if such customers chose to produce their own crude and semi-finished steel. When they let it be known that they intended to become self-sufficient the market situation looked precarious for Carnegie. Consequently he countered this lead by announcing plans to build at Conneaut, Ohio, the finest tube works in the world. It was announced, also, that he had plans to construct a railroad from Pittsburgh to the Atlantic seaboard.[3] Both of these moves, if consummated, spelled trouble for J. P. Morgan, whose interests lay not only in rival steel companies but also in the Pennsylvania Railroad, which carried Carnegie's products over its rails.

Carnegie was powerful. His company had large cash resources. It was exceptionally well equipped and highly organized to bring out the best efforts of its talented steel-makers. Its capital structure was devoid of water.

The Morgan companies, such as Federal Steel, National Tube, and American Bridge, had the financial support of the country's outstanding investment banker. This support was not as strong as it appeared, however, for it must be remembered that the House of Morgan had many irons in the financial fire. Its power could not, therefore, be concentrated on a steel war. Furthermore, the Morgan-controlled companies were badly over-capitalized, and would be vulnerable in a severe struggle.

Judge Moore's steel companies were so badly handicapped by this same weakness that competent economists have doubted if the Moore-controlled concerns could have withstood even the market effects of an opening battle.[4]

The Combination of Combinations

How some of Carnegie's rivals felt about the steel situation is revealed in the words of Judge Gary of Federal Steel, who told the Stanley Com-

---

[3] In one of his earlier threats against the Pennsylvania Railroad, Carnegie actually sent great crews of men into the mountains of Pennsylvania to construct roadbed and tunnels for a competing railway to the Atlantic seaboard. The project was, however, suddenly given up. Recently, highway engineers, constructing a highway along the same route from Harrisburg to Pittsburgh, found the tools which had been discarded in the tunnels when Carnegie abandoned the construction. See *The New York Times*, October 15, 1939, Section 10, p. 1.

[4] *Cf.* Seager and Gulick, *op. cit.*, pp. 220–221.

mittee that " . . . it is not at all certain that if the old management or the management which was in force at one time had continued, the Carnegie Company would not have driven entirely out of business every steel company in the United States."[5]

While it may be that Judge Gary was trying to excuse eventual combination, nevertheless Scotch determination and a full purse were dangerous. Morgan and his associates chose to be discreet rather than valorous, but did not find it easy to buy out Carnegie. Earlier attempts to acquire his interests had failed. Carnegie, it seems, did have ambitions to distribute his surplus wealth and die a relatively poor man. It appears, however, that he had no burning desire to distribute his surplus by making a poor bargain with those who already had large surpluses of their own. Budding financial deals languished, therefore, until the forceful and fluent Charles M. Schwab, right-hand man of Carnegie, revived hopes. Schwab, it is said, sat close by J. P. Morgan at a dinner one December evening in 1900. As guest of honor and chief speaker of the occasion, Mr. Schwab presented dramatically the case for complete integration in the steel industry. More advanced technical organization, assured markets, economies of larger-scale operations, expansion in international trade, and other variations of the same general theme incited great enthusiasm. Mr. Morgan was impressed by Schwab's arguments, and shortly thereafter he asked Mr. Schwab to discover on what terms Carnegie would be willing to sell.

Lincoln Steffens tells us that the man who ultimately brought Carnegie and Morgan into agreement was James B. Dill, an extraordinarily clever corporation lawyer, who had pushed through the New Jersey legislature the amendment to its incorporation laws permitting the charter grants to holding companies.[6] Dill told Steffens: "I put Morgan in one room, Carnegie in another, while I took the third room in between them with my clerks and stenographers. I knew that if they met they would blow up; so I played the part of buffer and negotiator. They could express their opinions of each other to me. I could agree with both of them, sympathize with the generosity and bigness of each one, and share his contempt for the narrow meanness of the other. I was sincere, uninsultable, and true to their agreeable purposes, the one to buy, the other to sell."[7]

What Elbert Gary dreamed about as President of Federal Steel, what Charles Schwab dramatized for Morgan's benefit, James B. Dill fashioned, for a fee, into the United States Steel Corporation. This "combination of combinations" acquired the Carnegie Steel Company and its

---

[5] Hearings before the Committee on Investigation of the U. S. Steel Corporation, H. R. No. 1127, 62nd Congress, 2nd Session, 1911, Vol. I, p. 220.

[6] *Autobiography of Lincoln Steffens* (New York, Harcourt, Brace and Co., 1931), p. 192.

[7] *Ibid.*, p. 192.

subsidiary, the Frick Coke Company, for $492,006,160 in securities.[8] Andrew Carnegie's share was $213,000,000.

Literally scores of corporations were amalgamated into the corporate personality created by James B. Dill and J. P. Morgan. Into U. S. Steel came Carnegie, Federal, American Steel and Wire of New Jersey, National Steel, National Tube, American Steel Hoop, American Sheet Steel, American Tin Plate, and their subsidiaries. In short order there followed American Bridge, Consolidated Iron Mines, Bessemer Steamship, and the Oliver Iron Mining Company. Later, other important concerns were acquired. Thus the threatening steel war was averted. Carnegie got his price. The House of Morgan realized promoter's profits of $62,500,000 net, and obtained control of the new combination. Complete integration in the steel industry was an accomplished fact.

U. S. Steel's inventory showed a varied list of assets: enormous quantities of raw materials such as coking coal, iron ore, limestone; railways and steamships; coking plants, blast furnaces, rolling mills, finishing mills, warehouses, and sales offices.[9] In addition to these tangible assets it was equipped with a corporate charter which allowed it to do almost everything except coin money.[10] And the Company did not remain satisfied with its great size. From surplus earnings and from the sale of securities it constructed additional plants, the most notable of which was the huge one at Gary, Indiana. Furthermore, it acquired competing concerns and either purchased or leased valuable ore properties. Union Steel was acquired in 1902. Clairton Steel, in receiver's hands, was absorbed in 1904. Both of these companies possessed valuable raw materials such as iron ore and coking coal. In November, 1907, it bought the Tennessee Coal, Iron, and Railroad Company, acquiring thereby enormous holdings of coal and iron ore.[11] Because this company's raw materials were all available in a relatively small but richly endowed area, pig iron could be manufactured there more cheaply than anywhere else.[12] Moreover, the market for open-hearth steel rails was developing rapidly. This made the Tennessee Company's iron ore, which did not convert properly into

[8] Seager and Gulick, op. cit., p. 223.

[9] The U. S. Steel Corporation acquired steel works of an annual capacity of 9,400,000 tons of crude steel; more than 7,700,000 tons capacity of finished rolled steel products; over 1000 miles of main track together with a large mileage of second track and sidings; more than 100 Lake ore vessels; iron ore reserves in the Lake region estimated at from 500,000,000 to 700,000,000 tons; over 50,000 acres of coking-coal lands; and many miscellaneous properties. Report of the Commissioner of Corporations on the Steel Industry, Part I, p. 13.

[10] For a copy of the charter of U. S. Steel see A. H. Stockder, Business Ownership Organization (New York, Henry Holt and Co., 1922), pp. 573–581.

[11] For the interesting details concerning this acquisition, see Seager and Gulick, op. cit., pp. 231–235.

[12] Cf. Eliot Jones, The Trust Problem in the United States (New York, The Macmillan Company, 1928), p. 209.

steel by the Bessemer process, much more attractive than formerly. By its acquisition the United States Steel also forestalled what would have been a formidable hundred-million-dollar integration of this property with the Republic Iron and Steel and the Sloss-Sheffield Steel and Iron Company.

In another move the Steel Corporation arranged with James J. Hill, head of the Great Northern Railway, to lease a large part of the railroad's ore lands. The terms of the lease were very unfavorable for the purchaser, and the Bureau of Corporations insisted that the lease was signed merely to check the growth of rival corporations. By 1910, the Corporation held ore reserves in excess of the combined holdings of all the other steel companies.

The Present Organization of the Industry

In 1920 an ill-informed prosecution and a befuddled court wiped away any taint of monopoly from the Steel Corporation and, by implication, from its competitors. Since then the leading company has grown, although meantime other large companies have made proportionately greater strides. The Steel Corporation's early start was so great that its dominant position has not been challenged; the industry has come to be almost completely dominated by a few large concerns. At the start of World War II, 80 per cent of the annual capacity of pig iron, steel ingots, and hot rolled steel products was concentrated in the hands of ten large corporations. About two hundred smaller concerns completed the roster of the industry. The size and relative importance of the leading companies is apparent in Table 17 showing the invested capital of the ten largest companies.

The ten companies accounted for 88 per cent of the industry, while the assets of the leading company alone made up 40 per cent of the total to give it a size two and a half times greater than its nearest rival. There is a considerable disparity in the importance of particular companies in the production of individual products, but these concerns dominate all branches of the industry. In manufacturing pig iron, steel ingots, and thirteen of the leading finished or semi-finished products, the five largest in the individual lines possessed between 43 and 94 per cent of the total capacity.[13] In the manufacture of some products, such as cold rolled sheets, the United States Steel Company was matched or nearly matched by other of the large companies. But its lead was commanding in pig iron and steel ingot capacity and in rails, finished hot rolled products, wire rods, hot rolled strip, and a number of other products.

---

[13] T. N. E. C., *Hearings*, Part 18, Table XVII, p. 10,409.

World War II produced a great growth in the capacity of the steel industry and a further increase in concentration. Between 1940 and 1945 steel-making capacity rose from 81.6 to 95.5 million tons annually, an increase of 17 per cent. Roughly 60 per cent of the increase in capacity was accounted for by the three leading corporations, United States Steel, Bethlehem, and Republic Steel. About half of the two and one-half billion

Table 17

INVESTED CAPITAL OF THE TEN LARGEST STEEL COMPANIES, 1937[14]

Company	Invested Capital in Millions of Dollars	Per Cent
Total Invested Capital for the Industry...................	$4281.26	100
1. United States Steel Corporation.........................	1717.92	40
2. Bethlehem Steel Corporation............................	656.68	15
3. Republic Steel Corporation..............................	329.50	8
4. Jones and Laughlin Steel Corporation....................	198.61	5
5. Youngstown Sheet and Tube Company..................	199.34	5
6. National Steel Corporation.............................	179.69	4
7. Inland Steel Company..................................	143.36	3
8. American Rolling Mills Company........................	132.62	3
9. Wheeling Steel Corporation.............................	110.37	3
10. Crucible Steel Company of America.....................	103.59	2
Total for the Ten Companies...........................	$3771.68	88

dollars spent on new plants was put up by the Government. A large part of the expenditures was for additions to existing plants, which, of course, adds to the pre-war concentration. Actually about half of government expenditures went into additions to existing plants, and a considerable part of the remainder went into plants that would have little chance of successful operation except in conjunction with existing producers.[15] Of new and independent operations resulting from the war, probably the major one results from continued operation in the post-war period of the Kaiser-owned Fontana plant, which cost about one hundred million dollars to build.

At the close of the war United States Steel was operating 35.1 per cent of the ingot capacity of the industry compared to 34.1 per cent before the war. The relative positions of the integrated companies and

---

[14] *Ibid.*, Table XVI, p. 10,408.
[15] Report of the Smaller War Plants Corporation, *Economic Concentration and World War II*, Senate Document No. 206, 79th Congress, 2nd Session, (Washington, D. C., U. S. Government Printing Office, 1946), p. 87.

the effect of war construction are reflected in the following tabulation showing the position of the companies in terms of ingot capacities.[16]

Table 18

RELATIVE CAPACITIES OPERATED BY INTEGRATED STEEL COMPANIES, 1940 AND 1945

Company	Jan. 1, 1940	Jan. 1, 1945
United States Steel Corp.	34.1%	35.1%
Bethlehem Steel Co.	14.1	13.5
Republic Steel Corp.	9.6	10.2
Jones & Laughlin Steel Corp.	6.0	5.3
Youngstown Sheet and Tube Co.	4.3	4.2
National Steel Corp.	4.7	4.1
Inland Steel Co.	3.8	3.6
American Rolling Mill Co.	3.7	3.4
Wheeling Steel Corp.	2.4	2.1
Crucible Steel Co.	1.1	1.6
Colorado Fuel & Iron Corp.	1.4	1.3
Pittsburgh Steel Co.	1.3	1.1
Ford Motor Co.	1.2	1.0
International Harvester Co.	0.9	0.9
Kaiser	......	0.8
Sharon Steel	0.6	0.7
Alan Wood	0.9	0.6
Wickwire Spencer	0.2	0.2
Other companies	9.7	10.3

In the production of iron and steel products, the construction undertaken during the war has either held the large companies in about their pre-war position or has increased the relative importance of these companies. The first ten possess 83 per cent of the total capacity.

WHY COMPETITION DECLINED

It was inevitable that competition would be affected by the concentration of business in the hands of these few large companies. Even if concerted action were not definitely planned by the producers, it must develop in some form or other. Where thousands of relatively small competitors are present in an industry the plans of any one are not of great importance, but where only four companies are found, as in the manufacture of heavy steel rails, the prices of any one, say the United States Steel, cannot be ignored by the Bethlehem Steel Company, the Inland Steel, and the Colorado Fuel and Iron Corporation. And it is equally true that the price and output plans of the smallest, the Inland Steel, must be carefully watched by the largest producer. Similarly, for other steel products where a few large companies are found, no one producer can go his own way independently planning his price and production policies.

---

[16] *Ibid.*, Table 23, pp. 85–86.

The Weakness of Small Companies

A very definite and planned coöperation developed with the appearance of the United States Steel Corporation. The smaller companies, then weaker than they now are, quite reasonably felt that coöperation would be far wiser than a competitive struggle with the giant concern. They faced a completely integrated company with a core of very efficient plants, giving it an output that was greater than their combined output in all the major lines except pig iron, where it almost equalled them.[17] And the president of this company, Judge Elbert H. Gary, at various times between 1907 and 1911 pointed out to officers of the smaller concerns that price competition would result in the survival of the fittest and "exhorted" them to avoid price-cutting.[18] It must have occurred to his listeners that Judge Gary was thinking of the billion-dollar United States Steel when he spoke of the fittest to survive.[19]

In later years, when rivals had attained a firmer position, the power of the Corporation was still great enough to make competitors walk warily. In 1928, Charles M. Schwab, President of the Bethlehem Steel Corporation, warned the industry that it could expect that the United States Steel would not much longer ignore the price-cutting being done by a number of independents.[20] Under the indicated conditions some action by the large concern would not be surprising, but it might seem strange that the president of the second largest company would see fit to use the leading producer as a "bogey" to scare his colleagues.

The Weakness of the Giant Concern

Strangely enough, in its early years the United States Steel also had reason to fear the effects of competition. It started out badly over-capitalized as the result of the high prices paid for its properties and the sixty-two and a half million dollars paid to the House of Morgan for promotion services. The Bureau of Corporations showed that its capitalization of $1,402,846,817 was clearly excessive. The stock market valued the securities of all the component parts at something under eight hundred millions, and the Bureau valued the physical properties of the giant concern at six hundred and eighty-two millions. It was clear that the corporation was so badly over-capitalized that all of its $508,222,394 of common stock and probably half of its preferred issue of $510,205,743

---

[17] *Report of the Comissioner of Corporations on the Steel Industry*, Part I, p. 365.
[18] Eliot Jones, *op. cit.*, pp. 225–230.
[19] *Cf.* United States *v.* United States Steel Corporation *et al.*, 223 Fed. Rep. 55, 154.
[20] Arthur Robert Burns, *The Decline of Competition* (New York, McGraw-Hill Book Company, 1936), p. 80.

were not backed by any assets. While this condition was almost commonplace among the big combines of the period, it called for special treatment. If the corporation operated under competitive conditions, it would be selling its products at costs which would include a reasonable profit only on the investment actually *used* for production. Obviously there would be no dividends for the common stock and little for the preferred. Only through coöperation that raised prices above the competitive level could a satisfactory financial record be maintained. By 1910 the Steel Corporation had used half a billion dollars of earnings to add to its plants and acquire new properties without increasing its capital stock or liabilities,[21] so all the water was squeezed out of its preferred stock and the common stock came to have assets equal to about half its par value.[22]

The Nature of Demand and Supply

While the dangers of over-capitalization were markedly diminished, the industry found a number of enduring characteristics that made price competition peculiarly unattractive. In general it appears that the demand for steel is inelastic and unit costs are not markedly reduced as output is increased, even from plants that are operating far short of capacity. A study made for the United States Steel Corporation under the supervision of Professor T. O. Yntema, then a member of the University of Chicago faculty, showed that the demand for steel going into the railway, automobile, and container industries was such as not to encourage price-cutting.[23] Products for these industries made up about 40 per cent of steel sales; and at least in any short period of time, a price reduction, say of 10 per cent, would bring something less than a 5 per cent increase in the volume of sales.[24] The major factors fixing this elasticity are found in the extent to which price affects the substitution of steel for other metals in various uses, the elasticity of demand for various finished products from which the demand for steel is derived, and the importance of steel prices in the cost of the finished article.[25] Automobile demand, for instance, between 1932 and 1938 took about 20 per cent of the steel produced in the United States, and, according to the economists of the United States Steel Corporation, showed a marked inelasticity. In the first place, technical and not price considerations mainly determine the metals used. Secondly, studies by the General Motors Corporation indicate that the demand for automobiles is only moderately elastic: for

---

[21] *Report of the Commissioner of Corporations on the Steel Industry,* Part I, p. 54.

[22] In 1901 intangible assets were valued by the United States Steel Corporation at $749,207,806, and in 1938 at $1; *cf.* T. N. E. C., *Hearings,* Part 26, p. 13,746.

[23] T. N. E. C., *Hearings,* Part 26, pp. 13,587–13,600.

[24] *Ibid.,* p. 13,594.

[25] *Ibid.,* pp. 13,895–13,898.

every decrease in price of 1 per cent, sales would increase 1½ per cent.[26]
Finally, price reductions in steel would have to be very large to make
significant reductions in the price of cars. In 1938, for example, there was
only $77.42 worth of steel in a Chevrolet sedan that sold in New York
for $730.[27] Steel costs have approximately the same importance in other
cars; it appears, then, that a 10 per cent reduction in the price of steel
would reduce car prices only 1 per cent. If the General Motors Corporation is correct in estimating the elasticity of demand for its product, the
10 per cent cut in steel prices would increase car sales and the demand
for steel by 1½ per cent.[28] To the steel producer this would mean that
for every ton he had been selling at an average price of sixty dollars, he
would now sell 1.015 tons at fifty-four dollars per ton. He would realize
$54.80 instead of $60.00.

It is probably true that the demand for other steel products is either
inelastic or at best of very moderate elasticity; cost studies suggest that
in any short period of time unit costs of production do not decrease
sufficiently with increased volume to balance the loss from reductions in
unit prices. The cost studies of the Steel Corporation directed by Yntema
used the tonnage figures and the total operating costs for each year between 1927 and 1938, and adjusted them to make them comparable to
the 1938 figures. For example, since more costly products might be
shipped in one year than in another, the actual tonnages sold each year
were converted into a weighted tonnage figure so as to allow a ton of
more or less average value to count more or less than one ton. And the
total costs for each year were adjusted to the 1938 cost level by making
adjustments for changes in pension, tax, wage and interest costs and for
changes in efficiency. The result was to show the relation between costs
and the varying volumes of business under 1938 conditions.

From the study it appeared that variable costs per unit change very
little as the volume of output increases in a partially utilized plant.
Fixed costs per unit of the product, of course, are favorably affected.[29]
The combined effect was to reduce unit costs by moderate amounts as
output increased toward capacity.[30] For the weighted average ton that
was used the total unit cost was about $86 for operations at 30 per cent

---

[26] *Ibid.,* p. 13,982; cited from C. F. Roos and Victor von Szeliski, "Factors
Governing Changes in Domestic Automobile Demand," *The Dynamics of Automobile
Demand,* New York, General Motors Corporation, 1939.

[27] T. N. E. C., *Hearings,* Part 26, page 13,998.

[28] If a 10 per cent reduction in price resulted in the construction of heavier cars
the demand might be favorably affected by this factor. If this were the case car
sales might be slightly greater than the estimate: *cf. ibid.,* Exhibit No. 1416, *An
Analysis of Steel Prices, Volume and Costs—Controlling Limitations on Price Reductions,* pp. 14,032 ff.

[29] Fixed costs make up about 25 per cent of the total cost when plants are operating at 50 per cent of capacity; *cf. ibid.,* Table 28, p. 14,058.

[30] *Ibid.,* Chart 13, p. 14,057.

of capacity, $72 at 60 per cent of capacity, and $67 at 90 per cent of capacity.[31]

If the large companies in the industry face approximately the same cost experience, and it is reasonable to assume they do, the industry as a whole cannot in any short period of time gain from price competition. Even with an elasticity of demand far greater than is indicated to be the case, price reductions would not bring comparable reductions in unit costs. An individual company can profit from price competition only by taking volume away from other companies. If buyers are price-conscious and competitors do not meet its small price reductions, it would enjoy a highly elastic demand and would get the benefit of unit cost reductions as its sales increased. But other companies would be forced to protect themselves, and any advantage would be lost unless prices were cut further and some sellers were slow in following.

Fluctuating Demand and Fixed Costs

In any industry where these cost and demand conditions are found there is danger of cut-throat competition. It is enhanced in the steel industry by the instability of demand. With changes in general business conditions the demand for steel fluctuates markedly as it does for the products of most of the capital goods industries.[32] And when total demand falls off badly, a general wave of price-cutting may occur that brings benefit to no one. Price reductions offered by one seller are met by others, and while revenue is sacrificed, the volume of sales does not respond sufficiently to reduce costs materially. If demoralization spreads badly enough, companies may get down to prices that do little more than cover their variable costs.

The organization of the industry and its economic characteristics inevitably made coöperation far more attractive than competition. The latter could only promise extreme dangers, while the former offered safety and possibly the chance of some measure of monopoly profits.

---

[31] These costs are derived from *ibid.*, Table 28, p. 14,058.

[32] This fluctuation is inevitable with the roundabout method of production, and may be described in an abstract illustration as follows: the yearly output of railway service may be represented as 100 and the cost of the fixed capital to produce this service as 500. It may be assumed that 10 per cent of this capital must be replaced each year, which means that demand for 100 units of railway service creates a demand for 50 units of capital equipment. If the demand for railway service increases 10 per cent, and the plant formerly was fully utilized, the demand for capital equipment will be 50 units for replacement and 50 units to increase the capital equipment to 550. That is, a 10 per cent increase in demand for railway services creates a 100 per cent increase in demand for capital equipment. Unfortunately this accelerated demand also works in reverse, and a 10 per cent decline in the demand for rail services will cause a much magnified decline in the equipment purchased by the railway industry. See Gottfried von Haberler, *Prosperity and Depression* (Geneva, League of Nations, 1939), pp. 89–98.

The very conditions that were the source of danger made monopoly control feasible. The few firms in the field made coöperation easy to plan. An inelastic demand permitted prices to be raised above the competitive level without serious reduction in the quantity of steel demanded. And unit costs would not increase very much as some restriction of sales did occur under high prices. Finally, the companies need not fear that large profits would attract new competitors. Entry into the industry has been made very difficult by the large original investment required to set up an operating company. In 1939, Ernest T. Weir of the National Steel Corporation commented at hearings of the Temporary National Economic Committee that a fully-equipped sheet mill would cost in the neighborhood of twenty-five million dollars. Integrated production of raw materials, pig iron, steel, and finished products would call for an investment of at least one hundred millions.[33] At postwar price levels this figure approaches two hundred and fifty millions. Until 1942 the only entrant of importance to break into the field has been the Ford Motor Company, which produces no pig iron, but has between 1 and 3 per cent of the industry's capacity in the production of steel ingots, hot rolled products, hot rolled black sheets, bars, and cold rolled sheets.[34] The war brought the Kaiser Company into the field, operating, as shown in a previous table, about 0.8 per cent of the industry's ingot capacity.

THE FORM OF COÖPERATION

From 1901 until 1904 companies in various branches of the industry worked together through pooling arrangements to fix prices and divide sales. These formal agreements were abandoned when the subsidiaries of the Steel Corporation dropped their use. Prices continued, however, to be fixed coöperatively in meetings attended by representatives of the larger companies.[35] Fear that these trade conferences might come under the ban of the Sherman Act led in turn to their abandonment.

When the short but severe depression of 1907 brought on a spasm of price-cutting the United States Steel management found a new device in the so-called Gary Dinners. While entertaining the officers of the leading companies, Mr. Gary persuaded them that competition was dangerous, while coöperation would be comfortable and profitable. To make their general agreement effective, representatives of approximately 90 per cent of the industry set up committees to make sure that the individual companies followed the prices set by the United States Steel. There was no need to reach formal agreements on prices as long as the

[33] T. N. E. C., Hearings, Part 19, p. 10,672.
[34] Ibid., Part 18, Table 17, p. 10,409.
[35] 223 Fed. Rep. 55, 173.

companies followed the lead given them and gave notice if they were going to initiate changes.[36] Judge Woolley of the New Jersey District Court was unquestionably correct in his observation that the United States Steel did not force a group of competitors into an unwilling coöperation. It merely assumed the responsibilities of its size for its own profit in becoming a leader for a group of willing followers.

Other individuals and other companies have taken over the rôle of Mr. Gary and the Steel Corporation. In 1928 Mr. Schwab, President of the Bethlehem Corporation, was the exhorter urging members of the American Iron and Steel Institute to avoid price-cutting. And four years later, in the depths of the depression, R. P. Lamont as head of the Institute assumed the rôle.[37] But generally the Steel Corporation kept its place. Mr. Weir of the National Steel Corporation testified that his company set its price for tin plate at the price fixed in the contract between the American Can Company and the United States Steel.[38] And Mr. Grace, President of Bethlehem Steel in 1939, testified that his company generally waited until the Steel Corporation published its prices, and commented that the "pace is set . . . by the Steel Corporation."[39]

In 1947, the Federal Trade Commission filed a complaint against the American Iron and Steel Institute and its members charging them with acting collectively and collusively to compare and publish prices. The Commission charged further that the existing multiple basing-point system insures that "the same identity of delivered prices will result as though the industry were operating under a single basing-point system and as though all mills were under one ownership and control." This complaint suggests that the trade association of the industry may have been used also as a means of establishing a pleasant and competitively peaceful coöperation.

From the viewpoint of the industry it is not very important who the leading personality or company happens to be, as long as coöperation is maintained. And its continuance is now protected not only by the organization and economic characteristics of the industry, but by well-established habit. Until 1924 its maintenance was made easy by the use of Pittsburgh as a basing-point for pricing in all regions of the country. Regardless of where steel was manufactured, it was sold to all buyers at delivered prices which were arrived at by taking the base-price set by the United States Steel at Pittsburgh and adding the railroad freight from there to the point of delivery. A buyer in Chicago would take steel from a producer located within a few miles of him, but the price would be set as if the shipment came from Pittsburgh. Aside from the obvious

[36] 223 Fed. Rep. 55, 157–161.
[37] Burns, *op. cit.*, pp. 77–81.
[38] T. N. E. C., *Hearings*, Part 19, p. 10,681.
[39] *Ibid.*, p. 10,601.

advantages the scheme had in grinding out sizable monopoly profits, it made a simple price structure for the whole continent. All the price leader need do was to set the base price and let the rest follow. Action of the Federal Trade Commission ended this pleasant situation in 1924, and until 1948 the industry used a number of bases from which delivery of various products was made. The pricing system was not as simple as before, but was still much easier to control than it might have been.

In 1948, probably as a result of various trials and tribulations which were threatening it, the industry gave up the basing-point system. A first trouble for the industry was an anti-trust suit instituted in 1944 against the stainless steel industry. It was charged that the possession of patents had left the Chemical Foundation in a position where it set prices for the industry using Pittsburgh as the basing-point, although no stainless steel was produced there. Actual prices were computed and published for the industry by the Sharon Steel Company. Later, when Chemical Foundation's patent had expired and producers were licensed under patents of the Carpenter Steel Company, the suit claimed, this Company acted as pricing agent for the industry, setting the base price. With this help it should have been easy enough for any one company to figure the delivered price to quote on any particular job, but according to the Government the industry took no chances on large orders from the Government. When bids on such orders were asked for, the final, delivered price was figured by the pricing agent and circulated to all possible suppliers. Some Government departments may have been astonished to receive quotations identical to the penny on orders running into hundreds of thousands of dollars and covering several hundred different articles. Or maybe they were not astonished. Anyway this somewhat idyllic situation ended in 1945, when the United States District Court of New Jersey (Trenton), after no contest pleas were entered by the defendants, fined eighteen companies and six individuals ten thousand dollars each. The industry gave up its Pittsburgh basing-point system.

A second tribulation was the suit instituted against the Iron and Steel Institute in 1949. A third came from outside the industry in the form of a Supreme Court decision in a suit instituted against basing-point systems in the cement industry. In 1948 the decision ended an attack started five years before by the Federal Trade Commission with an apparently sweeping condemnation of any artificial basing-point system. Precisely what the cement case would mean to various industries other than the cement industry could only be deduced from the decision. However, in October 1948, United States Steel gave up a long protracted struggle. The Company agreed in the Third Circuit Court of Appeals in Philadelphia that it would no longer contest an order of the Federal Trade Commission issued in 1924 which ordered the Company to cease and desist from quoting prices on any other basing-point than that where the products are manufactured or from which they are shipped. Thereafter the whole industry started a substantial shift to the quotation of prices f.o.b. the producing or shipping point.

One other possible source of price variation among companies had received the attention of the industry. When any price is announced, it applies to only one size and quality of each type of steel product. A buyer wanting some variation from the standard specification is charged an "extra."

For example, a base-price is quoted on sheet steel of a certain gauge, width, and finish, and an extra is added or a deduction is made for a customer who wants a finer surface than the hot rolled finish which may be the basic specification, or who takes something lighter than the basic gauge. If these charges were fixed independently by the various companies a considerable amount of price variation might appear. Coöperation, however, has been the rule here as in other phases of the pricing problem. Mr. Fairless described for the Temporary National Economic Committee the manner in which the United States Steel determines its extras.[40] In meetings with representatives of other companies its officers consider its own costs and those of the other companies to arrive at charges that are satisfactory to all. And the industry as a whole coöperates further through the use of cost studies made by the Iron and Steel Institute. Mr. Fairless was careful to deny that the Institute sets the extra charges, but in fixing costs which apparently are satisfactory to the whole industry it certainly helps coöperation between the companies.[41] In view of the small number of firms in the industry it is possible that no other pricing policy is feasible. But, necessary or not, coöperation left little room for competitive independence.

Similar conditions lead to similar results in the production of iron ore. In 1937, three companies made up over 70 per cent of the total shipments.[42] The largest, The Oliver Iron Mining Company, is a subsidiary of the United States Steel, and was responsible for over 40 per cent of the total. A base-price for ore of a certain analysis is set for the whole year at the price arrived at in the first large sale of the season. This price, with fixed deviations from it for ore of other quality, is accepted by all the large producers. There might be little harm or possibly some actual benefit in the practice if this first sale took place under competitive conditions. There is agreement, however, among the officials of the big companies as to the price that should be set.[43] Henry Ford as a

---

[40] *Ibid.*, p. 10,560.

[41] Examination by the Department of Justice of the extra charges listed in the extra books of twenty-five steel companies for sixteen different products showed additions and deductions to be identical for every manufacturer of each product. *Cf. ibid.*, pp. 10,724 ff.

[42] T. N. E. C., *Hearings*, Part 18, Exhibit No. 1352, p. 10,426.

[43] *Ibid.*, pp. 10,360–10,372.

large buyer of ore was frequently able to bargain for a particularly good price, but correspondence between officials of the ore companies showed that the price to Ford was not going to be the base-price whether it was the first sale or not.[44] The setting of lake freight rates on iron ore is done under approximately the same sort of conditions and shows the same lack of competitive determination.[45]

THE CONSEQUENCES OF LEADERSHIP

Leadership and its attendant coöperation have brought direct effects in the form of prices that are discriminatory, unusually stable, and, as a result, abnormally high and sometimes abnormally low. Earnings reported by the industry have not been as great as might be expected. It appears, however, that the reports understate the actual earnings, and certain inefficiencies brought in by coöperation have reduced profits.

The Effect on the Level of Prices

The formation of the United States Steel Corporation and the consequent pooling and leadership did not bring any sudden and unreasonable increases in prices until war influences affected the market after 1914. The first ten years, in fact, brought general and material reductions.[46] Bessemer steel rails offered the only outstanding exception. They remained at twenty-eight dollars a ton while prices of other fabricated products declined on the average by 19 per cent.[47] But prices were still above competitive levels, for costs were declining even more markedly. The price level maintained through the efforts of Judge Gary allowed the Steel Corporation to make average net earnings of 12 per cent on its actual investment.[48] In four of the first seven years after 1900, business conditions were good enough to let it earn over 14 per cent. Preferred dividends of seven dollars and common stock dividends ranging between $1.50 and $5.50 were paid in every year except one. When it is remembered that all the common stock and possibly half the preferred had no assets behind it, it is apparent that these dividend rates were very good.

Profits indicate that prices were particularly high in certain lines. The Bureau of Corporations estimated that ore prices were high enough to allow the Steel Corporation 10 per cent on its investment in ore lands

---

[44] *Ibid.*, pp. 10,370–10,371.

[45] *Ibid.*, pp. 10,372–10,381; p. 10,425.

[46] United States *v.* United States Steel Corporation, *et al.*, 223 Fed. Rep. 81 (1918); Defendants' Exhibit, Vol. II, p. 203.

[47] On a tonnage basis steel bars declined from $33 to $25; wire nails from $51 to $36; steel beams from $36 to $27; steel billets from $27 to $24. *Cf. ibid.*, Government Exhibit, Vol. XIV, pp. 2912–2922.

[48] *Report of the Commissioner of Corporations on the Steel Industry*, Part I, p. 54.

which included not only the properties actually operated but also vast idle reserves.[49] Two of the Company's railroads also showed remarkable profit records. The Duluth and Iron Range as well as the Duluth, Missabe, and Northern Railway were very efficiently run, but the spectacular earnings of the two roads came in part from exorbitant rates.[50] Since some other steel producers used this service, the high rates not only gave the Steel Corporation good profits, but gave it also a competitive advantage over these companies. The prices of steel rails were high enough to yield returns between 11 and 17 per cent.[51]

Prices for steel started upward in 1915, rising much more rapidly than the price index for all commodities.[52] Average earnings for the whole industry were 28 per cent on the capital investment in 1917 and approximately 20 per cent in 1916 and 1918.[53] Despite general reductions after the war, a number of prices stayed at monopoly levels until 1924. In September of that year the Steel Corporation agreed to obey the order of the Federal Trade Commission to abandon the use of Pittsburgh as the sole base for pricing. The effect showed how far prices had been from competitive levels. As might be expected, the prices for markets east and north of Pittsburgh were not affected, but to the west things were different. Chicago was established as a basing-point, with a differential of two dollars above the Pittsburgh base. Since the freight rate from Pittsburgh to Chicago of $6.80 had formerly been added to the Pittsburgh prices for deliveries in Chicago, the rearrangement lowered the base-price for the middle west by $4.80. What this meant in terms of finished products is shown by Frank Fetter in *The Masquerade of Monopoly*. Wire and wire nail prices per ton dropped overnight from twenty-two dollars to twenty at Spokane; from approximately eighteen to ten at Fargo; from twelve to two at Duluth, and from seven to one at Chicago.[54] As earnings were between 5 and 9 per cent on invested capital in the five years following these reductions, it is quite apparent that prices for the Middle and Far West had been exorbitant.

Until 1938 the industry used a very limited multiple basing-point system. For most products Birmingham, Chicago, and Bethlehem served

[49] *Ibid.*, Part II, p. xvii.
[50] *Ibid.*, Part I, p. 60.
[51] *Ibid.*, Part II, pp. 130–131.
[52] T. N. E. C., *Hearings*, Part 19, Exhibit 1379, p. 10,709.
[53] These percentages are figured before deduction of taxes, interest, and dividends. The Iron and Steel Institute reported earnings for 1916, 1917 and 1918 as 16.5%, 13.9%, and 9.0%. These percentages, however, are figured before deduction of interest and dividends, but after deduction of income and excess profit taxes, which were particularly heavy in the last two years. Since the interest here is in the level of prices and not in the realized profits of the industry, the larger figures are more significant.
[54] Frank Albert Fetter, *The Masquerade of Monopoly* (New York, Harcourt, Brace and Co., 1931), p. 159.

as additional bases from which delivered prices were figured. Their base-prices were usually two dollars a ton above the Pittsburgh level.[55] Two arbitrary features were maintained that could not have survived under competitive pricing. First, higher marketing costs might possibly have justified the higher base-price set for Birmingham, but neither production nor marketing costs could be used to justify the Chicago differential above Pittsburgh. Second, certain areas such as Buffalo and Detroit paid prices for certain products that could not be supported on any ground.[56]

The breakdown of its leadership in 1938 under the strain of business depression forced the United States Steel Corporation to reduce prices at Pittsburgh and to remove the differential at Chicago and Birmingham. Other companies then brought their price-cutting out into the open, and for many products established price bases at their own points of production.

It may seem strange that a non-competitive industry would deliberately hold prices below the level that would be established under competitive conditions, but this practice is not unknown in such industries. There is a good chance that it will occur where an unusual stability of prices is maintained. Apparently the stable price is satisfactory for the long run; and possibly price uniformity would be more difficult to maintain between companies if prices were moving up and down frequently. One of the most striking instances of a controlled and apparently deliberate underpricing occurred in steel after World War II. Demand for steel far outreached the capacity of the industry, yet prices did not react; in fact, United States Steel instituted price decreases in 1948. A very clear measure of the underpricing is apparent in the official prices and the black-market prices. The latter sort of price existed because steel was being allotted or rationed to buyers. And such buyers, if they could forego using the steel themselves, could obtain black-market prices. At one time these prices reached $295 per ton—for steel sold by the steel companies for $75. This is an extreme illustration, but lesser differentials were common. Further evidence of this strange phenomenon is found in a dual price system that developed in 1948. All the respectable oldtimers kept their decorous price stability, but the Kaiser Company went independent and raised prices as much as thirty dollars a ton over the mill quotations of other companies.

It is too early to see the detailed effects on prices which will result from the apparently complete abandonment of basing-points developing in the latter part of 1948. The changes will vary with the degree of

---

[55] From 1933 to 1935, under the National Recovery Administration code for the steel industry, about one-third of the leading steel products had only three basing-points; another third had from four to seven; and the remaining third had between eight and twenty-one. Cf. T. N. E. C., *Hearings*, Part 18, Table 20, p. 10,413.

[56] *Ibid.*, p. 10,412; also Fetter, *op. cit.*, p. 160.

artificiality previously maintained, and this varied greatly for different products and different areas. Needless to say various customers will be affected differently, and a considerable change may be expected in the customers buying from particular mills. In the past for many products it did not matter whether a buyer located in Illinois bought steel from Pennsylvania or Illinois. He paid the same delivered price in any event. But under f.o.b. mill pricing, the Pittsburgh mill would be forced to lower its mill price to all customers, near-by and distant, if that price plus the freight paid by the Illinois buyer is to be no higher than the cost of the same shipment from the Chicago mill.

In September 1948 the price of sheet was eighty-four dollars a ton at the Great Lakes Steel Company located in the environs of Detroit. At Pittsburgh and Chicago the mill price was eighty dollars; and freight to Detroit was slightly over nine dollars. In the past, steel companies at Pittsburgh and Chicago would have sold the delivered article in Detroit at eighty-four dollars, that is, they would have absorbed roughly five dollars of the freight costs. Now if they are going to meet the Detroit price, they must reduce the price at their mills to all buyers, near or far. If they do not reduce, and in many cases they cannot do so and cover costs, the buyer who formerly depended on them must switch to the Great Lakes Steel or pay higher prices than are paid by some of his competitors. It is easy to see why many buyers of products sold under basing-point systems are alarmed at the prospect of the disappearance of the pricing agreement.

The Effect of Leadership on Earnings

Despite their coöperation, the steel companies have not reported abnormally large earnings since 1920. Between 1923 and 1929, when industry was undisturbed by major depressions and the automobile and construction industries were expanding greatly, the American Iron and Steel Institute reported annual earnings for the whole industry to be between 5.0 and 9.4 per cent. And for the next nine years the average was under 2.5 per cent. In the early years after World War II profits were larger, averaging around 11 to 12 per cent; however, in the postwar inflation period, these profit rates were among the lowest averages for various large industry groups.[57]

General business conditions mainly account for the change after 1929, while several reasons explain the apparently moderate returns of the

---

[57] Net income before interest and dividends as a per cent of the capital stock, bonded debt, and surplus; cf. T. N. E. C., *Hearings*. Part 18, Table 26, p. 10,423; for an analysis of recent pricing policies and their effects on profits and investment in the industry, see Marvin Barloon, "The Question of Steel Capacity," *Harvard Business Review*, March 1949, pp. 209 ff.

earlier period. First, the earnings are probably greater than they appear.[58] In its study of the profits of the steel industry between 1915 and 1918, the Federal Trade Commission insisted that the investment figure for the industry was inflated and, as a result, earnings were made to appear smaller than they really were. And the Department of Justice in reporting to the Temporary National Economic Committee expressed the belief that the percentages reported for the twenties were no more reliable. It is certainly true that until 1938 the assets of the Steel Corporation were still inflated by at least two hundred and sixty million dollars.[59]

A second reason for moderate earnings lies in the fact that leadership has been responsible for some increases in the cost of producing steel. High prices have protected relatively inefficient plants and have allowed companies to sell outside their natural market areas. A great deal of cross-shipping has been common in the industry. A mill in Chicago would ship a large order into the East while plants located at Bethlehem would be shipping similar products into the Middle West.[60] In order to compete in distant markets each company must sell at delivered prices that do not include the full freight charge, and its costs are increased by this freight absorption.[61] In February, 1939, the United States Steel reported that it was adding an average of $1.99 to every ton sold to cover the freight absorptions on products it sold outside its natural market areas.[62] And it appears that the National Steel Company in figuring the cost of steel produced in Detroit for sale in Detroit added an amount to cover freight absorbed in other markets.[63]

Costs have also been adversely affected by unused capacity which is either supported or caused by high prices. In carrying integration back to the mining stage several companies, particularly the United States Steel, have accumulated very large reserves. In a number of instances it appears that mining properties have been acquired merely to prevent them from falling into the hands of other companies. In such circumstances their carrying costs are not a reasonable charge against present steel production, but nevertheless must be included in

---

[58] After deducting good-will, appreciation, and other intangibles from total investment, the Federal Trade Commission reported earnings before Federal taxes for the eleven large steel companies as ranging btween 6.45 and 11.53 in the years 1923 to 1929. Cf. T. N. E. C., *Hearings*, Part 31, *Investments, Profits, and Rates of Return for Selected Industries* (1941), Part III.

[59] In 1938 the United States Steel Corporation reduced its intangibles from two hundred and sixty millions to one dollar.

[60] Cf. Fetter, *op. cit.*, pp. 310–334.

[61] From the viewpoint of the one company this might appear to be a price reduction, but from the point of view of the consumer who pays the full price whether he buys from a nearby or distant producer, it is certainly not price-cutting.

[62] T. N. E. C., *Hearings*, Part 26, p. 13,839.

[63] Cf. testimony of Ernest T. Weir, Chairman of National Steel Corporation, T. N. E. C., *Hearings*, Part 19, p. 10,656.

current costs of production. And at times high and stable prices have forced a restriction of sales that has pushed plant costs up as production has fallen far short of capacity.[64] The level of prices through the twenties was such as to keep ingot production at about 70 per cent of capacity. It is reasonable to assume that high prices have either attracted excessive capital into the industry or have prevented the full use of a merely adequate capacity.[65] And finally, it will be noted that price stability has kept prices at times at levels lower than supply and demand conditions justified, and, of course, profits have suffered.

Discrimination as an Effect of Leadership

Before the modification of Pittsburgh Plus in 1924 the injury to Southern and Western buyers was very obvious. And when high steel prices forced manufacturers of other products to locate plants disadvantageously, or to hold their size below optimum, their costs would be increased by an amount greater than the added cost for steel. The Federal Trade Commission estimated that farm machinery prices were increased by an amount double the actual discrimination levied against Chicago manufacturers.[66]

The general geographical discrimination also led to personal discrimination of considerable importance. Western and Southern producers of finished steel products who were subsidiaries of the big steel companies had a tremendous advantage over their local competitors. The American Bridge Company with plants in Chicago could, as a subsidiary of the United States Steel Corporation, underbid a competing structural steel company, and still make large profits on its contracts. It would get its steel from another subsidiary located in Chicago, the Illinois Steel Company, and pay Chicago costs. An independent would pay the Pittsburgh price plus an artificial freight charge of $7.60 a ton. It is little wonder that independent finishing companies were small and of little importance in the South and Middle West.[67]

From 1924 to 1938 the differential maintained on most products at Chicago and Birmingham probably constituted discrimination. Certainly production and marketing costs in the Middle West did not justify the higher prices.[68] In the South the prices on at least some products were higher than costs warranted. It is probably true, however, that markets

---

[64] T. N. E. C., *Hearings*, Part 27, pp. 14, 588–14,590.

[65] For a fuller discussion of this topic see Chap. 29.

[66] F. T. C., *Annual Report*, 1924, p. 39.

[67] Artifically high prices for ore worked a similar injury on small steel companies purchasing ore in the open market.

[68] For structural shapes, plates, and merchant bars, Pittsburgh mill costs in 1921 were approximately $51 a gross ton, while Chicago costs for the three products were respectively $42.59, 47.56, 48.27; Birmingham costs were $55.55, 53.77, and 49.09. *Cf.*, T. N. E. C., *Hearings*, Part 27, pp. 14, 544–14,545.

were thin and selling expenses were high, particularly on certain items. When a number of new basing-points were established in 1938, the extent of past discrimination became apparent in the difference in the amount of price reductions at various points. Hot rolled sheets were reduced about 10 per cent at Pittsburgh, 20 per cent at Sparrows Point near Baltimore, and 19 per cent at Buffalo. Pig iron dropped 12 per cent at Pittsburgh, 17 at Buffalo, and 21 at Birmingham. With only two or three exceptions, all the major products of the industry showed a similarly unequal readjustment.

The Effect of Price Stability

Steel prices for the past forty years have shown a far greater stability than would be normal for a competitive industry. Demand has fluctuated sharply, but in many periods prices have not reacted. Between 1929 and 1932 the marked change in business conditions reduced the price index for semi-manufactured goods from 94 to 58, but a composite index of finished steel prices fell only twelve points.[69] In the years between the depression and the rearmament program unstable business conditions affected the price of semi-manufactured goods far more than steel prices. In general the industry has been both able and willing to control prices so that they have not moved upward as much as other comparable prices in good years and have not fallen as far in slack years.

Stability has been much more apparent in the prices of some of the products of the industry than in others. Steel rails remained at twenty-eight dollars a ton from 1901 to 1916. Then after a few years of irregularity they settled down in 1922 to a price of forty-three dollars, which was maintained until October, 1932. When it is remembered that the railways were suffering not only from very severe depression conditions but from highway competition, the maintenance of this price seems remarkable. It was only after considerable pressure from the government in 1932 that rail prices dropped to $37.75 a ton. Iron ore prices have shown a similar stability. From 1925 to 1928 the Lake Erie base price was set at $4.25 per ton, and from then until 1936 at $4.50. It was then maintained for some years at $4.95.[70] Freight rates from the head of Lake Superior have been even more stable.[71] Since ore costs contribute about ten dollars to the ton costs of finished products, their rigidity adds materially to the stability of finished prices.

Aside from the dangerous impact of stable prices on the cyclical fluctuation of business,[72] price rigidity tends generally to throw the influence

---

[69] *Ibid.*, Part 19, Exhibit No. 1383, p. 10,711.
[70] *Ibid.*, Part 18, Exhibit No. 1367, p. 10,439; p. 10,311.
[71] *Ibid.*, Exhibit No. 1368, p. 10,440.
[72] *Cf.* Chap. 29.

of changing demand conditions wholly on the volume of production. Even where demand is inelastic, competitive pricing allows both prices and output to absorb the shock of demand changes, so that the impact on either one is smaller than when one or the other is rigidly fixed. Co-operation on pricing, however, is more easily maintained when prices are stable, and the Steel Corporation has obviously discouraged both price increases when demand is strengthening and price decreases in periods of declining demand.[73]

Inadequate iron and steel capacities after World War II have pre-vented manufacturers of a number of products, such as automobiles, refrigerating equipment, building supplies, and so forth, from expanding their production to meet demand. As a result the steel industry has been exposed to highly vocal complaints from spokesmen for both big and little industry, from labor, and from a variety of government officials. The black market, previously mentioned, and the scramble for scarce steel provided irritations that the steel industry may live to regret. Strangely enough the failure to raise steel prices may have been a damaging fault. The index of steel prices rose 71 per cent from 1939 to 1948 as against a rise of 118 per cent in all commodities in the Bureau of Labor Statistics index. When prices of steel were held down during the shortage of supply, prices failed in one of their functions, that is, they failed to weed out the marginal demands and hence leave scarce supplies to highly necessitous buying. They may also have failed in another respect. Higher steel prices and the resultant profits might have led to expanded capacity in the industry. This can only be stated as a possibility, for, to a considerable extent, it would be forecasts of expected future profits and not current profits that would determine expansion plans. The industry is so completely integrated that no important expansion could be made in any one stage without requiring a related expansion all the way down the line, and large investments would be required.

Steel shortages have provided the drive behind a move to force added capacity on the industry whether or not it wants the added capac-ity. C. Girard Davidson, Assistant Secretary of the Interior, has proposed that loans be made by the Reconstruction Finance Corporation to the steel industry for plant expansion; and that, if such loans are not ac-cepted, the Government should undertake construction itself. This pro-posal was undoubtedly put up as a trial balloon. It appears that the balloon flew well, for President Truman recommended legislation to the Eighty-First Congress to authorize a study of the Davidson proposal. Meanwhile the industry added about five million tons to its ingot capacity in 1948 and 1949 and claimed that its capacity of 94 million tons was all that was economically justified. Opponents continued to claim that

---

[73] Cf. Burns, op. cit., pp. 211–216.

anywhere from ten to twenty-seven million tons of added capacity was required. It is virtually impossible to determine the relative merits of the conflicting claims, but the matter of import is the result that may come. An industry which has been able to maintain a high level of coöperation has apparently given up one of its most useful devices, the basing-point system, and is now threatened with the appearance of an intruder in the form of a Government company. Whether the threat becomes real will depend on a variety of political and economic factors.

24

The Meat Industry

Industries near to the consumer have not escaped their share of concentration and its effects. Large firms or associations of sellers play an important part in the processing or distribution of poultry, cheese products, canned salmon, flour, and milk. Other staples such as canned fruits, sugar, baking products, and vegetables are sold under similar conditions.[1] In the sale of butter, cheese, condensed milk, flour, and canned fruits, the sales of the three largest processors represent between 20 and 60 per cent of the total market.[2] Canned salmon is packed by relatively small companies, but it is marketed through a few brokers, and its prices are considerably affected by the Alaska Packers Association.[3] In the packing of fruits and vegetables the present importance of large distributors such as Libby, McNeill and Libby is relatively new, and the future seems to promise an ever larger place for the big company.

Both national and local markets for these and other food products have seen a small number of sellers introduce coöperation that has restrained competition. The presence of large firms seems to have allowed the flour millers to restrict production and exchange price information.[4] In June, 1941, two Federal grand juries returned indictments charging price-fixing and monopoly in the canning of fruits, vegetables, and sardines, and in the processing and marketing of dried fruits, rice, and dried milk. A typical indictment was one charging the Dried Fruit Association of California, eighteen packing companies belonging to the association, and thirty-one officers and directors with a conspiracy to cut prices paid

---

[1] Memorandum for the Assistant Attorney-General, Anti-trust Division, June 13, 1940; quoted in Thurman W. Arnold, *The Bottlenecks of Business* (New York, Reynal and Hitchcock, 1940), pp. 225–239.

[2] T. N. E. C., *Monograph No. 35, Large-Scale Organization in the Food Industries* (1940), p. 90.

[3] *Report of the Federal Trade Commission on Canned Foods* (1918), pp. 12, 66.

[4] *Preliminary Report of the Federal Trade Commission, Competitive Conditions in Flour Milling* (1926), Chap. 3.

THE MEAT INDUSTRY

to farmers for fruit and to raise prices to the consumer.[5] As large firms are coming to take a place of ever-increasing importance in food lines, competition unquestionably is being adversely affected. Coöperation among a few firms has not yet appeared in some industries, although conditions are present to make it possible. And in other fields agreements on price and output policies have been limited and temporary. It is possible, however, that the future of competitive individualism in these industries can be seen in the history of the meat-packing industry. Here a few large firms have towered over the rest of the field for almost fifty years, and the habit of coöperation seems to be firmly fixed.

ORGANIZATION OF THE MEAT-PACKING INDUSTRY

Until late in the nineteenth century the slaughter of cattle, sheep, and hogs and the marketing of dressed meats were done by many small operators scattered through the many market areas. Gustavus Swift, P. D. Armour, and Nelson Morris, founders of three of the four giant packing companies of the present, started before the Civil War as very small pork-packers and cattle dealers. Their businesses prospered and they went on to the slaughter of beef cattle in time to benefit from the technical revolution fostered by artificial refrigeration. During the seventies, various experiments had been made with carrying ice and dressed meats in railway box-cars, and by 1880 the modern refrigerator-car was ready for development. With its appearance the costly movement of cattle from the prairies to the big eastern markets was no longer necessary. Where formerly a thousand-pound steer would be shipped to the East to yield about six hundred pounds of meat, now only the valuable meat products needed to be moved. Geographical concentration of the industry was inevitable, and it settled in the Middle West at such centres as St. Louis and Chicago, where transport facilities offered an easy assembly of animals and easy distribution of meat products. And the concentration of a large volume of business in a few producing centres brought about the growth of large-scale plants using machinery, with an advanced division of labor, and made possible the utilization of valuable by-products.

In the midst of the shifting opportunities offered by these changes, a few companies established a clear leadership over their rivals. Between 1897 and 1907 the five largest companies almost trebled their facilities.[6] In 1919, when the total value of meat and meat products reached an all-time high of four billion dollars, they were slaughtering

---

[5] Reported in *The New York Times*, June 4, 1941.
[6] Swift and Company; Armour and Company; Morris and Company; Cudahy Packing Company; and Wilson and Company.

about 70 per cent of the total animals handled by the industry.[7] They were also important factors in the markets for fertilizers, hides, cottonseed oil, butter, eggs, and cheese. In addition, they used their widespread marketing organization to gain a place of outstanding importance in the sale of canned fruits, vegetables, and staple groceries. In 1917, Armour and Company, for example, undertook the marketing of rice, and quickly assumed the leading place. The Federal Trade Commission unkindly suggested that this development might not be unrelated to the 65 per cent increase in the wholesale price of rice that occurred at the same time.[8]

In 1923 Armour and Company increased its size materially by acquiring the properties of Morris and Company, one of the Big Five. The large companies, however, were temporarily endangered by the effects of another technical revolution. The rapid growth of motor trucking tended to decentralize the industry and increase the importance of local slaughtering. Small plants located in the hog and cattle-raising areas found a cheap means of transportation for their individually small outputs and avoided both the more costly shipment of livestock and the yardage and marketing costs of Chicago and other livestock centers. The following table suggests the influence of this development on the big packers.

Table 19

PROPORTION OF MEAT ANIMALS SLAUGHTERED BY THE FIVE LEADING PACKERS, 1908–1935[9]

Year	Cattle	Calves	Sheep and Lambs (including goats)	Hogs	All Animals
1908	74.9%	63.0%	71.6%	53.2%	59.7%
1916	82.2	76.6	86.4	61.2	70.5
1919	78.5	77.3	86.8	61.8	69.3
1924	73.2	72.9	83.2	52.7	60.6
1929	69.5	70.9	85.8	47.9	58.7
1935	67.1	71.0	85.3	51.9	66.2

By 1929, after steadily losing ground, the Big Five had dropped to the point where they were handling only 58 per cent of the total slaughter. Finding themselves unable to stop the decentralization, the large companies went along with it to regain much of the position they had lost. By

---

[7] *Report of the Federal Trade Commission on the Meat-Packing Industry* (1919). Part I, p. 33; cited hereafter as F. T. C., *Meat-Packing Report.*

[8] *Ibid.*, Part I, p. 36.

[9] T. N. E. C., *Monograph* No. 35, Table 5, p. 16.

1935 they had bought or built plants in the stock-raising regions, so as to lift their percentage to over 66.

The relatively important places held by Swift and Armour since the latter acquired Morris and Company show a marked disparity of size among the Big Four. The sales of these companies appearing in the following table show Swift and Armour to be of comparable size, while the Wilson and the Cudahy Packing Companies are markedly smaller.

Table 20[10]

SALES OF MEAT-PACKERS

Year	Total Value of Meat and Meat Products[a]	Sales of[a]			
		Swift and Co.	Wilson and Co.	Cudahy Packing Company	Armour and Co.
1919	$4,246,291[b]	$1,200,000		305,997	900,000
1925	3,050,286	875,000		224,491	900,000
1929	3,434,654	1,000,000	310,000	267,960	900,000
1933	1,490,085	500,000	141,093	124,278	452,000
1937	2,787,358	885,837	282,746	222,222	788,280
1942	7,946,000	1,409,000	517,000	367,000	1,300,000

a 000 omitted.

b Sales of the meat-packers include other products than meat, and are not strictly comparable with figures for the total value of meat and meat products.

It appears that technical changes and depression have not seriously affected the position of the large concerns. It is also apparent that a disproportionate concentration of business among these firms has become well-fixed. With the sales of Swift and Armour each exceeding a billion dollars in 1942, we may have reason to consider the industry today in terms of the Big Two.

THE CHARACTER OF COMPETITION

Before 1880 firms were small, entry into the industry was easy, and competition could work satisfactorily. In small local markets some monopoly unquestionably existed, but its powers were definitely limited, and the larger consuming areas had the protection of a number of competing sellers. The last sixty years, however, have seen competition seriously altered by the presence of the large producer. The alteration has appeared in two forms: first, an exchange of coöperation for inde-

[10] *Ibid.*, Table 6, p. 17; Report of the Smaller War Plants Corporation, *Economic Concentration and World War II*, p. 216.

pendence in the relations of the large companies; and second, the use of unfair competition against small rivals.

Coöperation of the Large Packers

From the very beginning of the modern meat-packing industry the various large companies showed no intention of maintaining a competitive independence. With one minor break, pooling agreements existed between 1885 and 1902. After agreeing for a few years on the quantities of meat to be shipped into certain markets, the large companies divided the country into territories, and in weekly meetings fixed quotas for each company.[11] Fines of forty cents per hundred pounds, collected from those who exceeded their allotted sales, were turned over to those who had not sold their quota. A uniform method of figuring costs led to price uniformity and eliminated any danger of price competition. These convenient arrangements lasted until attacks in newspapers and in Congressional speeches forced a slow-moving Department of Justice to take action. The Department was able to obtain an injunction restraining the large packers from continuing their illegal agreements, but failed in its criminal prosecution of those individuals responsible for the pooling arrangements.[12]

The injunction merely had the effect of driving the large companies into a more thorough-going coöperation. Armour and Company bought the property of one of the large members of the old pool and, in less than a fortnight after the injunction was issued, joined with Swift and Morris to merge all their properties. The three companies borrowed eight million dollars to acquire other plants, and induced the Cudahy interests to join the move. They abandoned the project only when they were unable to borrow sixty million dollars. A less ambitious scheme was then undertaken. All the properties that had been acquired were thrown together into the hands of a newly-formed holding corporation, the National Packing Company. Its stock was held in the names of a number of individuals, although the money used to acquire the properties had come from the Swift, Armour, and Morris companies. And strangely enough, the men who were now meeting weekly as directors were the same who had met before in weekly meetings to implement the old pooling arrangement.

Since two of the five large companies were not joint owners of the National Packing Company, some device had to be found, and inevitably was found, to bring all five into an arrangement so as to annul completely the injunction of the court. A new means with the old result was found in the so-called livestock pool. By agreement each of the companies pur-

---

[11] F. T. C., *Meat-Packing Report*, Part II, pp. 12–19.
[12] *Cf.* United States *v.* Swift and Co., 196 U. S. 375 (1902).

chased a set percentage of the stock bought at the principal markets and at country points.[13] Local buyers took detailed orders from the head buyers in Chicago, and were frequently prevented from buying to meet the needs of local plants when their purchases would upset the allocation arranged by their head offices. It was perfectly apparent that nothing was allowed to interfere with that agreement. And in the large central markets the buyers of the Big Five would buy at the same hours and offer identical prices. Each company kept a complete record of the amounts bought by the others, and daily compilations showed exactly how the sharing scheme was working.[14]

In 1911 the National Packing Company did not survive attacks of the Department of Justice, but this merely allowed the packers to prove that their coöperation did not depend on any particular organization.[15] Until at least 1920 they continued to divide the livestock market and, according to the Federal Trade Commission, exchanged cost and price information so as to avoid any price competition. And although there is now no evidence of regular meetings between representatives of the big companies, it seems that the habit of coöperation may continue. From 1919 to 1937 the evidence shows the Swift, Armour, Morris and Cudahy companies keeping their sales in a remarkably steady relation. There may be no written agreements, but at least a habitual division of livestock purchases exists and leads to a stable division of the market for meat products. From year to year tremendous changes occur in the total sale of meat, but each company holds its relative place.[16] The division of the market seems very slightly less stable than in the period of proved coöperation.[17]

In the past the packers argued that the maintenance of a fixed place

---

[13] Since between 75 and 85 per cent of cattle and calves are bought in a few public stockyards, the division of purchases was easy to arrange. In the case of hogs over 50 per cent of buying was done at country points; cf. T. N. E. C., *Monograph* No. 35, p. 19.

[14] F. T. C., *Meat-Packing Report*, Part II, pp. 46–99.

[15] In 1910 the Department of Justice started a civil suit for violation of the Sherman Act looking toward dissolution of the National Packing Company. This suit was dropped in favor of a criminal action against Louis F. Swift and ten other packers. In spite of weighty evidence against them, the packers won a favorable decision from the jury and then, in order to avoid resumption of the civil suit, divided the properties of the National Packing Company among Swift, Armour, and Morris; cf. U. S. v. National Packing Company et al., Circuit Court, Northern District of Illinois, December 27, 1910; and U. S. v. Louis F. Swift et al., No. 4509, District Court, Northern District of Illinois, March 26, 1912.

[16] In 1927, when the total sales of Swift, Wilson, Cudahy, and Armour were $2,-343,325,000, Swift sold 39.4% of the total and Armour 38.4%. In 1933, when the total had dropped to $1,217,371,000, Swift sold 41% and Armour 37%. The Wilson and Cudahy companies divide the remainder, with the sales of the former habitually 14 or 15% above those of the latter. Cf. T. N. E. C., *Monograph* No. 35, Table 6, p. 7.

[17] F. T. C., *Meat-Packing Report*, Part II, pp. 56–57.

by each company merely showed the existence of a very active competition and not coöperation. The rivalry was so severe that no one company could make any effort to increase its business without being matched by the others.[18] Unfortunately for the Big Five, this explanation failed to be completely convincing after the Federal Trade Commission unearthed certain correspondence between their officers. Letters discussed in detail both the operation of the market-sharing scheme and the adjustment of prices to the satisfaction of all concerned except the consumer. One rather revealing letter was written in 1916 by Phillip D. Armour to J. Ogden Armour about the Denver market. It read in part as follows: "Swift's plant, from what I hear and from the little I saw of it, is far ahead of ours both as to size and condition. Of course, as you know, everything here is done on a 50-50 basis, and with the facilities we have it is almost impossible to keep this ratio."[19]

It is possible that not mere habit but a planned coöperation may be the explanation of the present stability. On July 3, 1941, a Federal grand jury returned an indictment charging three meat-packing companies, seven officials, and two trade associations with a conspiracy to fix prices for hogs slaughtered in Chicago.[20] It was claimed that for the past three years the Wilson, Armour, and Swift companies had agreed on the prices they would offer for hogs and the hours at which their buyers would appear in the market. Two weeks earlier the same three companies had been named in an indictment charging a similar agreement in the purchase of sheep. If this measure of coöperation exists it is reasonable to assume that something other than a bitter and unyielding competition explains the present stability.

Relations With Independents

In recent years independent packers have managed to sell in the neighborhood of 30 per cent of the meat processed by all packing companies. They have had their good and bad periods, but, being located in both the urban areas and the cattle-raising regions, have generally been an important factor in the market. They have by no means been ignored by their giant competitors. When technical changes were just beginning to push a few companies to the forefront, they were hurt by exorbitant freight rates on cattle and the payment of rebates to their larger com-

---

[18] *Cf.* Burns, *op. cit.*, pp. 159–163.

[19] F. T. C., *Meat-Packing Report*, Part I, p. 53.

[20] These indictments were dismissed on February 15, 1949, at the request of the Government, on the ground that activities charged as illegal were included in and made a part of the civil suit for dissolution against the four major packers filed September 15, 1948. Commerce Clearing House, Inc., *Trade Regulation Service* (ninth edition), p. 61,065.

petitors by the Pennsylvania, New York Central, and Erie Railroads.[21] Railroad regulation put an end to this injury, but various forms of unfair competition continued to harass them.

In localities where they were making a nuisance of themselves by selling at competitive prices, they found the large packers cutting prices as low as necessary to bring them into line. Then prices would be raised.[22] Meat distributors who thought they could buy dressed meat from any packer they favored found they were mistaken. In an instance which was by no means an isolated one, Frank Aicher, a packer and distributor in Denver, was warned by an agent of Armour and Company to stop buying dressed meat from an independent. He chose not to obey, but soon found he could not stand the drastic price-cutting invoked by Armour. When called on again by an Armour representative, he decided to buy meat from Armour. The price-cuts were immediately removed, and an independent packer had lost another customer.[23] Independent rendering companies buying bones and waste meat products to produce edible and non-edible fats found themselves faced with an exactly opposite sort of cut-throat price competition. In New York, Chicago, Philadelphia, and other centres, the rendering business was dominated by subsidiaries of the large packers, and prices of the raw material were raised to destructive levels until smaller companies were eliminated.[24]

In markets where antipathy to the "meat trust" was strong, the large packers exposed independents to the competition of companies which they had secretly acquired, or which they controlled through stock ostensibly owned by some employee or attorney.[25] Former owners and former names were retained as a false front. In one case, Armour and Company bought a concern in Dallas, paid its former owner $25,000 a year to do nothing except act as its nominal head, and operated the company as an independent for nine years before even the other large companies knew of the change of control.[26] Dummy independents also gave the large companies the ability to use them for price-cutting forays in a market without involving their whole volume of business.

The threat of independents to introduce competition into meat-packing frequently forced the big companies to acquire the plants of troublemakers. The purchase was often made easier by a preliminary siege of price-cutting. And in other cases, small companies depending on the leaders for cold-storage facilities and refrigerator-cars found their de-

---

[21] *Report of the Federal Trade Commission on Agricultural Income Inquiry* (1938), Part I, p. 197 (cited hereafter as F. T. C., *Agricultural Income Inquiry*).

[22] F. T. C., *Meat-Packing Report*, Part I, pp. 484–488.

[23] F. T. C., *Meat-Packing Report*, Part III, pp. 136–137.

[24] *Ibid.*, pp. 156–177.

[25] *Ibid.*, pp. 264 ff.

[26] *Ibid.*, pp. 140–141.

pendence too great to permit them to survive.[27] At times small packers found, to their sorrow, that they had been depending for credit on banks controlled by their large rivals.

In addition to packing plants, Swift, Armour, and the others acquired a hold over strategic sections of the industry through purchase of organizations such as supply houses selling meats to hotels. Or they bought tanneries to which small packers could be forced to sell hides at ruinously low prices.[28] In the twenties the threatened uprising of small competitors in the cattle regions was checked by these moves.[29]

The financial power which made possible these acquisitions came as much from the influence of the large packers in a number of banks as from their own financial resources. The Federal Trade Commission found that members of the Morris, Wilson, Swift, and Armour families or employees of their companies were on the boards of sixty-one banks located in the livestock centres.[30]

Ownership of the stockyards handling almost all interstate commerce in stock yielded the large companies attractive profits and a considerable business advantage over smaller rivals. Most of these yards were originally developed by the railroads and acquired from time to time by the packing interests. By 1917 very few yards in any important centre were uncontrolled.[31] The resultant power of the Big Five to exclude banks and cattle loan companies from convenient locations near the yards increased their power over these financial agencies and made the lot of the small shipper and purchaser more unhappy. In addition, control of terminal railroad facilities, yardage services and charges, and other marketing factors, gave the large companies marked advantages. Even marketing information was controlled. When the shipper and the small packer turned to market papers for information they frequently took it from sources controlled by the Big Five. One supposedly independent paper, *The National Market Provisioner,* had an editor who received five thousand dollars a year subscribed jointly by Armour, Swift, and Morris.[32] It is only a fair presumption that services were rendered for the five thousand dollars.

In seeking transportation facilities for his dressed meat the small independent found an equally bad situation. In 1917 the Big Five owned over 90 per cent of the refrigerator-cars available for interstate packers.[33] When a small shipper did own a few cars he found he had to depend on his large competitors for icing service en route and his cars moved to

---

[27] F. T. C., *Meat-Packing Report,* Part I, p. 201.
[28] F. T. C., *Meat-Packing Report,* Part I, p. 488.
[29] T. N. E. C., *Monograph* No. 35, p. 17.
[30] F. T. C., *Meat-Packing Report,* Part I, p. 43.
[31] *Ibid.,* Part III, pp. 24–25.
[32] *Ibid.,* Part I, pp. 39–40.
[33] *Ibid.,* Part I, p. 34.

their destination much more slowly than those of large shippers. In addition, his cars might take months to return to him. When he had to depend on the cars of his large rivals he was in even worse straits. In part, of course, he was merely injured by his smallness and his lack of essential equipment, but, in part, he suffered discriminatory treatment at the hands of competitors who used their power to restrain troublesome competition.[34]

The Regulation of Competitive Conditions

Immediately after the First World War, relations between the large and small companies were considerably altered by government action. In 1919, the Department of Justice was preparing to prosecute the meat-packing combination, but on request of the large packers agreed to a compromise. By pre-arrangement a suit started in the Supreme Court of the District of Columbia was not contested, and the Big Five consented to accept the terms prescribed in a court decree. Among other things they agreed to dispose of their interest in public stockyards, stockyard railways and terminals, market newspapers, and public cold-storage warehouses.[35] The decree did not improve the situation in respect to the refrigerator-car service, but in time did give the mass of small packers a greater equality of opportunity. By 1924 Cudahy and Morris were fairly well out of stockyard ownership, but Swift and Armour had not as yet made any effective moves.[36] The next ten years, however, saw general compliance with the court order.[37]

Equality of treatment for all packers was further advanced by the Packers and Stockyards Act of 1921. Congress gave the Secretary of Agriculture two important powers. The first allowed the Secretary, after a complaint and hearing, to order packers to cease any form of discrimination practiced against persons or localities and to desist from attempts to restrain trade or achieve monopoly. Orders of the Secretary were made binding after thirty days unless appeal was brought to the Circuit Courts of Appeals. If they were then modified or confirmed, the order served as an injunction restraining the packer from the prohibited action.[38]

The second power transformed all stockyards using over 20,000 square feet of land into public utilities. All agents or dealers in such yards are required to register with the Secretary of Agriculture. Charges levied

[34] *Ibid.*, Part IV, pp. 70–84.
[35] U. S. *v.* Swift and Co. *et al.*, Consent Decree in the Supreme Court of the District of Columbia, February 27, 1920.
[36] F. T. C., Packer Consent Decree (1925), pp. 1–17.
[37] Subject to terms and conditions fixed by the Court, Swift continued to hold control of yards at Milwaukee, San Francisco, Newark, and Brighton.
[38] U. S. Code, Title 7, Sections 191–195.

by the stockyards for their services, and charges of agents buying or selling animals on commission, must be reasonable and non-discriminatory, and all schedules of rates must be open to the public and must be filed with the Department of Agriculture. The Secretary has power, after a hearing, to fix the maximum, minimum, or exact charges, and to order changes in service to prevent discrimination.[39]

A more basic attack on concentration and its effects was initiated in September 1948, when the Department of Justice let loose a real broadside at the Big Four. Attorneys for the Department filed suit against Armour, Swift, Cudahy, and Wilson aimed fundamentally at the source of industrial coöperation. The suit demands the break-up of the Big Four into fourteen independent companies. Time alone will prove whether an attack of this character possesses the legal and economic substance needed to restore an adequate measure of competitive controls. If the four large companies should be reorganized as sought by the government, many problems would still remain before real independence developed among the companies. However, a number of smaller meat packers now engaging in interstate sale of meat products would individually play a relatively more important part in the market. Such companies as Morrell, Hormel, Rath, Dold, and Kingan have sales ranging between one hundred and two hundred million annually, about half the volume of Cudahy, smallest of the Big Four. A lessening of the economic power of the large companies might well lead to a moderate measure of independence among some twenty or thirty producers which would not begin to create conditions required for perfect competition but would allow possibly at least the appearance of a tolerable substitute.

THE COMPETITIVE ADVANTAGE OF SIZE

While public controls have improved the competitive market, the large packers continue to enjoy economic advantages which have been a considerable source of power to them in the past. In varying measure large-scale operations bring advantages in the processing of by-products and in marketing. Non-edible portions amount to 45, 25, and 50 per cent respectively of the live weight of cattle, hogs, and sheep. And all these parts can be made to yield a commercial by-product.[40] But expensive equipment and laboratories must be operated to effect a complete utilization, and are feasible only if the packer is handling a large volume

---

[39] U. S. Code, Title 7, Section 211; penalties of $500 for each offense in disobedience of the Secretary's order are provided, and each day of continued violation constitutes a separate offense. The Attorney-General or any injured party may apply to district courts for enforcement of the Secretary's orders.

[40] C. V. Whalen, By-Products of the Slaughtering and Meat-Packing Industry, F. T. C., *Meat-Packing Report*, Part I, Exhibit XVII.

of materials. Almost all save the very small packers produce some by-products or sell materials to processors. Many small companies possess fertilizer equipment which allows them to utilize blood, skulls and jaw-bones, genital organs, and other non-edible materials. A number also have rendering plants using offal to produce fats and other materials they can sell to processing companies. Horns can be sold to fertilizer manu-facturers, skulls, cartilage, unborn calves, and so on to glue companies. But complete use of all the varied materials escapes the small packer. His large competitor uses glands, membranes, bones, intestines, hoofs and horns, hair and bristles, and other materials to produce medicinal preparations, knife and tooth-brush handles, fats, oils, glue stock, combs, mattresses, horse-collars, tallows, greases, fertilizers, and many other products.[41]

Their large volume of business also allows the leading companies, par-ticularly Swift and Armour, to operate a marketing system beyond the reach of small competitors. In order to cover the widely-scattered mar-kets for meat and to supply needed refrigeration, the Big Five added the operation of numerous cold-storage warehouses to their car service. From district warehouses salesmen cover the surrounding areas, and deliveries are made directly to retail stores. By 1916 both Armour and Swift were reaching approximately twenty-five thousand towns and cities through railway peddler cars and local deliveries from branch houses. All told, the Big Five were running eleven hundred out of the twelve hundred and fifty branch houses operated by the whole industry.[42] Ex-cept for some cured and processed pork products, their marketing organi-zation largely displaced the ordinary wholesaler in the industry.[43]

In order to expand this organization and to spread its overhead costs, the large companies became important factors in the sale of many food products.[44] By 1916, Swift had become the leading distributor of butter, and the Big Five handled about half the interstate sale of poultry, eggs, and cheese, a somewhat smaller part of the sales of canned milk and vegetable oil products, and approximately a quarter of the canned fruit and vegetable sales. In one year Armour and Company sold sixteen million pounds of rice and marketed important amounts of breakfast-foods and animal feeds. These and other excursions raised the spectre of a food monopoly, and the 1920 Consent Decree seriously checked the packers' expansion. They were ordered to discontinue the use of their facilities for the marketing of a number of commodities unrelated to

[41] F. T. C., *Meat-Packing Report*, Part I, pp. 369–389.
[42] *Ibid.*, pp. 143 ff.
[43] F. T. C., *Agricultural Income Inquiry*, Part I, pp. 194–195.
[44] The packers may also have seen the chance of monopoly profits in some other food lines, and may have desired to control the prices of some products which were competitive to meat.

meat packing and were forbidden to own, individually or collectively, as much as 50 per cent of the voting stock of any corporation or association engaged in marketing these lines. Various attempts were made to modify the decree, on the score that conditions had changed sufficiently in the distribution of foods to make the danger of monopoly negligible.[45] The Supreme Court remained unpersuaded. While they have thus been unable to realize all the possible advantages of their marketing organization, the large companies still retain some of their old superiority.

THE EFFECTS OF COÖPERATION

One of the most impressive effects of developments in the meat-packing field is the spreading to other fields of conditions that make difficulties for competitive individualism. From about 1900 to 1920 the importance of a few packing companies in by-product lines and in food distribution brought a considerable concentration of business in these fields. In leather production the four companies, along with two large leather companies, made up half the industry.[46] And shortly after 1900 Swift and Armour became very important factors in the tanning of leather. Almost inevitably the big slaughtering companies reached a similar position in the manufacture of fertilizers. Again, Armour and Swift stood well ahead of the Morris, Wilson, and Cudahy companies, but two non-packing companies towered over Armour and Swift. In the production of the important mixed fertilizer containing nitrogen, phosphorus and potash, five companies probably made up over 60 per cent of the industry. A few packers and cottonseed oil companies created about the same condition for the manufacture of cottonseed oil, lard compound and lard substitute. Eleven companies produced almost as much crude cottonseed oil as all others, and thirteen left only 10 per cent of the output of refined oil to smaller companies.

In general, this concentration has continued up to the present time. While the 1920 Consent Decree freed stockyards and marketing agencies from packer control, it also required the large packing companies to give up the marketing of some foods unrelated to the processing of meat. But it is probable that before their enforced withdrawal the slaughtering companies contributed to the appearance of concentration in the marketing of many of these food products. In their growth before 1920 they eliminated many small wholesalers and distributors and then left large organizations behind when they were forced to abandon their ownership of them. Libby, McNeill and Libby, for example, as a subsidiary of

[45] *Cf.* Swift and Co. *v.* U. S., 276 U. S. 311 (1927); U. S. *v.* California Canneries, 279 U. S. 553 (1928); U. S. *v.* Swift *et. al.*, 286 U. S. 106 (1931).
[46] F. T. C., *Meat-Packing Report*, Part I, p. 201.

Swift was the largest distributor of condensed and evaporated milk and now, under at least nominal independence, ranks as the largest company in the canning field.[47]

Prices, Costs, and Profits

To be really effective any control over the price level for dressed meats must be able to restrict the use of substitutes so as to make the demand for meat at least moderately inelastic and must, of course, be able to regulate the supply of meat. In 1918, the Federal Trade Commission found considerable evidence to support its contention that the packers used both means to enhance meat prices. The Big Five appeared to use their position in the sale of eggs, poultry, cheese, and fish to keep their prices in a satisfactory adjustment with meat prices.[48] In the action leading up to the 1920 Consent Decree the Department of Justice charged that as soon as the packers had eliminated competition in meat products they set out to end the competition of substitute foods. They undertook to control the supply of fish, vegetables, fresh or canned fruits, cereals, milk, poultry, butter, eggs, cheese and other substitutes for meat. On the other side of the picture, their controlling position and their cooperation in buying stock allowed them a considerable power to fix stock prices and hence control the supply brought onto the market. Lowered prices for livestock meant not only lower packing costs but smaller supplies of dressed meat which could be sold at higher prices. The 1941 indictments of Swift, Wilson, and Armour, charging price agreements in the purchase of sheep and hogs, suggest that circumstances have not changed much since 1920.

In spite of their obvious coöperation the large companies do not appear generally to have earned large profits. In the three years from 1912 to 1914 Armour, Swift, Morris, and Cudahy made in the neighborhood of 7 per cent on their net worth. The appearance of a large war demand from Europe improved earnings quite markedly. Until the United States entered the First World War, Swift made profits of 21 per cent and the other three approximately 14.[49] But during these same years sixty-five independents reported earnings that were 25 per cent larger. It is not possible to isolate with any certainty the factors that made these large profits for all. Unquestionably the war was bringing excess profits to many industries, as supply could not be expanded to match the jump in demand. It is impossible to tell to what extent an earlier restriction of stock production was responsible for the inflexibility of war-time supplies,

---

[47] T. N. E. C., *Monograph* No. 35, pp. 51–53.
[48] F. T. C., *Meat-Packing Report*, Part I, pp. 154–156.
[49] F. T. C., *Maximum Profit Limitation on Meat-Packing Industry* (Washington, D. C., 1919), p. 27.

and to what extent restrictive policies were deliberately followed during the period of war needs. It is quite probable that both influences were of importance.

The relative earning position of the Big Five and the independent companies appears in the following table. From this it is apparent that the whole industry suffered in the immediate post war readjustments, but

Table 21

MEAT PACKING PROFITS, 1918–1922[50]

Year	Return on Investment Excluding Appreciation	
	The Big Five	Independent Companies[a]
1918	12.8%	10.7
1919	6.1	5.3
1920	.3	2.1
1921	(loss) 10.3	1.3
1922	3.0[b]	5.9

a Forty-three companies all engaged in U. S. inspected slaughter.
b Includes surplus adjustment and appreciation.

the large companies showed far less ability to adjust to depression conditions than did independents.[51] During the twenties, when the large companies were reporting modest earnings below 3 per cent, their smaller rivals were making in the neighborhood of 9 per cent.[52] After very small returns in 1931 and 1932, the large packers have enjoyed better returns. According to the Federal Trade Commission, their earnings on an adjusted investment value have been averaging over 7 per cent.[53]

There are three possible explanations of the moderate earnings of these powerful companies, and the truth is probably to be found in some compound of the three. First, the large producers have at times used the profits of meat-packing to support less lucrative lines, and have sold by-products to subsidiaries at artificially low prices.[54] Profits have thus been put in the hands of these subsidiaries so as to hide the restriction of meat supplies and the elevation of dressed meat prices. Second, the returns reported by the large companies may have been distorted. They appear smaller than they frequently are. The Federal Trade Commission

[50] Packer Consent Decree, 68th Congress, 2nd Session, Senate Document No. 219, p. 21.
[51] See also Swift and Co. et al. v. U. S., 286 U. S. 106 (1931).
[52] Swift and Co. et al., 276 U. S. 311 (1928).
[53] F. T. C., Agricultural Income Inquiry, p. 871.
[54] F. T. C., Meat-Packing Report, Part I, p. 92.

has insisted that the packers' accounts hide numerous secret reserves, show artificial inter-company charges, and allow capital expenses to be charged against current operations.[55] Third, in spite of their efficient marketing systems the biggest companies cannot produce as cheaply as the independents. Their own admissions and the methods they have used against other companies would support this belief.[56] As a result they have been willing to use their great financial power merely to protect their position. Independents are left a comfortable place as long as they do not disturb the industry. And they, in their turn, having reason to fear cut-throat competition and enjoying attractive prices, are generally willing to follow along.

It is possible and even probable that the costs of the majority of both large and small firms have been adversely affected by the general decline of price competition. The pressure to improve production methods and the elimination of inefficient companies is at least retarded when prices are designed to maintain existing conditions. Cost-reducing improvements might still reward the innovator with increased profits, but the attraction of profits probably supplies a weaker incentive than the fear of competition. In addition, when everyone is being taken care of by the coöperation, change is something to be feared. The efficiency of plant operations was obviously harmed by the market-sharing arrangements. The purchase of stock was not set by the needs of the various packing plants, but by the arbitrary purchasing arrangement. It was obvious from the correspondence of Phillip Armour that the Armour plant in Denver was forced to operate beyond its optimum scale. All the evidence suggests that the division of purchases was set without regard to its effect on individual plant operations, so probably many plants operated at an uneconomical scale. Furthermore, a price level sufficiently high to satisfy the less efficient companies encourages the entry of additional firms. After 1921, when the large packers had lost their control of stockyard and refrigeration facilities, the number of small independents almost doubled. As the coöperating group lost ground it almost certainly suffered increased plant costs, as it handled a decreasing percentage of a total volume of business that was itself declining.

It appears that Swift or Armour might very well have taken over the rôle of price leader in the meat industry if certain conditions had not favored the market-sharing device. The results would not have been essentially different. A demand that is more elastic than the demand for steel, and the existence of thousands of small markets, would make the job of a price leader rather difficult. It would not be easy to publish prices for all markets and to maintain them for a period of time. As a

---

[55] *Ibid.*, p. 73.
[56] Swift and Co. *et al. v.* U. S., 276 U. S. 311 (1928). Brief for Swift and Co. *et al.*, pp. 9, 56.

result a leader would have difficulty in keeping his followers in line. Market-sharing, however, found a convenient industrial structure. Meat supplies went through the stockyard channel, which could be easily controlled by the coöperation of the large firms. And as long as there is agreement in the buying policies, each of the large companies is protected in the sale of meat from any possible competitive encroachment on the part of the others.

25

The Glass Container Industry

Although it is one of the oldest industries in America, glass manufacture has been one of the last of the larger fields to be mechanized. For over a century it continued to use raw materials and hand methods of manufacture substantially unchanged from the early Christian era.[1] Its basic raw material, silica, is an opaque sand which, melted and then cooled, turns into a transparent substance. The process is aided by soda ash acting in the mixture as a flux to reduce the melting point. Lime serves as a hardener and various metals may be added to give special qualities to the glass. The addition of lead, for example, makes the product more brilliant and more heat-resisting. These materials were melted in clay pots from which gobs of glass were dipped on the end of a four or five foot hollow tube. Skilful twirling of the rod and inflation of the gob gave a hollow ball of glass of the desired shape. When the mass hardened, it was re-heated to an even temperature to prevent strains from unequal cooling, and then allowed to cool gradually in some sort of oven.

The industry developed a considerable plant specialization long before specialized machinery appeared. Although the capital equipment was essentially similar, consisting only of a furnace and re-heating oven, the various factories showed a tendency to concentrate on only one type of product. Labor skills and market considerations tended to separate the manufacture of window-glass and tableware, and to group bottles, flasks and window-lamps in the hands of other producers.[2] When machinery displaced handwork in the middle stage between the melting and re-heating steps, specialization was further advanced. Factories were forced by the specialized and expensive equipment to produce only one type of product. And later, as large companies brought a number of

---

[1] Frances Rogers and Alice Beard, *5000 Years of Glass* (New York, Frederick A. Stokes Company, 1937), Chap. 2.

[2] Malcolm Keir, *Manufacturing* (New York, Ronald Press Company, 1928), p. 531.

plants under a single control, they rather generally continued the product specialization. As a result, glass manufacture is not a single industry, but consists of three fields with their characteristic products—glass containers, window and plate glass, electric bulbs and specialty glass. The divisions are not perfectly maintained, but they are clearly apparent. The presence of one or two very large and specialized companies in each field helps to maintain the divided appearance of the whole industry. In bottle-making the Owens-Illinois Glass Company can supply over 40 per cent of American bottle needs, but it buys its window glass from other producers. Similarly, the Libbey-Owens-Ford Glass Company and the Pittsburgh Plate Glass Company dominate the manufacture of window glass. And the Corning Glass Works maintains a clear supremacy in the production of electric light bulbs and a number of specialty lines such as signal and optical glass.

THE GLASS CONTAINER INDUSTRY

With the manufacture of some seven billion containers of all shapes and sizes, valued in the neighborhood of one hundred and twenty millions of dollars, the glass container industry annually accounts for almost half the value of glass products produced in the United States.[3] It has become thoroughly mechanized over the course of the last thirty years.[4] In 1899 the manufacture of a billion containers required the employment of over twenty-eight thousand wage-earners. In 1935 six billion were produced with four thousand fewer workers.[5] Mechanization has brought equally great changes to the organization of the industry. The need for large amounts of capital and the existence of important patents have contributed to the growth of large firms and have placed a few companies in strategic positions in the manufacture of various types of containers. The number of enterprises has been cut to one-third and a few of them tower over the others.[6] The same forces have been at work in the other glass industries with effects essentially similar to those apparent in the container field.

By 1895 certain improvements had been made in the art of bottle-making, but the essentially hand-made character of the product re-

---

[3] T. N. E. C., *Hearings*, Part II, Patents (1938), p. 755. Medicine and toilet wares make up over 30 per cent of the total volume; wide-mouth food containers and jars, over 18%; beer bottles, 8%, and milk bottles, 5%. See also, *Statistical Abstracts of the United States*, 1948, p. 872.

[4] Hand production accounts for approximately 2 per cent of the total value of glass containers.

[5] T. N. E. C., *Hearings*, Part II, Patents, p. 755.

[6] In the past thirty-five years the number of operating companies in the container field has fallen from 155 to 40, and five companies account for two-thirds of the total production.

mained. The viscous gob of glass on the end of a hollow tube was shaped by the skilled blower and then lowered into a mold. Another workman cut off the attenuated tail of glass and the gob was blown out to fit the conformation of the mold. Highly skilled labor was required to lift the proper amount of glass from the furnace and to shape the gob. While the labor was costly, the product was of variable quality. The high degree of skill required made the introduction of machine methods difficult. And, in addition to the difficulty of developing machinery to handle and measure exact quantities of molten glass, trouble came from the very strong glass-blowers' union. Its resistance to partial mechanization, however, only delayed the inevitable.

A glass blower, M. J. Owens, did more than anyone else to bring about the death of his own handicraft. Working for the Libbey Glass Company, and financially backed by E. D. Libbey, he developed the machine on which the present power of the great Owens-Illinois Glass Company was built. By 1903 Owens was ready to patent a machine which by suction drew molten glass from a melting-furnace into molds. There the glass was blown mechanically to the shape of the mold. Two years later he was successfully operating a machine that was completely automatic, using unskilled labor only for simple tasks.

The original machine was of massive circular construction, having iron molds mounted on four or six arms radiating from a central pillar. As each arm revolved, the rough mold which it held passed over a pot containing molten glass and was lowered until its open end touched the pool of glass. A charge of glass was sucked into the mold, and as the arm moved on, a knife cut the glass off from that in the pot and closed the lower opening. In the upper part of the mold a plug formed the neck-opening of the bottle. When the rough mold was then opened, the charge of glass hung suspended by the neck until a finished mold closed about it. The glass was then blown to its finished shape. After a journey lasting about twenty seconds the arm deposited the bottle on a conveyor and swung around to the pot for another charge. Later improvements increased the number of arms on the machine and allowed each arm to hold several molds.[7] With one unskilled operator the machine can now turn out as many as two hundred and forty small bottles in a minute and is capable of making bottles requiring as much as fifteen pounds of glass.

Until 1916 the Owens machine dominated the bottle industry. In return for royalty payments a few companies were licensed to use the machine, but after 1908 the Owens Bottle Machine Company began to produce bottles and ceased to put its machines into the hands of competitors. It followed a pricing policy that allowed hand production to survive, although it could have driven all but its own licensees from the

---

[7] For a discussion of earlier semi-automatic machinery see Keir, *op. cit.*, pp. 534 ff.

THE GLASS CONTAINER INDUSTRY

565

field. It is quite probable that its choice of high prices rested more on a desire for profits than on a concern for small independents.[8] Although the suction machine after ten years was only turning out one-third of the total of bottle production, the position of independents was precarious. Even if the Owens Company had not restricted the use of its machines, small companies would have found difficulty in paying the eighty thousand dollars which the machine cost or in carrying heavy royalty payments.[9] At best their lot was an unhappy one, and their very existence depended on the pricing policy of the Owens Company.

After 1916, however, this company was to meet a serious challenge from new machinery. The first opposition came from a stream feeding process which poured molten glass into molds. The stream of molten glass was shut off by a shearing device when the mold had received a proper quantity, and another mold moved into position. The machine was not completely satisfactory, as it was difficult to prevent the glass from thickening as it was poured, and air bubbles and laminations frequently appeared in the finished bottle. A second attack on the superiority of the Owens machine was more successful. Patents were granted on a machine using what was known as the plunger or gob process. A gob of viscous glass, forced out of a melting tank by a plunger, hung suspended until it was built up to the size required to fill a mold. It was then sheared off and the action was repeated on the next mold.[10] The Hartford-Fairmont Company acquired very broad patents over this feeding system and its machines, costing only thirteen thousand dollars each, were able to equal the performance of the much more costly suction machine.

About this time the Hartford-Fairmont Company improved its position in the industry still further by an exchange of patents with the Corning Glass Company. In 1915 the patent office found that patents held by a subsidiary of the latter interfered with some held by Hartford-Fairmont. Since Corning was interested in developing machinery for the manufacture of electric bulbs, the business interests of the two did not conflict, and a cross-licensing agreement allowed each company the patent scope it desired. Subsequent divisions of patents between the two allowed Corning the use of feeder equipment it needed, and gave it sole rights on patents covering the manufacture of bulbs, signal and optical glass, and heat-resisting ware. And Hartford-Fairmont, with its name now changed to the Hartford-Empire Company, continued to strengthen its position in the container industry by taking over a number of Corning patents.[11]

---

[8] *Cf.* Keir, *op. cit.*, pp. 538–539.

[9] Hartford-Empire Co. *v.* Hazel-Atlas Glass Co., 59 Fed. (2nd) 399, 402.

[10] For a description of the special features of various feeder machines see 59 Fed. (2nd) 404–411.

[11] T. N. E. C., *Hearings*, Part II, Patents, pp. 637–647.

All this left the Owens-Illinois Company in a very vulnerable position. Its machines were far less valuable and its bottle production was threatened by companies using the cheaper gob feeders under license from Hartford-Empire. It reacted by spending upwards of a million dollars to acquire patent rights on gob feeders. Coming into an inevitable and possibly intended patent conflict with Hartford-Empire, it fought its adversary until 1924. The two concerns then decided that coöperation would be much more profitable than competition. A mutually satisfactory settlement took the form of a cross-licensing agreement. Except for its suction patents, which were no longer important in licensing bottle producers, the Owens Bottle Company turned over its feeder and bottle-forming patents to the Hartford-Empire Company and agreed to pay royalties on the patented machines that it used. In return it was allowed the use of forty machines without license or royalty charge, and was to receive an annual sum roughly approximating one-half of the net profits which Hartford-Empire derived from patents.[12] Furthermore, for eight years it had the power to prevent the Hartford Company from licensing any bottle producer whom it found objectionable. In 1932 the Owens Company surrendered its rights to the royalty-free machines and took one-third instead of one-half of the patent income. Three years later, on the receipt of two and one-half millions, it gave up all claims to any share in that income.[13]

The Hartford-Empire Company meanwhile was enjoying its share of the benefits of the 1924 agreement. It escaped the considerable risks of patent infringement suits and became the important depository of bottle machinery patents for the whole industry. Its importance and power grew as patents from other sources were tossed into the pool. In 1932, the Hazel-Atlas Glass Company, second only to the Owens Company in the manufacture of glass containers, made an important contribution. Originally using the vacuum feeder under license, it developed a number of patents on other types of feeder equipment which brought it into conflict with Hartford-Empire. Between 1926 and 1932 it incurred burdensome legal expenses ranging between fifty and one hundred and fifty thousand dollars a year. Also, after it had suffered an adverse decision in the Circuit Court of Appeals, it faced the possibility of infringement damages which might have amounted to as much as two million dollars. Instead of testing the Circuit Court decision in the Supreme Court, it made peace on very satisfactory terms. Surrendering all its patents, it became, as had the Owens Company, a pensioner of Hartford-Empire.

[12] The income to be divided was defined in the agreement as including gross royalties, licensing fees in excess of cost, profits on parts, and damages collected in infringement suits, and from this $600,000 was to be deducted.

[13] During the period of the agreement the Owens Company paid Hartford-Empire $3,962,921 in royalties and received $4,815,093 as its share of the latter's income; T. N. E. C., *Hearings*, Part II, Patents, p. 494.

Although the patent suits had been dangerous and irritating, Hazel-Atlas was not just an unwilling victim of power. It was a company with considerable financial strength, and apparently had been able to adapt its feeder equipment so as to escape the coverage of Hartford-Empire's patents.[14] In part at least, it seems to have chosen a policy of coöperation to secure profits it could not get under competitive conditions. In addition to restraining competition in the sale of containers, the coöperation paid it between 1932 and 1938 the sum of six and one-half millions of dollars as its share of the patent profits. At the same time Hazel-Atlas paid into the coffers of the Hartford-Empire Company license and royalty payments amounting to five and three-quarters millions.[15] This development widened the power of the pool considerably in bringing in as licensees a number of smaller bottle companies which saw no hope for themselves except behind the shield of the Hartford-Empire Company.

In the meantime the Owens Bottle Company had effected a change in its name and strengthened its position in the production of bottles. It acquired the important Illinois Glass Company, formerly a licensee of both Hartford-Empire and the Owens Company. The merger united the two names to become the Owens-Illinois Glass Company.

The Organization of the Industry Before 1945

Patent pooling and the purchase and development of patents placed the Hartford-Empire Company in an unrivalled position. While it owned over seven hundred patents or patent rights on automatic glass-making machinery, it produced neither machines nor bottles. Its revenues came largely from license and royalty charges collected from bottle manufacturers licensed to use patented machines. The Owens-Illinois Glass Company no longer licensed other companies to use its machinery, but itself used an improved form of the vacuum feeder and equipment leased from Hartford-Empire. With seventeen plants located in various parts of the country, it outranked the largest of the other thirty-one container manufacturers who produced as licensees of Hartford-Empire. Only 4 per cent of the machine-made bottles produced in the United States were made by independents, and they struggled along, using outmoded equipment on which patents had expired.

Both intercorporate stockholding and interlocking directorates added to the network of connections in the bottle industry and between it and other glass industries. A holding company, Houghton Associates, Inc., representing the Houghton family, owned 40 per cent of the stock of the Corning Glass Works, which continued to manufacture specialty glass

[14] Cf. testimony of J. H. McNash, President, Hazel-Atlas Glass Company, ibid., pp., 536–545.
[15] Ibid., p. 543.

under license from the Hartford-Empire Company. In addition, the Houghton family owned 90 per cent of the stock of the Empire Machine Company, which in its turn owned 43 per cent of the stock of Hartford-Empire. A connection was established between these companies and the Owens group through joint ownership by Corning and Owens-Illinois of the Fiberglas Corporation, organized to manufacture glass wool. And Owens-Illinois and Hartford-Empire had close business relations with the Lynch Corporation, the largest producer of glass-forming machinery. In addition to all these ties, in 1938 four of the directors of the Corning Works were members of the Board of the Hartford-Empire Company; and Owens-Illinois had representatives on the boards of two companies producing containers in competition with it. In 1935, apparently to avoid attracting undesirable attention, William E. Levis, President of Owens-Illinois, resigned from the board of one ostensible competitor, the Hazel-Atlas Company. In writing to his uncle, however, he revealed that a representative of his company would take the place he vacated.[16]

Except for four very small producers, the whole of the container industry was brought under the central control of the Glass Container Association and by the licensing system of the Hartford-Empire Company. And the company used its patent power to plan some of the essential affairs of its licensees. The manner in which it used its power was apparent in a memorandum taken from its files by the Temporary National Economic Committee, and in the testimony of responsible officers appearing before the Committee. The following seemed to be settled features of its licensing policy:

(1) Machines were licensed only to selected manufacturers of the better type and were refused to many licensees who might be price-cutters;

(2) Licensees were restricted to the manufacture of certain specific types of containers in order to prevent too much competition;

(3) Licenses ran for a limited term, usually eight or ten years, so the Company could exercise continuing control over the situation;

(4) Licensees were frequently limited in the number of bottles of a certain type which they could produce in a year. For instance, only three milk-bottle producers could produce without limit;[17]

(5) Licensed producers were restricted as to the market in which they could sell;

(6) Certain licenses guaranteed the exclusive right to use Hartford-Empire machines to particular producers in certain lines. For example, the right to use the machines to manufacture fruit jars was limited to Hazel-Atlas, Owens-Illinois, and Ball Brothers.[18]

---

[16] *Ibid.*, p. 482.

[17] Thatcher Manufacturing Company, Owens-Illinois and Liberty Glass Company.

[18] The president of Hartford-Empire testified that a licensee would be violating his contract if he were licensed to produce jars for packers of food products and allowed his ware to be sold as fruit jars; *cf.* T. N. E. C., *Hearings*, Part II, Patents, p. 409.

Sources of Power

It is obvious that under these provisions the container industry was not organized to maintain the competitive independence of individual companies. The planning done for the whole industry by Hartford-Empire and a few large companies in the industry, notably Owens-Illinois, Thatcher Manufacturing Company, Hazel-Atlas, and Ball Brothers, grew out of the patent situation. It is a mistake, however, to ascribe the decline of competition to the presence of a simple patent monopoly. Patents were met wherever one turned, but no one invention or subsequent development by itself placed the Hartford-Empire Company in the position it held. In fact, patents in themselves tended to divide the industry. But competitive independence was prevented by various deliberately-used devices. The most important, of course, was patent pooling. The Corning and Owens-Illinois companies started it with the assignment of exclusive rights in a number of their patents to the Hartford-Empire. It is true that overlapping patents threatened to create conflict in the courts, but there is the persistent suggestion running through the history of the industry that pooling and the loss of independence were accepted willingly and were by no means always necessary. It is difficult to believe that Hartford-Empire would pay the Owens Bottle Company half of its royalty income for patents that it could eliminate in infringement proceedings. J. H. McNash, president of Hazel-Atlas, told the Temporary National Economic Committee that his company was satisfied its feeder equipment did not infringe Hartford patents. And even after the adverse court decision in 1932 it was going on with the fight with reasonable hopes of a successful conclusion. It threw its patents into the pool only when Hartford-Empire made it an offer that was far too attractive to be refused.

A year later and for no better reason the process was repeated with the large fruit jar manufacturer, Ball Brothers. This company did pay Hartford-Empire four hundred thousand dollars in absolution of its infringement sins, but it also received returns that suggest coöperation and not dictation. Hartford agreed not to issue to any manufacturer in the United States any further license on its feeder equipment for the making of fruit jars for household use. And Ball Brothers did not give the appearance of being in any great distress over the infringement situation, for it did not accept this considerable prize without further important concessions from its "competitors." Both the added pay that it wanted and the source of this are clearly revealed in a letter written by J. H. McNash, president of the Hazel-Atlas Company, to William E. Levis of Owens-Illinois. A paragraph reads as follows: "This Company, however, is willing to go pretty far, as I indicated in New York, to give Ball what he wants as long as that want does not actually cramp our style.

I don't mean by this that your Company or this Company should actually pay Ball to come in, but I believe the Hazel-Atlas Glass Company could restrict itself in such a way that there actually would not be a penalty."[19] Strange language to be exchanged between the officers of two supposedly competing companies with regard to a third competitor. The upshot was that Hazel-Atlas agreed to limit its annual production to three hundred thousand gross and Owens-Illinois gave oral assurance that it would not exceed one-third of that figure.[20] Ball was left as residual legatee.

These arrangements and others show that the ownership of patents was important in organization of the industry, but they also show that a general lack of competitive independence and a pervading willingness to coöperate played their part. Certainly, the coöperation of McNash and Levis was not quite what one might look for in a system of competitive individualism.

Its considerable financial strength, derived in large part from its valuable feeder patents, gave Hartford-Empire the power to acquire a large number of additional patents. Even its basic patents on the gob feeding machine, however, were not developed in its own organization, but were acquired by the purchase of a smaller company. Other important patents bought by the Owens Bottle Company were first turned down by Hartford-Empire, and later were influential in bringing the two into the cross-license arrangement. In a typical case the physical assets and patents of the O'Neill Machine Company were bought for the sake of valuable rights it possessed over feeding and forming machines. Its patents on gob feeding were tossed into Hartford's collection, while certain rights on suction machines went to Owens-Illinois.[21] A number of other cases suggest that Hartford-Empire had no particular superiority in developing new and improved methods.

Before the Temporary National Economic Committee, Lloyd T. Williams, patent counsel for Owens-Illinois, testified that one of the bottle machinery producers, Whitall Tatum Company, managed to present claims in the patent office which, if upheld, would have broadly overlain some of Hartford's basic machines. The claims were sufficiently well-founded to force Hartford first to purchase an option on rights to use the patents, and later to purchase the patent rights themselves. Between 1924 and 1933 a half-dozen other instances of the purchase of patents developed by others suggest that the financial strength of the patent pool was no inconsiderable source of its power.[22]

At times unsavory methods were used to persuade small companies

---

[19] T. N. E. C., *Hearings*, Part II, Patents, p. 561.
[20] *Ibid.*, pp. 564–567.
[21] *Ibid.*, p. 523.
[22] *Ibid.*, pp. 522–526.

to surrender their patents and come in under the licensing system. In
some cases small rivals were not able to afford the legal and business
costs involved in defending against infringement suits. With apparently
supportable patent claims they sold out to the great financial strength
of the Hartford-Empire organization. The president of Knox Glass Associates insisted that his organization had a suction feeding machine
developed by itself, but gave up a profitable business in the production
of fruit jars rather than fight infringement suits. On legal grounds he
believed it had an even chance of success, but on financial grounds the
great resources of its opponents made defense appear out of the question.[23]

The fortunes of the Amsler-Morton Company of Pittsburgh, a small
producer of melting and re-heating equipment, illustrate the tremendous weight that was thrown against small competitors. Around 1928 it
came into conflict with Hartford-Empire over its patented re-heating
ovens. It was selling ovens for $9500, and its large rival suggested that
there would be no patent troubles if it would raise its price to $13,500
and pay the added four thousand dollars to Hartford-Empire. Under
this arrangement things certainly would have been peaceful for Amsler-
Morton. It would have been trying to sell ovens for $13,500 that its
large rival was selling for $6500. It also would have been helping its
rival by giving it four thousand dollars on any unit it did sell. Amsler-
Morton did not think the proposition was very attractive. It turned down
a proposal to sell out completely, and still later refused to go into combination with one of its competitors, a licensee of Hartford-Empire. In
the proposed consolidation each of the two companies was to take a
third interest, and an unnamed party was to supply some working capital and take the other third. The new organization was promised a
license from Hartford and assured of all the construction business of the
Owens-Illinois Company. When Amsler-Morton held out for 51 per cent
of the stock of the proposed merger it was warned that its opponents "will
enter suit against you and . . . will continue to sue you until you are
out of business."[24]

Continuing the unequal fight, Amsler-Morton did not gain the chance
to test its patent claims in the courts. Hartford-Empire sued a manufacturer who used Amsler-Morton equipment for infringement damages.[25]
This producer also leased machines from Hartford-Empire, and was
bound by terms of the lease not to contest the validity of any of its
patents. As a result the basic issue concerning the validity of the two

[23] *Ibid.*, pp. 587–590.
[24] From the testimony of Paul L. Geer, Treasurer of the Amsler-Morton Company, *ibid.*, p. 599.
[25] Hartford-Empire Co. *v.* Swindell Bros., Inc. (Amsler-Morton Co., Intervener),
96 Fed. Rep. (2nd) 227.

conflicting patents could not be tested in a counter suit. Even fighting on grounds chosen by itself, the giant concern lost in the lower court, but on appeal managed to win a reversal. It then proceeded to warn all container manufacturers that use of the Amsler-Morton equipment would expose them to legal suits. The sales of the small company dropped from $800,000 in 1928 to $18,000 in 1937.

Two things seem rather striking in these proceedings. First, Owens-Illinois was sufficiently interested and sufficiently coöperative to assist in the attempts to eliminate the independent. And secondly, Hartford-Empire tied the hands of companies using their machines, so that any weakness in its patent position could not easily be revealed. It would seem that at least in some cases the financial and business power of the large company were more important than their patent powers. As late as 1930 a responsible patent official of the Owens-Illinois Company expressed the opinion that Hartford's patent position was anything but secure.[26] It was strengthened after 1932, but it seems that legal harassment of independents was still important in maintaining the company's control.

The financial resources backing a well-developed research organization aided Hartford-Empire in improving the machinery of the industry, and thereby helped contribute to its dominant position. But the research efforts of the large concern were also used to stifle the inventiveness of competitors. Whenever independents developed basic patents on a new machine, Hartford-Empire set its research organization at work to study its probable future development. It then surrounded the basic patent with specific patent claims over probable later applications of the machine. When it was successful, this "fencing" either prevented the improvement of the machine or forced the independent to apply for a license to use its own basic invention in the improved form. Officials of the Hartford-Empire Company defended the practice on both business and social grounds. Possibly it could be so defended. It might lead to improvements of basic claims that small companies would not develop. The defense in this particular instance, however, was made a bit difficult when the Temporary National Economic Committee uncovered an official memorandum of the Hartford-Empire Company, written in 1930.[27] In outlining its purpose in securing patents, the memorandum read in part as follows: "To secure patents on possible improvements of competing machines, so as to 'fence in' those and prevent their reaching an improved stage." The management officers of the company insisted that the memorandum had never been accepted by the Board of Directors, and hence

---

[26] From correspondence of Henry W. Carter, Vice-President in Charge of the Patent and License Department, Owens-Illinois Glass Co.; cf. T. N. E. C., *Hearings*, Part II, Patents, pp. 789–791.

[27] *Ibid.*, p. 776.

was not official. But the practice was sufficiently common to suggest that, officially recognized or not, it was of some importance in the industry.

Independent companies selling particular machines for some one part of container manufacture were harassed by attempts on the part of Hartford-Empire to force its customers to use its machines exclusively. It turned out a full line of bottle-making machinery, and some of its equipment was leased under tying clauses which permitted its use only with other machines of the company. Failure to observe this requirement exposed the licensee to revocation of the license and the loss of equipment that he needed and could not get elsewhere. In 1940, the provision still existed in all contracts written before 1936, so it continued to be a considerable source of injury to independents.[28]

Frequently the very great powers residing in patents have not been limited to the years envisaged in the patent law. The means used to extend patents beyond a seventeen-year period are not questionable as far as good business standards are concerned, but they do defeat the intention of the law. Various aspects of a specific invention are patented at different times, and in effect continue the monopoly for years. The important Hartford-Empire patents on feeder machines, covering the use of a plunger to force gobs of glass from a melting tank, expired in 1945. The machine, however, was not then free from control. A later patent covered the broad process of swelling a gob of glass in suspension and effectively covered the same machine.

Commonly the lengthening process was effected by the opposite arrangement of broad and specific patents. Frequently, as in the case of the Owens suction machine, the later rights covered improvements on the original machine. The initial Owens patents had expired, but the later machine embodied a number of specific improvements on which patents still existed. As long as the grant of monopoly as a reward for inventiveness seems a desirable social policy, the time extension associated with improvements must be sanctioned. But the mere juggling of general and specific claims has been common and seems to possess little social merit.

Slowness in the administration of the patent office has also been used to extend the period of control.[29] On the average, it takes between two and three years for the Patent Office to pass on the validity of applications. In this period while the patent is pending, the applicant possesses a fair measure of protection. If he runs into other claims in the Patent

---

[28] Cf. testimony of A. T. Safford, Secretary and Counsel, Hartford-Empire Company, ibid., p. 409.

[29] Cf. Leverett S. Lyon, Myron W. Watkins and Victor Abramson, Government and Economic Life, Vol. I (Washington, D. C.: The Brookings Institution, 1939), pp. 132–136.

Office which threaten to interfere with his application, he may have the patent pending protection for years and still, if successful in establishing his claim, may enjoy the seventeen years of assured monopoly. Where a company is large and powerful it possesses advantages over small rivals in appeals to the Patent Office and, if necessary, in appeals to the courts from rulings of that office. As a result, the pending protection may be a perfectly satisfactory safeguard for the claims of financially powerful companies.

One of the most important patents on feeder equipment held by the Hartford-Empire Company was applied for in 1910 and finally issued in 1937. For twenty-seven years independents could not manufacture or use the machine without considerable risk. Generally they chose to come in under Hartford-Empire licensing arrangements. In other words, the monopoly on an important machine was made to last for forty-four years instead of seventeen.[30]

It is obvious that the one big company had come to hold power immeasurably beyond that contained in any single patent right. Its position seemed so well bulwarked that independents had little chance of edging in with any sort of effective feeding and forming equipment. In fact, the wide coverage of its seven hundred patents and its financial strength tended to force new inventions into its hands. And, armed as it was, the company was able to dictate to the container industry. No enterpriser, however experienced and well-financed, could enter any branch of bottle manufacture without its permission. Officials of the company frankly admitted the situation. They were able to say whether the container industry would have a thousand or five hundred or fifty producing companies. They merely insisted that they were better judges of the needs of the bottle industry than any prospective enterpriser.[31] Possibly they were, but in their hands rested a tremendous power and responsibility that seems strange in a society dedicated in legal and economic theory to a system of competitive individualism.

Effects of the Patent Control

It is axiomatic that competition in any industry requires at least moderately free entry for new enterprisers. The patent pool operated so as to eliminate any chance of this requirement in the glass container industry. For some time Owens-Illinois had not been licensing any producers under its vacuum feeder patents, and Hartford-Empire carefully restricted the number of its licensees. Testimony of the president of the later company suggested that producers had little chance of gaining permission

---

[30] T. N. E. C., *Hearings*, Part II, Patents, pp. 436–441, 452–453.
[31] *Ibid.*, testimony of F. Goodwin Smith, President, Hartford-Empire Company, p. 413.

to enter. He commented that his company did "occasionally let people in," but the prospects were not very bright for applicants.[32]

In 1936 an investor, believing there were opportunities for a glass plant in Detroit, was not allowed to risk his capital. He was told that the industry had more than sufficient capacity, and he could argue if he liked, but he would not get a license.[33] Correspondence found by the Temporary National Economic Committee indicated how coöperation between Owens-Illinois and Hartford-Empire allowed the large companies already in the field to determine when new competitors were needed. At times various branches of the industry were overproducing and added investment would have been unwise. However, those already in the industry would have been more than human if they had not almost always believed that their field was crowded. They hardly could have been expected to welcome competitors with open arms. And as things were, they could maintain with relative ease a policy of restriction. All but a few large producers were licensed for only one particular kind of container. And many were limited in the amounts they could produce or the market areas in which they could sell.

With coöperation so far developed, there was inevitably little competitive independence in the pricing of glass containers. The large companies acted as the price-leaders for their fields—Thatcher for milk bottles, Ball Brothers for fruit jars, and Hazel-Atlas for wide-mouth containers. While setting prices for wide-mouth ware, Hazel-Atlas took its prices for its prescription ware and beer bottles from those listed by Owens-Illinois. Although the industry seemed constantly concerned with the improvement of glassware, the similarity in machinery prevented any important quality competition from arising to replace the absent price competition.

While over the long run prices declined materially, they showed a considerable rigidity in short periods. Between 1925 and 1929 the average price for containers dropped by about 10 per cent. In those years, however, technical changes were important, and it is almost certain that a competitive industry would have offered at least as large and probably larger reductions. In the face of depression conditions the industry was able to maintain prices much better than most. From 1929 to the depth of the depression, prices dropped by less than 10 per cent, and after 1933, when labor costs were increasing, they rose very little.[34]

At least in the sale of milk bottles the price control was strong enough to use price discrimination whenever it was worth while. One company, a licensee of Hartford-Empire, had been given the exclusive right to sell milk bottles in Texas. It also sold in other markets, notably St. Louis.

---

[32] T. N. E. C., *Hearings*, Part II, Patents, p. 423.

[33] *Ibid.*, p. 798.

[34] *Ibid.*, pp. 823, 827.

Here there were two other licensees. In Texas the company charged between eight and ten dollars a gross for bottles that it sold in St. Louis for about six dollars and fifty cents. The difference in supply conditions in the two markets, and not freight rates, accounted for the discrimination. The experience of an independent suggests how the discrimination was maintained. Seeing a promising opportunity in Texas, a small producer, the Knape-Coleman Company, located itself in the center of the state. For a time it did very well, and its competitor markedly lessened the discrimination by lowering Texas prices. But while the independent could make bottles successfully, it could not take care of the patent situation. It was sued for patent infringement on nine or ten claims, and resisted until one of the partners found himself and his one lawyer in court facing "a half-train-load of attorneys and equipment."[35] His attorney was so lost in the crowd that he asked for a recess and settled the case out of court. The license the company needed in order to continue could not be obtained, and it soon sold out to the Hartford-Empire licensee.

It is not surprising that a number of the operating companies in bottle manufacture showed earnings well above the average for competitive industry. Between 1934 and 1939, after all charges were met, the Hazel-Atlas Company made net profits on its net worth ranging between 11.61% and 17.63%, with an average well over 14%. Owens-Illinois managed to stay above this average in each of the years except one. Milk bottles brought the Thatcher Manufacturing Company returns that were above 20 per cent each year and above 30 in one year. Earnings of Hartford-Empire also were large. When the company was organizing the patent pool it made only between 3 and 8%. But its profits increased sharply as its power increased. It will be remembered that by 1934 three of the largest producing companies, Hazel-Atlas, Ball Brothers, and the Lynch Corporation, and many small companies, had exchanged independence for coöperation and taken out licenses. As a consequence the annual income of Hartford-Empire from license fees and royalties climbed from two million to over six million. In the years between 1934 and 1937 its approximate earnings were 16%, 23%, 48% and 67%.[36]

Recent Changes

World War II dealt kindly with the glass container companies, as metal containers for civilian supply were severely curtailed by war demands for metal products. Gross income of Owens-Illinois, for example, more than doubled, increasing from eighty-two million dollars in 1939

[35] *Ibid.*, p. 614.
[36] These percentages represent the relationship between the net income realized in operations and the net capital employed in operations; *cf. ibid.*, pp. 794–797.

to one hundred and sixty-nine million in 1945. In the pre-war year its net income before taxes was ten million dollars on assets of eighty-seven millions, a comparatively modest profit rate just below 12 per cent. In 1945 the net had risen to twenty-seven millions and assets to one hundred and twenty-three millions to yield 22 per cent on assets. War-time taxes left the Company a net slightly under nine millions, which was only a few hundred thousand dollars above the net after taxes received in 1939.[37] Meanwhile tin containers have returned to the market and glass bottle shipments have dropped, as can makers set out to recover their old markets. This inter-industry competition has been vigorous and unquestionably has curtailed the power of glass container producers. The extent to which it will react on the central patent holder, Hartford-Empire, is problematical. The bottle companies, particularly Owens-Illinois, have organized a vigorous use of non-price competition in sales and advertising. Owens-Illinois opened its new Duraglas Center in Toledo, Ohio, in 1948 and offered the research facilities of this plant to food processors. This research covers all aspects of food processing, bottling, advertising, and selling, and the offer of this complete marketing service is to be used to meet the competition of can companies.

Another unsettling factor in the industry was the defeat of Hartford-Empire and the leading producers of glass containers in the anti-trust suit brought against them.[38] Among other things, the court decree required the dissolution of Glass Container Association, the sale by Ball Brothers of one of its plants, and the disposal by Lynch Corporation of certain glass-making machinery. Corning Glass Works was required to divest itself of all stock owned in Hartford. The Government asked for the dissolution of Hartford-Empire, but instead the trial court required compulsory licensing, royalty-free of Hartford's patents. The Supreme Court refused to sanction dissolution and also objected to royalty-free licensing. Dissolution is reserved as a possible remedy if compulsory licensing at reasonable royalty rates does not correct effectively the monopoly conditions found to exist in the industry.

The effect of the decree has been to open the way to the entry of newcomers in the industry; to reduce the royalties of Hartford by more than 50 per cent; and to achieve substantial savings to manufacturers of glass containers, presumably to the benefit of consumers.[39]

---

[37] Moody's, *Industrials*, 1946, p. 1967.
[38] Hartford-Empire Co. *v.* U. S., 323 U. S. 386 (1945), 324 U. S. 570 (1945).
[39] House Committee on Small Business, *United States versus Economic Concentration and Monopoly* (Washington, D. C., U. S. Government Printing Office, 1946), pp. 243–244.

26

The Sugar Institute

For the last fifty years competition has been seriously constrained in the American sugar refining industry. It first gave way before a sweeping combination movement which placed a single company in a dominant position. Then, a few years after public prosecution was directed against the giant concern, it was throttled by the dozen large refiners refusing to maintain independent policies. Their coöperation was organized and directed by a trade association ostensibly formed to improve competitive practices and to supply statistical services to the members of the industry. In 1936 the Department of Justice and the Supreme Court of the United States ended the usefulness of the first association, but competition seems to have little chance in the industry. A second association immediately succeeded the first, and its efforts and the long tradition of coöperation will probably prevent any great degree of independence from appearing in the policies of the major companies.

Sugar-cane and beets constitute the plant materials from which sugar is produced. Except for small amounts of cane grown in Louisiana and Florida, the domestic refiners depend for sugar-cane on Cuba, Hawaii, the Philippine Islands and Puerto Rico. The cane is cut and taken directly to raw sugar mills, where it is crushed, and the liquid cleared of most of its impurities. This first processing yields raw sugar containing about 4 per cent of foreign matter. Most of the product is then shipped to American refineries, which remove the remaining impurities. In recent years less than six hundred thousand tons of the total consumption of six million tons has come into the United States as refined sugar.[1] Much of this came from Cuba, which for a few years enjoyed a preferential tariff rate. Tariffs have always existed to prevent the supplies from other than the insular possessions from being important, and in recent years quotas have fixed the size of all imports.[2]

---

[1] T. N. E. C., Monograph No. 18, *Trade Association Survey* (Washington, D. C., 1941), p. 107.

[2] For a summary of government intervention in the sugar industry, see United

Since most of the raw cane sugar refined in the United States is imported, refineries are located on the seaboard in or around New York, Philadelphia, San Francisco, New Orleans, Baltimore, Boston, and Savannah. They serve adjacent market areas and reach inland to come into competition with beet sugar produced in the Middle West and the South Central States. The sugar derived from beets is refined in the beet-growing areas and supplies close to one-fifth of the total sugar consumption. It differs in no respect from cane sugar, although it usually sells at slightly lower prices.

THE COMBINATION MOVEMENT

Until 1887 competition seemed to be the ruling condition in the refining industry. The number of companies was not large but appeared adequate to keep them independent of one another.[3] Twenty-six refineries were being operated by twenty-three companies, and the largest had only 17 per cent of the total production. Unfortunately for the future of competition, seventeen of the companies and twenty of the refineries were brought together in the newly-formed Sugar Refineries Company. Capitalized at fifty million dollars, this company exchanged its securities in the form of negotiable trust certificates for the capital stock of the acquired companies. The first action of the board of trustees, in whom control rested, was to close sixteen of the refineries. H. O. Havemeyer, who was largely responsible for the combination, insisted that excessive competition had so reduced profits before 1887 that some escape had to be found. And he freely admitted that very generous tariff protection against foreign competition made it possible to organize the monopoly trust.[4]

In 1890 New York State won a victory over the trust in successfully maintaining that one of the constituent companies had exceeded its charter powers when it entered the trust.[5] The only result, however, was to force the monopoly to change its name and its form of organization. The trustees incorporated the American Sugar Refining Company in New Jersey. Its capitalization was $50,000,000, the same as that of the trustee organization, and its shares were exchanged for the trustee certificates, while the former trustees moved over to become its board of directors. H. O. Havemeyer became its president. New York was unable to keep

States Cane Sugar Refiners' Association, *Sugar Economics, Statistics, and Documents* (1938), pp. 10–20.

[3] For a discussion of price determination where a small number of competitors is present, see Chap. 29.

[4] Industrial Commission, *Preliminary Report on Trusts and Industrial Combinations* (Washington, D. C., 1900), Testimony, pp. 133, 137.

[5] People *v.* North River Sugar Refining Co., 121 N. Y. 582 (1890).

even companies incorporated in the State out of the combination and, of course, could do nothing to disturb the national combine.

There remained four refineries located in Philadelphia which continued to compete with the combine. They were large, producing about one-third of the total for the country, but in time they also became cooperative. In 1892 their stockholders exchanged their stocks for those of the American Sugar Refining Company, and the combine now held over 90 per cent of the producing capacity of the United States. It will be remembered that the Department of Justice sued one of the Philadelphia companies, the E. C. Knight Company, seeking to upset the stock transfer so as to separate these companies from the combine, but the weird definition of interstate commerce by the Supreme Court defeated the attempt.[6] The Court recognized that "the American Sugar Refining Company acquired nearly complete control of the manufacture of refined sugar," but held that the Sherman Act was powerless to reach the monopoly. The Federal statute declared illegal any monopoly in the "trade or commerce among the several states," and the Court viewed the manufacture of sugar in a state for sale in other states as being distinct from trade or commerce in sugar.[7]

From this time until 1910 the combine was threatened now and then by the appearance of new cane sugar refineries and by the competition of beet sugar. At various times nearly a dozen independent companies built plants to refine raw cane sugar, but their independence was short-lived. Four companies were brought at one time into the combination through the organization of a holding company—the National Sugar Refining Company of New Jersey. The preferred stock of the holding company was exchanged for the capital stock of the independents, and the common stock, amounting to a par value of ten million dollars, was given to Mr. Havemeyer of American Sugar for his services in effecting the promotion. This stock was finally placed in a voting trust having officers of American Sugar as beneficiaries.[8] Other companies were forced to sell out to the combine after meeting cut-throat competition that drove prices below cost, and still others succumbed to attractive offers permitted by the large financial resources of the American Sugar Refining Company.

After 1897 tariff protection and improvements in the cultivation and processing of beets brought a marked growth in beet sugar refineries.[9] Output increased sixfold, and by 1907 sixty-three factories were in opera-

---

[6] United States v. E. C. Knight Company, 156 U. S. 1, 5 (1894).

[7] *Ibid.*

[8] For a description of the various combinations of this period, see Jones, *op. cit.*, pp. 92–102.

[9] S. Fabricant, *The Output of Manufacturing Industries, 1899–1937* (National Bureau of Economic Research, Inc., 1940), p. 139.

tion.[10] The factories were generally small, and the easy growth of their number promised a possible restoration of competition in the whole industry. The American Sugar Refining Company, however, could see that possibility and took effective action. It increased its capital stock from seventy-five to ninety million dollars so as to have the where-withal for acquisitions, obtained substantial amounts in rebates from a number of railroads, and flooded the markets of beet sugar producers with low-priced sugar. A considerable number of beet sugar refineries sold out to the combine, and others coöperated with it on prices and output matters. By 1910, probably half of the beet sugar industry was under control of the American Sugar Refining Company or of officers of that company.

In spite of its best efforts, the combine probably controlled only slightly more than 60 per cent of the output of sugar in 1910, when the Federal Government started suit under the Sherman Act. Independents had persisted in entering and staying in the field, so the dominant firm actually lost some ground in the decade after 1900. A considerable growth in the industry during the war prosperity of 1915 to 1920, the constraining effect of the anti-trust suit and the apparent efficiency of smaller companies very markedly reduced the proportion of the total business done by it. In 1922, when American Sugar accepted a consent decree which reduced its stock control over two beet sugar companies and one cane sugar company, it had fallen back into the position where it refined little more than a quarter of the total production.[11]

Competition After 1920

War-time price-fixing for sugar was ended in 1920, and the industry found itself with a sharply reduced demand and considerable over-capacity. The demand declined further in 1927, when the desire for slimness, taking on the proportions of a national campaign, markedly reduced the consumption. The capacity of the industry was large enough to turn out at least 50 per cent more than was being sold. Pressure from this source and a considerable lack of information on the amounts being produced and the size of inventories brought recurring surpluses onto the market. Since the product was highly standardized and brands were not of great importance, over-supplies had direct and material influences on price. The margin over the cost of raw sugar received by the refiner dropped from a high of 1.54 cents per pound in 1919 to just over one cent in 1927.[12]

---

[10] J. G. Glover and W. B. Cornell (editors), *The Development of American Industries* (New York, Prentice-Hall, Inc., 1933), p. 275.

[11] Jones, *op. cit.*, p. 108.

[12] The refiners' margin usually makes up about 14 per cent of the final price paid by the consumer.

In addition to suffering a one-third reduction in their margin, most of the refiners were forced by competition to cut prices in a number of hidden ways and to increase their costs by added services. They tended to match one another in the base price quoted, while cutting their effective prices in various ways. Where price concessions alone would gain a producer a particular sale, he might offer large commissions to brokers, lower freight charges, higher payments to customers for the use of their storage facilities or for the performance of services such as advertising.[13] Some refiners refused to depart from their basic prices, but by 1927, 30 per cent of sugar was sold with some sort of concession.

Competition also forced the refiners into a costly service and sales competition. In order to gain customers, a refiner would hold supplies of sugar at various consignment points for delivery into local market areas. His success would only result in the duplication of such facilities by his competitors with no resultant gain for anyone. The cost of this service, formerly borne by local jobbers and wholesalers, was markedly increased by the duplication, and fell on the refiners instead of on the local agencies. Sales campaigns undertaken to gain customers resulted in the same stalemate. The total consumption of sugar was not increased, while the costs of competition did increase.

Profits in the industry suffered. Until 1925 earnings were unsatisfactory, but it then appeared that possibly the industry was settling down to more stable policies. The net income of the cane sugar refiners rose to over 7 per cent of their net capital in 1926, but fell disastrously in the following year, when the industry reported no net income.[14] The fortunes of individual companies varied considerably, but the American Sugar Refining Company, with about a quarter of the capacity of the industry, showed fluctuations in income that were apparently typical. With operating deficits in three of the five years before 1926, it then made a substantial recovery, only to suffer in 1927 from the largest operating deficit of the whole post-war period.[15]

One large producer went out of business, and the existence of others was obviously threatened, as competitive forces worked through destructively low prices to remove over-capacity. The competitive process, however, was slow and painful where large firms were involved, and it disappeared before it had sufficient time to correct the over-capacity. In 1927 representatives of five large refineries met to find some means of protecting themselves against competition, and decided, as others had before them, to use the trade association device. Articles of incorporation and by-laws for the proposed association were drawn up, and early in 1928 the Sugar Institute began operations with the five promoters on the board

---

[13] Sugar Institute, Inc., *et al.*, *v.* United States, 297 U. S. 553, 574–575 (1936).
[14] U. S. Cane Sugar Refiners' Association, *op. cit.*, Table 72, p. 89.
[15] Poor's *Industrial Manual*, 1928, p. 1576.

of directors or in important managerial positions. Other refiners joined until 70 to 80 per cent of the industry was represented.[16] The actual administrative work of the Institute was performed by its executive secretary and a small staff of about twenty. During its first three years, annual administrative expenses amounted to about $200,000.[17] At the same time the beet sugar and the Louisiana cane sugar producers organized a similar association, the Domestic Sugar Bureau.[18]

ACTIVITIES OF THE SUGAR INSTITUTE

Prior to 1912, trade associations had been commonly nothing more than pooling devices which used some sort of central office to implement an agreement restricting competition. A more vigorous use of the Sherman Act after 1900 drove these associations to cover, along with some other monopoly organizations. In 1911 the clear statement of the Rule of Reason in the Supreme Court decisions on the Standard Oil and American Tobacco cases drew attention to the legality of a certain measure of coöperation between competitors in the same trade. And A. J. Eddy, in his book, *The New Competition,* showed the tremendous economic possibilities residing in a formally organized coöperation that aimed not to restrain competition, but to make it more informed and intelligent and less costly. When war-time economic controls were introduced after 1917, the desire of the War Industries Board to deal with

---

[16] 297 U. S. 553, 565. The high degree of concentration in the industry is apparent in the following table:

Cane Sugar Refiners	Per cent of 1927 production
American Sugar Refining Company (5 plants)	25.06
National Sugar Refining Company of New Jersey (3 plants)	22.07
California and Hawaiian Sugar Refining Corporation, Ltd.	10.84
Pennsylvania Sugar Company	6.73
Arbuckle Bros.	5.80
Western Sugar Refinery	4.46
Godchaux Sugars, Inc.	4.02
W. J. McCahan Sugar Refining and Molasses Co.	3.60
Savannah Sugar Refining Corporation	3.26
Revere Sugar Refinery	3.20
Imperial Sugar Company	3.00
Spreckels Sugar Corporation	2.66
Total For Twelve Companies	94.70

[17] T. N. E. C., *Monograph* No. 18, p. 116.

[18] Between 80% and 90% of beet sugar and about 30% of Louisiana cane sugar capacity was represented in the Bureau; *cf.* T. N. E. C., *ibid.*, p. 116.

associations representing a whole industry gave further impetus to trade association growth. By the end of the war there were probably some two thousand of these associations in existence. Some of them were weak or very limited in their functions, and their number declined during the following decade. By the time the Sugar Institute came into existence, there were probably between eight hundred and a thousand associations of importance in interstate industry.[19] The services performed by these organizations varied a great deal and in detail make up a long list.[20] It is possible, however, to classify the commonly performed services under a few headings, and the Sugar Institute undertook most of these general activities.

Promotion Services

Trade associations have undertaken various activities to promote the interests of the whole industry in a variety of connections. A number in the building trades have attempted to influence local building restrictions affecting the use of particular materials. Others have served as lobbying agents around state and Federal legislatures. Tariff hearings inevitably attract trade association officials to Washington. Advertising has been an important function, particularly where the product of an industry is directly exposed to the competition of substitutes produced in other industries.[21] Since the demand for sugar had been declining during the twenties, and had probably suffered in 1927 from the advertising of one of the large cigarette companies urging consumers to "Reach for a Lucky Instead of a Sweet," it was almost inevitable that the Sugar Institute would undertake advertising for the industry. Members paid the Institute an assessment of fifteen cents per ton to provide for an advertising campaign to increase the demand for sugar. In 1929 and again in 1930 nearly seven hundred thousand dollars were spent for this purpose.[22] The program did not bring any striking result. Consumption of cane sugar increased about 4 per cent from 1928 to 1929, and declined about 2 per cent in the following year.[23] It is quite possible that the expenditures prevented a further shrinkage in consumption, but at least the positive results were not great.

---

[19] National Industrial Conference Board, Inc., *Trade Associations* (New York, 1925), p. 326.

[20] Simon N. Whitney, *Trade Associations and Industrial Control* (New York, Central Book Co., 1934), Chap. 2.

[21] F. T. C., *Open-Price Trade Associations* (Washington, D. C., 1929), pp. 241–245.

[22] T. N. E. C., *Monograph* No. 18, p. 116.

[23] United States Cane Sugar Refiners' Association, *op. cit.*, p. 11.

Trade Statistics

To act intelligently in competitive surroundings the producer needs a great deal of market information that individual firms may be able to get only through coöperation with others. The present and future demand and supply conditions of the whole industry are difficult for the individual to estimate, and yet are important for intelligent planning. A number of trade associations have undertaken as an important part of their work the collection and reporting of trade statistics. Data collected have usually covered the productive capacity of the industry, production, stocks on hand, orders received, shipments, unfilled orders, and other matters of concern to a particular industry.[24] Individual companies report to the secretary of the trade association as frequently as the industry deems desirable, and the statistics are compiled and reported back to the member companies and may also be made available to the trade generally through journals or newspapers. The reports may or may not be detailed. In some instances the statistics are reported for the individual firms, where in others only state or national averages are returned to the reporting companies. In recent years associations have tended to keep the information more general in order to avoid any appearance that supposed competitors are revealing details of their business to one another in order to reach agreements restraining competition.[25]

With a dangerous over-capacity in the industry, the cane sugar refiners needed some means to adjust current production to demand if they were going to bring order and stability to their business. And through the Institute they undertook the collection of information on current trade conditions. Each company received weekly a report showing production and deliveries for the past week and stocks on hand, with its percentages of the totals noted. And in addition, each company was informed of the weekly production and deliveries of each of its competitors. Other sales data were collected and the capacity of each refinery was reported from time to time. The only information made available to buyers of sugar through trade journals concerned total production and deliveries. Later, when the Institute was threatened with prosecution under the anti-trust laws, it made public some additional figures showing per capita consumption by states.[26] Because several of the large refiners objected, the Institute did not collect information on new business. On the whole, the refiners' unwillingness to supply certain statistics and their desire for a direct control over price-cutting made the collection

---

[24] F. T. C., *Open-Price Trade Associations*, p. 85.
[25] *Cf.* 262 U .S. 371, 390.
[26] T. N. E. C., *Monograph* No. 18, p. 121.

of trade statistics a matter of secondary importance in the work of the Institute. Its primary work concerned the pricing of sugar.

Price Reporting

When the modern trade association was first gaining popularity its greatest promise was that it would offer a means to make prices open to the whole trade. Destructive price-cutting arising from ignorance of competitive prices would be eliminated, and buyers and sellers would possess information needed for intelligent pricing.[27] If the prices reported to the secretary and then sent by him to members of the association were actual prices on sales which had taken place, the coöperation would not restrain competition, but would eliminate hidden price-cutting in the form of secret concessions and rebates. Discrimination favoring large buyers who played one seller off against another by falsely reporting offers of low prices would disappear and prices would be held at normal levels by the open information available to all. At the time the Sugar Institute was organized, there were in the neighborhood of one hundred and fifty of such open-price associations, although they had even then begun the move to make prices open only to members of the association. It might seem only reasonable to refuse the price information to companies that did not support the association, but the scheme lost an important part of its claimed virtue when buyers ceased to be informed.

In this respect the Sugar Institute was free of guilt. Its open-price work merely continued reporting practices previously used by the individual firms that made "basis" prices open to all. Refiners posted on their bulletin boards a price representing the cost of raw sugar and the refining margin. Any change by one company was quickly made known to other sellers and to buyers. The basis price, however, was usually nothing more than a wishful thought on the part of the refiners. Certainly through the twenties the common use of rebates and direct or indirect price concessions to individual buyers robbed the quotations of any significance. Only the weakest or the most absent-minded buyer thought of paying the quoted price.

By agreeing to a so-called Code of Ethics members of the Institute set out to make the basis price really effective. Any form of price concessions was attacked by the following provisions:[28]

(1) All discriminations between customers should be abolished. To that end sugar should be sold only upon open prices and terms publicly announced;

---

[27] Eddy, *op. cit.*, Chap. 10.
[28] T. N. E. C., *Monograph* No. 18, pp. 119–120.

(2) The Institute condemns as unbusinesslike, uneconomic and unsound, any concessions made to purchasers on the basis of quantity purchased;

(3) The following trade practices are condemned as unethical, wasteful and unbusinesslike:

(i) special allowances to buyers for services performed such as brokerage, storage, or advertising;

(ii) split billings which allowed buyers to take delivery of sugar in carload lots and pay the carload freight rate while they paid for the sugar as if it were shipped at various times in less than carload lots;

(iii) concessions which allowed the buyer to pay less than the all-rail freight charge except where the buyer *insisted* on using a less costly form of transport;

(4) No options to purchase sugar at set prices should be given to buyers;

(5) Sugar should not be left on consignment in the hands of buyers but should always be kept under control of the refiner;

(6) Sugar should be sold under uniform sales contracts.

The Institute was not satisfied merely to formulate this Code, but set out to "raise" the morals of the industry. Personal pressure and persuasion were exerted to get management officers and directors to adhere to the Code, and frequent meetings of the officers of various companies were promoted in order to remove distrust. Its efforts were successful, and the industry sold sugar to all buyers at the published basis price. Rebating that had on the average kept the effective price about three cents per hundred pounds below the basis price was effectively stopped.

Services Affecting Production Costs

While trade associations have generally shown a considerable interest in pricing policies, they have not neglected the cost problems of their industries. Their services have been of two general types: assistance to the individual firms with cost accounting problems, and a variety of aids designed to reduce costs of production. In 1916 the Federal Trade Commission reported that investigation showed that not more than 10 per cent of manufacturers and merchants actually knew their costs.[29] And at least half of them did not even make estimates, but priced goods according to what they thought competitors were doing or were going to do. Government price-fixing and excess profits taxation during the war centered attention on this fact, and a number of trade associations undertook to improve conditions in their industries. Their work took two forms. They persuaded members of the association to adopt a recommended form of cost accounting in order to get some uniformity in cost computations. Probably one-fifth of the general trade associations in existence during the twenties undertook work of this sort. A smaller percentage went further in trying to get individual firms to adopt a

[29] F. T. C., *Annual Report*, 1916, p. 15.

standard practice in the treatment of a number of cost items such as depreciation, overhead, and interest on capital.[30] A still smaller number of associations circulated the cost of individual members throughout the membership.

This last service offered individual companies a chance to compare their own costs with those of other producers, and might serve the second purpose of the association in allowing high-cost firms to effect economies. Other cost-reducing services, however, were of greater importance. Under the guidance of trade associations a number of industries simplified or standardized their products so as to reduce materially costs of production or the costs of carrying very large inventories. The Associated Metal Lath Manufacturers, for instance, had been instrumental in reducing the varieties and sizes of metal laths from 128 to 24. Associations also performed a number of services for the industry which, if performed by individual firms, would have been very costly. Traffic bureaus were organized to advise individual companies on ways to reduce freight costs and to represent the industry at rate hearings. Credit bureaus have established credit ratings for customers and have given their members valuable information that individually they would find difficult and costly to collect. The Federal Trade Commission found a typical service of this sort being performed by the Music Industries Association. Past reports from members had given the Association data showing the reliability of some twenty thousand retail music dealers, and individual members constantly used this information in their dealings with retailers.[31]

The Sugar Institute claimed the creation of a credit bureau as one of the purposes of its organization, and it carried on research into possible non-food uses of sugar at the Mellon Institute of Industrial Research.[32] Such projects could have been pursued by individual firms, but duplication would have been costly, and probably would have achieved smaller results. The Institute also attacked the existing high cost of holding sugar stocks at a large number of consignment points. It was able to get refiners to drop a number of them in the North and the South, but failed completely in the central states, where cane sugar met the competition of beet sugar. On the whole its efforts were not very successful. Between 1927 and 1931 the number of consignment points actually increased from 344 to 468.[33] In general, the results achieved by the Institute in developing cost-reducing measures appear to have been very small—probably because it was not as interested in the work as were many other associations.

[30] F. T. C., *Open-Price Trade Associations,* Chap. 4.
[31] *Ibid.,* p. 223.
[32] *Cf.* 297 U. S. 553, 577.
[33] T. N. E. C., *Monograph* No. 18, p. 129.

EFFECTS OF THE INSTITUTE'S WORK

The economic services which the sugar industry performed coöperatively through the Institute largely concerned pricing policies. Producers in other fields found the trade association a much more valuable instrument than did the sugar refiners in improving the quality of market information, in eliminating costly and undesirable trade practices, and in the performance of a variety of cost-reducing services. The important Code of Ethics did not touch such matters as misrepresentation or the defamation of competitors, or any of the great list of competitive practices that may be deemed unfair and uneconomical. It aimed merely to eliminate price concessions. It is true that open price-cutting is more to be desired than hidden concessions, but the work of the Institute resulted in a uniform pricing practice that was likely to be settled coöperatively and not competitively. And in addition, once the basis price was fixed, buyers found they were facing the combination of producers whenever they tried for lower prices. The Institute examined the accounts of refiners and distributors and, according to the Department of Justice, held trials of refiners suspected of code violations.[34] As a result, before they could get a single price concession, buyers had to attack the whole price structure resting on the use of nothing but the published basis price.

The Basis Price

Through the coöperation of refiners responsible for 70 to 80 per cent of cane sugar production, the Institute was not only able to control the price-making methods of the industry, but it inevitably influenced the actual prices that were set. In pre-Institute days the refiners had announced their basis price, which applied to future sales until changed. They had customarily contracted to supply sugar at the current price for a period in the future running up to sixty days. Large buyers such as the manufacturers of Coca-Cola and Canada Dry ginger ale, and some chain stores and biscuit companies, were able to buy under even longer contracts. At the same time the refiners frequently gave the buyer a guarantee against price declines. Reduction in the basis price occurring before deliveries were made was extended to old contracts. These arrangements favorable to the buyer were ended about the time the Institute was organized. Contracts were limited to thirty days and the guarantee against price declines was withdrawn.

This pricing practice allowed the refiners to apply the former higher basis to all existing contracts when prices were reduced. And it allowed

[34] 297 U. S. 553, 565.

individual companies to experiment with higher prices without loss of trade. A refiner could post higher prices which would be reported by the Institute to his competitors. If they failed to follow, little harm was done. He merely returned to the former basis. There was no evidence that members of the Institute actually agreed on prices that should be charged, but the pricing arrangement served to protect the basis price against reduction. In addition, while members attending Institute meetings were careful not to make agreements concerning future prices, they certainly discussed the existing basis price, and by no very devious implication reflected their opinions on future price policies. According to the Department of Justice the Institute itself supplemented its information service with propaganda designed to raise prices.[35] In the Circuit Court Judge Mack commented that the results achieved were sufficient evidence to show collusion in price-fixing.[36] The Supreme Court observed that there was also a "high degree" of coöperation between the Institute and the Domestic Sugar Bureau, although again there was no evidence that the two reached specific agreements concerning the relative prices for cane and beet sugar.[37]

A comparison of sugar prices during the Institute period with those of earlier years suggests that coöperation paid well. There were fewer changes in the basis price, and the changes raised the level markedly. On the average, there had been forty-six changes a year in the five-year period before 1928, and only twenty-one in the five years before government prosecution of the Institute.[38] Some of this stability arose from smaller fluctuations in raw sugar prices, but coöperation seems to account for a considerable portion of it. And the margin between raw and refined sugar prices widened at the same time that stability was developing. This margin representing the refiners' income per hundred pounds of refined sugar had been dangerously low. In the latter part of 1927 it stood at 95 cents, and in January, 1928, with the appearance of the Institute, it jumped to $1.17 and then to $1.38. The companies coöperating in the Institute thereby transformed a 1927 loss of $250,000 into a profit for the following year of over sixteen millions of dollars.[39] When adjustments are made to the margins earned in various periods, so as to remove the influence of changed price and cost levels, it appears that during the Institute period the industry enjoyed a margin at least one-third greater than during the war period when the margin was regulated to yield a fair profit to the refiners.[40] In view of the fact that the industry was using only about 60 per cent of its capacity, the increase in

[35] *Loc. cit.*

[36] United States *v.* Sugar Institute, 15 Fed. Supp. 817, 888–890 (1934).

[37] 297 U. S. 553, 584.

[38] Whitney, *op. cit.*, p. 112.

[39] T. N. E. C., *Monograph* No. 18, p. 120.

[40] Whitney, *op. cit.*, p. 217.

margin is very striking. And since evidence suggests that the demand for sugar is elastic, the higher prices indicate a lack of interest in the long-run welfare of the industry.[41] Apparently the refiners merely desired an end of price competition.

Price Discrimination

One of the avowed aims of the promoters of the Sugar Institute was the elimination of discrimination. The industry, however, seemed to have a strange idea of just what constituted discriminatory treatment. Too often it was confused with competition. Price reductions were condemned because all buyers were not equally able in wringing concessions from the refiners. And a number of the steps ostensibly taken to remove discrimination actually created it. Quantity discounts were treated as unethical, in spite of the fact that the cost of handling and marketing was lower for large sales than for small. Furthermore, when contracts for the delivery of sugar were limited to thirty days, large concerns were injured. Small buyers were satisfied with such contracts and were not hurt by the disappearance of long-term arrangements, but manufacturing companies using large amounts of sugar faced the danger of greater fluctuation in one of their important costs. And the refiners themselves suffered. While they increased their ability to change prices they lost the steadying effect on production given by long-term contracts.[42] Other customers were injured by the elimination of any allowance for the use of their own bags or for the return of used bags. Previously some buyers had saved as much as ten cents per hundred pounds by supplying their own containers. For fairness to buyers who found an advantage in the practice and for its obvious economy the allowance should have been continued. But the Institute saw in it, as in quantity discounts and long-term contracts, a means by which concessions might be wrung out of refiners. To Judge Mack it seemed obvious that the refiners deliberately turned their backs on economical methods of marketing.[43]

More serious discrimination developed in connection with the shipping of sugar. In the past, whenever competitive conditions had permitted, the refiners had charged some buyers discriminately high freight rates. Very generally sugar was sold at delivered prices made up of the basis price with an added charge for delivery. The addition, however, did not always equal the actual freight cost. In certain areas refiners shipped by way of low-cost waterway hauls on rivers, canals, or the Great Lakes, but charged the all-rail rate. And in many instances where

---

[41] *Cf.* 15 Fed. Supp. 817, 869.
[42] *Ibid.*, p. 865.
[43] *Ibid.*, p. 879.

all-rail routes were used, the added charge for freight did not equal the actual shipping cost.

Buyers in the North central states[44] were supplied at delivered prices from refineries in Philadelphia, Baltimore, and New York. The actual freight costs per hundred pounds from Baltimore were one cent lower than from Philadelphia and three cents lower than from New York. But delivered prices from all three points were based on the freight cost from Philadelphia. Baltimore refiners made a profit of one cent on the freight charge, while those in New York had to use two cents of their refining income to cover their loss on the freight service. If the supply available from Baltimore for the central states were not sufficient to meet the demand at current prices, the Baltimore refiners with perfectly good reason could base their prices on the cost of marginal supplies coming from Philadelphia. If adequate supplies came from these two sources, and if New York refiners could sell in no other areas, they would be forced to make the best of a bad situation and sell at the Philadelphia delivered price. Until over-capacity became a problem in the twenties, no such excuse existed for the pricing arrangement which allowed New York refiners to charge discriminately high prices in their local market areas while they were dumping some part of their output at low prices in the central states. The refusal of refiners to stay in their natural market areas was a common phenomenon. Located on the seaboard, they persisted in reaching into the interior, where they met not only competition from the beet sugar producers of the Middle West and South central states, but competition from other seaboard refiners. At certain times and in certain areas the company selling in a distant market was able to get prices high enough to cover the basis price and the full freight cost, but generally the seller was forced to "absorb" some of the freight charge in order to reduce his delivered prices. But buyers in nearby markets were given no such concessions. They paid at least the full basis price and the actual cost of making delivery. For example, after 1917 Texas buyers were supplied from refineries located at New Orleans and from local refineries. They paid delivered prices covering the freight cost from New Orleans regardless of the origin of the sugar. Texas refiners, of course, made very attractive profits. If supplies from New Orleans were needed to meet the demand in Texas, the local refiners properly enjoyed profits from their location, and local buyers were not injured. But they were injured when Texas refineries sold some of their supply in distant markets at delivered prices that did not cover their full refining and distribution costs.

After 1920, traditional pricing policies were not maintained with any

[44] In Central Freight Association territory, which includes roughly the area lying east of the Mississippi River, west of a line from Buffalo to Pittsburgh and north of the Ohio River.

regularity, and by 1927 the refiners were engaged in a disorderly and planless price-cutting. The Institute went to work on the problem, and while it carefully refrained from acknowledging its work, it led the refiners to a restored use of the delivered-price practice. Its success was particularly marked in two areas where competition had been most unruly. In the market areas reached by the shipping facilities of the Erie Canal and the Great Lakes, buyers had been able to pay the basis price at Eastern refineries and ship wholly or in part by the cheap water routes. Counsel for the trade association advised the refiners that the Institute could not legally organize a delivered price system, but the refiners individually could do so. Early in 1929 the American Sugar Refining Company announced that it would no longer quote prices for delivery to the buyer at the refinery. Other producers followed the lead, and delivered prices for the Great Lakes region became the rule.

The freight charges levied were slightly below the all-rail rate, but markedly above the rates on alternate routes. The charge for delivery at Cleveland was set at thirty-nine cents per hundred pounds, and sugar could be delivered by barge for twenty-six cents. And apparently the refiners shipped sugar to Chicago for twenty-eight cents, but added fifty-one cents to the basic price when they sold it.[45] Buyers at Green Bay, Wisconsin, also paid their tribute. It cost them about eighteen cents per hundred pounds to lose the privilege of taking delivery at the refinery.

An outburst of competition in Alabama markets came to the same end under Institute tutelage. Buyers had been served from Savannah on the Atlantic coast and from New Orleans on the Gulf. Deliveries could be made from the latter point by barges using the Warrior River. Competition reduced prices to the New Orleans basis plus barge rates. But coöperation was able to alter things. For about six months the Institute managed to lead the refiners into the use of delivered prices based on all-rail rates. The arrangement, however, seems to have been too artificial even for the coöperating refiners. Buyers were eventually allowed the economic advantages which their location on water routes gave them.[46]

While these two organized systems of discrimination existed it is apparent that the use of delivered prices created a discrimination in favor of customers near the refineries and in favor of those distant buyers who lacked the advantage of cheap forms of transportation. The restraint of competition which coöperation effected was particularly striking in these two instances, for the areas discriminated against contained markets in which a number of refiners tried to maintain a foothold. In the Great Lakes area, for instance, not only did supplies come from Baltimore,

---

[45] 15 Fed. Supp. 817, 849–850.
[46] T. N. E. C., *Monograph* No. 18, pp. 124–128.

Philadelphia, and New York, but also from Western refineries. In commenting on the breakdown of coöperation in Alabama, Judge Mack expressed the belief that the discrimination would be restored unless the refiners were restrained by legal force.[47]

TRADE ASSOCIATIONS AND COMPETITION

The restraint of competition and the artificial pricing system achieved by the Sugar Institute are by no means typical results of all trade association activity. In industries where competition is protected by the presence of a large number of companies producing similar products, coöperation between producers has frequently improved the character of competition without lessening the independence of individual firms. But even under the most favorable circumstances some of the most valuable work of the trade association may be used to restrain competition. Cost accounting work, valuable in leading producers into an intelligent pricing policy, in some cases has been used to fix prices coöperatively. Associations have published average cost figures for the industry, and these figures have come to be accepted as satisfactory prices or as minimum prices. At one time the Federal Trade Commission found the Maple Flooring Manufacturers' Association actively pressing members to use its published average cost figures in setting their prices.[48] And other associations have not even used actual averages, but have published a "typical" cost, suggesting its use as a basic price. A trade association of flour millers in the Northwest collected cost figures and sent out to its members figures supposedly representing the average cost of milling flour in the area. Uniform prices based on these estimates were recommended, in spite of the fact that the reported average costs were above current prices which the millers were finding profitable.[49] In a number of other instances cost reporting has reduced price competition, and along with the use of specific cost figures has gone a considerable amount of propaganda against selling below cost. As a result prices have become more rigid, and the pricing independence of individual firms has been lessened.

The reporting of other statistics has also been used to suggest prices or certain output policies to members. Average price figures may be used in an obvious fashion, and production figures may be presented in such a manner as to check any expansion. The Southern Pine Association, with some three hundred members, collected current statistics on production, shipments, and orders, and in its reports to members showed how

---

[47] 15 Fed. Supp. 817, 856.

[48] F. T. C., *Open-Price Trade Associations*, p. 174.

[49] F. T. C., *Competition and Profits in Bread and Flour* (1928), p. 362.

these figures compared with so-called normal figures. The material was presented in such a fashion as to stress the comparison of actual production with this norm, so individual companies were pressed not to expand their production beyond certain limits. The Millers' National Federation made recommendations to its sizable membership directly urging that output be kept at 60 per cent of mill capacity.[50] Four associations in the furniture industry employed a representative to issue a price bulletin showing the selling values of furniture, and used him to exert direct pressure on their members to adhere to the suggested prices.[51]

While a great deal of association work has been directed toward uniform output and price policies, there has been in many cases extensive work done to standardize credit and sales terms. Codes of ethics have been common, and frequently they inveigh against practices that contain no fault save that they are competitive. It is difficult to determine the general success met by associations containing some hundreds of members. They frequently are not able to force acceptance of the cooperative policy on all the firms, and policing of recalcitrants is not always possible, or, if it is undertaken, may meet with varying success. In spite of the handicap offered by large numbers, many associations have diluted their valuable economic services with practices and pressures designed to control or eliminate various forms of competition.[52]

Where only a few companies are present in the industry, the trade association, in developing and shaping coöperation to restrain competition, will largely lose sight of the functions that might give it economic justification. It is obvious that the Sugar Institute had little interest in performing economic services for the sugar refiners. The emphasis on pricing practices and policy was not fortuitous. It grew out of the essential purpose of the association. Other associations in like circumstances show the same objective. In one instance twenty-five firms representing all the Florida and Georgia producers of wooden containers for fruits and vegetables organized the Standard Containers Manufacturers' Association with no other apparent purpose than the restraint of competition. Curtailed production allotments were made for each producer, and the Association policed its members by means of reports from the individual firms.[53] The possible economic advantages to be found in coöperation seemed of little or no interest to the Association or its members.

Either a partial or a thorough-going restraint of competition arises so frequently out of trade association activities that it cannot be considered

---

[50] F. T. C., *Conditions in the Flour Milling Business* (1932), p. 24.
[51] F. T. C., *Report on House Furnishings Industries*, Vol. I, Household Furniture (1923), p. 86.
[52] *Cf.* T. N. E. C., *Monograph* No. 21, *Competition and Monopoly in American Industry* (1940), pp. 234–267.
[53] F. T. C., *Order*, Docket 3289 (1940).

rare or exceptional. Between 1920 and 1940 there were instances in one hundred and thirty-five industries where the Federal Trade Commission or the Courts found trade associations setting price or output policies.[54] As this number includes no private suits and only one case under state anti-trust laws, and since a number of cases of illegal coöperation have unquestionably escaped prosecution, the extent of the restraint is considerably larger than the figure suggests. In spite of the important abuse represented, it is still true that the majority of trade associations direct their efforts to perfectly desirable ends. It is impossible to estimate the proportion of association work that leads to monopolistic results, but it seems safe to say that probably as high as 80 per cent of it is innocent of restraint.

It is possible that even when conditions are not favorably disposed for competition, legal force may direct the coöperation into valuable channels. The Sugar Institute was found guilty of unreasonable restraint of trade, but the Courts did not order its dissolution. They did, however, enjoin the association from using forty-five specifically named practices. The refusal to sell on any basis save delivered prices was enjoined along with a number of other practices that had been used to develop discrimination. The list of prohibitions is an extensive one, and the Court missed few of the restrictive practices of the past. Operating under such restrictions, the industry may give up the attempt to continue a formally organized coöperation, or it may continue in order to realize the real economic advantages of coöperation. Imperfect conditions for competition, of course, still exist. A mere dozen companies make up 95 per cent of the industry. The Court order is useful only because it makes difficult the organization of a rigid system of monopoly practices. In other circumstances, however, prosecution may eliminate the undesirable forms of coöperation and restore a fair measure of competitive independence.

---

[54] T. N. E. C., *Monograph* No. 21, pp. 235–240.

27

Milk, Anthracite Coal, and Automobiles

THE SALE OF FLUID MILK IN CHICAGO

In many instances, farming and the sale of farm products offer some of the best examples of competitive individualism at work, but various farm products have not escaped the effects of concentration. Cattle-producers and beet-growers and others have run into monopolistic or imperfect markets in the sale of their products. The sale of citrus fruits and various other fruits and vegetables has been controlled in varying degrees by selling associations. Recently, one of the most valuable farm products, milk, has come under non-competitive controls. It is a valuable prize for the monopolist. Its two-billion-dollar annual value not only exceeds that of any other farm product save meat animals, but compares favorably with the annual values produced by the major industries.[1]

Before 1900, milk production and sale were in the hands of a large number of small dairy farmers who produced milk, butter, and cheese for their local markets. Gradually, as cities came to require the pasteurization of milk, and consumers called for expensive delivery services, the industry came under the control of large incorporated businesses.[2] At present the two large distributors of milk, butter, ice cream, and cheese are the National Dairy Products Corporation and the Borden Company. The former was organized as a holding company in 1923. Twenty-five years later National Dairy Products had assets of $317,641,671 and in 1948 enjoyed sales that reached almost one billion dollars.[3] Its ownership of the capital stocks or the physical assets of operating companies throughout the country makes it practically a dairyland empire. Among

---

[1] For 1939 the cash income from farm marketing was 878 million dollars for all grains; 609 million for cotton and cotton seed; 413 million for fruits; 264 million for tobacco; 2.2 billion for meat animals; and 1.4 billion for dairy products. *Cf.* Bureau of Agricultural Economics, *Monthly Estimates of Cash Farm Income and Government Payments*, April, 1940, p. 11.

[2] Pasteurization was required by Chicago in 1910 and by New York in 1912.

[3] Standard and Poor's, *Corporation Records*, 1949.

these companies were the largest fluid milk and ice-cream distributor in the New York metropolitan market and the nationally important Kraft-Phenix Cheese Corporation. Its acquisitions allowed the company to handle about 10 per cent of the total milk sold in the United States, and gave it control over 20 to 60 per cent of the milk distributed in the cities where it operates.

Originally concerned with the manufacture and sale of condensed milk, the Borden Company also expanded into other dairy lines. In 1927, however, it was still comparatively small, owning three fluid milk distri-- buting companies, seven manufacturing and selling companies, and twenty-five other subsidiaries. In the next five years it acquired two hundred and seven separate enterprises engaged in producing and marketing various dairy products, issuing over two million shares of its common stock to make most of the acquisitions.[4] In 1936 it gave up the holding company organization and took over the actual assets of most of its subsidiaries.[5] At the end of 1948 Borden reported assets of $242,239,331. Its net sales for that year were well in excess of $600,000,000.

Since these two large concerns handle only about 15 per cent of the fluid milk marketed in the United States, they have not established any nation-wide monopoly control. In a number of specific markets, however, their combined control was too large to permit competition to work. Around 1939, they handled between 60 and 90 per cent of the fluid milk sold in Baltimore, Milwaukee, Detroit, Akron, and Madison.[6]

Under these conditions competitive independence is certainly lost, even if the companies do not develop definite agreements to restrain competition. Each seller in setting his price and output policies must not only consider his cost of production and the demand for milk, but also he must give due consideration to what the other large producer may do. When the firms are so large, change in their policies becomes the most important market factor. In this case, the two large firms are forced to coördinate their price and output policies very carefully. The result may not be outright monopoly, but it certainly is not competition in the traditional sense.[7] According to the Federal Trade Commission, there

---

[4] F. T. C., *Report on the Sale and Distribution of Milk and Milk Products Through Certain Farmers' Coöperatives in the New York Metropolitan Area and by Nation-Wide Distributors*, 1936, Appendix, Table III.

[5] *Report on the Sale and Distribution of Milk Products and Milk in the New York Milk Sales Area and on the Operations of Nation-Wide Processors and Distributors of Milk Products with Headquarters in New York;* House Document No. 95, 75th Congress, 1st Session (1936), p. 158.

[6] T. N. E. C., *Hearings*, Part 7, Exhibits 359 and 360, submitted by the Federal Trade Commission, pp. 3127–3128.

[7] Return on the invested capital of the National Dairy Products Corporation was 17.5% in 1929; 14.8% in 1931; 6.2% in 1933; and 8.5% in 1935.

is no price competition in these cities, either in the purchase of milk from farmers or in the sale of milk to consumers.[8]

In other markets the concentration of business has allowed producers to organize a thorough-going monopoly. Chicago presents itself as an unfortunately good example. The Borden subsidiary, Borden-Wieland, Incorporated, and the Bowman Dairy Company supply the city with about 50 per cent of its fluid milk.[9] This in itself need not have meant a complete throttling of competition. It did, however, create a base on which five organizations worked together to build an extensive coöperation.

Under an ordinance of the City of Chicago all farms producing milk for sale in the city must be approved by the Board of Health. Some fifteen thousand approved farms in Illinois, Indiana, Michigan, and Wisconsin supply Chicago's milk needs. The producers on these farms were organized in the Pure Milk Association, and this organization became the sole marketing agent for its members.

Approximately 65 per cent of the milk delivered to the city was taken by ten large dairy companies for pasteurization, bottling, and distribution in the Chicago area. These distributors were members of and controlled a second organization, the Associated Milk Dealers, Incorporated. They also controlled a third organization, the Milk Dealers Bottling Exchange, which collected and then distributed bottles and containers to their various owners.

Milkmen engaged in delivering milk were members of the Milk Wagon Drivers Union, an affiliate of the American Federation of Labor. Approximately 75 per cent of the Union members were employed by the large dairy companies.

The last group that appeared in the picture was the Chicago Board of Health. In administering the milk ordinances of the city it was in a position to influence seriously the number of farms permitted to supply milk, the individual farms that should be approved, and the particular dairy companies permitted to do business in the city.

After four months of study a Federal Grand Jury returned an indictment charging that these groups conspired to monopolize the milk industry in Chicago.[10] It was charged that the farm producers through the Pure Milk Association, and the large distributors through Milk Dealers, Incorporated, conspired to set both the prices which should be paid to all producers and the prices at which milk should be retailed in Chicago. Independent producers and distributors were forced to accept these same prices or suffer certain undesirable consequences. Distributors who

---

[8] House Document No. 95, 75th Congress, 1st Session (1936), pp. 67, 73, 106, 109–114.

[9] T. N. E. C., *Hearings*, Part 7, p. 3203.

[10] Department of Justice Release, November 15, 1938.

persisted in the mistaken belief that they had the right to determine their own policies found that they were unable to get their bottles back from the Bottling Exchange without considerable delay and trouble. They met threats and actual violence from the Milk Wagon Drivers Union, and discrimination from the Board of Health.

With this control established, the major distributors carefully fixed the total quantity of milk brought into Chicago, and refrained from competing with one another in the retail market. At the dictation of the large dairy companies, the Pure Milk Association refused to sell to any independents who were rash enough to try to sell to customers of their friends in the Associated Milk Dealers. And the labor union rallied to the cause with its contribution of violence.

Under this set-up the industry suffered the typical effects of oligopoly. The door was virtually closed to the entry of independent distributors and new farm producers. Prices to consumers remained high and were affected badly by the discrimination directed against the sale of milk in stores. The large distributors continued the expensive door-to-door delivery system and kept the retail price of milk for store sale at a high level so as to discourage this method of distribution.[11] In 1933 and 1934, before store sale was controlled, milk sold in stores for as low as six or six and one-half cents a quart, as against almost double this price for house delivery.[12]

Despite its participation in the coöperative scheme, the Pure Milk Association failed to improve the lot of its members. In spring and early summer, when supply was likely to increase, the big dairy companies did take the members' entire milk production, but they continued the common practice of paying a price below the fluid milk price for the surplus that was used for ice cream, butter, cheese and canned milk. And when he delivered his milk, the farmer was not permitted to know what average price he was receiving.

The monopolistic organization had an opportunity to make two valuable contributions to the Chicago milk industry. It made neither. First, it might have reduced the heavy competitive waste that exists when five, ten, or more companies send milkmen through the same districts. By consolidating routes and eliminating competitive distribution it could have reduced milk costs by at least two cents a quart. But the large distributors seemed little interested in such economies.

Second, it might have improved the adjustment of production to demand. Over-production and cut-throat competition have appeared in

---

[11] At times rocks were thrown through the windows of milk shops and red ink splashed over the properties. *Cf.* T. N. E. C., *Hearings*, Part, 7, pp. 2785–2786.

[12] Testimony of Doctor Frederic C. Howe, former Consumers' Counsel for the Agricultural Adjustment Administration, *ibid.*, Part 7, p. 2785.

almost all the metropolitan milk markets at one time or another, and the farm producers, in particular, have suffered.

A central control such as existed in Chicago could make a long-run adjustment of supply to demand. But the combine could not see any farther than its high prices. It did adjust production to the quantity of milk the buyers would take at ten to twelve cents a quart, but it never considered the possible quantities that might have been taken at prices between seven and ten cents. It is very probable that a price in the latter range, without expensive delivery service, would have permitted a far larger number of producers to remain in the field while satisfactory profits were earned by all.

The economic problems surrounding milk distribution in the Chicago area are duplicated in most large urban areas. A report of the Federal Trade Commission, *Milk Distribution, Prices, Spreads, and Profits,* made in 1945, reviews the national picture and shows certain widespread features. The general dependence of an urban center on an immediately surrounding area for its supplies of milk exposes the industry to wide fluctuations in supply from low- to high-yield seasons and creates difficulties for year-round marketing. Commonly the cost of distribution is very high, frequently being equal to the value paid the dairyman for the milk. The return being earned on investment by eighty-two fluid milk distributors, however, averaged only 5.4 per cent. This figure contrasts with returns of 14.7 per cent for sixty-two processors producing evaporated and condensed milk, ice cream, butter, and cheese. The higher profits here come from the depressed prices paid for milk which is bought in large part in periods of surplus supply. The Federal Trade Commission concludes that improvement in the distribution of milk is urgently required if the lots of both the distributor and consumer are to be improved.

When the Chicago milk organization was charged with monopoly in the Federal District Court (Northern District) the participants escaped.[13] They managed to persuade the Court that one small portion of the charge was invalidated by a defect in pleading and that the major charges were invalidated by the Agricultural Marketing Agreement Act of 1937. This legislation gave the Secretary of Agriculture the power to control and regulate the milk industry through marketing agreements entered into by the Secretary and producers. The Court held that the industry had been set aside for special treatment and hence could not be brought within the purview of the Sherman Act.

The Supreme Court could not be persuaded to take the same view. It commented that the judgment of the lower court expressly overruled any demurrers and motions to quash the charges so far as they chal-

---

[13] United States of America *v.* The Borden Company *et al.,* 28 Fed. Supp. 177 (1939).

lenged "the sufficiency of the allegations of unlawful conspiracy, and also so far as it was contended that interstate commerce was not involved. . . . "[14] And it maintained that only specific marketing agreements actually entered into by producers and the Secretary of Agriculture were beyond the reach of the Sherman Act. When the protection of the Secretary's supervision was absent, the anti-trust laws existed as the safeguard for the public against arbitrary and injurious agreements.

ANTHRACITE COAL

Approximately two billions of dollars are invested in American anthracite mining properties, but most of the industry is concentrated in only five counties of northeastern Pennsylvania. From this area covering less than five hundred square miles comes over 95 per cent of a product which in 1940 stood third in value among the minerals produced in the United States. The producing regions are not continuous. They are separated by mountains into three areas. The middle one, known as the Lehigh Field, is the smallest, and covers less than fifty square miles. Next in size is the northern or Wyoming Field, and the largest is the southern or Schuylkill Field.[15] Although the individual mines are concentrated geographically, they exist in sufficient number to make possible a considerable competitive independence. Competition, however, has appeared only sporadically. The industry came under the sway of four successive controls that brought the properties together in large ownership blocs and developed various forms of coöperation.

The Form of Coöperation

Canal companies were the first to suppress competition. The coal areas were situated near Eastern markets, being about two hundred and fifty miles from Pittsburgh and Buffalo and only about half that distance from New York and Philadelphia, but their exploitation depended on the development of cheap and dependable transport. This was provided in the early nineteenth century by canals. In 1820 the Lehigh River Canal carried a few hundred tons of coal to Philadelphia, and five years later the completion of canals on the Schuylkill River offered another route to that city.[16] When the Delaware & Hudson Canal was built from the northeastern section of the coal areas eastward to the Hudson River, markets were opened up in New York City and throughout New York

---

[14] United States v. Borden Company et al., 308 U. S. 188, 192 (1939).

[15] Anthracite deposits are found in small quantities in Colorado, New Mexico, Rhode Island, Massachusetts, Washington, Arkansas, and Alaska.

[16] Jules I. Bogen, The Anthracite Railroads (New York, The Ronald Press Co., 1927), pp. 7–10.

State. But no sooner did mining begin to expand than it came under the control of the strategically-placed canal companies. The Delaware & Hudson and the Lehigh Coal & Navigation companies were not satisfied to stay in the canal field, but expanded rapidly as owners of coal mines.[17] They acquired large reserves of coal and then charged excessive rates for transportation, so as to cripple the operations of independent mining companies.[18] Investigations by the Pennsylvania legislature showed the dangers resident in the union of canal and coal properties, but unfortunately nothing was done to prevent the development.

Between 1840 and 1860 railways successfully challenged the canals, but anthracite mining did not escape from control; it merely exchanged an old master for a new and stronger one. In 1842 the Philadelphia & Reading Railroad Company completed a line parallel to the Schuylkill Canal from the southern field to Philadelphia. In less than ten years it was carrying three times the volume of coal carried by its waterway competitor. For some years it confined its activities to transportation, but fear of competition, dissatisfaction with labor, and financial troubles in the mining companies led it into the coal business. Under its charter the railroad was unable to own coal properties, but through stock control of the Philadelphia & Reading Coal and Iron Company it tied up a number of mining companies. By 1880 it owned over one hundred thousand acres of coal lands, which it had bought at excessive prices, and was in bankruptcy. Despite its financial troubles, the railroad continued to aim at control of all mining in the southern field, and acquired a number of good and bad properties. Costly expansion forced it into two reorganizations. Before 1900 the railway and coal properties were under the control of a banking group headed by J. P. Morgan. A new corporation, the Reading Company, capitalized at one hundred and forty million dollars, was organized to hold the stocks and bonds of the Philadelphia & Reading Railroad and the Philadelphia & Reading Coal & Iron Company. The holding company also acquired control of the Central Railroad of New Jersey, which in its turn controlled important mining companies.[19]

Before the Philadelphia & Reading developed its control in the southern field a similar concentration had occurred in the other coal regions.[20] The pioneering railroad in the north, the Delaware, Lackawanna &

[17] Eliot Jones, *The Anthracite Coal Combination in the United States* (Cambridge, Mass., Harvard University Press, 1914), pp. 20–21.

[18] In contrast, the Schuylkill Navigation Company, having no charter rights to engage in mining, reduced its toll to develop its transportation business.

[19] In 1904 the Pennsylvania Railroad acquired control of the Philadelphia & Reading as a move toward bringing all the anthracite roads under a holding company. The Northern Securities decision ended the scheme and the distribution of shares left control of the Philadelphia & Reading in the hands of the Widener family of Philadelphia.

[20] Cf. United States v. Reading Company *et al.*, 253 U. S. 26, 30–48 (1920).

Western, was limited by its charter to the ownership of one thousand acres of coal lands, but by means of modifications in the charter and by stock ownership of coal companies it became an important operator. Similarly the Lehigh Valley Railroad, with no charter privileges to own coal properties, acquired a large area of coal lands and consolidated them in the Lehigh Valley Coal Company.

By 1910 railroad control was almost complete. Six companies owned close to 90 per cent of the existing reserves and marketed about three-quarters of the annual supplies of anthracite. As appears in the following table, three of the six far outstripped the others.[21]

Table 22

RAILROAD OWNERSHIP OF EXISTING ANTHRACITE COAL RESERVES, 1910

Name of Controlling Company	Percentage of Unmined Area of Anthracite
The Reading Company	44.00
Central Railroad of New Jersey	19.00
Lehigh Valley Company	16.87
Delaware, Lackawanna and Western Company	6.55
Erie Railroad	2.59
New York, Susquehanna and Western Railroad	.54
Total	89.55

These companies avoided any possible competitive conflicts by various means. Between 1873 and 1898 a succession of pooling agreements assigned allotments to each of the carriers, with penalties for those carrying in excess of their quotas. The output was restricted and prices were held up to monopoly levels, except in short periods when the agreements broke down.[22] In 1898, to prevent the construction of a railroad by independent coal companies, the railroad-coal companies utilized the Temple Iron Company to acquire coal properties from which traffic would originate for the proposed railway. After stifling the threatened competition, the large operators used this commonly-owned company as a coördinating agency. Their officers made up its board of directors, and it continued a coöperation similar to that effected during the period of pooling.

Agreements were reached with independent coal companies whereby their supplies of coal, representing about 20 per cent of the total sales, were marketed by the dominant railroad companies. The small operators were paid 65 per cent of the price realized on the market, which was more than they could have obtained if they had paid transportation

---

[21] United States v. Reading Company, 226 U. S. 324, 339 (1912).

[22] Jones, op. cit., pp. 40–58.

and handling costs and sold independently at the seaboard. Payment of a favorable price was apparently worth while from the viewpoint of the carriers, since the arrangement gave them complete control of the market.

In 1906 the commodities clause of the Hepburn Act forbade railroads to transport in interstate commerce goods which they produced or owned. A government suit against the Reading Company reached the Supreme Court, and that Company and the Central Railroad of New Jersey were forced to give up their ownership of coal properties.[23] A similar decision was rendered against the Lehigh Valley Railroad. The Pennsylvania and the Delaware & Hudson voluntarily disposed of their holdings. In the meantime, suit under the Sherman Act had forced dissolution of the Temple Iron Company.[24]

These developments shook the anthracite mines free of railroad control, but a community of interest between the large coal companies merely replaced railroad control in subduing any competitive impulses the industry might have had. Coal companies producing about 15 per cent of the annual output of anthracite continued after 1920 under railroad control, and these and other mining railroad companies continued to be connected through common financial control. Financial interrelations, working through a confusing mass of inter-related directorates, maintained the coöperation formerly organized by direct railroad ownership of the mining properties.[25] In the twenties, various consolidations increased the predominance of a few large mining companies.[26] Coöperation in pricing seems to have been accepted by these large concerns through acceptance of the Reading Company as a price leader.[27] At times smaller producers sold at prices above or below those of the large companies, but their pricing policies were shaped considerably by those of the leader.[28]

In 1939, informal coöperation gave way to a well-organized procedure. With the assistance of the governor of the state, the large coal operators set up an organization to control the output of the various companies. Working through a committee, they limited production by regulating the number of days the mines could operate each week. In at least two weeks the decision was reached that no mining should be done, and in

[23] 253 U. S. 26 (1920).

[24] 266 U. S. 324.

[25] T. N. E. C., Monograph No. 21, *Competition and Monopoly in American Industry* (1940), p. 180.

[26] In the early twenties the Morgan financial interests had representatives on the boards of all the coal-carrying railroads and of all the large coal companies.

[27] Common practice seems to have been the issuance on the first of April of a price list by the Philadelphia & Reading Coal & Iron Company. These prices were accepted by the other large companies as base prices for the year. *Cf.* Bogen, *op. cit.*, p. 237.

[28] Burns, *The Decline of Competition*, p. 129.

other weeks production was carried on for a varying number of days. Governor James played an important part in the maintenance of this coöperation. All the independents were not coöperative, but they found the Governor able and apparently willing to persuade them to accept the virtues of coöperation. In March, 1939, *The Black Diamond,* trade journal for the industry, showed the value of the Governor to the large mining companies. All the operators knew that the state Bureau of Mines would not find it difficult to discover grounds on which a mine might be closed for failing to observe exactly all the requirements of the mining laws of the state. And apparently without bothering with any subtlety, the head of the state indicated that companies refusing to coöperate in the restriction plan would find that their mines did not pass inspection by the Bureau.[29]

In January, 1940, with the continued assistance of Governor James and with new aid coming from the United Mine Workers, a carefully administered market-sharing arrangement was organized. To a control committee of nine the Governor appointed three representatives and chose six members from lists presented by the operators and the labor union. Proposals for production quotas for the whole industry are made weekly by another committee representing the operators. Of the fourteen members on this production committee, at least seven are named by the large companies. The total quota is broken down into specific weekly production allotments for each company, on the basis of the percentage of the total production which the company mined in the two or three years before 1940. Although there is no price-fixing machinery in the set-up, it is inevitable that the coöperation will affect prices. The committees have no legal standing, but with the Pennsylvania Bureau of Mines and the United Mine Workers promising trouble for any nonconformist, they possess sufficient power to enforce their decisions.

The Effects of Coöperation

It is apparent that independent coal companies have controlled a sufficiently small portion of the industry to allow the railroad coal companies to ignore them. Limited ownership of coal lands has prevented the small company from being much of a danger, so coöperation has been shaped by the interests of the few large producers. Since there is a considerable difference in the cost of mining and in the financial strength of the several coöperating companies, their interests might be variously served. But any possible conflict on price or output matters has been successfully resolved. Peace seems to have been maintained by granting the place of price leader to the Philadelphia & Reading Coal & Iron Company. The mines of this company are among the most costly to

---
[29] T. N. E. C., *Monograph* No. 21, pp. 181–182.

operate, and being a large producer, it would have to be satisfied before coöperation would be successful.[30] It is quite possible that lower prices and larger sales would have better served the interest of others in the group, but results that did not satisfy the Reading Company almost certainly would put an end to coöperation.

Prices among the large companies have been uniform, and have been higher in periods when coöperation was effected than in the few periods of competitive pricing.[31] From 1900 to 1913, except for seasonal variations, the price of domestic anthracite remained remarkably stable, and then rose very sharply until 1924, when a new level was maintained until the middle of 1929. Severe depression conditions in 1932 only reduced the wholesale price of anthracite by 10 per cent, and high prices were current after the depression.[32] At various times it was quite obvious that the large companies were maintaining prices that did not equate demand to supply. In certain periods independents have been able to get prices measurably above those of the coöperating group, and in others have cut prices in order to move their supplies.[33]

Coöperation has brought to most of the large companies earnings that are more than normal. Some of the largest returns have been earned on the coal holdings of the Delaware, Lackawanna & Western Railroad. Before the sharp increase in coal prices after 1913, the railway was earning dividends of almost 30 per cent. Two-fifths of its revenue came from coal properties. In 1921 its holdings were organized in the Glen Alden Coal Company, and prices were good enough to permit dividends of ten dollars a year on stock that had been sold to the railroad shareholders at five dollars a share.[34] The earnings of the leader have been more modest. But in spite of operating high-cost mines, it was able for years to carry excessive holdings of reserve ore and pay to its railway associate transportation rates high enough to allow very profitable operations.[35] Since 1930 the large companies have generally been in trouble, but competition has come from outside the industry to affect adversely the total sales of anthracite.[36]

The coal operators have been able to prevent price competition in their industry and to apportion sales satisfactorily, but they have not been able to prevent their total sales from declining. Normal commer-

[30] Report of the United States Coal Commission (Washington, D. C., 1923), Part I, p. 85.
[31] Cf. Jones, op. cit., p. 44; Burns, op. cit., pp. 118–120.
[32] T. N. E. C., Monograph No. 21, p. 181.
[33] Burns, op. cit., p. 126.
[34] Harry W. Laidler, Concentration of Control in American Industry (New York, T. Y. Crowell Company, 1931), pp. 58–59.
[35] Report of the United States Coal Commission, Part I, p. 85.
[36] Richard Ramsay Mead, An Analysis of the Decline of the Anthracite Industry since 1921 (Philadelphia, Ph.D. Thesis, University of Pennsylvania, privately printed, 1935), p. 35.

cial production in the years before 1926 stood close to eighty million tons; since then sales have declined steadily. By 1932 only forty-six million tons were marketed, and although some improvement occurred with better business conditions, the trend seems to have continued. The reason for the decline is found in the growing importance of competitive fuels.[37] Coke, fuel oil, and bituminous coal are offering the competition that the large coal companies have prevented in the sale of anthracite. Coke produced from bituminous coal has been made more cheaply in recent years, as a result of lower prices for bituminous and increased realization from the sale of by-products. The improvement of oil-furnaces and the strong marketing efforts of furnace manufacturers have made fuel oil a strong competitor, while lower prices and improvements in the form of automatic stokers have strengthened the position of bituminous coal.

Improvements in utilization, aggressive marketing, and relative prices account for the rise of these competitive fuels, and in large part account for the decline of anthracite.[38] And coöperation in the anthracite industry unquestionably has prevented anthracite from checking the last two causes. Prices have been held at unreasonable levels and market-sharing has almost surely blunted the marketing aggressiveness of the large anthracite companies.

The producers responsible for coöperation have borne much of the brunt of the declining market. In 1923, the eight "railway" coal operators produced close to 74 per cent of the total commercial production, but in 1937 less than 65 per cent.[39] Independents probably improved their position by the use of price reductions which were not met by the coöperating group.[40] Their amicable arrangements have not solved the problems presented by the rise of competitive fuels and the growth of independent production, but the large companies have managed to keep their positions relative to one another. In good years and bad each company continues to produce about the same percentage of the total produced by the whole group.[41] Unfortunately, while competition at present is disturbing the coöperation, it may be preparing more restraints for the future. Independents are using their coal reserves more rapidly than are the large companies, and the day may not be far distant when the large companies may more than regain their losses of recent years.

---

[37] Cf. National Industrial Conference Board, The Competitive Position of Coal in the United States (New York, 1931).

[38] Improvement in the quality of anthracite accounts for some of the trends, while mild winters and depression conditions would explain some of the decline in particular years.

[39] T. N. E. C., Monograph No. 21, p. 181.

[40] Over a ten-year period the output of railway mining companies dropped from approximately fifty-two million tons to thirty-two, while the output of independent companies dropped from 18.6 millions to 17 millions.

[41] Mead, op. cit., Table V, p. 30.

AUTOMOBILES

Early Development

As a relative youngster in the industrial family of the United States, the automobile industry has outstripped many of its elders. It is less than sixty years since the Duryea brothers produced at Springfield, Mass., the first gasoline engine vehicle built in the country. Something of its origins and much of its appearance was suggested by its name, "The Buggyaut." By 1948 the industry had turned out its first hundred million assemblies and was keeping on American roads about thirty-six million vehicles out of the world total of forty-five millions. Current annual outputs of cars and trucks are running close to the five million mark, not far off the 5,358,420 units built in the peak year of 1929.[42] With its 700,-000 employees the assembly industry uses over 1 per cent of the entire working population of the country, and its six billion dollar output is an important part of the nation's total manufactures. The production of automobile and truck parts adds about 350,000 to the list of employees. In addition, some 40,000 auto dealers employ hundreds of thousands of men and women. All told, these lines and many closely related servicing and selling jobs bring the total employment to around the eight million mark.[43]

In general structure the automobile manufacture is made up of two industries, the assembly of cars and the manufacture of parts. Motor vehicle assembly plants, 113 in number, are scattered through twenty-four states, with the greatest concentration in Michigan. Auto part manufacturers are spread even more widely over the country. Packard Motor Car Company, for example, buys from over one thousand suppliers of parts scattered over twenty-five states and Canada. Michigan cities inevitably make the largest contribution, but Worcester, Mass., more than five hundred miles from Detroit, makes some sixty-five parts. Ford Motor Company purchases of parts account for 58 per cent of the total cost of the car.[44] A wide range of suppliers in various parts of the country look to Ford for an outlet for their manufactures. Some companies in the parts industry are as large as some of the assembly companies, while others only employ a few dozen workers.

The turn of the century saw the start of a mushroom growth of automobile manufacturing companies. Thirty companies were in production

---

[42] "The First 100-Million Cars Were The Hardest," *Business Week*, August 21, 1948, pp. 26 ff.

[43] The Automobile Manufacturers Association reports that immediately before the war out of the total U. S. consumption the automotive industry took 18% of the steel; 51% of the iron; 80% of the rubber; 75% of plate glass; 34% of lead.

[44] "Auto Parts Makers Expand," *Business Week*, August 21, 1948, p. 36 ff.

before 1900. Production, however, frequently meant nothing more than the turning out of a car or two a year. By 1910 three hundred companies had appeared on the scene. But most of them played only brief walk-on rôles in the drama of the industry. Over 270 of them had left the stage by the end of the first decade.[45] The next twenty years saw many more brief appearances. In his *Motor Memories*, Eugene W. Lewis said that in the history of the industry there have been eleven hundred companies "whose heads believed they were manufacturers of motor cars."[46] Commonly accepted statistics have discounted these beliefs considerably and record only 181 companies producing passenger cars between 1899 and 1928.[47] Out of this number 137 fell by the wayside before 1926.[48] Forty-eight lasted only three years. The average life of the failures was brief, being approximately five years.

Present Structure

Between 1920 and 1940, failures and the continuance of an earlier combination movement left only eleven companies. In this period the present structure of the industry was set. It developed the concentration which in this field as in others has given rise to the nomenclature, commonly used in the industry, classifying General Motors, Ford, and Chrysler as the "Big Three" and the other eight companies as "independents." These latter were Crosley, Graham Paige, Hudson, Hupp, Nash, Packard, Studebaker, and Willys-Whippet.

Concentration in the industry is most marked in its most important field, the production of passenger cars.[49] In 1925 when Chrysler Corporation was formed, the Big Three managed to gather in 64 per cent of the total car sales. In the peak year 1929 this percentage was 72 and rose steadily in the following six years of depression conditions to 90.[50]

At the opening of World War II when the industry began to turn to war production the independents were in no stronger position, holding

---

[45] Eugene W. Lewis, *Motor Memories* (Detroit, Mich.: Alved of Detroit, Inc., 1947) Chaps. 2 and 3.

[46] A partial list of once well-known cars contains only a few familiar names: Atlas: Autocar: Bartholomew: Berkshire: Blomstrom: Chalmers: Chandler: Cleveland: Cole: Corbin: Daniels: Deere: Diamond T: Dorris: Durant: Elmore: Erskine: Essex: Everett: Flanders: Franklin: Graham: Haynes: Herreshoff: Jackson: Jeffery: Jewett: Jordan: Kissel: K-R-I-T: Kline: Knox: Marion: Maxwell: Mitchell: Moline: Moon: Northern: Oakland: Overland: Paige: Pope-Hartford: Premier: Pullman: Rambler: Regal: Reo: Rickenbacker: Saxon: Stoddart-Dayton: Velie: Wescott: Winton.

[47] T. N. E. C., Monograph No. 27, *The Structure of Industry*, p. 243.

[48] Report of the Smaller War Plants Corporation, *Economic Concentration and World War II* (Washington, D. C., U. S. Government Printing Office, 1946).

[49] Except for war years the value of passenger car output is approximately 70% of the total value of automobiles and trucks. See Automobile Manufacturers Association, *Automobile Facts and Figures*, 1946 and 1947.

[50] F. T. C., *Report on the Motor Vehicle Industry* (1939), p. 29.

about the same 10 per cent they had managed in 1935. But they have done somewhat better since the war, enlarging their place steadily, so that the Big Three were trimmed down by 1948 to approximately 78 per cent. A new entrant, Kaiser-Frazer was accounting for close to 6 per cent of total sales. The more seasoned Studebaker, apparently setting a postwar style pattern for the industry, helped itself to a bigger share, being a close runner-up to Kaiser-Frazer.[51]

In the sale of passenger cars the relative fortunes of the Big Three have altered materially over the course of time. Ford Motor Company was the leader until it made the change from its Model T to Model A in 1927. Its best year on a percentage basis was 1921, when it sold 845,000 units out of a total for the industry of 1,518,000 to take 55 per cent of the market. Two years later its sales reached an all-time peak of 1,669,298, which was 46 per cent of a boom year for the industry. The shutdown in 1927, required for the change in model, cost Ford heavily—sales fell to 274,000. The Company never regained its old place. The opening of World War II saw it holding just slightly over 20 per cent of total sales. In 1948 the combined sales of Ford and Mercury cars came to 22 per cent.[52]

General Motors Corporation and Ford Motor Company followed wholly different paths to reach their present size. The growth of General Motors is essentially a product of the combination of formerly independent companies. The present-day Ford Company is the product of the growth of a single firm. Expansion of Chrysler Corporation cannot be attributed preponderantly to either of these two methods but must be credited to the use of both.

The Buick car provided the nucleus around which was gathered the many and varied components of the gigantic General Motors Corporation. After a period of experimentation with automobiles, David D. Buick, a manufacturer of plumbers' supplies, put a small single-cylinder car on the market in 1903. Expansion of the company brought William C. Durant, a recognized leader in the automobile industry, into the enterprise in 1904. The affairs of the company prospered so well that Durant set out to merge all the principal car manufacturers in one holding company. For this purpose General Motors Company was formed in 1908. Its first holding was the Buick properties. By the end of the following year the holding company had acquired or controlled, usually through exchange of stock, more than twenty automobile and accessory companies, including Cadillac, Oldsmobile, and Oakland.

Durant's purpose inevitably led him into attempts to acquire the

---

[51] *Business Week*, August 21, 1948, p. 33.
[52] F. T. C., *Report on Motor Vehicle Industry* (1939), p. 29; *Business Week*, January 22, 1949, p. 72.

Ford Motor Company. Only the lack of three million dollars in cash stopped him. Henry Ford was not willing to accept an exchange of Ford stock for General Motors stock but apparently was willing to sell out for stock and cash.[53] The rapid growth of the combine had placed it in a potentially strong market position but in a financial position where its current needs for cash were embarrassingly heavy. At the same time that the Ford company was lost to the combine, an equally important company slipped away when R. E. Olds insisted that he would not take less for his Reo car than Ford was demanding.

The combine's need for cash not only lost it the Ford and Reo companies but pushed Durant out of the company he had organized. A twelve million dollar loan was found, but the bankers supplying it took control of the company and Durant could salvage only a position as director. However, Durant was not through with the combine. He joined Louis Chevrolet in the organization of the Chevrolet Motor Company in 1911. Their two cars, the Chevrolet and the Little, enjoyed tremendous success, and Durant returned to his old technique, the exchange of corporate stocks, to turn the tables on the combine which had ousted him. The Chevrolet properties were placed in a holding company without any change in corporate name, and Durant set out to trade at first five shares and later four shares of its stock for one share of General Motors common. In the stockholders' meeting of General Motors of 1915, he demonstrated the success of his trading. The meeting found Durant had acquired a majority of the voting shares, and as newly restored president he was once again in the driver's seat. Events were to prove, however, that the ride was not too comfortable and was relatively short. Within five years Durant was ousted again, this time permanently, by the same set of circumstances that removed him in the first instance.

Between 1916 and 1920 General Motors merged its more important subsidiaries into the parent company. A number of companies—Buick, Oldsmobile, Cadillac, Oakland, General Motors Truck, Northway, Weston-Mott, and others—were set up as operating divisions, and General Motors took on more the aspect of an operating and less the appearance of a holding company.

In 1920 the company was in the midst of a large expansion program which called for large sales of stock. A declining stock market created troubles, and Durant threw his own fortune and tremendous borrowings into market support of General Motors stock. His borrowings were reputed to have reached thirty-five million dollars, and the market still remained weak. If Durant had been forced to sell his holdings, the effect on General Motors would likely have been catastrophic, so the cash was found to cover his commitments. The du Ponts, with the aid of J. P.

---

[53] F. T. C., *Report on Motor Vehicle Industry* (1939), p. 422.

Morgan and Company, took over his obligations. Durant resigned the presidency of the company on November 30, 1920.

Under the new control Pierre S. Du Pont held the chairmanship of the board of directors and, after 1923, Alfred P. Sloan the presidency of the Company. Expansion in 1919 and in the years under the new control has brought a tremendous list of enterprises under the General Motors mantle. Expansion was undertaken in three directions. The first was into foreign markets, which resulted in the appearance of General Motors subsidiaries in New Zealand, Egypt, South Africa, Denmark, Argentina, Canada, Spain, and various other countries. The second line of expansion led the Company into the manufacture of almost every part and accessory used in car assembly.[54] The third has made the Company an important element in the manufacture of a number of products not associated with car manufacture, such as Diesel motors, air-conditioning and refrigerating equipment, electric household appliances, and so forth.[55]

War-time operations of General Motors added materially to the capital resources concentrated under the control of the Company. In 1939 its gross capital assets of $769,000,000 were just under 50 per cent of the industry total. Between 1940 and 1945 the Company added facilities estimated as usable in post-war production of $897,000,000.[56] Proportionate gains were made by the other automobile manufacturers, however, notably Ford, Chrysler, and Packard, and the relative position of General Motors has not changed materially.

The growth of the Ford Motor Company from its incorporation in Michigan in 1903 with $100,000 in subscribed capital stock to the present Delaware-incorporated company with assets exceeding $850,000,000 at the end of World War II offers some essential contrasts to the development of General Motors.[57] Where in considerable part the latter was built up from a combination of plants effected through exchange of the parent company's stocks for those of subsidiaries, the Ford expansion horizontally and vertically rests fundamentally on earnings accumulated from the Ford car. Horizontal expansion of the Ford enterprise has been limited to the purchase of one company in 1922, the Lincoln Motor Company, which was then in receivership. It is by no means certain that expansion of this sort should be termed horizontal, since it links, as did various acquisitions of General Motors, two cars in wholly different price classes. Expansion which can be clearly classified as vertical in-

---

[54] Among the part and accessory activities are Fisher Body Division, AC Spark Plug Division, Delco Products Division, Hyatt Bearing Division, Saginaw Malleable Iron Division, Delco Brake Division, Guide Lamp Division, etc.

[55] For description of corporate organization and list of operations and products in 1939, see F. T. C., *Report on Motor Vehicle Industry*, pp. 432 ff.

[56] Report of the Smaller War Plants Corporation, *Economic Concentration and World War II*, Table 49, p. 150.

[57] Report of the Smaller War Plants Corporation, *Economic Concentration and World War II*, Table 49, p. 150.

tegration has left the Ford Company as the most highly integrated of any in the automobile field, through its ownership of coal and iron mines, steel plants, glass factories, tire factories, and so on. The Company, however, follows the same policy as the other integrated automobile companies in producing for itself only a portion of the materials and parts needed. In this position it is able to buy the rest of its needs on favorable terms from independent companies.

The outstanding feature in the development of the Ford business is the extent to which the large capital required has been accumulated out of the profits of the Company. Starting with $100,000 of subscribed capital in 1903, the Company began immediately to plow back a goodly portion of its earnings into its expanding operations. In the fifteen months ending September 30, 1904, out of earnings of $246,000 the sum of $146,000 was reinvested in the business. The balance, $100,000, was paid in cash dividends. This policy might be considered a very conservative one, but it nevertheless allowed for very handsome dividends. The same policy was followed in the succeeding years. Up to the end of World War I, the best year from the point of view of reinvestment was 1916, when net earnings after taxes were approximately $60,000,000, cash dividends were slightly over $6,000,000, and reinvested earnings were $53,000,000. All told, the reinvested earnings in the first sixteen years of the Company's life were $258,860,000 and the cash dividends $99,390,000. Until the depth of the depression in 1933, the same policy was continued, with even larger sums being retained in business. In the thirteen years after 1920 the earnings reinvested annually ranged from a low of $42,000,000 to a high of $102,000,000.

In 1916 this reinvestment policy received a setback when the two Dodge brothers and other minority stockholders brought suit to restrain the Ford management from proceeding with certain of its expansion plans and to compel the Company to distribute a considerable part of its cash surplus in dividends. Early in 1919 the decision of the Supreme Court of Michigan required the Company to declare a cash dividend of $19,275,000. One sequel of this action was the purchase by the Ford Company of the shares owned by the minority holders. For this purpose the Company borrowed $75,000,000 from New York and Boston bankers. A second sequel was the end of the already strained business relations between the Dodge brothers and Ford. Up to this time the former had been manufacturing certain car parts for Ford, but the Ford policy increasingly led it into its own manufacture and placed the Dodge brothers in a very vulnerable position. In 1914, the Dodge brothers started independent production of the car which bears their name, being considerably aided by the cash dividend which they had forced on Ford and the money received from sale of their Ford stock.

In spite of these interruptions, the Ford policy of reinvestment continued on a large scale until 1933. In 1927 and 1928, when the Company was involved in a virtual reconstruction of its plants to effect the change from the legendary Model T to the Model A, it suffered a loss for the two years of over $100,000,000; and in three years, 1931–1933, depression conditions created another loss of $118,000,000. Until the depth of the depression, however, anywhere from forty to a hundred million dollars were reinvested almost every year.

The Chrysler Corporation rushed its way into the ranks of the Big Three both by combination and by development of the combined plants and the related reinvestment of profits. Between 1912 and 1920 Walter P. Chrysler served in the General Motors combine as president of the Buick Company and vice-president of the parent organization. In spite of its size the General Motors organization apparently was not big enough to contain both Durant and Chrysler, and in 1920 Chrysler left it.[58] In the same year he undertook to reorganize the bankrupt Maxwell Motor Company. A banking group was heavily involved in the Company and was looking for a way of recovering its loans. As described by the Federal Trade Commission, the prospects of the enterprise were not very attractive. It had a twenty-five million dollar debt, 26,000 unsold cars, a lease on properties of Chalmers Motor Corporation, and fifty discouraged distributors.[59]

Modernization of the Maxwell plant and a vigorous and successful sales program lifted sales of the Maxwell car by 1923 to nearly sixty thousand and the Chalmers to over nine thousand. Loans were repaid, cash reserves were built up, and the Chalmers plant was acquired by exchanging Maxwell stock and a certain amount of cash for notes of Chalmers Corporation held by creditors of the Company.

By 1924 Chrysler was ready to cash in on past research and experimentation with a new type of high-compression engine, and the Chrysler car appeared. Manufacture of the Chalmers car was discontinued in 1924, of the Maxwell in 1925. The Chrysler Corporation was formed as a Delaware corporation and exchanged its stock for that of the Maxwell Company. The other major unit brought into the Chrysler organization was Dodge Brothers, Inc., in 1928. After the death of the Dodge brothers, the latter company had been organized under the sponsorship of the financial house Dillon, Read and Co., but after 1926 it suffered a severe decline in sales despite a generally good market for cars. The remainder of the basic units of the Chrysler organization was organized, and production of the Plymouth car was undertaken.

Before World War II the gross capital assets of Chrysler Corporation

[58] Eugene W. Lewis, *Motor Memories*, Chaps. 8 and 9.
[59] F. T. C., *Report on Motor Vehicle Industry*, Chap. XIII.

were reported as $115,000,000,[60] a good part of which came from reinvested profits, which by that time amounted to $82,700,000.[61]

Concentration and Competition

The effects of concentration on competition in the automobile industry can be traced in various fashions. The whole enquiry, however, can be developed in brief form by tracing the effect on purchasers of automobiles and on retail automobile dealers. In considerable part the latter may properly be viewed as constituting a large buying group who have first dealings with the small number of large producers. Certainly the whole story would not be told if the enquiry were limited to the effects of concentration on the final buyer.

The effects of concentration significant to the automobile owner are those common to fields dominated by a few large producers. In general, major emphasis has been placed on a vigorous non-price competition and minor emphasis on price competition. The former is apparent in many forms—large advertising programs, highly developed sales organizations, automobile shows, style changes, and so forth. In spite of the small number of producers in the field, this competition does not appear to have been restrained by active or passive coöperation. At the close of World War II and the resumption of passenger car production, the major companies were apparently loath to undertake costly style changes and continued old models with only slight modification. Studebaker, however, seized on this as an opportunity and presented a car of new design. The results were twofold. Studebaker took a large percentage of the market, and the rest of the industry hurried to meet this competition with their own design changes.

It is very difficult to describe briefly and yet accurately the degree of price competition that has been maintained in the industry. Until Henry Ford turned to the production of heavier and more expensive cars in the 1930's, he had been responsible for the presence of a degree of price competition that is unusual in a highly concentrated industry. In the early years of development Ford had been almost alone in appreciating that a mass market could be found for the automobile. When other producers were thinking in terms of costly cars for wealthy buyers, he was developing the Model T and, after its appearance in 1908, consistently following a price-reducing policy which could not be ignored by other producers.[62] The Ford touring car, sold by the manufacturer for $950 in 1909, declined year by year to a low of $360 in 1916. From that

[60] Report of Smaller War Plants Corporation, *Economic Concentration and World War II*, Table 49, p. 150.

[61] F. T. C., *Report on Motor Vehicle Industry*, p. 1060.

[62] T. N. E. C., Monograph No. 21, *Competition and Monopoly In American Industry*, pp. 194–198.

point the price rose to $575 by 1920 and then started downward again to an all-time low of $290 in 1924.[63]

World War II left car production far behind demand and imposed consistently rising costs on the industry, so that price increases were inevitably the order of the day. It may be significant that the first break in the upward spiral of prices was made by General Motors, who initiated price reductions in the spring of 1949. If the Ford Company has dropped its vigorous, independent pricing policies which were a major factor for years in the industry, price competition may play a less important rôle in the future.

The profit record of the automobile industry throws a great deal of light on pricing policies. In the period between 1927 and 1937, which contains boom and depression years, General Motors earned an average rate of return of 32 per cent on its investment in the motor-vehicle business. Its best year was 1927, when the rate of return was 61 per cent; its poorest was 1932, when a 2 per cent loss was suffered. However, 1931 and 1933, which were also years of severe depression, show returns of 25 per cent and 17 per cent. In the same period Chrysler was earning an average of 27 per cent, with its high of 49 per cent also appearing in 1927 and its low, a loss of 9 per cent, in 1932.[64] The consolidated motor vehicle operations of the Ford and Lincoln companies show an over-all loss of 0.8 per cent for the same eleven years. The best rate of return was 15 per cent in 1929, and the poorest a 14 per cent loss in 1932.

Viewed from the standpoint of the automobile dealer, the concentration of automobile production has ranged a few very powerful suppliers opposite a large number of relatively small dealers. The latter are independent merchants who pay cash for cars f.o.b. factory or manufacturer's wholesale warehouse. The independence of the dealer, however, has been seriously curtailed.[65] For some years the operation of finance companies by the Big Three resulted in a situation where dealers as well as car buyers were virtually forced to do any required financing through designated financing companies at rates that were probably above competitive levels. At times dealers also were forced to buy cars in amounts that were dictated by the manufacturer to suit his supply situation and his need for money. This resulted in the dealer taking cars that he had to sell at a loss. In general the Big Three impose an exclusive dealer agreement on the retailer respecting not only vehicles but also parts and accessories. Where the manufacturer can supply cars in the several price classes, the arrangement may not be inequitable and may constitute

---

[63] F. T. C., *Report on Motor Vehicle Industry*, Table 60, p. 632.

[64] F. T. C., *Report on Motor Vehicle Industry*, Table 17, p. 491, and Table 58, p. 618.

[65] T. N. E. C., Monograph No. 21, *Competition and Monopoly In American Industry*, pp. 170–172.

protection the producer reasonably feels he needs to assure that the full selling effort of the retailer is concentrated on his products. Nevertheless, a relatively poor-selling car may be tied to a popular car and the dealer be forced to taken a certain proportion of the former in order to obtain adequate supplies of the latter.

Although the dealer may suffer in a variety of ways, the essential weakness in the manufacturer-dealer market consists of the one-sidedness that allows the few manufacturers to find freely the needed retail outlets but does not allow a dealer much opportunity to find alternative sources of supply. The dealer invests in show rooms and garages which have adequate earning power only so long as he possesses a contract with the supplier. These contracts generally are for short terms, and the threat of cancellation inevitably restricts the independence of the dealer.[66]

Concentration in the motor vehicle industry rests fundamentally on the advantages of large-scale production and the attendant large capital required for entry into the field. Patents have been valuable business assets, but patent pooling has prevented them from being a source of power leading to concentration. The National Automobile Chamber of Commerce was formed in 1914 by 136 companies to implement an agreement for exchange of patents. Ford has never entered the agreement. The ability of Ford to operate successfully outside the patent pool and the continuance of pooling in somewhat changed form up to the present by most other companies supplying the United States market suggest that patents have not been injurious to competitive organization of the industry.[67]

In the early days entry into the industry was relatively free, and competitive forces worked vigorously if not ruthlessly to eliminate submarginal producers. The present-day advantages attaching to integration, assembly-line manufacture, and an extensive marketing organization support large-scale organizations and make entry difficult.

Combination has created a certain degree of the present concentration, and the economic value of combining potentially independent plants may be seriously questioned. Certain economies are achieved, particularly in marketing, but offsets also occur as administrative organization is developed to handle the operation of a capital structure running into hundreds of millions of dollars.

---

[66] See F. T. C., *Report on Motor Vehicle Industry*, Chaps. III to VIII.
[67] T. N. E. C., *Hearings*, Part 31–A, p. 18,035.

28

Sulphur, Export Associations, and Cartels

INTRODUCTION

Sulphur is a chemical element of prime importance in the manufacture of rubber, chemical products, pulp and paper, explosives, insecticide, paint and varnish, and many other commodities.

It is obtained from three domestic sources and from the importation of pyrites.[1] The principal domestic source of supply is natural sulphur coming from deposits in Texas and Louisiana, with minor contributions from California and Utah. Domestic pyrites constitute the second source of supply. And some sulphur is obtained from the chemical treatment of other sulphide ores, such as copper and zinc; from sulphate ores, such as barite and gypsum; and from various fuel gases.

In 1946, private enterprise in the United States produced about 3,860,-000 long tons of sulphur, exclusive of relatively small amounts recovered as sulphuric acid. About four-fifths of this production was sulphur in its native state. The balance came from domestic and imported pyrites and gas by-product. Domestic production was sufficiently large to permit the exportation of 1,245,820 tons of crude and refined sulphur and, at the same time, to add considerable tonnage to the industry's stock pile.

Fifty years ago the situation was quite different. American industry was using much less sulphur, and it relied heavily on foreign sources for its supply. Pyrites came largely from Spain and natural sulphur from Italy. At that time the chemical industry relied on pyrites for the production of sulphuric acid and, consequently, was dependent on the Spanish supplies. Other industries, using natural sulphur, bought their requirements from the rich Sicilian mines where Anglo-Italian interests maintained a virtual world monopoly.

Our dependence on foreign supplies was due neither to the lack of sulphur in the United States nor to ignorance as to its location. We had long known that rich deposits underlay the doming of the strata of the

---

[1] Compounds of iron and sulphur, copper and sulphur, etc.

Gulf Coastal Plain in Louisiana and Texas.[2] The geophysical conditions were such, however, that the sulphur was inaccessible. The treacherous quicksand which overlay the layers of natural sulphur and the poisonous gases which exuded from the deposits made the known methods of shaft mining impracticable.

In the nineties real progress was made towards the ultimate exploitation of the Texas-Louisiana deposits. A petroleum research worker, Herman Frasch, devised a method in 1891, and constant experimentation and improvement brought it into actual use in 1903. Frasch's method consists of sinking a structure of four concentric pipes into the sulphur deposits far below the surface. Superheated water is then carried down and forced through perforations in the pipe structure to the sulphur strata. Subjected to the heat, the sulphur, which has a low melting point, dissolves and flows to the base of the well. The molten sulphur is then raised to the surface through the free annular space in the pipes by the suction of escaping hot air, which is forced downward under tremendous pressure through the innermost pipe. As the liquid sulphur appears at the surface it is drained into gigantic wooden vats where evaporation eliminates the water and leaves great blocks of solid sulphur.[3]

Early Organization and Control of the Industry

For many years the production and sale of American natural sulphur was controlled by a single firm, the Union Sulphur Company. In 1903, it was reorganized and, using Frasch's mining experience, the Frasch process, and cheap fuel from oil discovered near the then known sulphur deposits, it stepped up production considerably.[4] By 1906 Union's production approached 300,000 long tons. It quickly captured the domestic market from the Anglo-Sicilian interests, and started with considerable success to invade the northern European markets.[5]

The severe damage which the Union Sulphur Company did to the Anglo-Sicilian monopoly in the world market caused much distress in Italy. Large accumulated stocks in Italy could only be sold at a loss, and poverty existed among the unemployed Sicilians. The Italian government

[2] Joseph E. Pogue, *The Mineral Industries of the United States*, United States National Museum, Bulletin 102, Part 3, Sulphur (Washington, D. C. 1917), p. 6.

[3] Some of these sulphur blocks are more than a quarter of a mile long, 200 feet wide, and more than 50 feet high. For an illustration of these and the plant and equipment for sulphur mining, see *Chemical and Metallurgical Engineering*, Vol. XLVIII, No. 3 (March, 1941), p. 70.

[4] Testimony of Dr. R. H. Montgomery of the University of Texas, T. N. E. C., *Hearings*, Part 5, p. 1988.

[5] R. H. Montgomery, *The Brimstone Game* (New York, The Vanguard Press, 1940), p. 45.

sent a commission to Louisiana to study the production methods of the American company. The commission estimated that the Union Sulphur Company could produce at the mine for $3.48 per long ton and could deliver anywhere in the American market for a maximum price of $7.72. This delivered price precluded Italian sales in the American market, for it was about 50 per cent of the Italian cost of production. Furthermore it constituted, as experience showed, a dire threat to Italy's European market. In order to meet this situation, the Italian government organized a *consorzio* or pool in the hard-hit Sicilian sulphur industry, and a year later reached an agreement with the Union Sulphur Company through its German affiliate and agency, the German Union Sulphur Company. The agreement was known as the Consortium of 1907.

The Consortium was an arrangement whereby the participants allocated markets and controlled prices. In the main, the North American market was to be exploited exclusively by Union Sulphur. The Italian market was reserved for the Sicilian producers. The northern European was to be divided between the two groups according to plan.[6] The American company's interest in this market area was to be handled through the German Union Sulphur Company. Prices, it was agreed, should be raised from the low levels to which they had fallen due to the price competition which had resulted from the previous competitive struggle. The minimum figure to be reached by 1908 was $18.50 per ton, which was more than 50 per cent above the lowest price their previous competition had established. And by June 1, 1909, the price was to reach $22.50 per ton.[7]

In a span of four years the American users of natural sulphur had exchanged a foreign monopoly for a domestic monopoly whose price policy was curbed only by competition of Spanish pyrites. Natural sulphur imports, which had been dropping rapidly, became a mere trickle (from Japan) after the Consortium of 1907. Assured of no foreign interference, and with potential domestic competition restrained because Frasch was identified with the Union Sulphur Company and the original Frasch process patents did not expire until 1908, the Union Sulphur Company was the sole seller of natural sulphur. It held all industrial markets except that of the chemical industry, which still relied on Spanish pyrites as raw material for sulphuric acid. Consequently the mine price of sulphur was fixed and maintained at a high level for a considerable period of time.

---

[6] T. N. E. C., *Hearings*, Part 5, p. 2220.

[7] Montgomery, *op. cit.*, pp. 46–47. Presumably these dollar prices or their lira equivalent were per long ton at the exporter's chief marine shipping point. The price goal which Dr. Montgomery claims the Consortium was to reach in 1909 is slightly above the 1908 agreement entered into by the Italian Consorzio and the German Union Sulphur Company. In that agreement the long ton price at New York was set at a minimum of $22.00, including cost, insurance, and freight.

Profits per ton were very large. In 1913, for example, earnings per share reached a peak of $3400 and dividends were exceptional.[8]

But this pleasant situation for the monopoly was not completely undisturbed. Two factors appeared to threaten the established order. In 1908, the Freeport Sulphur Company was organized to exploit sulphur deposits at Bryanmound, Texas. For five years Union delayed the newcomer's production by suing it for infringement of the Frasch process. In 1913, nevertheless, Freeport began actual production in quantity sufficient to offer Union real competition. And in 1919 the patent situation was cleared when certain Frasch apparatus patents were declared invalid as lacking characteristics of invention. The court was unwilling to recognize process patents which extended the control of the Frasch process beyond the original seventeen-year period.[9] The second disturbing factor was the action taken by New Jersey to improve its incorporation and anti-trust laws. Under the revised laws it was illegal for a New Jersey corporation to enter into combination with international competitors. Frasch, who was head of the Union Sulphur Company, cancelled the contract which the Union's affiliated German company had made with the Italian Consorzio, stating in a telegram that the New Jersey law required his company to maintain a position absolutely free of any combination.[10]

These events pointed toward a revival of competition abroad and the construction of competition in the American market. The outbreak of the First World War in Europe and the subsequent entry of the United States sharply changed the situation. The demands of the munitions industry for sulphuric acid greatly increased. The unrestricted submarine warfare cut off the supplies of Spanish pyrites and forced the use of natural sulphur. This added another very real increase in demand for natural sulphur to the real increases that had occurred from other industrial markets. Union and Freeport could both sell in the widening domestic market without serious interference with each other.

The war also introduced several other features. The War Industries Board sharply restricted the export of sulphur and pegged the long ton price at $22.50. Neither of these actions inflicted any great damage on the two companies, because the domestic market was able to absorb all the supply, and the cost of producing sulphur was far under $22.50 a ton. A far more disturbing factor was the drilling for production by the Gulf Sulphur Company in 1917. Originally incorporated in Texas in 1909, this company apparently had remained inactive. In 1918 it changed its name to the Texas Gulf Sulphur Company, and began active production in March, 1919.

---

[8] *Cf.* Montgomery, *op. cit.*, p. 49.
[9] 255 Fed. 961, 980 (1919). The Supreme Court denied certiorari, 249 U. S. 618.
[10] T. N. E. C., *Hearings*, Part 5, p. 2226.

Organization and Control After 1920

The immediate post-war period found in the field the three companies, Union, Freeport, and Texas Gulf. Well equipped with a new plant, Texas Gulf acted like a maverick. When the War Industries Board lifted its price controls, Texas started to cut prices sharply. Union and Freeport retaliated by undercutting Texas, and within a short time the price of natural sulphur per long ton had tumbled to $12.50.[11] But this downward trend did not continue for long. The mine price moved upward, and in 1928 was pegged at $18.00 per ton, where it remained for a long period of time.

In 1922, the three companies entered into an agreement and formed the Sulphur Export Corporation under the protection of the Webb-Pomerene Act. This Act, it will be recalled, conditionally freed such organizations from the operation of the Federal anti-trust laws when they combined to do business in the export markets. Under the terms of the agreement were included the stock participation in the Export Corporation, selection of its directors from the directorates of the three companies, allocation and fulfillment of export orders, power to fix export prices, recording of shipments, the method of withdrawal from the agreement, and other matters of lesser importance. And, in accordance with the law,[12] copies of the agreement were filed with the Federal Trade Commission.

In 1920, the Union Sulphur Company found its underground supplies of sulphur exhausted. Upon exhaustion of its large surface stock of sulphur it proceeded to wind up its active participation in the sulphur markets. This left Texas Gulf Sulphur and Freeport Sulphur to share the market.

When Union Sulphur wound up its affairs it turned over its stock-holding in the Export Corporation to Texas Gulf and Freeport. One of the first moves made by the Export Corporation was to enter into an agreement, dated March 14, 1923, with the Italian Consorzio.[13] By the terms of this agreement the Italian domestic market was not to be molested by the American organization. And the American market, composed of North America, islands off the coast of Canada, Cuba, and the United States insular possessions, was to be served exclusively from American production. An elaborate plan was developed to share the remaining world demand. This was divided on a basis roughly approximating 75 per cent for the Export Corporation and 25 per cent for the Consorzio. Several other provisions of major interest appear in the agree-

---

[11] Montgomery, *op. cit.*, pp. 56, 62; T. N. E. C., *Hearings*, Part 5, p. 1991.

[12] Webb-Pomerene Act of 1918, Section 5 (U. S. C., Title 15, Sec. 61).

[13] For a copy of the agreement, see T. N. E. C., *Hearings*, Part 5, Exhibit No. 381-A, pp. 2214–2217.

ment. Under the heading of *Price* it was agreed that prices, terms, and conditions of sale in the commonly shared markets would be fixed from time to time by the parties in such a manner as best to serve their mutual interest. And, in a paragraph dealing with *Manufactured Sulphur,* it was agreed that the sulphur manufacturing industry should be maintained as it was then; that actions designed to disturb the situation should be considered jointly; and that both parties should use their best efforts to prevent any alteration. This original agreement, it appears, lasted four years and was twice renewed thereafter. In 1932, it became ineffective when the Italian Consorzio was dissolved.

Two facts concerning the agreement deserve special consideration. First, the Export Corporation failed to file a copy of the agreement with the Federal Trade Commission until nearly eighteen months after the agreement was in force. Second, such agreements with foreign competitors were not given legal status by the Commission until August 6, 1924,[14] which was more than a year after the agreement went into effect. The presumption is strong, therefore, that the Export Corporation purposely kept its agreement under cover until concealment was made unnecessary by the Commission's rulings.

Evidently the Italian-American interests found their association satisfactory. Although the original agreement ended with the dissolution of the Consorzio in 1932, a new one was drawn up very soon between the Export Corporation and the Ufficio per la Vendita dello Zolfo Italiano, a new central sales organization created by Royal Italian decree in 1933. This agreement in the main followed its predecessor, with some important additions which reflected the trend of developments in the sulphur industry. Moreover, the Montecatini interests in Italy, producers of by-product sulphur, were compelled by the Italian government to join the new central sales organization established by Royal decree.

Again, home markets were reserved to each of the signatories, and their participation in other markets was divided according to plan. The agreement specifically recognized the return of the competition of pyrites as a source of sulphur. In a paragraph dealing with *Sulphur for the Manufacture of Sulphuric Acid,* the agreement stated: "It is the judgment of both parties that the sale of a certain tonnage of sulphur *at a special price* solely for the manufacture of sulphuric acid is in their mutual interest. Any such sales of sulphur for the manufacture of sul-

---

[14] At this time the Federal Trade Commission ruled that an export association might adopt a trade agreement with non-nationals reaching the same market, providing this was not the domestic market of the United States and the action of the combination did not reflect unlawfully upon our domestic market. The Commission also ruled that export trade associations need not actually sell in foreign commerce, but might be formed solely for the purpose of fixing prices in foreign trade. For a sharp criticism of both these rulings, see Leslie T. Fournier, "Webb-Pomerene Law," *American Economic Review,* Vol. XXII, No. 1 (March, 1932), pp. 18–33.

phuric acid shall be made only by mutual agreement of the parties and the terms and conditions thereof shall likewise be mutually agreed."[15] Apparently both signatories recognized that the competition of pyrites might force discrimination according to the uses to which the sulphur was put. This is further apparent in a section dealing with prices, wherein the companies again recognized that competition from other sources placed limits on their price-fixing powers.[16]

During the thirties the Sulphur Export Corporation's situation was disturbed by the appearance in the domestic market of two small natural sulphur-producing companies in the United States—the Duval Texas Sulphur Company and the Jefferson Lake Oil Company—and the development of a Norwegian firm, Orkla Grube, Aktiebolag, known popularly as Orkla. The Export Corporation solved the domestic producer problem by allocating to the newcomers an annual export tonnage to be sold largely in the Scandinavian, Baltic, French, and Australasian markets through the medium of the Export Corporation.[17] Arrangements were made also with Orkla to prevent any undue disturbance in the industry.

Orkla had acquired patents on a new process for extracting sulphur from pyrites and had to be satisfied. It was allotted annual sales of 70,000 long tons in the world market, providing it confined its sales to the Scandinavian and Finnish markets. Control over the use of its newly patented process in the United States was allocated to the Texas Gulf Sulphur Company. These arrangements have limited effectively the expansion of Orkla, and have controlled its patents so as to prevent the growth of new and effective competition in the United States market. To ward off further the growth of competition, Texas Gulf Sulphur has acquired usable pyrites deposits in Peru and Newfoundland.[18] The original agreement with Orkla was modified, effective January 1, 1937, to accomplish two additional objectives: (1) to allow Orkla to participate to a certain degree with the Sulphur Export Corporation on the continents of Europe, Asia, Africa, and adjacent islands; and (2) to enter into a patent control agreement whereby basic patents of by-product competition developing in the jointly shared market areas would be ac-

---

[15] T. N. E. C., *Hearings*, Part 5, p. 2210 (italics added).

[16] This agreement was suspended by the outbreak of World War II in 1939. It was cancelled finally on February 21, 1945, by action of the directorate of the Sulphur Export Corporation. See F. T. C., *Report on the Sulphur Industry and International Cartels* (Washington D. C., U. S. Government Printing Office, 1947), p. 11.

[17] *Ibid.*, Exhibits No. 384 and 385, pp. 2236–2238. After 1935 there appear to have been no definite arrangements with the two American non-members of the Export Corporation. However, they appear to have found the experience of cartel price leadership worth following in sales in the European markets. See the F. T. C., *Report on the Sulphur Industry, etc.*, p. 14.

[18] T. N. E. C., *Hearings*, Part 5, testimony of Dr. R. H. Montgomery, p. 1944.

quired by purchase or otherwise. The cost of acquisition was to be shared by the two organizations, and the patent titles were to be held by a subsidiary of Orkla.[19] The Sulphur Export Corporation–Orkla agreement was subject to the concurrence of the Italian government-sponsored Ufficio per La Vendita dello Zolfo Italiano thus making it a part of the sulphur triumvirate. The outbreak of World War II suspended the Sulphur Export Corporation–Orkla arrangement, and in February 1945 it was cancelled by action of the directors of the Sulphur Export Corporation.

International Economic Effects

What have been the international economic effects of such agreements? The original Union Sulphur–Italian Consorzio for a long while protected the competitively weak, high-cost Italian sulphur industry by means of a controlled price structure. Foreign and domestic users of sulphur and—what often passes unobserved—the many buyers of products in which sulphur or its derivatives are used subsidized the Italian sulphur industry and other high-cost producers by the payment of prices above competitive levels. And at the same time the market paid tribute to Union Sulphur.

Later developments in these world arrangements through the members of the Sulphur Export Association–Italian Ufficio–Orkla economic alliance continued the controls to the outbreak of World War II and provided in addition the means to throttle any by-product and pyrites reduction competition which might arise to disturb the organization's price leadership and market arrangements. For example, when Orkla patent licensees in Spain and Portugal sought to widen their markets by export to France, the powerful alliance (a world cartel) extended its restraining influence through the Sulphur Export Corporation. Moreover, the sulphur cartel used its influence further to support a weak cartel of French sulphur grinders by refusing to sell to particular French grinders who deviated from the policies of the grinders' cartel.[20]

The more conspicuous economic effects of these private international agreements were: (1) the elimination of price competition in sulphur; (2) the enhancement of sulphur prices above competitive levels in all markets of consequence; (3) additions to the cost of products of which sulphur is a component; (4) the control and suppression of by-product sulphur production at lower costs through a policy of patent control. To the extent that the last effect was realized by the sulphur cartel, the world lost recoverable by-product sulphur;[21] and to that extent the

---

[19] F. T. C., *Report on the Sulphur Industry, etc.*, p. 12.
[20] See *Ibid.*, p. 14.
[21] *Ibid.*, p. 81.

practice added to the more rapid exhaustion of the world's natural sulphur and pyrites-bearing sulphur supply.

The sulphur industry reveals how low-cost American producers through the Sulphur Export Association, organized legally under the Webb-Pomerene Act of 1918, an Italian government-sponsored cartel, and a Norwegian firm owning patents on the best method to recover sulphur from pyrites combined to exercise world-wide control over an industry.[22] Restraints on the cartel were negligible.[23]

The Domestic Scene: Costs, Prices and Profits

Considerable attention has been directed toward the completeness and care with which American natural sulphur producers organized and protected themselves in the sale of sulphur in foreign markets. The entire philosophy underlying the foreign market arrangement was market-sharing without price competition. It would be naïve, indeed, to assume that this philosophy was not applicable to the domestic scene, despite the absence of concrete evidence in the form of written agreements or understandings. Since the domestic market is the larger and more important market, certainly production and domestic sales and

---

[22] It should be recalled that the Sulphur Export Association in 1939 suspended, and in February 1945 cancelled, its agreements with Orkla and the Italian Ufficio. A much-delayed Federal Trade Commission investigation of the activities of the Sulphur Export Corporation resulted in several recommendations by the Commission in February 1947 calling for the readjustment of the Export Association's business. Specifically, the recommendations were that the Association refrain from formulating, promoting, or participating in any plan or agreement whereby it: (1) deducts from its tonnage quota of shipments abroad the shipments made by American producers who are not members of the Association; (2) guarantees the right of foreign producers to sell a specified minimum tonnage of sulphur in a designated period on a priority basis over and above the tonnage to be sold by the Sulphur Export Association in the same territory in the same period; (3) agrees with foreign producers to maintain the *status quo* in the manufactured sulphur industry in the trade territories to which such agreements applied and to do nothing which would encourage any alteration in the competitive trade situation in the areas of the manufactured sulphur industry; (4) enters into agreements, and obligates itself financially, to acquire and share in the control over patents or processes useful in the production of sulphur for commercial purposes; (5) handles American non-member exports or agrees with American non-member exporters not to sell in certain markets or to sell only at previously agreed upon, non-competitive prices and terms. The foregoing practices and arrangements had composed the main substance of the agreements between the Export Association, the Italian cartel, and Orkla. The Commission furthermore recommended that: (1) the Export Corporation in the future cease and desist from handling in any way the sulphur of any American producer who is not a regular member of the Export Corporation; (2) the Export Corporation in the future seasonably file with the Commission all information required under the Webb-Pomerene Act together with the documentary evidence required or requested by the Commission under the Act.

[23] Reclaimed elemental (natural) sulphur, some Chilean and Japanese sulphur outside the cartel, and deviations from price leadership by the few independent American producers may have exercised some slight restraint.

prices could not be neglected in any discussion that the Export Corporation's directors might have had about foreign market prices and policies. This is but a natural consequence of any arrangement which permits world competitors, whether domestic or foreign, to assemble legally to discuss prices and policy in other than domestic markets. To conclude otherwise is to be extremely unrealistic about market relations and human nature.

In regard to the domestic markets, conditions have not and do not favor thorough-going competition. There are but four natural sulphur producers of any importance. Texas Gulf produces roughly 50 per cent of the total output and Freeport Sulphur about 40 per cent. Duval Texas and Jefferson Lake Oil are responsible for the remainder. But these smaller companies are not completely independent. They operate on properties owned or controlled by one of the leaders. And they were permitted to sell abroad through the Export Corporation, in which they owned[24] no shares. With the foreign competition in our domestic market effectively estopped by agreement, and with but few firms of very unequal strength supplying the domestic market, it would be unusual, indeed, to find vigorous price competition.

The use of pyrites as material for sulphuric acid in place of sulphur did appear to inject a competitive element into the picture. Investigation shows, however, that it was not very helpful. The price of pyrites remained rigid for the most part. Texas Gulf Sulphur has long controlled the American rights for the Orkla process. The use of this process might have made pyrites a more popular source of material for the sulphuric acid industry. This development, in turn, might have exerted some downward pressure on the price of natural sulphur. The prevailing conditions inevitably force the conclusion, however, that the natural sulphur industry could not be competitive, and costs, prices, and profits in the industry support that conclusion.

As computed by the Federal Trade Commission, the cost of production of natural sulphur during the period 1929–1937 has averaged $5.64 per long ton for one of the leading companies and $6.13 for the other. Annual averages for each company during this period have not fluctuated more than 10 per cent above or below the period averages for each. And for one of these companies, the Commission's computed costs closely approximate the cost per ton reported by the company itself to Moody's investment service.[25]

The quoted price of natural sulphur during this same period has been $18.00 a long ton, save for very slight deviations on a few occasions.

---

[24] Under present arrangements they are entitled to this service only by direct membership in the Export Association.

[25] T. N. E. C., *Hearings*, Part 5, Exhibit No. 376, p. 2204.

This price, f.o.b. mine, seems to have been quoted as a basis for all sales, whether domestic or foreign.[26]

The margin of price over cost was, therefore, a large one. The leading producers have enjoyed on the average, and from one year to another, exceptional profits. Freeport Sulphur averaged 16.35 per cent before and 13.64 per cent after Federal taxes on its investment between 1919 and 1938, despite three years of losses experienced in the early 1920's, when it ran into certain technical production difficulties. At times this company has approximated 30 per cent on its investment. Texas Gulf Sulphur has done even better. Over the period 1919–1946, Texas Gulf has averaged on its investment 26.1 per cent before and 22 per cent after Federal taxes. In one very lush year, return on investment reached slightly under 68 per cent after Federal taxes. And the entry of Duval Texas and Jefferson Lake Oil—both very profitable but smaller firms— has not greatly changed the situation for either of the two older companies.

In view of the unusual profit-making opportunities that the natural sulphur industry afforded, it would seem that competitive capital and other productive resources would have been attracted quickly to the industry, particularly between 1930 and 1940, when capital was hard put to find attractive opportunities. Investment has increased in the industry, but it has been largely the reinvestment of earnings by the older companies. Why have more new companies not come in? Why have the powerful oil companies that own most of the sulphur-bearing lands not undertaken production on their own account? The answer to both questions is to be found in the relations that exist between the oil companies and the present sulphur producers, and in the large accumulations of surface stocks of sulphur arising from the unusually low ratio of annual sales to inventory.

Freeport Sulphur leases its Texas production areas from the Texas Corporation and pays to the lessor 75 per cent of its net profits. Freeport's Louisiana production areas are leased from the Gulf Refining Company, Humble Oil & Refining Company, and the Shell Petroleum Corporation, and the net profits are shared equally by lessor and lessee. Texas Gulf Sulphur is also associated with such companies as Texas, Sun Oil, Humble Oil & Refining, Standard of Louisiana, Gulf Refining, and others through lease, profit-sharing, and royalty arrangements which are very lucrative for the oil companies. Since a goodly share of the sulphur industry's exceptional returns has already accrued and continues to go to these oil companies, it is unnecessary for them to enter directly into sulphur production and sale. And certainly it would be unwise for them to destroy the geese that lay the golden eggs by competing directly

---

[26] The price per long ton moved downward in 1938 and hovered around $16.00 from 1938 to 1942.

or by leasing lands to others to compete. The threat that the latter might be done is an excellent way of maintaining lucrative leases with the existing sulphur companies. Under the existing relationships the conclusion follows that competition in the rich sulphur-bearing Texas-Louisiana area is not likely to appear. The supply of sulphur will be forthcoming from present producers in such amounts as customers are willing to take at the established price.

Conditions on the demand side of the market are such that there seems to be little likelihood of buyers forcing lower competitive prices. Sulphur is a component of great chemical importance in the manufacture of many commodities, but as an element of cost in the final product, it is of minor importance. As a result, a substantial reduction in the price of sulphur would not materially affect the price of the product in which it is one of many components. Consequently, unless price competition is very severe for the products made in part from sulphur, there is no great pressure to reduce the price of sulphur. As a matter of fact, one of the important sulphur producers believes that purchasers like the stable price system.[27] Buyers feel reasonably sure that in terms of price they are all on the same footing. They are relieved of the burden of maintaining inventories to protect themselves against price increases, and they need not worry about possible price declines reducing the value of what inventories they do maintain.

Analysis of the natural sulphur industry leads to the conclusion that, despite the attractive price-cost relationships in the field, new domestic competition is not to be expected. Furthermore, the existence of so few producers of very unequal strength makes price competition between existing companies dangerous and therefore improbable. Pyrites are unlikely to be important for two reasons: first, Texas Gulf Sulphur holds control of a patent on a new process of extracting sulphur from pyrites, and the use of this patent might upset the pyrites market; second, the suppliers of pyrites operate under a rigid price system which they are unlikely to abandon. If they did, they would find themselves in competition with natural sulphur producers who enjoy a wide margin between prices and costs with which to combat the disturbers. Rather remote potential competition lies with the oil companies, who have no desire to upset their pleasant relations simply to create competition in another field. The cancellation of the international arrangements in 1945 and the recommendations of the Federal Trade Commission in regard to the relations which the Sulphur Export Corporation may have abroad and with non-member domestic companies may inject some greater degree of competition into the international scene. It is quite unlikely that this

---

[27] Malcolm P. McNair and Richard S. Meriam, *Problems in Business Economics* (New York and London, McGraw-Hill Book Co., 1941), p. 415.

will happen with any rapidity, however, if at all, since long-established relations often coast along on their own momentum for a considerable period of time, barring severe economic depression. So far as the domestic market is concerned, conditions of oligopoly—in fact almost duopoly—prevail; hence price competition is likely to be sporadic and occasional. Consequently, unless disturbed by public controls, the domestic natural sulphur producers, competing only in terms of service, will continue to earn returns considerably above competitive levels.

Other Export Associations and Cartels

In its international aspects the case history of the natural sulphur industry is not uncommon. As we have indicated earlier, Copper Exporters, Inc., was organized in 1926 by the leading American copper producers. It immediately associated itself by agreement with practically all the important copper producers and dealers in the world. The resulting international cartel fixed prices and allocated sales quotas on a world basis, and the domestic price of copper adjusted itself upward to world prices very shortly. This version of the copper cartel, however, broke down in the period of the great world depression owing to the rigid copper prices and faulty production controls, which created an artificial surplus problem.[28] In another instance, the United States Alkali Export Association (Alkasso), a Webb-Pomerene Association formed in 1919, was the main organization in the United States serving as a means for coöperation in the world alkali cartel. The California Alkali Export Association (Calkex), formed in 1936, coöperated with it. Membership in the export associations included all the important American producers until 1941, when the Solvay Process withdrew.[29] Across the Atlantic, the Imperial Chemical Industries, Ltd. (ICI), of England assumed the function of negotiator with Alkasso. ICI, a great industrial power in itself, represented such financial and industrial giants as I. G. Farbenindustrie, Solvay et Cie, Aussiger Verein, and others long associated with one of the oldest European cartels, established by the Solvay brothers in 1872. The purpose of this private industrial alliance was complete coöperation among the parties so as to avoid competition anywhere in the world. More specifically, exclusive markets were assigned to each cartel member and the cartel served as a price-fixing agency. Non-exclusive markets endured controlled competition by assignment of sales quotas to the cartel membership.

---

[28] See F. T. C., *Report on the Copper Industry*, Part I, (Washington, D. C., U. S. Government Printing Office, 1947), p. 15.

[29] G. W. Stocking and M. W. Watkins, *Cartels in Action*, (New York, The *Twentieth Century Fund*, 1946, p. 434).

The Department of Justice brought suit against Alkasso to obtain injunctive relief from a combination and conspiracy to restrain interstate and foreign commerce in alkalis by agreement to divide foreign markets, establish export quotas, control foreign prices, and eliminate competition from foreign producers in the United States market. The defendant organizations sought protection on jurisdictional grounds, claiming that exclusive jurisdiction over export associations was vested in the Federal Trade Commission, and, until the Federal Trade Commission investigated and referred its findings and recommendations to the Attorney-General, action under the Sherman Act could not be taken. The lower court rejected this contention, holding that powers conferred on the Federal Trade Commission under the Webb-Pomerene Act (Section 5) to investigate export trade associations believed to be in restraint of trade do not preclude the institution of government suits in the Federal district courts to enjoin violators of the Sherman Act before the Commission has acted. The Supreme Court affirmed the order of the lower court.[30] In rendering the court's decision, Mr. Chief Justice Stone stated that there was nothing in the legislative history to show a Congressional purpose to restrict the authority of the United States to maintain suits for every kind of violation of the anti-trust laws. Referring to Congressional hearings on the Webb-Pomerene Act, the Chief Justice cited the remark of Senator Pomerene that the proposed law did not preclude suits by the United States before the Federal Trade Commission has made an investigation.[31] In view of the comfort to monopoly supplied by the law the decision is a welcome one.

One should not conclude, however, that American participation in cartels is solely through the medium of export trade associations.[32] Within the confines of a single country the cartel in its broadest sense is nothing more than one of our old friends, the trust, the combine, the unreasonable restraint of competition, oligopolistic coöperation, the proponent of industrial power economics, or the advocate of "rationalization" of industry. When it jumps national boundaries it becomes the international cartel in full bloom with no real change in its purposes but much more dangerous in its economic and political implications and far more difficult to handle.

---

[30] United States Alkali Export Association, Inc., et al. v. U. S., 325 U. S. 196 (1945). The lower court contended that the investigatory procedure by the F. T. C. was merely auxiliary and was not a substitute for the provisions of the Sherman Act, hence it did not in any way interfere with or prevent maintenance of action under the Sherman Act.

[31] Ibid., pp. 210–211.

[32] See T. N. E. C., Investigation of Concentration of Economic Power, Monograph No. 6, Export Prices and Export Cartels (Webb-Pomerene Associations) (Washington, D. C., U. S. Government Printing Office, 1941), for a more extended report on export trade associations.

Cartel Forms

In their formation, international cartels commonly utilize three methods of organization—the association, the combine, and patent licensing arrangements.

The association, as the name implies, is a loose form of organization. Structurally and functionally it resembles our trade association—more particularly our export trade associations, such as those for sulphur, copper, and alkali. Its activities may or may not be in the public interest. Usually its policies represent from the public viewpoint a mixture of good and bad economics. Association rules and regulations are established; these may be supplemented by informal (unwritten) or formal arrangements designed to develop market opportunities successfully with a minimum of pain for any one of the cartel members. The degree of exploitation varies with market conditions and public quiescence.

The combine is the closely knit organization. Common ownership or management welds together the organizations either through corporate structure or intercorporate contract, or through dominant personalities and blood relations or interlocking directorates. A few examples will suffice to illustrate the leading patterns. The International Telephone and Telegraph Company by means of stock ownership controls a variety of telephone, radio, and cable communications companies throughout the world. Furthermore, it dominates by its security holdings the International Standard Electric Corporation, which controls a worldwide network of communications equipment manufacturers. By similar control devices the N. V. Philips organization of Holland had a firm hold on electronics and illumination equipment and supplies in eighteen countries.[33] World War II upset the arrangements of this vast organization, but the Philips group was sufficiently far-sighted to anticipate Nazi intent; by means of trust agreements in England and the United States, it put a part of its organizations beyond threatening Axis control. Furthermore, it provided a post-war arrangement by means of which the Philips network could be dominated by a Philips holding company with only ten voting shares.[34]

Consider also the case of one of our most venerable firms—E. I. du Pont de Nemours Company. It had some interesting connections of an international character which illustrate another phase of cartelization. With a subsidiary of the German giant, I. G. Farbenindustrie, du Pont

---

[33] For the ramifications of the Philips industrial empire, see A Study Made for the Subcommittee on War Mobilization of the Committee on Military Affairs, United States Senate, *Economic and Political Aspects of International Cartels*, (Washington, D. C., U. S. Government Printing Office, 1944), pp. 70–71, and the chart facing p. 70. This study was made by Dr. Corwin Edwards and will be cited hereafter as the Edwards Report.

[34] Edwards Report, p. 8.

owned Bayer-Semesan Company, supplier of seed disinfectant for farmers and market gardeners. All I. G. and du Pont seed disinfectant business passed through Bayer-Semesan. Similarly du Pont and the great
British Imperial Chemical Industries, Ltd., sold their products in Brazil
and Argentina through subsidiaries known in each country as Duperial.

Sometimes dominant personalities and blood relationship bind organizations together and bring about uniformity of policy. Thus the president
of Rohm and Haas of Philadelphia was a former official of Rohm and
Haas of Darmstadt in Germany. The significance of this was dramatized
on November 18, 1948, when Attorney-General Tom C. Clark announced
an anti-trust judgment against the Philadelphia Rohm and Haas terminat-
ing an illegal conspiracy among this American company, Rohm and
Haas of Darmstadt, I. G. Farbenindustrie, and Imperial Chemical Industries, Ltd., of England whereby they divided world sales territories and
suppressed competition in the manufacture and sale of plastics.[35] And it
is not purely accidental that the same families which dominate the Aluminum Company of America (Alcoa) also dominate the Aluminum
Company, Ltd., of Canada (Alted). Alcoa, once a member of an international combine until it was prohibited from such participation by the
1912 consent decree, later operated through its *alter ego,* Alted, in the
great Aluminum Alliance by means of family stockholdings and common
officers and directors.[36]

Confusing and intricate as the corporate structural relations may be,
the patent licensing arrangements are, perhaps, even more so. Such
arrangements are most likely to exist in industries where the pace of
technological development has been or can be exceedingly swift. Here
managerial life is far more comfortable, and corporate profits are far
more regular, if the hazards of progress can be controlled privately. In
the interest of science—not to mention private economic gains and private economic security—dominant firms coöperate through their leaders
who can then truly agree that "it is always fair weather when good
fellows get together." What usually follows is to be expected. The world
market is shared, and, *within limits,* scientific results are exchanged. Each
party agrees to share its past, present, and future scientific developments
with the others provided each is permitted a peaceful existence in the
home market, plus, if possible, an aliquot part of the remaining unas-
signed world market. Sometimes a portion of the world is favored by
being designated non-exclusive territory. In this territory licensees may
compete for business. Obviously, really rich territories are not thrown
open to competition, or, if they are, competition soon becomes controlled

---

[35] Department of Justice release dated November 18, 1948.
[36] For a summary description of these maneuvers, see G. W. Stocking and M. W.
Watkins, *Cartels in Action,* pp. 255–256; and for a chart of the Alliance, see *ibid.,*
p. 263.

privately when the potential richness of the market area approaches reality.

The licensing arrangement has extensive ramifications. It may include specifications as to prices, distribution channels, production quotas, and other arrangements deemed necessary in the orderly exploitation of an opportunity. As Dr. Corwin Edwards has observed "the peculiarity of the device is the fact that patents and processes agreements may be effective without covering all companies and all territories."[37]

Economic Consequences of Cartels

In the first place cartels maintain prices above the levels which prices would attain under more vigorous competition. A favorable price-cost ratio is an important objective of cartel policy. As a member of the Steel Export Association observed, "under cartels, prices are good, otherwise there is no good reason for a cartel." Similarly, an official of I. G. Farbenindustrie wrote, "the maintaining of a certain price level would be to the advantage of all competitive companies." And evidence has been submitted to a Congressional committee of investigation revealing that, after General Electric and the German Krupp interests pooled their patents, tungsten carbide, a hard metal composition of vital importance in cutting tools and in wear-resistant surfaces, rose from $50 to $453 per pound in the United States. During the nineteen thirties our industries paid prices ranging from $225 to $453 per pound for this substance. In 1942, however, after the General Electric Company had been indicted under our antitrust laws, the range in price was between $27 and $45 per pound.[38]

Cartels control quality improvement also. Under competition, customers who are dissatisfied with the quality of a supplier's product may buy elsewhere. Under cartelization, however, the dissatisfied customers find they cannot shift easily to new supply sources. The cartelists agree not to cater to one another's dissatisfied customers. And occasionally painful evidence is adduced showing that some powerful firms spend time and money on research to impair rather than improve quality. An illuminating example is found in the case of lamp bulbs. An engineer of a large, well-known company wrote his superior officers as follows:

Two or three years ago we proposed a reduction in the life of flashlight lamps from the old basis on which one lamp was supposed to outlast three batteries to a point where the life of the lamp and a battery under service conditions would be approximately equal. . . . We have continued our studies and efforts to bring about the use of one battery-life lamps. . . . If this were done, we

[37] Edwards Report, p. 4.
[38] Ibid., pp. 12–13.

estimate it would result in increasing our flashlight business approximately 60 per cent. We can see no logical reason either from our standpoint or that of the battery manufacturers why such a change should not be made at this time.[39]

The engineer then urged that a deal be made with battery manufacturers. One cannot help but observe that this disturbing illustration of negative research is highly inconsistent with the advertised versions of industrial scientists at work. Why doesn't competition prevent such things? The answer lies in cartel organization and protection. The United States market is reserved for two large domestic producers, who, in turn, control companies licensed to make lamps according to the control companies' specifications. Accordingly, such uneconomic research can be subsidized safely by the control companies while the public foots the bills.

Cartels foster improper investment of productive resources. This occurs in at least two ways: (1) by underinvestment through exclusion of investment funds which should go into cartelized fields for the employment of productive factors which are used elsewhere less effectively or not at all; or (2) by overinvestment through the "protection" offered the cartel membership by means of controlled price-cost relations. In the first instance, new venture capital is kept out by the usual cartel techniques—typical of any private monopoly—and cartel membership reinvestment of profits is controlled carefully so as not to reduce greatly the desired return on investment. In the second instance, overinvestment results in usable capacity which is kept idle purposely so that price-cost relations are made favorable to all the cartel members at the expense of consumers, who are forced to subsidize idle resources. The economic motivations are principally the reduction of economic uncertainty among the participating members of the cartels while profits are maintained at levels satisfactory to them. Furthermore, both *under- and over-investment* have adverse economic effects on other industries operating in freer markets. And the results are not limited to restricted areas. The effects —economic, political, and social—are world-wide in scope.

The international economic effects of cartels, however, are extremely difficult to estimate. Each cartel poses its own special problems and results. By agreement, members of a cartel might choose to exploit the domestic market and do so without sacrificing domestic employment and production. In this instance it might choose to maintain high and rigid domestic prices for its products, the amounts untaken at the controlled domestic prices would be sold in foreign "free" markets at prices equal to or somewhat above the out-of-pocket (prime) costs per unit of the products of the highest cost members. Such a policy would preclude the rise of competition in the foreign "free" markets—unless the foreign

---

[39] *Ibid.*, p. 16.

governments in those "free" markets resented the "dumping" and erected tariff barriers high enough to exclude the cartel's goods so as to support infant home industries.

On the other hand, if the cartel controlled a world-wide necessity, its members, for domestic political reasons, might choose to favor the home markets and full production while they exploited unprotected foreigners. This policy would be popular at home, since the prices in the home market might be set at levels which would yield fair profit margins while "all-the-traffic-will-bear" prices might be obtained in the unprotected foreign areas. Obviously, however, such a policy could not be undertaken successfully unless the cartel controlled a product through patent arrangements or by absorption of the major sources of supply of raw materials, e.g., tin, quebracho, natural sulphur, and so on. Otherwise competition might arise in the exploited areas.

In each of the aforementioned cases, the cartelists do not exploit fully their preferred positions because it is not expedient to do so. Nevertheless they are better off than they would be under vigorous competition. Hence the difference between full and partial exploitation of a situation may be computed for them as a cost of maintaining a relatively peaceful existence free from either governmental interference or private competition at home or elsewhere.

A third possibility is implied in the preceding examples. The cartelists might exploit all markets to the degree necessary to obtain the maximum total net gain—the theoretical ideal from the viewpoint of the international monopolistic combine. In this instance, productive resources would be excluded from the field; the industry would be under-invested in terms of competitive standards; and there might even be under-utilization of the restricted productive capacity until expanding real changes in demand made it expedient to use existing plant facilities fully.

This third possibility, however, is likely to be a temporary condition in most instances. Somewhere in the world, venture capital—attracted by the exceptional gains—would enter the field if only for the purpose of forcing the cartelists to absorb the newcomers and make them a part of the favored groups. Such developments would lead to over-investment and under-utilization of productive resources in the cartelized industry. In view of the latter developments, internal troubles are likely to appear in the rough periods of depression and economic distress. The cartel is faced then with temporary disintegration and turmoil, which in turn lead to careful reorganization to strengthen the cartel and recover a monopoly profit position.

The twin motivating forces—private economic security and private net gain—which determine cartel formation and policy seem to lead inevitably to national and international economic developments of an unfortunate nature. Some markets will be underdeveloped; others over-developed. Some groups will be favored; others exploited. Terms and conditions of trade domestically and internationally will be artificially established and maintained. Even in the face of governmental attempts to lower world trade barriers, cartel markets will be respected and protected by cartel membership.[40] The amount and direction of capital investment will be guided artificially and often restricted in accordance with the "sound" objectives of cartel leadership.

Despite the economic arguments against cartelization, there is in the world of today a strong undercurrent of support for international cartels. Much of this support comes from big business organization and leadership in European countries where the philosophy and the ideal of the free and open market have been in the discard for many decades.[41] Various proposals rise to the surface from time to time. In England, for example, world cartelization has had the support of the Federation of British Industries—the British counterpart of our National Association of Manufacturers. In the Federation's scheme, private cartels would coördinate and regulate international markets, while trade associations and other private industrial organizations would control domestic markets. Governments would have a hand in this form of economic planning and administration of world production and trade, but their rôle would be extremely limited. And Sir Edgar R. Jones, a tycoon in the British iron and steel industry, has advocated a World Trade Alliance as *sole regulator* of all international trade. The basic organization in this Alliance would be the privately controlled cartel.[42] Deepened by the problems of post-war overcapacity, the prevailing philosophy in the areas of support for cartelization seems to be that *independent* decisions and *free* markets can lead only to unfortunate consequences in trade; that private coöperation to control investment, production, sales quotas, and market areas is synonymous with economic welfare for all. To express it more vividly —the real issue of its sponsors is "cartels or chaos" rather than "cartels or competition." Accordingly, cartels are international agencies for the promotion and preservation of world peace rather than, as has been claimed, devices to encourage international strife. Other factors which have buttressed this private support of the cartel are the twentieth century development of trading nation-states, such as Russia and its satellites, and the apparent necessity of government-sponsored interna-

---

[40] *Cf.* Edwards Report, p. 44.

[41] It is somewhat assuring to note that the International Chamber of Commerce went on record in opposition to cartels in its 1949 annual meeting held in Montreal, Canada. *The New York Times*, June 18, 1949, p. 20. The Charter of the International Trade Organization, negotiated in Havana in the winter of 1947–1948 by the delegates of fifty-six countries, expresses opposition to cartels and provides procedures to deal with them. The charter has yet to be ratified.

[42] See G. W. Stocking and M. W. Watkins, *Cartels or Competition*, pp. 360–361.

tional commodity agreements concerning the production of certain agricultural products.

Experiences revealed by the vast body of material on the development and operations of international cartels[43] should serve as a deterrent to ready acceptance of these assertions and plans in support of cartelization as the solution of public economic problems and world peace. As Professor Ben W. Lewis has observed: despite the rationalizations to the contrary, cartels mean the restriction of production, monopoly prices, and protection of the vested interests of closed groups of producers.[44] And international *regulation* of cartels is not the obvious answer. In present circumstances, international regulation would be frustrated by conflicts in culture and in political and economic interests. Even in more favorable circumstances, regulation would supply the regulators with an almost impossible task. The answer to monopolization does not lie in more monopolization, even in the guise of benevolent cartels.[45]

---

[43] See G. W. Stocking and M. W. Watkins, *Cartels or Compensation,* pp. 493–505. for a list of the outstanding works on the subject of cartels.

[44] See B. W. Lewis, "No! to International Cartels," *The Antioch Review,* Summer Issue, 1946, p. 298.

[45] The Charter of the International Trade Organization recognizes this and provides that each member, under the charter after its ratification, will take all possible steps to see that enterprises in its jurisdiction do not engage in restrictive business practices affecting international trade harmfully. A procedure is established by means of which the ITO may receive complaints, conduct investigations, and make findings. The ITO also tolerates intergovernmental commodity agreements of a temporary nature but limits and governs their use.

29

The Economics of Coöperation Under Oligopoly

Several cases have been studied in which the concentration of business in the hands of a few large companies has been followed by some form or other of coöperation. Twelve refineries are responsible for 95 per cent of our cane sugar supplies; ten steel companies produce only a slightly smaller percentage of our steel. In such diverse fields as bottle manufacture, meat-packing, milk distribution, and the production of natural sulphur two or three companies had reached a dominant position. And frequently a single company towered over the others. In all these industries the mixture of interdependence and conflict left by this concentration has led to coöperative arrangements. Coöperation has been formally organized or has become a conventional thing without the benefit of obvious organization. During its life the Sugar Institute provided a centralized mechanism to transform interdependence into coöperation. Carefully tended and long-established arrangements in the meat industry create a market-sharing result. Traditional "follow-the-leader" policies in steel and in the various fields of bottle manufacture have brought unity soon after concentration left a small number of firms in the industries.

THE EXTENT OF COÖPERATION

Coöperation in these forms has appeared in many other parts of American industry. Since the break-up of the Standard Oil monopoly a number of the "successor" companies in their respective territories have set both the price paid for crude petroleum and the selling price of gasoline. Smaller companies have accepted their leadership.[1] In the processing of copper and lead the American Smelting and Refining Company far exceeds other companies, and its prices are taken by them without question. The conditions under which newsprint paper is pro-

---

[1] Burns, *The Decline of Competition*, pp. 93ff.

duced and sold necessitate coöperation in some form or other. Four large companies serve various sections of the country, and heavy investments in timber reserves and in machinery make the entry of competitors difficult and raise the danger that heavy fixed charges may lead to destructive price competition. Demand is inelastic, but is subject to considerable fluctuation as business conditions affect the advertising volume and circulation of newspapers. It is not surprising that some one company takes the lead in setting prices. At times the International Paper Company, and recently the Great Northern Paper Company of Maine, have acted for the industry. Uniform prices are found between the National Biscuit and Loose-Wiles Biscuit companies, and their prices are accepted by some three hundred and thirty smaller bakery companies who, in the aggregate, produce less than the two large firms. After the American Viscose Company lost its complete monopoly hold over the manufacture of rayon with the lapse of patent protection, it retained slightly less than a third of the American market, while three other large organizations[2] and about two dozen small companies appeared. Until 1931 Viscose and du Pont showed a uniformity in instituting price changes that hardly could be accidental, and their prices were accepted by the industry. Then, until stopped by the Federal Trade Commission in 1937, eight of the largest producers entered an agreement to fix prices coöperatively. In several other large industries the presence of a small number of large concerns has led to unity reached through the leadership of some one company. And local markets have by no means escaped. Only a few retail stores handling such products as meats, groceries, clothing and so forth are found in many towns, and their mutual welfare has not infrequently been safeguarded by coöperation effected through some accepted price leader.

Where, as in the meat-packing industry, a very small number of enterprises exists, their interdependence has resulted in some form of market-sharing. By means of patents two companies, the International Business Machine Corporation and Remington Rand, completely control the sale of a number of business machines such as electric accounting equipment. They find a highly profitable business in the sale of cards for their machines, and each company agrees to sell cards only to its own lessees.[3]

Patents permit a similar coöperation in the sale of oxyacetylene equipment. The Union Carbide and Carbon Corporation and the Air Reduction Company do not let price competition disturb their respective places in the market. More formal arrangements exist in the case of the Westinghouse Air Brake and the New York Air Brake companies, the sole

---

[2] E. I. du Pont de Nemours and Co.; the Celanese Corporation of America; and a group under common ownership—the North American Rayon Corporation.

[3] Until stopped by Supreme Court Decree in 1936 the companies achieved the same division of the market by tying clauses in their leases on machines.

producers of brake equipment for the railroads. Coöperation first took place in the way of a cross-licensing patent agreement, which appears to be in a form to effect a lasting division of the market. Payments are made by each company to the other on the basis of its use of the patents of the other, and it seems that the royalty rate paid by the New York Company increases sharply when its sales take over a certain portion of the market. The logical and apparently intended effect is to leave a fairly assured place to each.

While market-sharing in the anthracite field has only recently achieved its most formal and respectable position, it occurred a number of times between 1870 and the turn of the century in the form of temporary pooling agreements. In the same period a number of other products, notably cordage, salt, whiskey, nails, explosives, iron and steel, iron ore, and cast-iron pipe, came under the sway of agreements fixing the specific output or the regional markets of individual producers. In 1899 prosecution of the Addyston Pipe and Steel Company revealed that pipe manufacturers responsible for three-quarters of the production agreed among themselves on the prices to be quoted on bids, and then held private auctions among themselves to determine what company would fill the bid. The price paid in this auction by the company gaining the business was distributed to the other producers who carefully tendered bids above the agreed price.[4]

Another old form of market-sharing which is very common in American business today possibly allows some advantage to the buyer. A producer of industrial equipment, such as the General Electric, may buy all its gasoline and oil supplies from one gasoline distributor, and in turn the refining company purchases all or an important part of its electrical equipment from the General Electric Company. At the same time, one of its competitors will have similar understandings with some other refining company. As a result of arrangements that are little more than habitual, the companies establish well-fixed lines between themselves that effectively divide the market for certain products.

The association between supposed competitors that allows them to coöperate on important aspects of their business policies is frequently developed or implemented by trade associations. It can and does appear, however, without the aid of any independent organization. Particularly where only two or three enterprises are found in the field, the association may be developed directly between the companies. The United Fruit Company and its marketing subsidiary, the Fruit Dispatch Company, handle about 60 per cent of the bananas imported into the United States, while the Standard Fruit and Steamship Company is responsible for about 30 per cent. They are not disturbed seriously by any rivals, and

---

[4] Addyston Pipe and Steel Co., et al. v. U. S., 175 U. S. 237.

operate in a friendly and understanding fashion. The cross-licensing of a number of patents allows the Corning Glass Works and the General Electric Company to coöperate in controlling the manufacture of tungsten lamps. The General Electric licenses six companies to produce lamps, and these companies follow its prices. Before 1940, foreign supplies from all sources were kept out of the United States by agreement between foreign producers and the General Electric. Until 1932, when the General Electric and the Westinghouse Electric and Manufacturing Company were forced by court decree to give up their stock ownership in the Radio Corporation of America, these companies controlled and coöperated happily in the manufacture and sale of radios.

The existence of delivered price systems often bears witness to the presence of an association between producers where there is no evidence of any formal organization. After the Chicago area had developed a steel capacity equal to and beyond the needs of the surrounding market, the fixing of prices on the Pittsburgh Plus basis offered incontrovertible evidence of coöperation. In cement manufacture the same evidence was apparent. There were a number of basing-points, but base prices were set so that mills were able to sell at delivered prices in distant markets where other mills were located. The general refusal of producers to set prices so as to dominate their natural market areas was a mark of coöperation that might have been aided by the formal machinery offered by the Cement Institute. The Cast Iron Soil Pipe Association apparently can take considerable credit for the maintenance of an artificial delivered price system in the sale of cast-iron pipe. Two-thirds of the producers are located in or around Birmingham, and prices for the country as a whole are set at the Birmingham level plus freight costs. Since the commodity is very heavy for its value, the acceptance of this pricing formula yields considerable profits to producers in other areas, but in return they allow Birmingham producers to enter their nearby markets.

THE EFFECTS OF COÖPERATION

It is very dangerous to generalize about the effects of industrial coöperation. The strength of association, the motives of sellers, and the position of individual firms vary so much in the specific instances that any theory of industrial coöperation would be inapplicable or only partially applicable to some of the cases it attempted to describe. It is possible, however, to point out the general nature of the results that tend to develop. Coöperation has affected the level and the character of prices in a distinctive fashion, and a number of its important economic effects may be traced through its effects on prices.

The Level of Prices and Profits

In the cases which have been studied there is plentiful evidence that prices were held above competitive levels. The profits of the Hartford-Empire Company, ranging between 16% and 67%, reflected the effect of the pooling of patents. Individual patents might have been expected to yield more than normal returns, but the very large profits of Hartford-Empire came only after concerted action had thrown all the important glass machinery patents into its hands. Coöperation in the various fields of bottle manufacture was strong enough to bring to Hazel-Atlas and Thatcher and other companies returns ranging between 10% and 30%. For years steel prices were at an extortionate level for many consuming areas, and the continued existence of the differential between the Pittsburgh and Chicago bases after 1924, though it was much lower, marked the continuance of prices above cost. The Federal Trade Commission apparently had forced the large steel companies to abandon what they had considered to be their best monopoly price, but it had by no means been able to bring prices down to competitive levels.

In various urban areas as well as in Chicago there is plentiful evidence to suggest that coöperation has made the price of at least certain dairy products artificially high. In other cases it is evident that it has brought only moderate profits. During the twenties the large meat-packers earned average returns in the neighborhood of 3%. However, since the more important independents, by following the price leadership of the big packers, were able to earn approximately 9%, it would appear that high costs and not reasonable prices account for the moderate earnings of the leading packers. In the case of the National Cash Register Company dividends have been moderate, and some portion of the profits has been diverted to profit-sharing among the employees of the company.

In the many other industries where coöperation has developed in one form or another, prices and earnings have varied considerably, but have generally been well above competitive levels. Rayon paid liberal profits to Viscose. When Viscose was in a monopoly position from 1915 to 1920, rayon brought annual returns ranging from approximately 25 to 110% on the stockholders' investment.[5] In the next nine years, when other producers were in the field, its annual earnings were somewhat lower, ranging between 18% and 50%. From 1930 to 1938 they reached a low of 1% and a high of 12%. From 1925 to 1938 the other large rayon companies earned a little less than Viscose, with averages slightly above 10% on the original investment. Earnings of other companies have not reached some of the magnificent heights of Viscose, but show averages that are com-

---

[5] For earnings of various companies see T. N. E. C., *Monograph* No. 21, index.

parable. Even in 1933 the International Business Machine Company earned 13% on net worth. The Westinghouse Air Brake Company suffered a deficit in the depression, but in fifteen years it has ploughed back sufficient earnings to increase its capital assets from $500,000 to fifty million. Coöperation does not serve all alike, however, for its colleague, the New York Air Brake Company, has not enjoyed comparable affluence.

It is evident that the dissolution of the old American Tobacco Company did not restore competitive conditions. From 1917 to 1937, Liggett and Myers, Reynolds, and the present American Tobacco made annual earnings on their total investment of 16.70%, 23.05%, and 17.16% respectively. In addition, very sizable bonuses and salaries have been paid to their chief officers.

In general, earnings actually seemed to have approached and frequently equalled those enjoyed by monopoly organizations. Profits may at times be larger than indicated, and where accurately reported they do not always indicate the real height of prices and the full restriction of output. They undoubtedly are reduced by the higher costs frequently invoked by the high price policy. In the production of sugar, coal, steel, and other products coöperation has been associated with over-capacity in the industry, which burdens the restricted production with the cost of idle investment and the inefficient partial use of existing plants. Average costs for the industry as a whole are increased by the support given to high-cost firms which would otherwise be eliminated. It is possible and even probable that management will take less care in searching for improved methods of production and other economy measures. When the coöperation concentrates on price policies, there may develop a considerable rivalry in various forms of non-price competition, which will add to the costs borne by the industry.

In conclusion, it seems that prices approximate the level that allows the larger or more efficient firms to earn returns that approach or equal those of monopoly. The smaller or less efficient members of the coöperating group usually, but not always, seem to find the prices at a level that yields slightly smaller returns which are still markedly above the competitive level.

The Stability of Prices

Rather commonly, coöperation holds prices unchanged over sufficiently long periods of time to indicate that alterations in demand or supply conditions are not allowed to disturb the price level for the industry. While all commodities were dropping from a wholesale price index of approximately ninety-seven in 1929 to a low of sixty in 1933, many of the commodities affected by coöperation showed very small declines. Cement prices were allowed to drop 16 per cent and production fell off by 55 per cent. Banana prices fell 3 per cent. The popular forty-watt tungsten lamp sold all through the depression at 1929 levels, and all sizes kept the same price levels between 1930 and 1934. Steel rails showed no decline until 1933, when government pressure and wide-spread publicity were brought to bear on the steel companies. It was undoubtedly difficult for the industry to think of changing rail prices. They had remained at $28 a ton from 1901 to 1916, and after a period of irregularity were maintained at forty-three dollars from 1922 to 1933. Many other steel products showed no changes for periods of three and four years, but none was able to approach the distance record established by rails.

Newsprint paper, natural sulphur, plate glass, cigarettes, business machines and most of the goods produced under conditions of coöperation show prices that commonly remained unchanged for periods of two to four years. Even when some irregularity is noticed there is still, as in the sale of anthracite, evidence of an artificial stability. After a decade of marked rigidity, save for seasonal declines, anthracite prices since 1913 have been irregular. But at times independents are found selling above the prices of the "railroad" coal companies, and at other times below. The large companies obviously seek stability, even though demand changes would allow the exaction of higher prices. And they are willing at other times to suffer serious losses in volume rather than readjust prices.

The effects that price stabilization will have on the efficiency of production will vary with the extent of supply or demand changes occurring in the period of stability and with the elasticity of demand and supply. If the demand were very inelastic and some improvement in production lowered supply prices, the selling prices could be lowered. The inelastic demand, however, would mean that the volume of production would not increase greatly. It follows, then, that the maintenance of the old prices, while it injures buyers, will not be responsible for a serious curtailment of production and consequent inefficiencies in the industry itself. The repercussion on the efficiency of other industries which suffer from the reduced buying power of consumers may be more serious. Similarly, if unit costs are such that the quantities producers can offer profitably at various prices are much the same, the stability of prices over a period in which demand is changing will not affect the volume of production seriously.

It is apparent, of course, that there is nothing artificial or harmful in stability itself. Perfect competition would yield stable prices, as long as demand and supply conditions are unchanged. And it is possible that coöperation may improve on the results yielded by competition as it operates in some markets. About September the large packers of salmon, probably with the assistance of the Alaska Packers Association, set the price of canned salmon; and the price is maintained until the new pack is ready for the market in the following year. If the prices accurately reflect the size of the pack and the strength of the demand throughout the year, the coöperation prevents prices from dropping, and stops wasteful consumption from developing in the fall and winter when supplies are plentiful. Consequently it prevents high prices and scarcity in the late spring and summer. In the absence of the price stabilization it is possible that supplies would be smoothed out over the whole year by speculators, but at least stabilization under these conditions would do no harm. There is a danger, however, that rigidity may continue even when it becomes apparent that the annual supply and demand have not been equated by the stabilized prices.

Stability is particularly injurious in the frequently violent changes characteristic of the business cycle. In recovery and prosperity periods, the demand for all goods is growing as unemployed labor and resources are put to work and there occurs a magnified demand for the various forms of capital equipment. If the prices of some materials and equipment rise while others remain stable, there develops the general danger of distortions in the allocation of labor and capital that may later be eliminated only by insolvencies and bankruptcies that constitute a harsh and dangerous corrective.

There is also a more specific and certain danger. If the prices for materials such as steel, rubber, or cement that constitute the costs of capital expansion are held down, the so-called heavy industries are in danger of serious over-expansion. They are enjoying a marked increase in demand, and its effects will be magnified by artificially low costs. Very high profit margins and a consequent encouragement to dangerous over-expansion are almost inevitable. Since various changes will in time reduce the demand for capital goods, the dangers are particularly acute.

Sooner or later growth in the demand for mass-produced consumers' goods will be checked. In the first place, it is based on increased production from fuller employment. Secondly, tremendous amounts of purchasing power are being diverted into investment in the expanding capital goods industries. And thirdly, an increasing proportion of consumer purchasing will probably be directed toward products and services that are not the result of mass production. As soon as the rate of growth of the demand for mass-produced consumer goods declines, even though the absolute amount is still increasing, there occurs an actual decline in the demand for the products of the so-called heavy industries.[6]

---

[6] In terms of the illustration in the footnote, Chap. 23, note 32: a demand for railway service represented by 100 requires 500 units of capital equipment. But 10 per cent of this equipment has to be replaced each year, which creates a demand for 50 units of equipment. If demand for railway service increases to 110 the demand for equipment jumps to 100 units, an increase of 100%. Then in the next

The situation rapidly becomes critical, and sweeping unemployment and general business collapse can only be avoided by drastic measures. For two reasons prices of heavy goods must be cut. Production and employment must be kept as large as possible, so as to support consumer buying power. And cost reductions must be offered the consumer goods industries in order to assist the price reductions that will increase the volume of their production. In that fashion expansion of the light industries will ease the effects of contraction in the heavy industries. The process will not be painless for either labor or capital, but it would avoid long periods of stagnation such as occurred from 1931 to 1933. However, it cannot work if price stabilization exists.

In the steel industry and in others where similar demand and cost conditions are found there has developed the belief that price stabilization tends not to accentuate but to minimize the seriousness of recession and depression periods. Spokesmen have argued that price reductions would actually reduce demand by encouraging buyers to delay their buying until prices are lowered further. It is true that buying is frequently delayed in a period of falling prices, and it is true that a considerable portion of the buying of materials and equipment for the replacement or expansion of capital equipment can be delayed. However, if the prices are reduced drastically there is no reason to believe buyers would speculate on the chance of further reductions.

Even with the demand and cost conditions apparent in the steel industry, price stabilization does not serve the best interests of either the industry or the national economy. It is apparently true that a 10 per cent decrease in steel prices in a recession period would increase the quantities demanded by amounts that would reduce unit costs by less than 10 per cent. In considerable part the cause lies in the inelasticity of demand. A 10 per cent decrease in prices of steel going into automobiles would allow something in the neighborhood of a 1 per cent decrease in the price of automobiles. The sale of automobiles would be affected very little and would improve the sale of steel by insignificant amounts. This is a trenchant argument against price reductions, if it is assumed that in a world of price stability the steel companies alone reduce prices. But if costs in the form of prices for iron ore, coal, shipping services, capital and labor can be reduced materially, the steel industry can reduce prices considerably without any burden. If it, and all the other industries supplying the materials that go into automobiles, contribute their reduction, and if labor and capital in the automobile industry are willing to adjust their prices downward, they can offer significant price

---

period, if demand for railway service grows to 115, the amount of equipment needed is 55 units (10% of 550) for replacement and 25 units (5/110 of 550) for new equipment. The total equipment needed is only 80 units—an actual decrease in spite of the fact that the demand for railway service is still growing.

reductions. Certainly the adjustment is not going to be painless. But the choice between it and protracted depression should be easy to make, whether the outstanding consideration is business profits or the welfare of the mass of people.

Price stabilization occurring over very long periods of time, as in the case of steel rails, may seriously injure the adjustment of the industry to demand. When the commodity is used for the production of other goods or of services, harm of varying seriousness will be done to other industries, depending on the extent to which supply and demand conditions change. In addition, the prices will be far above competitive levels. Unless the power of some leading company is very strong, the long-enduring coöperation demands that prices be high enough to satisfy any possible recalcitrants.

Discrimination

A considerable amount of discrimination against buyers has developed out of industrial coöperation. Where it is wide-spread and continuing it grows out of the presence of delivered price systems. In the marketing of steel and sugar, buyers in a number of locations have been denied the advantages of their locations, while other buyers are able to get deliveries at prices that do not reflect the relative cost. Other outstanding examples of discriminatory delivered price systems are found in the sale of cast-iron soil pipe and cement.[7] Some 35 per cent of the national production of soil pipe occurs in plants widely scattered over the United States, but buyers located near these plants do not pay the cost at the factory plus freight. They pay the cost at Birmingham plus an imaginary freight from Birmingham. As a result a plumbing supply house located across the street from a factory will pay a higher price than buyers who are located hundreds of miles away but nearer to Birmingham. And also, as in the case of marketing sugar, certain buyers who could reduce delivery costs by the use of highway or waterway carriage are required to pay delivered prices based on the all-rail rate.

Cement was sold from sixty basing points at which about half the mills were actually located. At each basing point one company usually took the lead in setting prices, and was followed not only by nearby producers, but by those located at non-basing points who sold in the same markets. The small number of competitors forced the latter to coöperate. If they undertook to sell in their nearby markets at prices representing their mill cost plus the actual freight paid, they faced the almost certain risk that the coöperating mills would establish a base at their locations. Their price-cutting brought them no benefit. As in other cases, transport by boat or truck was not open to the buyer.

---

[7] Cf. T. N. E. C., *Monograph* No. 21, pp. 153–160.

Systems in which delivered prices are the same in a large zone may create a similar geographic discrimination.[8] Thus, after 1928, markets east of the Mississippi for newsprint paper were grouped into four zones. All buyers in a zone paid the same delivered price, although the actual freight charges varied on different shipments. When the zone is large and freight costs are an important part of the price, the amount of discrimination against buyers near the producing points will be material. And where the price levels in the several zones are different, strange results will appear along their borders. The steel industry used this system before Pittsburgh Plus was inaugurated, with the result that in one instance buyers on one side of the Mississippi River paid two or three dollars more per ton than those on the other side. Among the products selling at various times under zone systems that failed to accord equal treatment to buyers are such essentials as enamel-ware, alcohol, coffee, soap, and gasoline.[9]

It seems probable that the discriminating systems are created not only to increase profits, but to simplify and preserve the coöperation of oligopolies. Where sellers need not fear competition, they can increase their profits by discrimination, if there is a difference in the elasticity of demand on the part of buyers or groups of buyers. Prices at a high level will yield high profits where the quantity demanded will not be greatly restricted; for other buyers, who would reduce their buying materially, lower prices would yield better returns. These systems, however, possess another advantage. They make pricing simple. With simplicity the coöperating group can easily reach agreements, and can clearly see the extent to which individual companies may be cutting prices.

Whatever their virtues in the way of simplifying the pricing problems of the coöperating managements, the systems entail wasteful production and marketing. Since the discrimination is designed to adjust prices to different buyers so as to minimize the sales restriction caused by high price levels, it is not in itself responsible for a wasteful restriction of

---

[8] Cf. Burns, The Decline of Competition, pp. 282–290.

[9] Clair Wilcox has listed the following commodities as selling at one time or another under discriminatory delivered price systems: asphalt roofing, bathtubs, nuts and bolts, cast-iron pipe, cement, coffee, copper, corn products, denatured alcohol, fertilizer, gasoline, gypsum board, industrial rivets, lead, linseed oil, lumber, metal lath, newsprint paper, pig-iron, power cable and wire, range boilers, salt, snow-fence, soap, steel, stoves, sugar, tiles, turbine generators and condensers, and zinc; and during the period that industry operated under the codes of the National Recovery Act, automobiles, automobile parts, bearings, builders' supplies, business furniture, china and porcelain, coal, construction machinery, cordage and twine, farm equipment, food and grocery products, glass containers, ice, ladders, liquefied gas, lime, lye, paint and varnish, paper and pulp, paper bags, ready-mixed concrete, refractory products, reinforcing materials, road machinery, shovels, draglines and cranes, storage and filing equipment, structural clay products, valves and fittings, and vitrified clay sewer pipe. Cf. T. N. E. C., Monograph No. 21, pp. 147–148.

production among the coöperating producers. The waste here grows out of the high level of prices and not the discrimination. The systems, however, are wasteful in allowing producers to sell out of their natural market areas. Freight costs are increased for the industry as shipments from sellers in distant parts of the country cross one another to reach their market destinations. This cross-freighting has seriously increased the costs of marketing a number of the products sold under zone or basing point systems.

More serious harm is done when the goods are bought by industries as part of the supplies needed for their production. The producers that are denied their natural market advantages are held down in size, while the buyers who are benefited are allowed to expand beyond the size that is economically justified. Or if some producers locate their plants so as to escape the discrimination, they probably surrender real economic advantages that could be found in other locations.

NON-PRICE COMPETITION

It is apparent that competitively-determined prices have ceased to perform their planning functions in a considerable sector of American industry. As they are administered by various forms of coöperation, they no longer regulate the entry or exit of individual firms, and no longer serve as the instrument by which the superior producers assume a large rôle in the market at the expense of the less efficient. The end of price competition, however, has not meant the disappearance of market competition. Firms coöperating to control prices have struggled frequently to improve their position in the market by the use of a number of devices designed to increase their sales. Instead of trying to attract a large volume of business by the offer of price concessions, the individual firm adds selling costs to its production costs. Its selling efforts may be put into advertising, the employment of salesmen, changes in style, alterations in the quality of the article, personal endorsements, and so forth.

The purpose is a double one: to increase the quantities it can sell at any current price; and to increase the inelasticity of demand for its product. These objectives may be sought coöperatively with other members of the industry. To achieve the first, the sugar industry attempted through trade association efforts to increase the demand for sugar. Coöperative action may also help to achieve the second purpose. When the citrus fruit growers support the advertising of their trade association which stresses the vitamin value of citrus fruits, they may persuade buyers that their products are very necessary for health. Then, even if prices are raised, buyers may be sufficiently convinced to sacrifice their purchases of other products rather than reduce seriously their buying of citrus fruits. To the extent that the industry demand becomes more inelastic, the demand enjoyed by the individual producer assumes a greater inelasticity as long as the prices of all the producers of citrus fruits move up or down together. In the market, however, the individual producer is commonly more concerned with rivals near him—those selling products which buyers view as direct substitutes. And it is frequently against these that he directs his competitive efforts.

By assuming selling costs he attempts to increase his sales and insulate himself against similar attempts on the part of producers of physically similar goods. If he is able to persuade buyers that his product is distinctive, the demand for his product ceases to depend directly on the prices asked by other producers. He may be able to raise his prices above the current level for intrinsically similar products and still suffer a sufficiently small loss in volume that his income is increased by an amount greater than the increased selling cost. If so, he would continue to enlarge his selling efforts until any further additions would not bring increases in income to balance the growth of selling costs.

With competition of this sort, just as with price competition, a producer may reach a monopoly situation. Price competition, by eliminating all competitors, may lead to monopoly. Non-price competition, by sharply and permanently differentiating a particular product, also may allow an individual seller to set his prices so as to yield the maximum monopoly profit. In general, however, price competition has not been self-destructive, and there is no reason to believe that the mass of better producers will extend their non-price competition to the point where it is ruinous.

Even where there is a sufficient interdependence between producers to prevent pricing independence, there is an opportunity for non-price competition. Although the cost of advertising, style changes, and so forth may reach dismayingly large totals, the cost per unit of the commodity is small. A large tobacco company can make a tremendous advertising effort with the addition of a very small fraction of a cent to the cost of a package of cigarettes. The reduction of price by a similar fraction would pass almost unnoticed.

These additions to cost act as a competitive instrument between sellers. They lay cost burdens on a company, and they exert a continuing pressure to divert demand from one producer to another. And in many industries they constitute the only form of competition. How well they can serve in the place of price competition becomes a question of considerable importance. In particular cases when the demand is not sufficient to maintain all the existing firms, this competition may be able to eliminate the inefficient firms; and in general, it may be able to force all companies to produce as efficiently as possible. If it possesses these powers it may take over the planning rôle lost by price competition. Where coöperation between supposed rivals has resulted in market-sharing schemes, non-price competition will not be very important. What importance it possesses will be derived from the efforts directed by the coöperating group against independents producing a similar product and against goods that are effective substitutes.

The competitive force of non-price competition resides in the threat it develops against the sales volume of rivals and in the added cost that it forces producers to assume. If coöperation has been able to hold the invested capacity of an industry down to the level required merely to produce the restricted amounts sold under the high prices of coöperation, non-price competition can do little to correct the diseconomy arising out of the deliberate under-investment. It can increase the demand for the products of the coöperating group, but it possesses no great power to force any change in the policy of restricted investment. It may have some influence if style competition, advertising, or the employment of sales forces requires a sizable expenditure that varies little with the volume of business. Although the coöperating firms will have kept the size of their plants adjusted to the restricted output, they may now be forced to expand their sales in order to produce at the point where the combined production and selling cost per unit of the product is lowest. If they fail to expand, they will be surrendering some profits they might make.

The coöperatively controlled industries are very commonly over-invested, and the restriction of output following from high price levels forces individual plants to operate at less than their capacity. Here, non-price competition may act as a corrective. The added costs it lays on all the firms may be sufficient to force weaker ones out of the industry. This process will be slow, unless the expenditures bulk very large in the total costs. It may be aided, however, by a shift in demand away from the marginal concerns. If so, the process of elimination will be much more rapid. Some producers will be burdened not only with the costs of non-price competition, but with increases in the unit cost of production as their plants are less fully utilized. As some firms are eliminated the survivors will enjoy lower unit production costs as their volume increases. The decreases may be greater than the expenditures on non-price competition, and social gains would be inherent in the use of such competition.

Where there is pressure working for the elimination of some firms it is impossible to generalize regarding the certainty of results. There is no assurance that the marginal firm, from the point of view of production costs, will also be marginal in the use of non-price competition. There is some connection between production efficiency and success with certain forms of marketing competition. Particularly as specialists take over these activities, the element of chance may be reduced. The company which is able to spend the most money on advertising campaigns, for example, may get the best results. And if its methods cannot be quickly copied by rivals, it may exert serious pressure on marginal concerns whose financial situation will not permit similar expenditures. But chance is still too large a factor to allow any generalization.

A producer may expend relatively small sums in developing such things as new styles, a new package, new advertising ideas, and have a sweeping success. Not only does the presence of a large element of luck remove any assurance that inefficient producers will be eliminated, but it may militate against any reduction in the number of producing units. As non-price competition takes on the aspect of a horse-race where long shots may pay off at any moment, sub-marginal producers are encouraged to stay in the field.

It will be apparent that the costs laid on the coöperating firms by non-price competition will tend to force them to seek ways and means of reducing production costs. If the competitive efforts of the several producers do not result in any shift in demand, each one must still continue his expenditures or suffer loss of sales. A considerable pressure may be exerted on each seller to reduce production costs by the use of better techniques or more efficient plant operation. Where a shift in demand occurs, the firms losing sales must improve their production situation or be eliminated.

There is some evidence that non-price competition is contributing to the concentration of business with undesirable results. It is possible that the necessity of spreading the cost of huge sales organizations over a large output forced Swift and Armour to maintain a combination of producing units beyond the most efficient size. And entry into industry becomes increasingly difficult as huge expenditures must be made to popularize a product or establish the reputation of a company before financial success is possible.

It is apparent that non-price competition has some merit. Where coöperation has removed price competition, non-price competition is generally better than none at all. It is, however, markedly inferior to price competition. It uses resources that otherwise could be used in producing goods and services. This disadvantage is only slightly offset by the incidental benefits sometimes yielded the consumer by such things as free samples, cheaper newspapers supported by advertising, or entertaining radio programs. And its results are uncertain and slow as compared to price competition. There are too many circumstances in which it exerts only slight pressure to reduce inefficiency. Lastly, it is costly; moreover, the incidence of this cost is largely on the consumer.

30

Public Control of Industrial Coöperation

The pervasiveness of coöperation between members of industrial and trade groups has been indicated. Numerous practices and devices have been developed to relieve traders of the rigors of competition. Direct price competition, upon which the public has long relied for the best allocation and most efficient use of economic resources, has been supplanted in many industries. Sales promotion and quality and service competition are unsatisfactory substitutes. It is very clear that the decline of price competition is a source of real difficulty in the operation of the American economy.

Present legal controls have not been able to prevent the coöperation. The main attack has stemmed from the Sherman Act, so most of the discussion of the adequacy of our existing governmental controls must relate to the construction of that statute as applied to loose combinations. The Federal Trade Commission has also concerned itself with monopolistic agreements and coöperative devices. These cases were reviewed in connection with the work of the Commission, hence it will be sufficient simply to refer to them and to fit them into the general picture.

The legal status of the several types or aspects of coöperation may be treated under the following headings: (1) Price-fixing agreements; (2) Control of output and investment; (3) Price uniformity and trade association activity; (4) Market-sharing; (5) Price leadership; (6) Coercion and boycotts. Not all of these have been thoroughly explored by the courts. The law with respect to some is well established; in other instances there is a paucity of legal pronouncement. There is a good prospect that the legality of many business arrangements will be clarified within the next few years. The intensified drive against trade restraints on numerous fronts which has been carried on by the Department of Justice during the last fifteen years, interrupted only by the war, is bound to yield a harvest of court decisions giving a fuller construction of the law.[1] Nearly all of the cases being prosecuted relate to coöpera-

---

[1] An idea of the degree to which the enforcement of the anti-trust laws has been revitalized may be ascertained from the appropriations which have been allowed

tion.[2] In this respect the law is keeping pace with modern industrial development. It is attacking, as the major danger to competition, the coöperation that frequently replaces huge monopolistic combinations.

PRICE-FIXING AGREEMENTS

From the very first, the Supreme Court has condemned price-fixing agreements and understandings as illegal restraints of trade. The Trans-Missouri Freight Association[3] and the Joint Traffic Association[4] cases, it will be recalled, involved the fixing of railway rates. Group price-fixing was found to be unlawful, even though the purpose was to prevent ruinous competition and to maintain rates which were reasonable. A similar decision was rendered in the Addyston Pipe case,[5] where prices on cast-iron pipe were maintained within a wide area through a system of collusive bidding.

Even after the "rule of reason" was enunciated in 1911, direct price-fixing was not tolerated. A scheme to fix prices entered into by the manufacturers of 85 per cent of enameled bathroom fixtures was outlawed in the Standard Sanitary case[6] of 1912. Patents were assigned to the secretary of their trade association, and the licenses granted manufacturers to use the patents required adherence to selling prices fixed by

---

the Anti-trust Division of the Department of Justice during the last forty-five years. The amount appropriated annually from 1903 to 1935 ranged from $100,000 to $300,000. Recent appropriations have been as follows for the fiscal years:

1936	$ 435,000	1944	1,760,000
1937	435,000	1945	1,540,000
1938	413,894	1946	1,875,000
1939	780,060	1947	2,170,500
1940	1,309,000	1948	2,400,000
1941	1,421,600	1949	3,569,500
1942	2,325,000	1950	3,750,000
1943	$1,800,000		

(*Annual Report of the Attorney-General of the U. S.*, 1941, pp. 63–64; House Committee on Small Business, *United States versus Economic Concentration and Monopoly*, p. 51; and *House Hearings on Department of Justice Appropriation Bills for 1948, 1949, and 1950.*)
The number of attorneys employed by the Anti-trust Division has grown correspondingly. During the classic "trust-busting" era instituted by President Theodore Roosevelt, 1903–1913, there were only five lawyers in the Anti-trust Division. From 1914 to 1935, the number varied from 15 to 33. On January 28, 1949, there were 296 attorneys in the Division. The total personnel numbered 325 on June 30, 1941, and an estimated 658 in 1950.
    [2] For citations of recent indictments, decisions, and consent decrees under the Sherman Act, see Commerce Clearing House, *Trade Regulation Service.*
    [3] 166 U. S. 290 (1897).
    [4] 171 U. S. 505 (1898).
    [5] 175 U. S. 211 (1899).
    [6] U. S. *v.* Standard Sanitary Manufacturing Co., 226 U. S. 20 (1912).

the association. It was held that rights conferred by the patent law could not be used as a subterfuge for the suppression of price competition in the field. Further confirmation of the illegality of horizontal price-fixing was had in the American Hardwood Manufacturers' Association case[7] in 1921. Producers of one-third of the total output of hardwood lumber operated an "open competition plan" through their trade association. No specific agreement as regards price or output was proved. On the strength of the elaborate statistical program, the pressure exerted on members to maintain harmonious policies, and the extraordinary increases in prices, however, the Supreme Court found evidence of concerted action to curtail production and increase prices. Only a minority control of the industry was held by the association, yet it was declared an illegal restraint of trade.

But the leading case with respect to the private control of prices is United States v. Trenton Potteries Company,[8] decided in 1927. The manufacturers of 82 per cent of the vitreous pottery bathroom fixtures produced in the United States had combined to fix prices and to restrict sales to certain jobbers. The question before the Supreme Court was whether or not the trial court had erred when it charged the jury that the defendants could be found guilty if the alleged agreement or combination were found to exist irrespective of their good intentions, the reasonableness of the prices fixed, or whether prices had actually been raised or lowered. The trial court had said: " . . . The law is clear that an agreement on the part of the members of a combination controlling a substantial part of an industry, upon the prices which the members are to charge for their commodity, is in itself an undue and unreasonable restraint of trade and commerce."[9]

The Supreme Court rendered a clear and emphatic answer to the question. It is the existence of power and not the manner of its exercise that determines the legality of coöperative arrangements. Price-fixing agreements are unreasonable restraints in and of themselves because they restrict competition. It is immaterial whether the prices fixed are reasonable or not. The logic of the decision was carefully stated by Justice Stone as follows:

The aim and result of every price-fixing agreement, if effective, is the elimination of one form of competition. The power to fix prices, whether reasonably exercised or not, involves power to control the market and to fix arbitrary and unreasonable prices. The reasonable price fixed today may through economic and business changes become the unreasonable price of tomorrow. Once established, it may be maintained unchanged because of the absence of competition secured by the agreement for a price reasonable when fixed. Agreements which create such potential power may well be held to be in them-

[7] American Column & Lumber Co. v. U. S., 257 U. S. 377 (1921).

[8] 273 U. S. 392 (1927).

[9] Ibid., 396.

selves unreasonable or unlawful restraints, without the necessity of minute inquiry whether a particular price is reasonable or unreasonable as fixed and without placing on the government in enforcing the Sherman Law the burden of ascertaining from day to day whether it has become unreasonable through the mere variation of economic conditions. Moreover, in the absence of express legislation requiring it, we should hesitate to adopt a construction making the difference between legal and illegal conduct in the field of business relations depend upon so uncertain a test as whether prices are reasonable—a determination which can be satisfactorily made only after a complete survey of our economic organization and a choice between rival philosophies.[10]

It should have been noticed that the Supreme Court has not regarded the degree of market control of the coöperating group as of any legal consequence in the foregoing cases. Most of the decided cases have involved combinations embracing a very substantial percentage of productive capacity, but others, notably the Hardwood Association, were minority groups that had nothing approaching complete monopoly power.

The decision in the Appalachian Coals[11] case of 1933 casts some doubt on the general rule holding invalid all agreements between competitors relating to price. This case involved an exclusive sales agency created by 137 producers of bituminous coal operating in the so-called Appalachian territory. These firms mined about 12 per cent of all the bituminous coal produced east of the Mississippi River, and approximately 64 per cent of the commercial production in the Appalachian territory and the immediately surrounding area. The common selling agency was to fix the prices at which coal would be sold, and was to seek to eliminate marketing abuses and other conditions which contributed to the distress of the coal industry.

The Supreme Court upheld the joint selling agency on the ground that the defendants did not have monopoly power and could not fix the market price of coal. It emphasized that the fact that active competition from producers in other areas was met in the consuming markets, and that the enormous undeveloped deposits of coal afforded potential competition. Extensive notice was taken of the depressed condition of the industry and the existence of certain trade abuses. To improve conditions in the industry by coöperative action was not regarded as an unreasonable trade restraint, even though it might stabilize business or produce "fairer price levels." Reference was made to the Steel and Harvester cases, and the Court appeared to accept the defendants' contention that under these decisions no legal objection could have been made if the mining companies had eliminated competition between themselves by a complete integration of their properties in a single ownership. In other words, the test of legality in cases involving coöperation of independent firms

---

[10] *Ibid.*, pp. 397–398.
[11] Appalachian Coals, Inc., *v.* U. S., 288 U. S. 344 (1933).

was the same as in merger cases, namely, whether or not monopoly power is sought or attained. Finally, it may be noted that the lower court was instructed to retain jurisdiction over the case, so that if the plan in actual operation impaired "fair competitive opportunities" appropriate action might be taken. This suggests the Court's concern over the possibility that such arrangements may lead to abuses, even in a highly competitive industry, unless constant vigilance is maintained.

The Appalachian Coals decision, which had been suggested by rulings in a few earlier cases,[12] produced much speculation as to the course of future decisions regarding price-fixing. While it was realized that the Supreme Court was probably influenced by the fact that it was dealing with an over-invested industry whose plight was aggravated by the severe business depression of 1929, there was an indication that minority groups might be given considerable freedom as regards coöperative pricing. But this has not happened. Recent pronouncements of the Court

---

[12] Chief of these was Standard Oil Co. (Indiana) v. U. S., 283 U. S. 163 (1931). It involved a pooling and cross-licensing arrangement of competing patents relating to the "cracking" process for producing gasoline. The Government alleged that the fixing of royalty rates by the defendants was tantamount to the fixing of prices and a restraint of trade. But the Court insisted that this would be true only if the combine effectively dominated the industry and had the power to limit the supply or fix the price of gasoline. Since the output of "cracked" gasoline was only about 26 per cent of the output of all gasoline, it was found that dominant control of the market did not exist. The agreement respecting royalty charges to licensees was therefore upheld.

Another case that is often cited as a qualification of the rule holding all price-fixing arrangements illegal is Board of Trade of the City of Chicago v. U. S., 246 U. S. 231 (1918). The Government challenged a rule of the Chicago Board of Trade that all dealings in grain "to arrive" during the part of the day when the exchange was not in session had to be made at the closing bid price. In upholding the trading regulation, the Court found that its purpose was not to suppress competition, and that it helped to improve market conditions in a variety of ways. The operation of the rule had no appreciable effect on general market prices and no material effect on the volume of grain moving into Chicago. Justice Brandeis said (p. 238): " . . . The legality of an agreement or regulation cannot be determined by so simple a test as whether it restrains competition. Every agreement concerning trade, every regulation of trade, restrains. To bind, to restrain, is of their very essence. The true test of legality is whether the restraint imposed is such as merely regulates and perhaps thereby promotes competition or whether it is such as may suppress or even destroy competition. To determine that question the court must ordinarily consider the facts peculiar to the business to which the restraint is applied; its condition before and after the restraint was imposed; the nature of the restraint and its effect, actual or probable. The history of the restraint, the evil believed to exist, the reason for adopting the particular remedy, the purpose or end sought to be attained, are all relevant facts. This is not because a good intention will save an otherwise objectionable regulation or the reverse; but because knowledge of intent may help the court to interpret facts and to predict consequences." The case is more famous for this oft-quoted statement of the rule of reason than as a precedent in price-fixing decisions. As Professor Handler has pointed out (T. N. E. C., Monograph No. 38, p. 31), the "case dealt with a special situation and the tendency of the Court has been to limit it to its facts." The situation presented was quite unlike that which exists in most industrial markets.

have confirmed the doctrine of the Trenton Potteries case and have left no doubt as to the illegality of price-fixing agreements in any circumstance.

Strong statements to this effect were made in United States *v.* Socony-Vacuum Oil Co. in 1940.[13] A conviction of twelve oil companies operating in the Mid-Western area for the concerted purchasing of "spot" gasoline from independent refiners for the purpose of raising prices was sustained. After stating that the Appalachian Coals case was not in point, and after reviewing other precedents, the Court said:

> Thus for over forty years this Court has consistently and without deviation adhered to the principle that price-fixing agreements are unlawful *per se* under the Sherman Act and that no showing of so-called competitive abuses or evils which those agreements were designed to eliminate or alleviate may be interposed as a defense. . . . Any combination which tampers with price structures is engaged in an unlawful activity. Even though the members of the price-fixing group were in no position to control the market, to the extent that they raised, lowered, or stabilized prices they would be directly interfering with the free play of market forces. The Act places all such schemes beyond the pale and protects that vital part of our economy against any degree of interference.[14]

And it is stated even more positively in another part of the opinion that the economic strength of the group is immaterial. Justice Douglas said:

> The group making those agreements may or may not have power to control the market. But the fact that the group cannot control the market prices does not necessarily mean that the agreement as to prices has no utility to the members of the combination. . . . Whatever economic justification particular price-fixing agreements may be thought to have, the law does not permit an inquiry into their reasonableness. They are all banned because of their actual or potential threat to the central nervous system of the economy.[15]

In 1942, in condemning the fixing of re-sale prices by patent-holders through agency and patent-licensing agreements,[16] the Court reaffirmed its position in the Trenton Potteries and Socony-Vacuum cases. Citing these decisions, the Court declared that price-fixing agreements are illegal *per se* under the Sherman Act. They are unreasonable restraints "because they eliminate competition."

A troublesome question in the matter of price-fixing agreements has been the extent to which owners of patents might, through license agreements, fix the prices at which licensees could sell the patented article without violating the anti-trust laws. Under the older Bement and Gen-

---

[13] 310 U. S. 150 (1940).
[14] *Ibid.*, pp. 218, 221.
[15] *Ibid.*, pp. 225–226, note 59.
[16] U.S. *v.* Univis Lens Co., 316 U. S. 241 (1942); U. S. *v.* Masonite Corp., 316 U. S. 265 (1942).

eral Electric cases,[17] an exception to the general rule against price-fixing agreements was maintained on the ground that the holder of a patent was simply obtaining the rewards for his patent monopoly when he fixed the terms of sale of the patented product. In the United States Gypsum and Line Material Company cases,[18] decided in 1948, the Supreme Court virtually closed the door to price-fixing in patent licenses. The Court did not expressly overrule the General Electric case, but the decisions holding that the license agreements were merely devices to effect a conspiracy or agreement among producers to fix prices on patented products reduce the doctrine to little or no practical significance.

On the basis of these decisions, therefore, it can be confidently asserted that price-fixing arrangements are definitely outlawed. Any agreement or understanding between competitors relating to prices, whether for the purpose of raising, lowering, or stabilizing them, is banned. No inquiry will be made into the reasonableness of the prices fixed or the economic desirability of price-fixing schemes. They may not be justified on the grounds of ruinous competition or competitive evils, nor will the intentions of the parties, whether good or bad, save them. The rule is applicable both to minority and to majority combinations. Degree of market control is not a factor.

In eliminating this legal test, the Court has avoided a troublesome and difficult problem. Its failure to determine successfully the existence of monopoly power is well illustrated in the merger cases. A blanket prohibition is by far the best policy. Any concessions, even to a minority group, are very apt to lead to a progressive weakening of competitive forces throughout the economy. If a group in one area or section of the market is allowed to organize for the purpose of restricting price competition among its members, other groups will seek and obtain the same privilege. Once each section has become organized, it will be an easy step to agreements and understandings embracing whole industries. Even if this is not the eventual outcome, limited agreements usually affect the market in some measure, particularly in those areas served by local producers. If any interference with competitive forces is to be permitted, it must be brought about only under the supervision of government. Until administrative machinery is established to control the prices fixed by private groups, it is the part of wisdom to allow no exceptions to the general rule.

The adequacy of public control is a function not only of the status of

---

[17] Bement v. National Harrow Co., 186 U. S. 70 (1902); U. S. v. General Electric Co., 272 U. S. 476 (1926).

[18] U. S. v. United States Gypsum Co., 333 U. S. 364 (1948); U. S. v. Line Material Co., 333 U. S. 282 (1948).

the law, but of the machinery available for detecting violations and prosecuting them. A major difficulty in enforcing the law against price-fixing is the discovery and proof of illegal agreements and understandings. Obviously, every effort is made to conceal them from the public and governmental agencies. If evidence of overt acts does exist, and if sufficient resources are made available to those governmental agencies responsible for law enforcement, they can be detected and prosecuted successfully. The recent achievements of the Department of Justice and the Federal Trade Commission show this to be true. These agencies rely in part upon investigations undertaken on their motion to uncover violations of law, but a fruitful source of information is found in the complaints registered by injured competitors and large buyers.[19] Now that the Government has displayed a serious interest in eliminating threats to the competitive system, and has backed this up with substantial resources, there appears to be no difficulty either in detecting violations or in obtaining the necessary evidence to convict offenders.

CONTROL OF OUTPUT AND INVESTMENT

So long as there is any elasticity in the demand curve for a particular product, it is obvious that any agreement which raises the price of the product will result in reduced sales. A like result will follow if prices are stabilized when demand for a product is declining. Output is restricted and fewer productive resources are used in the industry. Price-fixing and curtailment of production go hand in hand, therefore, and are two aspects of the same general industrial policy; only the methods differ.

A restriction of output may be effected by reducing hours of operation of plants, shutting down certain plants, or simply agreeing not to produce more than a given amount. Or, if the combining group controls patents, the number of firms licensed to use the patents may be restricted, and those licensed may be required to limit production to fixed quotas. Investment in the field is thus controlled. Whatever the method of control, output is limited, and prices may be maintained as effectively as if they were fixed by agreement.

It would seem to follow that, if direct price-fixing is unconditionally illegal, output control is likewise banned under the Sherman Law. The

---

[19] For an interesting account of the origin of complaints and their investigation, see E. P. Hodges, F. Hamilton, and C. L. Terrel, "Complaints of Anti-trust Law Violations and Their Investigation," *Law and Contemporary Problems*, Vol. VII (1940), pp. 90–103.

courts have so held. Few cases involving this question have been decided, but several early lower court decisions have pointed the way.[20] The authoritative Supreme Court decision is the American Hardwood Manufacturers' Association[21] case, which was considered in the section on price-fixing. No agreement was shown to exist among these manufacturers of one-third of the hardwood lumber produced in the country, but the Court found that detailed statistical information and persuasion were used to effect a coöperative control of production. One of the prime purposes of the meetings and reports, in the opinion of the Court, "was to induce members to coöperate in restricting production, thereby keeping the supply low and the prices high, and that whenever there was any suggestion of running the mills to an extent which would bring up the supply to a point which might affect prices, the advice against operations which might lead to such result was put in the strongest possible terms. The coöperation is palpable and avowed, its purpose is clear, and we shall see that it was completely realized."[22] The scheme to curtail output and thereby enhance prices was condemned.

Subsequent judicial statements indicate no change in doctrine.[23] In upholding a common selling agency in the Appalachian Coals case, the Court emphasized the absence of any attempt to limit production.[24] An important aspect of the decision adverse to the Socony-Vacuum Oil Co. and others was the "restriction of (the) supply of gasoline by removal of a surplus."[25] And it is noteworthy that the Federal Trade Commission

---

[20] Chesapeake & Ohio Fuel Co. v. U. S., 115 Fed. 610 (1902); Gibbs v. McNeeley, 118 Fed. 120 (1902). Involved in the Gibbs case was an association of manufacturers and wholesale dealers in Washington red-cedar shingles that undertook to fix prices and "to order the closing down of all mills, and to take other necessary steps to curtail the output of Washington red-cedar shingles, when in their judgment the supply should exceed the demand." The arrangement was condemned in unmistakable terms, the Court saying: "The combination in the case before the court is more than a combination to regulate prices; it is a combination to control the production of a manufactured article more than four-fifths of which is made for interstate trade, and to diminish competition in its production, as well as to advance its price. These features, we think, determine its object, and bring it under the condemnation of the law."

[21] American Column & Lumber Co. v. U. S., 257 U. S. 377 (1921).

[22] Ibid., p. 404.

[23] In this connection reference is sometimes made to National Association of Window Glass Manufacturers v. U. S., 263 U. S. 403 (1923). An arrangement was made whereby producers of hand-blown window glass would operate only during specified periods, the periods being staggered so that, while some were operating full scale, others would be idle. The purpose was to allow each firm, when operating, to obtain a full complement of the limited available supply of skilled labor. There was no curtailment of production, hence the Court found it to be a reasonable restraint. Because of the peculiar situation involved and the absence of output curtailment, the case would seem not to qualify the general rule holding restriction of output unlawful.

[24] 288 U. S. 344, 367 (1933).

[25] 310 U. S. 150, 220, (1940).

also has acknowledged the illegal nature of output restrictions by issuing orders against such concerted action.[26]

Coöperative action by holders of process patents to curtail the output of a product which is itself unpatented is unlawful. It is sufficient to quote the rule stated in the "cracking" case: "Where domination exists, a pooling of competing process patents, or an exchange of licenses for the purpose of curtailing the manufacture and supply of an unpatented product, is beyond the privileges conferred by the patents and constitutes a violation of the Sherman Act."[27]

An outstanding application of this rule was in the case of the Hartford-Empire Company.[28] This patent pool violated the law in a number of ways, not the least of which were the restriction of the production and distribution of glass-making machinery and the curtailment of the output of glassware. The courts declined to dissolve the Hartford-Empire Company, but the Supreme Court, for the first time, gave its approval to an anti-trust decree requiring the compulsory licensing of the misused patents. The Court was unwilling to compel the licensing of patents royalty free; rather, it required that licenses be extended at a reasonable royalty to all who applied for them without discrimination or restriction. As a result of the decree, Hartford royalties were reduced by more than 50 per cent, and the number of manufacturers of glassware of various kinds has been increased substantially.[29] Compulsory licensing, royalty-free or more commonly at a reasonable royalty, has been provided for in a large number of consent decrees and can be said to have become a firmly established remedy in cases where patents have been used to maintain prices or restrict entry unlawfully.[30]

In its sustained assault against the participation of American firms in international cartels, the Department of Justice has found patent licensing agreements the most common basis for monopolistic controls embracing allocations of markets, output restrictions, and price maintenance. A number of consent decrees were effective in breaking international pooling and licensing arrangements that restricted American production of strategic materials during World War II. The magnesium decree required the cancellation of all existing patent licenses and agreements and the free licensing of production and fabrication patents "without any

---

[26] See, for example, California Rice Industry, 26 F. T. C. 968 (1938); American Veneer Package Assn., Inc., 30 F. T. C. 665 (1940).

[27] Standard Oil Co. (Indiana) v. U. S., 283 U. S. 163, 174 (1931).

[28] Hartford-Empire Co. v. U. S., 323 U. S. 386 (1945); 324 U. S. 570 (1945).

[29] House Committee on Small Business, United States versus Economic Concentration and Monopoly, pp. 243–244.

[30] See, for example, U. S. v. Bendix Aviation Corp., D. C. N. J. 1946; U. S. v. Diamond Match Co., D. C. N. Y. 1946; U. S. v. Dick & Co., D. C. Ohio 1948. These and many other cases are reported in Commerce Clearing House, Trade Regulation Service.

restrictions or conditions whatsoever" during the war emergency.[31] Reasonable royalties could be charged after the war. The consent decree entered into by the Standard Oil Company of New Jersey declared unlawful certain agreements with I. G. Farbenindustrie, the German chemical trust, which had the effect of suppressing patented processes for the production of synthetic rubber and gasoline from petroleum and coal.[32] Free public licensing and technical information necessary for operations under the patents were required for the duration of the war. Among other things, the defendants were forbidden "to divide sales territories, or restrict production or agree not to manufacture." Another decree that was upheld by the Supreme Court in 1947 involved the control of the production of titanium products by the National Lead Company and du Pont.[33] Through an exchange of patents, the two firms controlled the entire American market and participated in a world cartel that allocated sales territories for titanium pigments. The companies were enjoined from further illegal conduct and required to divest themselves of financial interests in certain foreign companies and to grant licenses on a reciprocal basis at reasonable royalties. Justice Douglas, with whom Justices Murphy and Rutledge joined, believed the decree gave inadequate relief. It is not clear whether the three favored divestiture of plants, which the majority had refused, but they were emphatic in their stand that licensing should be compelled royalty-free and without restrictions.

PRICE UNIFORMITY AND TRADE ASSOCIATION ACTIVITY

Uniformity of prices among sellers in a given market is characteristic of price-fixing arrangements. But uniformity is also characteristic of markets wherein competitive forces operate freely. Because of this seeming paradox, it is most difficult to enforce a public policy against price uniformity arising from collusion. The fact of price uniformity in industrial markets, however, is evidence usually of concerted efforts to maintain price. Where neither buyers nor sellers are fully informed, where sellers produce under diverse conditions, and where disparities in size, financial strength and efficiency make for unequal bargaining power as between sellers and buyers, absolute uniformity in prices is not the

---

[31] U.S. v. Aluminum Co. of America et al., U. S. District Court for Southern District of New York, April 15, 1942. The defendants pleaded nolo contendere to the indictment charging violation of the anti-trust laws, and were fined $140,000.

[32] U. S. v. Standard Oil Co. et al., U. S. District Court of New Jersey, March 25, 1942. Fines of $50,000 were imposed upon the defendants when they pleaded nolo contendere in the criminal proceedings. The consent decree terminated the civil suit.

[33] U. S. v. National Lead Co., 332 U. S. 319 (1947).

natural result of competition. Suspicion is aroused particularly when the prices are maintained for long periods of time and fail to move in accordance with the trend of all prices.

Special attention is given to price uniformity apart from the consideration of price-fixing by agreement, because of the numerous devices and practices whereby organizations of business men have sought to attain this goal without formal agreements. The policies of trade associations, for example, have been directed in large measure to the curtailment of price-cutting. Price-cutting, particularly in periods of declining demand and excessive productive capacity, is greatly feared, and every effort is made to build up a code of business ethics which brands price-cutters as unethical sellers or "chiselers." Trade associations, as indicated in an earlier chapter, have not been satisfied to perform their avowed functions of making competition more informed and intelligent by the gathering and dissemination of significant trade statistics. They have gone further and instituted coöperative control to insure the elimination of price-cutting. To the extent that they have been successful, they have induced a uniformity and stability in prices and terms of sale which have interfered seriously with the control functions of prices.

The Supreme Court has decided five cases relating to the statistical activities of trade associations. Adverse decisions were rendered in three of them, and the programs of the associations were sustained in the other two. The procedure of the Court has been to scrutinize the facts of each particular case to ascertain whether the operation of the plan as a whole has the effect of so limiting competition as to constitute an unreasonable restraint of trade. Such an approach makes it difficult to determine just what parts of a general program are unlawful and to state with certainty what an association may legitimately do by way of interchanging trade information.

The two earliest proceedings in which so-called "open price" or "open competition" plans were reviewed were the American Hardwood Manufacturers' Association[34] case of 1921 and the Linseed Oil[35] case of 1923. "Concerted action" to restrain trade was found in both cases. Repeated reference has already been made to the Hardwood Association case. It is sufficient to point out here that the statistics exchanged as to prices, sales, and production were very detailed, and were accompanied by interpretive comments and strong suggestions respecting future price and production policies. The information collected was not made available to buyers or the general public, hence it did not contribute to the full knowledge essential for the proper functioning of competition. Important elements in the plan of the twelve "crushers" of flaxseed and producers of linseed oil, cake and meal, were the exchange of all price sched-

---

[34] American Column & Lumber Co. v. U. S., 257 U. S. 377 (1921).
[35] U. S. v. American Linseed Oil Co., 262 U. S. 371 (1923).

ules and terms of sale, an agreement to adhere to published prices and to give immediate notice of any quotations at prices lower than these, a zone pricing system, and the interchange of detailed information respecting sales, purchasers, inventories, and other matters. No publicity was given to the statistical information. The business conduct of members was carefully watched, and fines were imposed for failure to live up to their obligations. The Court found that "prices of oil became more stable," and concluded that the "necessary tendency" of the whole plan was "to destroy the kind of competition to which the public has long looked for protection."[36]

In 1925, in the Maple Flooring[37] and Cement Manufacturers[38] cases, the Supreme Court again had occasion to scrutinize elaborate trade association plans for the collection and dissemination of market data. This time, however, the Court found that the facts revealed no agreement or concerted action with respect to prices or output. Several facts served to distinguish the Maple Flooring case from prior decisions. One was that the reports of sales and prices related exclusively to past and closed transactions and did not disclose current prices, the names of purchasers, or the identity of producers rendering specific information. Another was the wide publicity given to the statistics which were gathered. But there were also facts which should have given the Court pause. A basing-point system of pricing was involved. Maple flooring was sold on a delivered price basis, and to aid in the calculation of these prices a freight-rate book giving rates from a basing point to numerous points in the United States was distributed by the association. The association also compiled and circulated the average cost of production of all types of flooring. The Court acknowledged that these data might be used as a basis for fixing prices, but found no evidence of it. On the contrary, prices were found to have exhibited no "abnormality" and were "fair and reasonable."[39]

Justice Stone was greatly impressed with the economic benefits to be had from a wide distribution of market information, and rightly so. Having reduced the issues in the case to the question of the legality of combining for the purpose of collecting and disseminating business

---

[36] U. S. v. American Linseed Oil Co., 262 U. S. 371, 390 (1923).

[37] Maple Flooring Manufacturers Assn. v. U. S., 268 U. S. 563 (1925).

[38] Cement Manufacturers Assn. v. U. S., 268 U. S. 588 (1925).

[39] Monthly meetings were also held, but the Court found that prices were not discussed. The following is significant (p. 575): "It was admitted by several witnesses, however, that upon occasion the trend of prices and future prices became the subject of discussion outside the meeting among individual representatives of the defendants attending the meeting." One is reminded of Adam Smith's classic remark to the effect that "people of the same trade seldom meet together, even for merriment and diversion, but the conversation ends in a conspiracy against the public, or in some contrivance to raise prices." *Wealth of Nations* (ed. Cannan), Vol. I, p. 130.

statistics, he could reach but one decision. He said: "Persons who unite in gathering and disseminating information in trade journals and statistical reports on industry . . . are not engaged in unlawful conspiracies in restraint of trade merely because the ultimate result of their efforts may be to stabilize prices or limit production through a better understanding of economic laws and a more general ability to conform to them."[40] But here the Court was treading on dangerous ground, for the logical result of full information in a market is not stability of price and restriction of production. In purely competitive markets a restriction of production is occasioned by falling prices. A freely determined price adjusts production to demand and cannot be stable in a dynamic economy. The Court seems here to have placed its stamp of approval upon the unfortunate philosophy of many trade associations.[41]

In the Cement Manufacturers[42] case, the members received a variety of trade statistics as well as credit information and data designed to prevent buyers from fraudulently obtaining more cement than they were entitled to under their contracts. Periodic meetings were held, but there was no discussion of current prices or production policies. Not all of the statistics were disseminated to the general public. Cement was sold on a delivered-price basis, and the association distributed freight-rate books giving rates from established basing-points to nearly all destinations in the Northeastern section of the United States. Despite a finding of a "substantial uniformity in the price of cement," the Court held that no inference could be drawn from the Association's activities of a conspiracy to control prices or output. There were some variations in price, and the general uniformity was explained as arising not out of price-fixing, but from the speed with which sellers met changes in price. The Court did admit that price uniformity at artificial levels might in some circumstances be evidence of an agreement, an understanding, or concerted action by sellers.

The facts of the Sugar Institute[43] case, decided in 1936, have been reviewed in detail in an earlier chapter. Comment here will be confined to a few significant matters relating to the Court's decision. The Court found that a dominant purpose of the Institute was to suppress price competition by maintaining a uniform price structure at relatively high levels. A price-reporting plan designed allegedly to eliminate secret discrimination was a part of its arrangement. Members agreed to adhere

---

[40] 268 U. S. 563, 584.

[41] Justice McReynolds, dissenting, said (p. 587): "It seems to me that ordinary knowledge of human nature and of the impelling force of greed ought to permit no serious doubt concerning the ultimate outcome of the arrangements. . . . Pious protestations and smug preambles but intensify distrust when men are found busy with schemes to enrich themselves through circumventions."

[42] 268 U. S. 588 (1925).

[43] U. S. v. Sugar Institute, Inc., 297 U. S. 553 (1936).

strictly to their filed prices until changes, which became effective the following day, were publicly announced and the Institute was notified. The requirement to adhere to published prices was unqualifiedly condemned because it precluded independent negotiations between buyers and sellers and caused prices to be uniform, rigid, and unduly high. The lower court had also objected to the filing and dissemination of prices to be applied in the future. This was in accordance with views expressed in earlier cases. But the Supreme Court sanctioned the reporting of current and future prices because established marketing practices in the trade required the public announcement of prices in advance of sales. It was believed that competitive forces would be freed if the rule requiring sellers to adhere to published prices was eliminated. The Court based this part of its decision on the facts peculiar to the sugar industry, and seems not to have intended to formulate a general rule. There is a real danger that the reporting of current and future prices may be used in some circumstances to facilitate price leadership and harmonious price policies.

Another interesting feature of the Sugar Institute case concerned the statistical services of the trade association. The Institute was enjoined from disseminating statistics on sales, stocks, and similar matters unless they were made available to the purchasing and distributing trade. This was limited by the Supreme Court, however, on the ground that some information which was of a confidential nature might be obtained from refiners. It may be conceded that credit information and the like cannot be given wide publicity, but there would seem to be no reason to permit the withholding of any purely statistical data that an association finds it worth while to gather.

Most of the efforts of the Sugar Institute were directed at obtaining uniformity in terms of sale and in business methods. Its regulations prevented secret concessions and discrimination, but they had the effect also of blocking all opportunities for individual competitive action. Having eliminated any alternative means for rivalry or any indirect price competition, it could then concentrate on the maintenance of uniform prices at satisfactory levels. Accordingly, the Court enjoined concerted action designed either to maintain a delivered price system and uniform credit terms, or to prohibit quantity discounts and long-term contracts. The economic effects of these and numerous other practices were clearly perceived by the courts. In view of the generous treatment accorded basing-point systems in the Maple Flooring and Cement cases, it is particularly noteworthy that concerted action to support a delivered price system was found to be illegal.

The review of the cases involving trade associations suggests that there is no legal objection to the interchange of statistical information between competitors or to numerous other coöperative activities. But certain features of trade association programs are condemned because they yield results which are at variance with competition. Since the courts have determined the legality of plans according to their purposes or effects as a whole, it is not altogether clear which features are lawful and which unlawful. On the basis of the facts stressed in the court opinions and the comments respecting specific parts of plans, the following summary of illegal features may be ventured: (1) Agreements to adhere to published prices and to make no changes in prices without notice; (2) agreements or concerted action to maintain uniform terms and conditions of sales; (3) failure to disseminate statistical information to purchasers and the general public; (4) discussion of prices and production policies at meetings of competitors; (5) interpretive comments and persuasion which might effect uniform action regarding output and prices; (6) the identification of purchasers or sellers in connection with data distributed to competing firms. It is also quite certain that statistical data must be confined to past and closed transactions, but the holding in the Sugar Institute case permitting the filing of current and future prices suggests that peculiar trade conditions may justify legal qualification of this rule. The status of delivered-price systems as a device for maintaining uniformity of prices was also uncertain in the Sherman Act cases, but the Sugar Institute decision did cast doubt on their legality. Ultimate clarification of the legality of delivered prices calculated on accepted basing-points had to await court review of decisions under the Federal Trade Commission and Clayton Acts.

In condemning undesirable aspects of trade association activity, the courts have established certain barriers to the abuse of functions which have a legitimate place in a competitive society.[44] To assure observance of these rules requires vigilance and constant administrative supervision.[45] Trade associations have been prone to stress price stabilization rather than larger profits through increased production and greater vol-

---

[44] A substantial number of consent decrees have been entered in recent years in which trade associations have been forbidden to engage in such practices as price-fixing, adhering to announced prices and terms of sale, disseminating current and future prices, failing to disclose statistical information to purchasers and the public, and the sponsoring of meetings to discuss price and production policies. See, for example, U. S. v. National Container Assn., Southern District, New York, 1940; U. S. v. Southern California Marble Assn., Southern District, California, 1940; U. S. v. California Rice Industry, Northern District, California, 1941; U. S. v. National Retail Lumber Dealers Assn., District, Colorado, 1942. These and other cases are reported in Commerce Clearing House, *Trade Regulation Service*.

The Federal Trade Commission has also issued numerous orders against trade associations, prohibiting the practices enumerated above. See, for example, American Veneer Package Assn., Inc., 30 F. T. C. 665 (1940); Hardwood Institute, Complaint No. 3418 (1942).

[45] For an excellent analysis of the legality of the statistical activities of trade associations and well-considered proposals for strengthening public control, see Milton Handler, T. N. E. C., *Monograph* No. 38, pp. 18–29.

ume of sales. There is a considerable temptation, therefore, to use the trade association as a device for secret understandings and price leadership. Such organizations are apt to bring to industries that "friendly coöperative spirit" about which the Court remarked in the Sugar Institute case. In view of the ease with which trade association functioning may pass from the legitimate to the unlawful, it would seem wise to require each association to register with the Federal Trade Commission and to disclose in great detail its organization, functions, and plan of operation. They should then be required to file all statistical data that have been gathered, as well as to disseminate them to buyers and the general public. Full authority should be given the Commission to require the filing of other reports, to attend meetings, and to scrutinize records. Equipped with adequate authority and information, a vigilant administrative agency would be in a position to detect and to bring appropriate legal action against coöperative control of prices and production.

MARKET-SHARING

There seems to be no doubt that the artificial sharing of markets is illegal under the Sherman Act. The leading decision of the Supreme Court is the Addyston Pipe[46] case. Involved in this case, it will be recalled, was a pooling arrangement between producers of cast-iron pipe. Prices were fixed by the association and business was divided between the members by a complicated system of collusive bidding. The whole arrangement was condemned in such terms as to make it clear that where agreements rather than price competition determine the distribution of sales between firms, the law is violated. The manner in which shares are determined, whether by allocating fixed quotas, customers, or regional areas, is immaterial, since in every case competition between the firms is suppressed. Thus, in the Continental Wall Paper[47] case, a coöperative selling scheme embracing producers of 98 per cent of the wall paper sold in the country was condemned. Among other things, the company fixed the prices of wall paper and determined the output of the contributing firms.

Where the existence of market-sharing agreements or understandings has been established, both the Federal courts and the Federal Trade Commission have declared them illegal.[48] It is difficult, however, to establish the fact that an explicit agreement or conspiracy exists. Where

---

[46] Addyston Pipe & Steel Co. v. U. S., 175 U. S. 211 (1899).

[47] Continental Wall Paper Co. v. Voigt and Sons Co., 212 U. S. 227 (1909).

[48] See, for example, Butchart v. U. S., 295 Fed. 577 (1924); Consent decree in U. S. v. National Container Assn., Southern District, New York (1940); Fyr-Fyter Co., 21 F. T. C. 257 (1935).

coöperation is effected by general consent or convention, as seems to have been the case in the sale of anthracite coal and in meat-packing, the burden of proof is particularly difficult. Unless the courts are willing to infer the existence of tacit agreements from statistical evidence showing uniformity in percentage distribution of business for protracted periods, actual market-sharing may persist.

In the international field, the sharing of markets has been disclosed to be one of the most common methods utilized by cartels to control competition in world trade. The agreements in the case against the Alkali Export Association, for example, contained provisions dividing and allocating foreign markets, establishing export quotas, and preserving the domestic market for American producers. Sales territories and customers were assigned in the agreements involved in the titanium products cartel. Similar arrangements have been revealed in the case of aluminum, electrical equipment, matches, chemicals, and other products. Such agreements are clearly illegal to the extent that they restrain foreign and domestic commerce.[49]

PRICE LEADERSHIP

The attitude of the Supreme Court toward the legality of price leadership was indicated in the Steel[50] and International Harvester[51] cases. In those cases, it will be recalled, evidence of price leadership had been introduced to support the charge of monopoly. But the Court refused to give weight to the evidence as establishing illegal dominance and suppression of competition. Imitation of a leader's price was looked upon as being no more improper than the imitation of a competitor's designs or styles. In the International Harvester case, the Court said:

It has not . . . attempted to dominate or in fact controlled or dominated the harvesting machinery industry by the compulsory regulation of prices. The most that can be said as to this, is that many of its competitors have been accustomed, independently and as a matter of business expediency, to follow approximately the prices at which it has sold its harvesting machines. . . . And the fact that competitors may see proper, in the exercise of their own judgment, to follow the prices of another manufacturer, does not establish any suppression of competition or show any sinister domination.[52]

Price leadership as such is lawful. Simply following the prices of a leader may involve no agreement or conspiracy, hence cannot be inter-

---

[49] U. S. Alkali Export Association v. U. S., 325 U. S. 196 (1945); U. S. v. National Lead Co., 332 U. S. 319 (1947); U. S. v. Diamond Match Co., consent decree, D. C. N. Y. 1946.

[50] U. S. v. United States Steel Corp., 251 U. S. 417 (1920).

[51] U. S. v. International Harvester Co., 274 U. S. 693 (1927).

[52] Ibid., pp. 708–709.

dicted by a statute which outlaws these devices for restraining competition. Yet leadership activity with respect to prices, production or other trade matters can be as effective in controlling prices and output as confederation. A secret understanding, rather than established habit or convention, may underlie the smooth and profitable operation of a leadership scheme. If the evidence of price leadership, and uniform and inflexible prices associated with it, established the presence of conspiracy, the law could move effectively.

It is clear that any understanding is unlawful which permits a firm to make the decisions respecting price policy for an industry group. In the Masonite case, the Court said: "The fixing of prices by one member of a group pursuant to express delegation, acquiescence, or understanding is just as illegal as the fixing of prices by direct, joint action."[53] Agency agreements between a manufacturer and his competitors for the sale of a patented product had been separately negotiated, and the patentee had retained the right to fix the price without consulting the agents. And it is also noteworthy that the Court, on the strength of intimations in a recent decision concerning conspiracy in the motion picture field,[54] might give considerable weight to leadership activity and price uniformity as evidence of conspiracy to fix prices. After pointing out that there was no direct testimony as to unlawful agreement, and that inferences had to be drawn from the conduct of the defendants, the Court said: "It taxes credulity to believe that the several distributors would, in the circumstances, have accepted and put into operation with substantial unanimity such far-reaching changes in their business methods without some understanding that all were to join, and we reject as beyond the range of probability that it was the result of mere chance."[55] This was not a price leadership case, but the conclusion reached does suggest possibilities regarding an attack upon the subtler forms of modern industrial coöperation.

What can be done about price leadership? The most direct attack upon the problem would be to remove the economic conditions which make possible such behavior. Leadership is most apt to be found in industries where there are relatively few large firms and where a single firm is considerably larger than its rivals. Breaking up the dominant concerns would contribute to the restoration of competitive conditions. It might not create immediately a sufficiently large number of firms for pure competition, but it would certainly be a salutary step in that direction. Such action would not be desirable if it were to entail a net loss in productive efficiency, but it has still to be demonstrated that overwhelming size is necessary to the greatest efficiency. The benefits of

---

[53] U. S. v. Masonite Corp., 316 U. S. 265 (1942).

[54] Interstate Circuit, Inc. v. U. S., 306 U. S. 208 (1939).

[55] *Ibid.*, p. 223.

mass production can be obtained from units which now constitute parts of many large horizontal combinations.

There are other and more conservative proposals. Professor Handler has suggested that a "statutory presumption of illegality arising from proof of price uniformity" be created.[56] This would force alleged conspirators to come forward with evidence in their possession to explain why prices were uniform and to show that uniformity was not the result of a definite agreement. He would also make leadership *prima facie* evidence that the leader has a monopoly. This might help to discourage the practice, and would, if leadership by the dominant firm persists, make it easier to prove illegal domination and force the dissolution of the firm. The suggested remedy for leadership which results from convention rather than agreement is administrative control. Control by an administrative agency would be designed, as Professor Handler has put it, "to eliminate the causes of and conditions favorable to the practice, and to restore, invigorate, and protect competition" in industries where leadership is prevalent.[57] Such flexible administrative regulation could be of some aid in removing devices which facilitate leadership, but to remove the fundamental causes would require reorganization of the concentrated industries. If the large dominant firms are to be allowed to exist and to exercise managerial powers, any regulation must necessarily inquire into the reasonableness of prices and undertake to control them. This would entail the assumption of the numerous and difficult tasks presently associated with the regulation of transportation and public utility rates.

One specific practice upon which the smooth operation of leadership and uniform price policies seems to depend is the quotation of delivered prices.[58] Formula prices calculated by means of basing-points or zones produces identical delivered prices from all points of origin. It is a simple matter, therefore, to detect price-cutting by any seller. The leader may exercise his power in the selection of the basing-points and in the quotation of prices at the various bases. Coöperators have little difficulty in calculating delivered prices on the basing-point quotations.

What will be the actual effect on price leadership in the steel industry of introducing f.o.b. pricing, for example, remains to be seen. It is even uncertain whether the modified pricing methods occasioned by recent administrative and judicial decrees will be permanently maintained. Congress has found it inadvisable to require a rigid f.o.b. pricing system, and is inclined to allow delivered pricing and freight ab-

---

[56] T. N. E. C., *Monograph* No. 38, p. 44.

[57] *Ibid.*, p. 45.

[58] For an analysis of the relation of formula prices to price leadership, see George P. Comer, "Price Leadership," *Law and Contemporary Problems*, Vol. VII (1940), pp. 61–73.

sorption where independently practiced. How such a policy will work out in relation to price leadership, it is difficult to predict. Leadership could still persist with respect to uniform f.o.b. prices, but it would be unlikely when competitors were confined to selling in their natural market areas. Competitors located at the same producing points could, of course, follow uniform pricing policies to advantage. If prices were quoted on an f.o.b. mill basis, the prices of differently situated sellers would tend to vary at each point of delivery, and, assuming equal production costs, the business would go to the seller having the lowest freight charges.

COERCION AND BOYCOTTS

One further type of coöperation deserves brief consideration. It is not uncommon for a trade group to take concerted action to force others to conform to business policies which are desired by the combining firms. The method used to obtain compliance with the demands of the coöperating group is usually some form of boycotting. They refuse to deal with the obnoxious firms. Since such concerted action must necessarily impair the economic welfare of the non-conforming firms and may actually force them out of business, the courts have invariably found the boycott to be an unreasonable restraint of trade.

The leading decision by the Supreme Court is Eastern States Retail Lumber Dealers' Association v. United States.[59] Members of the association were required to report the names of wholesalers who sold lumber directly to consumers. A blacklist of offending wholesalers was then circulated among the retailers. There was no agreement requiring the withholding of patronage from these firms, but the obvious purpose and effect were just that. The retailers contended that their action was necessary to protect the retail trade and that their continued existence was in the public interest, but the Court held that this constituted no defense for the use of means that violated the law. It was conceded that an individual or firm acting alone might for any reason stop his dealings with another. In no circumstances, however, could he conspire with others to take action which had the effect of unduly suppressing competition.

A long series of cases has been decided on the authority of the above decision. Three may be mentioned. In the Paramount[60] case, the ten leading producers and distributors of motion picture films agreed to refuse to contract for the display of films except on the terms of a standard contract. Exhibitors objected to the provision requiring arbitration of

---

[59] 234 U. S. 600 (1914).
[60] Paramount-Famous-Lasky Corp. v. U. S., 282 U. S. 30 (1930).

all disputes. The Court found no justification of the arrangement in the fact that arbitration was "well adapted to the needs" of the industry, and condemned it because it coerced exhibitors and limited the freedom of trade. In the Fashion Originators' Guild[61] case, the Court upheld an order of the Federal Trade Commission against a boycott program designed to protect the participating firms from so-called "style piracy." The plan violated the law in several respects, chief of which was the fact that it subjected "all retailers and manufacturers who decline to comply with the Guild's program to an organized boycott." Again the Court refused to entertain evidence offered in extenuation of the boycotting scheme. And in the Associated Press[62] case, the Court found that the restrictions upon membership in the newsgathering association violated the law. The bylaws of the AP, as actually administered over the years, made it impossible for a newspaper to acquire membership over the objection of a competing member newspaper in the same city and field. Applicants who did not compete with members were freely admitted. Contentions that other competing news agencies were available and that application of the law interfered with the freedom of the press were of no avail. The Court ruled that consideration could not be given to the competitive effect upon any member when applications for admission were passed upon.[63]

The law with respect to boycotts and other coercive restraints is eminently satisfactory. Such interferences with competition are unlawful in all circumstances. It is immaterial how good the intentions of the combining group are and what facts may be adduced by way of justification.

CONCLUSION

The anti-trust laws are effectual instruments for removing impediments to competition where they are effected by means of agreement, understanding, or conspiracy. There has been no sustained weakening of the law relating to loose combinations that have as their objective the fixing of prices, the control of output, the sharing of markets, or the exclusion of competitors. A handful of decisions reflect the "rule of reason," but the great body of cases manifests an uncompromising attitude toward any coöperation which threatens the operation of competitive individualism.

---

[61] Fashion Originators' Guild v. F. T. C., 312 U. S. 457 (1941).

[62] Associated Press v. U. S., 326 U. S. 1 (1945).

[63] See also American Medical Association v. U. S., 317 U. S. 519 (1943), in which the Court, without deciding whether a physician's practice of his profession constitutes trade, upheld the charge that the Association conspired to obstruct and restrain the business of Group Health Association, Inc., a coöperative organized to provide medical care and hospitalization in Washington, D. C.

There is in this respect a decided contrast to the liberal rules which have been adopted in some of the merger cases. And the effect has not been altogether wholesome, for the disparity in treatment has undoubtedly encouraged the elimination of competition through merger and consolidation. With this added stimulus to concentration in many fields, the relations between firms have become such that harmonious price and production policies are inevitable, even apart from any formal coöperation. The attitude of the courts toward price leadership indicates the difficulty of attacking such market behavior under statutes that deal with agreements and conspiracies. Where the number of firms is large it becomes necessary to resort to agreements and understandings, and these can be detected and prosecuted under the law.

Some changes in the law are advisable, but they need not be revolutionary. The creation of statutory presumptions with respect to price leadership and price uniformity would lighten the burden of proof and facilitate prosecution. The elimination of collusive and discriminatory basing-point and zoning systems is desirable. Administrative supervision of trade associations is necessary. The main problem, however, is that of more adequate enforcement of the anti-trust laws. The generally accepted objectives of these laws cannot be realized if their enforcement is sporadic and half-hearted. Marked progress has already been made because of the provision of larger appropriations and more adequate staffs for the Department of Justice and the Federal Trade Commission. If these provisions are continued and increased to meet the expanding needs of these enforcement agencies, there is hope for the survival of the competitive system.

CONCLUSION
Possible Public Policies

31

The Reconstruction of Competitive Individualism

It is perfectly apparent that in sizable areas of the American economy the concentration of business in very large corporate units has created conditions inimical to competitive control of production. The planning of business affairs is left supposedly to individuals who risk their property in return for the profit rewards paid for successful direction. And profits, along with the other two members of the ruling triumvirate—prices and costs—serve to show how the scarce productive resources of the country should be allocated among all the possible uses, and exercise a pressure to force them to be used efficiently. But the planning process cannot work if property does not exercise its control functions, and if the individual producer is not held in check by the competition of other producers. And all too frequently these prerequisites are missing, with results that should not be tolerated.

Concentration frequently has removed corporate control from the mass of owners and placed it in the hands of either minority groups with small property interests, or management groups who have exchanged their positions as employees for places of control. Frequently the stockholder is unable to protect his rights to control, but in many instances he is perfectly willing to surrender a right that entails obligations. Regardless of the stockholder's attitude, the planning machinery will work badly if his duties are assumed by some group possessing a different position and interest in the corporation.

Neither management nor minority groups have the same point of view toward corporate affairs as do the majority of stockholders, and management officers are in an essentially different position in the corporate structure. They are not in the position of residual income receivers who take large or small returns as the corporation is successful or unsuccessful. Once in control, they are able to perpetuate their power and set payments for their services that may have little connection with their efficiency. It is impossible to operate an individualistic system in which the power of some individuals is not subject to any quickly effective check. That is obvious in the realm of political individualism, and it must be equally true that an arrangement of checks and balances is required in any system of economic individualism. Or if unlimited power is granted to the executive, the system must provide for the immediate dismissal of the executive when he loses the confidence of the electorate. And that provision we do not have. Even if production plans are well laid, and the rewards paid to themselves by control groups are moderate, we cannot depend on a planning system that may be upset at any time by the actions of one group in the system. The presence of a benign and intelligent autocrat does not create a system of economic or political democracy.

In the study of monopoly and industrial coöperation it appears that concentrated power has not brought satisfactory planning. The economic results of monopoly are not tolerable. Production is commonly restricted for the sake of high profits or stability, and the incentive for improvement may be lessened as producers are no longer exposed to competitive pressures.

From its beginning the system of competitive individualism has been shaped by political controls. It is commonplace to recognize that the state must authoritatively define and protect the rights of the various classes of individuals that coöperate in competitive production. To the American common law a great many statutory controls have been added. In very recent years Federal legislation has materially altered the rules that apply in the sale of corporate securities and in the organization of public utility holding companies. And for a number of decades the Federal power has been directed against monopoly. The older controls have not been notably successful in preventing either the faulty operation or the partial disappearance of competition. But solution for these problems must be sought in a more intense application of social controls.

POSSIBLE PUBLIC POLICIES

Public policy may take one of three divergent lines, or may try for some compromise among the three. It may attack the general conditions and the specific industrial practices that are inimical to competitive individualism; it may replace private planning with social planning; it may allow unchecked power to remain in the hands of the economic interests that can seize it. Up to the present time our public supervision of economic affairs has allowed all three lines of policy to develop. Spasmodic opposition to monopoly has brought a measure of the first. Despair over competitive individualism has brought forth some amount of government planning or government operation in certain fields of industry. And certainly many corporations and many industries are directed by groups that are subject to no effective and direct economic or political check.

It is possible to find an economic philosophy that would justify any one of these alternatives. Even the last is to a few people an acceptable economic application of the Fascist philosophy. It would bring the organization of individuals into conflicting economic groups. Inevitably the conflict would become political, and the victor would hold his position through a Fascistic political organization of the State. Since the philosophy is unacceptable to American ideals, there is no need to prepare any bill of particulars against its economic application.

Social planning as an alternative would substitute some form of collective planning for economic individualism. Political power would be organized so as to make directly the necessary economic decisions as to where and how labor and material resources were to be utilized. The authority of the people concentrated in the machinery of the State would be used to control the concentration of economic power that modern business has developed. The planning rôle now held by prices, costs, and profits would be taken over by government officials. Controversy over the merits of socialism has waged for many years and cannot be settled here. Probably the values to be gained and lost in the abandonment of the system of private enterprise for some form of socialism are too varied and too susceptible to varying measurement for any logical answer. Only a zealot finds the clear and indisputable answer, and he finds it in his own dogma.

Three considerations seem to appear logically out of study of the problem. First, the present system, which has become largely a lack of system, is not going to remain unchanged. The stand-patter who can see no wrong in the system and no reason in the force of circumstances for inevitable change is living in a pleasant dream-world.

Second, there is a danger that we may lose cherished political values in turning to social planning as an alternative to economic individualism. It was not by chance that in the Western world economic and political individualism came to the fore together. From the rise of the medieval town to the Industrial Revolution their growth was linked. And it may even be possible for such a nation as Russia, if she would accept thorough-going international coöperation, to replace authoritarianism by a really democratic Communism. But the task entailed in planning the infinitely detailed economic affairs of a huge nation is a dangerously heavy one for popular government. As individualism is replaced, groups are organized to protect their collective interests, and the danger to political individualism becomes very great.

Third, we have been slow to recognize and take consistent action against the economic developments that are unfavorable to the competitive system. There is much that can be done through political controls to give competitive individualism an opportunity to survive and to plan satisfactorily our economic affairs. Possible measures to revitalize competition and to improve its operation in control of production constitute the subject matter of this chapter.

Most of the many varieties of socialists and social planners will dismiss this project as hopeless tinkering. But if the logic of our industrial circumstances has any force, it surely would support the proposal that we give our present system the best possible trial before we move on into all the uncertainties of some undefined system of social planning. There are certain areas of private industry where competition has become so weakened or distorted that the attempt to continue competitive controls would be a mistake. The following chapter discusses the special treatment that might be afforded these "problem" industries.

THE RECONSTRUCTION OF COMPETITIVE CONTROLS

Public controls merely designed to alter the production pattern will not suffice for the revitalization of the competitive system. They must reach into other areas of our economy where private regulation of our economic affairs is working unsatisfactorily. The dangers for competitive individualism which have been displayed in banking instability, in economic nationalism, in severe inequality in incomes, must be met adequately by social controls. These problems, however, have been beyond the scope of this work, and their correctives certainly cannot be dealt with here. The measures discussed here are only those designed to protect and improve directly the competitive control of production. They comprise a considerable program affecting our public policy in respect to economic investigations, the corporate form, intercorporate relations, administration, the legal monopoly contained in patent privileges, and the area of competition.

Public Investigation

In the light of industrial developments in the United States it appears that there are segments of the economy which are still highly competitive; segments which contain a mixture of competitive and monopolistic elements; and segments in which competition has not worked and probably cannot work satisfactorily. Before any intelligent policy can be undertaken we must be able to locate these varying conditions, and we must determine those industries in which the revitalization of competition does not appear feasible. And where it appears that positive public controls will protect and improve the operation of competitive controls, further investigation is needed to reveal the specific weaknesses and faults of competition.

There are various ways of securing this information. Congress can appropriate funds periodically to conduct prolonged investigations. The study of the concentration of economic power by the Temporary National Economic Committee was of great value. Or the Anti-trust Division of the Department of Justice, in preparing to prosecute alleged violators of the anti-trust laws, may get a fairly clear and complete picture of the competitive-monopolistic elements in an industry. The Federal Trade Commission may learn a good deal about the plane of competition through the medium of trade practice conferences or through prosecutions conducted against particular violators of the Trade Commission Act, the Clayton Act, or other legislation under its jurisdiction.

No one of these ways is completely satisfactory. Nor do they in combination fill the bill. Sound public policy requires that at least the leading industries be the objects of continuing and not occasional study and observation. The Economic Division of the Federal Trade Commission might be expanded for this purpose. Manned by trained economic analysts and granted sufficient funds to do a thorough piece of work, this division could discover and organize the facts concerning the growth of an industry and current policies bearing on prices, market areas, market practices, the use of patents, corporate structures and corporate interrelations, and other matters affecting the quality and vigor of competition.

The advantages of this arrangement are evident. Within a comparatively short time the public would have a fairly comprehensive idea of the segments of industry which are largely competitive and appear likely to remain so. Likewise the public would learn of the nature and extent of monopoly elements in other segments of industry. A more effective and intelligent public approach to each situation could be formulated. In the event that the proper regulatory agency wished to conduct anti-trust prosecution on a broad scale against an entire industry or against individual malefactors, up-to-date and pertinent information would always be available. Certainly economic study and analysis should reveal the danger-points of monopolistic infection and the specific areas of monopoly. It would be unnecessary for a regulatory agency to await the accumulation of complaints by the public or to conduct preliminary investigations of its own before applying the law. On the other hand, should it appear that the possibilities of restoring real competition are remote, public funds would not be spent in attempts to win futile paper victories in court. A more effective and immediate attack on the problem could be recommended for Congressional action.

Corporate Organization

The growth of large corporations has supplied the basic condition out of which many of the faults of the competitive economy have arisen. Recent public controls administered by the Securities Exchange Commission have been directed against exploitation in the sale of new and old securities, and in some measure against the loss of control by security owners. Increased publicity for corporate affairs and control of proxy solicitation may assist the owner in exercising control over corporate affairs. But owners coming, as they usually do, into a corporation after it has been organized are affected by evils that creep in with incorporation. Complex financial structures make it difficult for the owner even to know, much less maintain any fixed position in respect to, the income and assets of the corporation. And similarly, incorporation provisions frequently make it very easy for a group in control to disfranchise large numbers of owners through the use of such devices as weighted and non-voting stock. When control in the individual corporation can be so easily concentrated in the hands of a small group, and when large powers are granted to the corporation, the growth of monopoly and industrial coöperation is made easy.

It appears certain that improved controls over the corporation through simpler and more rigidly supervised charter provisions are not going to come from the individual states. Federal incorporation of all interstate companies is required. Incorporation fees may be left largely to the states, but the prescription of uniform and clearly delimited powers for the corporation and for each of the groups comprising the corporation must be made by some Federal agency. It is a function that might well be assigned to an enlarged Federal Trade Commission.

The tremendous size of a number of corporations makes grave problems for competitive individualism. A fifty-million or a five-hundred-million-dollar corporation is a powerful individual, and its presence creates a number of the strains that bother the individualistic system. It has been proposed that Federal incorporation should be used to place a maximum on the size of corporations.

Legislation might prescribe the general standard as being that volume of business for the individual firm which would be compatible with workable, thorough-going competition. The duty of setting the specific maxima for different industries could be given to some administrative body such as the Federal Trade Commission. Administration of a control of this sort would not be easy nor wholly satisfactory. The maxima might be sufficiently small to reduce companies in some industries below their optimum size, thereby sacrificing something in economic efficiency. Furthermore, competition itself might suffer as individual firms, through vigorous competition, increased their volume of business up to the maximum.[1] But if other measures are insufficient to insure competition, a choice must be made between (1) the administrative difficulties and possible economic sacrifices of a measure of this sort; (2) the much greater administrative burden and possible economic sacrifices of a "planned" economy; and (3) the consequences, political, economic, and social, that may flow from the further concentration of economic power.

Inter-corporate Relations

The relations developed among corporations have been responsible for both the faulty operation and the decline of competition. The holding company has created certain corporate problems, and a number of inter-corporate relations have been important in the development of monopoly and industrial coöperation. Repeal or amendment of certain public controls and the creation of new controls would be beneficial.

The Miller-Tydings Act legalizing re-sale price maintenance, and the Webb-Pomerene Act permitting the association of American producers in export associations, unquestionably "tend to substantially lessen competition." The desirability of these acts needs the careful reconsideration of the Congress.

The policy embodied in the Sherman Act must be clarified and sharpened. As interpreted by the Supreme Court, the Act has been directed only at completed monopoly, and varying weight has been given to the criteria used to establish the existence of monopoly. As a result the control has had little or no preventive value, and its application has been inconsistent and unpredictable. The emphasis upon the behavior of dominant manufacturing combinations toward accomplices or small survivors has too frequently allowed the continued existence of actual monopolies. A more realistic view seems to have been shown by the courts in recent cases. With less weight accorded to specific intent and the abuse of power as tests of illegality, the prospect of a successful attack upon combinations that hold substantial power is enhanced. But it is still true that the Sherman Act is a weak instrument for the prevention of monopoly growth. The control should move positively to protect competition, and should not wait for the full development of monopoly power. In applying the anti-trust laws to exclusionary tactics of powerful firms and to the innumerable devices used for purposes of coöperation, the courts have left little to be desired in recent years. A like awareness of the dangers inherent in the extension of economic power through mergers

---

[1] For a most interesting discussion of the whole problem of concentration of economic power and, in particular, the problems arising from attempts to impose rigid limits upon permissible size of business organizations, see Corwin D. Edwards, *Maintaining Competition*, (New York, McGraw-Hill Book Company, Inc., 1949), Chap. IV. For an intriguing plan to limit size, see Fred I. Raymond, *The Limitist*, (New York, W. W. Norton and Company, 1947).

and the reduction in the number of competing firms would be a welcome development in the judicial interpretation of the anti-trust laws.

The damaging loophole now in Section 7 of the Clayton Act should be closed, and added strength to prevent undesirable concentration should be given to the Section. In this connection the following recommendation of the Temporary National Economic Committee, transmitted to Congress in March 1941, would provide satisfactory corrections.[2] No corporation should be allowed to acquire the capital assets and property of competing corporations unless it could be shown:

(a) That the acquisition is in the public interest and will be promotive of greater efficiency and economy of production, distribution, and management;

(b) That it will not substantially lessen competition, restrain trade, or tend to create a monopoly (either in a single section of the country or in the country as a whole) in the trade, industry, or line of commerce in which such corporations are engaged;

(c) That the corporations involved in such acquisition do not control more than such proportion of the trade, industry, or line of commerce in which they are engaged as Congress may determine;

(d) That the size of the acquiring company after the acquisition will not be incompatible with the existence and maintenance of vigorous and effective competition in the trade, industry, or line of commerce in which it is engaged;

(e) That the acquisition will not so reduce the number of competing companies in the trade, industry, or line of commerce as materially to lessen the effectiveness and vigor of competition in such trade, industry, or line of commerce;

(f) That the acquiring company has not, to induce the acquisition, indulged in any unlawful methods of competition or has not otherwise violated the provisions of the Federal Trade Commission Act, as amended.

In addition, the Committee recommended legislation to prohibit all acquisition of stock in competing companies except when made for *bona fide* investment purposes or for the control of true subsidiaries.

Section 8 of the Clayton Act, designed to prevent competing corporations which exceed a certain size from developing a community of interest through the use of interlocking directorates, has been practically useless. Means of evasion are too numerous. Wealthy individuals, members of a single wealthy family, or the management of a family corporation may own legally a controlling stock interest in more than one apparently competing company. Similarly, this section does not prevent competing enterprises from having identical officers or from using identical service agencies—accounting, banking, law—through which acceptable common policies pertaining to competition might be established. The Federal Trade Commission and an appropriate Congressional committee should study thoroughly the existing administrative and legal weaknesses of Section 8 and design appropriate legislation for Congres-

---

[2] T. N. E. C., *Final Report and Recommendations of the Temporary National Economic Committee* (March 31, 1941), p. 39.

sional action. If this section of the law is not to be improved it should be eliminated entirely. It is unfair to expect the Commission to enforce the unenforceable. And certainly laws, or parts of them, which can so easily be flouted add little to the respect for law.

The use of two devices instrumental in organizing industrial coöperation should be curtailed: basing-point and zone price systems have been used too frequently to prevent the appearance of competitive independence in an industry. Progress in this direction has been made in such heavy industries as steel and cement. Outright prohibition of delivered-pricing is probably impracticable and unnecessary, but the collusive use of the device in industries where transportation charges are significant must be prevented through administrative action.

The trade association, although used to restrain competition, has too many valuable and legitimate functions to be driven out of use. The illegal coöperation which it may organize must be attacked, however, and supervision would at least reduce the problem. Legislation should require all interstate trade associations to register with and give regular and full accounts of their activities and policies to the Federal Trade Commission. In this fashion at least the easy organization of illegal restraints will be prevented.

Administrative Changes

At the present time the two Federal agencies dealing with monopoly in industry are the Federal Trade Commission and the Anti-trust Division of the Department of Justice. To date the latter has borne the brunt of this work under the Sherman Act, although the Commission has assumed some of the burden under Section 5 of its organic act and under the Clayton Act. The work of the two agencies should be consolidated. Logically the entire job should rest with the Federal Trade Commission, and the proper changes in legislation should be made to make this possible. That portion of the Department of Justice legal staff which has devoted most of its attention to monopoly prosecution should be transferred to the Trade Commission. Along with it should go the economic staff (with which the Anti-trust Division has been implemented during the past few years) and the accumulated data on anti-trust activity of the last half-century. Consolidation of the agencies dealing with competitive methods and industrial monopoly would foster a more effective treatment of the whole problem. The entire task would fall squarely on the shoulders of a single agency. Responsibility could not be shifted easily. Moreover, there would be somewhat less chance for political favoritism or spite to permeate Federal policy and administration, since the Commission is a bi-partisan organization.

In certain respects the penalties for violations of the anti-trust laws should be increased. The present maximum fine of $5,000 is not a sufficient deterrent to individuals responsible for the actions of corporate bodies. Since the courts will rarely apply existing imprisonment penalties, a much higher maximum should be set for fines to discourage violations of the law. The importance of $5,000 today is much less than it was when the Sherman Act was passed in 1890. It is not at all uncommon for alleged violators of the law to plead *nolo contendere* and accept the relatively puny fines presently imposed.[3] In sections of industry that are not too competitive, allowances can easily be made in costs to cover the imposition of such fines, or the fines can be paid from monopoly gains without great injury to the company. An upper limit of $50,000 was proposed by the Temporary National Economic Committee.[4] The T. N. E. C. recommendation is not unreasonable in the light of modern conditions and past results.

It must be recognized, however, that markedly increased appropriations must be made for continuing investigations and for enforcement of anti-trust controls. Legislative and administrative changes are useless until adequate funds are provided for administration.[5] The problems are surely of sufficient import to the American system to allow the most economy-minded Congressman a pure conscience in supporting materially greater appropriations.

Certain administrative changes should be made to strengthen the Federal Trade Commission and the Department of Justice in their battle against violators of the laws. The request of the Commission should be granted to amend the Clayton Act so that cease and desist orders entered thereunder shall become final in the same manner as similar orders now do under the Federal Trade Commission Act. The hand of the Department of Justice should be strengthened in civil cases under the Sherman Act by granting the Department the right to subpoena evidence to improve its investigatory powers. And in the formulation of decrees arising from civil action under the Sherman Act, it should be mandatory for the courts to use the advisory services of the Federal Trade Commission when negotiating a decree with the prosecution and defense.[6]

An alternate proposal designed to improve the operations of both the Anti-trust Division of the Department of Justice and the Federal Trade Commission is the establishment of a Joint Policy Committee of the two

---

[3] For supporting evidence, see Department of Justice releases dated March 1, 1949, April 18 and 20, 1949, May 3 and 9, 1949, and June 9, 1949.

[4] T. N. E. C., *Final Report and Recommendations*, p. 40.

[5] Cf. M. C. Estes Kefauver, "Needed Changes in Legislation," *American Economic Review*, Papers and Proceedings, Vol. XXXVIII, No. 2 (May 1948), pp. 185–188.

[6] Cf. Edwards, *op. cit.*, pp. 298–303. For an extended treatment of administrative procedures of antitrust, see Walton Hamilton and Irene Till, T. N. E. C. Monograph No. 16, *Antitrust in Action* (Washington, D. C., U. S. Government Printing Office, 1941).

agencies.[7] This proposal disturbs neither agency. It also retains the desirable principle of checks and balances; at the same time it would encourage closer coöperation and unity of purpose. Furthermore, it could be accomplished much more easily than a more drastic change. This Joint Policy Committee should be represented on an *inter-agency* committee which would include all important agencies whose work impinges on the maintenance of competition.[8] In this way a more concerted attack could be made on the various monopolistic elements and injurious competitive methods found in American industry.

Two civil remedies might be developed to deter the growth of monopoly or to aid in its elimination. Where a company or a group of companies has been found controlling the market, any tariff protection existing for its products and any patent rights which it possesses should be revoked. Tariffs have been money-making aids for many enterprises, and the threatened loss of tariff protection would act as a strong deterrent to monopolists in a number of industries. Similarly, the patent privilege granted by society to the individual has been the source of success for many companies, and its withdrawal would represent a severe penalty. Not only would these measures seem to lessen the attacks made on competition, but they would aid materially in the restoration of competition wherever patents or tariffs had been used as a source of power to build illegal coöperation or monopoly.

Patents and Patent Control

There is clearly a need to revise the present patent system. In the cigarette, aluminum, shoe machinery, glass container, and other important industries it has been the source of anti-social results. Industrialists have extended the legal monopoly granted under letters patent far beyond what the law originally intended. And usually the consequences are not apparent until the situation is well out of control and remedies are relatively ineffective.

In approaching patent law reforms, two thoughts should be kept constantly in mind. First, inventive genius and collective research should be encouraged, protected, and rewarded in the interests of the common welfare. Second, common welfare is enhanced where the results of inventive genius are made available to society on reasonable terms and free of abusive practices which interfere unduly with the operations of a political economy dedicated to the maintenance of reasonably free competition. There is good reason to believe that these two objectives are not fundamentally incompatible.

---

[7] *Task Force Report on Regulatory Commissions*, Appendix N, p. 132.
[8] *Ibid.*, p. 132.

The Temporary National Economic Committee[9] and others have made several proposals which deserve thoughtful consideration. To prevent patent suppression and at the same time provide the patentee with an equitable return for inventive genius, it has suggested that patent legislation be enacted which will make any future patent available for use by any person or organization upon payment of a fair price for the privilege.

A less drastic proposal along similar lines is that a patentee should be prevented from unreasonably holding inventions out of use, since such action is not in harmony with the basic purpose of the patent grant, viz., to promote progress of the arts. The law should be reformulated so as to require a patentee to put the patent to use within a reasonable period of time or make it available by license to those who are willing to pay a fair royalty for its use.

Whatever form compulsory licensing takes, immediate or conditional, such legislation should be implemented by administrative machinery to which patentee and licensed users of the patent might turn to determine the fairness of royalty rates. In the interest of all parties, including the public, appeal from questionable decisions of the administrative body should be carried to the Circuit Court of Appeals for adjudication, and, if necessary, to the Supreme Court itself.

In recent years the courts have required holders of patents, in certain circumstances involving violation of the anti-trust laws, to make their patents available to all comers upon payment of reasonable royalties.[10] This is a step in the right direction. And, in event immediate or conditional compulsory licensing is not attainable through a change in the law, the Congress should at least make compulsory, unrestricted licensing the right of government when patentees abuse the anti-trust and the patent laws. It might well be that patent suppression and withholding from use unreasonably could be defined as abuses. By making this type of penalty statutory, its imposition upon proved violation becomes a certainty.

Licenses to use patents should be granted on an unrestricted basis. Where restrictions can be imposed, there is a very strong possibility that a double toll can be exacted from the public. The licensee may be restricted in the amount of goods he produces with the patented machine or process. He may also have to sell his product at prices dictated by the patentee or confine the sale of his product to designated market areas. The effect would be restricted production and sale, monopoly prices for the final products, and an inordinately high royalty rate based

---

[9] T. N. E. C., *Final Report and Recommendations*, pp. 36–37.

[10] Court judgments and consent decrees have imposed both royalty-free and reasonable royalty compulsory licensing of patents, depending upon the conditions. See *Antitrust Law Symposium*, p. 82.

on the monopoly price of the final product. The glass container industry illustrates the consequences of the present inequitable system.

The supervision of royalty contracts and license arrangements might be added to the duties of the Federal Trade Commission. Patentees should be required to file attested copies of licenses, assignments, sales contracts, and the like with the Commission within thirty days after execution. Failure to file would be indicative of lack of good faith, and should subject the delinquent to a substantial penalty. If the Trade Commission becomes the future central agency for the control of industrial monopoly, as well as the conservator of fair competition in interstate trade and commerce, there should be little dispute over giving it the power to supervise the patent situation, once patents are granted and registered in the Patent Office.

Another feature of the patent problem which is in need of remedial action has to do with the duration of actual protection under the law. It is assumed that the patentee is protected legally for seventeen years, but actually he may be protected for a longer period of time. The case of the Hartford-Empire Company illustrates the point. This company applied for a patent in 1910, which was granted in 1937. A powerful company thus enjoys considerable protection for twenty-seven years and then gets full measure of protection for an additional seventeen years. Professor Walton Hamilton's proposal, adopted by the Temporary National Economic Committee, would limit the period of patent monopoly to not more than twenty years from the date of initial filing.[11] Where applications are held pending in the Patent Office longer than three years, the usual seventeen-year term of patent protection would be decreased to that extent. The arrangement would discourage deliberate retardation on the part of the applicant, and would encourage quick and efficient handling by the Patent Office. Furthermore, Congress would have to meet squarely the problem of proper appropriations for Patent Office purposes, or else undergo increased public censure for failing to provide an adequate staff for this important office.

For years infringement suits have been a very potent weapon in the hands of large firms. Litigation or the threat of it has been an instrument of aggression rather than a method of protection. It is not easy to solve the problem of retaining the defensive features of the action while curbing its use as a weapon to cripple or destroy potential competition. On several occasions the Federal Trade Commission has attempted with no success to prevent firms from using threats of infringement litigation as a device to achieve monopoly positions. Two orders to cease and desist were appealed to the courts, and in each case the Federal Trade

---

[11] T. N. E. C., Monograph No. 31, *Patents and Free Enterprise*, p. 146. See also T. N. E. C., *Final Report and Recommendations*, p. 37.

Commission was defeated. It was unable to prove that the threats to sue were not made in good faith.[12] The adoption of the unrestricted license to use patents at terms which are fair to the patentee and to the licensee may reduce the volume of infringement suits and deflate the importance of the threat of litigation. Furthermore, one important improvement can be made. Legislation should prevent the directing of any charge of infringement against the licensee until the plaintiff has secured a judgment against the holder of the conflicting patent right. In this fashion a clear adjudication of the conflicting claims can be obtained, and the action cannot be used to harass defenseless licensees while judicial consideration of the basic conflict is avoided.

Market Area Restrictions

With low-cost transportation, a great many products can move economically to distant producing and consuming areas. Their free movement is essential to a desirable economic specialization, and can also provide important protections for competition. Just as in the past many local monopolies disappeared with the development of a national economy, so in a number of cases can national monopolies be weakened by the competition of foreign supplies. But while we have spent a great deal of emotion over the preservation of the American system, we have made things easy for monopolies by protecting them against foreign competition. The tariff has been the mother of many monopolies. For a number of the products which have been afforded protection, the removal of this tariff protection would introduce a healthy competition. For some it would mean the weakening of a firmly entrenched monopoly. It is difficult to overcome the interests of industrial groups who benefit from tariff protection, but even they must recognize the lack of social logic in withholding competition from industries in which monopolistic arrangements are admittedly public problems.

Removal of tariff protection *per se* obviously will not be effective where international cartels prevail. Hence it is imperative that continued attacks be made on American firms participating in such agreements. Furthermore, the United States should continue to assert its influence and exercise its leadership in the United Nations organizations to decrease the power of cartels in international trade.

There is a danger that state interests may result in a further narrowing of the area of competition. State trade barriers, in the form of protective measures against infection from out-of-state grain, cattle, vegetables and fruits, have not always been innocent of a business purpose. And certainly severe limitations in some states on the maximum weight and length allowed to highway carriers have been designed frequently to

---

[12] *Supra*, Chap. 22, note 156.

protect railways from competition. If we accept a national trade barrier as economically justified, we can hardly complain if individual states set up their own barrier. But, aside from the dubious economics involved, the danger of further weakening competition is too great to be ignored. In the interest of preserving the competitive system we must maintain as wide a market as economic factors will permit.

OTHER PROPOSALS

The power of concentration can be markedly lessened in many industries where it has developed. Consumer coöperation, without government aid, now possesses some power and may develop much greater power to prevent the spread of collusion, even where a few large sellers are present in the market. As in England and in Sweden, consumers may find in union a strength to match that of monopolies or oligopolies. As the power of consumer organizations increases, due care must be exercised to prevent crippling legislation designed to interfere with their development. And until the problem of increasing size in business organization has been solved satisfactorily, consumer coöperation should not be discouraged from the backward integration necessary in many fields to cope with market rivals.

Ways and means short of direct subsidy should be devised to promote small business organizations. A positive approach would be through the supply of services not available or not within the financial reach of small organizations. For example, acquisition of investment capital is now difficult and expensive for small business, since investment bankers find it unattractive to do business in small-scale lots. Furthermore, the mortality among small businesses is greatest in the period of infancy, when the babes in the commercial woods lack the knowledge of the pitfalls in the various paths they may follow. What has been done for farmers to improve research, technology, and management might well be furnished to small businesses, thereby enhancing their chances of survival. And, in the formulation of tax programs to meet the financial burdens of a huge public debt and the markedly increased costs of modern government, due care should be taken at all times to avoid tax laws unwittingly, or even purposely, designed to bear too heavily on small business concerns.

The status of labor under the antitrust laws should be re-examined. In 1945, in the Allen Bradley–International Brotherhood of Electrical Workers case, the Supreme Court held that a combination of labor unions and business groups in restraint of trade violated the anti-trust laws. In so holding, the Court maintained an interpretative view consistent with earlier cases of like character. The Court went on, however, to argue that the net effect of this interpretation was, in fact, to leave labor unions—when acting alone—free to engage in conduct which restrains trade in commercial markets. The Court then proceeded to throw on the Congress responsibility for remedial action dealing with this sensitive and intricate problem. The desirability of such exemption of labor unions, it said, is a matter for Congressional determination except as limited by the Taft-Hartley Act[13] discussed above. Therefore, a labor organization by itself may enjoy anti-trust immunity on the grounds that its restrictive actions are related directly to the labor market and bargaining power over wage and working conditions and relate only incidentally to the commercial markets. The strategy and tactics of John L. Lewis illustrate the point. By ordering the coal workers to work only three days a week so as to reduce coal stock piles prior to the expiration of a contract, Mr. Lewis' labor organization can restrict production and affect the commercial market at public expense in order to gain bargaining objectives in the labor market. Thus an industry union can maintain or raise consumer prices in the interests of a particular labor group as effectively as can a combination of producers—and in the case of labor the anti-trust laws cannot be successfully invoked to protect the remaining public. When other unions are in a position to imitate this technique on a wide scale, real national income will suffer greatly. A solution of the problem, however, will not be easy, since labor markets and commercial markets and practices related to each are not clearly defined.

Conclusion

The evidence of concentration and the problems it creates for competitive control of production support our proposals. No sweeping cures of all ills are offered, but the proposals which are made hold real promise for improvement. Competitive individualism can survive successfully in a large portion of the American economy if the public will subscribe to the vigorous application of the principle of checks and balances in the economic as well as in the political field. It appears logical to support the competitive system with adequate controls. But there is little that can be said for the continuation of a policy that constitutes no more than a rear-guard, delaying action. Greater public awareness of the nature and depth of the issues involved and the consequences that may flow from indifference would be helpful in gaining popular support of a positive program. Yet in spite of the best we can do to revitalize competition, there will be many industries where competitive controls cannot

---

[13] Public Law 101, 80th Congress, 1st session, § 208. Prentice-Hall, Inc., *Labor Relations,* ¶ 36,414.

or should not be restored. For these particular fields special forms of governmental intervention must be used.

In the international field continued and consistent efforts should be made to promote greater freedom in trade. The pace of change should be adapted to the ability of other nations to accept the changes. A policy which does not require them to accept too abrupt a distortion of their domestic and international economic relations may encourage their coöperation.

32

The Abandonment of Competitive Individualism

In some industries it is probable that a vigorous and effective competition cannot be restored by public controls. Dissolution of the tobacco monopoly in 1911 did not create conditions under which competitive forces could work successfully. The improvement of public regulation may allow this industry to be altered so as to restore a thorough-going competition, but in others experience may suggest that a sufficiently large number of firms cannot be restored. Concentration in the manufacture of aluminum has gone so far and is now so firmly based on the scarcity of cheap sources of power that it would seem beyond the ability of anti-trust controls to create the fifty or a hundred independent companies required for competition. Yet it seems within the realm of possibility that reconstruction might be successfully undertaken in some of the problem industries which have been studied. The proposals made in the previous chapter concerning patents may allow competitive controls to be tried in the manufacture of shoe machinery, ethyl gasoline, glass containers, and in other industries where patents have been the basis of monopoly or oligopoly. Attack on the inter-corporate relations and collusive policies responsible for restraint of competition may free other industries. It seems, however, that the aluminum industry and possibly the steel industry are beyond reconstruction. And experience will reveal others where the best of public controls will be powerless to restore competition. For these industries, other public policies must be prepared.

In this study it has been assumed that economic power cannot be left in the hands of any group without some system of checks and balances. As a result, schemes in which the planning is left to management or labor or any other interest group are considered unsatisfactory. And any attempt to balance the power of one concentrated interest group against that of another will fail. The failure will be apparent in destructive conflict between the groups and the eventual dominance of one. Only one power can be used to match and to check the strength of great economic concentrations, and that is the power of the state. Where it seems impossible to revitalize competition in privately controlled industries, one of two courses of action may be taken: private ownership may be continued, but private management may be subjected to extensive regulation by a governmental administrative agency; producing properties may be acquired by the state and the industry may be operated as a state monopoly, or government plants may compete with privately operated plants. Consideration of these policies will show that they are available for our use, and that each offers a possible regulatory mechanism to fill any gaps left by the disappearance of competitive controls.

REGULATION BY COMMISSION

In a number of American industries public controls have been created not merely to supervise the competitive control but to replace it. These are the industries commonly recognized as public utilities or as being "affected with a public interest." The term "public utility" has been used in a variety of ways. It may include only those industries operating in municipal areas under some form of special franchise to supply water, gas, electric, or transit services. In a broader sense it may include the industries of transport and communication, such as the railways and telegraph. In a still looser sense it has encompassed the indeterminate group of operations like banking, commercial airways, boards of trade, insurance, and so forth. In general, these industries are distinguishable from private industry only by the fact that they are subjected to more rigorous regulation.

The Nature of Public Utility Regulation

Where price decisions are made by private management, an industry may be considered a private field of enterprise. But where price decisions are made by public authority through franchise terms, legislative acts, or administrative commissions, the industry may properly be considered a public utility. Price-fixing inevitably brings in its wake other aspects of regulation, particularly service regulation to define the product or service to which price-fixing is applied. In private industries—competitive or monopolistic—the price and the product offered by sellers are the instruments which reveal the working of competitive effort or monopolistic control. Prices play such an important rôle in the organization of the capitalistic system that any industry subjected to public price-fixing may reasonably be considered a public utility.

Certain obligations are laid on the public utility. The primary one, which is enforced and defined by some form of price-fixing, is that the prices of the product be "reasonable." Secondary obligations also are commonly created. First, whereas a private industry may offer different prices to different buyers, the public utility is forbidden to discriminate between buyers.[1] Second, the producer may be required to prepare adequate facilities to meet the foreseeable demand of the buyer, and he is required to serve all who apply. Finally, control of a public utility may fix definite standards respecting the quality of the commodity or service sold by the industry.

These controls will clearly affect the earnings and, as a result, the property values of privately-owned and publicly-regulated industry. With private property protected by constitutional guarantees, the mere act of a legislature does not expose a private industry to public price-fixing. The courts must find reason for the constriction of private property. In a review of price-fixing and wage-fixing controls set up by the state of Kansas, the Supreme Court made the following observation:

> The mere declaration by a legislature that a business is affected with a public interest is not conclusive of the question whether its attempted regulation on that ground is justified. The circumstances of its alleged change from the status of a private business and its freedom from regulation into one in which the public have come to have an interest are always a subject of judicial review.[2]

The legislative step which leads to regulation of a public utility will usually follow after public complaints have accumulated against the private industry. If the complaints of consumers are serious two things are implied: first, that the commodity is considered to be of more than average importance and there is no readily available substitute; second, that the producer is at least partially free from the competition of other producers. There is likely to be little reason for seeking a corrective in legislation if effective competition exists in the form of substitute commodities or competing producers. Complaints from producers, on the other hand, will have their origin in excessive competition. They may find that cut-throat competition keeps making their lives intolerable, and they may seek for remedy in public utility regulation.

It is hard to say what specific circumstances will allow regulation to hurdle the obstacles of the Fifth and Fourteenth Amendments. The courts have mentioned many specific reasons and combinations of reasons for subordinating private rights to the public control. In the Wolff Packing Company case, Chief Justice Taft found justification for doing so in three industrial categories. The first includes industries, such as the railroads, which are operating under special privileges granted by the public; the second, industries such as innkeeping, for which public regu-

---

[1] Section 2 of the Clayton Act forbids discrimination in private industry only when the effect of the discrimination is to lessen competition substantially.

[2] Wolff Packing Co. *v.* Kansas Industrial Court, 262 U. S. 536 (1923).

lation has been continued from "earliest times" up to the present; the third, industries which have come into a "peculiar relation" to the public.

More recent rulings of the Supreme Court have broadened and clarified the definition of public industries. In 1934, five members of the Court subscribed to a statement of public interest written by Justice Roberts:

The touchstone of public interest in any business, its practices and charges, clearly is not the enjoyment of any franchise from the state. . . . Nor is it the enjoyment of a monopoly. . . .

It is clear that there is no closed category of business affected with a public interest, and the function of the courts in the application of the Fifth and Fourteenth Amendments is to determine in each case whether circumstances vindicate the challenged regulation as a reasonable exertion of governmental authority. . . . [3]

The regulation challenged in this case was a New York law giving a Milk Control Board the power, among other things, to fix maximum and minimum prices for milk. In the following excerpt from the majority opinion the Court presents the socially unsatisfactory result of competitive regulation as the single criterion which properly places certain industries outside the control of competitive forces:

If the law-making body within its sphere of government concludes that the conditions or practices in an industry make unrestricted competition an inadequate safeguard of the consumer's interest, produce waste harmful to the public, threaten ultimately to cut off the supply of a commodity needed by the public, or portend the destruction of the industry itself, appropriate statutes passed in an honest effort to correct the threatened consequences may not be set aside because the regulation adopted fixes prices reasonably deemed by the legislature to be fair to those engaged in the industry and to the consuming public.

The opinion does not conclusively reveal—and no judicial dictum can reveal—the precise conditions under which the safeguard of competition will be considered "inadequate," or the occasions when the inadequacy may affect "the public," or what constitutes "a commodity needed by the public." These missing specifications are really of little importance. The chief requirement is this: a belief of the public (attested by five members of the Supreme Court) that competition fails to bring satisfactory regulation to an industry.

Problems of Regulation

The problems of government regulation arise from the application of administrative controls relating to the fairness of prices and the adequacy of the quantity and quality of goods and services being supplied by the regulated industry. In the light of established legal and economic

[3] Nebbia v. People of the State of New York, 291 U. S. 502, 534, 536 (1934).

standards, the regulators must reconcile satisfactorily the interests of the various parties involved. Since the prime reason for regulation is to reduce the costs to society because of the lack or ineffectiveness of private competition, it follows that the regulatory body must strive constantly for the prices and quality of product obtained under effective competition. In terms of price, quantity, and quality of the product, it must satisfy not only the consumer group, but also all those who are responsible for the production of the article. Failure to keep this fundamental principle in mind leads inevitably to legal strife between the regulated and the regulators. And even though the regulators do keep the principle ever before them, regulation breeds a heavy docket of court cases, for the very simple reason that the concepts of fair price and service adequacy are subject to varying interpretations.

The fairness of the price of a product and the adequacy of service in supplying that product in the right amounts and of the right quality require the establishment of standards for each that are inseparable.[4] From the consumer's point of view the price of a product of a given quality, when made available on the market in a given quantity, is fair if the regulated firm covers all its fairly-determined costs. In short, deviations from fairness occur when the supplying company receives a monopoly gain as shown by comparing its return on capital investment with returns on capital in competitive fields, or fails to receive a return on capital equivalent to the earning power of capital in competitive opportunities elsewhere. It must be admitted, however, that the consumer shows less concern with the latter than with the former. Consumer notions of quantity, quality, and continuity of service are even more difficult to define accurately. Needless to say, any deterioration of service without a downward adjustment of price will elicit complaints. On the other hand, improvements of service without change of price are accepted gladly. Any increase in price must be justified by costs, however, if public censure is to be avoided.

From the producer's viewpoint, prices are fair only when they are high enough to cover all the valid costs of production, including a rate of return on capital investment comparable to what the invested capital might get in the best of competitive alternatives of comparable risk. Assuming that the costs of productive agents are determined competitively, it is obvious that regulated prices set at too low a level will bring losses to producers and the diversion of capital to more lucrative fields. On the other hand, a price set too high will stimulate consumer cries that the regulators are collaborating with the regulated; are negligent and ignorant of their jobs; or are guilty on both charges.

---

[4] *Cf.* L. S. Lyon, Victor Abramson, and associates, *Government and Economic Life* (Washington, D. C., The Brookings Institution, 1940), Vol. II, p. 672.

And the horns of the regulatory dilemma are made even more uncomfortable when regulation involves more than a single product and service and more than a single price. Here the regulators must concern themselves with a pricing pattern as well as a level of prices. They might be fortunate enough to establish a level of prices that would satisfy the requirements of an adequate return on capital, and yet be subject to justifiable censure because of the discriminatory nature of the pricing pattern. In short, the over-all conditions might be met very nicely, but the total burden of consumer payments might be distributed inequitably in terms of the service rendered. Corrections would have to be made, or the regulatory body would have to prove that the apparent discrimination actually benefited the complainants by relieving them of higher costs arising from any other basis of cost allocation. For example, a two-price system of household and industrial electric power rates, for various reasons, might favor the industrial users. Failure to establish such differentials might mean a diminution of industrial uses of power, with the consequence that higher rates would result for household service. On the other hand, unjustifiable differentials would mean that one group was subsidizing the other. Keen knowledge of costs and of demand schedules is required if regulators are to handle adequately all the problems relating to reasonable prices, adequate service, and non-discriminatory rates.

From the price problem spring many other related problems. A price which is fair covers accurately determined costs and yields a fair return on capital investment. But costs must be computed accurately and fairly. And a fair return on capital investment necessitates the establishment of a standard upon which to compute the value of the investment, and impels a decision as to what is a fair return. Moreover, little can be accomplished toward the solution of the major or the related problems without careful development and recording of the facts and careful control of an accepted system of accounts.

In 1898, in Smyth v. Ames,[5] the Supreme Court made the first announcement of its famous rule to the effect that the basis of all calculations as to the reasonableness of rates must be the fair value of the property being used for public convenience. Concerning the computation of fair value the Court indicated that the original cost of construction, the amount spent in permanent improvements, the amount and market value of the bonds and stocks, the present as compared with the original cost of construction, the probable earning capacity of the property under particular rates prescribed by statute, and the sum required to meet operating expenses, were all matters for consideration, and were to be given such weight as might be just and right in each case. And it concluded that there might be other matters to be considered in estimating

---

[5] 169 U. S. 466.

the value of the property.[6] The Court obviously offered little help by setting forth this conglomerate rule.

Over the years and out of a welter of disputes, two methods of valuation have received the most attention and support: original cost or prudent investment, and present or reproduction cost. Both methods have had their staunch supporters. Among regulatory commissions, however, the Smyth v. Ames ruling of the Supreme Court has forced the use of a hybrid method of calculation of the earnings base. One authority calls this the "trance" method, and describes the process as follows. The commission examines the evidence relating to reproduction cost and prudent investment. It views the evidence with respect to intangible values and considers the condition of the property. Then, arriving at a judgment which defies analysis or description, it produces a valuation figure which bears no relation to any figures appearing in the evidence it has reviewed. This process is accompanied by denials of the use of formulae or compromise, and an expression of the commission's inability to explain just how it reached the final figure.[7] The whole process, it appears, is an obvious attempt to counter with vagueness the Court's lack of clarity in its Smyth v. Ames pronouncement.

The original cost (prudent investment) method is the more precise. It requires the computation of the amounts wisely and honestly spent in the construction of the existing used and usable plant and facilities. To this end records and accounts are extremely vital. If they are lacking, the gaps must be filled by estimates. Once the records are established, the regulatory body must insist upon proper maintenance of the information. If this is accomplished, the regulatory body is able at all times to furnish a valuation figure speedily and inexpensively after the first costs of computation have been incurred. In terms of administrative expediency, the prudent investment valuation ranks as the superior method. It exhibits, however, a serious weakness. Valuations may be too high or too low, depending on the price level at the time the properties were constructed, as compared with the existing price level. In some cases this weakness may not be over-serious, since the investment in property may be the summation of many investments made at different periods of time and at varying price levels. Hence the prudent investment figures may approximate what they would be if the properties were valued at current prices.[8] The occasional appearance of this result, however, is not enough to erase the fundamental weakness of the method.

When reproduction or present cost is used as a measure of fair value, whether or not the reproduction involves an identical plant or a modern

---

[6] *Ibid.*, pp. 546–547.

[7] *Cf.* Lyons, Abramson, and associates, *op. cit.*, p. 692.

[8] E. M. Bernstein, *Public Utility Rate Making and the Price Level* (Chapel Hill, N. C., University of North Carolina Press, 1937), pp. 123–124.

substitute, it necessitates engineering appraisals. These often require years to complete. Moreover, qualified appraisers on both sides attain results which differ widely. Experience shows that the method is conducive to great controversy, long delays in arriving at a decision, and heavy legal expenses on the part of both the regulators and the regulated. Agreements as to pricing, labor performance, overhead costs, construction conditions, and the like are not reached quickly or easily. Nevertheless, if competitive results are the objectives of regulation, as they admittedly are, the reproduction or present cost method of valuation (particularly if it relates to a substitute modern plant performing the same service) more closely approximates the competitive conditions. The present cost method is adjusted to current price levels, and the fair return is based on the current value of the property.

It is unnecessary here to pursue further the relative merits of the two leading methods of determining property values to establish a price or rate base. The important point is that there is great controversy over the vital problem of valuation, and the Supreme Court failed over a long period of years to bring order out of the chaos it created in its Smyth v. Ames pronouncement. At times, it seemed to favor present costs. At other times, prudent investment caught its fancy. At no time, however, was it forthright in prescribing a definite rule of valuation which indicated the precise weights to be accorded the various elements to be considered in arriving at a valuation figure. Consequently, regulatory commissions tossed all the different value elements into the hopper, turned on the power, and turned out a valuation figure which they hoped would appeal to the judiciary as just and reasonable. This was hardly a satisfying procedure from anyone's viewpoint, and it certainly did not add to the popularity of public regulation.

But the Supreme Court has finally taken a position on the question of valuation which has stabilized the regulatory process. It did not do so, however, by adopting either original cost or reproduction cost. Rather, it left the matter of choice up to the individual commissions. The Court said in the Natural Gas Pipeline case of 1942: "The Constitution does not bind rate-making bodies to the service of any single formula or combination of formulas. . . . Once a fair hearing has been given, proper findings made and other statutory requirements satisfied, the courts cannot intervene in the absence of a clear showing that the limits of due process have been overstepped. If the Commission's order, as applied to the facts before it and viewed in its entirety, produces no arbitrary result, our inquiry is at an end."[9] Under this new dispensation, the commissions are no longer compelled to consider reproduction cost in determining a rate base and may choose to adopt prudent investment

---

[9] Federal Power Commission v. Natural Gas Pipeline Co., 315 U. S. 575 (1942). See also Federal Power Commission v. Hope Natural Gas Co., 320 U. S. 591 (1945).

if they so desire. The courts retain the right, however, to review rates fixed by regulatory agencies to ascertain whether the end result is fair and the return adequate to maintain the credit of the regulated enterprises.

Once the valuation question is settled, there emerges the coördinate problem of the fairness of the rate of return on capital. In competitive markets the "going" rate of return represents two elements, risk and capital productivity. The rate of return in regulated industries should approximate the competitive return and include allowances for risk and capital productivity, though not necessarily in the same proportions. (Under proper regulation the risk factor is undoubtedly less because the industry is more sheltered.) The legal concept of the Supreme Court coincides with the economic concept if one of the Court's pronouncements in the Bluefield Water case is maintained. Therein the Court said:[10] "A public utility is entitled to such rates as will permit it to earn a return on the value of the property . . . equal to that generally being made at the same time and in the same general part of the country on investments in other business undertakings which are attended by corresponding risks and uncertainties; . . . "[11]

Since the competitive return is the guide to the return in the regulated industry, it follows that the latter should parallel the variations in the former. Furthermore, the conditions under which various firms in a regulated industry operate may require frequently that regulated companies be allowed different rates of return at the same time as well as at different times. For example, a large utility company with strongly established financial connections would find it easier and less costly to raise new capital than would a smaller company further removed from that market. Size and location factors as well as earnings have some bearing on the ability of competitive companies to raise new capital. It is no less true in the case of firms falling under the supervision of regulating agencies. Consequently, it seems that any precise measurement as to what constitutes a fair rate of return is not feasible. It should follow competitive returns in the area in which the regulated firm is located. And it should be high enough to attract new capital through both stock and bond sales whenever the need for further investment is justified economically.

Troublesome as they are, these direct pricing problems lead to other

---

[10] Bluefield Water Works Co. v. Public Service Commission, 262 U. S. 679, 692 (1923).

[11] In practice, the average allowable rate of return in the public utility field, over the period 1915–1930, was about 7.4 per cent. The range varied roughly between 5 and 9 per cent, with a fringe of instances below and above. So far as the Court is concerned, 6 per cent appears to be the low point for fairness, and 8 per cent the upper level.

difficulties of regulation. Extensive accounting requirements must be laid on the regulated industry. The fair return formula requires a careful supervision of the income and the costs of the public companies; prices must not be maintained at a high level merely because the operators are wasteful and inefficient. Since the financial practices of regulated companies may inflate costs or create risks of insolvency, the public utility commission must exercise a thorough-going control over financial policies. Maintenance costs may be artificially inflated or may be neglected by private management, with injury to the consumer in the form of artificially high prices or eventual deterioration in the producing properties. As a result the sums set aside for maintenance and depreciation must be supervised carefully by the regulatory body. And last but not least among the problems of regulation are matters concerning the quality and quantity of the service or product. Somehow the regulating commission must be able to determine whether or not changes in the production of the industry are called for by demand for the product. It can see the prices at which the existing quantity and quality is being sold, but it faces almost insuperable difficulties in determining the effect of changes in the quality and quantity on the price of the product. Yet these matters are of essential concern. The present output may sell at prices that allow a fair return on the proper value of the property, but possibly a larger output selling at lower prices would yield as good or better return. Only through very difficult estimates of the effect of changed output on costs and prices can the regulatory body reach proper price decisions.

Conclusion

It is evident that there exists in administrative price-fixing an available control for industries in which monopoly or oligopoly conditions cannot be corrected. It must be obvious, however, that administration of the control offers many serious difficulties. In addition, two faults are inseparable from the control. The first, price inflexibility, develops out of the administrative problems. The prices of the great mass of products rise and fall under the influence of various factors, and administered prices should move with them. The administrative procedure is so complicated, however, that the regulated prices almost inevitably lag behind. After business prosperity has given way to recession, they commonly continue to rise as the cost and price situations of the prosperity period bring about delayed changes. The same delay is apparent in other phases of the business cycle, and is an important factor in preventing the price adjustments required by changed business conditions. To solve this problem, regulatory commissions have developed the practice of issuing temporary rate orders. But such temporary orders may be maintained only through agreement with the regulated companies. As a result, where price reductions are needed, uncoöperative firms can insist on their legal rights and force the use of the unwieldly process of formal hearings. Furthermore, though various states have incorporated emergency rate provisions in their laws, the process has not yet received judicial approval. The lower courts have viewed these provisions as violations of due process, and the Supreme Court has not settled the issue.[12]

The second fault of commission control is an inherent one. It appears in the form of a divided managerial responsibility. The great mass of management decisions are left to the private management, but the commission control interferes in all aspects of the business through its control over prices. It is difficult for the private management to act efficiently in the sphere allotted to it when it cannot control future price policies.

It is possible that extensive public interference is incompatible with private operation. In the opinion of Joseph B. Eastman, the inevitable division of responsibility creates a serious problem. He suggests the nature and the consequences of the divided authority in the following paragraphs:

Public regulation is necessarily an interference with management and it involves divided responsibility to a considerable degree. The industry has two masters. One is the private management responsible to the stockholders, and the other is the commission responsible to the legislative branch of the Government. Initial authority rests with the management, but final authority not infrequently rests with the commission. The division of authority has the usual result that when things go wrong, the blame may be shifted, and it is difficult to concentrate responsibility.

A regulated industry is in danger of loss of enterprise and efficiency. . . . The tendency of the industry is to look to the Government for relief or help, where self-help would be the better policy. There is a tendency, also, to magnify the virtues of high rates, and to look to increase in rates for relief from low earnings. . . . [13]

In spite of its costliness and its faults, public utility regulation offers a possible planning device for use where competitive controls fail. With all its weaknesses, it affords an alternative that is markedly superior to private monopoly. It is possible, however, that some form of government operation in the problem industries would prevent the abuses of

---

[12] In 1940 the Supreme Court had an opportunity to settle this issue in the case of Driscoll v. Edison Light and Power Company, but avoided it in finding that an order of the Pennsylvania Commission was reasonable regardless of the procedural matters involved.

[13] Document No. 119, 73rd Congress, 2nd Session (1934), p. 12.

industrial monopoly and coöperation without developing the problems created by public utility regulation.

GOVERNMENT OPERATION

In the United States, Federal, state, and local governments have never been as much involved in government industries as some foreign governments. Nevertheless, for a variety of reasons they have had a considerable experience with public ownership and operation of industry. War and military preparedness have forced the Federal Government to supply housing for defense workers, operate shipyards, direct a large merchant marine, and produce a varied list of war supplies. In peace-time it has extended its activities to cover the production of electric power, reclamation and irrigation services, housing, highway improvements, and other services. In addition, the political organization of the state has brought the government into a number of lines of production. For example, one of the largest and most successful publishing enterprises in the world is found in the United States Government Printing Office.

Among the several states a considerable amount of government operation of industry also can be found. At one time or another, states have owned and operated banks, railroads, canals, turnpikes, bridges, and grain elevators. In recent years, certain social problems arising out of the sale of liquor and insurance have brought several states into these fields as enterprisers. Local governments also have been important operators. They have commonly operated sewage disposal facilities, water systems, docks, airport facilities, and are found operating street railways and urban bus systems in a number of communities.

The Nature of Government Operation

The legal right of government to own and operate industrial properties is well established in the United States. Referring to this right in the Kansas Industrial Court controversy, Chief Justice Taft said in effect that the state might engage in almost any business, providing the legislature believed such activity would help the general public, and providing the state would assume the cost of acquiring and operating the properties.[14] This opinion has been upheld in a number of cases. The Court ruled favorably when the city of Portland, Maine, undertook a fuel yard venture.[15] It did likewise in supporting the legitimacy of the North Dakota Mill and Elevator Act permitting that state to participate in a

---

[14] Chas. Wolff Packing Co. v. Court of Industrial Relations of Kansas, 262 U. S. 522, 537 (1920).

[15] Jones v. City of Portland, 245 U. S. 217 (1917).

wide variety of industries.[16] And the Court saw no reason to change its viewpoint in a case involving municipal ownership and operation of a wholesale and retail gasoline business by the city of Lincoln, Nebraska.[17]

Federal ownership and participation in business is predicated on its enumerated powers. How far the Federal Government may go depends on the social, economic, and legal views of a majority of the members of the Supreme Court. For, after all, judges interpret the broad language of that guiding instrument of social relations, the Constitution, in the light of their own social philosophy. And, in recent years, the supreme judiciary has broadened its notions of Federal powers to such an extent that the Federal Government has adequate grounds for participation and ownership in many lines of business. The Supreme Court has upheld the Tennessee Valley Authority program under the constitutional powers of the Federal Government to provide for national defense and promote navigation. And it acknowledged the Federal Government's right to dispose of electric energy as the right of disposal of any government property.[18] Furthermore, the Court validated government purchase of private plants and distributing lines, on the grounds that the protesting utilities had no standing in court because they did not have exclusive franchises for their operations, and hence had no legal claim of damages.[19]

Under these broad powers American governmental units may organize various forms of public industries. Government ownership probably will be used, but it is perfectly possible to allow private investment to supply funds for government industry. The control rights of private investors would have to be very definitely restricted, so as to leave the management responsible to the governmental authority. Operating conditions may also be varied. The public enterprise may be operated as a competitor to private companies, or may be granted an exclusive monopoly.

Problems of Government Operation

Since government operation of industry is viewed as a replacement for faulty competitive controls, it must have as its outstanding objective the economic results attained by effective competitive controls. Other objectives than productive efficiency may be sought. National defense, conservation, the correction of undesirable social conditions, and other concerns may alter the primary objective, but must not be allowed to obscure it.

---

[16] Green v. Frazier, 253 U. S. 233, 242–243 (1920).
[17] Standard Oil Co. et al. v. City of Lincoln, 275 U. S. 504 (1927).
[18] Ashwander v. T. V. A., 297 U. S. 288, 330 (1936).
[19] Tennessee Electric Power Co. v. T. V. A., 306 U. S. 118, 139 (1939).

It is important that the objectives of government enterprise be stated clearly at the outset and maintained throughout the operation of the enterprise. Thus, if the operations are undertaken to replace a private industry which has failed to maintain satisfactory price and cost relations, the government enterprise must be obliged to maintain purely economic standards and to render a proper account of its performance. On the other hand, if the purpose is to perform a broad public service in the interests of health, safety, and the like, without regard to the recovery of the full costs of the service, the difference in objective must be made clear. Failure to do this will endanger the operations of both types of project. Citizens and taxpayers need to be just as careful about the objectives and scope of a government industry as of a private industry. Too liberal use of vague "blanket charters" will lead to distressing situations in both cases.

If government operations are undertaken in an industry either to replace or to compete with a private monopoly, the objective would be an economic one—attainment of the price and cost conditions of perfect competition. There is no reason to believe that other social aims would be entailed. If this is so, the difficulties presented by complex objectives can be avoided. The public company can be made to stand on its own feet without the aid of subsidy from the state. This is desirable in the case of government monopoly, and absolutely necessary where the public company competes with private companies. As a device to force competition into an industry and to measure the efficiency of the private companies in the industry, public operation must not be subsidized. Its prices must be set at the level that covers all its costs of production. Even then, the danger of unfair competition for the private companies is present if the public company has difficulty in allocating its fixed costs among the various products it produces. This danger is present to an unusual degree in the operations of the Tennessee Valley Authority. This corporation, headed by a three-man board chosen by the President, operates vast properties on the Tennessee River for flood control, navigation, and the generation of electric power. Its competition with power companies will be unfair unless fixed costs are properly proportioned among the several services. Unfortunately, there is no scientific basis for the distribution of fixed costs, and the costs and prices of power sold by the T. V. A. will always be suspect.

Fixed costs do not offer a corresponding difficulty in the ordinary fields of industry; a fairly clear determination of costs would be feasible for public companies in the problem industries which we have studied. And government companies operating either as monopolies or in competition with private companies must be made to price their products on their costs of production.

Perhaps the leading problem concerning public ownership is to prevent political considerations from interfering with the attainment of economic results. Politics interferes with economics in two ways. It works through the application of the spoils system in selecting government personnel, and through political pressure groups. Under the spoils system, government personnel is selected not for its knowledge, skill, and experience in the work to be done, but rather for the contribution that the appointee made to the election of the existing administration.[20] Uncertainty of tenure accompanies such appointments, as a rule; consequently high-grade men are unwilling to leave better-paying jobs in private industry to undertake the temporary management of government enterprise. Furthermore, selections based on political favoritism rather than on merit do not carry with them prestige values large enough to offset the sacrifice that the more competent men would have to make in annual income. In addition, even though a competent individual might receive the appointment, he may find his competence impaired by the type of subordinate he is able to hire. While extension of civil service qualifications may be helpful in overcoming this problem, it is not always a complete or satisfactory solution. Except for such causes as extreme incompetence or outright dishonesty, civil service employees are not easily removed. This is especially unfortunate where the relatively incompetent are holding key positions in the higher salary brackets. Competent subordinates, if they recognize the situation, as they surely will, lose interest and drop out, or stay in and adapt their pace to that of the incompetent leaders.

Where government-owned industry handled by political appointees is an island in a sea of private industry, there is a strong presumption that its purchases of materials, supplies, and the like will follow political connections, rather than selection based on a careful analysis of prices and quality. Costs are likely, therefore, to be higher than they need be. This form of graft prevails in privately owned industry to some extent, but it cannot survive for long where thorough-going competition is present.

Another adverse influence on efficiency and costs is the political pressure group. The chief factor in locating government industry may be the strongest pressure group rather than economic considerations. If organized labor is politically strong, it may influence legislators to encourage a wage policy not fairly commensurate with labor's contribution to the productive process. Pressure politics may lead to expansion beyond optimum size at the expense of costs. Prices may be depressed below costs to curry the political favor of pressure groups or in response to

---

[20] It is interesting to note that politics exercised no great influence in the appointment of T. V. A. personnel. *Cf.* Leonard D. White, *Survey of the Personnel Department of T. V. A.*, Senate Document 56, Part 2, Appendix A, p. 66 (76th Congress, 1st Session).

their influence. In such circumstances, deficit appropriations must be made to balance income and outgo. The incidence of the burden then depends on the taxing structure.

As an offset to some of these unhealthy possibilities, controls in government over specific government enterprises might be and are established by the more public-spirited legislators and administrators. These controls, however, constitute additional costs in two ways: through the direct costs of supervision and the indirect costs of interfering with and delaying administration. Not only is there an elaboration of procedural red tape if the control is lodged with another governmental agency such as the office of the Comptroller-General, but governmental investigation by Congressional committees also may impede the management of the government enterprise. Hindrances such as these, whether or not they are deserved, cannot help but impair for shorter or longer periods the quantity and quality of the government-produced product or service.

Assuming that the political factor can be handled so that it does not greatly impair productive efficiency in a government enterprise, can efficiency be maintained on a plane comparable to that found under private ownership? To argue that it would be maintained is to contend that there is a driving force to efficiency under a government monopoly that is not present under a privately-owned monopoly. And this is not completely true in an economic sense. Under private monopoly, there should be an urge to keep expense of operation down to as low a point as possible, once the monopolist has adjusted production or price to the point where the total gain over expenses is the largest. That is the way to maximum private gain. But if there is truth to the common charge that the monopolist grows careless in regard to costs because of the security of his position, may not the charge be made that a government monopoly has less reason to be concerned about its level of costs where there is no private gain? It does not necessarily follow, however, that the level of costs under government operation would be higher than the level of costs under a private monopoly. Some costs doubtless would be lower. The government would be less inclined to restrict production artificially, and would enjoy the economies of larger-scale operations. Yet the costs of government operation might not be as low as they could be, because the incentive of private gain is not there. A substitute for this must be found and encouraged. In public recognition of outstanding service, pride of performance, and the instinct of good workmanship lies the answer, with the fear of dismissal or demotion operating as a supporting factor.

Favoring government operation are several facts that must not be overlooked. Government enterprise has ready access to capital markets. The machinery of distribution through the Federal Reserve banks is available to sell Federal Government securities. Moreover, the government is able to borrow at interest rates lower than those available to private business. Government ownership may unify operations and avoid duplication of facilities. It is conceivable also that, in a given state of technological development, government ownership might permit the adoption of the most efficient size of plant. Furthermore, government-owned industry would have at its disposal (at relatively low costs) the services of experts from other government agencies. It would not need to go beyond the government's own pools of legal, financial, engineering, and scientific talent maintained for other governmental purposes. And finally, government ownership would eliminate the costs of government regulation of private industry.

Conclusion

It is obvious that government operation of industry is an available alternative to private industry, but it must be equally clear that it offers no easy solution for the industries where competitive controls have broken down. It is surrounded by many political dangers, and it may not possess a satisfactory motivation to replace that of private enterprise.

None of the controls that could be used to regulate industry in the absence of competitive controls offers an easy solution for the problems of industrial monopoly and collusion. Consequently, every effort should be directed first toward the protection of competitive controls, and toward their reconstruction where they are endangered. The economic and political results of private monopoly cannot be tolerated, so difficult alternatives to the competitive control must be used if monopoly replaces competition.

All the measures that can be directed against the decline of competition should be used, and used with extreme vigor. Resources employed in corporate regulation and in protection of competition are well spent. The funds now being used on anti-trust measures can be better utilized, but they must be materially increased if we are to avoid still greater expenditures called for by the breakdown of competitive regulation. Although the spread of public utility regulation or government operation should be avoided, we do have in them a means of fitting monopolized industries into the general competitive pattern. The failure of competition in isolated fields can be met with public controls, and competition can thus be maintained in the great mass of American industry.

We are always tempted to turn from the difficulties of the day-to-day administration of a policy to a new program. It is all too easy to see how difficult it is to implement effectively the present plan, while the administrative difficulties of novel programs are obscure enough to be glossed over. The program for the revitalization of competitive controls is an extensive and difficult one. Our traditional policy has been only negatively administered, and the proposals to prepare positive conditions under which competition may work will create serious administrative and economic difficulties. Furthermore, even though these are vigorously developed, they will not create the conditions of perfect competition. They do offer, however, an opportunity to create a workable competition for the mass of American industry. And there is no reason to believe that the imperfections of such a system would be greater than those developed in the actual administration of novel programs. If socialistic or fascistic policies were given the inadequate implementation which we have given our anti-trust policy, they would result in hopeless chaos. Until our traditional policy has been really tried, it should not be condemned as a failure.

Index

Index